Get Connected.

FEATURES

LearnSmart™

McGraw-Hill LearnSmart is an adaptive learning program that identifies what an individual student knows and doesn't know. LearnSmart's adaptive learning path helps students learn faster, study more efficiently, and retain more knowledge. Reports available for both students and instructors indicate where students need to study more and assess their success rate in retaining knowledge.

Graphing Tool

The graphing tool within Connect Economics provides opportunities for students to draw, interact with, manipulate, and analyze graphs in their online auto-graded assignments, as they would with pencil and paper. The Connect graphs are identical in presentation to the graphs in the book, so students can easily relate their assignments to their reading material.

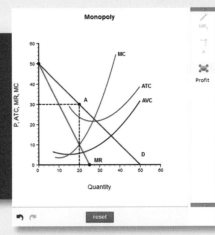

Get Engaged.

eBooks

Connect Plus includes a media-rich eBook that allows you to share your notes with your students. Your students can insert and review their own notes, highlight the text, search for specific information, and interact with media resources. Using an eBook with Connect Plus gives your students a complete digital solution that allows them to access their materials from any computer. Videos of key Demonstration Problems are linked next to the applicable Demonstration Problems within each of the chapters.

Lecture Capture

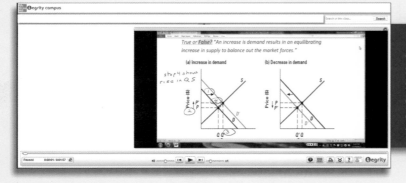

Make your classes available anytime, anywhere. With simple, one-click recording, students can search for a word or phrase and be taken to the exact place in your lecture that they need to review.

Managerial Economics and
Business Strategy

The McGraw-Hill Series Economics

EIGHTH EDITION

Managerial Economics and Business Strategy

Michael R. Baye
Bert Elwert Professor of Business Economics & Public Policy
Kelley School of Business
Indiana University

Jeffrey T. Prince
Associate Professor of Business Economics & Public Policy
Kelley School of Business
Indiana University

The McGraw-Hill Companies

McGraw-Hill Irwin

MANAGERIAL ECONOMICS AND BUSINESS STRATEGY

Published by McGraw-Hill/Irwin, a business unit of The McGraw-Hill Companies, Inc., 1221 Avenue of the Americas, New York, NY, 10020. Copyright © 2014 by The McGraw-Hill Companies, Inc. All rights reserved. Printed in the United States of America. Previous editions © 2010, 2008, and 2006. No part of this publication may be reproduced or distributed in any form or by any means, or stored in a database or retrieval system, without the prior written consent of The McGraw-Hill Companies, Inc., including, but not limited to, in any network or other electronic storage or transmission, or broadcast for distance learning.

Some ancillaries, including electronic and print components, may not be available to customers outside the United States.

This book is printed on acid-free paper.

3 4 5 6 7 8 9 0 DOC/DOC 1 0 9 8 7 6 5 4 3

ISBN 978-0-07-352322-4
MHID 0-07-352322-4

Senior Vice President, Products & Markets: *Kurt L. Strand*
Vice President, Content Production & Technology Services: *Kimberly Meriwether David*
Managing Director: *Douglas Reiner*
Executive Brand Manager: *Michele Janicek*
Executive Director of Development: *Ann Torbert*
Managing Development Editor: *Christina Kouvelis*
Director of Digital Content: *Doug Ruby*
Marketing Manager: *Katie Hoenicke*
Content Project Manager: *Marianne L. Musni*
Buyer II: *Debra R. Sylvester*
Senior Designer: *Lisa King*
Cover/Interior Designer: *Lisa King*
Cover Image: *©Design Pics / Kristy-Anne Glubish*
Typeface: *10/12 Times Roman*
Compositor: *Laserwords Private Limited*
Printer: *R. R. Donnelley*

All credits appearing on page or at the end of the book are considered to be an extension of the copyright page.

Library of Congress Cataloging-in-Publication Data

Baye, Michael R., 1958-
  Managerial economics and business strategy / Michael R. Baye, Bert Elwert Professor of Business
 Economics & Public Policy Kelley, School of Business, Indiana University, Jeffrey T. Prince, Associate
 Professor of Business Economic & Public Policy Kelly, School of Business, Indiana University.—
 Eighth edition.
    pages cm.—(The McGraw-Hill series economics)
  Includes index.
  ISBN-13: 978-0-07-352322-4 (alk.paper)
  ISBN-10: 0-07-352322-4 (alk. paper)
  1. Managerial economics. 2. Strategic planning. I. Prince, Jeffrey T. II. Title.
 HD30.22.B38 2014
 338.5024'658—dc23

                                                                                   2012048859

The Internet addresses listed in the text were accurate at the time of publication. The inclusion of a website does not indicate an endorsement by the authors or McGraw-Hill, and McGraw-Hill does not guarantee the accuracy of the information presented at these sites.

www.mhhe.com

DEDICATION

To my former students.
—Michael R. Baye

To Annie and Kate.
—Jeffrey T. Prince

ABOUT THE AUTHORS

Michael R. Baye is the Bert Elwert Professor of Business Economics & Public Policy at Indiana University's Kelley School of Business, and served as the Director of the Bureau of Economics at the Federal Trade Commission from July 2007 to December 2008. He received his B.S. in economics from Texas A&M University in 1980 and earned a Ph.D. in economics from Purdue University in 1983. Prior to joining Indiana University, he taught graduate and undergraduate courses at The Pennsylvania State University, Texas A&M University, and the University of Kentucky. He has held a variety of editorial posts in economics, marketing, and business, and currently serves as a co-editor for the *Journal of Economics and Management Strategy*.

Professor Baye has won numerous awards for his outstanding teaching and research, and teaches courses in managerial economics and industrial organization at the undergraduate, M.B.A., and Ph.D. levels. His research has been published in the *American Economic Review, Journal of Political Economy, Econometrica,* the *Review of Economic Studies,* the *Economic Journal,* and *Management Science.* It has also been featured in the *Wall Street Journal, Forbes,* the *New York Times*, and numerous other outlets. When he is not teaching or engaged in research, Mike enjoys activities ranging from camping to shopping for electronic gadgets.

Jeffrey T. Prince is Associate Professor of Business Economics & Public Policy at Indiana University's Kelley School of Business. He received his B.A. in economics and B.S. in mathematics and statistics from Miami University in 1998 and earned a Ph.D. in economics from Northwestern University in 2004. Prior to joining Indiana University, he taught graduate and undergraduate courses at Cornell University.

Professor Prince has won top teaching honors as a faculty member at both Indiana University and Cornell, and as a graduate student at Northwestern. He has a broad research agenda within applied economics, having written and published on topics that include demand in technology markets, Internet diffusion, regulation in health care, risk aversion in insurance markets, and quality competition among airlines. He is one of a small number of economists to have published in both the top journal in economics (*American Economic Review*) and the top journal in management (*Academy of Management Journal*). He currently serves on the editorial board for *Information Economics and Policy*. In his free time, Jeff enjoys activities ranging from poker and bridge to running and racquetball.

PREFACE TO THE EIGHTH EDITION

Thanks to feedback from users around the world, *Managerial Economics and Business Strategy* remains the best-selling managerial text in the market. We are grateful to all of you for allowing us to provide this updated and improved edition. Before highlighting some of the new features of the eighth edition, we would like to stress that the fundamental goal of the book—providing students with the tools from intermediate microeconomics, game theory, and industrial organization that they need to make sound managerial decisions—has not changed. What *has* changed is the examples used to make managerial economics come to life for this generation of students and—thanks to the addition of Jeff Prince to this edition—the utilization of new technologies (such as *Connect*) for enhancing the teaching and learning experiences of instructors and their students.

This book begins by teaching managers the practical utility of basic economic tools such as present value analysis, supply and demand, regression, indifference curves, isoquants, production, costs, and the basic models of perfect competition, monopoly, and monopolistic competition. Adopters and reviewers also praise the book for its real-world examples and because it includes modern topics not contained in any other single managerial economics textbook: oligopoly, penetration pricing, multistage and repeated games, foreclosure, contracting, vertical and horizontal integration, networks, bargaining, predatory pricing, principal–agent problems, raising rivals' costs, adverse selection, auctions, screening and signaling, search, limit pricing, and a host of other pricing strategies for firms enjoying market power. This balanced coverage of traditional and modern microeconomic tools makes it appropriate for a wide variety of managerial economics classrooms. An increasing number of business schools are adopting this book to replace (or use alongside) managerial strategy texts laden with anecdotes but lacking the microeconomic tools needed to identify and implement the business strategies that are optimal in a given situation.

This eighth edition of *Managerial Economics and Business Strategy* has been revised to include updated examples and problems, but it retains all of the basic content that made previous editions a success. The basic structure of the textbook is unchanged to ensure a smooth transition to this edition.

KEY PEDAGOGICAL FEATURES

The eighth edition retains all of the class-tested features of previous editions that enhance students' learning experiences and make it easy to teach from this book. But this edition includes a number of new features available to those using McGraw-Hill's wonderful interactive learning products, *Connect* and *LearnSmart*. *Connect* offers hundreds of variations of end-of-chapter problems that may be electronically graded and provide students with immediate, detailed, feedback. Students and instructors can access these and other powerful resources directly from their laptops, tablets and phones. For more information, please refer to pp. xiv–xvii of the preface.

Headlines

As in previous editions, each chapter begins with a *Headline* that is based on a real-world economic problem—a problem that students should be able to address after completing the chapter. These *Headlines* are essentially hand-picked "mini-cases" designed to motivate students to learn the material in the chapter. Each *Headline* is answered at the end of the relevant chapter—when the student is better prepared to deal with the complications of real-world problems. Reviewers as well as users of previous editions praise the *Headline*s not only because they motivate students to learn the material in the chapter, but also because the answers at the end of each chapter help students learn how to use economics to make business decisions.

Learning Objectives

Each chapter includes learning objectives designed to enhance the learning experience. A listing is provided at the end of the chapter that identifies select end of chapter problems to the learning objective(s) to which they relate.

Demonstration Problems

The best way to learn economics is to practice solving economic problems. So, in addition to the *Headlines*, each chapter contains many *Demonstration Problems* sprinkled throughout the text, along with detailed answers. This provides students with a mechanism to verify that they have mastered the material, and reduces the cost to students and instructors of having to meet during office hours to discuss answers to problems. One key demonstration problem in each chapter has an accompanying video tutorial, which walks through the solution step-by-step. These videos are available via the eBook included in Connect® Plus and the Online Learning Center, www.mhhe.com/baye8e. For more information please refer to p. xiv of the Preface.

Inside Business Applications

Most chapters contain boxed material (called *Inside Business* applications) to illustrate how theories explained in the text relate to a host of different business situations. As in previous editions, we have tried to strike a balance between applications drawn from the current economic literature and the popular press.

Calculus and Non-Calculus Alternatives

Users can easily include or exclude calculus-based material without losing content or continuity. That's because the basic principles and formulae needed to solve a particular class of economic problems (e.g., $MR = MC$) are first stated without appealing to the notation of calculus. Immediately following each stated principle or formula is a clearly marked *Calculus Alternative*. Each of these calculus alternatives states the preceding principle or formula in calculus notation, and explains the relation between the calculus and non-calculus based formula. More detailed calculus derivations are relegated to chapter *Appendices*. Thus, the book is designed for use by instructors who want to integrate calculus into managerial economics and by those who do not require students to use calculus.

Key Terms and Marginal Definitions

Each chapter ends with a list of key terms and concepts. These provide an easy way for professors to glean material covered in each chapter, and for students to check their mastery of terminology. In addition, marginal definitions are provided throughout the text.

End-of-Chapter Problems

Three types of problems are offered. Highly structured but nonetheless challenging *Conceptual and Computational Questions* stress fundamentals. These are followed by *Problems and Applications,* which are far less structured and, like real-world decision environments, may contain more information than is actually needed to solve the problem. Many of these applied problems are based on actual business events.

Additionally, the Time Warner case that follows Chapter 14 includes 14 problems called Memos that have a "real-world feel" and complement the text. All of these case-based problems may be assigned on a chapter-by-chapter basis as specific skills are introduced, or as part of a capstone experience. Solutions to all of the memos are contained online at www.mhhe.com/baye8e.

Detailed answers to all problems—including *Problems and Applications* and the Time Warner case *Memos*, are available to instructors on the password-protected website (www.mhhe.com/baye8e).

Case Study

A case study in business strategy—*Challenges at Time Warner*—follows Chapter 14 and was prepared especially for this text. It can be used either as a capstone case for the course or to supplement individual chapters. The case allows students to apply core elements from managerial economics to a remarkably rich business environment. Instructors can use the case as the basis for an "open-ended" discussion of business strategy, or they can assign specific "memos" (contained at the end of the case) that require students to apply specific tools from managerial economics to the case. Teaching notes, as well as solutions to all of the memos, are provided on the book's website.

Flexibility

Instructors of managerial economics have genuinely heterogeneous textbook needs. Reviewers and users continue to praise the book for its flexibility, and they assure us that sections or even entire chapters can be excluded without losing continuity. For instance, an instructor wishing to stress microeconomic fundamentals might choose to cover Chapters 2, 3, 4, 5, 8, 9, 10, 11, and 12. An instructor teaching a more applied course that stresses business strategy might choose to cover Chapters 1, 2, 3, 5, 6, 7, 8, 10, 11, and 13. Each may choose to include additional chapters (for example, Chapter 14 or the Time Warner case) as time permits. More generally, instructors can easily omit topics such as present value analysis, regression, indifference curves, isoquants, or reaction functions without losing continuity.

CHANGES IN THE EIGHTH EDITION

We have made every effort to update and improve *Managerial Economics and Business Strategy* while assuring a smooth transition to the eighth edition. Following is a summary of the pedagogical improvements, enhanced supplements, and content changes that make the eighth edition an even more powerful tool for teaching and learning managerial economics and business strategy.

- McGraw-Hill's homework management platform system, Connect®, is now offered for the eighth edition. This allows students to access video tutorials for selected demonstration problems through an electronic version of the book available in Connect® Plus, and gives instructors the ability to assign (and automatically grade) literally hundreds of end-of-chapter problems (including algorithmic variants), and options to provide students with immediate, detailed feedback and answers. In our experience, this allows both students and instructors to economize on the time required to set up one-on-one appointments.

- Also new to the eighth edition, LearnSmart is an adaptive learning tool that allows students to continually test their mastery of basic and more complex concepts.

- Over 100 new variations of the class-tested problems from the previous edition plus several new end-of-chapter problems. Where appropriate, problems from the previous edition have been updated to reflect the current economic climate.

- Suggested end-of-chapter problems for each learning objective, to help foster targeted learning.

- The updated *Test Bank* has been rigorously quality tested, and now contains over 100 new, challenging problems.

- New and updated *Headlines*.

- New and updated *Inside Business* applications.

Chapter-by-Chapter Changes

- **Chapter 1** contains new and updated examples, and an updated *Inside Business* application. It also contains twenty refreshed end-of-chapter problems.

- **Chapter 2** contains new and updated examples and *Inside Business* applications. This chapter has fourteen refreshed end-of-chapter problems.

- **Chapter 3** contains new and updated examples as well as an updated *Inside Business* application. It also has improved discussion of regression analysis. This chapter has twenty refreshed end-of-chapter problems.

- **Chapter 4** contains updated examples, and two new *Inside Business* applications; the first examines the relationship between the budget constraint and credit card usage, and the second examines output-oriented incentives. It also has two new and sixteen refreshed end-of-chapter problems.

- **Chapter 5** contains updated *Inside Business* applications, as well as a new demonstration problem. It also has sixteen refreshed end-of-chapter problems.
- **Chapter 6** offers a new *Headline*, and new examples. It also has four new and three refreshed end-of-chapter problems.
- **Chapter 7** contains thoroughly updated examples and industry data, as well as updated *Inside Business* applications. It also includes updates that account for the new 2010 *Horizontal Merger Guidelines*, and nine refreshed end-of-chapter problems.
- **Chapter 8** contains an updated *Headline* and several new examples. It also has fifteen refreshed end-of-chapter problems.
- **Chapter 9** provides improved exposition of contestable markets, and a new *Inside Business* application examining OPEC and the temptation to cheat on collusive arrangements. It also includes thirteen refreshed end-of-chapter problems.
- **Chapter 10** contains a new *Inside Business* application examining cola wars in India, as well as improved exposition of equilibrium strategies. It also has sixteen refreshed end-of-chapter problems.
- **Chapter 11** contains an updated *Headline*, updated *Inside Business* applications, and a new *Inside Business* application examining whether price discrimination is necessarily bad for consumers. There are fifteen refreshed end-of-chapter problems.
- **Chapter 12** includes an improved explanation of the merits of standard deviation as a measure of risk, and a new *Inside Business* application that examines adverse selection in the context of a famous quote by Groucho Marx. It also has eleven refreshed end-of-chapter problems.
- **Chapter 13** contains a new *Headline* and new examples for commitment mechanisms and network effects. It also has eight refreshed end-of-chapter problems.
- **Chapter 14** contains updated discussion of the 2010 *Horizontal Merger Guidelines*, the *Dodd-Frank Wall Street Reform and Consumer Protection Act*, and updated *Inside Business* applications. It also has seven refreshed end-of-chapter problems.

ORGANIZED LEARNING IN THE EIGHTH EDITION

Chapter Learning Objectives

Students and instructors can be confident that the organization of each chapter reflects common themes outlined by four to seven learning objectives listed on the first page of each chapter. These objectives, along with AACSB and Bloom's taxonomy learning categories, are connected to all end-of-chapter material and test bank questions to offer a comprehensive and thorough teaching and learning experience.

Assurance of Learning Ready

Many educational institutions today are focused on the notion of *assurance of learning*, an important element of some accreditation standards. *Managerial Economics and Business Strategy* is designed specifically to support your assurance of learning initiatives with a simple, yet powerful solution.

Each test bank question for *Managerial Economics and Business Strategy* maps to a specific chapter learning outcome/objective listed in the text. You can use our test bank software, EZ Test, or *Connect Economics* to easily query for learning outcomes/objectives that directly relate to the learning objectives for your course. You can then use the reporting features of EZ Test to aggregate student results in similar fashion, making the collection and presentation of assurance of learning data simple and easy.

AACSB Statement

The McGraw-Hill Companies is a proud corporate member of AACSB International. Understanding the importance and value of AACSB accreditation, *Managerial Economics and Business Strategy*, Eighth edition, recognizes the curricula guidelines detailed in the AACSB standards for business accreditation by connecting questions in the test bank and end-of-chapter material to the general knowledge and skill guidelines found in the AACSB standards.

The statements contained in *Managerial Economics and Business Strategy,* Eighth edition, are provided only as a guide for the users of this textbook. The AACSB leaves content coverage and assessment within the purview of individual schools, the mission of the school, and the faculty.

SUPPLEMENTS FOR THE INSTRUCTOR

We are pleased to report that the eighth edition of *Managerial Economics and Business Strategy* truly offers adopters the most comprehensive and easily accessible supplements in the market. Below we discuss popular features of some of the supplements that have been greatly expanded for this edition. The following ancillaries are available for quick download and convenient access via the book website at www.mhhe.com/baye8e and are password protected for security.

Cases

In addition to the Time Warner case, nearly a dozen full-length cases were prepared to accompany *Managerial Economics and Business Strategy.* These cases complement the textbook by showing how real-world businesses use tools like demand elasticities, markup pricing, third-degree price discrimination, bundling, Herfindahl indices, game theory, and predatory pricing to enhance profits or shape business strategies. The cases are based on actual decisions by companies that include Microsoft, Heinz, Visa, Staples, American Airlines, Sprint, and Kodak. Expanded teaching notes and solutions for all of the cases—including the Time Warner case—are also provided.

PowerPoint Slides

Thoroughly updated and fully editable PowerPoint presentations with animated figures and graphs, prepared by Patrick Scholten of Bentley University, make teaching and learning a snap. For instance, a simple mouse click reveals the firm's demand curve. Another click reveals the associated marginal revenue curve. Another click shows the firm's marginal cost. A few more clicks, and students see how to determine the profit-maximizing output, price, and maximum profits. Animated graphs and tables are also provided for all other relevant concepts (like Cournot and Stackelberg equilibrium, normal form and extensive form games, and the like).

Solutions Manual

We have prepared a solutions manual that provides detailed answers to all end-of-chapter problems, all of which have been class-tested for accuracy.

Test Bank

An updated test bank, prepared by the authors, offers well over 1,000 multiple-choice questions categorized by learning objectives, AACSB learning categories, Bloom's taxonomy objectives, and level of difficulty.

Computerized Test Bank

McGraw-Hill's EZ Test is a flexible and easy-to-use electronic testing program that allows you to create tests from book-specific items, customized to your needs. It accommodates a wide range of question types, and you can add your own questions. Multiple versions of the test can be created, and any test can be exported for use with course management systems such as BlackBoard. EZ Test Online gives you a place to administer your EZ-Test created exams and quizzes online. The program is available for Windows and Macintosh environments.

Digital Image Library

All the figures and tables presented in the book have been made available in electronic format, providing flexibility to integrate art from the textbook into PowerPoint presentations, or to directly print the figures on overhead transparencies.

SUPPLEMENTS FOR THE STUDENT

Study Guide

We have prepared a study guide that offers a wealth of additional resources to master the course. The study guide includes a study outline, a review of key concepts, a variety of questions for additional practice, and the solutions to the questions so you can check your answers.

Online Learning Center www.mhhe.com/baye8e

The book website is a central resource for students and instructors alike. Students can access a glossary, Time Warner Case Study materials, data for key chapters, Inside Business assets, chapter overviews, and PowerPoint presentations. Students can also test their knowledge of chapter concepts with auto-gradable practice quizzes.

MCGRAW-HILL CONNECT® ECONOMICS

Less Managing. More Teaching. Greater Learning.

McGraw-Hill *Connect*® *Economics* is an online assignment and assessment solution that connects students with the tools and resources they'll need to achieve success.

McGraw-Hill *Connect Economics* helps prepare students for their future by enabling faster learning, more efficient studying, and higher retention of knowledge.

McGraw-Hill *Connect*® *Economics* features

Connect Economics offers a number of powerful tools and features to make managing assignments easier, so faculty can spend more time teaching. With *Connect Economics*, students can engage with their coursework anytime and anywhere, making the learning process more accessible and efficient. *Connect Economics* offers the features described here.

Simple assignment management

With *Connect Economics*, creating assignments is easier than ever, so you can spend more time teaching and less time managing. The assignment management function enables you to:

- Create and deliver assignments easily with selectable end-of-chapter questions and test bank items.
- Streamline lesson planning, student progress reporting, and assignment grading to make classroom management more efficient than ever.
- Go paperless with the eBook and online submission and grading of student assignments.

Smart grading

When it comes to studying, time is precious. *Connect Economics* helps students learn more efficiently by providing feedback and practice material when they need it, where they need it. When it comes to teaching, your time also is precious. The grading function enables you to:

- Have assignments scored automatically, giving students immediate feedback on their work and side-by-side comparisons with correct answers.

- Access and review each response; manually change grades or leave comments for students to review.
- Reinforce classroom concepts with practice tests and instant quizzes.

Instructor library

The *Connect Economics* Instructor Library is your repository for additional resources to improve student engagement in and out of class. You can select and use any asset that enhances your lecture.

Student study center

The *Connect Economics* Student Study Center is the place for students to access additional resources. The Student Study Center:

- Offers students quick access to lectures, practice materials, eBooks, and more.
- Provides instant practice material and study questions, easily accessible on the go.

Diagnostic and adaptive learning of concepts: LearnSmart

Students want to make the best use of their study time. The LearnSmart adaptive self-study technology within *Connect Economics* provides students with a seamless combination of practice, assessment, and remediation for every concept in the textbook. LearnSmart's intelligent software adapts to every student response and automatically delivers concepts that advance the student's understanding while reducing time devoted to the concepts already mastered. The result for every student is the fastest path to mastery of the chapter concepts. LearnSmart:

- Applies an intelligent concept engine to identify the relationships between concepts and to serve new concepts to each student only when he or she is ready.
- Adapts automatically to each student, so students spend less time on the topics they understand and practice more those they have yet to master.
- Provides continual reinforcement and remediation, but gives only as much guidance as students need.
- Integrates diagnostics as part of the learning experience.
- Enables you to assess which concepts students have efficiently learned on their own, thus freeing class time for more applications and discussion.

Student progress tracking

Connect Economics keeps instructors informed about how each student, section, and class is performing, allowing for more productive use of lecture and office hours. The progress-tracking function enables you to:

- View scored work immediately and track individual or group performance with assignment and grade reports.

- Access an instant view of student or class performance relative to learning objectives.
- Collect data and generate reports required by many accreditation organizations, such as AACSB and AICPA.

Lecture capture

Increase the attention paid to lecture discussion by decreasing the attention paid to note taking. For an additional charge, Lecture Capture offers new ways for students to focus on the in-class discussion, knowing they can revisit important topics later. Lecture Capture enables you to:

- Record and distribute your lecture with a click of a button.
- Record and index PowerPoint presentations and anything shown on your computer so it is easily searchable, frame by frame.
- Offer access to lectures anytime and anywhere by computer, iPod, or mobile device.
- Increase intent listening and class participation by easing students' concerns about note-taking. Lecture Capture will make it more likely you will see students' faces, not the tops of their heads.

MCGRAW-HILL CONNECT® PLUS ECONOMICS

McGraw-Hill reinvents the textbook learning experience for the modern student with *Connect® Plus Economics*. A seamless integration of an eBook and *Connect Economics*, *Connect Plus Economics* provides all of the *Connect Economics* features plus the following:

- An integrated eBook, allowing for anytime, anywhere access to the textbook.
- Dynamic links between the problems or questions you assign to your students and the location in the eBook where that problem or question is covered.
- A powerful search function to pinpoint and connect key concepts in a snap.

In short, *Connect Economics* offers you and your students powerful tools and features that optimize your time and energies, enabling you to focus on course content, teaching, and student learning. *Connect Economics* also offers a wealth of content resources for both instructors and students. This state-of-the-art, thoroughly tested system supports you in preparing students for the world that awaits.

For more information about Connect, please visit www.mcgrawhillconnect.com, or contact your local McGraw-Hill sales representative.

TEGRITY CAMPUS: LECTURES 24/7

 Tegrity Campus is a service that makes class time available 24/7 by automatically capturing every lecture in a searchable format for students to review when they study and complete assignments. With a simple one-click start-and-stop process, you capture all computer screens and corresponding audio. Students can replay any part of any class with easy-to-use browser-based viewing on a PC or Mac.

Educators know that the more students can see, hear, and experience class resources, the better they learn. In fact, studies prove it. With Tegrity Campus, students quickly recall key moments by using Tegrity Campus's unique search feature. This search helps students efficiently find what they need, when they need it, across an entire semester of class recordings. Help turn all your students' study time into learning moments immediately supported by your lecture.

To learn more about Tegrity, watch a two-minute Flash demo at http://tegritycampus.mhhe.com.

MCGRAW-HILL CUSTOMER CARE CONTACT INFORMATION

At McGraw-Hill, we understand that getting the most from new technology can be challenging. That's why our services don't stop after you purchase our products. You can e-mail our Product Specialists 24 hours a day to get product training online. Or you can search our knowledge bank of Frequently Asked Questions on our support website. For Customer Support, call 800-331-5094, e-mail hmsupport@mcgraw-hill.com, or visit www.mhhe.com/support. One of our Technical Support Analysts will be able to assist you in a timely fashion.

COURSESMART

 CourseSmart is a new way for faculty to find and review eTextbooks. It's also a great option for students who are interested in accessing their course materials digitally. CourseSmart offers thousands of the most commonly adopted textbooks across hundreds of courses from a wide variety of higher education publishers. It is the only place for faculty to review and compare the full text of a textbook online. At CourseSmart, students can save up to 50% off the cost of a print book, reduce their impact on the environment, and gain access to powerful web tools for learning including full text search, notes and highlighting, and e-mail tools for sharing notes between classmates. Your eBook also includes tech support in case you ever need help.

Finding your eBook is easy. Visit www.CourseSmart.com and search by title, author, or ISBN.

ACKNOWLEDGMENTS

We thank the many users of *Managerial Economics and Business Strategy* who provided both direct and indirect feedback that has helped improve *your* book. This includes thousands of students at Indiana University's Kelley School of Business and instructors worldwide who have used this book in their own classrooms, colleagues who unselfishly gave up their own time to provide comments and suggestions, and reviewers who provided detailed suggestions to improve this and previous editions of the book. We especially thank the following professors for enlightening us on the market's diverse needs and for providing suggestions and constructive criticisms to improve this book:

Fatma Abdel-Raouf, *Goldey-Beacom College*
Burton Abrams, *University of Delaware*
Rashid Al-Hmoud, *Texas Tech University*
Anthony Paul Andrews, *Governors State University*
Sisay Asefa, *Western Michigan University*
Simon Avenell, *Murdoch University*
Joseph P. Bailey, *University of Maryland*
Dale G. Bails *Christian Brothers University*
Dean Baim, *Pepperdine University*
Sheryl Ball, *Virginia Polytechnic University*
Klaus Becker, *Texas Tech University*
Richard Beil, *Auburn University*
Barbara C. Belivieu, *University of Connecticut*
Dan Black, *University of Chicago*
Louis Cain, *Northwestern University*
Kerem Cakirer, *Indiana University*
Leo Chan, *University of Kansas*
Robert L. Chapman, *Florida Metropolitan University*
Joni Charles, *Texas State University—San Marcos*
Basanta Chaudhuri, *Rutgers University—New Brunswick*
Shuo Chen, *State University of New York at Geneseo*
Xiujian Chen, *State University of New York—Binghamton University*
Kwang Soo Cheong, *Johns Hopkins University*
Christopher B. Colburn, *Old Dominion University*
Daniel Patrick Condon, *Dominican University*
Michael Conlin, *Syracuse University*
Keith Crocker, *Penn State University*
Ian Cromb, *University of Western Ontario*
Dean Croushore, *Federal Reserve*
Wilffrid W. Csaplar Jr., *Bethany College*
Shah Dabirian, *California State University, Long Beach*
Joseph DaBoll-Lavioe, *Nazareth College of Rochester*

George Darko, *Tusculum College*
Tina Das, *Elon University*
Ron Deiter, *Iowa State University*
Jonathan C. Deming, *Seattle Pacific University*
Casey Dirienzo, *Appalachian State University*
Eric Drabkin, *Hawaii Pacific University*
Martine Duchatelet, *Barry University*
Keven C. Duncan, *University of Southern Colorado*
Yvonne Durham, *Western Washington University*
Eugene F. Elander, *Brenau University*
Ibrahim Elsaify, *Goldey-Beacom College*
Mark J. Eschenfelder, *Robert Morris University*
David Ely, *San Diego State University*
Li Feng, *Texas State University–San Marcos*
David Figlio, *University of Florida*
Ray Fisman, *Graduate School of Business, Columbia University*
Silke Forbes, *University of California—San Diego*
David Gerard, *Carnegie Mellon University*
Sharon Gifford, *Rutgers University*
Lynn G. Gillette, *Northeast Missouri State University*
Otis Gilley, *Louisiana Tech University*
Roy Gobin, *Loyola University*
Stephan Gohmann, *University of Louisville*
Steven Gold, *Rochester Institute of Technology*
Julie Hupton Gonzalez, *University of California–Santa Cruz*
Thomas A. Gresik, *Mendoza College of Business (University of Notre Dame)*
Andrea Mays Griffith, *California State University*
Madhurima Gupta, *University of Notre Dame*
Carl Gwin, *Pepperdine University*
Gail Heyne Hafer, *Lindenwood College*
Karen Hallows, *George Mason University*
William Hamlen Jr., *SUNY Buffalo*
Shawkat Hammoudeh, *Drexel University*

Mehdi Harian, *Bloomsburg University*

Nile W. Hatch, *Marriott School (Brigham Young University)*

Clifford Hawley, *West Virginia University*

Ove Hedegaard, *Copenhagen Business School*

Steven Hinson, *Webster University*

Robert L. Holland, *Purdue University*

Hart Hodges, *Western Washington University*

Jack Hou, *California State University–Long Beach*

Lowel R. Jacobsen, *William Jewell College*

Thomas D. Jeitschko, *Michigan State University*

Jaswant R. Jindia, *Southern University*

Russell Kashian, *University of Wisconsin—Whitewater*

Paul Kattuman, *Judge Business School (Cambridge University)*

Brian Kench, *University of Tampa*

Kimberley L. Kinsley, *University of Mary Washington*

Peter Klein, University of Georgia, *University of Missouri–Columbia*

Audrey D. Kline, *University of Louisville*

Robert A. Krell, *George Mason University*

Paul R. Kutasovic, *New York Institute of Technology*

W. J. Lane, *University of New Orleans*

Daniel Lee, *Shippensburg University*

Dick Leiter, *American Public University*

Canlin Li, *University of California–Riverside*

Chung-Ping Loh, *University of North Florida*

Vahe Lskavyan, *Ohio University–Athens*

Heather Luea, *Newman University*

Nancy L. Lumpkin, *Georgetown College*

Thomas Lyon, *University of Michigan*

Richard Marcus, *University of Wisconsin—Milwaukee*

Vincent Marra, *University of Delaware*

Wade Martin, California State University, *Long Beach*

Catherine Matraves, *Michigan State University–East Lansing*

John Maxwell, *Indiana University*

David May, *Oklahoma City University*

Alan McInnes, *California State University, Fullerton*

Christopher McIntosh, *University of Minnesota Duluth*

Kimberly L. Merritt, *Oklahoma Christian University*

Edward Millner, *Virginia Commonwealth University*

John Moran, *Syracuse University*

Shahriar Mostashari, *Campbell University*

John Morgan, *Haas Business School (University of California–Berkeley)*

Ram Mudambi, *Temple University*

Francis Mummery, *California State University–Fullerton*

Inder Nijhawan, *Fayetteville State University*

Albert A. Okunade, *University of Memphis*

Walton M. Padelford, Union University

Darrell Parker, *Georgia Southern University*

Stephen Pollard, California State University, *Los Angeles*

Dwight A. Porter, *College of St. Thomas*

Stanko Racic, *University of Pittsburgh*

Eric Rasmusen, *Indiana University*

Matthew Roelofs, *Western Washington University*

Christian Roessler, *National University of Singapore*

Bansi Sawhney, *University of Baltimore*

George L. Schatz, *Maine Maritime Academy*

Craig Schulman, *University of Arkansas*

Karen Schultes, *University of Michigan–Dearborn*

Peter M. Schwartz, *University of North Carolina*

Richard Alan Seals Jr., *Oklahoma City University*

Edward Shinnick, *University College Ireland*

Dean Showalter, *Southwest Texas State University*

Chandra Shrestha, *Virginia Commonwealth University*

Karen Smith, *Columbia Southern University*

John Stapleford, *Eastern University*

Mark Stegeman, *University of Arizona*

Ed Steinberg, *New York University*

Barbara M. Suleski, *Cardinal Stritch College*

Caroline Swartz, *University of North Carolina Charlotte*

Joseph K. Tanimura, *San Diego State University*

Bill Taylor, *New Mexico Highlands University*

Roger Tutterow, *Kennesaw State College*

Nora Underwood, *University of Central Florida*

Lskavyan Vahe, *Ohio University*

Lawrence White, *Stern School of Business (New York University)*

Leonard White, *University of Arkansas*

Keith Willett, *Oklahoma State University—Stillwater*

Mike Williams, *Bethune Cookman College*

Richard Winkelman, *Arizona State University*

Eduardo Zambrano, *University of Notre Dame*

Rick Zuber, *University of North Carolina, Charlotte*

We thank Michele Janicek, Christina Kouvelis, Douglas Reiner, and Scott Smith at McGraw-Hill for all they have done to make this project a success. We also thank Mitchell Baye, Patrick Scholten, Eric Schmidbauer, Susan Kayser, and Vikram Ahuja for suggestions and assistance during various stages of the revision, and Ellie Mafi-Kreft, Haizhen Lin, and Steven Kreft, who graciously agreed to class test the Connect Plus features in their classrooms. Finally, we thank our families for their continued love and support.

As always, we welcome your comments and suggestions for the next edition. Please feel free to write to us directly at *mbaye@indiana.edu* or *jeffprin@indiana.edu*.

Michael R. Baye
Jeffrey T. Prince

BRIEF CONTENTS

CONTENTS

CHAPTER TWO
Market Forces: Demand and Supply 37

CHAPTER THREE
Quantitative Demand Analysis   77

CHAPTER FOUR
The Theory of Individual Behavior   123

CHAPTER FIVE
The Production Process and Costs   163

CHAPTER SIX
The Organization of the Firm   210

CHAPTER SEVEN
The Nature of Industry   245

CHAPTER EIGHT

Managing in Competitive, Monopolistic, and Monopolistically Competitive Markets   274

CHAPTER NINE
Basic Oligopoly Models   325

CHAPTER TEN
Game Theory: Inside Oligopoly   364

CHAPTER ELEVEN
Pricing Strategies for Firms with Market Power   409

CHAPTER TWELVE

The Economics of Information   447

CHAPTER THIRTEEN
Advanced Topics in Business Strategy   487

CHAPTER FOURTEEN

A Manager's Guide to Government in the Marketplace   523

CHAPTER ONE

The Fundamentals of Managerial Economics

Amcott Loses $3.5 Million; Manager Fired

On Tuesday software giant Amcott posted a year-end operating loss of $3.5 million. Reportedly, $1.7 million of the loss stemmed from its foreign language division.

    With short-term interest rates at 7 percent, Amcott decided to use $20 million of its retained earnings to purchase three-year rights to Magicword, a software package that converts generic word processor files saved as French text into English. First-year sales revenue from the software was $7 million, but thereafter sales were halted pending a copyright infringement suit filed by Foreign, Inc. Amcott lost the suit and paid damages of $1.7 million. Industry insiders say that the copyright violation pertained to "a very small component of Magicword."

    Ralph, the Amcott manager who was fired over the incident, was quoted as saying, "I'm a scapegoat for the attorneys [at Amcott] who didn't do their homework before buying the rights to Magicword. I projected annual sales of $7 million per year for three years. My sales forecasts were right on target."

    Do you know why Ralph was fired?[1]

Learning Objectives

After completing this chapter, you will be able to:

LO1 Summarize how goals, constraints, incentives, and market rivalry affect economic decisions.

LO2 Distinguish economic versus accounting profits and costs.

LO3 Explain the role of profits in a market economy.

LO4 Apply the five forces framework to analyze the sustainability of an industry's profits.

LO5 Apply present value analysis to make decisions and value assets.

LO6 Apply marginal analysis to determine the optimal level of a managerial control variable.

LO7 Identify and apply six principles of effective managerial decision making.

---

[1]Each chapter concludes with an answer to the question posed in that chapter's opening headline. After you read each chapter, you should attempt to solve the opening headline on your own and then compare your solution to that presented at the end of the chapter.

INTRODUCTION

Many students taking managerial economics ask, "Why should I study economics? Will it tell me what the stock market will do tomorrow? Will it tell me where to invest my money or how to get rich?" Unfortunately, managerial economics by itself is unlikely to provide definitive answers to such questions. Obtaining the answers would require an accurate crystal ball. Nevertheless, managerial economics is a valuable tool for analyzing business situations such as the ones raised in the headlines that open each chapter of this book.

In fact, if you surf the Internet, browse a business publication such as *BusinessWeek* or *The Wall Street Journal,* or read a trade publication like *Restaurant News* or *Supermarket Business News,* you will find a host of stories that involve managerial economics. A recent search generated the following headlines:

"The Dodge Dart marks Chrysler's renaissance"

"ConocoPhillips completes spinoff of refining business"

"Charles Schwab cuts some of its ETF fees. Will rivals match?

"Apple accused of price-fixing"

"Competition heats up for Northwest wine shipping"

"U.S. Government steps up challenges to hospital mergers"

"Brands rethink social media strategy"

"Google buys QuickOffice"

Sadly, billions of dollars are lost each year because many existing managers fail to use basic tools from managerial economics to shape pricing and output decisions, optimize the production process and input mix, choose product quality, guide horizontal and vertical merger decisions, or optimally design internal and external incentives. Happily, if you learn a few basic principles from managerial economics, you will be poised to drive the inept managers out of their jobs! You will also understand why the latest recession was great news to some firms and why some software firms spend millions on the development of applications for smart phones but permit consumers to download them for free.

Managerial economics is not only valuable to managers of *Fortune* 500 companies; it is also valuable to managers of not-for-profit organizations. It is useful to the manager of a food bank who must decide the best means for distributing food to the needy. It is valuable to the coordinator of a shelter for the homeless whose goal is to help the largest possible number of homeless, given a very tight budget. In fact, managerial economics provides useful insights into every facet of the business and nonbusiness world in which we live—including household decision making.

Why is managerial economics so valuable to such a diverse group of decision makers? The answer to this question lies in the meaning of the term *managerial economics.*

The Manager

manager
A person who directs resources to achieve a stated goal.

A *manager* is a person who directs resources to achieve a stated goal. This definition includes all individuals who (1) direct the efforts of others, including those who delegate tasks within an organization such as a firm, a family, or a club; (2) purchase inputs to be used in the production of goods and services such as the output of a firm, food for the needy, or shelter for the homeless; or (3) are in charge of making other decisions, such as product price or quality.

A manager generally has responsibility for his or her own actions as well as for the actions of individuals, machines, and other inputs under the manager's control. This control may involve responsibilities for the resources of a multinational corporation or for those of a single household. In each instance, however, a manager must direct resources and the behavior of individuals for the purpose of accomplishing some task. While much of this book assumes the manager's task is to maximize the profits of the firm that employs the manager, the underlying principles are valid for virtually any decision process.

Economics

economics
The science of making decisions in the presence of scarce resources.

The primary focus of this book is on the second word in *managerial economics. Economics* is the science of making decisions in the presence of scarce resources. *Resources* are simply anything used to produce a good or service or, more generally, to achieve a goal. Decisions are important because scarcity implies that by making one choice, you give up another. A computer firm that spends more resources on advertising has fewer resources to invest in research and development. A food bank that spends more on soup has less to spend on fruit. Economic decisions thus involve the allocation of scarce resources, and a manager's task is to allocate resources so as to best meet the manager's goals.

One of the best ways to comprehend the pervasive nature of scarcity is to imagine that a genie has appeared and offered to grant you three wishes. If resources were not scarce, you would tell the genie you have absolutely nothing to wish for; you already have everything you want. Surely, as you begin this course, you recognize that time is one of the scarcest resources of all. Your primary decision problem is to allocate a scarce resource—time—to achieve a goal—such as mastering the subject matter or earning an A in the course.

Managerial Economics Defined

managerial economics
The study of how to direct scarce resources in the way that most efficiently achieves a managerial goal.

Managerial economics, therefore, is the study of how to direct scarce resources in the way that most efficiently achieves a managerial goal. It is a very broad discipline in that it describes methods useful for directing everything from the resources of a household to maximize household welfare to the resources of a firm to maximize profits.

To understand the nature of decisions that confront managers of firms, imagine that you are the manager of a *Fortune* 500 company that makes computers. You must make a host of decisions to succeed as a manager: Should you purchase components such as disk drives and chips from other manufacturers or produce them within your own firm? Should you specialize in making one type of computer or produce several different types? How many computers should you produce, and at what price should you sell them? How many employees should you hire, and how should you compensate them? How can you ensure that employees work hard and produce quality products? How will the actions of rival computer firms affect your decisions?

The key to making sound decisions is to know what information is needed to make an informed decision and then to collect and process the data. If you work for a large firm, your legal department can provide data about the legal ramifications of alternative decisions; your accounting department can provide tax advice and basic cost data; your marketing department can provide you with data on the characteristics of the market for your product; and your firm's financial analysts can provide summary data for alternative methods of obtaining financial capital. Ultimately, however, the manager must integrate all of this information, process it, and arrive at a decision. The remainder of this book will show you how to perform this important managerial function by using six principles that comprise effective management.

THE ECONOMICS OF EFFECTIVE MANAGEMENT

The nature of sound managerial decisions varies depending on the underlying goals of the manager. Since this course is designed primarily for managers of firms, this book focuses on managerial decisions as they relate to maximizing profits or, more generally, the value of the firm. Before embarking on this special use of managerial economics, we provide an overview of the basic principles that comprise effective management. In particular, an effective manager must (1) identify goals and constraints; (2) recognize the nature and importance of profits; (3) understand incentives; (4) understand markets; (5) recognize the time value of money; and (6) use marginal analysis.

Identify Goals and Constraints

The first step in making sound decisions is to have well-defined *goals* because achieving different goals entails making different decisions. If your goal is to maximize your grade in this course rather than maximize your overall grade point average, your study habits will differ accordingly. Similarly, if the goal of a food bank is to distribute food to needy people in rural areas, its decisions and optimal distribution network will differ from those it would use to distribute food to needy inner-city residents. Notice that in both instances, the decision maker faces *constraints* that affect the ability to achieve a goal. The 24-hour day affects your ability to earn an A in this course; a budget affects the ability of the food bank to distribute food to the needy. Constraints are an artifact of scarcity.

Different units within a firm may be given different goals; those in a firm's marketing department might be instructed to use their resources to maximize sales or market share, while those in the firm's financial group might focus on earnings growth or risk-reduction strategies. Later in this book we will see how the firm's overall goal—maximizing profits—can be achieved by giving each unit within the firm an incentive to achieve potentially different goals.

Unfortunately, constraints make it difficult for managers to achieve goals such as maximizing profits or increasing market share. These constraints include such things as the available technology and the prices of inputs used in production. The goal of maximizing profits requires the manager to decide the optimal price to charge for a product, how much to produce, which technology to use, how much of each input to use, how to react to decisions made by competitors, and so on. This book provides tools for answering these types of questions.

Recognize the Nature and Importance of Profits

The overall goal of most firms is to maximize profits or the firm's value, and the remainder of this book will detail strategies managers can use to achieve this goal. Before we provide these details, let us examine the nature and importance of profits in a free-market economy.

Economic versus Accounting Profits

When most people hear the word *profit*, they think of accounting profits. *Accounting profit* is the total amount of money taken in from sales (total revenue, or price times quantity sold) minus the dollar cost of producing goods or services. Accounting profits are what show up on the firm's income statement and are typically reported to the manager by the firm's accounting department.

economic profits
The difference between total revenue and total opportunity cost.

opportunity cost
The explicit cost of a resource plus the implicit cost of giving up its best alternative use.

A more general way to define profits is in terms of what economists refer to as economic profits. *Economic profits* are the difference between the total revenue and the total opportunity cost of producing the firm's goods or services. The *opportunity cost* of using a resource includes both the *explicit* (or *accounting*) *cost* of the resource and the *implicit cost* of giving up the best alternative use of the resource. The opportunity cost of producing a good or service generally is higher than accounting costs because it includes both the dollar value of costs (explicit, or accounting, costs) and any implicit costs.

Implicit costs are very hard to measure and therefore managers often overlook them. Effective managers, however, continually seek out data from other sources to identify and quantify implicit costs. Managers of large firms can use sources within the company, including the firm's finance, marketing, and/or legal departments, to obtain data about the implicit costs of decisions. In other instances managers must collect data on their own. For example, what does it cost you to read this book? The price you paid the bookseller for this book is an explicit (or accounting) cost, while the implicit cost is the value of what you are giving up by reading the book. You could be studying some other subject or watching TV, and each of these alternatives has some value to you. The "best" of these alternatives is your implicit cost of reading this book; you are giving up this alternative to read the book. Similarly, the opportunity cost of going to school is much higher than the cost of tuition and books; it also includes the amount of money you would earn had you decided to work rather than go to school.

In the business world, the opportunity cost of opening a restaurant is the best alternative use of the resources used to establish the restaurant—say, opening a hairstyling salon. Again, these resources include not only the explicit financial resources needed to open the business but any implicit costs as well. Suppose you own a building in New York that you use to run a small pizzeria. Food supplies are your only accounting costs. At the end of the year, your accountant informs you that these costs were $20,000 and that your revenues were $100,000. Thus, your accounting profits are $80,000.

However, these accounting profits overstate your economic profits, because the costs include only accounting costs. First, the costs do not include the time you spent running the business. Had you not run the business, you could have worked for someone else, and this fact reflects an economic cost not accounted for in accounting profits. To be concrete, suppose you could have worked for someone else for $30,000. Your opportunity cost of time would have been $30,000 for the year. Thus, $30,000 of your accounting profits are not profits at all but one of the implicit costs of running the pizzeria.

Second, accounting costs do not account for the fact that, had you not run the pizzeria, you could have rented the building to someone else. If the rental value of the building is $100,000 per year, you gave up this amount to run your own business. Thus, the costs of running the pizzeria include not only the costs of supplies ($20,000) but the $30,000 you could have earned in some other business *and* the $100,000 you could have earned in renting the building to someone else. The economic cost of running the pizzeria is $150,000—the amount you gave up to run your business. Considering the revenue of $100,000, you actually lost $50,000 by running the pizzeria; your *economic profits* were −$50,000.

Throughout this book, when we speak of costs, we mean economic costs. Economic costs are opportunity costs and include not only the explicit (accounting) costs but also the implicit costs of the resources used in production.

The Role of Profits

A common misconception is that the firm's goal of maximizing profits is necessarily bad for society. Individuals who want to maximize profits often are considered self-interested, a quality that many people view as undesirable. However, consider Adam Smith's classic line from *The Wealth of Nations:* "It is not out of the benevolence of the butcher, the brewer, or the baker, that we expect our dinner, but from their regard to their own interest."[2]

---

[2]Adam Smith, *An Inquiry into the Nature and Causes of the Wealth of Nations,* 1776.

INSIDE BUSINESS 1–1

The Goals of Firms in Our Global Economy

Recent trends in globalization have forced businesses around the world to more keenly focus on profitability. This trend is also present in Japan, where historical links between banks and businesses have traditionally blurred the goals of firms. For example, the Japanese business engineering firm, Mitsui & Co. Ltd., launched "Challenge 21," a plan directed at helping the company emerge as Japan's leading business engineering group. According to a spokesperson for the company, "[This plan permits us to] create new value and maximize profitability by taking steps such as renewing our management framework and prioritizing the allocation of our resources into strategic areas. We are committed to maximizing shareholder value through business conduct that balances the pursuit of earnings with socially responsible behavior."

Ultimately, the goal of any continuing company must be to maximize the value of the firm. This goal is often achieved by trying to hit intermediate targets, such as minimizing costs or increasing market share. If you—as a manager—do not maximize your firm's value over time, you will be in danger of either going out of business, being taken over by other owners (as in a leveraged buyout), or having stockholders elect to replace you and other managers.

Source: "Mitsui & Co., Ltd. UK Regulatory Announcement: Final Results," *Business Wire*, May 13, 2004.

Smith is saying that by pursuing its self-interest—the goal of maximizing profits—a firm ultimately meets the needs of society. If you cannot make a living as a rock singer, it is probably because society does not appreciate your singing; society would more highly value your talents in some other employment. If you break five dishes each time you clean up after dinner, your talents are perhaps better suited for filing paperwork or mowing the lawn. Similarly, the profits of businesses signal where society's scarce resources are best allocated. When firms in a given industry earn economic profits, the opportunity cost to resource holders outside the industry increases. Owners of other resources soon recognize that, by continuing to operate their existing businesses, they are giving up profits. This induces new firms to enter the markets in which economic profits are available. As more firms enter the industry, the market price falls, and economic profits decline.

Thus, profits signal the owners of resources where the resources are most highly valued by society. By moving scarce resources toward the production of goods most valued by society, the total welfare of society is improved. As Adam Smith first noted, this phenomenon is due not to benevolence on the part of the firms' managers but to the self-interested goal of maximizing the firms' profits.

Principle	**Profits Are a Signal**
	Profits signal to resource holders where resources are most highly valued by society.

FIGURE 1–1   The Five Forces Framework

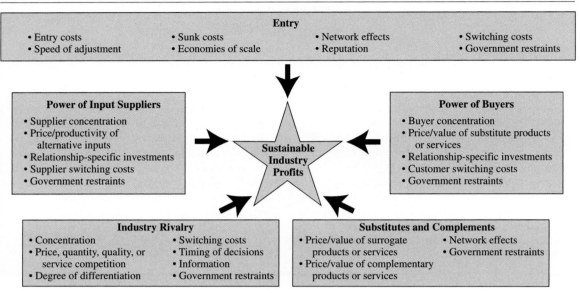

The Five Forces Framework and Industry Profitability

A key theme of this textbook is that many interrelated forces and decisions influence the level, growth, and sustainability of profits. If you or other managers in the industry are clever enough to identify strategies that yield a windfall to shareholders this quarter, there is no guarantee that these profits will be sustained in the long run. You must recognize that profits are a signal—if your business earns superior profits, existing and potential competitors will do their best to get a piece of the action. In the remaining chapters we will examine a variety of business strategies designed to enhance your prospects of earning and sustaining profits. Before we do so, however, it is constructive to provide a conceptual framework for thinking about some of the factors that impact industry profitability.

Figure 1–1 illustrates the *"five forces" framework* pioneered by Michael Porter.[3] This framework organizes many complex managerial economics issues into five categories or "forces" that impact the sustainability of industry profits: (1) entry, (2) power of input suppliers, (3) power of buyers, (4) industry rivalry, and (5) substitutes and complements. The discussion below explains how these forces influence industry profitability and highlights the connections among these forces and material covered in the remaining chapters of the text.

Entry.   As we will see in Chapters 2, 7, and 8, entry heightens competition and reduces the margins of existing firms in a wide variety of industry settings. For this reason, the ability of existing firms to sustain profits depends on how barriers to

---

[3]Michael Porter, *Competitive Strategy* (New York: Free Press, 1980).

entry affect the ease with which other firms can enter the industry. Entry can come from a number of directions, including the formation of new companies (Wendy's entered the fast-food industry in the 1970s after its founder, Dave Thomas, left KFC); globalization strategies by foreign companies (Toyota sold vehicles in Japan since the 1930s but waited until the middle of the last century to enter the U.S. automobile market); and the introduction of new product lines by existing firms (computer manufacturer Apple now also sells the popular iPhone).

As shown in Figure 1–1, a number of economic factors affect the ability of entrants to erode existing industry profits. In subsequent chapters, you will learn why entrants are less likely to capture market share quickly enough to justify the costs of entry in environments where there are sizeable sunk costs (Chapters 5, 9), significant economies of scale (Chapters 5, 8), or significant network effects (Chapter 13), or where existing firms have invested in strong reputations for providing value to a sizeable base of loyal consumers (Chapter 11) or to aggressively fight entrants (Chapters 10, and 13). In addition, you will gain a better appreciation for the role that governments play in shaping entry through patents and licenses (Chapter 8), trade policies (Chapters 5 and 14), and environmental legislation (Chapter 14). We will also identify a variety of strategies to raise the costs to consumers of "switching" to would-be entrants, thereby lowering the threat that entrants will erode your profits.

Power of Input Suppliers. Industry profits tend to be lower when suppliers have the power to negotiate favorable terms for their inputs. Supplier power tends to be low when inputs are relatively standardized and relationship-specific investments are minimal (Chapter 6), input markets are not highly concentrated (Chapter 7), or alternative inputs are available with similar marginal productivities per dollar spent (Chapter 5). In many countries, the government constrains the prices of inputs through price ceilings and other controls (Chapters 2 and 14), which limits to some extent the ability of suppliers to expropriate profits from firms in the industry.

Power of Buyers. Similar to the case of suppliers, industry profits tend to be lower when customers or buyers have the power to negotiate favorable terms for the products or services produced in the industry. In most consumer markets, buyers are fragmented and thus buyer concentration is low. Buyer concentration and hence customer power tend to be higher in industries that serve relatively few "high-volume" customers. Buyer power tends to be lower in industries where the cost to customers of switching to other products is high—as is often the case when there are relationship-specific investments and hold-up problems (Chapter 6), imperfect information that leads to costly consumer search (Chapter 12), or few close substitutes for the product (Chapters 2, 3, 4, and 11). Government regulations, such as price floors or price ceilings (Chapters 2 and 14), can also impact the ability of buyers to obtain more favorable terms.

Industry Rivalry. The sustainability of industry profits also depends on the nature and intensity of rivalry among firms competing in the industry. Rivalry tends to be less intense (and hence the likelihood of sustaining profits is higher) in concentrated industries—that is, those with relatively few firms. In Chapter 7 we will take a closer look at various measures that can be used to gauge industry concentration.

The level of product differentiation and the nature of the game being played—whether firms' strategies involve prices, quantities, capacity, or quality/service attributes, for example—also impact profitability. In later chapters you will learn why rivalry tends to be more intense in industry settings where there is little product differentiation and firms compete in price (Chapters 8, 9, 10, and 11) and where consumer switching costs are low (Chapters 11 and 12). You will also learn how imperfect information and the timing of decisions affect rivalry among firms (Chapters 10, 12, and 13).

Substitutes and Complements.   The level and sustainability of industry profits also depend on the price and value of interrelated products and services. Porter's original five forces framework emphasized that the presence of close substitutes erodes industry profitability. In Chapters 2, 3, 4, and 11 you will learn how to quantify the degree to which surrogate products are close substitutes by using elasticity analysis and models of consumer behavior. We will also see that government policies (such as restrictions limiting the importation of prescription drugs from Canada into the United States) can directly impact the availability of substitutes and thus industry profits.

More recent work by economists and business strategists emphasizes that complementarities also affect industry profitability.[4] For example, Microsoft's profitability in the market for operating systems is enhanced by the presence of complementary products ranging from relatively inexpensive computer hardware to a plethora of Windows-compatible application software. Analogously, Apple's profitability in the cell phone market is enhanced by the tens of thousands of complementary applications ("apps") that are compatible with its iPhone. In Chapters 3, 5, 10, and 13 you will learn how to quantify these complementarities or "synergies" and identify strategies to create and exploit complementarities and network effects.

In concluding, it is important to recognize that the many forces that impact the level and sustainability of industry profits are interrelated. For instance, the U.S. automobile industry suffered a sharp decline in industry profitability during the 1970s as a result of sharp increases in the price of gasoline (a complement to automobiles). This change in the price of a complementary product enabled Japanese automakers to *enter* the U.S. market through a differentiation strategy of marketing their fuel-efficient cars, which sold like hotcakes compared to the gas-guzzlers American automakers produced at that time. These events, in turn, have had a profound impact on industry rivalry in the automotive industry—not just in the United States, but worldwide.

It is also important to stress that the five forces framework is primarily a tool for helping managers see the "big picture"; it is a schematic you can use to organize various industry conditions that affect industry profitability and assess the efficacy of alternative business strategies. However, it would be a mistake to view it as a comprehensive list of all factors that affect industry profitability. The five forces

---

[4]See, for example, Barry J. Nalebuff and Adam M. Brandenburger, *Co-Opetition* (New York: Doubleday, 1996) as well as R. Preston McAfee, *Competitive Solutions* (Princeton: Princeton University Press, 2002).

INSIDE BUSINESS 1–2

Profits and the Evolution of the Computer Industry

When profits in a given industry are higher than in other industries, new firms will attempt to enter that industry. When losses are recorded, some firms will likely leave the industry. This sort of "evolution" has changed the global landscape of personal computer markets.

At the start of the PC era, personal computer makers enjoyed positive economic profits. These higher profits led to new entry and heightened competition. Over the past two decades, entry has led to declines in PC prices and industry profitability despite significant increases in the speed and storage capacities of PCs. Less efficient firms have been forced to exit the market.

In the early 2000s, IBM—the company that launched the PC era when it introduced the IBM PC in the early 1980s—sold its PC business to China-based Lenovo. Compaq—an early leader in the market for PCs—has since been acquired by Hewlett-Packard. A handful of small PC makers have enjoyed some success competing against the remaining traditional players, which include Dell and Hewlett-Packard. By the late 2000s, Dell's strategy switched from selling computers directly to consumers to entering into relationships with retailers such as BestBuy and Staples. While only time will tell how these strategies will impact the long-run viability of traditional players, competitive pressures continue to push PC prices and industry profits downward.

---

framework is not a substitute for understanding the economic principles that underlie sound business decisions.

Understand Incentives

In our discussion of the role of profits, we emphasized that profits signal the holders of resources when to enter and exit particular industries. In effect, changes in profits provide an incentive to resource holders to alter their use of resources. Within a firm, *incentives* affect how resources are used and how hard workers work. To succeed as a manager, you must have a clear grasp of the role of incentives within an organization such as a firm and how to construct incentives to induce maximal effort from those you manage. Chapter 6 is devoted to this special aspect of managerial decision making, but it is useful here to provide a synopsis of how to construct proper incentives.

The first step in constructing incentives within a firm is to distinguish between the world, or the business place, as it is and the way you wish it were. Many professionals and owners of small establishments have difficulties because they do not fully comprehend the importance of the role incentives play in guiding the decisions of others.

A friend of ours—Mr. O—opened a restaurant and hired a manager to run the business so he could spend time doing the things he enjoys. Recently, we asked him how his business was doing, and he reported that he had been losing money ever since the restaurant opened. When asked whether he thought the manager was doing a good job, he said, "For the $75,000 salary I pay the manager each year, the manager *should* be doing a good job."

Mr. O believes the manager "should be doing a good job." This is the way he wishes the world was. But individuals often are motivated by self-interest. This is not to say that people never act out of kindness or charity, but rather that human nature is such that people naturally tend to look after their own self-interest. Had Mr. O taken a managerial economics course, he would know how to provide the manager with an incentive to do what is in Mr. O's best interest. The key is to design a mechanism such that if the manager does what is in *his* own interest, he will indirectly do what is best for Mr. O.

Since Mr. O is not physically present at the restaurant to watch over the manager, he has no way of knowing what the manager is up to. Indeed, his unwillingness to spend time at the restaurant is what induced him to hire the manager in the first place. What type of incentive has he created by paying the manager $75,000 per year? The manager receives $75,000 per year regardless of whether he puts in 12-hour or 2-hour days. The manager receives no reward for working hard and incurs no penalty if he fails to make sound managerial decisions. The manager receives the same $75,000 regardless of the restaurant's profitability.

Fortunately, most business owners understand the problem just described. The owners of large corporations are shareholders, and most never set foot on company ground. How do they provide incentives for chief executive officers (CEOs) to be effective managers? Very simply, they provide them with "incentive plans" in the form of bonuses. These bonuses are in direct proportion to the firm's profitability. If the firm does well, the CEO receives a large bonus. If the firm does poorly, the CEO receives no bonus and risks being fired by the stockholders. These types of incentives are also present at lower levels within firms. Some individuals earn commissions based on the revenue they generate for the firm's owner. If they put forth little effort, they receive little pay; if they put forth much effort and hence generate many sales, they receive a generous commission.

The thrust of managerial economics is to provide you with a broad array of skills that enable you to make sound economic decisions and to structure appropriate incentives within your organization. We will begin under the assumption that everyone with whom you come into contact is greedy, that is, interested only in his or her own self-interest. In such a case, understanding incentives is a must. Of course, this is a worst-case scenario; more likely, some of your business contacts will not be so selfishly inclined. If you are so lucky, your job will be all the easier.

Understand Markets

In studying microeconomics in general, and managerial economics in particular, it is important to bear in mind that there are two sides to every transaction in a market: For every buyer of a good there is a corresponding seller. The final outcome of the market process, then, depends on the relative power of buyers and sellers in the marketplace. The power, or bargaining position, of consumers and producers in the market is limited by three sources of rivalry that exist in economic transactions: consumer–producer rivalry, consumer–consumer rivalry, and producer–producer rivalry. Each form of rivalry serves as a disciplining device to guide the market process, and each affects different markets to a different extent. Thus, your ability as a manager to meet performance objectives will depend on the extent to which your product is affected by these sources of rivalry.

Consumer–Producer Rivalry

Consumer–producer rivalry occurs because of the competing interests of consumers and producers. Consumers attempt to negotiate or locate low prices, while producers attempt to negotiate high prices. In a very loose sense, consumers attempt to "rip off" producers, and producers attempt to "rip off" consumers. Of course, there are limits to the ability of these parties to achieve their goals. If a consumer offers a price that is too low, the producer will refuse to sell the product to the consumer. Similarly, if the producer asks a price that exceeds the consumer's valuation of a good, the consumer will refuse to purchase the good. These two forces provide a natural check and balance on the market process even in markets in which the product is offered by a single firm (a monopolist). An illustrative example of this type of rivalry is the common haggling over price between a potential car buyer and salesperson.

Consumer–Consumer Rivalry

A second source of rivalry that guides the market process occurs among consumers. *Consumer–consumer rivalry* reduces the negotiating power of consumers in the marketplace. It arises because of the economic doctrine of scarcity. When limited quantities of goods are available, consumers will compete with one another for the right to purchase the available goods. Consumers who are willing to pay the highest prices for the scarce goods will outbid other consumers for the right to consume the goods. Once again, this source of rivalry is present even in markets in which a single firm is selling a product. A good example of consumer–consumer rivalry is an auction, a topic we will examine in detail in Chapter 12.

Producer–Producer Rivalry

A third source of rivalry in the marketplace is *producer–producer rivalry.* Unlike the other forms of rivalry, this disciplining device functions only when multiple sellers of a product compete in the marketplace. Given that customers are scarce, producers compete with one another for the right to service the customers available. Those firms that offer the best-quality product at the lowest price earn the right to serve the customers. For example, when two gas stations located across the street from one another compete on price, they are engaged in producer–producer rivalry.

Government and the Market

When agents on either side of the market find themselves disadvantaged in the market process, they frequently attempt to induce government to intervene on their behalf. For example, the market for electricity in most towns is characterized by a sole local supplier of electricity, and thus there is no producer–producer rivalry. Consumer groups may initiate action by a public utility commission to limit the power of utilities in setting prices. Similarly, producers may lobby for government assistance to place them in a better bargaining position relative to consumers and foreign producers. Thus, in modern economies government also plays a role in disciplining the market process. Chapter 14 explores how government affects managerial decisions.

Recognize the Time Value of Money

The timing of many decisions involves a gap between the time when the costs of a project are borne and the time when the benefits of the project are received. In these instances it is important to recognize that $1 today is worth more than $1 received in the future. The reason is simple: The opportunity cost of receiving the $1 in the future is the forgone interest that could be earned were $1 received today. This opportunity cost reflects the *time value of money.* To properly account for the timing of receipts and expenditures, the manager must understand present value analysis.

Present Value Analysis

present value
The amount that would have to be invested today at the prevailing interest rate to generate the given future value.

The *present value (PV)* of an amount received in the future is the amount that would have to be invested today at the prevailing interest rate to generate the given future value. For example, suppose someone offered you $1.10 one year from today. What is the value today (the present value) of $1.10 to be received one year from today? Notice that if you could invest $1.00 today at a guaranteed interest rate of 10 percent, one year from now $1.00 would be worth $1.00 × 1.1 = $1.10. In other words, over the course of one year, your $1.00 would earn $.10 in interest. Thus, when the interest rate is 10 percent, the present value of receiving $1.10 one year in the future is $1.00.

A more general formula follows:

Formula (Present Value).   The present value (*PV*) of a future value (*FV*) received *n* years in the future is

$$PV = \frac{FV}{(1 + i)^n} \tag{1–1}$$

where *i* is the rate of interest, or the opportunity cost of funds.

For example, the present value of $100.00 in 10 years if the interest rate is at 7 percent is $50.83, since

$$PV = \frac{\$100}{(1 + .07)^{10}} = \frac{\$100}{1.9672} = \$50.83$$

This essentially means that if you invested $50.83 today at a 7 percent interest rate, in 10 years your investment would be worth $100.

Notice that the interest rate appears in the denominator of the expression in Equation 1–1. This means that the higher the interest rate, the lower the present value of a future amount, and conversely. The present value of a future payment reflects the difference between the *future value (FV)* and the *opportunity cost of waiting (OCW)*: $PV = FV - OCW$. Intuitively, the higher the interest rate, the higher the opportunity cost of waiting to receive a future amount and thus the lower the present value of the future amount. For example, if the interest rate is zero, the opportunity cost of waiting is zero, and the present value and the future value coincide. This is consistent with Equation 1–1, since $PV = FV$ when the interest rate is zero.

The basic idea of the present value of a future amount can be extended to a series of future payments. For example, if you are promised FV_1 one year in the future, FV_2 two years in the future, and so on for n years, the present value of this sum of future payments is

$$PV = \frac{FV_1}{(1 + i)^1} + \frac{FV_2}{(1 + i)^2} + \frac{FV_3}{(1 + i)^3} + \cdots + \frac{FV_n}{(1 + i)^n}$$

Formula (Present Value of a Stream). When the interest rate is i, the present value of a stream of future payments of $FV_1, FV_2, \ldots, FV_n$ is

$$PV = \sum_{t=1}^{n} \frac{FV_t}{(1 + i)^t}$$

net present value
The present value of the income stream generated by a project minus the current cost of the project.

Given the present value of the income stream that arises from a project, one can easily compute the net present value of the project. The *net present value (NPV)* of a project is simply the present value (PV) of the income stream generated by the project minus the current cost (C_0) of the project: $NPV = PV - C_0$. If the net present value of a project is positive, then the project is profitable because the present value of the earnings from the project exceeds the current cost of the project. On the other hand, a manager should reject a project that has a negative net present value, since the cost of such a project exceeds the present value of the income stream that project generates.

Formula (Net Present Value). Suppose that by sinking C_0 dollars into a project today, a firm will generate income of FV_1 one year in the future, FV_2 two years in the future, and so on for n years. If the interest rate is i, the net present value of the project is

$$NPV = \frac{FV_1}{(1 + i)^1} + \frac{FV_2}{(1 + i)^2} + \frac{FV_3}{(1 + i)^3} + \cdots + \frac{FV_n}{(1 + i)^n} - C_0$$

Demonstration Problem 1-1

The manager of Automated Products is contemplating the purchase of a new machine that will cost $300,000 and has a useful life of five years. The machine will yield (year-end) cost reductions to Automated Products of $50,000 in year 1, $60,000 in year 2, $75,000 in year 3, and $90,000 in years 4 and 5. What is the present value of the cost savings of the machine if the interest rate is 8 percent? Should the manager purchase the machine?

Answer:

By spending $300,000 today on a new machine, the firm will reduce costs by $365,000 over five years. However, the present value of the cost savings is only

$$PV = \frac{50,000}{1.08} + \frac{60,000}{1.08^2} + \frac{75,000}{1.08^3} + \frac{90,000}{1.08^4} + \frac{90,000}{1.08^5} = \$284,679$$

Consequently, the net present value of the new machine is

$$NPV = PV - C_0 = \$284,679 - \$300,000 = -\$15,321$$

Since the net present value of the machine is negative, the manager should not purchase the machine. In other words, the manager could earn more by investing the $300,000 at 8 percent than by spending the money on the cost-saving technology.

Present Value of Indefinitely Lived Assets

Some decisions generate cash flows that continue indefinitely. For instance, consider an asset that generates a cash flow of CF_0 today, CF_1 one year from today, CF_2 two years from today, and so on for an indefinite period of time. If the interest rate is i, the value of the asset is given by the present value of these cash flows:

$$PV_{Asset} = CF_0 + \frac{CF_1}{(1 + i)} + \frac{CF_2}{(1 + i)^2} + \frac{CF_3}{(1 + i)^3} + \cdots$$

While this formula contains terms that continue indefinitely, for certain patterns of future cash flows one can readily compute the present value of the asset. For instance, suppose that the current cash flow is zero ($CF_0 = 0$) and that all future cash flows are identical ($CF_1 = CF_2 = \ldots$). In this case the asset generates a perpetual stream of identical cash flows at the end of each period. If each of these future cash flows is CF, the value of the asset is the present value of the *perpetuity*:

$$PV_{Perpetuity} = \frac{CF}{(1 + i)} + \frac{CF}{(1 + i)^2} + \frac{CF}{(1 + i)^3} + \cdots$$
$$= \frac{CF}{i}$$

Examples of such an asset include perpetual bonds and preferred stocks. Each of these assets pays the owner a fixed amount at the end of each period, indefinitely. Based on the above formula, the value of a perpetual bond that pays the owner $100 at the end of each year when the interest rate is fixed at 5 percent is given by

$$PV_{Perpetual\ bond} = \frac{CF}{i} = \frac{\$100}{.05} = \$2,000$$

Present value analysis is also useful in determining the value of a firm, since the value of a firm is the present value of the stream of profits (cash flows) generated by the firm's physical, human, and intangible assets. In particular, if π_0 is the firm's current level of profits, and π_1 is next year's profit, and so on, then the value of the firm is

$$PV_{Firm} = \pi_0 + \frac{\pi_1}{(1 + i)} + \frac{\pi_2}{(1 + i)^2} + \frac{\pi_3}{(1 + i)^3} + \cdots$$

In other words, the value of the firm today is the present value of its current and future profits. To the extent that the firm is a "going concern" that lives on even after its founder dies, firm ownership represents a claim to assets with an indefinite profit stream.

Notice that the *value of a firm* takes into account the long-term impact of managerial decisions on profits. When economists say that the goal of the firm is to maximize profits, it should be understood to mean that the firm's goal is to maximize its value, which is the present value of current and future profits.

Principle	**Profit Maximization** Maximizing profits means maximizing the value of the firm, which is the present value of current and future profits.

While it is beyond the scope of this book to present all the tools Wall Street analysts use to estimate the value of firms, it is possible to gain insight into the issues involved by making a few simplifying assumptions. Suppose a firm's current profits are π_0, and that these profits have not yet been paid out to stockholders as dividends. Imagine that these profits are expected to grow at a constant rate of g percent each year, and that profit growth is less than the interest rate ($g < i$). In this case, profits one year from today will be $(1 + g)\pi_0$, profits two years from today will be $(1 + g)^2\pi_0$, and so on. The value of the firm, under these assumptions, is

$$PV_{Firm} = \pi_0 + \frac{\pi_0(1 + g)}{(1 + i)} + \frac{\pi_0(1 + g)^2}{(1 + i)^2} + \frac{\pi_0(1 + g)^3}{(1 + i)^3} + \cdots$$

$$= \pi_0 \left(\frac{1 + i}{i - g} \right)$$

For a given interest rate and growth rate of the firm, it follows that maximizing the lifetime value of the firm (long-term profits) is equivalent to maximizing the firm's current (short-term) profits of π_0.

You may wonder how this formula changes if current profits have already been paid out as dividends. In this case, the present value of the firm is the present value of future profits (since current profits have already been paid out). The value of the firm immediately after its current profits have been paid out as dividends (called the *ex-dividend date*) may be obtained by simply subtracting π_0 from the above equation:

$$PV_{Firm}^{Ex\text{-}dividend} = PV_{Firm} - \pi_0$$

This may be simplified to yield the following formula:

$$PV_{Firm}^{Ex\text{-}dividend} = \pi_0\left(\frac{1+g}{i-g}\right)$$

Thus, so long as the interest rate and growth rate are constant, the strategy of maximizing current profits also maximizes the value of the firm on the ex-dividend date.

Principle	**Maximizing Short-Term Profits May Maximize Long-Term Profits** If the growth rate in profits is less than the interest rate and both are constant, maximizing current (short-term) profits is the same as maximizing long-term profits.

Demonstration Problem 1–2

Suppose the interest rate is 10 percent and the firm is expected to grow at a rate of 5 percent for the foreseeable future. The firm's current profits are $100 million.

(a) What is the value of the firm (the present value of its current and future earnings)?

(b) What is the value of the firm immediately after it pays a dividend equal to its current profits?

Answer:

(a) The value of the firm is

$$PV_{Firm} = \pi_0 + \frac{\pi_0(1+g)}{(1+i)} + \frac{\pi_0(1+g)^2}{(1+i)^2} + \frac{\pi_0(1+g)^3}{(1+i)^3} + \cdots$$

$$= \pi_0\left(\frac{1+i}{i-g}\right)$$

$$= \$100\left(\frac{1+.1}{.1-.05}\right) = (\$100)(22) = \$2,200 \text{ million}$$

(b) The value of the firm on the ex-dividend date is this amount ($2,200 million) less the current profits paid out as dividends ($100 million), or $2,100 million. Alternatively, this may be calculated as

$$PV_{Firm}^{Ex\text{-}dividend} = \pi_0\left(\frac{1+g}{i-g}\right)$$

$$= (\$100)\left(\frac{1+.05}{.1-.05}\right) = (\$100)(21) = \$2,100 \text{ million}$$

INSIDE BUSINESS 1–3

Joining the Jet Set

Recently, US Airways offered a standard one-year membership into its US Airways Club for $450. Alternatively, one could purchase a three-month membership for $120. Many managers and executives join air clubs because they offer a quiet place to work or relax while on the road; thus, productivity is enhanced.

Let's assume you wish to join the club for one year. Should you pay the up-front $450 fee for a one-year membership or buy four three-month memberships at $120 each, for total payments of $480? For simplicity, let's suppose the airline will not change the three-month fee of $120 over the next year.

On the surface it appears that you save $30 by paying for a one-year membership in advance. But this approach ignores the time value of money. Is paying for a full year in advance profitable when you take the time value of money into account?

The present value of the cost of membership if you pay for one year in advance is $450, since all of that money is paid today. If you pay every three months, you pay $120 today, $120 in three months, $120 in six months, and $120 in nine months. Given an interest rate of 8 percent per year, which translates into a quarterly rate of 2 percent, the present value of payments is

$$PV = \$120 + \frac{\$120}{1.02} + \frac{\$120}{(1.02)^2} + \frac{\$120}{(1.02)^3}$$

or

$$PV = 120 + 117.65 + 115.34 + 113.08$$
$$= \$466.07$$

Thus, in present value terms, you save $16.07 if you pay for an annual membership in advance. If you wish to join for one year and expect three-month fees to either remain constant or rise over the next year, it is better to pay in advance. Given the current interest rate, the airline is offering a good deal, but the present value of the savings is $16.07, not $30.

While the notion of the present value of a firm is very general, the simplified formula presented above is based on the assumption that the growth rate of the firm's profits is constant. In reality, however, the investment and marketing strategies of the firm will affect its growth rate. Moreover, the strategies used by competitors generally will affect the growth rate of the firm. In such instances, there is no substitute for using the general present value formula and understanding the concepts developed in later chapters in this book.

Use Marginal Analysis

Marginal analysis is one of the most important managerial tools—a tool we will use repeatedly throughout this text in alternative contexts. Simply put, *marginal analysis* states that optimal managerial decisions involve comparing the marginal (or incremental) benefits of a decision with the marginal (or incremental) costs. For example, the optimal amount of studying for this course is determined by comparing (1) the improvement in your grade that will result from an additional hour of studying and (2) the additional costs of studying an additional hour. So long as the benefits of studying an additional hour exceed the costs of studying an additional hour, it is profitable to continue to study. However, once an additional hour of studying adds more to costs than it does to benefits, you should stop studying.

More generally, let $B(Q)$ denote the total benefits derived from Q units of some variable that is within the manager's control. This is a very general idea: $B(Q)$ may be the revenue a firm generates from producing Q units of output; it may be the benefits associated with distributing Q units of food to the needy; or, in the context of our previous example, it may represent the benefits derived by studying Q hours for an exam. Let $C(Q)$ represent the total costs of the corresponding level of Q. Depending on the nature of the decision problem, $C(Q)$ may be the total cost to a firm of producing Q units of output, the total cost to a food bank of providing Q units of food to the needy, or the total cost to you of studying Q hours for an exam.

Discrete Decisions

We first consider the situation where the managerial control variable is discrete. In this instance, the manager faces a situation like that summarized in columns 1 through 3 in Table 1–1. Notice that the manager cannot use fractional units of Q; only integer values are possible. This reflects the discrete nature of the problem. In the context of a production decision, Q may be the number of gallons of soft drink produced. The manager must decide how many gallons of soft drink to produce (0, 1, 2, and so on), but cannot choose to produce fractional units (for example, one pint). Column 2 of Table 1–1 provides hypothetical data for total benefits; column 3 gives hypothetical data for total costs.

Suppose the objective of the manager is to maximize the net benefits

$$N(Q) = B(Q) - C(Q),$$

which represent the premium of total benefits over total costs of using Q units of the managerial control variable, Q. The net benefits—$N(Q)$—for our hypothetical

TABLE 1–1   Determining the Optimal Level of a Control Variable: The Discrete Case

(1) Control Variable Q	(2) Total Benefits $B(Q)$	(3) Total Costs $C(Q)$	(4) Net Benefits $N(Q)$	(5) Marginal Benefit $MB(Q)$	(6) Marginal Cost $MC(Q)$	(7) Marginal Net Benefit $MNB(Q)$ $\Delta(4)$ or
Given	Given	Given	(2) – (3)	$\Delta(2)$	$\Delta(3)$	(5) – (6)
0	0	0	0	—	—	—
1	90	10	80	90	10	80
2	170	30	140	80	20	60
3	240	60	180	70	30	40
4	300	100	200	60	40	20
5	350	150	200	50	50	0
6	390	210	180	40	60	−20
7	420	280	140	30	70	−40
8	440	360	80	20	80	−60
9	450	450	0	10	90	−80
10	450	550	−100	0	100	−100

example are given in column 4 of Table 1–1. Notice that the net benefits in column 4 are maximized when net benefits equal 200, which occurs when 5 units of Q are chosen by the manager.[5]

To illustrate the importance of marginal analysis in maximizing net benefits, it is useful to define a few terms. *Marginal benefit* refers to the additional benefits that arise by using an additional unit of the managerial control variable. For example, the marginal benefit of the first unit of Q is 90, since the first unit of Q increases total benefits from 0 to 90. The marginal benefit of the second unit of Q is 80, since increasing Q from 1 to 2 increases total benefits from 90 to 170. The marginal benefit of each unit of Q—$MB(Q)$—is presented in column 5 of Table 1–1.

Marginal cost, on the other hand, is the additional cost incurred by using an additional unit of the managerial control variable. Marginal costs—$MC(Q)$—are given in column 6 of Table 1–1. For example, the marginal cost of the first unit of Q is 10, since the first unit of Q increases total costs from 0 to 10. Similarly, the marginal cost of the second unit of Q is 20, since increasing Q from 1 to 2 increases total costs by 20 (costs rise from 10 to 30).

Finally, the *marginal net benefits* of Q—$MNB(Q)$—are the change in net benefits that arise from a one-unit change in Q. For example, by increasing Q from 0 to 1, net benefits rise from 0 to 80 in column 4 of Table 1–1, and thus the marginal net benefit of the first unit of Q is 80. By increasing Q from 1 to 2, net benefits increase from 80 to 140, so the marginal net benefit due to the second unit of Q is 60. Column 7 of Table 1–1 presents marginal net benefits for our hypothetical example. Notice that marginal net benefits may also be obtained as the difference between marginal benefits and marginal costs:

$$MNB(Q) = MB(Q) - MC(Q)$$

Inspection of Table 1–1 reveals a remarkable pattern in the columns. Notice that by using 5 units of Q, the manager ensures that net benefits are maximized. At the net-benefit-maximizing level of Q (5 units), the marginal net benefits of Q are zero. Furthermore, at the net-benefit-maximizing level of Q (5 units), marginal benefits equal marginal costs (both are equal to 50 in this example). There is an important reason why $MB = MC$ at the level of Q that maximizes net benefits: So long as marginal benefits exceed marginal costs, an increase in Q adds more to total benefits than it does to total costs. In this instance, it is profitable for the manager to increase the use of the managerial control variable. Expressed differently, when marginal benefits exceed marginal costs, the net benefits of increasing the use of Q are positive; by using more Q, net benefits increase. For example, consider the use

marginal benefit
The change in total benefits arising from a change in the managerial control variable Q.

marginal cost
The change in total costs arising from a change in the managerial control variable Q.

---

[5]Actually, net benefits are equal to 200 for either 4 or 5 units of Q. This is due to the discrete nature of the data in the table, which restricts Q to be selected in one-unit increments. In the next section, we show that when Q can be selected in arbitrarily small increments (for example, when the firm can produce fractional gallons of soft drink), net benefits are maximized at a single level of Q. At this level of Q, marginal net benefits are equal to zero, which corresponds to 5 units of Q in Table 1–1.

of 1 unit of Q in Table 1–1. By increasing Q to 2 units, total benefits increase by 80 and total costs increase by only 20. Increasing the use of Q from 1 to 2 units is profitable, because it adds more to total benefits than it does to total costs.

Principle	**Marginal Principle**
	To maximize net benefits, the manager should increase the managerial control variable up to the point where marginal benefits equal marginal costs. This level of the managerial control variable corresponds to the level at which marginal net benefits are zero; nothing more can be gained by further changes in that variable.

Notice in Table 1–1 that while 5 units of Q maximizes net benefits, it does not maximize total benefits. In fact, total benefits are maximized at 10 units of Q, where marginal benefits are zero. The reason the net-benefit-maximizing level of Q is less than the level of Q that maximizes total benefits is that there are costs associated with achieving more total benefits. The goal of maximizing net benefits takes costs into account, while the goal of maximizing total benefits does not. In the context of a firm, maximizing total benefits is equivalent to maximizing revenues without regard for costs. In the context of studying for an exam, maximizing total benefits requires studying until you maximize your grade, regardless of how much it costs you to study.

Continuous Decisions

The basic principles for making decisions when the control variable is discrete also apply to the case of a continuous control variable. The basic relationships in Table 1–1 are depicted graphically in Figure 1–2. The top panel of the figure presents the total benefits and total costs of using different levels of Q under the assumption that Q is infinitely divisible (instead of allowing the firm to produce soft drinks only in one-gallon containers as in Table 1–1, it can now produce fractional units). The middle panel presents the net benefits, $B(Q) - C(Q)$, and represents the vertical difference between B and C in the top panel. Notice that net benefits are maximized at the point where the difference between $B(Q)$ and $C(Q)$ is the greatest in the top panel. Furthermore, the slope of $B(Q)$ is $\Delta B/\Delta Q$, or marginal benefit, and the slope of $C(Q)$ is $\Delta C/\Delta Q$, or marginal cost. The slopes of the total benefits curve and the total cost curve are equal when net benefits are maximized. This is just another way of saying that when net benefits are maximized, $MB = MC$.

Principle	**Marginal Value Curves Are the Slopes of Total Value Curves**
	When the control variable is infinitely divisible, the slope of a total value curve at a given point is the marginal value at that point. In particular, the slope of the total benefit curve at a given Q is the marginal benefit of that level of Q. The slope of the total cost curve at a given Q is the marginal cost of that level of Q. The slope of the net benefit curve at a given Q is the marginal net benefit of that level of Q.

FIGURE 1–2 Determining the Optimal Level of a Control Variable: The Continuous Case

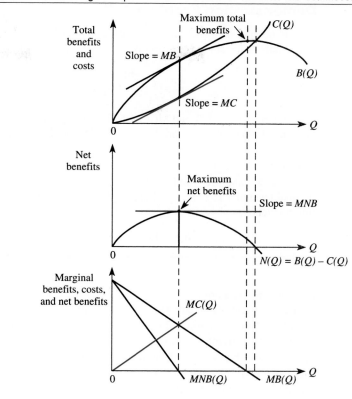

A Calculus Alternative

Since the slope of a function is the derivative of that function, the preceding principle means that the derivative of a given function is the marginal value of that function. For example,

$$MB = \frac{dB(Q)}{dQ}$$

$$MC = \frac{dC(Q)}{dQ}$$

$$MNB = \frac{dN(Q)}{dQ}$$

The bottom panel of Figure 1–2 depicts the marginal benefits, marginal costs, and marginal net benefits. At the level of Q where the marginal benefit curve intersects the marginal cost curve, marginal net benefits are zero. That level of Q maximizes net benefits.

For a video
walkthrough of
this problem, visit
www.mhhe.com/
baye8e

Demonstration Problem 1–3

An engineering firm recently conducted a study to determine its benefit and cost structure. The results of the study are as follows:

$$B(Y) = 300Y - 6Y^2$$
$$C(Y) = 4Y^2$$

so that $MB = 300 - 12Y$ and $MC = 8Y$. The manager has been asked to determine the maximum level of net benefits and the level of Y that will yield that result.

Answer:

Equating MB and MC yields $300 - 12Y = 8Y$. Solving this equation for Y reveals that the optimal level of Y is $Y^* = 15$. Plugging $Y^* = 15$ into the net benefit relation yields the maximum level of net benefits:

$$NB = 300(15) - (6)(15^2) - (4)(15^2) = 2,250$$

Incremental Decisions

Sometimes managers are faced with proposals that require a simple thumbs up or thumbs down decision. Marginal analysis is the appropriate tool to use for such decisions; the manager should adopt a project if the additional revenues that will be earned if the project is adopted exceed the additional costs required to implement the project. In the case of yes-or-no decisions, the additional revenues derived from a decision are called *incremental revenues*. The additional costs that stem from the decision are called *incremental costs*.

incremental revenues
The additional revenues that stem from a yes-or-no decision.

incremental costs
The additional costs that stem from a yes-or-no decision.

To illustrate, imagine that you are the CEO of Slick Drilling Inc. and you must decide whether or not to drill for crude oil around the Twin Lakes area in Michigan. You are relatively certain there are 10,000 barrels of crude oil at this location. An accountant working for you prepared the information in Table 1–2 to help you decide whether or not to adopt the new project.

While the accountant supplied you with a lot of information in Table 1–2, the only data relevant for your decision are the incremental revenues and costs of adopting the new drilling project. In particular, notice that your direct and indirect fixed costs are the same regardless of whether you adopt the project and therefore are irrelevant to your decision. In contrast, note that your revenues increase by $183,200 if you adopt the project. This change in revenues stemming from the adoption of the project represents your incremental revenues. To earn these additional revenues, however, you must spend an additional $90,000 for drill augers and $75,000 for additional temporary workers. The sum of these costs—$165,000—represents the incremental cost of the new drilling project. Since your incremental revenues of $183,200 exceed the incremental costs of $165,000, you should give your "thumbs up" to the new project. Doing so adds $18,200 to your bottom line.

As another example, suppose the first unit of a control variable adds more to benefits than costs ($MB > MC$), but the second unit adds more to costs than benefits

TABLE 1–2 Incremental Costs and Revenues of the New Drilling Project

	Current Situation	After New Drilling Project	Incremental Revenues and Costs
Total revenue	$1,740,400	$1,923,600	**$183,200**
Variable cost			
Drill augers	750,000	840,000	90,000
Temporary workers	500,000	575,000	75,000
Total variable cost	1,250,000	1,415,000	**165,000**
Direct fixed costs			
Depreciation—equipment	120,000	120,000	
Total direct fixed cost	120,000	120,000	0
Indirect fixed costs			
Supervisors' salaries	240,000	240,000	
Office supplies	30,000	30,000	
Total indirect fixed cost	270,000	270,000	0
Profit	$ 100,400	$ 118,600	**$18,200**

($MB < MC$). In this case, the manager should give a "thumbs down" to the second unit, since it adds more to costs than benefits.

LEARNING MANAGERIAL ECONOMICS

Before we continue our analysis of managerial economics, it is useful to provide some hints about how to study economics. Becoming proficient in economics is like learning to play music or ride a bicycle: The best way to learn economics is to practice, practice, and practice some more. Practicing managerial economics means practicing making decisions, and the best way to do this is to work and rework the problems presented in the text and at the end of each chapter. Before you can be effective at practicing, however, you must understand the language of economics.

The terminology in economics has two purposes. First, the definitions and formulas economists use are needed for precision. Economics deals with very complex issues, and much confusion can be avoided by using the language economists have designed to break down complex issues into manageable components. Second, precise terminology helps practitioners of economics communicate more efficiently. It would be difficult to communicate if, like Dr. Seuss, each of us made words mean whatever we wanted them to mean. However, the terminology is not an end in itself but simply a tool that makes it easier to communicate and analyze different economic situations.

Understanding the definitions used in economics is like knowing the difference between a whole note and a quarter note in music. Without such an understanding, it would be very difficult for anyone other than an extremely gifted musician to learn to play an instrument or to communicate to another musician how to play a new song. Given an understanding of the language of music, anyone who is willing to take the time to practice can make beautiful music. The same is true of economics:

Anyone who is willing to learn the language of economics and take the time to practice making decisions can learn to be an effective manager.

ANSWERING THE HEADLINE

Why was Ralph fired from his managerial post at Amcott? As the manager of the foreign language division, he probably relied on his marketing department for sales forecasts and on his legal department for advice on contract and copyright law. The information he obtained about future sales was indeed accurate, but apparently his legal department did not fully anticipate all the legal ramifications of distributing Magicword. Sometimes, managers are given misinformation.

The real problem in this case, however, is that Ralph did not properly act on the information that was given him. Ralph's plan was to generate $7 million per year in sales by sinking $20 million into Magicword. Assuming there were no other costs associated with the project, the projected net present value to Amcott of purchasing Magicword was

$$NPV = \frac{\$7,000,000}{(1 + .07)^1} + \frac{\$7,000,000}{(1 + .07)^2} + \frac{\$7,000,000}{(1 + .07)^3} - \$20,000,000$$

$$= -\$1,629,788$$

which means that Ralph should have expected Amcott to lose over $1.6 million by purchasing Magicword.

Ralph was not fired because of the mistakes of his legal department but for his managerial ineptness. The lawsuit publicized to Amcott's shareholders, among others, that Ralph was not properly processing information given to him: He did not recognize the time value of money.

KEY TERMS AND CONCEPTS

accounting cost	manager
accounting profits	managerial economics
constraints	marginal analysis
consumer–consumer rivalry	marginal benefit
consumer–producer rivalry	marginal cost
economic profits	marginal net benefit
economics	net present value (NPV)
ex-dividend date	opportunity cost
explicit cost	perpetuity
five forces framework	present value (PV)
future value (FV)	producer–producer rivalry
goals	profit
implicit cost	resources
incentives	time value of money
incremental cost	value of a firm
incremental revenue	

END-OF-CHAPTER PROBLEMS BY LEARNING OBJECTIVE

Every end-of-chapter problem addresses at least one learning objective. Below is a nonexhaustive sample of end-of-chapter problems for each learning objective.

LO1 Summarize how goals, constraints, incentives, and market rivalry affect economic decisions.
Try these problems: 1, 13

LO2 Distinguish economic versus accounting profits and costs.
Try these problems: 8, 14

LO3 Explain the role of profits in a market economy.
Try these problems: 7, 21

LO4 Apply the five forces framework to analyze the sustainability of an industry's profits.
Try these problems: 21, 22

LO5 Apply present value analysis to make decisions and value assets.
Try these problems: 2, 12

LO6 Apply marginal analysis to determine the optimal level of a managerial control variable.
Try these problems: 3, 15

LO7 Identify and apply six principles of effective managerial decision making.
Try these problems: 20, 23

CONCEPTUAL AND COMPUTATIONAL QUESTIONS

connect
|ECONOMICS

1. Southwest Airlines begins a "Bags Fly Free" campaign, charging no fees for a first and second checked bag. Does this situation best represent producer–producer rivalry, consumer–consumer rivalry, or consumer–producer rivalry? Explain.

2. What is the maximum amount you would pay for an asset that generates an income of \$250,000 at the end of each of five years if the opportunity cost of using funds is 8 percent?

3. Suppose that the total benefit and total cost from a continuous activity are, respectively, given by the following equations: $B(Q) = 100 + 36Q - 4Q^2$ and $C(Q) = 80 + 12Q$. [Note: $MB(Q) = 36 - 8Q$ and $MC(Q) = 12$.]
   a. Write out the equation for the net benefits.
   b. What are the net benefits when $Q = 1$? $Q = 5$?
   c. Write out the equation for the marginal net benefits.
   d. What are the marginal net benefits when $Q = 1$? $Q = 5$?
   e. What level of Q maximizes net benefits?
   f. At the value of Q that maximizes net benefits, what is the value of marginal net benefits?

4. A firm's current profits are $400,000. These profits are expected to grow indefinitely at a constant annual rate of 4 percent. If the firm's opportunity cost of funds is 6 percent, determine the value of the firm
   a. The instant before it pays out current profits as dividends.
   b. The instant after it pays out current profits as dividends.

5. What is the value of a preferred stock that pays a perpetual dividend of $125 at the end of each year when the interest rate is 5 percent?

6. Complete the following table and answer the accompanying questions.
   a. At what level of the control variable are net benefits maximized?
   b. What is the relation between marginal benefit and marginal cost at this level of the variable?

Control Variable Q	Total Benefits B(Q)	Total Cost C(Q)	Net Benefits N(Q)	Marginal Benefit MB(Q)	Marginal Cost MC(Q)	Marginal Net Benefit MNB(Q)
100	1200	950		210	60	
101	1400				70	
102	1590				80	
103	1770				90	
104	1940				100	
105	2100				110	
106	2250				120	
107	2390				130	
108	2520				140	
109	2640				150	
110	2750				160	

7. It is estimated that over 100,000 students will apply to the top 30 M.B.A. programs in the United States this year.
   a. Using the concept of net present value and opportunity cost, explain when it is rational for an individual to pursue an M.B.A. degree.
   b. What would you expect to happen to the number of applicants if the starting salaries of managers with M.B.A. degrees remained constant but salaries of managers without such degrees decreased by 20 percent? Why?

8. Jaynet spends $30,000 per year on painting supplies and storage space. She recently received two job offers from a famous marketing firm—one offer was for $110,000 per year, and the other was for $80,000. However, she turned both jobs down to continue a painting career. If Jaynet sells 25 paintings per year at a price of $8,000 each
   a. What are her accounting profits?
   b. What are her economic profits?

9. Suppose the total benefit derived from a continuous decision, Q, is $B(Q) = 20Q - 2Q^2$ and the corresponding total cost is $C(Q) = 4 + 2Q^2$, so that $MB(Q) = 20 - 4Q$ and $MC(Q) = 4Q$.
    a. What is total benefit when $Q = 2$? $Q = 10$?
    b. What is marginal benefit when $Q = 2$? $Q = 10$?
    c. What level of Q maximizes total benefit?
    d. What is total cost when $Q = 2$? $Q = 10$?
    e. What is marginal cost when $Q = 2$? $Q = 10$?
    f. What level of Q minimizes total cost?
    g. What level of Q maximizes net benefits?

10. An owner can lease her building for $120,000 per year for three years. The explicit cost of maintaining the building is $40,000, and the implicit cost is $55,000. All revenues are received, and costs borne, at the end of each year. If the interest rate is 5 percent, determine the present value of the stream of
    a. Accounting profits.
    b. Economic profits.

PROBLEMS AND APPLICATIONS

11. You have recently learned that the company where you work is being sold for $300,000. The company's income statement indicates current profits of $11,000, which have yet to be paid out as dividends. Assuming the company will remain a "going concern" indefinitely and that the interest rate will remain constant at 9 percent, at what constant rate does the owner believe that profits will grow? Does this seem reasonable?

12. You are in the market for a new refrigerator for your company's lounge, and you have narrowed the search down to two models. The energy-efficient model sells for $700 and will save you $45 at the end of each of the next five years in electricity costs. The standard model has features similar to the energy-efficient model but provides no future saving in electricity costs. It is priced at only $500. Assuming your opportunity cost of funds is 6 percent, which refrigerator should you purchase?

13. You are the human resources manager for a famous retailer, and you are trying to convince the president of the company to change the structure of employee compensation. Currently, the company's retail sales staff is paid a flat hourly wage of $20 per hour for each eight-hour shift worked. You propose a new pay structure whereby each salesperson in a store would be compensated $10 per hour, plus 1 percent of that store's daily profits. Assume that, when run efficiently, each store's maximum daily profits are $25,000. Outline the arguments that support your proposed plan.

14. Jamie is considering leaving her current job, which pays $75,000 per year, to start a new company that develops applications for smart phones. Based on market research, she can sell about 50,000 units during the first year at a price of $4 per unit. With annual overhead costs and operating expenses amounting to $145,000, Jamie expects a profit margin of 20 percent. This margin is 5 percent larger than that of her largest competitor, Apps, Inc.

   a. If Jamie decides to embark on her new venture, what will her accounting costs be during the first year of operation? Her implicit costs? Her opportunity costs?

   b. Suppose that Jamie's estimated selling price is lower than originally projected during the first year. How much revenue would she need in order to earn positive accounting profits? Positive economic profits?

15. Approximately 14 million Americans are addicted to drugs and alcohol. The federal government estimates that these addicts cost the U.S. economy $300 billion in medical expenses and lost productivity. Despite the enormous potential market, many biotech companies have shied away from funding research and development (R&D) initiatives to find a cure for drug and alcohol addiction. Your firm—Drug Abuse Sciences (DAS)—is a notable exception. It has spent $200 million to date working on a cure, but is now at a crossroads. It can either abandon its program or invest another $60 million today. Unfortunately, the firm's opportunity cost of funds is 5 percent, and it will take another five years before final approval from the Food and Drug Administration is achieved and the product is actually sold. Expected (year-end) profits from selling the drug are presented in the accompanying table. Should DAS continue with its plan to bring the drug to market, or should it abandon the project? Explain.

Year 1	Year 2	Year 3	Year 4	Year 5	Year 6	Year 7	Year 8	Year 9
$0	$0	$0	$0	$12,000,000	$13,400,000	$17,200,000	$20,700,000	$22,450,000

16. As a marketing manager for one of the world's largest automakers, you are responsible for the advertising campaign for a new energy-efficient sports utility vehicle. Your support team has prepared the following table, which summarizes the (year-end) profitability, estimated number of vehicles sold, and average estimated selling price for alternative levels of advertising. The accounting department projects that the best alternative use for the funds used in the advertising campaign is an investment returning 9 percent. In light of the staggering cost of advertising (which accounts for the lower projected profits in years 1 and 2 for the high and moderate advertising intensities), the team leader recommends a low advertising intensity in order to maximize the value of the firm. Do you agree? Explain.

Profitability by Advertising Intensity

	Profits (in millions)			Units Sold (in thousands)			Average Selling Price		
	Year 1	Year 2	Year 3	Year 1	Year 2	Year 3	Year 1	Year 2	Year 3
Advertising Intensity									
High	$20	$ 80	$300	10	60	120	$35,000	$36,500	$38,000
Moderate	40	80	135	5	12.5	25	35,800	36,100	36,300
Low	75	110	118	4	6	7.2	35,900	36,250	36,000

17. The head of the accounting department at a major software manufacturer has asked you to put together a pro forma statement of the company's value under several possible growth scenarios and the assumption that the company's many divisions will remain a single entity forever. The manager is concerned that, despite the fact that the firm's competitors are comparatively small, collectively their annual revenue growth has exceeded 50 percent over each of the last five years. She has requested that the value projections be based on the firm's current profits of $3.2 billion (which have yet to be paid out to stockholders) and the average interest rate over the past 20 years (6 percent) in each of the following profit growth scenarios:
    a. Profits grow at an annual rate of 9 percent. (This one is tricky.)
    b. Profits grow at an annual rate of 2 percent.
    c. Profits grow at an annual rate of 0 percent.
    d. Profits decline at an annual rate of 4 percent.

18. Suppose one of your clients is four years away from retirement and has only $2,500 in pretax income to devote to either a Roth or traditional IRA. The traditional IRA permits investors to contribute the full $2,500 since contributions to these accounts are taxdeductible, but they must pay taxes on all future distributions. In contrast, contributions to a Roth IRA are not tax-deductible. For example, if a person's tax rate is 25 percent, an investor is able to contribute only $1,875 after taxes; however, the earnings of a Roth IRA grow tax-free. Your company has decided to waive the one-time set-up fee of $50 to open a Roth IRA; however, investors opening a traditional IRA must pay the $50 setup fee. Assuming that your client anticipates that her tax rate will remain at 19 percent in retirement and will earn a stable 7 percent return on her investments, will she prefer a traditional or Roth IRA?

19. You are the manager in charge of global operations at BankGlobal—a large commercial bank that operates in a number of countries around the world. You must decide whether or not to launch a new advertising campaign in the U.S. market. Your accounting department has provided the accompanying statement, which summarizes the financial impact of the advertising campaign

Financial Impact on U.S. Operations

	Pre-Advertising Campaign	Post-Advertising Campaign
Total Revenues	$18,610,900	$31,980,200
Variable Cost		
TV Airtime	5,750,350	8,610,400
Ad development labor	1,960,580	3,102,450
Total variable costs	7,710,930	11,712,850
Direct Fixed Cost		
Depreciation—computer equipment	1,500,000	1,500,000
Total direct fixed cost	1,500,000	1,500,000
Indirect Fixed Cost		
Managerial salaries	8,458,100	8,458,100
Office supplies	2,003,500	2,003,500
Total indirect fixed cost	$10,461,600	$10,461,600

on U.S. operations. In addition, you recently received a call from a colleague in charge of foreign operations, and she indicated that her unit would lose $8 million if the U.S. advertising campaign were launched. Your goal is to maximize BankGlobal's value. Should you launch the new campaign? Explain.

20. According to *The Wall Street Journal*, merger and acquisition activity in the first quarter rose to $5.3 billion. Approximately three-fourths of the 78 first-quarter deals occurred between information technology (IT) companies. The largest IT transaction of the quarter was EMC's $625 million acquisition of VMWare. The VMWare acquisition broadened EMC's core data storage device business to include software technology enabling multiple operating systems—such as Microsoft's Windows, Linux, and Novell Inc.'s netware—to simultaneously and independently run on the same Intel-based server or workstation. Suppose that at the time of the acquisition a weak economy led many analysts to project that VMWare's profits would grow at a constant rate of 2 percent for the foreseeable future, and that the company's annual net income was $39.60 million. If EMC's estimated opportunity cost of funds is 9 percent, as an analyst, how would you view the acquisition? Would your conclusion change if you knew that EMC had credible information that the economy was on the verge of an expansion period that would boost VMWare's projected annual growth rate to 4 percent for the foreseeable future? Explain.

21. Brazil points to its shrimp-farming industry as an example of how it can compete in world markets. One decade ago, Brazil exported a meager 400 tons of shrimp. Today, Brazil exports more than 58,000 tons of shrimp, with

approximately one-third of that going to the United States. Brazilian shrimp farmers, however, potentially face a new challenge in the upcoming years. The Southern Shrimp Alliance—a U.S. organization representing shrimpers—filed a dumping complaint alleging that Brazil and five other shrimp-producing countries are selling shrimp below "fair market value." The organization is calling for the United States to impose a 300 percent tariff on all shrimp entering the United States' borders. Brazilian producers and the other five countries named in the complaint counter that they have a natural competitive advantage such as lower labor costs, availability of cheap land, and a more favorable climate, resulting in a higher yield per acre and permitting three harvests per year. In what many see as a bold move, the American Seafood Distributors Association—an organization representing supermarkets, shrimp processors, and restaurants—has supported Brazilian and other foreign producers, arguing that it is the Southern Shrimp Alliance that is engaging in unfair trade practices. Describe the various rivalries depicted in this scenario, and then use the five forces framework to analyze the industry.

22. You are the manager of Local Electronics Shop (LES), a small brick-and-mortar retail camera and electronics store. One of your employees proposed a new online strategy whereby LES lists its products at Pricesearch.com—a price comparison Web site that allows consumers to view the prices of dozens of retailers selling the same items. Would you expect this strategy to enable LES to achieve sustainable economic profits? Explain.

23. Two months ago, the owner of a car dealership (and a current football star) significantly changed his sales manager's compensation plan. Under the old plan, the manager was paid a salary of $6,000 per month; under the new plan, she receives 2 percent of the sales price of each car sold. During the past two months, the number of cars sold increased by 40 percent, but the dealership's margins (and profits) significantly declined. According to the sales manager, "Consumers are driving harder bargains and I have had to authorize significantly lower prices to remain competitive." What advice would you give the owner of the dealership?

CONNECT EXERCISES

If your instructor has adopted Connect for the course and you are an active subscriber, you can practice with the questions presented above, along with many alternative versions of these questions. Your instructor may also assign a subset of these problems and/or their alternative versions as a homework assignment through Connect, allowing for immediate feedback of grades and correct answers.

CASE-BASED EXERCISES

Your instructor may assign additional problem-solving exercises (called *memos*) that require you to apply some of the tools you learned in this chapter to make a recommendation based on an actual business scenario. Some of these memos accompany the Time Warner case (pages 561–597 of your textbook). Additional memos, as well as data that may be useful for your analysis, are available online at www.mhhe.com/baye8e.

SELECTED READINGS

Anders, Gary C.; Ohta, Hiroshi; and Sailors, Joel, "A Note on the Marginal Efficiency of Investment and Related Concepts." *Journal of Economic Studies* 17(2), 1990, pp. 50–57.

Clark, Gregory, "Factory Discipline." *Journal of Economic History* 54(1), March 1994, pp. 128–63.

Fizel, John L., and Nunnikhoven, Thomas S., "Technical Efficiency of For-profit and Non-profit Nursing Homes." *Managerial and Decision Economics* 13(5), Sept.–Oct. 1992, pp. 429–39.

Gifford, Sharon, "Allocation of Entrepreneurial Attention." *Journal of Economic Behavior and Organization* 19(3), December 1992, pp. 265–84.

McNamara, John R., "The Economics of Decision Making in the New Manufacturing Firm." *Managerial and Decision Economics* 13(4), July–Aug. 1992, pp. 287–93.

Mercuro, Nicholas; Sourbis, Haralambos; and Whitney, Gerald, "Ownership Structure, Value of the Firm and the Bargaining Power of the Manager." *Southern Economic Journal* 59(2), October 1992, pp. 273–83.

Parsons, George R., and Wu, Yangru, "The Opportunity Cost of Coastal Land-Use Controls: An Empirical Analysis." *Land Economics* 67, Aug. 1991, pp. 308–16.

Phillips, Owen R.; Battalio, Raymond C.; and Kogut, Carl A., "Sunk Costs and Opportunity Costs in Valuation and Bidding." *Southern Economic Journal* 58, July 1991, pp. 112–28.

Pindyck, Robert S., "Irreversibility, Uncertainty, and Investment." *Journal of Economic Literature* 29, Sept. 1991, pp. 1110–48.

Appendix
The Calculus of Maximizing Net Benefits

This appendix provides a calculus-based derivation of the important rule that to maximize net benefits, a manager must equate marginal benefits and marginal costs.

Let $B(Q)$ denote the benefits of using Q units of the managerial control variable, and let $C(Q)$ denote the corresponding costs. The net benefits are $N(Q) = B(Q) - C(Q)$. The objective is to choose Q so as to maximize

$$N(Q) = B(Q) - C(Q)$$

The first-order condition for a maximum is

$$\frac{dN}{dQ} = \frac{dB}{dQ} - \frac{dC}{dQ} = 0$$

But

$$\frac{dB}{dQ} = MB$$

is nothing more than marginal benefits, while

$$\frac{dC}{dQ} = MC$$

is simply marginal costs. Thus, the first-order condition for a maximum implies that

$$\frac{dB}{dQ} = \frac{dC}{dQ}$$

or $MB = MC$.

The second-order condition requires that the function $N(Q)$ be concave in Q or, in mathematical terms, that the second derivative of the net benefit function be negative:

$$\frac{d^2N}{dQ^2} = \frac{d^2B}{dQ^2} - \frac{d^2C}{dQ^2} < 0$$

Notice that $d^2B/dQ^2 = d(MB)/dQ$, while $d^2C/dQ^2 = d(MC)/dQ$. Thus, the second-order condition may be rewritten as

$$\frac{d^2N}{dQ^2} = \frac{d(MB)}{dQ} - \frac{d(MC)}{dQ} < 0$$

In other words, the slope of the marginal benefit curve must be less than the slope of the marginal cost curve.

Demonstration Problem 1–4

Suppose $B(Q) = 10Q - 2Q^2$ and $C(Q) = 2 + Q^2$. What value of the managerial control variable, Q, maximizes net benefits?

Answer:
Net benefits are

$$N(Q) = B(Q) - C(Q) = 10Q - 2Q^2 - 2 - Q^2$$

Taking the derivative of $N(Q)$ and setting it equal to zero gives

$$\frac{dN}{dQ} = 10 - 4Q - 2Q = 0$$

Solving for Q gives $Q = 10/6$. To verify that this is indeed a maximum, we must check that the second derivative of $N(Q)$ is negative:

$$\frac{d^2N}{dQ^2} = -4 - 2 = -6 < 0$$

Therefore, $Q = 10/6$ is indeed a maximum.

CHAPTER TWO

Market Forces: Demand and Supply

Samsung and Hynix Semiconductor to Cut Chip Production

Sam Robbins, owner and CEO of PC Solutions, arrived at the office and glanced at the front page of *The Wall Street Journal* waiting on his desk. One of the articles contained statements from executives of two of South Korea's largest semiconductor manufacturers—Samsung Electronic Company and Hynix Semiconductor—indicating that they would suspend all their memory chip production for one week. The article went on to say that another large semiconductor manufacturer was likely to follow suit. Collectively, these three chip manufacturers produce about 30 percent of the world's basic semiconductor chips.

PC Solutions is a small but growing company that assembles PCs and sells them in the highly competitive market for "clones." PC Solutions experienced 100 percent growth last year and is in the process of interviewing recent graduates in an attempt to double its workforce.

After reading the article, Sam picked up the phone and called a few of his business contacts to verify for himself the information contained in the *Journal.* Satisfied that the information was correct, he called the director of personnel, Jane Remak.

What do you think Sam and Jane discussed?

Learning Objectives

After completing this chapter, you will be able to:

LO1 Explain the laws of demand and supply, and identify factors that cause demand and supply to shift.

LO2 Calculate consumer surplus and producer surplus, and describe what they mean.

LO3 Explain price determination in a competitive market, and show how equilibrium changes in response to changes in determinants of demand and supply.

LO4 Explain and illustrate how excise taxes, *ad valorem* taxes, price floors, and price ceilings impact the functioning of a market.

LO5 Apply supply and demand analysis as a qualitative forecasting tool to see the "big picture" in competitive markets.

INTRODUCTION

This chapter describes *supply* and *demand,* which are the driving forces behind the market economies that exist in the United States and around the globe. As suggested in this chapter's opening headline, supply and demand analysis is a tool that managers can use to visualize the "big picture." Many companies fail because their managers get bogged down in the day-to-day decisions of the business without having a clear picture of market trends and changes that are on the horizon.

To illustrate, imagine that you manage a small retail outlet that sells PCs. A magic genie appears and says, "Over the next month, the market price of PCs will decline and consumers will purchase fewer PCs." The genie revealed the big picture: PC prices and sales will decline. If you worry about the *details* of your business without knowledge of these future trends in prices and sales, you will be at a significant competitive disadvantage. Absent a view of the big picture, you are likely to negotiate the wrong prices with suppliers and customers, carry too much inventory, hire too many employees, and—if your business spends money on informative advertising—purchase ads in which your prices are no longer competitive by the time they reach print.

Supply and demand analysis is a qualitative tool which, like the above genie, empowers managers by enabling them to see the "big picture." It is a qualitative forecasting tool you can use to predict trends in competitive markets, including changes in the prices of your firm's products, related products (both substitutes and complements), and the prices of inputs (such as labor services) that are necessary for your operations. As we will see in subsequent chapters, after you use supply and demand analysis to see the big picture, additional tools are available to assist with details—determining *how much* the price will change, *how much* sales and revenues will change, and so on.

For those of you who have taken a principles-level course in economics, some parts of this chapter will be a review. However, make sure you have complete mastery of the tools of supply and demand. The rest of this book will assume you have a thorough working knowledge of the material in this chapter.

DEMAND

Suppose a clothing manufacturer desires information about the impact of its pricing decisions on the demand for its jeans in a small foreign market. To obtain this information, it might engage in market research to determine how many pairs of jeans consumers would purchase each year at alternative prices per unit. The numbers from such a market survey would look something like those in Table 2–1. The market research reveals that if jeans were priced at $10 per pair, 60,000 pairs of jeans would be sold per year; at $30 per pair, 20,000 pairs of jeans would be sold annually.

When there is no ambiguity, it is sometimes convenient to say simply "price" rather than "price per pair" or "price per unit." For instance, if one of your classmates says gasoline is priced at $3.99 in Indianapolis, you understand that she means $3.99 per gallon. Looking at the rows in Table 2-1, notice that the only difference in the entries is the price of jeans and the quantity of jeans sold. Everything else that might influence buyer decisions, such as consumer income, advertising, and

TABLE 2–1   The Demand Schedule for Jeans in a Small Foreign Market

Price of Jeans	Quantity of Jeans Sold	Average Consumer Income	Advertising Expenditure	Average Price of Shirts
$ 0	80,000	$25,000	$50,000	$20
5	70,000	25,000	50,000	20
10	60,000	25,000	50,000	20
15	50,000	25,000	50,000	20
20	40,000	25,000	50,000	20
25	30,000	25,000	50,000	20
30	20,000	25,000	50,000	20
35	10,000	25,000	50,000	20
40	0	25,000	50,000	20

the prices of other goods such as shirts, is held constant. In effect, the market survey does not ask consumers how much they would buy at alternative levels of income or advertising; it simply seeks to determine how much would be purchased at alternative prices. The market research reveals that, holding all other things constant, the quantity of jeans consumers are willing and able to purchase goes down as the price rises. This fundamental economic principle is known as the *law of demand:* Price and quantity demanded are inversely related. That is, as the price of a good rises (falls) and all other things remain constant, the quantity demanded of the good falls (rises).

Figure 2–1 plots the data in Table 2–1. The straight line connecting those points, called the *market demand curve,* interpolates the quantities consumers would be willing and able to purchase at prices not explicitly dealt with in the market

market demand curve
A curve indicating the total quantity of a good all consumers are willing and able to purchase at each possible price, holding the prices of related goods, income, advertising, and other variables constant.

FIGURE 2–1   The Demand Curve

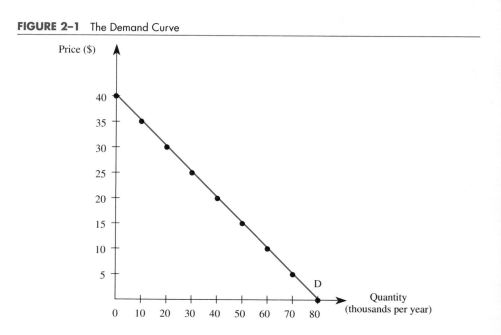

research. For example, using this market demand curve, we conclude that consumers would be willing and able to purchase 35,000 pairs of jeans when the price is $22.50 (and all other variables stay the same). Notice that the line is downward sloping, which reflects the law of demand, and that all other factors that influence demand are held constant at each point on the line.

Demand Shifters

Economists recognize that variables other than the price of a good influence demand. For example, the number of pairs of jeans individuals are willing and financially able to buy also depends on the price of shirts, consumer income, advertising expenditures, and so on. Variables other than the price of a good that influence demand are known as *demand shifters.*

change in quantity demanded
Changes in the price of a good lead to a change in the quantity demanded of that good. This corresponds to a movement along a given demand curve.

When we graph the demand curve for good X, we hold everything but the price of X constant. A representative demand curve is given by D^0 in Figure 2–2. The movement along a demand curve, such as the movement from A to B, is called a *change in quantity demanded.* Whenever advertising, income, or the price of related goods changes, it leads to a *change in demand;* the position of the entire demand curve shifts. A rightward shift in the demand curve is called an *increase in demand,* since more of the good is demanded at each price. A leftward shift in the demand curve is called a *decrease in demand.*

Now that we understand the general distinction between a shift in a demand curve and a movement along a demand curve, it is useful to explain how five demand shifters—consumer income, prices of related goods, advertising and consumer tastes, population, and consumer expectations—affect demand.

change in demand
Changes in variables other than the price of a good, such as income or the price of another good, lead to a change in demand. This corresponds to a shift of the entire demand curve.

FIGURE 2–2   Changes in Demand

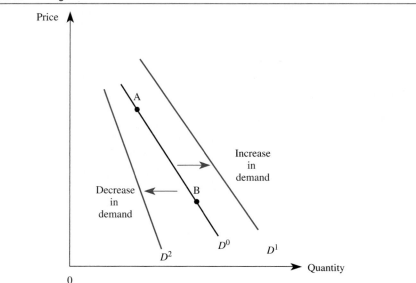

INSIDE BUSINESS 2–1

Asahi Breweries Ltd. and the Asian Recession

During a recent recession, Japan saw many business failures. Even businesses that traditionally do well during economic downturns, such as the beer brewing industry, were hit hard. Analysts blame the downturn in the beer market on two factors: (1) Japanese incomes (GDP) declined significantly as a result of the recession, and (2) Japan's government imposed a beer tax in an effort to raise revenue.

As a result of these events, top Japanese breweries such as Kirin Brewery Company, Ltd., and Sapporo Breweries Ltd. experienced a sharp decline in domestic beer sales. Meanwhile, their competitor—Asahi Breweries—touted double-digit growth and increased its market share. Asahi attributes its growth in sales to its superior sales network and strong marketing campaign for its best-selling beer, *Asahi Super Dry*.

While part of Asahi's growth and success is attributable to the company's sales force and marketing activities—both create greater consumer awareness—this does not fully explain why Asahi has done especially well during the recent Asian recession. One possibility is that Asahi beer is an inferior good. This does not mean that Asahi beer is "skunky" or of low quality; indeed, its *Super Dry* is the beer of choice for many Japanese beer drinkers. The term *inferior good* simply means that when Japanese incomes decline due to a recession, the demand for Asahi beer increases.

Sources: Annual Reports for Asahi Breweries Ltd., Sapporo Breweries Ltd., and Kirin Brewery Company, Ltd.

Income

Because income affects the ability of consumers to purchase a good, changes in income affect how much consumers will buy at any price. In graphical terms, a change in income shifts the entire demand curve. Whether an increase in income shifts the demand curve to the right or to the left depends on the nature of consumer consumption patterns. Accordingly, economists distinguish between two types of goods: normal and inferior goods.

A good whose demand increases (shifts to the right) when consumer incomes rise is called a *normal good.* Normal goods may include goods such as steak, airline travel, and designer jeans: As income goes up, consumers typically buy more of these goods at any given price. Conversely, when consumers suffer a decline in income, the demand for a normal good will decrease (shift to the left).

Changes in income tend to have profound effects on the demand for durable goods, and these effects are typically amplified in developing countries and rural areas. In 2004, for instance, farmers in India enjoyed higher incomes thanks to the impact on crops of beneficial monsoons. As a result, the demand in rural areas of India for tractors and motorcycles surged, almost tripling the level of demand in the previous year. By 2009, this surge in demand reversed due to significant reductions in consumer incomes stemming from a global economic recession. The demand for durables in developed countries also declined dramatically, and automakers were especially hard hit.

In some instances, an increase in income reduces the demand for a good. Economists refer to such a good as an *inferior good.* Bologna, bus travel, and "generic" jeans are possible examples of inferior goods. As income goes up, consumers typically consume less of these goods at each price. It is important to point out that

normal good
A good for which an increase (decrease) in income leads to an increase (decrease) in the demand for that good.

inferior good
A good for which an increase (decrease) in income leads to a decrease (increase) in the demand for that good.

by calling such goods *inferior,* we do not imply that they are of poor quality; we use this term simply to define products that consumers purchase less of when their incomes rise and purchase more of when their incomes fall.

Prices of Related Goods

Changes in the prices of related goods generally shift the demand curve for a good. For example, if the price of a Coke increases, most consumers will begin to substitute Pepsi, because the relative price of Coke is higher than before. As more and more consumers substitute Pepsi for Coke, the quantity of Pepsi demanded at each price will tend to increase. In effect, an increase in the price of Coke increases the demand for Pepsi. This is illustrated by a shift in the demand for Pepsi to the right. Goods that interact in this way are known as *substitutes.*

substitutes
Goods for which an increase (decrease) in the price of one good leads to an increase (decrease) in the demand for the other good.

Many pairs of goods readily come to mind when we think of substitutes: chicken and beef, cars and trucks, raincoats and umbrellas. Such pairs of goods are substitutes for most consumers. However, substitutes need not serve the same function. For example, televisions and patio furniture could be substitutes; as the price of televisions increases, you may choose to purchase additional patio furniture rather than an additional television. Goods are substitutes when an increase in the price of one good increases the demand for the other good.

complements
Goods for which an increase (decrease) in the price of one good leads to a decrease (increase) in the demand for the other good.

Not all goods are substitutes; in fact, an increase in the price of a good such as computer software may lead consumers to purchase fewer computers at each price. Goods that interact in this manner are called *complements.* Beer and pretzels are another example of complementary goods. If the price of beer increased, most beer drinkers would decrease their consumption of pretzels. Notice that when good X is a complement to good Y, a reduction in the price of Y actually increases (shifts to the right) the demand for good X. More of good X is purchased at each price due to the reduction in the price of the complement, good Y.

Advertising and Consumer Tastes

Another variable that is held constant when drawing a given demand curve is the level of advertising. An increase in advertising shifts the demand curve to the right, from D^1 to D^2, as in Figure 2–3. Notice that the impact of advertising on demand can be interpreted in two ways. Under the initial demand curve, D^1, consumers would buy 50,000 units of high-style clothing per month when the price is $40. After the advertising, the demand curve shifts to D^2, and consumers will now buy 60,000 units of the good when the price is $40. Alternatively, when demand is D^1, consumers will pay a price of $40 when 50,000 units are available. Advertising shifts the demand curve to D^2, so consumers will pay a higher price—$50—for 50,000 units.

Why does advertising shift demand to the right? Advertising often provides consumers with information about the existence or quality of a product, which in turn induces more consumers to buy the product. These types of advertising messages are known as *informative advertising.*

Advertising can also influence demand by altering the underlying tastes of consumers. For example, advertising that promotes the latest fad in clothing may increase the demand for a specific fashion item by making consumers perceive it as "the" thing to buy. These types of advertising messages are known as *persuasive advertising.*

FIGURE 2–3 Advertising and the Demand for Clothing

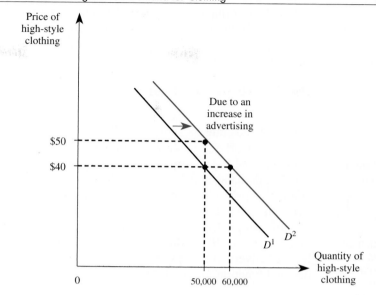

Population

The demand for a product is also influenced by changes in the size and composition of the population. Generally, as the population rises, more and more individuals wish to buy a given product, and this has the effect of shifting the demand curve to the right. Over the twentieth century, the demand curve for food products shifted to the right considerably with the increasing population.

It is important to note that changes in the composition of the population can also affect the demand for a product. To the extent that middle-aged consumers desire different types of products than retirees, an increase in the number of consumers in the 30- to 40-year-old age bracket will increase the demand for products like real estate. Similarly, as a greater proportion of the population ages, the demand for medical services will tend to increase.

Consumer Expectations

Changes in *consumer expectations* also can change the position of the demand curve for a product. For example, if consumers suddenly expect the price of automobiles to be significantly higher next year, the demand for automobiles today will increase. In effect, buying a car today is a substitute for buying a car next year. If consumers expect future prices to be higher, they will substitute current purchases for future purchases. This type of consumer behavior often is referred to as *stockpiling* and generally occurs when products are durable in nature. We often see this behavior for less expensive durables, too; consumers may stockpile laundry detergent in response to temporary sales at grocery stores. The current demand for a perishable product such as bananas generally is not affected by expectations of higher future prices.

Other Factors

In concluding our list of demand shifters, we simply note that any variable that affects the willingness or ability of consumers to purchase a particular good is a potential demand shifter. Health scares affect the demand for cigarettes. The birth of a baby affects the demand for diapers.

The Demand Function

By now you should understand the factors that affect demand and how to use graphs to illustrate those influences. The final step in our analysis of the demand side of the market is to show that all the factors that influence demand may be summarized in what economists refer to as a *demand function*.

demand function
A function that describes how much of a good will be purchased at alternative prices of that good and related goods, alternative income levels, and alternative values of other variables affecting demand.

The demand function for good X describes how much X will be purchased at alternative prices of X and related goods, alternative levels of income, and alternative values of other variables that affect demand. Formally, let Q_x^d represent the quantity demanded of good X, P_x the price of good X, P_y the price of a related good, M income, and H the value of any other variable that affects demand, such as the level of advertising, the size of the population, or consumer expectations. Then the demand function for good X may be written as

$$Q_x^d = f(P_x, P_y, M, H)$$

Thus, the demand function explicitly recognizes that the quantity of a good consumed depends on its price and on demand shifters. Different products will have demand functions of different forms. One very simple but useful form is the linear representation of the demand function: Demand is *linear* if Q_x^d is a linear function of prices, income, and other variables that influence demand. The following equation is an example of a *linear demand function*:

linear demand function
A representation of the demand function in which the demand for a given good is a linear function of prices, income levels, and other variables influencing demand.

$$Q_x^d = \alpha_0 + \alpha_x P_x + \alpha_y P_y + \alpha_M M + \alpha_H H$$

The α_is are fixed numbers that the firm's research department or an economic consultant typically provides to the manager. (Chapter 3 provides an overview of the statistical techniques used to obtain these numbers.)

By the law of demand, an increase in P_x leads to a decrease in the quantity demanded of good X. This means that $\alpha_x < 0$. The sign of α_y will be positive or negative depending on whether goods X and Y are substitutes or complements. If α_y is a positive number, an increase in the price of good Y will lead to an increase in the consumption of good X; therefore, good X is a substitute for good Y. If α_y is a negative number, an increase in the price of good Y will lead to a decrease in the consumption of good X; hence, good X is a complement to good Y. The sign of α_M also can be positive or negative depending on whether X is a normal or an inferior good. If α_M is a positive number, an increase in income (M) will lead to an increase in the consumption of good X, and good X is a normal good. If α_M is a negative number, an increase in income will lead to a decrease in the consumption of good X, and good X is an inferior good.

Demonstration Problem 2–1

An economic consultant for X Corp. recently provided the firm's marketing manager with this estimate of the demand function for the firm's product:

$$Q_x^d = 12{,}000 - 3P_x + 4P_y - 1M + 2A_x$$

where Q_x^d represents the amount consumed of good X, P_x is the price of good X, P_y is the price of good Y, M is income, and A_x represents the amount of advertising spent on good X. Suppose good X sells for $200 per unit, good Y sells for $15 per unit, the company utilizes 2,000 units of advertising, and consumer income is $10,000. How much of good X do consumers purchase? Are goods X and Y substitutes or complements? Is good X a normal or an inferior good?

Answer:

To find out how much of good X consumers will purchase, we substitute the given values of prices, income, and advertising into the linear demand equation to get

$$Q_x^d = 12{,}000 - 3(200) + 4(15) - 1(10{,}000) + 2(2{,}000)$$

Adding up the numbers, we find that the total consumption of X is 5,460 units. Since the coefficient of P_y in the demand equation is $4 > 0$, we know that a $1 increase in the price of good Y will increase the consumption of good X by 4 units. Thus, goods X and Y are substitutes. Since the coefficient of M in the demand equation is $-1 < 0$, we know that a $1 increase in income will decrease the consumption of good X by 1 unit. Thus, good X is an inferior good.

The information summarized in a demand function can be used to graph a demand curve. Since a demand curve is the relation between price and quantity, a representative demand curve holds everything but price constant. This means one may obtain the formula for a demand curve by inserting given values of the demand shifters into the demand function, but leaving P_x in the equation to allow for various values. If we do this for the demand function in Demonstration Problem 2–1 (where $P_y = \$15$, $M = \$10{,}000$, and $A_x = 2{,}000$), we get

$$Q_x^d = 12{,}000 - 3P_x + 4(15) - 1(10{,}000) + 2(2{,}000)$$

which simplifies to

$$Q_x^d = 6{,}060 - 3P_x \tag{2–1}$$

Because we usually graph this relation with the price of the good on the vertical axis, it is useful to represent Equation 2–1 with price on the left-hand side and everything else on the right-hand side. This relation is called an *inverse demand function*. For this example, the inverse demand function is

$$P_x = 2{,}020 - \frac{1}{3}Q_x^d$$

FIGURE 2–4 Graphing the Inverse Demand Function

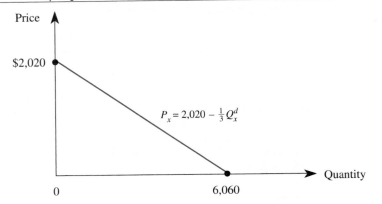

It reveals how much consumers are willing and able to pay for each additional unit of good X. This demand curve is graphed in Figure 2–4.

Consumer Surplus

We now show how a manager can use the demand curve to ascertain the value a consumer or group of consumers receives from a product. The concepts developed in this section are particularly useful in marketing and other disciplines that emphasize strategies such as *value pricing* and *price discrimination.*

By the law of demand, the amount a consumer is willing to pay for an additional unit of a good falls as more of the good is consumed. For instance, imagine that the demand curve in Figure 2–5(a) represents your demand for water immediately after participating in a 10K run. Initially, you are willing to pay a very high price—in this case, $5 per liter—for the first drop of water. As you consume more water, the amount you are willing to pay for an additional drop declines from $5.00 to $4.99 and so on as you move down the demand curve. Notice that after you have consumed an entire liter of water, you are willing to pay only $4 per liter for another drop. Once you have enjoyed 2 liters of water, you are willing to pay only $3 per liter for another drop.

To find your total value (or benefit) of 2 liters of water, we simply add up the maximum amount you were willing to pay for each of these drops of water between 0 and 2 liters. This amount corresponds to the area underneath the demand curve in Figure 2–5(a) up to the quantity of 2 liters. Since the area of this region is $8, the total value you receive from 2 liters of water is $8.

Fortunately, you don't have to pay different prices for the different drops of water you consume. Instead, you face a per-unit price of, say, $3 per liter and get to buy as many drops (or even liters) as you want at that price. Given the demand curve in Figure 2–5(a), when the price is $3 you will choose to purchase 2 liters of water. In this case, your total out-of-pocket expense for the 2 liters of water is $6. Since you value 2 liters of water at $8 and only have to pay $6 for it, you are getting $2 in value over and above the amount you have to pay for water. This "extra" value is known as *consumer surplus*—the value consumers get from a good but do not have to pay for. This concept

consumer surplus
The value consumers get from a good but do not have to pay for.

FIGURE 2–5 Consumer Surplus

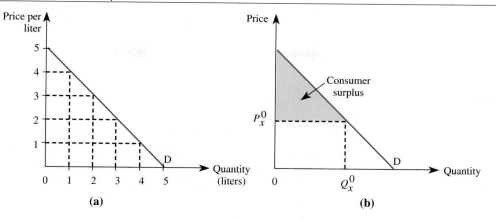

(a)

(b)

is important to managers because it tells how much extra money consumers would be willing to pay for a given amount of a purchased product.

More generally, consumer surplus is the area above the price paid for a good but below the demand curve. For instance, the shaded triangle in Figure 2–5(b) illustrates the consumer surplus of a consumer who buys Q_x^0 units at a price of P_x^0. To see why, recall that each point on the demand curve indicates the value to the consumer of another unit of the good. The difference between each price on the demand curve and the price P_x^0 paid represents surplus (the value the consumer receives but does not have to pay for). When we add up the "surpluses" received for each unit between 0 and Q_x^0 (this sum equals the shaded region), we obtain the consumer surplus associated with purchasing Q_x^0 units at a price of P_x^0 each.

Managers can use the notion of consumer surplus to determine the total amount consumers would be willing to pay for multiunit packages. While this will be discussed in detail in Chapter 11 where we examine pricing strategies, we illustrate the basic idea in the following problem.

Demonstration Problem 2–2

A typical consumer's demand for the Happy Beverage Company's product looks like that in Figure 2–5(a). If the firm charges a price of $2 per liter, how much revenue will the firm earn and how much consumer surplus will the typical consumer enjoy? What is the most a consumer would be willing to pay for a bottle containing exactly 3 liters of the firm's beverage?

Answer:

At a price of $2 per liter, a typical consumer will purchase 3 liters of the beverage. Thus, the firm's revenue is $6 and the consumer surplus is $4.50 [the area of the consumer surplus triangle is one-half the base times the height, or .5(3)($5 − $2) = $4.50]. The total value of 3 liters of the firm's beverage to a typical consumer is thus $6 + $4.50, or $10.50. This is also the maximum amount a consumer would be willing to pay for a bottle containing exactly 3 liters of the firm's beverage. Expressed differently, if the firm sold the product in 3-liter bottles rather than in smaller units, it could sell each bottle for $10.50 to earn higher revenues and extract all consumer surplus.

SUPPLY

market supply curve
A curve indicating the total quantity of a good that all producers in a competitive market would produce at each price, holding input prices, technology, and other variables affecting supply constant.

In the previous section we focused on demand, which represents half of the forces that determine the price in a market. The other determinant is market supply. In a competitive market there are many producers, each producing a similar product. The *market supply curve* summarizes the total quantity all producers are willing and able to produce at alternative prices, holding other factors that affect supply constant.

While the market supply of a good generally depends on many things, when we graph a supply curve, we hold everything but the price of the good constant. The movement along a supply curve, such as the one from A to B in Figure 2–6, is called a *change in quantity supplied.* The fact that the market supply curve slopes upward reflects the inverse *law of supply:* As the price of a good rises (falls) and other things remain constant, the quantity supplied of the good rises (falls). Producers are willing to produce more output when the price is high than when it is low.

Supply Shifters

change in quantity supplied
Changes in the price of a good lead to a change in the quantity supplied of that good. This corresponds to a movement along a given supply curve.

Variables that affect the position of the supply curve are called *supply shifters,* and they include the prices of inputs, the level of technology, the number of firms in the market, taxes, and producer expectations. Whenever one or more of these variables changes, the position of the entire supply curve shifts. Such a shift is known as a *change in supply.* The shift from S^0 to S^2 in Figure 2–6 is called an *increase in supply* since producers sell more output at each given price. The shift from S^0 to S^1 in Figure 2–6 represents a *decrease in supply* since producers sell less of the product at each price.

change in supply
Changes in variables other than the price of a good, such as input prices or technological advances, lead to a change in supply. This corresponds to a shift of the entire supply curve.

FIGURE 2–6 Changes in Supply

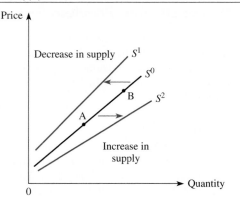

The Trade Act of 2002, NAFTA, and the Supply Curve

Over the past two decades, presidents from both political parties have signed trade agreements and laws that include provisions designed to reduce the cost of producing goods at home and abroad. These cost reductions translate into increases in the supply of goods and services available to U.S. consumers.

The North American Free Trade Agreement (NAFTA) between the United States, Canada, and Mexico was signed into law by Bill Clinton and contained provisions to eliminate or phase out tariffs and other barriers in industrial products (such as textiles and apparel) and agricultural products. NAFTA also included provisions designed to reduce barriers to investment in Mexican petrochemicals and financial service sectors.

The Trade Act of 2002 was enacted under George W. Bush and gives the President the ability to negoti-

ate additional international agreements (subject to an up-or-down vote by Congress).

During his campaign and early in his presidency, Barack Obama pledged to renegotiate NAFTA. However, the deep recession during that time caused him to postpone that effort. Only time will tell whether the current and future administrations will continue on the course set by Presidents Clinton and Bush.

Sources: "NAFTA Renegotiation Must Wait, Obama Says," *Washington Post*, February 20, 2009; *Economic Report of the President*, Washington, D.C.: U.S. Government Printing Office, February 2007, p. 60; *Economic Report of the President*, Washington, D.C.: U.S. Government Printing Office, February 2006, p. 153; *Economic Report of the President*, Washington, D.C.: U.S. Government Printing Office, February 1995, pp. 220–21.

Input Prices

The supply curve reveals how much producers are willing to produce at alternative prices. As production costs change, the willingness of producers to produce output at a given price changes. In particular, as the price of an input rises, producers are willing to produce less output at each given price. This decrease in supply is depicted as a leftward shift in the supply curve.

Technology or Government Regulations

Technological changes and changes in government regulations also can affect the position of the supply curve. Changes that make it possible to produce a given output at a lower cost, such as the ones highlighted in Inside Business 2–2, have the effect of increasing supply. Conversely, natural disasters that destroy existing technology and government regulations, such as emissions standards that have an adverse effect on businesses, shift the supply curve to the left.

Number of Firms

The number of firms in an industry affects the position of the supply curve. As additional firms enter an industry, more and more output is available at each given price. This is reflected by a rightward shift in the supply curve. Similarly, as firms leave an industry, fewer units are sold at each price, and the supply decreases (shifts to the left).

Substitutes in Production

Many firms have technologies that are readily adaptable to several different products. For example, automakers can convert a truck assembly plant into a car assembly plant by altering its production facilities. When the price of cars rises, these firms can convert some of their truck assembly lines to car assembly lines to increase the quantity of cars supplied. This has the effect of shifting the truck supply curve to the left.

Taxes

The position of the supply curve is also affected by taxes. An *excise tax* is a tax on each unit of output sold, where the tax revenue is collected from the supplier. For example, suppose the government levies a tax of $.20 per gallon on gasoline. Since each supplier must now pay the government $.20 per gallon for each gallon of gasoline sold, each must receive an additional $.20 per gallon to be willing to supply the same quantity of gasoline as before the tax. An excise tax shifts the supply curve up by the amount of the tax, as in Figure 2–7. Note that at any given price, producers are willing to sell less gasoline after the tax than before. Thus, an excise tax has the effect of decreasing the supply of a good.

Another form of tax often used by a government agency is an ad valorem tax. *Ad valorem* literally means "according to the value." An *ad valorem tax* is a percentage tax; the sales tax is a well-known example. If the price of a good is $1 and a 10 percent ad valorem tax is attached to that good, the price after the tax is $1.10. Because an ad valorem tax is a percentage tax, it will be higher for high-priced items.

In Figure 2–8, S^0 represents the supply curve for backpacks before the inception of a 20 percent ad valorem tax. Notice that 1,100 backpacks are offered for sale when the price of a backpack is $10 and 2,450 backpacks are offered when the price is $20.

FIGURE 2–7   A Per Unit (Excise) Tax

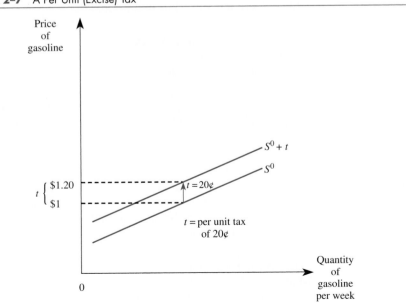

FIGURE 2–8 An Ad Valorem Tax

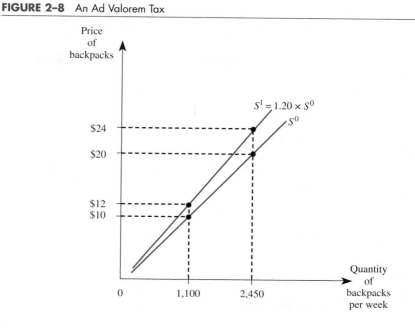

Once the 20 percent tax is implemented, the price required to produce each unit goes up by 20 percent at any output level. Therefore, price will go up by $2 at a quantity of 1,100 and by $4 at a quantity of 2,450. An ad valorem tax will rotate the supply curve counterclockwise, and the new curve will shift farther away from the original curve as the price increases. This explains why S^1 is steeper than S^0 in Figure 2–8.

Producer Expectations

Producer expectations about future prices also affect the position of the supply curve. In effect, selling a unit of output today and selling a unit of output tomorrow are substitutes in production. If firms suddenly expect prices to be higher in the future and the product is not perishable, producers can hold back output today and sell it later at a higher price. This has the effect of shifting the current supply curve to the left.

The Supply Function

supply function
A function that describes how much of a good will be produced at alternative prices of that good, alternative input prices, and alternative values of other variables affecting supply.

You should now understand the difference between supply and quantity supplied and recognize the factors that influence the position of the supply curve. The final step in our analysis of supply is to show that all the factors that influence the supply of a good can be summarized in a supply function.

The *supply function* of a good describes how much of the good will be produced at alternative prices of the good, alternative prices of inputs, and alternative values of other variables that affect supply. Formally, let Q_x^s represent the quantity supplied of a good, P_x the price of the good, W the price of an input (such as the wage rate on labor), P_r the price of technologically related goods, and H the value of some other variable that affects supply (such as the existing technology, the number of firms in the market, taxes, or producer expectations). Then the supply function for good X may be written as

$$Q_x^s = f(P_x, P_r, W, H)$$

Thus, the supply function explicitly recognizes that the quantity produced in a market depends not only on the price of the good but also on all the factors that are potential supply shifters. While there are many different functional forms for different types of products, a particularly useful representation of a supply function is the linear relationship. Supply is *linear* if Q_x^s is a linear function of the variables that influence supply. The following equation is representative of a linear supply function:

$$Q_x^s = \beta_0 + \beta_x P_x + \beta_r P_r + \beta_w W + \beta_H H$$

linear supply function
A representation of the supply function in which the supply of a given good is a linear function of prices and other variables affecting supply.

The coefficients (the β_is) represent given numbers that have been estimated by the firm's research department or an economic consultant.

Demonstration Problem 2–3

Your research department estimates that the supply function for television sets is given by

$$Q_x^s = 2,000 + 3P_x - 4P_r - P_w$$

where P_x is the price of TV sets, P_r represents the price of a computer monitor, and P_w is the price of an input used to make television sets. Suppose TVs are sold for $400 per unit, computer monitors are sold for $100 per unit, and the price of an input is $2,000. How many television sets are produced?

Answer:
To find out how many television sets are produced, we insert the given values of prices into the supply function to get

$$Q_x^s = 2,000 + 3(400) - 4(100) - 1(2,000)$$

Adding up the numbers, we find that the total quantity of television sets produced is 800.

The information summarized in a supply function can be used to graph a supply curve. Since a supply curve is the relationship between price and quantity, a representative supply curve holds everything but price constant. This means one may obtain the formula for a supply curve by inserting given values of the supply shifters into the supply function, but leaving P_x in the equation to allow for various values. If we do this for the supply function in Demonstration Problem 2–3 (where $P_r = \$100$ and $P_w = 2,000$), we get

$$Q_x^s = 2,000 + 3P_x - 4(100) - 1(2,000)$$

which simplifies to

$$Q_x^s = 3P_x - 400 \qquad (2-2)$$

Since we usually graph this relation with the price of the good on the vertical axis, it is useful to represent Equation 2–2 with price on the left-hand side and everything else on the right-hand side. This is known as an *inverse supply function*. For this example, the inverse supply function is

$$P_x = \frac{400}{3} + \frac{1}{3} Q_x^s$$

which is the equation for the supply curve graphed in Figure 2–9. This curve reveals how much producers must receive to be willing to produce each additional unit of good X.

Producer Surplus

Just as consumers want price to be as low as possible, producers want price to be as high as possible. The supply curve reveals the amount producers will be willing to produce at a given price. Alternatively, it indicates the price firms would have to receive to be willing to produce an additional unit of a good. For example, the supply curve in Figure 2–9 indicates that a total of 800 units will be produced when the price is $400. Alternatively, if 800 units are produced, producers will have to receive $400 to be induced to produce another unit of the good.

producer surplus
The amount producers receive in excess of the amount necessary to induce them to produce the good.

 Producer surplus is the producer analogue to consumer surplus. It is the amount of money producers receive in excess of the amount necessary to induce them to produce the good. More specifically, note that producers are willing to sell each unit of output below 800 units at a price less than $400. But if the price

FIGURE 2–9 Producer Surplus

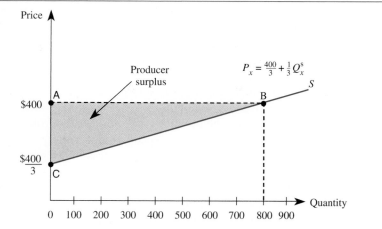

is $400, producers receive an amount equal to $400 for each unit of output below 800, even though they would be willing to sell those individual units for a lower price.

Geometrically, producer surplus is the area above the supply curve but below the market price of the good. Thus, the shaded area in Figure 2–9 represents the surplus producers receive by selling 800 units at a price of $400—an amount above what would be required to produce each unit of the good. The shaded area, ABC, is the producer surplus when the price is $400. Mathematically, this area is one-half of 800 times $266.67, or $106,668.

Producer surplus can be a powerful tool for managers. For instance, suppose the manager of a major fast-food restaurant currently purchases 10,000 pounds of ground beef each week from a supplier at a price of $1.25 per pound. The producer surplus the meat supplier earns by selling 10,000 pounds at $1.25 per pound tells the restaurant manager the dollar amount that the supplier is receiving over and above what it would be willing to accept for meat. In other words, the meat supplier's producer surplus is the maximum amount the restaurant could save in meat costs by bargaining with the supplier over a package deal for 10,000 pounds of meat. Chapters 6 and 10 will provide details about how managers can negotiate such a bargain.

MARKET EQUILIBRIUM

The equilibrium price in a competitive market is determined by the interactions of all buyers and sellers in the market. The concepts of market supply and market demand make this notion of interaction more precise: The price of a good in a competitive market is determined by the interaction of market supply and market demand for the good.

Since we will focus on the market for a single good, it is convenient to drop subscripts at this point and let P denote the price of this good and Q the quantity of the good. Figure 2–10 depicts the market supply and demand curves for such a good. To see how the competitive price is determined, let the price of the good be P^L. This price corresponds to point B on the market demand curve; consumers wish to purchase Q^1 units of the good. Similarly, the price of P^L corresponds to point A on the market supply curve; producers are willing to produce only Q^0 units at this price. Thus, when the price is P^L, there is a *shortage* of the good; that is, there is not enough of the good to satisfy all consumers willing to purchase it at that price.

In situations where a shortage exists, there is a natural tendency for the price to rise; consumers unable to buy the good may offer producers a higher price in an attempt to get the product. As the price rises from P^L to P^e in Figure 2–10, producers have an incentive to expand output from Q^0 to Q^e. Similarly, as the price rises, consumers are willing to purchase less of the good. When the price rises to P^e, the quantity demanded is Q^e. At this price, just enough of the good is produced to satisfy all consumers willing and able to purchase at that price; quantity demanded equals quantity supplied.

Suppose the price is at a higher level—say, P^H. This price corresponds to point F on the market demand curve, indicating that consumers wish to purchase

FIGURE 2-10 Market Equilibrium

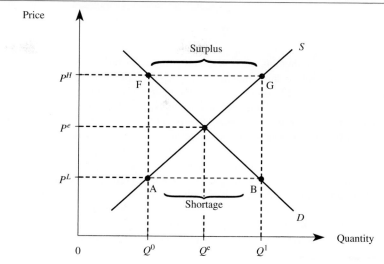

Q^0 units of the good. The price P^H corresponds to point G on the market supply curve; producers are willing to produce Q^1 units at this price. Thus, when the price is P^H, there is a *surplus* of the good; firms are producing more than they can sell at a price of P^H.

Whenever a surplus exists, there is a natural tendency for the price to fall to equate quantity supplied with quantity demanded; producers unable to sell their products may ask for a lower price in an attempt to reduce their unsold inventories. As the price falls from P^H to P^e, producers have an incentive to reduce quantity supplied to Q^e. Similarly, as the price falls, consumers are willing to purchase more of the good. When the price falls to P^e, the quantity demanded is Q^e; quantity demanded equals quantity supplied.

Thus, the interaction of supply and demand ultimately determines a competitive price, P^e, such that there is neither a shortage nor a surplus of the good. This price is called the *equilibrium price* and the corresponding quantity, Q^e, is called the *equilibrium quantity* for the competitive market. Once this price and quantity are realized, the market forces of supply and demand are balanced; there is no tendency for prices either to rise or to fall.

Principle	**Competitive Market Equilibrium**

Equilibrium in a competitive market is determined by the intersection of the market demand and supply curves. The equilibrium price is the price that equates quantity demanded with quantity supplied. Mathematically, if $Q^d(P)$ and $Q^s(P)$ represent the quantity demanded and supplied when the price is P, the equilibrium price, P^e, is the price such that

$$Q^d(P^e) = Q^s(P^e)$$

The equilibrium quantity is simply $Q^d(P^e)$ or, equivalently, $Q^s(P^e)$.

INSIDE BUSINESS 2–3

Unpopular Equilibrium Prices

For a recent college graduation, each graduating student was directed to pick up three free tickets any time between April 9 and April 20. After April 20, remaining tickets were given to those desiring additional tickets, on a first come, first served basis. Once the free tickets were fully distributed, any trades between ticket holders and ticket demanders were left to market forces—which led to a very unpopular equilibrium price.

With several concurrent events competing for students' attention during this time, many students did not claim their three free tickets by the deadline. As graduation approached, students who did not claim their tickets were willing to pay large sums of money to purchase tickets for visiting family members and friends. Since the demand for tickets was great and only a limited number of tickets were available, some sellers were asking as much as $400 for a ticket!

Several students expressed outrage over the high prices. However, the high prices are merely a symptom of the high value many students placed on graduation tickets coupled with the limited supply. Had graduating seniors without tickets better forecasted this market outcome, they would have picked up their free tickets on time.

Source: "$400? Ticket Scalpers Cash in on IU Kelley's Commencement," *The Herald-Times*, May 3, 2012.

Demonstration Problem 2–4

According to an article in *China Daily,* China recently accelerated its plan to privatize tens of thousands of state-owned firms. Imagine that you are an aide to a senator on the Foreign Relations Committee of the U.S. Senate, and you have been asked to help the committee determine the price and quantity that will prevail when competitive forces are allowed to equilibrate the market. The best estimates of the market demand and supply for the good (in U.S. dollar equivalent prices) are given by $Q^d = 10 - 2P$ and $Q^s = 2 + 2P$, respectively. Determine the competitive equilibrium price and quantity.

Answer:

Competitive equilibrium is determined by the intersection of the market demand and supply curves. Mathematically, this simply means that $Q^d = Q^s$. Equating demand and supply yields

$$10 - 2P = 2 + 2P$$

or

$$8 = 4P$$

Solving this equation for P yields the equilibrium price, $P^e = 2$. To determine the equilibrium quantity, we simply plug this price into either the demand or the supply function (since, in equilibrium, quantity supplied equals quantity demanded). For example, using the supply function, we find that

$$Q^e = 2 + 2(2) = 6$$

PRICE RESTRICTIONS AND MARKET EQUILIBRIUM

The previous section showed how prices and quantities are determined in a free market. In some instances, government places limits on how much prices are allowed to rise or fall, and these restrictions can affect the market equilibrium. In this section, we examine the impact of price ceilings and price floors on market allocations.

Price Ceilings

One basic implication of the economic doctrine of scarcity is that there are not enough goods to satisfy the desires of all consumers at a price of zero. As a consequence, some method must be used to determine who gets to consume goods and who does not. People who do not get to consume goods are essentially discriminated against. One way to determine who gets a good and who does not is to allocate the goods based on hair color: If you have red hair, you get the good; if you don't have red hair, you don't get the good.

The price system uses price to determine who gets a good and who does not. The price system allocates goods to consumers who are willing and able to pay the most for the goods. If the competitive equilibrium price of a pair of jeans is $40, consumers willing and able to pay $40 will purchase the good; consumers unwilling or unable to pay that much for a pair of jeans will not buy the good.

It is important to keep in mind that it is not the price system that is "unfair" if one cannot afford to pay the market price for a good; rather, it is unfair that we live in a world of scarcity. Any method of allocating goods will seem unfair to someone because there are not enough resources to satisfy everyone's wants. For example, if jeans were allocated to people on the basis of hair color instead of the price system, you would think this allocation rule was unfair unless you were born with the "right" hair color.

Often individuals who are discriminated against by the price system attempt to persuade the government to intervene in the market by requiring producers to sell the good at a lower price. This is only natural, for if we were unable to own a house because we had the wrong hair color, we most certainly would attempt to get the government to pass a law allowing people with our hair color to own a house. But then there would be too few houses to go around, and some other means would have to be used to allocate houses to people.

price ceiling
The maximum legal price that can be charged in a market.

Suppose that, for whatever reason, the government views the equilibrium price of P^e in Figure 2–11 as "too high" and passes a law prohibiting firms from charging prices above P^c. Such a price is called a *price ceiling.*

Do not be confused by the fact that the price ceiling is below the initial equilibrium price; the term *ceiling* refers to that price being the highest permissible price in the market. It does not refer to a price set above the equilibrium price. In fact, if a ceiling were imposed above the equilibrium price, it would be ineffective; the equilibrium price would be below the maximum legal price.

Given the regulated price of P^c, quantity demanded exceeds quantity supplied by the distance from A to B in Figure 2–11; there is a shortage of $Q^d - Q^s$ units. The reason for the shortage is twofold. First, producers are willing to produce less at the lower price, so the available quantity is reduced from Q^e to Q^s. Second, consumers wish to purchase more at the lower price; thus, quantity demanded increases from Q^e to Q^d. The result is that there is not enough of the good to satisfy all consumers willing and able to purchase it at the price ceiling.

How, then, are the goods to be allocated now that it is no longer legal to ration them on the basis of price? In most instances, goods are rationed on the basis of "first come, first served." As a consequence, price ceilings typically result in long lines such as those created in the 1970s due to price ceilings on gasoline. Thus, price ceilings discriminate against people who have a high opportunity cost of time and do not like to wait in lines. If a consumer has to wait in line two hours to buy 10 gallons of gasoline and his or her time is worth $5 per hour, it costs the consumer $2 \times \$5 = \$10$ to wait in line. Since 10 gallons of gasoline are purchased, this amounts to spending $1 per gallon waiting in line to purchase the good.

This basic idea can be depicted graphically. Under the price ceiling of P^c, only Q^s units of the good are available. Since this quantity corresponds to point F on the demand curve in Figure 2–11, we see that consumers are willing to pay P^F for another unit of the good. By law, however, they cannot pay the firm more than P^c. The difference, $P^F - P^c$, reflects the price per unit consumers are willing to pay by waiting in line. The *full economic price* paid by a consumer (P^F) is thus the amount paid to the firm (P^c), plus the implicit amount paid by waiting in line ($P^F - P^c$). The latter price is paid not in dollars but through opportunity cost and thus is termed the *nonpecuniary price*.

full economic price
The dollar amount paid to a firm under a price ceiling, plus the nonpecuniary price.

$$
\begin{array}{ccccc}
P^F & = & P^c & + & (P^F - P^c) \\
\text{Full} & & \text{Dollar} & & \text{Nonpecuniary} \\
\text{economic} & & \text{price} & & \text{price} \\
\text{price} & & & &
\end{array}
$$

As Figure 2–11 shows, P^F is greater than the initial equilibrium price, P^e. When opportunity costs are taken into account, the full economic price paid for a good is actually higher after the ceiling is imposed.

Since price ceilings reduce the quantity available in the market, such regulations reduce social welfare even if they do not result in long lines. The dollar value of the lost social welfare is given by the shaded triangle in Figure 2–11. Intuitively, each point on the demand curve represents the amount consumers would be willing to pay

FIGURE 2–11 A Price Ceiling

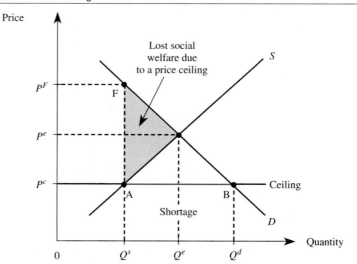

for an additional unit, while each point on the supply curve indicates the amount producers would have to receive to induce them to sell an additional unit. The vertical difference between the demand and supply curves at each quantity therefore represents the change in social welfare (consumer value less relevant production costs) associated with each incremental unit of output. Summing these vertical differences for all units between Q^e and Q^s yields the shaded triangle in Figure 2–11 and thus represents the total dollar value of the lost social welfare due to a price ceiling. The triangle in Figure 2–11 is sometimes called "deadweight loss."

Demonstration Problem 2–5

Based on your answer to the Senate Foreign Relations Committee (Demonstration Problem 2–4), one of the senators raises a concern that the free market price might be too high for the typical Chinese citizen to pay. Accordingly, she asks you to explain what would happen if the Chinese government privatized the market, but then set a price ceiling at the Chinese equivalent of $1.50. How do you answer? Assume that the market demand and supply curves (in U.S. dollar equivalent prices) are still given by

$$Q^d = 10 - 2P \text{ and } Q^s = 2 + 2P$$

Answer:

Since the price ceiling is below the equilibrium price of $2, a shortage will result. More specifically, when the price ceiling is $1.50, quantity demanded is

$$Q^d = 10 - 2(1.50) = 7$$

and quantity supplied is

$$Q^s = 2 + 2(1.50) = 5$$

Thus, there is a shortage of $7 - 5 = 2$ units.

To determine the full economic price, we simply determine the maximum price consumers are willing to pay for the five units produced. To do this, we first set quantity equal to 5 in the demand formula:

$$5 = 10 - 2P^F$$

or

$$2P^F = 5$$

Next, we solve this equation for P^F to obtain the full economic price, $P^F = \$2.50$. Thus, consumers pay a full economic price of $2.50 per unit; $1.50 of this price is in money, and $1 represents the nonpecuniary price of the good.

Based on the preceding analysis, one may wonder why the government would ever impose price ceilings. One answer might be that politicians do not understand the basics of supply and demand. This probably is not the answer, however.

The answer lies in who benefits from and who is harmed by ceilings. When lines develop due to a shortage caused by a price ceiling, people with high opportunity

INSIDE BUSINESS 2–4

Price Ceilings and Price Floors around the Globe

Federal, state, and local authorities around the world are often persuaded to enact laws that restrict the prices that businesses can legally charge their customers. Many states in the United States have usury laws—price ceilings on interest rates—that restrict the rate that banks and other lenders can legally charge their customers. In 2005, Poland passed the Anti-Usury Act, which limited the consumer interest rate to quadruple the security rate of the National Bank of Poland; violators of the Act can face a fine or up to two years of imprisonment. Thailand allowed gasoline prices to be determined by market forces during the 1990s, but its Commerce Ministry imposed a price ceiling in an attempt to hold down the rapidly rising gasoline prices during the early 2000s.

All but five states in the United States have enacted minimum wage legislation—that is, a price floor on the hourly rate a business can legally pay its employees. These restrictions are in addition to the minimum wage set by the federal government, and as of 2012, state minimum wages were higher than the federal minimum wage in 18 states. The effect of these minimum wages is similar to that shown in Figure 2–12. However, since governments do not hire workers who are unable to find employment at the artificially high wage, the "surplus" of labor translates into unemployment. Over a dozen Canadian provinces also have enacted minimum wage laws. In addition, Ontario, British Columbia, and Quebec have established floor prices (called "minimum retail prices") on beer to keep prices artificially high in an attempt to discourage alcohol consumption and to protect Canadian brewers from inexpensive U.S. brands.

Sources: "Oil Sales: Ceiling Set on Retail Margin," *The Nation,* June 15, 2002; "An Oil Shock of Our Own Making," *The Nation,* May 20, 2004; "Italian Usury Laws: Mercy Strain'd" *The Economist,* November 23, 2000; "Democrats Look to Keep Minimum Wage on Table," *The Wall Street Journal,* June 20, 2006; "Beer Price War Punishes Mom-and-Pop Shops," *The Gazette,* November 4, 2005; "EU Lawmakers Pass Credit Directive," *Krakow Post,* May 15, 2012; and United States Department of Labor, www.dol.gov/whd/ minwage/america.htm, accessed May 15, 2012.

costs are hurt, while people with low opportunity costs may actually benefit. For example, if you have nothing better to do than wait in line, you will benefit from the lower dollar price; your nonpecuniary price is close to zero. On the other hand, if you have a high opportunity cost of time because your time is valuable to you, you are made worse off by the ceiling. If a particular politician's constituents tend to have a lower than average opportunity cost, that politician naturally will attempt to invoke a price ceiling.

Sometimes when shortages are created by a ceiling, goods are not allocated on the basis of lines. Producers may discriminate against consumers on the basis of other factors, including whether or not consumers are regular customers. During the gasoline shortage of the 1970s, many gas stations sold gas only to customers who regularly used the stations. In California during the late 1990s, price ceilings were imposed on the fees that banks charged nondepositors for using their automatic teller machines (ATMs). The banks responded by refusing to let nondepositors use their ATM machines. In other situations, such as ceilings on loan interest rates, banks may allocate money only to consumers who are relatively well-to-do.

The key point is that in the presence of a shortage created by a ceiling, managers must use some method other than price to allocate the goods. Depending on which method is used, some consumers will benefit and others will be worse off.

Price Floors

In contrast to the case of a price ceiling, sometimes the equilibrium competitive price may be considered too low for sellers. In these instances, individuals may lobby for the government to legislate a minimum legal price for a good. Such a price is called a *price floor*. Perhaps the best-known price floor is the minimum wage, the lowest legal wage that can be paid to workers.

price floor
The minimum legal price that can be charged in a market.

If the equilibrium price is above the price floor, the price floor has no effect on the market. But if the price floor is set above the competitive equilibrium level, such as P^f in Figure 2–12, there is an effect. Specifically, when the price floor is set at P^f, quantity supplied is Q^s and quantity demanded is Q^d. In this instance, more is produced than consumers are willing to purchase at that price, and a surplus develops. In the context of the labor market, there are more people looking for work than there are jobs to go around at that wage, and unemployment results. In the context of a product market, the surplus translates into unsold inventories. In a free market, price would fall to alleviate the unemployment or excess inventories, but the price floor prevents this mechanism from working. Buyers end up paying a higher price and purchasing fewer units.

What happens to the unsold inventories? Sometimes the government agrees to purchase the surplus. This is the case with price floors on many agricultural products, such as cheese. Under a price floor, the quantity of unsold products is given by the distance from G to F in Figure 2–12, or $Q^s - Q^d$. If the government purchases this surplus at the price floor, the total cost to the government is $P^f(Q^s - Q^d)$. Since the area of a rectangle is its base times its height, the cost to the government of buying the surplus is given by the shaded area FGQ^sQ^d in Figure 2–12.

FIGURE 2–12 A Price Floor

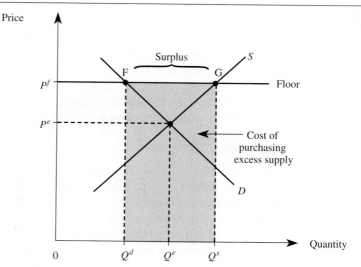

Demonstration Problem 2–6

One of the members of the Senate Foreign Relations Committee has studied your analysis of Chinese privatization (Demonstration Problems 2–4 and 2–5) but is worried that the free-market price might be too low to enable producers to earn a fair rate of return on their investment. He asks you to explain what would happen if the Chinese government privatized the market, but agreed to purchase unsold units of the good at a floor price of $4. What do you tell the senator? Assume that the market demand and supply curves (in U.S. dollar equivalent prices) are still given by

$$Q^d = 10 - 2P \text{ and } Q^s = 2 + 2P$$

Answer:

Since the price floor is above the equilibrium price of $2, the floor results in a surplus. More specifically, when the price is $4, quantity demanded is

$$Q^d = 10 - 2(4) = 2$$

and quantity supplied is

$$Q^s = 2 + 2(4) = 10$$

Thus, there is a surplus of $10 - 2 = 8$ units. Consumers pay a higher price ($4), and producers have unsold inventories of 8 units. However, the Chinese government must purchase the amount consumers are unwilling to purchase at the price of $4. Thus, the cost to the Chinese government of buying the surplus of 8 units is $4 \times 8 = \$32$.

COMPARATIVE STATICS

You now understand how equilibrium is determined in a competitive market and how government policies such as price ceilings and price floors affect the market. Next, we show how managers can use supply and demand to analyze the impact of changes in market conditions on the competitive equilibrium price and quantity. The study of the movement from one equilibrium to another is known as *comparative static analysis*. Throughout this analysis, we assume that no legal restraints, such as price ceilings or floors, are in effect and that the price system is free to work to allocate goods among consumers.

Changes in Demand

Suppose that *The Wall Street Journal* reports that consumer incomes are expected to rise by about 2.5 percent over the next year, and the number of individuals over 25 years of age will reach an all-time high by the end of the year. We can use our supply and demand apparatus to examine how these changes in market conditions will affect car rental agencies like Avis, Hertz, and National. It seems reasonable to presume that rental cars are normal goods: A rise in consumer incomes will most likely increase the demand for rental cars. The increased number of consumers aged 25 and older will also increase demand, since at many locations those who rent cars must be at least 25 years old.

FIGURE 2–13 Effect of a Change in Demand for Rental Cars

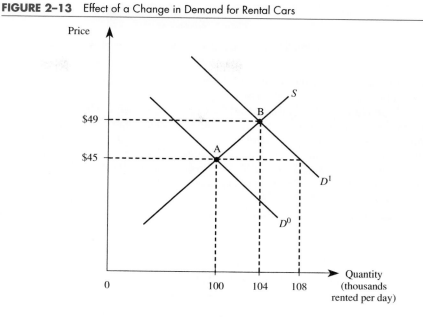

We illustrate the ultimate effect of this increase in the demand for rental cars in Figure 2–13. The initial equilibrium in the market for rental cars is at point A, where demand curve D^0 intersects the market supply curve S. The changes reported in *The Wall Street Journal* suggest that the demand for rental cars will increase over the next year, from D^0 to some curve like D^1. The equilibrium moves to point B, where car rental companies rent more cars and charge a higher price than before the demand increase.

The reason for the rise in rental car prices is as follows: The growing number of consumers aged 25 or older, coupled with the rise in consumer incomes, increases the demand for rental cars. At the old price of $45 per day, there are only 100,000 cars available. This is less than the 108,000 cars that customers want to rent at that price. Car rental companies thus find it in their interest to raise their prices and to increase their quantity supplied of rental cars until ultimately enough cars are available at the new equilibrium price of $49 to exactly equal the quantity demanded at this higher price.

Demonstration Problem 2–7

The manager of a fleet of cars currently rents them out at the market price of $49 per day, with renters paying for their own gasoline and oil. In a front-page newspaper article, the manager learns that economists expect gasoline prices to rise dramatically over the next year, due to increased tensions in the Middle East. What should she expect to happen to the price of the cars her company rents?

Answer:

Since gasoline and rental cars are complements, the increase in gasoline prices will decrease the demand for rental cars. To see the impact on the market price and quantity of rental cars, let D^1 in Figure 2–13 represent the initial demand for rental cars, so that the initial

---

INSIDE BUSINESS 2–5

Globalization and the Supply of Automobiles

In today's global economy, the number of firms in the market critically depends on the entry and exit decisions of foreign firms. Recently, several Chinese automakers—including the country's biggest domestic brand, Chery Automobile Co.—announced ambitious plans to expand abroad. Chery already exports to 70 developing countries in Asia, the Middle East, and Latin America, and is eyeing further expansion into more developed markets.

Entry by Chery and other Chinese manufacturers into a developed market such as the U.S. automobile market would shift the supply curve to the right. Other things equal, this will negatively impact the bottom lines of firms that currently sell in these markets: The increase in supply will reduce the equilibrium prices of automobiles and the profits of existing U.S. automakers.

Source: "Chinese Automakers Aim for Global Expansion," Manufacturing.Net, April 23, 2010.

---

equilibrium is at point B. An increase in the price of gasoline will shift the demand curve for rental cars to the left (to D^0), resulting in a new equilibrium at point A. Thus, she should expect the price of rental cars to fall.

Changes in Supply

We can also use our supply and demand framework to predict how changes in one or more supply shifters will affect the equilibrium price and quantity of goods or services. For instance, consider a bill before Congress that would require all employers, small and large alike, to provide health care to their workers. How would this bill affect the prices charged for goods at retailing outlets?

This health care mandate would increase the cost to retailers and other firms of hiring workers. Many retailers rely on semiskilled workers who earn relatively low wages, and the cost of providing health insurance to these workers is large relative to their annual wage earnings. While firms might lower wages to some extent to offset the mandated health insurance costs paid, the net effect would be to raise the total cost to the firm of hiring workers. These higher labor costs, in turn, would decrease the supply of retail goods. The final result of the legislation would be to increase the prices charged by retailing outlets and to reduce the quantity of goods sold there.

We can see this more clearly in Figure 2–14. The market is initially in equilibrium at point A, where demand curve D intersects the market supply curve, S^0. Higher input prices decrease supply from S^0 to S^1, and the new competitive equilibrium moves to point B. In this instance, the market price rises from P^0 to P^1, and the equilibrium quantity decreases from Q^0 to Q^1.

Simultaneous Shifts in Supply and Demand

Managers in both the private and public sectors sometimes encounter events that lead to simultaneous shifts in both demand and supply. A tragic example occurred at the end of the last century when an earthquake hit Kobe, Japan. The earthquake did considerable damage to Japan's sake wine industry, and the nation's supply of

---

INSIDE BUSINESS 2–6

Using a Spreadsheet to Calculate Equilibrium in the Supply and Demand Model

The Web site for the eighth edition of *Managerial Economics and Business Strategy*, www.mhhe.com/baye8e, contains a file named SupplyandDemandSolver.xls. With a few clicks of a mouse, you can use this tool to determine equilibrium in the linear supply and demand model under different scenarios by accessing different tabs in the file. You can also use this program to see how equilibrium prices and quantities change through "real-time" comparative static exercises.

Additionally, this tool permits you to calculate both producer and consumer surplus and investigate how their magnitudes change when demand and supply parameters change. You can also use it to examine the quantitative impact of price regulations, such as price ceilings and price floors, and the resulting lost

social welfare (or deadweight loss) associated with prices that are regulated at levels above or below the equilibrium price.

It is important to stress that this tool is not a substitute for being able to perform these tasks without the aid of the tool. But the tool will help you visualize how different demand and supply parameters lead to different quantitative effects. Just as important, you can create a never-ending number of practice problems and solve them by hand, and then use this tool to check your answers. For Connect users, the algorithmic versions of the end-of-chapter problems will allow you to solve many versions of these types of equilibrium problems with immediate feedback on your performance.

---

sake wine decreased as a result. Unfortunately, the stress caused by the earthquake led many to increase their demand for sake and other alcoholic beverages. We can use the tools of this chapter to examine how these simultaneous changes in supply and demand affected the equilibrium price and quantity of sake.

In Figure 2–15, the market is initially in equilibrium at point A, where demand curve D^0 intersects market supply curve S^0. Since the earthquake led to a simultaneous

FIGURE 2–14 Effect of a Change in Supply

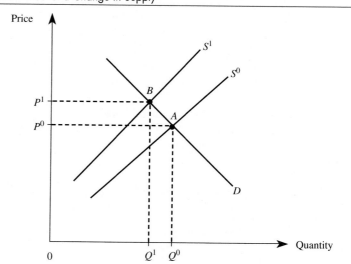

FIGURE 2–15   A Simultaneous Increase in Demand and Decrease in Supply Raises the Equilibrium Price

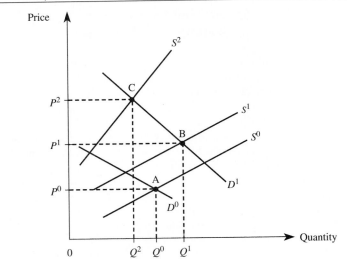

decrease in supply and increase in demand for sake, suppose supply decreases from S^0 to S^1 and demand increases from D^0 to D^1. In this instance, a new competitive equilibrium occurs at point B; the price of sake increases from P^0 to P^1, and the quantity consumed increases from Q^0 to Q^1.

As the curves are drawn in Figure 2–15, the effect of the decrease in supply and increase in demand was to increase both the price and the quantity. But what if instead of shifting from S^0 to S^1, the supply curve shifted much farther to the left to S^2 so that it intersected the new demand curve at point C instead of B? In this instance, price would still be higher than the initial equilibrium price, P^0. But the resulting quantity would be lower than the initial equilibrium (point C implies a lower quantity than point A). Thus, we have seen that when demand increases and supply decreases, the market price rises, but the market quantity may rise or fall depending on the relative magnitude of the shifts.

When using supply and demand analysis to predict the effects of simultaneous changes in demand and supply, you must be careful that the predictions are not artifacts of how far you have shifted the curves. As shown in Table 2–2, simultaneous changes in demand and supply generally lead to ambiguities regarding whether the equilibrium price or quantity will rise or fall. A valuable exercise is to draw various simultaneous shifts in supply and demand to verify the results summarized in Table 2–2.

Demonstration Problem 2–8

For a video walkthrough of this problem, visit www.mhhe.com/ baye8e

Suppose you are the manager of a chain of computer stores. For obvious reasons you have been closely following developments in the computer industry, and you have just learned that Congress has passed a two-pronged program designed to further enhance the U.S. computer industry's position in the global economy. The legislation provides increased funding

TABLE 2-2 Equilibrium Price and Quantity: The Impact of Simultaneous Shifts in Demand and Supply

Nature of the Change	Increase in Demand	Decrease in Demand
Increase in Supply	Price: Ambiguous Quantity: Increases	Price: Decreases Quantity: Ambiguous
Decrease in Supply	Price: Increases Quantity: Ambiguous	Price: Ambiguous Quantity: Decreases

for computer education in primary and secondary schools, as well as tax breaks for firms that develop computer software. As a result of this legislation, what do you predict will happen to the equilibrium price and quantity of software?

Answer:

The equilibrium quantity certainly will increase, but the market price may rise, remain the same, or fall, depending on the relative changes in demand and supply. To see this, note that the increased funding for computer education at primary and secondary schools will lead to an increase in the demand for computer software, since it is a normal good. The reduction in taxes on software manufacturers will lead to an increase in the supply of software. You should draw a figure to verify that if the rightward shift in supply is small compared to the rightward shift in demand, both the equilibrium price and quantity will increase. If supply increases by the same amount as demand, there will be no change in the price but the equilibrium quantity will rise. Finally, if supply increases more than the increase in demand, the resulting equilibrium will entail a lower price and a greater quantity. In all cases, the equilibrium quantity increases. But the effect on the market price depends on the relative magnitudes of the increases in demand and supply.

ANSWERING THE HEADLINE

Now that we have developed a formal apparatus for understanding how markets work, we will return to the story that opened this chapter.

Sam recognized that a cut in chip production will ultimately lead to higher chip prices. Since chips are a key input in the production of PCs, an increase in the price

FIGURE 2-16 Rising Chip Prices Decrease the Supply of PCs

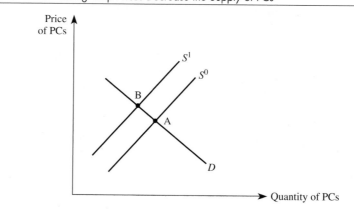

of chips would in turn lead to a decrease in the market supply of PCs, as indicated by the change in supply from S^0 to S^1 in Figure 2–16. Notice that total quantity of PCs sold in the market falls as the equilibrium moves from point A to point B. In light of this anticipated decline in PC sales, Sam and Jane discussed the wisdom of going ahead with their plan to double PC Solutions' workforce at this time.

SUMMARY

This chapter provided an overview of supply and demand and the interaction of these forces. We covered applications of demand, supply, price ceilings, price floors, and comparative statics. By reading this chapter and working through the demonstration problems presented, you should have a basic understanding of how to analyze the workings of a competitive market.

The model of supply and demand is just a starting point for this book. Throughout the remainder of the book, we assume you have a thorough understanding of the concepts presented in this chapter. In the next chapter, we will present the concepts of elasticity and show how to use them in making managerial decisions. We will also present some additional quantitative tools to help managers make better decisions.

KEY TERMS AND CONCEPTS

ad valorem tax
change in demand
change in quantity demanded
change in quantity supplied
change in supply
comparative static analysis
complements
consumer expectations
consumer surplus
decrease in demand
decrease in supply
demand
demand function
demand shifters
equilibrium price
equilibrium quantity
excise tax
full economic price
increase in demand
increase in supply
inferior good
informative advertising

inverse demand function
inverse supply function
law of demand
law of supply
linear demand function
linear supply function
market demand curve
market supply curve
nonpecuniary price
normal good
persuasive advertising
price ceiling
price floor
producer expectations
producer surplus
shortage
stockpiling
substitutes
supply
supply function
supply shifters
surplus

END-OF-CHAPTER PROBLEMS BY LEARNING OBJECTIVE

Every end-of-chapter problem addresses at least one learning objective. Below is a nonexhaustive sample of end-of-chapter problems for each learning objective.

LO1 Explain the laws of demand and supply, and identify factors that cause demand and supply to shift.

Try these problems: 1, 3

LO2 Calculate consumer surplus and producer surplus, and describe what they mean.

Try these problems: 5, 9

LO3 Explain price determination in a competitive market, and show how equilibrium changes in response to changes in determinants of demand and supply.

Try these problems: 6, 14

LO4 Explain and illustrate how excise taxes, *ad valorem* taxes, price floors, and price ceilings impact the functioning of a market.

Try these problems: 2, 18

LO5 Apply supply and demand analysis as a qualitative forecasting tool to see the "big picture" in competitive markets.

Try these problems: 11, 19

CONCEPTUAL AND COMPUTATIONAL QUESTIONS

1. The X-Corporation produces a good (called X) that is a normal good. Its competitor, Y-Corp., makes a substitute good that it markets under the name Y. Good Y is an inferior good.
   a. How will the demand for good X change if consumer incomes decrease?
   b. How will the demand for good Y change if consumer incomes increase?
   c. How will the demand for good X change if the price of good Y increases?
   d. Is good Y a lower-quality product than good X? Explain.

2. Good X is produced in a competitive market using input A. Explain what would happen to the supply of good X in each of the following situations:
   a. The price of input A decreases.
   b. An excise tax of $3 is imposed on good X.
   c. An ad valorem tax of 7 percent is imposed on good X.
   d. A technological change reduces the cost of producing additional units of good X.

3. Suppose the supply function for product X is given by $Q_x^s = -30 + 2P_x - 4P_z$.
   a. How much of product X is produced when $P_x = \$600$ and $P_z = \$60$?
   b. How much of product X is produced when $P_x = \$80$ and $P_z = \$60$?
   c. Suppose $P_z = \$60$. Determine the supply function and inverse supply function for good X. Graph the inverse supply function.

4. The demand for good X is given by

$$Q_x^d = 6,000 - \frac{1}{2}P_x - P_y + 9P_z + \frac{1}{10}M$$

Research shows that the prices of related goods are given by $P_y = \$6,500$ and $P_z = \$100$, while the average income of individuals consuming this product is $M = \$70,000$.

a. Indicate whether goods Y and Z are substitutes or complements for good X.

b. Is X an inferior or a normal good?

c. How many units of good X will be purchased when $P_x = \$5,230$?

d. Determine the demand function and inverse demand function for good X. Graph the demand curve for good X.

5. The demand curve for product X is given by $Q_x^d = 300 - 2P_x$.

a. Find the inverse demand curve.

b. How much consumer surplus do consumers receive when $P_x = \$45$?

c. How much consumer surplus do consumers receive when $P_x = \$30$?

d. In general, what happens to the level of consumer surplus as the price of a good falls?

6. Suppose demand and supply are given by $Q^d = 60 - P$ and $Q^s = P - 20$.

a. What are the equilibrium quantity and price in this market?

b. Determine the quantity demanded, the quantity supplied, and the magnitude of the surplus if a price floor of $50 is imposed in this market.

c. Determine the quantity demanded, the quantity supplied, and the magnitude of the shortage if a price ceiling of $32 is imposed in this market. Also, determine the full economic price paid by consumers.

7. Suppose demand and supply are given by

$$Q_x^d = 14 - \frac{1}{2}P_x \text{ and } Q_x^s = \frac{1}{4}P_x - 1$$

a. Determine the equilibrium price and quantity. Show the equilibrium graphically.

b. Suppose a $12 excise tax is imposed on the good. Determine the new equilibrium price and quantity.

c. How much tax revenue does the government earn with the $12 tax?

8. Use the accompanying graph to answer these questions.

a. Suppose demand is D and supply is S^0. If a price ceiling of $6 is imposed, what are the resulting shortage and full economic price?

b. Suppose demand is D and supply is S^0. If a price floor of $12 is imposed, what is the resulting surplus? What is the cost to the government of purchasing any and all unsold units?

c. Suppose demand is D and supply is S^0 so that the equilibrium price is $10. If an excise tax of $6 is imposed on this product, what happens to the equilibrium price paid by consumers? The price received by producers? The number of units sold?

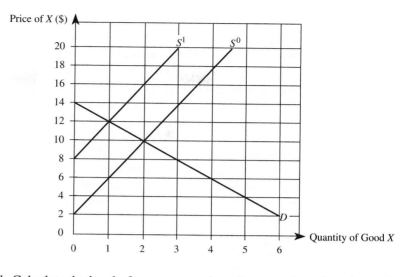

d. Calculate the level of consumer and producer surplus when demand and supply are given by D and S^0 respectively.

e. Suppose demand is D and supply is S^0. Would a price ceiling of $2 benefit any consumers? Explain.

9. The supply curve for product X is given by $Q_x^s = -520 + 20P_x$.

a. Find the inverse supply curve.

b. How much surplus do producers receive when $Q_x = 400$? When $Q_x = 1,200$?

10. Consider a market where supply and demand are given by $Q_x^s = -16 + P_x$ and $Q_x^d = 92 - 2P_x$. Suppose the government imposes a price floor of $40, and agrees to purchase any and all units consumers do not buy at the floor price of $40 per unit.

a. Determine the cost to the government of buying firms' unsold units.

b. Compute the lost social welfare (deadweight loss) that stems from the $40 price floor.

PROBLEMS AND APPLICATIONS

11. You are the manager of a midsized company that assembles personal computers. You purchase most components—such as random access memory (RAM)—in a competitive market. Based on your marketing research, consumers earning over $80,000 purchase 1.5 times more RAM than consumers with lower incomes. One morning, you pick up a copy of *The Wall Street Journal* and read an article indicating that input components for RAM are expected to rise in price, forcing manufacturers to produce RAM at a higher unit cost. Based on this information, what can you expect to happen to the price you pay for random access memory?

Would your answer change if, in addition to this change in RAM input prices, the article indicated that consumer incomes are expected to fall over the next two years as the economy dips into recession? Explain.

12. You are the manager of a firm that produces and markets a generic type of soft drink in a competitive market. In addition to the large number of generic products in your market, you also compete against major brands such as Coca-Cola and Pepsi. Suppose that, due to the successful lobbying efforts of sugar producers in the United States, Congress is going to levy a $0.50 per pound tariff on all imported raw sugar—the primary input for your product. In addition, Coke and Pepsi plan to launch an aggressive advertising campaign designed to persuade consumers that their branded products are superior to generic soft drinks. How will these events impact the equilibrium price and quantity of generic soft drinks?

13. Some have argued that higher cigarette prices do not deter smoking. While there are many arguments both for and against this view, some find the following argument to be the most persuasive of all: "The laws of supply and demand indicate that higher prices are ineffective in reducing smoking. In particular, higher cigarette prices will reduce the demand for cigarettes. This reduction in demand will push the equilibrium price back down to its original level. Since the equilibrium price will remain unchanged, smokers will consume the same number of cigarettes." Do you agree or disagree with this view? Explain.

14. You are the manager of an organization in America that distributes blood to hospitals in all 50 states and the District of Columbia. A recent report indicates that nearly 50 Americans contract HIV each year through blood transfusions. Although every pint of blood donated in the United States undergoes a battery of nine different tests, existing screening methods can detect only the antibodies produced by the body's immune system—not foreign agents in the blood. Since it takes weeks or even months for these antibodies to build up in the blood, newly infected HIV donors can pass along the virus through blood that has passed existing screening tests. Happily, researchers have developed a series of new tests aimed at detecting and removing infections from donated blood before it is used in transfusions. The obvious benefit of these tests is the reduced incidence of infection through blood transfusions. The report indicates that the current price of decontaminated blood is $60 per pint. However, if the new screening methods are adopted, the demand and supply for decontaminated blood will change to $Q^d = 210 - 1.5P$ and $Q^s = 2.5P - 150$. What price do you expect to prevail if the new screening methods are adopted? How many units of blood will be used in the United States? What is the level of consumer and producer surplus? Illustrate your findings in a graph.

15. As a result of increased tensions in the Middle East, oil production is down by 1.21 million barrels per day—a 5 percent reduction in the world's supply of crude oil. Explain the likely impact of this event on the market for gasoline and the market for small cars.

16. You are an assistant to a senator who chairs an ad hoc committee on reforming taxes on telecommunication services. Based on your research, AT&T has spent over $15 million on related paperwork and compliance costs. Moreover, depending on the locale, telecom taxes can amount to as much as 25 percent of a consumer's phone bill. These high tax rates on telecom services have become quite controversial, due to the fact that the deregulation of the telecom industry has led to a highly competitive market. Your best estimates indicate that, based on current tax rates, the monthly market demand for telecommunication services is given by $Q^d = 300 - 4P$ and the market supply (including taxes) is $Q^s = 3P - 120$ (both in millions), where P is the monthly price of telecommunication services. The senator is considering tax reform that would dramatically cut tax rates, leading to a supply function under the new tax policy of $Q^s = 3.2P - 120$. How much money per unit would a typical consumer save each month as a result of the proposed legislation?

17. G.R. Dry Foods Distributors specializes in the wholesale distribution of dry goods, such as rice and dry beans. The firm's manager is concerned about an article he read in this morning's *Wall Street Journal* indicating that the incomes of individuals in the lowest income bracket are expected to increase by 10 percent over the next year. While the manager is pleased to see this group of individuals doing well, he is concerned about the impact this will have on G.R. Dry Foods. What do you think is likely to happen to the price of the products G.R. Dry Foods sells? Why?

18. From California to New York, legislative bodies across the United States are considering eliminating or reducing the surcharges that banks impose on non-customers who make $12 million in withdrawals from other banks' ATM machines. On average, noncustomers earn a wage of $24 per hour and pay ATM fees of $3.00 per transaction. It is estimated that banks would be willing to maintain services for 5 million transactions at $1.25 per transaction, while noncustomers would attempt to conduct 19 million transactions at that price. Estimates suggest that, for every 1 million gap between the desired and available transactions, a typical consumer will have to spend an extra minute traveling to another machine to withdraw cash. Based on this information, use a graph to carefully illustrate the impact of legislation that would place a $1.25 cap on the fees banks can charge for noncustomer transactions.

19. Rapel Valley in Chile is renowned for its ability to produce high-quality wine at a fraction of the cost of many other vineyards around the world. Rapel Valley produces over 20 million bottles of wine annually, of which 5 million are exported to the United States. Each bottle entering the United States is subjected to a $0.50 per bottle excise tax, which generates about $2.5 million in tax revenues. Strong La Niña weather patterns have caused unusually cold temperatures, devastating many of the wine producers in that region of Chile. How will La Niña affect the price of Chilean wine? Assuming La Niña does not impact the California wine-producing region, how will La Niña impact the market for Californian wines?

20. Viking InterWorks is one of many manufacturers that supplies memory products to original equipment manufacturers (OEMs) of desktop systems. The CEO recently read an article in a trade publication that reported the projected demand for desktop systems to be $Q^d_{desktop} = 1{,}600 - 2P_{desktop} + .6M$ (in millions of units), where $P_{desktop}$ is the price of a desktop system and M is consumer income. The same article reported that the incomes of the desktop systems' primary consumer demographic would increase 4.2 percent this year to $61,300 and that the selling price of a desktop would decrease to $980, both of which the CEO viewed favorably for Viking. In a related article, the CEO read that the upcoming year's projected demand for 512 MB desktop memory modules is $Q^d_{memory} = 11{,}200 - 100P_{memory} - 2P_{desktop}$ (in thousands of units), where P_{memory} is the market price for a 512 MB memory module and $P_{desktop}$ is the selling price of a desktop system. The report also indicated that five new, small start-ups entered the 512 MB memory module market, bringing the total number of competitors to 100 firms. Furthermore, suppose that Viking's CEO commissioned an industrywide study to examine the industry capacity for 512 MB memory modules. The results indicate that when the industry is operating at maximum efficiency, this competitive industry supplies modules according to the following function: $Q^S_{memory} = 1{,}000 + 25P_{memory} + N$ (in thousands), where P_{memory} is the price of a 512 MB memory module and N is the number of memory module manufacturers in the market. Viking's CEO provides you, the production manager, with the above information and requests a report containing the market price for memory modules and the number of units to manufacture in the upcoming year based on the assumption that all firms producing 512 MB modules supply an equal share to the market. How would your report change if the price of desktops were $1,080? What does this indicate about the relationship between memory modules and desktop systems?

21. Seventy-two percent of the members of the United Food and Commercial Workers Local 655 voted to strike against Stop 'n Shop in the St. Louis area. In fear of similar union responses, two of Stop 'n Shop's larger rivals in the St. Louis market—Dierberg's and Schnuck's—decided to lock out their union employees. The actions of these supermarkets, not surprisingly, caused Local 655 union members to picket and boycott each of the supermarkets' locations. While the manager of Mid Towne IGA—one of many smaller competing grocers—viewed the strike as unfortunate for both sides, he was quick to point out that the strike provided an opportunity for his store to increase market share. To take advantage of the strike, the manager of Mid Towne IGA increased newspaper advertising by pointing out that Mid Towne employed Local 655 union members and that it operated under a different contract than "other" grocers in the area. Use a graph to describe the expected impact of advertising on Mid Towne IGA (how the equilibrium price and quantity change). Identify the type of advertising in which Mid

Towne IGA engaged. Do you believe the impact of advertising will be permanent? Explain.

22. Florida, like several other states, has passed a law that prohibits "price gouging" immediately before, during, or after the declaration of a state of emergency. Price gouging is defined as " . . . selling necessary commodities such as food, gas, ice, oil, and lumber at a price that grossly exceeds the average selling price for the 30 days prior to the emergency." Many consumers attempt to stock up on emergency supplies, such as bottled water, immediately before and after a hurricane or other natural disaster hits an area. Also, many supply shipments to retailers are interrupted during a natural disaster. Assuming that the law is strictly enforced, what are the economic effects of the price gouging statute? Explain carefully.

23. In a recent speech, the governor of your state announced: "One of the biggest causes of juvenile delinquency in this state is the high rate of unemployment among 16 to 19 year olds. The low wages offered by employers in the state have given fewer teenagers the incentive to find summer employment. Instead of working all summer, the way we used to, today's teenagers slack off and cause trouble. To address this problem, I propose to raise the state's minimum wage by $1.50 per hour. This will give teens the proper incentive to go out and find meaningful employment when they are not in school." Evaluate the governor's plan to reduce juvenile delinquency.

CONNECT EXERCISES

If your instructor has adopted Connect for the course and you are an active subscriber, you can practice with the questions presented above, along with many alternative versions of these questions. Your instructor may also assign a subset of these problems and/or their alternative versions as a homework assignment through Connect, allowing for immediate feedback of grades and correct answers.

CASE-BASED EXERCISES

Your instructor may assign additional problem-solving exercises (called *memos*) that require you to apply some of the tools you learned in this chapter to make a recommendation based on an actual business scenario. Some of these memos accompany the Time Warner case (pages 561–597 of your textbook). Additional memos, as well as data that may be useful for your analysis, are available online at www.mhhe.com/baye8e.

SELECTED READINGS

Ault, Richard W.; Jackson, John D.; and Saba, Richard P., "The Effect of Long-Term Rent Control on Tenant Mobility." *Journal of Urban Economics* 35(2), March 1994, pp. 140–58.

Espana, Juan R., "Impact of the North American Free Trade Agreement (NAFTA) on U.S.–Mexican Trade and Investment Flows." *Business Economics* 28(3), July 1993, pp. 41–47.

Friedman, Milton, *Capitalism and Freedom.* Chicago: University of Chicago Press, 1962.

Katz, Lawrence F., and Murphy, Kevin M., "Changes in Relative Wages, 1963–1987: Supply and Demand Factors." *Quarterly Journal of Economics* 107(1), February 1992, pp. 35–78.

Olson, Josephine E., and Frieze, Irene Hanson, "Job Interruptions and Part-Time Work: Their Effect on MBAs' Income." *Industrial Relations* 28(3), Fall 1989, pp. 373–86.

O'Neill, June, and Polachek, Solomon, "Why the Gender Gap in Wages Narrowed in the 1980s." *Journal of Labor Economics* 11(1), January 1993, pp. 205–28.

Simon, Herbert A., "Organizations and Markets." *Journal of Economic Perspectives* 5(2), Spring 1991, pp. 25–44.

Smith, Vernon L., "An Experimental Study of Competitive Market Behavior." *Journal of Political Economy* 70(2), April 1962, pp. 111–39.

Williamson, Oliver, *The Economic Institutions of Capitalism.* New York: Free Press, 1985.

CHAPTER THREE

Quantitative Demand Analysis

Winners of Wireless Auction to Pay $7 Billion

The CEO of a regional telephone company picked up the March 14 *New York Times* and began reading on page D1:

> The Federal Government completed the biggest auction in history today, selling off part of the nation's airwaves for $7 billion to a handful of giant companies that plan to blanket the nation with new wireless communications networks for telephones and computers . . .

The CEO read the article with interest because his firm is scrambling to secure loans to purchase one of the licenses the FCC plans to auction off in his region next year. The region serviced by the firm has a population that is 7 percent greater than the average where licenses have been sold before, yet the FCC plans to auction the same number of licenses. This troubled the CEO, since in the most recent auction 99 bidders coughed up a total of $7 billion—an average of $70.7 million for a single license.

Fortunately for the CEO, the *New York Times* article contained a table summarizing the price paid per license in 10 different regions, as well as the number of licenses sold and the population of each region. The CEO quickly entered this data into his spreadsheet, clicked the regression tool button, and found the following relation between the price of a license, the quantity of licenses available, and regional population size (price and population figures are expressed in millions of dollars and people, respectively):

$$\ln P = 2.23 - 1.2 \ln Q + 1.25 \ln Pop$$

Learning Objectives

After completing this chapter, you will be able to:

LO1 Apply various elasticities of demand as a quantitative tool to forecast changes in revenues, prices, and/or units sold.

LO2 Illustrate the relationship between the elasticity of demand and total revenues.

LO3 Discuss three factors that influence whether the demand for a given product is relatively elastic or inelastic.

LO4 Explain the relationship between marginal revenue and the own price elasticity of demand.

LO5 Show how to determine elasticities from linear and log-linear demand functions.

LO6 Explain how regression analysis may be used to estimate demand functions, and how to interpret and use the output of a regression.

Based on the CEO's analysis, how much money does he expect his company will need to buy a license? How much confidence do you place in this estimate? (The data required to answer the second question are available online at www.mhhe.com/baye8e in the file named AUCTION_DATA.XLS.)

INTRODUCTION

In Chapter 2 we saw that the demand for a firm's product (Q_x^d) depends on its price (P_x), the prices of substitutes or complements (P_y), consumer incomes (M), and other variables (H) such as advertising, the size of the population, or consumer expectations:

$$Q_x^d = f(P_x, P_y, M, H)$$

Until now, our analysis of the impact of changes in prices and income on consumer demand has been qualitative rather than quantitative; that is, we focused on the "big picture" to identify only the directions of the changes and said little about their magnitude.

While seeing the big picture is an important first step to sound managerial decisions, the successful manager is also adept at providing "detailed" quantitative answers to questions like these:

- How much do we have to cut our price to achieve 3.2 percent sales growth?

- If we cut prices by 6.5 percent, how many more units will we sell? Do we have sufficient inventories on hand to accommodate this increase in sales? If not, do we have enough personnel to increase production? How much will our revenues and cash flows change as a result of this price cut?

- How much will our sales change if rivals cut their prices by 2 percent or a recession hits and household incomes decline by 2.5 percent?

The first half of this chapter shows how a manager can use elasticities of demand as a quantitative forecasting tool to answer these and hundreds of other questions asked each day by managers in charge of pricing decisions, inventory management, yield (revenue) management, production decisions, strategic (competitor) analysis, and other operations including human resource management.

The second half of the chapter describes regression analysis, which is the technique economists use to estimate the parameters of demand functions. The primary focus is on how a manager can use managerial economics to evaluate information available in the library or provided by the firm's research department. Accordingly, we will explain how to interpret regression results and how managers can use regression tools contained in spreadsheet programs like Excel to actually estimate simple demand relationships.

THE ELASTICITY CONCEPT

Suppose some variable, such as the price of a product, increased by 10 percent. What would happen to the quantity demanded of the good? Based on the analysis in Chapter 2 and the law of demand, we know that the quantity demanded would fall.

It would be useful for a manager to know whether the quantity demanded would fall by 5 percent, 10 percent, or some other amount.

The primary tool used to determine the magnitude of such a change is elasticity analysis. Indeed, the most important concept introduced in this chapter is elasticity. Elasticity is a very general concept. An *elasticity* measures the responsiveness of one variable to changes in another variable. For example, the elasticity of your grade with respect to studying, denoted $E_{G,S}$, is the percentage change in your grade ($\%\Delta G$) that will result from a given percentage change in the time you spend studying ($\%\Delta S$). In other words,

elasticity
A measure of the responsiveness of one variable to changes in another variable; the percentage change in one variable that arises due to a given percentage change in another variable.

$$E_{G,S} = \frac{\%\Delta G}{\%\Delta S}$$

Since $\%\Delta G = \Delta G/G$ and $\%\Delta S = \Delta S/S$, we may also write this as $E_{G,S} = (\Delta G/\Delta S)$ (S/G). Notice that $\Delta G/\Delta S$ represents the slope of the functional relation between G and S; it tells the change in G that results from a given change in S. By multiplying this by S/G, we convert each of these changes into percentages, which means that the elasticity measure does not depend on the units in which we measure the variables G and S.

A Calculus Alternative

If the variable G depends on S according to the functional relationship $G = f(S)$, the elasticity of G with respect to S may be found using calculus:

$$E_{G,S} = \frac{dG}{dS}\frac{S}{G}$$

---

own price elasticity
A measure of the responsiveness of the quantity demanded of a good to a change in the price of that good; the percentage change in quantity demanded divided by the percentage change in the price of the good.

Two aspects of an elasticity are important: (1) whether it is positive or negative and (2) whether it is greater than 1 or less than 1 in absolute value. The sign of the elasticity determines the relationship between G and S. If the elasticity is positive, an increase in S leads to an increase in G. If the elasticity is negative, an increase in S leads to a decrease in G.

Whether the absolute value of the elasticity is greater or less than 1 determines how responsive G is to changes in S. If the absolute value of the elasticity is greater than 1, the numerator is larger than the denominator in the elasticity formula, and we know that a small percentage change in S will lead to a relatively large percentage change in G. If the absolute value of the elasticity is less than 1, the numerator is smaller than the denominator in the elasticity formula. In this instance, a given percentage change in S will lead to a relatively small percentage change in G. It is useful to keep these points in mind as we define some specific elasticities.

OWN PRICE ELASTICITY OF DEMAND

We begin with a very important elasticity concept: the *own price elasticity of demand,* which measures the responsiveness of quantity demanded to a change in price. Later in this section we will see that managers can use this measure to determine the quantitative impact of price hikes or cuts on the firm's sales and revenues. The own price elasticity of demand for good X, denoted E_{Q_x, P_x}, is defined as

$$E_{Q_x, P_x} = \frac{\% \Delta Q_x^d}{\% \Delta P_x}$$

If the own price elasticity of demand for a product is -2, for instance, we know that a 10 percent increase in the product's price leads to a 20 percent decline in the quantity demanded of the good, since $-20\%/10\% = -2$.

A Calculus Alternative

The own price elasticity of demand for a good with a demand function $Q_x^d = f(P_x, P_y, M, H)$ may be found using calculus:

$$E_{Q_x, P_x} = \frac{\partial Q_x^d}{\partial P_x} \frac{P_x}{Q_x}$$

Recall that two aspects of an elasticity are important: (1) its sign and (2) whether it is greater or less than 1 in absolute value. By the law of demand, there is an inverse relation between price and quantity demanded; thus, the own price elasticity of demand is a negative number. The absolute value of the own price elasticity of demand can be greater or less than 1 depending on several factors that we will discuss next. However, it is useful to introduce some terminology to aid in this discussion.

elastic demand
Demand is elastic if the absolute value of the own price elasticity is greater than 1.

First, demand is said to be *elastic* if the absolute value of the own price elasticity is greater than 1:

$$|E_{Q_x, P_x}| > 1$$

inelastic demand
Demand is inelastic if the absolute value of the own price elasticity is less than 1.

Second, demand is said to be *inelastic* if the absolute value of the own price elasticity is less than 1:

$$|E_{Q_x, P_x}| < 1$$

Finally, demand is said to be *unitary elastic* if the absolute value of the own price elasticity is equal to 1:

unitary elastic demand
Demand is unitary elastic if the absolute value of the own price elasticity is equal to 1.

$$|E_{Q_x, P_x}| = 1$$

Conceptually, the quantity consumed of a good is relatively responsive to a change in the price of the good when demand is elastic and relatively unresponsive to changes in price when demand is inelastic. This means that price increases will reduce consumption very little when demand is inelastic. However, when demand is elastic, a price increase will reduce consumption considerably.

Elasticity and Total Revenue

Table 3–1 shows the hypothetical prices and quantities demanded of software, the own price elasticity, and the total revenue ($TR = P_x Q_x$) for the linear demand function, $Q_x^d = 80 - 2P_x$. Notice that the absolute value of the own price elasticity gets larger as

TABLE 3–1 Total Revenue and Elasticity ($Q_x^d = 80 - 2P_x$)

	Price of Software (P_x)	Quantity of Software Sold (Q_x)	Own Price Elasticity (E_{Q_x, P_x})	Total Revenue ($P_x Q_x$)
A	$ 0	80	0.00	$ 0
B	5	70	−0.14	350
C	10	60	−0.33	600
D	15	50	−0.60	750
E	20	40	−1.00	800
F	25	30	−1.67	750
G	30	20	−3.00	600
H	35	10	−7.00	350
I	40	0	−∞	0

price increases. In particular, the slope of this linear demand function is constant ($\Delta Q_x^d / \Delta P_x = -2$), which implies that $E_{Q_x, P_x} = (\Delta Q_x^d / \Delta P_x)(P_x / Q_x)$ increases in absolute value as P_x increases. Thus, the own price elasticity of demand varies along a linear demand curve.

When the absolute value of the own price elasticity is less than 1 (points A through D in Table 3–1), an increase in price increases total revenue. For example, an increase in price from $5 to $10 per unit increases total revenue by $250. Notice that for these two prices, the corresponding elasticity of demand is less than 1 in absolute value.

When the absolute value of the own price elasticity is greater than 1 (points F through I in Table 3–1), an increase in price leads to a reduction in total revenue. For example, when the price increases from $25 (where the own price elasticity is −1.67) to $30 (where the own price elasticity is −3), we see that total revenue decreases by $150. The price–quantity combination that maximizes total revenue in Table 3–1 is at point E, where the own price elasticity equals −1.

The demand curve corresponding to the data in Table 3–1 is presented in the top panel of Figure 3–1, while the total revenue associated with each price–quantity combination on the demand curve is graphed in the lower panel. As we move up the demand curve from point A to point I, demand becomes increasingly elastic. At point E, where demand is unitary elastic, total revenue is maximized. At points to the northwest of E, demand is elastic and total revenue decreases as price increases. At points to the southeast of E, demand is inelastic and total revenue increases when price increases. This relationship among the changes in price, elasticity, and total revenue is called the *total revenue test*.

Principle	**Total Revenue Test** If demand is elastic, an increase (decrease) in price will lead to a decrease (increase) in total revenue. If demand is inelastic, an increase (decrease) in price will lead to an increase (decrease) in total revenue. Finally, total revenue is maximized at the point where demand is unitary elastic.

FIGURE 3–1 Demand, Elasticity, and Total Revenue

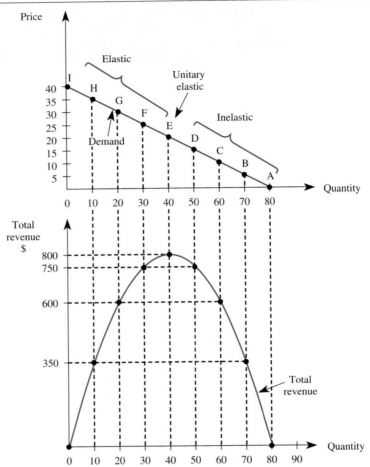

Businesses around the globe use the total revenue test to help manage cash flows. For instance, Dell recently faced a dilemma regarding its pricing strategy for computers: Should it increase prices to boost cash flow or adopt a "cut price and make it up in volume" strategy? Based on a careful analysis of its demand, the company decided to adopt the latter strategy and reduced prices in order to increase revenues.

To see why, suppose the research department of a computer company estimates that the own price elasticity of demand for a particular desktop computer is -1.7. If the company cuts prices by 5 percent, will computer sales increase enough to increase overall revenues? We can answer this question by setting $-1.7 = E_{Q_x, P_x}$ and $-5 = \%\Delta P_x$ in the formula for the own price elasticity of demand:

$$-1.7 = \frac{\%\Delta Q_x^d}{-5}$$

Solving this equation for $\%\Delta Q_x^d$ yields $\%\Delta Q_x^d = 8.5$. In other words, the quantity of computers sold will rise by 8.5 percent if prices are reduced by 5 percent. Since the percentage increase in quantity demanded is greater than the percentage decline in prices ($|E_{Q_x, P_x}| > 1$), the price cut will actually raise the firm's sales revenues. Expressed differently, since demand is elastic, a price cut results in a greater than proportional increase in sales and thus increases the firm's total revenues.

In extreme cases the demand for a good may be perfectly elastic or perfectly inelastic. Demand is *perfectly elastic* if the own price elasticity of demand is infinite in absolute value. Demand is *perfectly inelastic* if the own price elasticity of demand is zero.

perfectly elastic demand
Demand is perfectly elastic if the own price elasticity is infinite in absolute value. In this case the demand curve is horizontal.

When demand is perfectly elastic, a manager who raises price even slightly will find that none of the good is purchased. In this instance the demand curve is horizontal, as illustrated in Figure 3–2(a). Producers of generic (unbranded) products, such as aspirin, may face a demand curve that is perfectly elastic; a small increase in price may induce their customers to stop buying their product, in favor of a competing generic version of the product. In contrast, when demand is perfectly inelastic, consumers do not respond at all to changes in price. In this case the demand curve is vertical, as shown in Figure 3–2(b). Many perceive products and services in the health care industry (such as life-saving drugs) to have demand curves that are perfectly inelastic. While many have highly inelastic demand curves, they generally are not perfectly inelastic (see Inside Business 3–2 for a more thorough discussion).

perfectly inelastic demand
Demand is perfectly inelastic if the own price elasticity is zero. In this case the demand curve is vertical.

Usually, demand is neither perfectly elastic nor perfectly inelastic. In these instances knowledge of the particular value of an elasticity can be useful for a manager. Large firms, the government, and universities commonly hire economists or statisticians to estimate the demand for products. The manager's job is to know how to interpret and use such estimates.

FIGURE 3–2 Perfectly Elastic and Inelastic Demand

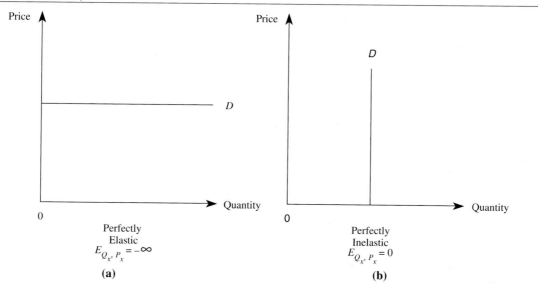

(a) Perfectly Elastic $E_{Q_x, P_x} = -\infty$

(b) Perfectly Inelastic $E_{Q_x, P_x} = 0$

INSIDE BUSINESS 3–1

Calculating and Using the Arc Elasticity: An Application to the Housing Market

While in many instances managers can obtain estimates of elasticities from the library or the firm's research staff, sometimes managers are confronted with situations where elasticity estimates are not readily available. Fortunately, all is not lost in these instances thanks to a concept called the *arc elasticity of demand.*

To be specific, suppose a manager has data that show when the price of some good was P_1, consumers purchased Q_1 units of the good, and when the price changed to P_2, Q_2 units were purchased. Other things equal, these data can be used to approximate the own price elasticity of demand for the good by using the arc elasticity formula:

$$E^{Arc} = \frac{\Delta Q^d}{\Delta P} \times \frac{Average\ P}{Average\ Q}$$

In the formula, the average Q is $(Q_1 + Q_2)/2$ and the average P is $(P_1 + P_2)/2$.

In order to illustrate how this formula can be used to compute an elasticity based on real world data, we can analyze data on sales and price for existing single-family homes in the United States. According to the National Association of Realtors, the median sales price for such homes in October was $160,800, and at this price 343,000 homes were sold. Thus, $P_1 = $160,800$ and $Q_1 = 343,000$ represent one point on the demand curve—the price and quantity of existing single-family homes in October.

Similarly, $P_2 = $164,000$ and $Q_2 = 335,000$ represent the price and quantity of existing single-family homes one month later. Interest rates and income—the two primary determinants of the demand for housing—were roughly constant between October and November. Thus, it is reasonable to assume that demand was stable (did not shift) over this one-month period, and that this price–quantity pair represents another point on the demand curve for single-family homes in the United States.

Based on these two points on the demand curve, we may approximate the own price elasticity of demand for existing single-family homes in the United States by using the arc elasticity formula:

$$
\begin{aligned}
E^{Arc} &= \frac{(Q_1 - Q_2)(P_1 + P_2)/2}{(P_1 - P_2)(Q_1 + Q_2)/2} \\
&= \frac{343{,}000 - 335{,}000}{160{,}800 - 164{,}000} \\
&\quad \times \frac{(160{,}800 + 164{,}000)/2}{(343{,}000 + 335{,}000)/2} \\
&= -1.2
\end{aligned}
$$

The own price elasticity of demand is greater than 1 in absolute value, so by the total revenue test we know that the increase in housing prices over the period resulted in lower total expenditures on housing. We might also speculate that the incomes of real estate agents fell over this period, due to the lower real estate commissions generated by these reduced expenditures on housing.

It is important to point out that the arc elasticity technique described here only approximates the true elasticity of demand for housing. The accuracy of the approximation depends crucially on the assumption that the demand curve did not shift between October and November. If the demand for single-family housing in the United States shifted over the period, due to unusually good house-hunting weather, for instance, then the true elasticity of demand will differ from our approximation.

Source: www.realtor.org/topics/existing-home-sales/data

Factors Affecting the Own Price Elasticity

Now that you understand what the own price elasticity is and how it can be used to assess the impact of price changes on sales volume and revenues, we will discuss three factors that affect the magnitude of the own price elasticity of a good: available substitutes, time, and expenditure share.

Available Substitutes

One key determinant of the elasticity of demand for a good is the number of close substitutes for that good. Intuitively, the more substitutes available for the good, the more elastic the demand for it. In these circumstances, a price increase leads consumers to substitute toward another product, thus reducing considerably the quantity demanded of the good. When there are few close substitutes for a good, demand tends to be relatively inelastic. This is because consumers cannot readily switch to a close substitute when the price increases.

A key implication of the effect of the number of close substitutes on the elasticity of demand is that the demand for broadly defined commodities tends to be more inelastic than the demand for specific commodities. For example, the demand for food (a broad commodity) is more inelastic than the demand for beef. Short of starvation, there are no close substitutes for food, and thus the quantity demanded of food is much less sensitive to price changes than is a particular type of food, such as beef. When the price of beef increases, consumers can substitute toward other types of food, including chicken, pork, and fish. Thus, the demand for beef is more elastic than the demand for food.

Table 3–2 shows some own price elasticities from market studies in the United States. These studies reveal that broader categories of goods indeed have more inelastic demand than more specifically defined categories. The own price elasticity of food is slightly inelastic, whereas the elasticity of cereal, a more specific type of food, is elastic. We would expect this outcome because there are many substitutes for cereal, but no substitutes exist for food. Table 3–2 also reveals that the demand for women's clothing is more elastic than the demand for clothing in general (a broader category).

Finally, consider the reported estimates of the own price elasticities for motorcycles and bicycles, motor vehicles, and transportation. Transportation is the most broadly defined group, followed by motor vehicles and then motorcycles and bicycles. Therefore, we would expect the demand for motorcycles and bicycles to be more elastic than the demand for motor vehicles and the demand for motor vehicles to be more elastic than the demand for transportation. The numbers in Table 3–2 are

TABLE 3–2 Selected Own Price Elasticities

Market	Own Price Elasticity
Transportation	−0.6
Motor vehicles	−1.4
Motorcycles and bicycles	−2.3
Food	−0.7
Cereal	−1.5
Clothing	−0.9
Women's clothing	−1.2

Sources: M. R. Baye, D. W. Jansen, and J. W. Lee, "Advertising Effects in Complete Demand Systems," *Applied Economics* 24 (1992), pp. 1087–96; W. S. Commanor and T. A. Wilson, *Advertising and Market Power* (Cambridge, MA: Harvard University Press, 1974).

consistent with these expectations; market studies support the statement that demand is more elastic when there are more close substitutes for a product.

Time

Demand tends to be more inelastic in the short term than in the long term. The more time consumers have to react to a price change, the more elastic the demand for the good. Conceptually, time allows the consumer to seek out available substitutes. For example, if a consumer has 30 minutes to catch a flight, he or she is much less sensitive to the price charged for a taxi ride to the airport than would be the case if the flight were several hours later. Given enough time, the consumer can seek alternative modes of transportation such as a bus, a friend's car, or even on foot. But in the short term, the consumer does not have time to seek out the available substitutes, and the demand for taxi rides is more inelastic.

Table 3–3 presents short-term and long-term own price elasticities for transportation, food, alcohol and tobacco, recreation, and clothing. Notice that all the short-term elasticities are less (in absolute value) than the corresponding long-term elasticities. In the short term, all the own price elasticities are less than 1 in absolute value, with the exception of the own price elasticity for recreation. The absolute values of the long-term own price elasticities are all greater than 1, except for alcohol and tobacco.

Expenditure Share

Goods that comprise a relatively small share of consumers' budgets tend to be more inelastic than goods for which consumers spend a sizable portion of their incomes. In the extreme case, where a consumer spends her or his entire budget on a good, the consumer must decrease consumption when the price rises. In essence, there is nothing to give up but the good itself. When a good comprises only a small portion of the budget, the consumer can reduce the consumption of other goods when the price of the good increases. For example, most consumers spend very little on salt; a small increase in the price of salt would reduce quantity demanded very little, since salt constitutes a small fraction of consumers' total budgets.

Would you expect the own price elasticity of demand for food to be more or less elastic than that for transportation? Since food is a much greater necessity than

TABLE 3–3   Selected Short- and Long-Term Own Price Elasticities

Market	Short-Term Own Price Elasticity	Long-Term Own Price Elasticity
Transportation	−0.6	−1.9
Food	−0.7	−2.3
Alcohol and tobacco	−0.3	−0.9
Recreation	−1.1	−3.5
Clothing	−0.9	−2.9

Source: M. R. Baye, D. W. Jansen, and J. W. Lee, "Advertising Effects in Complete Demand Systems," *Applied Economics* 24 (1992), pp. 1087–96.

transportation (after all, you cannot live without food), you might expect the demand for food to be more inelastic than the demand for transportation. However, Table 3–3 reveals that the demand for transportation is more inelastic (in both the short- and long-term) than the demand for food. How can this be true?

The answer lies in the percentage of income Americans spend on food and transportation. The average U.S. consumer spends almost four times as much on food as on transportation. Even though food is more "important" in a biological sense than transportation, the demand for food tends to be more elastic because a much larger proportion of people's budgets is spent on food.

Marginal Revenue and the Own Price Elasticity of Demand

We learned in Chapter 1 that *marginal revenue (MR)* is the change in total revenue due to a change in output, and that to maximize profits a firm should produce where marginal revenue equals marginal cost. We will explore profit-maximizing output and pricing decisions in detail later in this book, but it is useful at this point to show how a firm's marginal revenue is linked to the own price elasticity of demand for the firm's product.

The line labeled *MR* in Figure 3–3 is the marginal revenue associated with each price–output pair on the demand curve. Notice that for a linear demand curve, the marginal revenue schedule lies exactly halfway between the demand curve and the vertical axis. Furthermore, marginal revenue is less than the price for each unit sold.

Why is marginal revenue less than the price charged for the good? To induce consumers to purchase more of a good, a firm must lower its price. When the firm charges the same price for each unit sold, this lower price is received not only on the

FIGURE 3–3 Demand and Marginal Revenue

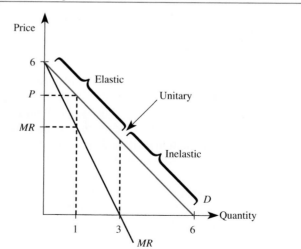

INSIDE BUSINESS 3–2

Inelastic Demand for Prescription Drugs

Many people perceive the demand for prescription drugs and other pharmaceutical products to be perfectly inelastic. After all, a patient needing an expensive cardiovascular drug might die in the absence of treatment. Moreover, in many instances the cost of medication is paid by an insurance company and not by the patient. These two factors do tend to make the demand for many pharmaceutical products relatively inelastic. However, since surgery and lifestyle changes are substitutes for many life-saving drugs, economic theory predicts that the demand for such products is unlikely to be perfectly inelastic.

The accompanying table summarizes results from two recent studies that confirm this prediction: The demand for pharmaceutical products is inelastic, but not perfectly so. For instance, the own price elasticity of demand for anti-ulcer drugs is −0.7, while the own price elasticity of demand for cardiovascular drugs is slightly more inelastic at −0.4. Consequently, a 10 percent increase in the price of anti-ulcer drugs reduces their use by 7 percent. A 10 percent increase in the price of cardiovascular drugs results in only a 4 percent reduction in quantity demanded.

The own price elasticities of demand reported here are based on the industry demand for each type of drug. The demand for particular brands within each industry is even more responsive to price changes.

Type of Drug	Own Price Elasticity
Cardiovascular	−0.4
Anti-infective	−0.9
Psychotherapeutic	−0.3
Anti-ulcer	−0.7

Sources: M. Baye, R. Maness, and S. Wiggins, "Demand Systems and the True Subindex of the Cost of Living for Pharmaceuticals," *Applied Economics* 29 (1997), pp. 1179–89; and E. Berndt, L. Bui, D. Reiley, and G. Urban, "Information, Marketing, and Pricing in the U.S. Anti-ulcer Drug Market," *American Economic Review* 85, no. 2 (May 1995), pp. 100–5.

---

last unit sold, but also on those units that could have been sold at a higher price had the firm not lowered its price. To be concrete, suppose consumers purchase 1 unit of output at a price of $5 per unit, for total expenditures (revenues to producers) of $5 \times 1 = $5. Consumers will purchase an additional unit of the good only if the price falls, say from $5 to $4 per unit. Now the firm receives $4 on the first unit sold, and $4 on the second unit sold. In effect, the firm loses $1 in revenue because the first unit now brings $4 instead of $5. Total revenue rises from $5 to $8 as output is increased by 1 unit, so marginal revenue is $8 − $5 = $3, which is less than price.

Notice in our example that by decreasing price from $5 to $4, quantity demanded increased from 1 unit to 2 units, and total revenues increased from $5 to $8. By the total revenue test, this means that demand is elastic over this range. In contrast, had the price reduction increased quantity demanded but decreased total revenues, demand would be inelastic over the range and marginal revenue would be negative. In fact, the more inelastic the demand for a product, the greater the decline in revenue that results from a price cut, despite the increased quantity demanded.

This intuition leads to the following general relationship between marginal revenue and the elasticity of demand:

$$MR = P\left[\frac{1 + E}{E}\right]$$

This formula, which is formally derived in Chapter 8, simplifies notation by dropping subscripts: P is the price of the good and E is the own price elasticity of demand for the good. Notice that when $-\infty < E < -1$, demand is elastic, and the formula implies that MR is positive. When $E = -1$, demand is unitary elastic, and marginal revenue is zero. As we learned in Chapter 1, the point where marginal revenue is zero corresponds to the output at which total revenue is maximized. Finally, when $-1 < E < 0$, demand is inelastic, and marginal revenue is negative. These general results are consistent with what you saw earlier in Table 3–1 for the case of linear demand.

CROSS-PRICE ELASTICITY

cross-price elasticity
A measure of the responsiveness of the demand for a good to changes in the price of a related good; the percentage change in the quantity demanded of one good divided by the percentage change in the price of a related good.

Another important elasticity is the *cross-price elasticity* of demand, which reveals the responsiveness of the demand for a good to changes in the price of a related good. This elasticity helps managers ascertain how much its demand will rise or fall due to a change in the price of another firm's product. The cross-price elasticity of demand between goods X and Y, denoted E_{Q_x, P_y}, is mathematically defined as

$$E_{Q_x, P_y} = \frac{\% \Delta Q_x^d}{\% \Delta P_y}$$

For instance, if the cross-price elasticity of demand between Corel WordPerfect and Microsoft Word word processing software is 3, a 10 percent hike in the price of Word will increase the demand for WordPerfect by 30 percent, since $30\%/10\% = 3$. This increase in demand for WordPerfect occurs because consumers substitute away from Word and toward WordPerfect, due to the price increase.

A Calculus Alternative

When the demand function is $Q_x^d = f(P_x, P_y, M, H)$, the cross-price elasticity of demand between goods X and Y may be found using calculus:

$$E_{Q_x, P_y} = \frac{\partial Q_x^d}{\partial P_y} \frac{P_y}{Q_x}$$

More generally, whenever goods X and Y are substitutes, an increase in the price of Y leads to an increase in the demand for X. Thus, $E_{Q_x, P_y} > 0$ whenever goods X and Y are substitutes. When goods X and Y are complements, an increase in the price of Y leads to a decrease in the demand for X. Thus, $E_{Q_x, P_y} < 0$ whenever goods X and Y are complements.

Table 3–4 provides some representative cross-price elasticities. For example, clothing and food have a cross-price elasticity of -0.18. This means that if the price of food increases by 10 percent, the demand for clothing will decrease by 1.8 percent; food and clothing are complements. More important, these data provide a quantitative measure of the impact of a change in the price of food on the consumption of clothing.

Based on the data summarized in Table 3–4, are food and recreation complements or substitutes? If the price of recreation increased by 15 percent, what would happen to the demand for food? These questions are embedded in the following problem.

TABLE 3–4   Selected Cross-Price Elasticities

	Cross-Price Elasticity
Transportation and recreation	−0.05
Food and recreation	0.15
Clothing and food	−0.18

Source: M. R. Baye, D. W. Jansen, and J. W. Lee, "Advertising Effects in Complete Demand Systems," *Applied Economics* 24 (1992), pp. 1087–96.

Demonstration Problem 3–1

You have just opened a new grocery store. Every item you carry is generic (generic beer, generic bread, generic chicken, etc.). You recently read an article in the *Wall Street Journal* reporting that the price of recreation is expected to increase by 15 percent. How will this affect your store's sales of generic food products?

Answer:

Table 3–4 reveals that the cross-price elasticity of demand for food and recreation is 0.15. If we insert the given information into the formula for the cross-price elasticity, we get

$$0.15 = \frac{\% \Delta Q_x^d}{15}$$

Solving this equation for $\% \Delta Q_x^d$, we get

$$\% \Delta Q_x^d = 2.25$$

Thus, food and recreation are substitutes. If the price of recreation increases by 15 percent, you can expect the demand for generic food products to increase by 2.25 percent.

Cross-price elasticities play an important role in the pricing decisions of firms that sell multiple products. Indeed, many fast-food restaurants offer hamburgers for under $1.00 because their managers realize that hamburgers and sodas are complements: When consumers buy a hamburger, a soda typically accompanies the purchase. Thus, by lowering the price of burgers, a restaurant affects its revenues from both burger sales and soda sales. The precise impact on these revenues depends on the own price and cross-price elasticities of demand.

Specifically, we know from the total revenue test that a reduction in the price of hamburgers will increase (decrease) revenues from hamburger sales when the own price elasticity of demand for hamburgers is elastic (inelastic). In addition, since hamburgers and sodas are complements, reducing the price of hamburgers increases the quantity demanded of sodas, thus increasing soda revenues. The magnitude of the increase in soda revenues will depend on the magnitude of the cross-price elasticity of demand between burgers and soda.

INSIDE BUSINESS 3-3

Using Cross-Price Elasticities to Improve New Car Sales in the Wake of Increasing Gasoline Prices

At the close of the last century, increases in the price of gasoline led to decreases in demand for products that are complements for gasoline, such as automobiles. The reason was that higher gasoline prices moved consumers to substitute toward public transportation, bicycling, and walking. An econometric study by Patrick McCarthy provides quantitative information about the impact of fuel costs on the demand for automobiles. One of the more important determinants of the demand for automobiles is the fuel operating cost, defined as the cost of fuel per mile driven. The study reveals that for each 1 percent increase in fuel costs, the demand for automobiles will decrease by 0.214 percent. A 10 percent increase in the price of gasoline increases the cost of fuel per mile driven by 10 percent and thus reduces the demand for a given car by 2.14 percent.

What did automakers do during this period to mitigate the negative impact of rising gasoline prices

on the demand for new automobiles? They made cars more fuel efficient. The results just summarized imply that for every 10 percent increase in fuel efficiency (measured by the increase in miles per gallon), the demand for automobiles increases by 2.14 percent. Auto manufacturers could completely offset the negative impact of higher gasoline prices by increasing the fuel efficiency of new cars by the same percentage as the increase in gasoline prices. In fact, by increasing fuel efficiency by a greater percentage than the increase in gasoline prices, they would actually *increase* the demand for new automobiles.

Source: Patrick S. McCarthy, "Consumer Demand for Vehicle Safety: An Empirical Study," *Economic Inquiry* 28 (July 1990), pp. 530–43.

More generally, suppose a firm's revenues are derived from the sales of two products, X and Y. We may express the firm's revenues as $R = R_x + R_y$, where $R_x = P_x Q_x$ denotes revenues from the sale of product X and $R_y = P_y Q_y$ represents revenues from product Y. The impact of a small percentage change in the price of product X ($\%\Delta P_x = \Delta P_x / P_x$) on the total revenues of the firm is[1]

$$\Delta R = [R_x(1 + E_{Q_x, P_x}) + R_y E_{Q_y, P_x}] \times \%\Delta P_x$$

To illustrate how to use this formula, suppose a restaurant earns $4,000 per week in revenues from hamburger sales (product X) and $2,000 per week from soda sales (product Y). Thus, $R_x = \$4,000$ and $R_y = \$2,000$. If the own price elasticity of demand for burgers is $E_{Q_x, P_x} = -1.5$ and the cross-price elasticity of demand between sodas and hamburgers is $E_{Q_y, P_x} = -4.0$, what would happen to the firm's total revenues if it reduced the price of hamburgers by 1 percent? Plugging these numbers into the above formula reveals

---

[1]This formula is an approximation for large changes in price.

$$\Delta R = [\$4,000(1 - 1.5) + \$2,000(-4.0)](-1\%)$$
$$= \$20 + \$80$$
$$= \$100$$

In other words, lowering the price of hamburgers 1 percent increases total revenues by $100. Notice that $20 of this increase comes from increased burger revenues (the demand for burgers is elastic, so the reduction in the price of burgers increases hamburger revenues) and $80 of the increase is from additional soda sales (the demand for soda increases by 4 percent, resulting in additional revenues of $80 from soft drink sales).

INCOME ELASTICITY

Income elasticity is a measure of the responsiveness of consumer demand to changes in income. Mathematically, the income elasticity of demand, denoted $E_{Q_x, M}$, is defined as

$$E_{Q_x, M} = \frac{\%\Delta Q_x^d}{\%\Delta M}$$

A Calculus Alternative

The income elasticity for a good with a demand function $Q_x^d = f(P_x, P_y, M, H)$ may be found using calculus:

$$E_{Q_x, M} = \frac{\partial Q_x^d}{\partial M} \frac{M}{Q_x}$$

income elasticity
A measure of the responsiveness of the demand for a good to changes in consumer income; the percentage change in quantity demanded divided by the percentage change in income.

When good X is a normal good, an increase in income leads to an increase in the consumption of X. Thus, $E_{Q_x, M} > 0$ when X is a normal good. When X is an inferior good, an increase in income leads to a decrease in the consumption of X. Thus, $E_{Q_x, M} < 0$ when X is an inferior good.

Table 3–5 presents some classic estimates of income elasticities for various products. Consider, for example, the income elasticity for transportation, 1.8. This number gives us two important pieces of information about the relationship between income and the demand for transportation. First, since the income elasticity is positive, we know that consumers increase the amount they spend on transportation when their incomes rise. Transportation thus is a normal good. Second, since the income elasticity for transportation is greater than 1, we know that expenditures on transportation grow more rapidly than income.

The second row of Table 3–5 reveals that food also is a normal good, since the income elasticity of food is 0.8. Since the income elasticity is less than 1, an increase in income will increase the expenditure on food by a lower percentage than the

TABLE 3–5 Selected Income Elasticities

	Income Elasticity
Transportation	1.80
Food	0.80
Ground beef, nonfed	−1.94

Sources: M. R. Baye, D. W. Jansen, and J. W. Lee, "Advertising Effects in Complete Demand Systems," *Applied Economics* 24 (1992), pp. 1087–96; G. W. Brester and M. K. Wohlsenant, "Estimating Interrelated Demands for Meats Using New Measures for Ground and Table Cut Beef," *American Journal of Agricultural Economics* 73 (November 1991), p. 21.

percentage increase in income. When income declines, expenditures on food decrease less rapidly than income.

The third row of Table 3–5 presents the income elasticity for nonfed ground beef. Nonfed beef comes from cattle that have not been fed a special diet. Most cattle are fed corn for 90 to 120 days before going to market and thus produce more tender beef than nonfed cattle. The income elasticity for nonfed ground beef is negative; hence, we know that nonfed ground beef is an inferior good. The consumption of nonfed ground beef will decrease by 1.94 percent for every 1 percent rise in consumer income. Therefore, managers of grocery stores should decrease their orders of nonfed ground beef during economic booms and increase their orders during recessions.

Demonstration Problem 3–2

Your firm's research department has estimated the income elasticity of demand for nonfed ground beef to be −1.94. You have just read in *the Wall Street Journal* that due to an upturn in the economy, consumer incomes are expected to rise by 10 percent over the next three years. As a manager of a meat-processing plant, how will this forecast affect your purchases of nonfed cattle?

Answer:

Set $E_{Q_x, M} = -1.94$ and $\%\Delta M = 10$ in the formula for the income elasticity of demand to obtain

$$-1.94 = \frac{\%\Delta Q_x^d}{10}$$

Solving this equation for $\%\Delta Q_x^d$ yields −19.4. Since nonfed ground beef has an income elasticity of −1.94 and consumer income is expected to rise by 10 percent, you can expect to sell 19.4 percent less nonfed ground beef over the next three years. Therefore, you should decrease your purchases of nonfed cattle by 19.4 percent, unless something else changes.

OTHER ELASTICITIES

Given the general notion of an elasticity, it is not difficult to conceptualize how the impact of changes in other variables, such as advertising, may be analyzed in elasticity terms. For example, the *own advertising elasticity* of demand for good X is the ratio of the percentage change in the consumption of X to the percentage change in advertising spent on X. The *cross-advertising elasticity* between goods X and Y would measure the percentage change in the consumption of X that results from a 1 percent change in advertising directed toward Y.

TABLE 3–6   Selected Long-Term Advertising Elasticities

	Advertising Elasticity
Clothing	0.04
Recreation	0.25

Source: M. R. Baye, D. W. Jansen, and J. W. Lee, "Advertising Effects in Complete Demand Systems," *Applied Economics* 24 (1992), pp. 1087–96.

Table 3–6 shows estimates of the advertising elasticities for clothing and recreation. Both elasticities are positive and less than 1. The fact that they are positive reveals, as you might expect, that increases in advertising lead to an increase in the demand for the products; that is, if clothing manufacturers increase their advertising, they can expect to sell more clothing at any given price. However, the fact that the advertising elasticity of clothing is 0.04 means that a 10 percent increase in advertising will increase the demand for clothing by only .4 percent. As a broad category, clothing is not very advertising elastic.

To illustrate how managers can use estimates such as these, imagine that you have just been hired by the U.S. Department of Commerce to help direct the tourist trade in the United States. Your boss knows you recently took a course in managerial economics and asks you how much she should increase advertising to increase the demand for recreation in the United States by 15 percent.

From Table 3–6, we know that $E_{Q_x, A_x} = 0.25$. Plugging this and $\%\Delta Q_x^d = 15$ into the general formula for the elasticity of Q_x^d with respect to A_x yields

$$0.25 = \frac{\%\Delta Q_x^d}{\%\Delta A_x} = \frac{15}{\%\Delta A_x}$$

Solving this equation for the percentage change in advertising shows that advertising must increase by a hefty 60 percent to increase the demand for recreation by 15 percent.

OBTAINING ELASTICITIES FROM DEMAND FUNCTIONS

Now that you understand what elasticities are and how to use them to make managerial decisions, we will examine how to calculate elasticities from demand functions. First, we will consider elasticities based on linear demand functions. Then we will see how to calculate elasticities from particular nonlinear demand functions.

Elasticities for Linear Demand Functions

Given an estimate of a linear demand function, it is quite easy to calculate the various elasticities of demand.

Formula: Elasticities for Linear Demand. If the demand function is linear and given by

$$Q_x^d = \alpha_0 + \alpha_x P_x + \alpha_y P_y + \alpha_M M + \alpha_H H$$

the elasticities are

own price elasticity: $\qquad E_{Q_x, P_x} = \alpha_x \dfrac{P_x}{Q_x}$

cross-price elasticity: $\qquad E_{Q_x, P_y} = \alpha_y \dfrac{P_y}{Q_x}$

income elasticity: $\qquad E_{Q_x, M} = \alpha_M \dfrac{M}{Q_x}$

A Calculus Alternative

The elasticities for a linear demand curve may be found using calculus. Specifically,

$$E_{Q_x, P_x} = \frac{\partial Q_x^d}{\partial P_x} \frac{P_x}{Q_x} = \alpha_x \frac{P_x}{Q_x}$$

and similarly for the cross-price and income elasticities.

Thus, for a linear demand curve, the elasticity of demand with respect to a given variable is simply the coefficient of the variable multiplied by the ratio of the variable to the quantity demanded. For instance, the own price elasticity of demand is simply the coefficient of P_x (which is α_x in the demand function) multiplied by the ratio of the price of X to the quantity consumed of X.

For a linear demand curve, the value of an elasticity depends on the particular price and quantity at which it is calculated. This means that the own price elasticity is not the same as the slope of the demand curve. In fact, for a linear demand function, demand is elastic at high prices and inelastic at lower prices. To see this, note that when $P_x = 0$, $|E_{Q_x, P_x}| = |\alpha_x \frac{0}{Q_x}| = 0 < 1$. In other words, for prices near zero, demand is inelastic. On the other hand, when prices rise, Q_x decreases and the absolute value of the elasticity increases.

For a video walkthrough of this problem, visit www.mhhe.com/baye8e

Demonstration Problem 3–3

The daily demand for Invigorated PED shoes is estimated to be

$$Q_x^d = 100 - 3P_x + 4P_y - .01M + 2A_x$$

where A_x represents the amount of advertising spent on shoes (X), P_x is the price of good X, P_y is the price of good Y, and M is average income. Suppose good X sells at $25 a pair, good Y sells at $35, the company utilizes 50 units of advertising, and average consumer income is $20,000. Calculate and interpret the own price, cross-price, and income elasticity of demand.

Answer:

To calculate the own price elasticity for linear demand, we use the formula

$$E_{Q_x, P_x} = \alpha_x \frac{P_x}{Q_x}$$

Here $\alpha_x = -3$, and $P_x = 25$. The only other information we need to calculate the elasticity is the quantity consumed of X. To find Q_x, we substitute the given values of prices, income, and advertising into the demand equation to get

$$Q_x^d = 100 - 3(25) + 4(35) - .01(20{,}000) + 2(50) = 65 \text{ units}$$

Hence the own price elasticity of demand is given by

$$E_{Q_x, P_x} = -3\left(\frac{25}{65}\right) = -1.15$$

If Invigorated PED raises shoe prices, the percentage decline in the quantity demanded of its shoes will be greater in absolute value than the percentage rise in price. Consequently, demand is elastic: Total revenues will fall if it raises shoe prices.

Similarly, the cross-price elasticity of demand is

$$E_{Q_x, P_y} = 4\left(\frac{35}{65}\right) = 2.15$$

Since this is positive, good Y is a substitute for Invigorated PED shoes. The income elasticity of demand for Invigorated PED's shoes is

$$E_{Q_x, M} = -0.01\left(\frac{20{,}000}{65}\right) = -3.08$$

Invigorated PED's shoes are inferior goods, since this is a negative number.

Elasticities for Nonlinear Demand Functions

Managers frequently encounter situations where a product's demand is not a linear function of prices, income, advertising, and other demand shifters. In this section we demonstrate that the tools we developed can easily be adapted to these more complex environments.

Suppose the demand function is not a linear function but instead is given by

$$Q_x^d = cP_x^{\beta_x} P_y^{\beta_y} M^{\beta_M} H^{\beta_H}$$

where c is a constant. In this case, the quantity demanded of good X is not a linear function of prices and income but a nonlinear function. If we take the natural logarithm of this equation, we obtain an expression that is linear in the logarithms of the variables:[2]

$$\ln Q_x^d = \beta_0 + \beta_x \ln P_x + \beta_y \ln P_y + \beta_M \ln M + \beta_H \ln H$$

where $\beta_0 = \ln(c)$ and the β_i's are arbitrary real numbers. This relation is called a *log-linear demand* function.

log-linear demand
Demand is log-linear if the logarithm of demand is a linear function of the logarithms of prices, income, and other variables.

As in the case of linear demand, the sign of the coefficient of $\ln P_y$ determines whether goods X and Y are substitutes or complements, whereas the sign of the coefficient of $\ln M$ determines whether X is a normal or an inferior good. For example, if β_y is a positive number, an increase in the price of good Y will lead to an increase in the consumption of good X; in this instance, X and Y are substitutes. If β_y is a negative number, an increase in the price of good Y will lead to a decrease in the consumption of good X; in this instance, goods X and Y are complements. Similarly, if β_M is a positive number, an increase in income leads to an increase in the consumption of good X, and X is a normal good. If β_M is a negative number, an increase in income leads to a decrease in the consumption of good X, and X is an inferior good.

Formula: Elasticities for Log-Linear Demand. When the demand function for good X is log-linear and given by

$$\ln Q_x^d = \beta_0 + \beta_x \ln P_x + \beta_y \ln P_y + \beta_M \ln M + \beta_H \ln H$$

the elasticities are

own price elasticity:	$E_{Q_x, P_x} = \beta_x$
cross-price elasticity:	$E_{Q_x, P_y} = \beta_y$
income elasticity:	$E_{Q_x, M} = \beta_M$

A Calculus Alternative

The above result may also be derived using calculus. Taking the antilogarithm of the equation for log-linear demand gives

$$Q_x^d = cP_x^{\beta_x} P_y^{\beta_y} M^{\beta_M} H^{\beta_H}$$

where c is a constant. Using the calculus formula for an elasticity yields

$$E_{Q_x, P_x} = \frac{\partial Q_x^d}{\partial P_x}\left(\frac{P_x}{Q_x}\right) = \beta_x cP_x^{\beta_x - 1} P_y^{\beta_y} M^{\beta_M} H^{\beta_H}\left(\frac{P_x}{cP_x^{\beta_x} P_y^{\beta_y} M^{\beta_M} H^{\beta_H}}\right) = \beta_x$$

and similarly for the cross-price and income elasticities.

Notice that when demand is log-linear, the elasticity with respect to a given variable is simply the coefficient of the corresponding logarithm. The own price elasticity of

____
[2]Here, ln denotes the *natural logarithm*. In some spreadsheets (such as Excel), this function is denoted LN.

TABLE 3–7 The Log-Linear Demand for Breakfast Cereal

$$\ln(Q_c) = -7.256 - 1.647 \ln(P_c) + 1.071 \ln(M) + 0.146 \ln(A)$$

Q_c = per capita consumption of breakfast cereal

P_c = price of cereal

M = per capita income

A = a measure of advertising by the top four cereal firms

Source: Adapted from Michael R. Baye, *The Economic Effects of Proposed Regulation of TV Advertising Directed at Children: A Theoretical and Empirical Analysis,* senior honors thesis, Texas A&M University, 1980.

demand is the coefficient of $\ln(P_x)$, and in fact, the coefficient of *any* other logarithm on the right-hand side of the log-linear demand relation tells us the elasticity of demand with respect to that demand shifter. Since all of these coefficients are constants, none of the elasticities depend on the value of variables like prices, income, or advertising.

Table 3–7 shows the results of a statistical study that found the demand for breakfast cereal to be log-linear. Since this is a log-linear demand relation, we know that the coefficients may be interpreted as elasticities.

The study summarized in Table 3–7 focused primarily on the effect of advertising on the demand for breakfast cereal. Other factors affecting the demand for cereal include its price and the average (per capita) income of consumers. Surprisingly, the study found that the price of milk was not an important determinant of the demand for breakfast cereal.

In Table 3–7, the coefficient of the logarithm of price is -1.647. This shows that the demand for cereal is elastic and downward sloping. Furthermore, a decrease of 10 percent in the price of cereal will increase the quantity of cereal demanded by 16.47 percent, and therefore raise the sales revenues of cereal manufacturers. The coefficient of the logarithm of income is $+1.071$, indicating that cereal is a normal good. A 10 percent increase in consumers' per capita income would result in a 10.7 percent increase in cereal demand. The coefficient of the logarithm of advertising is positive, indicating that an increase in cereal advertising will increase cereal demand. However, notice that the advertising elasticity is relatively small. A 10 percent increase in cereal advertising increases the demand for cereal by only 1.46 percent. Apparently, cereal advertising does not induce consumers to eat cereal for lunch and dinner.

As a final check of your ability to utilize elasticities, try to work the following problem.

Demonstration Problem 3–4

An analyst for a major apparel company estimates that the demand for its raincoats is given by

$$\ln Q_x^d = 10 - 1.2 \ln P_x + 3 \ln R - 2 \ln A_y$$

where R denotes the daily amount of rainfall and A_y represents the level of advertising on good Y. What would be the impact on demand of a 10 percent increase in the daily amount of rainfall? What would be the impact of a 10 percent reduction in the amount of advertising directed toward good Y? Can you think of a good that might be good Y in this example?

Answer:

We know that for log-linear demand functions, the coefficient of the logarithm of a variable gives the elasticity of demand with respect to that variable. Thus, the elasticity of demand for raincoats with respect to rainfall is

$$E_{Q_x, R} = \beta_R = 3$$

Furthermore,

$$E_{Q_x, R} = \beta_R = \frac{\% \Delta Q_x^d}{\% \Delta R}$$

Hence,

$$3 = \frac{\% \Delta Q_x^d}{10}$$

Solving this equation yields $\% \Delta Q_x^d = 30$. In other words, the 10 percent increase in rainfall will lead to a 30 percent increase in the demand for raincoats.

To examine the impact on the demand for raincoats of a 10 percent reduction in advertising spent on good Y, again note that for log-linear demand functions, each coefficient gives the elasticity of demand with respect to that variable. Thus, the elasticity of demand for raincoats with respect to advertising directed toward good Y is

$$E_{Q_x, A_y} = \beta_{A_y} = -2$$

Furthermore,

$$E_{Q_x, A_y} = \beta_{A_y} = \frac{\% \Delta Q_x^d}{\% \Delta A_y}$$

Hence,

$$-2 = \frac{\% \Delta Q_x^d}{-10}$$

Solving this equation yields $\% \Delta Q_x^d = 20$. In other words, the 10 percent reduction in advertising directed toward good Y leads to a 20 percent increase in the demand for raincoats. Perhaps good Y is umbrellas, for one would expect the demand for raincoats to increase whenever fewer umbrella advertisements are made.

REGRESSION ANALYSIS

The preceding analysis assumes the manager knows the demand for the firm's product. We pointed out several studies that provide explicit estimates of demand elasticities and functional forms for demand functions. As a manager, you may obtain estimates of demand and elasticity from published studies available in the library or from a consultant hired to estimate the demand function based on the specifics of your product. Or, you might enter data into a spreadsheet program and click the regression toolbar to obtain an estimated demand function, along with some regression diagnostics. Regardless of how the manager obtains the estimates, it is useful to have a general understanding of how demand functions are estimated and what the various diagnostic statistics that accompany the reported output mean. This entails knowledge of a branch of economics called econometrics.

Econometrics is simply the statistical analysis of economic phenomena. It is far beyond the scope of this book to teach you how to estimate demand functions, but it is possible to convey the basic ideas econometricians use to obtain such information. Your primary job as a manager is to use the information to make decisions similar to the examples provided in previous sections of this chapter.

Let us briefly examine the basic ideas underlying the estimation of the demand for a product. Suppose there is some underlying data on the relation between a dependent variable, Y, and some explanatory variable, X. Suppose that when the values of X and Y are plotted, they appear as points A, B, C, D, E, and F in Figure 3–4. Clearly, the points do not lie on a straight line, or even a smooth curve (try alternative ways of connecting the dots if you are not convinced).

The job of the econometrician is to find a smooth curve or line that does a "good" job of approximating the points. For example, suppose the econometrician believes that, on average, there is a linear relation between Y and X, but there is also some random variation in the relationship. Mathematically, this would imply that the true relationship between Y and X is

$$Y = a + bX + e$$

FIGURE 3–4 The Regression Line

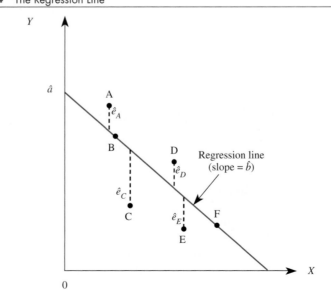

where a and b are unknown parameters and e is a random variable (an error term) that has a zero mean. Because the parameters that determine the expected relation between Y and X are unknown, the econometrician must find out the values of the parameters a and b.

Note that for any line drawn through the points, there will be some discrepancy between the actual points and the line. For example, consider the line in Figure 3–4, which does a reasonable job of fitting the data. If a manager used the line to approximate the true relation, there would be some discrepancy between the actual data and the line. For example, points A and D actually lie above the line, while points C and E lie below it. The deviations between the actual points and the line are given by the distance of the dashed lines in Figure 3–4, namely $\hat{e}_A$, $\hat{e}_C$, $\hat{e}_D$, and $\hat{e}_E$. Since the line represents the expected, or average, relation between Y and X, these deviations are analogous to the deviations from the mean used to calculate the variance of a random variable.

The econometrician uses a regression software package to find the values of a and b that minimize the sum of the squared deviations between the actual points and the line. In essence, the *regression line* is the line that minimizes the squared deviations between the line (the expected relation) and the actual data points. These values of a and b, which frequently are denoted $\hat{a}$ and $\hat{b}$, are called *parameter estimates,* and the corresponding line is called the *least squares regression.*

least squares regression
The line that minimizes the sum of squared deviations between the line and the actual data points.

The least squares regression line for the equation

$$Y = a + bX + e$$

is given by

$$Y = \hat{a} + \hat{b}X$$

The parameter estimates, $\hat{a}$ and $\hat{b}$, represent the values of a and b that result in the smallest *sum of squared errors* between a line and the actual data.

Spreadsheet software packages, such as Excel, make it easy to use regression analysis to estimate demand functions. To illustrate, suppose a television manufacturer has data on the price and quantity of TVs sold last month at 10 outlets in Pittsburgh. Here we use price and quantity as our explanatory and dependent variables, respectively. When the data are entered into a spreadsheet, it looks like the first 11 rows in Table 3–8. A few clicks of the mouse, and the spreadsheet calculates the average price and quantity reported in row 12. Furthermore, clicking the regression toolbar produces the regression output reported in rows 16 through 33. Cell 32-B shows that the intercept of the estimated demand function for TVs is 1631.47, and cell 33-B shows that the estimated coefficient of price is −2.60. Thus, the linear demand function for TVs that minimizes the sum of squared errors between the actual data points and the line through the points is

$$Q = 1631.47 - 2.60P$$

Notice that the spreadsheet program also produces detailed information about the regression and the estimated coefficients as a by-product of the regression. As discussed below, these statistics enable the manager to test for the statistical significance of the estimated coefficients and to assess the performance of the overall regression.

TABLE 3–8   Using a Spreadsheet to Perform a Regression

	A	B	C	D	E	F	G
1	**Observation**	**Quantity**	**Price**				
2	1	180	475				
3	2	590	400				
4	3	430	450				
5	4	250	550				
6	5	275	575				
7	6	720	375				
8	7	660	375				
9	8	490	450				
10	9	700	400				
11	10	210	500				
12	**Average**	450.50	455.00				
13							
14							
15							
16	**Regression Statistics**						
17							
18	Multiple R	0.87					
19	R-Square	0.75					
20	Adjusted R-Square	0.72					
21	Standard Error	112.22					
22	Observations	10.00					
23							
24	**Analysis of Variance**						
25		**df**	**Sum of Squares**	**Mean Square**	**F**	**Significance F**	
26	Regression	1.00	301470.89	301470.89	23.94	0.0012	
27	Residual	8.00	100751.61	12593.95			
28	Total	9.00	402222.50				
29							
30		**Coefficients**	**Standard Error**	**t-Statistic**	**P-Value**	**Lower 95%**	**Upper 95%**
31							
32	Intercept	1631.47	243.97	6.69	0.0002	1068.87	2194.07
33	Price	−2.60	0.53	−4.89	0.0012	−3.82	−1.37

Evaluating the Statistical Significance of Estimated Coefficients

Rows 30 through 33 of the regression output in Table 3–8 provide information about the precision with which the parameters of the demand function are estimated. The coefficients reported in cells 32-B and 33-B are merely the parameter estimates— estimates of the true, unknown coefficients. Given different data generated from the same true demand relation, different estimates of the true coefficients would be obtained. The *standard error* of each estimated coefficient is a measure of how much each estimated coefficient would vary in regressions based on the same underlying true demand relation, but with different observations. The smaller the standard error of an estimated coefficient, the smaller the variation in the estimate given data from different outlets (different samples of data).

Given a set of standard, but somewhat technical, assumptions about the regression model, data sampling, and means of the errors, the least squares estimates are unbiased estimators of the true demand parameters. If, in addition, the e_i's are independently and identically distributed normal random variables (in short, *iid normal* random variables) with constant variance, the reported standard errors of the estimated coefficients can be used to construct confidence intervals and to perform significance tests. These techniques are discussed below.

Confidence Intervals

Given a parameter estimate, its standard error, and the necessary technical assumptions mentioned above, the firm manager can construct upper and lower bounds on the true value of the estimated coefficient by constructing a 95 percent *confidence interval*. A useful rule of thumb is presented in the principle below, but fortunately regression packages compute precise confidence intervals for each coefficient estimated in a regression. For instance, cells 33-F and 33-G in Table 3–8 indicate that the upper and lower bounds of the 95 percent confidence interval for the coefficient of price are −3.82 and −1.37. The parameter estimate for the price coefficient, −2.60, lies in the middle of these bounds. Thus, we know that the best estimate of the price coefficient is −2.60, and we are 95 percent confident that the true value lies between −3.82 and −1.37.

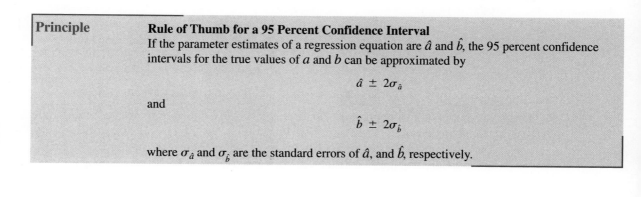

Principle

Rule of Thumb for a 95 Percent Confidence Interval
If the parameter estimates of a regression equation are $\hat{a}$ and $\hat{b}$, the 95 percent confidence intervals for the true values of a and b can be approximated by

$$\hat{a} \pm 2\sigma_{\hat{a}}$$

and

$$\hat{b} \pm 2\sigma_{\hat{b}}$$

where $\sigma_{\hat{a}}$ and $\sigma_{\hat{b}}$ are the standard errors of $\hat{a}$, and $\hat{b}$, respectively.

The *t*-Statistic

t-statistic
The ratio of the value of a parameter estimate to the standard error of the parameter estimate.

The t-*statistic* of a parameter estimate is the ratio of the value of the parameter estimate to its standard error. For example, if the parameter estimates are $\hat{a}$ and $\hat{b}$ and the corresponding standard errors are $\sigma_{\hat{a}}$ and $\sigma_{\hat{b}}$, the *t*-statistic for $\hat{a}$ is

$$t_{\hat{a}} = \frac{\hat{a}}{\sigma_{\hat{a}}}$$

and the t-statistic for $\hat{b}$, is

$$t_{\hat{b}} = \frac{\hat{b}}{\sigma_{\hat{b}}}$$

When the t-statistic for a parameter estimate is large in absolute value, then you can be confident that the true parameter is not zero. The reason for this is that when the absolute value of the t-statistic is large, the standard error of the parameter estimate is small relative to the absolute value of the parameter estimate. Thus, one can be more confident that, given a different sample of data drawn from the true model, the new parameter estimate will be in the same ballpark.

A useful rule of thumb is that if the absolute value of a t-statistic is greater than or equal to 2, then the corresponding parameter estimate is statistically different from zero. Regression packages report *P-values,* which are a much more precise measure of statistical significance. For instance, in cell 33-E of Table 3–8 we see that the P-value for the estimated coefficient of price is .0012. This means that there is only a 12 in 10,000 chance that the true coefficient of price is actually 0. Notice that the lower the P-value for an estimated coefficient, the more confident you are in the estimate.

Usually, P-values of .05 or lower are considered low enough for a researcher to be confident that the estimated coefficient is statistically significant. If the P-value is .05, we say that the estimated coefficient is statistically significant at the 5 percent level. Notice that the P-value reported in Table 3–8 for the coefficient of price implies that it is statistically significant at the .12 percent level: The estimated coefficient is highly significant.

Principle	**Rule of Thumb for Using *t*-Statistics**
	When the absolute value of the *t*-statistic is greater than 2, the manager can be 95 percent confident that the true value of the underlying parameter in the regression is not zero.

Evaluating the Overall Fit of the Regression Line

In addition to evaluating the statistical significance of one or more coefficients, one can also measure the precision with which the overall regression line fits the data. Two yardsticks frequently used to measure the overall fit of the regression line—the R-square and the F-statistic—are discussed next.

The R-Square
Rows 18 through 20 of Table 3–8 provide diagnostics that indicate how well the regression line explains the sample of observations of the dependent variable (in the example, quantity is the dependent variable and price is the explanatory variable). The *R-square* (also called the *coefficient of determination*) tells the fraction of the total variation in the dependent variable that is explained by the

regression. It is computed as the ratio of the sum of squared errors from the regression ($SS_{Regression}$) to the total sum of squared errors (SS_{Total}):

$$R^2 = \frac{Explained\ Variation}{Total\ Variation} = \frac{SS_{Regression}}{SS_{Total}}$$

For instance, in cell 26-C of Table 3–8 we see that the sum of squared errors from the regression is 301470.89, while cell 28-C reveals that the total sum of squared errors is 402222.50. Thus, the R-square is .75 ($= 301470.89/402222.50$). This means that the estimated demand equation (the regression line) explains 75 percent of the total variation in TV sales across the sample of 10 outlets. Most spreadsheet regression packages automatically calculate the R-square, as seen in cell 19-B of Table 3–8.[3]

The value of an R-square ranges from 0 to 1:

$$0 \leq R^2 \leq 1$$

The closer the R-square is to 1, the "better" the overall fit of the estimated regression equation to the actual data. Unfortunately, there is no simple cutoff that can be used to determine whether an R-square is close enough to 1 to indicate a "good" fit. With time series data, R-squares are often in excess of .9; with cross-sectional data, R-squares below .2 are not uncommon. Thus, a major drawback of the R-square is that it is a subjective measure of goodness of fit.

Another problem with the R-square is that it cannot decrease when additional explanatory variables are included in the regression. Thus, if we included income, advertising, and other explanatory variables in our regression, but held other things constant, we would almost surely get a higher R-square. Eventually, when the number of estimated coefficients increased to the number of observations, we would end up with an R-square of 1. Sometimes, the R-square is very close to 1 merely because the number of observations is small relative to the number of estimated parameters. This situation is undesirable from a statistical viewpoint because it can provide a very misleading indicator of the goodness of fit of the regression line. For this reason, many researchers use the adjusted R-square reported in cell 20-B of Table 3–8 as a measure of goodness of fit.

The *adjusted R-square* is given by

$$\overline{R^2} = 1 - (1 - R^2)\frac{(n-1)}{(n-k)}$$

where n is the total number of observations and k is the number of estimated coefficients. In performing a regression, the number of parameters to be estimated cannot exceed the number of observations. The difference, $n - k$, represents the *residual degrees of freedom* after conducting the regression. Notice that the adjusted R-square "penalizes" the researcher for performing a regression with only

---

[3]The square root of the R-square, called the Multiple R, is also reported by most spreadsheet regression programs. It is given in cell 18-B of Table 3–8.

a few degrees of freedom (that is, estimating numerous coefficients from relatively few observations). In fact, the penalty can be so high that, in some instances, the adjusted R-square is actually negative.

In our example, cell 22-B in Table 3–8 shows us that $n = 10$. Cells 32-B and 33-B indicate that we estimated 2 parameters, so $k = 2$. With 8 residual degrees of freedom, the adjusted R-square of our regression is $1 - (1 - .75)(9/8) = .72$. This number is reported in cell 20-B. For these data, there is little difference between the R-square and the adjusted R-square, so it does not appear that the "high" R-square is a result of an excessive number of estimated coefficients relative to the sample size.

The F-Statistic

While the R-square and adjusted R-square of a regression both provide a gauge of the overall fit of a regression, we note that there is no universal rule for determining how "high" they must be to indicate a good fit. An alternative measure of goodness of fit, called the *F-statistic,* does not suffer from this shortcoming. The F-statistic provides a measure of the total variation explained by the regression relative to the total unexplained variation. The greater the F-statistic, the better the overall fit of the regression line through the actual data. In our example, the F-statistic is reported as 23.94 in cell 26-E of Table 3–8.

The primary advantage of the F-statistic stems from the fact that its statistical properties are known. Thus, one can objectively determine the statistical significance of any reported F value. The significance value for our regression, .0012, is reported in cell 26-F of Table 3–8. This low number means that there is only a .12 percent chance that the estimated regression model fit the data purely by accident.

As with P-values, the lower the significance value of the F-statistic, the more confident you can be of the overall fit of the regression equation. Regressions that have F-statistics with significance values of 5 percent or less are generally considered significant. Based on the significance value reported in cell 26-F of Table 3–8, our regression is significant at the .12 percent level. The regression is therefore highly significant.

Regression for Nonlinear Functions and Multiple Regression

The techniques described above to estimate a linear demand function with a single explanatory variable can also be used to estimate nonlinear demand functions. These same tools can be used to estimate demand functions in which the quantity demanded depends on several explanatory variables, such as prices, income, advertising, and so on. These issues are discussed below.

Regression for Nonlinear Functions

Sometimes, a plot of the data will reveal nonlinearities in the data, as seen in Figure 3–5. Here, it appears that price and quantity are not linearly related: The demand function is a curve. The log-linear demand curve we examined earlier in this chapter has such a curved shape.

INSIDE BUSINESS 3–4

Shopping Online in Europe: Elasticities of Demand for Personal Digital Assistants Based on Regression Techniques

Thanks to the Internet, consumers can let their mouse do the shopping instead of paying bus fares or filling their cars with gasoline to visit brick-and-mortar stores. How responsive are the demands of online shoppers to the prices charged by online retailers? Recently, economists working at the Haas School of Business at Berkeley, Cambridge University, and the Kelley School of Business at Indiana University used regression techniques and online data from Europe to answer this question.

The economists estimated demand functions for a variety of different brands and models of personal digital assistants (PDAs) sold by different online retailers at the leading European shopping site, Kelkoo.com. This site permits shoppers in Europe to purchase a wide array of products online, ranging from electronic gadgets to vacuum cleaners and washing machines. While Kelkoo.com may not be familiar to shoppers on the American side of the pond, its parent company—Yahoo!—is a household name worldwide.

The accompanying table summarizes the author's econometric estimates of the elasticity of demand facing firms selling six different models of PDAs. Notice that an online retailer selling the IPAQ 1940 faces the most elastic demand (-14.7), while a firm selling the Clié SJ22 faces the least elastic demand (-3.3). Depending on the brand and model, an online retailer that reduced price by 10 percent would enjoy a 33 to 147 percent increase in online sales. The t-statistics all exceed 2 in absolute value, which indicates that the estimates are statistically significant at the 5 percent level.

Brand/Model	Elasticity	t-statistic
HP Compaq IPAQ 1940	−14.7	−20.39
HP Compaq IPAQ 2210	−11.7	−10.54
Palm Tungsten T2	−6.1	−11.9
Palm Zire 71	−11.1	−11.47
Sony Clié NX73V	−5.9	−10.82
Sony Clié SJ22	−3.3	−8.65

Source: Michael R. Baye, J. Rupert J. Gatti, Paul Kattuman, and John Morgan, "Clicks, Discontinuities, and Firm Demand Online," *Journal of Economics and Management Strategy*, vol. 18, no. 4, 2009, pp. 935–75.

FIGURE 3–5   Log-Linear Regression Line

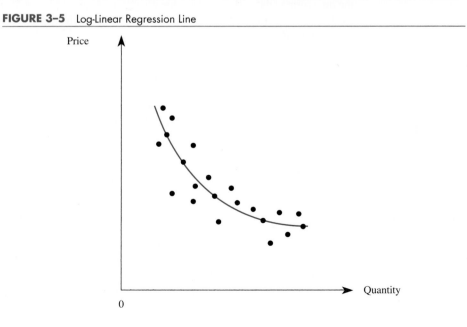

To estimate a log-linear demand function, the econometrician takes the natural logarithm of prices and quantities before executing the regression routine that minimizes the sum of squared errors (e):

$$\ln Q = \beta_0 + \beta_P \ln P + e$$

In other words, by using a spreadsheet to compute $Q' = \ln Q$ and $P' = \ln P$, this demand specification can be viewed equivalently as

$$Q' = \beta_0 + \beta_P P' + e$$

which is linear in Q' and P'. Therefore, one can use procedures identical to those described earlier and regress the transformed Q' on P' to obtain parameter estimates. Recall that the resulting parameter estimate for β_P in this case is the own price elasticity of demand, since this is a log-linear demand function.

Demonstration Problem 3–5

During the 31 days this past March, an online ticket agent offered varying price discounts on Broadway tickets in order to gather information needed to estimate the demand for its tickets. A file named Demo_3_5.xls is available online at www.mhhe.com/baye8e. If you open this file and view the tab labeled *Data*, you will find information about the quantity of Broadway tickets the company sold at various prices in March. Use these data to estimate a log-linear demand function. Use an equation to summarize your findings.

Answer:

The first step is to transform the price and quantity data into natural logarithms, using the relevant spreadsheet command. You can see how to do this step by viewing the tab labeled *Transformed* in the Demo_3_5.xls file. The second step is to perform a linear regression on the transformed data. These regression results are displayed in the *Results* tab of the file. The final step is to summarize the regression results in a demand equation. In this case, the estimates in the *Results* tab imply the following log-linear demand function:

$$\ln Q^d = 8.44 - 1.58 \ln P$$

Written in this manner, the *logarithm* of quantity demanded is a linear function of the *logarithm* of price, and the company's elasticity of demand for tickets is -1.58. Alternatively, one can express the actual quantity demanded as a *nonlinear* function of price by taking the exponential of both sides of the above equation:

$$\exp[\ln Q^d] = \exp[8.44] \exp[-1.58 \ln P]$$
$$Q^d = \exp[8.44]P^{-1.58}$$
$$Q^d = 4629P^{-1.58}$$

Multiple Regression

In general, the demand for a good will depend not only on the good's price, but also on demand shifters. Regression techniques can also be used to perform *multiple regressions*—regressions of a dependent variable on multiple explanatory variables. For the case of a linear demand relation, one might specify the demand function as

$$Q_x^d = \alpha_0 + \alpha_x P_x + \alpha_y P_y + \alpha_M M + \alpha_H H + e$$

where the α's are the parameters to be estimated, P_y, M, and H are demand shifters, and e is the random error term that has a zero mean. Alternatively, a log-linear specification might be appropriate if the quantity demanded is not linearly related to the explanatory variables:

$$\ln Q_x^d = \beta_0 + \beta_x \ln P_x + \beta_y \ln P_y + \beta_M \ln M + \beta_H \ln H + e$$

Provided the number of observations is greater than the number of parameters to be estimated, one can use standard regression packages included in spreadsheet programs to find the values of the parameters that minimize the sum of squared errors of the regression. The R-square, F-statistic, t-statistics, and confidence intervals for multiple regressions have the same use and interpretations described earlier for the case of a simple regression with one explanatory variable. The following demonstration problem illustrates this fact.

Demonstration Problem 3–6

FCI owns 10 apartment buildings in a college town, which it rents exclusively to students. Each apartment building contains 100 rental units, but the owner is having cash flow problems due to an average vacancy rate of nearly 50 percent. The apartments in each building have comparable floor plans, but some buildings are closer to campus than others. The owner of FCI has data from last year on the number of apartments rented, the rental price (in dollars), and the amount spent on advertising (in hundreds of dollars) at each of the 10 apartments. These data, along with the distance (in miles) from each apartment building to campus, are presented in rows 1 through 11 of Table 3–9. The owner regressed the quantity demanded of apartments on price, advertising, and distance. The results of the regression are reported in rows 16 through 35 of Table 3–9. What is the estimated demand function for FCI's rental units? If FCI raised rents at one complex by $100, what would you expect to happen to the number of units rented? If FCI raised rents at an average apartment building, what would happen to FCI's total revenues? What inferences should be drawn from this analysis?

Answer:

Letting P, A, and D represent price, advertising, and distance from campus, the estimated coefficients imply the following demand for rental units at an apartment building:

$$Q_x^d = 135.15 - 0.14P + 0.54A - 5.78D$$

Since the coefficient of price is -0.14, a $100 increase in price reduces the quantity demanded at an apartment building by 14 units. The own price elasticity of demand for FCI's rental units, calculated at the average price and quantity, is $(-.14)$ $(420/53.10) = -1.11$. Since demand is elastic, raising the rent at an average apartment building would decrease not only the number of units rented, but total revenues as well.

The R-square of .79 indicates that the regression explains 79 percent of the variation in the quantity of apartments rented across the 10 buildings. The F-statistic suggests that the regression is significant at the 1.82 percent level, so the manager can be reasonably confident that the good fit of the equation is not due to chance. Notice that all the estimated parameters are statistically significant at the 5 percent level, except for the coefficient of advertising. Thus, it does not appear that advertising has a statistically significant effect on the demand for the rental units.

TABLE 3–9 Input and Output from a Multiple Regression

	A	B	C	D	E	F	G
1	**Observation**	**Quantity**	**Price**	**Advertising**	**Distance**		
2	1	28	250	11	12		
3	2	69	400	24	6		
4	3	43	450	15	5		
5	4	32	550	31	7		
6	5	42	575	34	4		
7	6	72	375	22	2		
8	7	66	375	12	5		
9	8	49	450	24	7		
10	9	70	400	22	4		
11	10	60	375	10	5		
12	**Average**	53.10	420.00	20.50	5.70		
13							
14							
15							
16	**Regression Statistics**						
17							
18	Multiple R	0.89					
19	R-Square	0.79					
20	Adjusted R-Square	0.69					
21	Standard Error	9.18					
22	Observations	10.00					
23							
24	**Analysis of Variance**						
25		**df**	**Sum of Squares**	**Mean Square**	**F**	**Significance F**	
26	Regression	3.00	1920.99	640.33	7.59	0.0182	
27	Residual	6.00	505.91	84.32			
28	Total	9.00	2426.90				
29							
30		**Coefficients**	**Standard Error**	**t-Statistic**	**P-Value**	**Lower 95%**	**Upper 95%**
31							
32	Intercept	135.15	20.65	6.54	0.0006	84.61	185.68
33	Price	−0.14	0.06	−2.41	0.0500	−0.29	0.00
34	Advertising	0.54	0.64	0.85	0.4296	−1.02	2.09
35	Distance	−5.78	1.26	−4.61	0.0037	−8.86	−2.71

Distance from campus appears to be a very significant determinant of the demand for apartments. The t-statistic for this coefficient is in excess of 4 in absolute value, and the P-value is .37 percent. Based on the lower and upper bound of its confidence interval, the owner can be 95 percent confident that for every mile an apartment is away from campus, FCI loses between 2.71 and 8.86 renters.

Since FCI can't relocate its apartments closer to campus, and advertising does not have a statistically significant impact on units rented, it would appear that all FCI can do to reduce its cash flow problems is to lower rents at those apartment buildings where demand is elastic.

A Caveat

You now know how to interpret the output of a regression and how to use the output to summarize the demand for a product in a simple equation. Demand functions are not fictitious textbook constructs—they are equations that managers may actually obtain by using appropriate econometric techniques and data.

It is important to stress, however, that econometrics is a specialized field of economics that takes years of study to master. For the same reason it would not be prudent for you to perform LASIK eye surgery after merely reading a section called "The Eye" in your biology textbook, prudent managers rely on the expertise of "specialists" (economic experts or consultants) to obtain demand estimates. Unless you invest in the coursework required to master a host of econometric issues that are beyond the scope of any managerial economics textbook or spreadsheet program (e.g., endogeneity, sample selection, heteroskedacity, autocorrelation, and unobserved effects), it is probably best for you to use your econometric knowledge primarily as a tool for communicating with (and interpreting the output provided by) econometric specialists.

ANSWERING THE HEADLINE

At the beginning of the chapter we asked how much money the CEO of a regional telephone company would need to win a new license in an FCC auction. Based on the provided regression, the expected price paid for a license is negatively related to the number of licenses available and positively related to the size of the population in the region:

$$\ln P = 2.23 - 1.2 \ln Q + 1.25 \ln Pop$$

Since this is a log-linear demand equation, the coefficients are elasticities. In particular, the coefficient of $\ln Pop$ (1.25) tells us the percentage change in price resulting from each 1 percent change in population. Since the population in the relevant region is 7 percent higher than the average, this means $1.25 = \%\Delta P / 7$, or $\%\Delta P = 8.75$. In other words, the price the CEO expects to pay in his region is 8.75 percent higher than the average price paid in the March 14 auction. Since that price was \$70.7 million, the expected price needed to win the auction in his region is, other things equal, \$76.9 million. The CEO's model predicts that the demand for licenses will be greater in his region due to the greater size of the market ultimately serviced by the holders of the licenses.

The CEO should exercise caution in using this estimate, however. The regression does not include information about regional income and the number of bidders—two pieces of information that might be useful for predicting the price. One would expect the average income of a region to have a positive effect on the price firms are willing to pay, since ultimately higher incomes in a region will translate into higher prices for wireless communication services. In addition, the greater the number of bidders for licenses, the greater the competition and thus the higher one would expect the price to be. If these two variables differ significantly across regions, then the CEO's regression estimates will be biased.

Subject to these caveats, however, the regression results summarized in Table 3–10 suggest that the CEO's model does a good job of explaining the prices of licenses. The R-square of .85 indicates that 85 percent of the total variation in prices is explained by the model, and the F-statistic indicates that the regression is highly significant (at the .13 percent level). The absolute values of the t-statistics are all well in excess of 2, with P-values all below 5 percent. This suggests that the CEO can be reasonably confident that the true coefficients are different from zero, and in fact reasonably close to the estimated ones.

Nonetheless, the predictions based on this regression equation will not perfectly reveal the price the CEO's firm will have to pay next year to win a license. Since the upper bound of the 95 percent confidence interval for the coefficient of ln Pop is 1.73, the CEO can be 95 percent confident that $79.3 million will be enough to win a license. This is because $1.73 = \%\Delta P/7$, so $\%\Delta P = 12.11$. In other words, he will need 12.11 percent more than the $70.7 million paid for a license during the March 14 auction to be 95 percent confident. Given the magnitude of the amount involved, the CEO might want to get his research department or an economic consultant to perform a more detailed analysis of the situation.

TABLE 3–10 Regression Output Based on Data from the FCC Auction

	A	B	C	D	E	F	G
1	**Regression Statistics**						
2							
3	Multiple R	0.92					
4	R-Square	0.85					
5	Adjusted R-Square	0.81					
6	Standard Error	0.32					
7	Observations	10.00					
8							
9	**Analysis of Variance**						
10		*df*	*Sum of Squares*	*Mean Square*	*F*	*Significance F*	
11	Regression	2.00	4.02	2.01	19.95	0.0013	
12	Residual	7.00	0.71	0.10			
13	Total	9.00	4.73				
14							
15		*Coefficients*	*Standard Error*	*t-Statistic*	*P-Value*	*Lower 95%*	*Upper 95%*
16							
17	Intercept	2.23	0.43	5.24	0.0012	1.23	3.24
18	ln Pop	1.25	0.20	6.11	0.0005	0.77	1.73
19	ln Q	−1.20	0.20	−6.10	0.0005	−1.66	−0.73

SUMMARY

In this chapter we covered quantitative aspects of demand analysis, including the own price elasticity, income elasticity, and cross-price elasticity of demand. We examined functional forms for demand functions, including linear and log-linear specifications, and discussed the regression procedures used to estimate demand relationships. Armed with these tools, a manager can predict not only the direction of changes in demand but how far demand will move when one of the determinants of demand changes. Knowing the concepts of elasticity and the use of *t*-statistics and confidence intervals is extremely important when making decisions about how much inventory to hold, how many employees to schedule, and how many units of a product to produce when different determinants of demand change.

In this chapter, we saw that increasing price does not always increase revenues. If the absolute value of own price elasticity is greater than 1, an increase in price will decrease total revenue. We also covered the magnitude of changes caused by a change in the price of a substitute or a complement.

Finally, we introduced the concepts of regression and confidence intervals. By utilizing the elasticities based on an estimated demand function and constructing a confidence interval, a manager can be 95 percent certain about the amount by which demand will move when a variable like income or advertising changes.

KEY TERMS AND CONCEPTS

adjusted *R*-square
arc elasticity of demand
coefficient of determination
confidence interval
cross-advertising elasticity
cross-price elasticity
econometrics
elastic demand
elasticity
F-statistic
iid normal assumption
income elasticity
inelastic demand
least squares regression
log-linear demand
multiple regression

own advertising elasticity
own price elasticity of demand
P-value
parameter estimates
perfectly elastic demand
perfectly inelastic demand
R-square
regression analysis
regression line
residual degrees of freedom
standard error
sum of squared errors
t-statistic
total revenue test
unitary elastic demand

END-OF-CHAPTER PROBLEMS BY LEARNING OBJECTIVE

Every end-of-chapter problem addresses at least one learning objective. Below is a nonexhaustive sample of end-of-chapter problems for each learning objective.

LO1 Apply various elasticities of demand as a quantitative tool to forecast changes in revenues, prices, and/or units sold.
Try these problems: 5, 14

LO2 Illustrate the relationship between the elasticity of demand and total revenues.
Try these problems: 6, 15

LO3 Discuss three factors that influence whether the demand for a given product is relatively elastic or inelastic.
Try these problems: 13, 22

LO4 Explain the relationship between marginal revenue and the own price elasticity of demand. Try these problems: 1, 11

LO5 Show how to determine elasticities from linear and log-linear demand functions.
Try these problems: 2, 10

LO6 Explain how regression analysis may be used to estimate demand functions, and how to interpret and use the output of a regression.
Try these problems: 7, 20

CONCEPTUAL AND COMPUTATIONAL QUESTIONS

connect
|ECONOMICS

1. Answer the following questions based on the accompanying diagram.

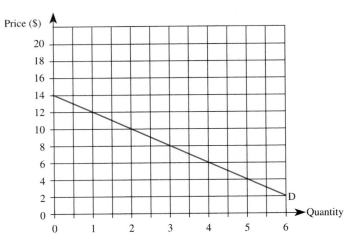

    a. How much would the firm's revenue change if it lowered the price from $12 to $10? Is demand elastic or inelastic in this range?

    b. How much would the firm's revenue change if it lowered the price from $4 to $2? Is demand elastic or inelastic in this range?

    c. What price maximizes the firm's total revenues? What is the elasticity of demand at this point on the demand curve?

2. The demand curve for a product is given by $Q_x^d = 1{,}200 - 3P_x - 0.1P_z$ where $P_z = \$300$.

    a. What is the own price elasticity of demand when $P_x = \$140$? Is demand elastic or inelastic at this price? What would happen to the firm's revenue if it decided to charge a price below $140?

    b. What is the own price elasticity of demand when $P_x = \$240$? Is demand elastic or inelastic at this price? What would happen to the firm's revenue if it decided to charge a price above $240?

    c. What is the cross-price elasticity of demand between good X and good Z when $P_x = \$140$? Are goods X and Z substitutes or complements?

3. Suppose the demand function for a firm's product is given by

$$\ln Q_x^d = 7 - 1.5 \ln P_x + 2 \ln P_y - 0.5 \ln M + \ln A$$

where

    $P_x = \$15,$
    $P_y = \$6,$
    $M = \$40{,}000$, and
    $A = \$350.$

    a. Determine the own price elasticity of demand, and state whether demand is elastic, inelastic, or unitary elastic.

    b. Determine the cross-price elasticity of demand between good X and good Y, and state whether these two goods are substitutes or complements.

    c. Determine the income elasticity of demand, and state whether good X is a normal or inferior good.

    d. Determine the own advertising elasticity of demand.

4. Suppose the own price elasticity of demand for good X is -3, its income elasticity is 1, its advertising elasticity is 2, and the cross-price elasticity of demand between it and good Y is -4. Determine how much the consumption of this good will change if:

    a. The price of good X decreases by 5 percent.

    b. The price of good Y increases by 8 percent.

    c. Advertising decreases by 4 percent.

    d. Income increases by 4 percent.

5. Suppose the cross-price elasticity of demand between goods X and Y is 4. How much would the price of good Y have to change in order to increase the consumption of good X by 20 percent?

6. You are the manager of a firm that receives revenues of $40,000 per year from product X and $90,000 per year from product Y. The own price elasticity of demand for product X is -1.5, and the cross-price elasticity of demand between product Y and X is -1.8. How much will your firm's total revenues (revenues from both products) change if you increase the price of good X by 2 percent?

7. A quant jock from your firm used a linear demand specification to estimate the demand for its product and sent you a hard copy of the results. Unfortunately, some entries are missing because the toner was low in her printer. Use the information presented below to find the missing values labeled '1' through '7' (round your answer to the nearest hundredth). Then, answer the accompanying questions.

   a. Based on these estimates, write an equation that summarizes the demand for the firm's product.

   b. Which regression coefficients are statistically significant at the 5 percent level?

   c. Comment on how well the regression line fits the data.

SUMMARY OUTPUT						
Regression Statistics						
Multiple R	0.38					
R-Square	'1'					
Adjusted R-Square	'2'					
Standard Error	20.77					
Observations	150					
Analysis of Variance						
	Degrees of Freedom	**Sum of Squares**	**Mean Square**	**F**	**Significance F**	
Regression	2	'3'	5199.43	12.05	0.00	
Residual	147	63,408.62	431.35			
Total	'4'	73,807.49				
	Coefficients	**Standard Error**	**t-Statistic**	**P-Value**	**Lower 95%**	**Upper 95%**
Intercept	58.87	'5'	3.84	0.00	28.59	89.15
Price of X	−1.64	0.85	'6'	0.06	−3.31	0.04
Income	'7'	0.24	4.64	0.00	0.63	1.56

8. Suppose the true inverse demand relation for good X is $Q_x^d = a + bP_x + cM + e$, and you estimated the parameters to be $\hat{a} = 22$, $\hat{b} = -1.8$, $\sigma_{\hat{a}} = 2.5$, and $\sigma_{\hat{b}} = 0.7$. Find the approximate 95 percent confidence interval for the true values of a and b.

9. The demand function for good X is $Q^d_x = a + bP_x + cM + e$, where P_x is the price of good X and M is income. Least squares regression reveals that $\hat{a} = 8.27$, $\hat{b} = -2.14$, $\hat{c} = 0.36$, $\sigma_{\hat{a}} = 5.32$, $\sigma_{\hat{b}} = 0.41$, and $\sigma_{\hat{c}} = 0.22$. The R-squared is 0.35.

   a. Compute the t-statistic for each of the estimated coefficients.

   b. Determine which (if any) of the estimated coefficients are statistically different from zero.

   c. Explain, in plain words, what the R-square in this regression indicates.

10. The demand function for good X is $\ln Q^d_x = a + b \ln P_x + c \ln M + e$, where P_x is the price of good X and M is income. Least squares regression reveals that $\hat{a} = 7.42$, $\hat{b} = -2.18$, and $\hat{c} = 0.34$.

   a. If $M = 55,000$ and $P_x = 4.39$, compute the own price elasticity of demand based on these estimates. Determine whether demand is elastic or inelastic.

   b. If $M = 55,000$ and $P_x = 4.39$, compute the income elasticity of demand based on these estimates. Determine whether X is a normal or inferior good.

PROBLEMS AND APPLICATIONS

11. Revenue at a major cellular telephone manufacturer was $2.3 billion for the nine months ending March 2, up 85 percent over revenues for the same period last year. Management attributes the increase in revenues to a 108 percent increase in shipments, despite a 21 percent drop in the average blended selling price of its line of phones. Given this information, is it surprising that the company's revenue increased when it decreased the average selling price of its phones? Explain.

12. You are the manager of a firm that sells a leading brand of alkaline batteries. A file named Q12.xls with data on the demand for your product is available online at www.mhhe.com/baye8e. Specifically, the file contains data on the natural logarithm of your quantity sold, price, and the average income of consumers in various regions around the world. Use this information to perform a log-linear regression, and then determine the likely impact of a 3 percent decline in global income on the overall demand for your product.

13. For the first time in two years, Big G (the cereal division of General Mills) raised cereal prices by 4 percent. If, as a result of this price increase, the volume of all cereal sold by Big G dropped by 5 percent, what can you infer about the own price elasticity of demand for Big G cereal? Can you predict whether revenues on sales of its Lucky Charms brand increased or decreased? Explain.

14. If Starbucks's marketing department estimates the income elasticity of demand for its coffee to be 2.6, how will the prospect of an economic boom (expected to increase consumers' incomes by 6 percent over the next year) impact the quantity of coffee Starbucks expects to sell?

15. You are a division manager at Toyota. If your marketing department estimates that the semiannual demand for the Highlander is $Q = 150,000 - 1.5P$, what price should you charge in order to maximize revenues from sales of the Highlander?

16. You are a manager in charge of monitoring cash flow at a company that makes photography equipment. Traditional photography equipment comprises 40 percent of your revenues, which grow about 2 percent annually. You recently received a preliminary report that suggests consumers take three times more digital photographs than photos with traditional film, and that the cross-price elasticity of demand between digital and disposable cameras is -0.3. In 2012, your company earned about $600 million from sales of digital cameras and about $400 million from sales of disposable cameras. If the own price elasticity of demand for disposable cameras is -2, how will a 4 percent decrease in the price of disposable cameras affect your overall revenues from both disposable and digital camera sales?

17. As newly appointed "Energy Czar," your goal is to reduce the total demand for residential heating fuel in your state. You must choose one of three legislative proposals designed to accomplish this goal: (a) a tax that would effectively increase the price of residential heating fuel by $1; (b) a subsidy that would effectively reduce the price of natural gas by $3; or (c) a tax that would effectively increase the price of electricity (produced by hydroelectric facilities) by $4. To assist you in your decision, an economist in your office has estimated the demand for residential heating fuel using a linear demand specification. The regression results are presented on page 119. Based on this information, which proposal would you favor? Explain.

18. As the owner of Barney's Broilers—a fast-food chain—you see an increase in the demand for broiled chicken as consumers become more health conscious and reduce their consumption of beef and fried foods. As a result, you believe it is necessary to purchase another oven to meet the increased demand. To finance the oven you go to the bank seeking a loan. The loan officer tells you that your revenues of $750,000 are insufficient to support additional debt. To qualify for the loan, Barney's Broilers's revenue would need to be $50,000 higher. In developing a strategy to generate the additional revenue, you collect data on the price (in cents) per pound you charge customers and the related quantity of chicken consumed per year in pounds. This information is contained in the file called Q18.xls available online at www.mhhe.com/baye8e. Use these data and a log-linear demand specification to obtain least squares estimates of the demand for broiled chicken. Write an equation that summarizes the demand for broiled chicken, and then determine the percentage price increase or decrease that is needed in order to boost revenues by $50,000.

19. Suppose the Kalamazoo Brewing Company (KBC) currently sells its microbrews in a seven-state area: Illinois, Indiana, Michigan, Minnesota, Mississippi, Ohio, and Wisconsin. The company's marketing department has collected data from its distributors in each state. These data consist of the

	A	B	C	D	E	F	G
1	**SUMMARY OUTPUT**						
2							
3	*Regression Statistics*						
4	Multiple *R*	0.76					
5	*R*-Square	0.57					
6	Adjusted *R*-Square	0.49					
7	Standard Error	47.13					
8	Observations	25					
9							
10	*Analysis of Variance*						
11		*Degrees of Freedom*	*Sum of Squares*	*Mean Square*	*F*	*Significance F*	
12	Regression	4	60936.56	15234.14	6.86	.03	
13	Residual	20	44431.27	2221.56			
14	Total	24	105367.84				
15							
16		*Coefficients*	*Standard Error*	*t-Statistic*	*P-Value*	*Lower 95%*	*Upper 95%*
17	Intercept	136.96	43.46	3.15	0.01	50.60	223.32
18	Price of Residential Heating Fuel	−91.69	29.09	−3.15	0.01	−149.49	−33.89
19	Price of Natural Gas	43.88	9.17	4.79	0.00	25.66	62.10
20	Price of Electricity	−11.92	8.35	−1.43	0.17	−28.51	4.67
21	Income	−0.050	0.3500	−0.14	0.90	−0.75	0.65

quantity and price (per case) of microbrews sold in each state, as well as the average income (in thousands of dollars) of consumers living in various regions of each state. The data for each state are available online at www.mhhe.com/baye8e under the filename Q19.xls, where there are multiple tabs at the bottom of the spreadsheet, each referring to one of the seven states selling the Kalamazoo Brewing Company's microbrews. Assuming that the underlying demand relation is a linear function of price and income, use your spreadsheet program to obtain least squares estimates of the state's demand for KBC microbrews. Print the regression output and provide an economic interpretation of the regression results.

20. According to CNN, two dairy farmers challenged the legality of the funding of the "Got Milk?" campaigns. They argued that the "Got Milk?" campaigns do little to support milk from cows that are not injected with hormones and other sustainable agriculture products, and therefore violate their (and other farmers') First Amendment rights. The 3rd U.S. Circuit Court of Appeals agreed and concluded that dairy farmers cannot be required to pay to fund the advertising campaigns. One of the obvious backlashes to the National Dairy

Promotion and Research Board is reduced funding for advertising campaigns. To assess the likely impact on milk consumption, suppose that the National Dairy Promotion and Research Board collected data on the number of gallons of milk households consumed weekly (in millions), weekly price per gallon, and weekly expenditures on milk advertising (in hundreds of dollars). These data, in forms to estimate both a linear model and log-linear model, are available online at www.mhhe.com/baye8e in a file named Q20.xls. Use these data to perform two regressions: a linear regression and a log-linear regression. Compare and contrast the regression output of the two models. Comment on which model does a better job fitting the data. Suppose that the weekly price of milk is $3.40 per gallon and the National Dairy Promotion and Research Board's weekly advertising expenditures fall 35 percent after the court's ruling to $150 (in hundreds). Use the best-fitting regression model to estimate the weekly quantity of milk consumed after the court's ruling.

21. A few years ago, the Federal Communications Commission (FCC) eliminated a rule that required Baby Bells to provide rivals access and discounted rates to current broadband facilities and other networks they may build in the future. Providers of digital subscriber lines (DSL) that use the local phone loop are particularly affected. Some argue that the agreement will likely raise many DSL providers' costs and reduce competition. Providers of high-speed Internet services utilizing cable, satellite, or wireless technologies will not be directly affected, since such providers are not bound by the same facilities-sharing requirements as firms using the local phone networks. In light of the FCC ruling, suppose that News Corp., which controls the United States' largest satellite-to-TV broadcaster, is contemplating launching a Spaceway satellite that could provide high-speed Internet service. Prior to launching the Spaceway satellite, suppose that News Corp. used least squares to estimate the regression line of demand for satellite Internet services. The best-fitting results indicate that demand is $Q_{sat}^d = 152.5 - .8P_{sat} + 1.2P_{DSL} + .5P_{cable}$ (in thousands), where P_{sat} is the price of satellite Internet service, P_{DSL} is the price of DSL Internet service, and P_{cable} is the price of high-speed cable Internet service. Suppose that after the FCC's ruling the price of DSL, P_{DSL}, is $25 per month and the monthly price of high-speed cable Internet, P_{cable}, is $50. Furthermore, News Corp. has identified that its monthly revenues need to be at least $15 million to cover its monthly costs. If News Corp. set its monthly subscription price for satellite Internet service at $55, would its revenue be sufficiently high to cover its cost? Is it possible for News Corp. to cover its cost given the current demand function? Justify your answer.

22. Recently, Pacific Cellular ran a pricing trial in order to estimate the elasticity of demand for its services. The manager selected three states that were representative of its entire service area and increased prices by 5 percent to customers in those areas. One week later, the number of customers enrolled in Pacific's cellular plans

declined 4 percent in those states, while enrollments in states where prices were not increased remained flat. The manager used this information to estimate the own price elasticity of demand and, based on her findings, immediately increased prices in all market areas by 5 percent in an attempt to boost the company's 2012 annual revenues. One year later, the manager was perplexed because Pacific Cellular's 2012 annual revenues were 10 percent lower than those in 2011—the price increase apparently led to a reduction in the company's revenues. Did the manager make an error? Explain.

23. The owner of a small chain of gasoline stations in a large Midwestern town read an article in a trade publication stating that the own price elasticity of demand for gasoline in the United States is −0.2. Because of this highly inelastic demand in the United States, he is thinking about raising prices to increase revenues and profits. Do you recommend this strategy based on the information he has obtained? Explain.

CONNECT EXERCISES

If your instructor has adopted Connect for the course and you are an active subscriber, you can practice with the questions presented above, along with many alternative versions of these questions. Your instructor may also assign a subset of these problems and/or their alternative versions as a homework assignment through Connect, allowing for immediate feedback of grades and correct answers.

CASE-BASED EXERCISES

Your instructor may assign additional problem-solving exercises (called *memos*) that require you to apply some of the tools you learned in this chapter to make a recommendation based on an actual business scenario. Some of these memos accompany the Time Warner case (pages 561–597 of your textbook). Additional memos, as well as data that may be useful for your analysis, are available online at www.mhhe.com/baye8e.

SELECTED READINGS

Chiles, Ted W., Jr., and Sollars, David L., "Estimating Cigarette Tax Revenue." *Journal of Economics and Finance* 17(3), Fall 1993, pp. 1–15.

Crandall, R., "Import Quotas and the Automobile Industry: The Cost of Protectionism." *Brookings Review* 2(4), Summer 1984, pp. 8–16.

Houthakker, H., and Taylor, L., *Consumer Demand in the United States: Analyses and Projections,* 2nd ed. Cambridge, MA: Harvard University Press, 1970.

Maxwell, Nan L., and Lopus, Jane S., "The Lake Wobegon Effect in Student Self-Reported Data." *American Economic Review* 84(2), May 1994, pp. 201–5.

Pratt, Robert W., Jr., "Forecasting New Product Sales from Likelihood of Purchase Ratings: Commentary." *Marketing Science* 5(4), Fall 1986, pp. 387–88.

Sawtelle, Barbara A., "Income Elasticities of Household Expenditures: A U.S. Cross Section Perspective." *Applied Economics* 25(5), May 1993, pp. 635–44.

Stano, Miron, and Hotelling, Harold, "Regression Analysis in Litigation: Some Overlooked Considerations." *Journal of Legal Economics* 1(3), December 1991, pp. 68–78.

Williams, Harold R., and Mount, Randall I., "OECD Gasoline Demand Elasticities: An Analysis of Consumer Behavior with Implications for U.S. Energy Policy." *Journal of Behavioral Economics* 16(1), Spring 1987, pp. 69–79.

CHAPTER FOUR

The Theory of Individual Behavior

Packaging Firm Uses Overtime Pay to Overcome Labor Shortage

Boxes Ltd. produces corrugated paper containers at a small plant in Sunrise Beach, Texas. Sunrise Beach is a retirement community with an aging population, and over the past decade the size of its working population has shrunk. In 2012, this labor shortage hampered Boxes Ltd.'s ability to hire enough workers to meet its growing demand and production targets. This is despite the fact that it pays $10 per hour—almost 30 percent more than the local average—to its workers.

Last year, Boxes Ltd. hired a new manager who instituted an overtime wage plan at the firm. Under her plan, workers earn $10 per hour for the first eight hours worked each day, and $15 per hour for each hour worked in a day in excess of eight hours. This plan eliminated the firm's problems, as the firm's production levels and profits are up by 20 percent this year.

Why did the new manager institute the overtime plan instead of simply raising the wage rate in an attempt to attract more workers to the firm?

Learning Objectives

After completing this chapter, you will be able to:

LO1 Explain four basic properties of a consumer's preference ordering and their ramifications for a consumer's indifference curves.

LO2 Illustrate how changes in prices and income impact an individual's opportunities.

LO3 Illustrate a consumer's equilibrium choice and how it changes in response to changes in prices and income.

LO4 Separate the impact of a price change into substitution and income effects.

LO5 Show how to derive an individual's demand curve from indifference curve analysis and market demand from a group of individuals' demands.

LO6 Illustrate how "buy one, get one free" deals and gift certificates impact a consumer's purchase decisions.

LO7 Apply the income–leisure choice framework to illustrate the opportunities, incentives, and choices of workers and managers.

INTRODUCTION

This chapter develops tools that help a manager understand the behavior of individuals, such as consumers and workers, and the impact of alternative incentives on their decisions. This is not as simple as you might think. Human beings use complicated thought processes to make decisions, and the human brain is capable of processing vast quantities of information. At this very moment your heart is pumping blood throughout your body, your lungs are providing oxygen and expelling carbon dioxide, and your eyes are scanning this page while your brain processes the information on it. The human brain can do what even supercomputers and sophisticated "artificial intelligence" technology are incapable of doing.

Despite the complexities of human thought processes, managers need a model that explains how individuals behave in the marketplace and in the work environment. Of course, attempts to model individual behavior cannot capture the full range of real-world behavior. Life would be simpler for managers of firms if the behavior of individuals were not so complicated. On the other hand, the rewards for being a manager of a firm would be much lower. If you achieve an understanding of individual behavior, you will gain a marketable skill that will help you succeed in the business world.

Our model of behavior will necessarily be an abstraction of the way individuals really make decisions. We must begin with a simple model that focuses on essentials instead of dwelling on behavioral features that would do little to enhance our understanding. Keep these thoughts in mind as we begin our study of an economic model of consumer behavior.

CONSUMER BEHAVIOR

Now that you recognize that any theory about individual behavior must be an abstraction of reality, we may begin to develop a model to help us understand how consumers will respond to the alternative choices that confront them. A *consumer* is an individual who purchases goods and services from firms for the purpose of consumption. As a manager of a firm, you are interested not only in who consumes the good but in who purchases it. A six-month-old baby consumes goods but is not responsible for purchase decisions. If you are employed by a manufacturer of baby food, it is the parent's behavior you must understand, not the baby's.

In characterizing consumer behavior, there are two important but distinct factors to consider: consumer opportunities and consumer preferences. *Consumer opportunities* represent the possible goods and services consumers can afford to consume. *Consumer preferences* determine which of these goods will be consumed. The distinction is very important: While I can afford (and thus have the opportunity to consume) one pound of beef liver each week, my preferences are such that I would be unlikely to choose to consume beef liver at all. Keeping this distinction in mind, let us begin by modeling consumer preferences.

In today's global economy literally millions of goods are offered for sale. However, to focus on the essential aspects of individual behavior and to keep things manageable, we will assume that only two goods exist in the economy. This assumption is made purely to simplify our analysis: All of the conclusions that we draw from this two-good setting remain valid when there are many goods. We will let X represent the quantity of one good and Y the quantity of the other good. By using this notation to represent the two goods, we have a very general model in the sense that X and Y can be any two goods rather than restricted to, say, beef and pork.

Assume a consumer is able to order his or her preferences for alternative bundles or combinations of goods from best to worst. We will let $>$ denote this ordering and write $A > B$ whenever the consumer prefers bundle A to bundle B. If the consumer views the two bundles as equally satisfying, we will say she or he is indifferent between bundles A and B and use $A \sim B$ as shorthand notation. If $A > B$, then, if given a choice between bundle A and bundle B, the consumer will choose bundle A. If $A \sim B$, the consumer, given a choice between bundle A and bundle B, will not care which bundle he or she gets. The preference ordering is assumed to satisfy four basic properties: completeness, more is better, diminishing marginal rate of substitution, and transitivity. Let us examine these properties and their implications in more detail.

Property 4–1: Completeness. For any two bundles—say, A and B—either $A > B$, $B > A$, or $A \sim B$.

By assuming that preferences are *complete*, we assume the consumer is capable of expressing a preference for, or indifference among, all bundles. If preferences were not complete, there might be cases where a consumer would claim not to know whether he or she preferred bundle A to B, preferred B to A, or was indifferent between the two bundles. If the consumer cannot express her or his own preference for or indifference among goods, the manager can hardly predict that individual's consumption patterns with reasonable accuracy.

Property 4–2: More Is Better. If bundle A has at least as much of every good as bundle B and more of some good, bundle A is preferred to bundle B.

If *more is better,* the consumer views the products under consideration as "goods" instead of "bads." Graphically, this implies that as we move in the northeast direction in Figure 4–1, we move to bundles that the consumer views as being better than bundles to the southwest. For example, in Figure 4–1 bundle A is preferred to bundle D because it has the same amount of good X and more of good Y. Bundle C is also preferred to bundle D, because it has more of both goods. Similarly, bundle B is preferred to bundle D.

indifference curve
A curve that defines the combinations of two goods that give a consumer the same level of satisfaction.

While the assumption that more is better provides important information about consumer preferences, it does not help us determine a consumer's preference for all possible bundles. For example, note in Figure 4–1 that the "more is better" property does not reveal whether bundle B is preferred to bundle A or bundle A is preferred to bundle B. To be able to make such comparisons, we will need to make some additional assumptions.

An *indifference curve* defines the combinations of goods X and Y that give the consumer the same level of satisfaction; that is, the consumer is indifferent between

FIGURE 4–1 The Indifference Curve

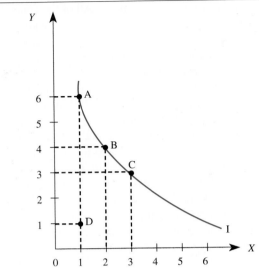

any combination of goods along an indifference curve. A typical indifference curve is depicted in Figure 4–1. By definition, all combinations of X and Y located on the indifference curve provide the consumer with the same level of satisfaction. For example, if you asked the consumer, "Which would you prefer—bundle A, bundle B, or bundle C?" the consumer would reply, "I don't care," because bundles A, B, and C all lie on the same indifference curve. In other words, the consumer is indifferent among the three bundles.

The shape of the indifference curve depends on the consumer's preferences. Different consumers generally will have indifference curves of different shapes. One important way to summarize information about a consumer's preferences is in terms of the marginal rate of substitution. The *marginal rate of substitution (MRS)* is the absolute value of the slope of an indifference curve. The marginal rate of substitution between two goods is the rate at which a consumer is willing to substitute one good for the other and still maintain the same level of satisfaction.

The concept of the marginal rate of substitution is actually quite simple. In Figure 4–1, the consumer is indifferent between bundles A and B. In moving from A to B, the consumer gains 1 unit of good X. To remain on the same indifference curve, she or he gives up 2 units of good Y. Thus, in moving from point A to point B, the marginal rate of substitution between goods X and Y is 2.

The careful reader will note that the marginal rate of substitution associated with moving from A to B in Figure 4–1 differs from the rate at which the consumer is willing to substitute between the two goods in moving from B to C. In particular, in moving from B to C, the consumer gains 1 unit of good X. But now he or she is willing to give up only 1 unit of good Y to get the additional unit of X. The reason is that this indifference curve satisfies the property of *diminishing marginal rate of substitution*.

marginal rate of substitution (MRS)
The rate at which a consumer is willing to substitute one good for another good and still maintain the same level of satisfaction.

Property 4–3: Diminishing Marginal Rate of Substitution. As a consumer obtains more of good X, the amount of good Y he or she is willing to give up to obtain another unit of good X decreases.

This assumption implies that indifference curves are convex from the origin; that is, they look like the indifference curve in Figure 4–1. To see how the locations of various indifference curves can be used to illustrate different levels of consumer satisfaction, we must make an additional assumption: that preferences are *transitive*.

Property 4–4: Transitivity. For any three bundles, A, B, and C, if $A > B$ and $B > C$, then $A > C$. Similarly, if $A \sim B$ and $B \sim C$, then $A \sim C$.

The assumption of transitive preferences, together with the more-is-better assumption, implies that indifference curves do not intersect one another. It also eliminates the possibility that the consumer is caught in a perpetual cycle in which she or he never makes a choice.

To see this, suppose Billy's preferences are such that he prefers jelly beans to licorice, licorice to chocolate, and chocolate to jelly beans. He asks the clerk to fill a bag with jelly beans, because he prefers jelly beans to licorice. When the clerk hands him a bagful of jelly beans, Billy tells her he likes chocolate even more than jelly beans. When the clerk hands him a bagful of chocolate, he tells her he likes licorice even more than chocolate. When the clerk hands him a bagful of licorice, Billy tells her he likes jelly beans even more than licorice. The clerk puts back the licorice and hands Billy a bagful of jelly beans. Now Billy is right back where he started! He is unable to choose the "best" kind of candy because his preferences for kinds of candy are not transitive.

The implications of these four properties are conveniently summarized in Figure 4–2, which depicts three indifference curves. Every bundle on indifference curve III is preferred to those on curve II, and every bundle on indifference curve II is preferred to those on curve I. The three indifference curves are convex and do not cross. Curves farther from the origin imply higher levels of satisfaction than curves closer to the origin.

FIGURE 4–2 A Family of Indifference Curves

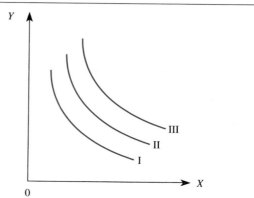

Indifference Curves and Risk Preferences

Have you ever wondered why some individuals choose to undertake risky prospects, such as skydiving and investing in risky financial assets, while others choose safer activities? Indifference curve analysis provides an answer to this question.

The accompanying figures plot three potential investment options (represented by points A, B, and C), each with different expected returns and risks. Option A is the safest investment, but it offers the lowest return (2.94 percent); option B is of medium safety, with a moderate return (4.49 percent); and fund C is the least safe, but it carries the highest potential return (6.00 percent).

Investors view safety and the level of the return on an investment as "goods"; investments with higher returns and higher levels of safety are preferred to investments with lower returns and lower levels of safety. Investors are willing to substitute between the level of return and the level of safety. Given the three options, from an investor's viewpoint, there is a tradeoff between a higher reward (return) and the level of safety of the investment.

The relatively steep indifference curves drawn in panel (a) describe an investor who has a high marginal rate of substitution between return and safety; she or he must receive a large return to be induced to give up a small amount of safety. The relatively flat indifference curves drawn in panel (b) indicate an investor with a low marginal rate of substitution between return and safety. This individual is willing to give up a lot of safety to get a slightly higher return. An investor with indifference curves such as those in panel (a) finds investment option A most attractive, because it is associated with the highest indifference curve. In contrast, an investor with indifference curves such as those in panel (b) achieves the highest indifference curve with investment option C. Both types of investors are rational, but one investor is willing to give up some additional financial return for more safety.

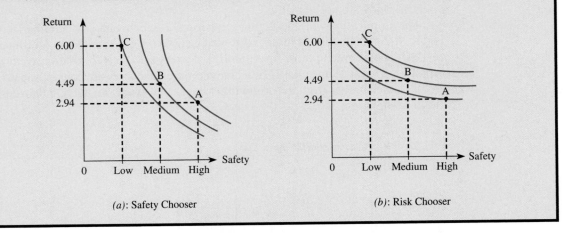

(a): Safety Chooser

(b): Risk Chooser

CONSTRAINTS

In making decisions, individuals face *constraints*. There are legal constraints, time constraints, physical constraints, and, of course, budget constraints. To maintain our focus on the essentials of managerial economics without delving into issues beyond the scope of this course, we will examine the role prices and income play in constraining consumer behavior.

The Budget Constraint

Simply stated, the *budget constraint* restricts consumer behavior by forcing the consumer to select a bundle of goods that is affordable. If a consumer has only $30 in his or her pocket when reaching the checkout line in the supermarket, the total value of the goods the consumer presents to the cashier cannot exceed $30.

To demonstrate how the presence of a budget constraint restricts the consumer's choice, we need some additional shorthand notation. Let M represent the consumer's income, which can be any amount. By using M instead of a particular value of income, we gain generality in that the theory is valid for a consumer with any income level. We will let P_x and P_y represent the prices of goods X and Y, respectively. Given this notation, the opportunity set (also called the *budget set*) may be expressed mathematically as

budget set
The bundles of goods a consumer can afford.

$$P_x X + P_y Y \leq M$$

In words, the budget set defines the combinations of goods X and Y that are affordable for the consumer: The consumer's expenditures on good X, plus her or his expenditures on good Y, do not exceed the consumer's income. Note that if the consumer spends his or her entire income on the two goods, this equation holds with equality. This relation is called the *budget line*:

budget line
The bundles of goods that exhaust a consumer's income.

$$P_x X + P_y Y = M$$

In other words, the budget line defines all the combinations of goods X and Y that exactly exhaust the consumer's income.

It is useful to manipulate the equation for the budget line to obtain an alternative expression for the budget constraint in slope-intercept form. If we multiply both sides of the budget line by $1/P_y$, we get

$$\frac{P_x}{P_y} X + Y = \frac{M}{P_y}$$

Solving for Y yields

$$Y = \frac{M}{P_y} - \frac{P_x}{P_y} X$$

Note that Y is a linear function of X with a vertical intercept of M/P_y and a slope of $-P_x/P_y$.

The consumer's budget constraint is graphed in Figure 4–3. The shaded area represents the consumer's budget set, or opportunity set. In particular, any combination of goods X and Y within the shaded area, such as point G, represents an affordable combination of X and Y. Any point above the shaded area, such as point H, represents a bundle of goods that is unaffordable.

FIGURE 4–3 The Budget Set

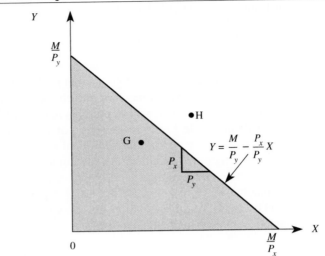

The upper boundary of the budget set in Figure 4–3 is the budget line. If a consumer spent her or his entire income on good X, the expenditures on good X would exactly equal the consumer's income:

$$P_x X = M$$

By manipulating this equation, we see that the maximum affordable quantity of good X consumed is

$$X = \frac{M}{P_x}$$

This is why the horizontal intercept of the budget line is

$$\frac{M}{P_x}$$

Similarly, if the consumer spent his or her entire income on good Y, expenditures on Y would exactly equal income:

$$P_y Y = M$$

market rate of substitution
The rate at which one good may be traded for another in the market; slope of the budget line.

Consequently, the maximum quantity of good Y that is affordable is

$$Y = \frac{M}{P_y}$$

The slope of the budget line is given by $-P_x/P_y$ and represents the *market rate of substitution* between goods X and Y. To obtain a better understanding of the market rate of substitution between goods X and Y, consider Figure 4–4, which presents a

FIGURE 4-4 The Budget Line

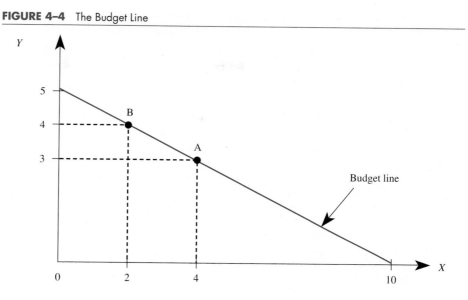

budget line for a consumer who has $10 in income and faces a price of $1 for good X and a price of $2 for good Y. If we substitute these values of P_x, P_y, and M into the formula for the budget line, we observe that the vertical intercept of the budget line (the maximum amount of good Y that is affordable) is $M/P_y = 10/2 = 5$. The horizontal intercept is $M/P_x = 10/1 = 10$ and represents the maximum amount of good X that can be purchased. The slope of the budget line is $-P_x/P_y = -(1/2)$.

The reason the slope of the budget line represents the market rate of substitution between the two goods is as follows: Suppose a consumer purchased bundle A in Figure 4-4, which represents the situation where the consumer purchases 3 units of good Y and 4 units of good X. If the consumer purchased bundle B instead of bundle A, she would gain one additional unit of good Y. But to afford this, she must give up 2 units $(4 - 2 = 2)$ of good X. For every unit of good Y the consumer purchases, she must give up 2 units of good X in order to be able to afford the additional unit of good Y. Thus the market rate of substitution is $\Delta Y/\Delta X = (4 - 3)/(2 - 4) = -1/2$, which is the slope of the budget line.

Changes in Income

The consumer's opportunity set depends on market prices and the consumer's income. As these parameters change, so will the consumer's opportunities. Let us now examine the effects on the opportunity set of changes in income by assuming prices remain constant.

Suppose the consumer's initial income in Figure 4-5 is M^0. What happens if M^0 increases to M^1 while prices remain unchanged? Recall that the slope of the budget line is given by $-P_x/P_y$. Under the assumption that prices remain unchanged, the increase in income will not affect the slope of the budget line.

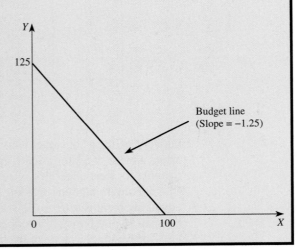

INSIDE BUSINESS 4–2

The Budget Constraints and Credit Cards

In today's economy, many consumers choose to make purchases using credit cards rather than cash. How does access to a credit card affect a consumer's budget constraint? A key aspect of credit cards is that they allow us to consume today and pay later. We can capture this feature of credit cards within our framework by considering a consumer's decision about purchasing a product, e.g., music downloads, at different points in time.

Let X be music downloads today (period 1) and Y be music downloads one period later (period 2). For simplicity, let the price of a music download in both periods be $1. Suppose in period 1 Kate is considering purchasing some music downloads, but has no more cash on hand. However, she has access to $100 of credit on her credit card, which she must pay off in period 2. The interest rate on her card is 25 percent. Since, regardless of her purchase timing, she does not make any payments until period 2, we can construct her budget line in terms of income and prices in period 2. The price of a music download in period 2 is $1; however, the price of a music download in period 1 will cost her $1.25 in period 2 money since she must borrow the $1 price at an interest rate of 25 percent.

From the preceding discussion, Kate's budget line in terms of period 2 money has the following features: $M = 125, $P_x = 1.25, and $P_y = 1. This budget line is illustrated in the accompanying figure. The slope of -1.25 represents the amount of music downloads she must give up from period 2 to buy one more in period 1.

However, the vertical and horizontal intercepts of the budget line both increase as the consumer's income increases, because more of each good can be purchased at the higher income. Thus, when income increases from M^0 to M^1, the budget line shifts to the right in a parallel fashion. This reflects an increase in

FIGURE 4–5   Changes in Income Shrink or Expand Opportunities

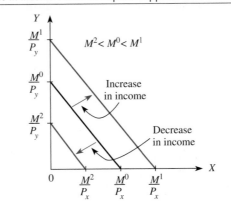

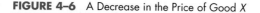

FIGURE 4–6   A Decrease in the Price of Good X

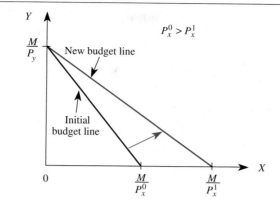

the consumer's opportunity set, because more goods are affordable after the increase in income than before. Similarly, if income decreases to M^2 from M^0, the budget line shifts toward the origin and the slope of the budget line remains unchanged.

Changes in Prices

Now suppose the consumer's income remains fixed at M, but the price of good X decreases to $P_x^1 < P_x^0$. Furthermore, suppose the price of good Y remains unchanged. Since the slope of the budget line is given by $-P_x/P_y$, the reduction in the price of good X changes the slope, making it flatter than before. Since the maximum amount of good Y that can be purchased is M/P_y, a reduction in the price of good X does not change the Y intercept of the budget line. But the maximum amount of good X that can be purchased at the lower price (the X intercept of the budget line) is M/P_x^1, which is greater than M/P_x^0. Thus, the ultimate effect of a reduction in the price of good X is to rotate the budget line counterclockwise, as in Figure 4–6. Similarly, an increase in the price of good X leads to a clockwise rotation of the budget line, as the next demonstration problem indicates.

Demonstration Problem 4–1

A consumer has initial income of \$100 and faces prices of $P_x = \$1$ and $P_y = \$5$. Graph the budget line, and show how it changes when the price of good X increases to $P_x^1 = \$5$.

Answer:

Initially, if the consumer spends his entire income on good X, he can purchase $M/P_x = 100/1 = 100$ units of X. This is the horizontal intercept of the initial budget line in Figure 4–7. If the consumer spends his entire income on good Y, he can purchase $M/P_y = 100/5 = 20$ units of Y. This is the vertical intercept of the initial budget line. The slope of the initial budget line is $-P_x/P_y = -1/5$.

FIGURE 4–7   An Increase in the Price of Good X

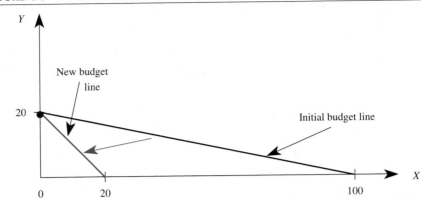

When the price of good X increases to 5, the maximum amount of X the consumer can purchase is reduced to $M/P_x = 100/5 = 20$ units of X. This is the horizontal intercept of the new budget line in Figure 4–7. If the consumer spends his entire income on good Y, he can purchase $M/P_y = 100/5 = 20$ units of Y. Thus, the vertical intercept of the budget line remains unchanged; the slope changes to $-P_x^1/P_y = -5/5 = -1$.

CONSUMER EQUILIBRIUM

The objective of the consumer is to choose the consumption bundle that maximizes his or her utility, or satisfaction. If there was no scarcity, the more-is-better property would imply that the consumer would want to consume bundles that contained infinite amounts of goods. However, one implication of scarcity is that the consumer must select a bundle that lies inside the budget set, that is, an affordable bundle. Let us combine our theory of consumer preferences with our analysis of constraints to see how the consumer goes about selecting the best affordable bundle.

Consider a bundle such as A in Figure 4–8. This combination of goods X and Y lies on the budget line, so the cost of bundle A completely exhausts the consumer's income. Given the income and prices corresponding to the budget line, can the consumer do better—that is, can the consumer achieve a higher indifference curve? Clearly, if the consumer consumed bundle B instead of bundle A, she or he would be better off since the indifference curve through B lies above the one through A. Moreover, bundle B lies on the budget line and thus is affordable. In short, it is inefficient for the consumer to consume bundle A because bundle B both is affordable and yields a higher level of well-being.

Is bundle B optimal? The answer is no. Bundle B exhausts the consumer's budget, but there is another affordable bundle that is even better: bundle C. Note that there are bundles, such as D, that the consumer prefers more than bundle C, but

FIGURE 4–8 Consumer Equilibrium

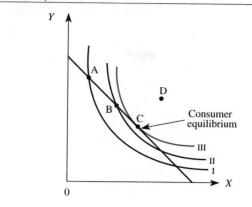

consumer equilibrium
The equilibrium consumption bundle is the affordable bundle that yields the greatest satisfaction to the consumer.

those bundles are not affordable. Thus, we say bundle *C* represents the consumer's *equilibrium choice.* The term *equilibrium* refers to the fact that the consumer has no incentive to change to a different affordable bundle once this point is reached.

An important property of consumer equilibrium is that at the equilibrium consumption bundle, the slope of the indifference curve is equal to the slope of the budget line. Recalling that the absolute value of the slope of the indifference curve is called the *marginal rate of substitution* and the slope of the budget line is given by $-P_x/P_y$, we see that at a point of consumer equilibrium,

$$MRS = \frac{P_x}{P_y}$$

If this condition did not hold, the personal rate at which the consumer is willing to substitute between goods *X* and *Y* would differ from the market rate at which he or she is able to substitute between the goods. For example, at point *A* in Figure 4–8, the slope of the indifference curve is steeper than the slope of the budget line. This means the consumer is willing to give up more of good *Y* to get an additional unit of good *X* than she or he actually has to give up, based on market prices. Consequently, it is in the consumer's interest to consume less of good *Y* and more of good *X*. This substitution continues until ultimately the consumer is at a point such as C in Figure 4–8, where the *MRS* is equal to the ratio of prices.

COMPARATIVE STATICS

Price Changes and Consumer Behavior

A change in the price of a good will lead to a change in the equilibrium consumption bundle. To see this, recall that a reduction in the price of good *X* leads to a counterclockwise rotation of the budget line. Thus, if the consumer initially is at equilibrium at point A in Figure 4–9, when the price of good *X* falls to P_x^1, his or her

Price Changes and Inventory Management for Multiproduct Firms

One of the more important decisions a manager must make is how much inventory to have on hand. Too little inventory means an insufficient quantity of products to meet the demand of consumers, in which case your customers may defect to another store. The opportunity cost of inventory is the forgone interest that could be earned on the money tied up in inventory, storage costs, and so on. In performing inventory management, an effective manager recognizes the relationship that exists among products in the store and the impact of a change in the price of one product on the required inventories of other products. For example, a decline in the price of video game *consoles* not only increases the quantity demanded of game consoles, but also increases the demand for video *games,* which are complementary goods. This result has obvious implications for inventory management.

A more subtle aspect of a reduction in the price of a product is its impact on the demand for, and optimal inventories of, substitute goods. If a retailer sells many products, and some of the products are substitutes, a reduction in the price of one product will lead to a reduction in the retailer's sales of these substitute goods. For instance, when the price of Xbox 360 game consoles is reduced, the consumption of Xbox 360 consoles increases as a direct consequence of the price reduction. However, note that the consumption of substitutes like PlayStation3 game consoles will decrease as a result of the reduction in the price of Xbox 360 game consoles. If the manager does not account for the impact of a price reduction on the consumption of substitute goods, he or she is likely to face a buildup of inventories of PlayStation3 consoles when the price of Xbox 360 game consoles decreases.

opportunity set expands. Given this new opportunity set, the consumer can achieve a higher level of satisfaction. This is illustrated as a movement to the new equilibrium point, B, in Figure 4–9.

FIGURE 4–9   Change in Consumer Equilibrium Due to a Decrease in the Price of Good X (Note that good Y is a substitute for X.)

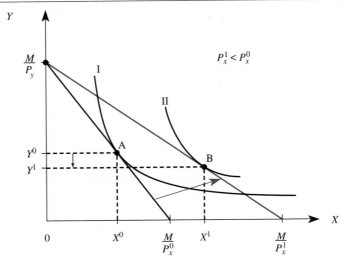

Precisely where the new equilibrium point lies along the new budget line after a price change depends on consumer preferences. Accordingly, it is useful to recall the definitions of substitutes and complements that were introduced in Chapter 2.

First, goods X and Y are called *substitutes* if an increase (decrease) in the price of X leads to an increase (decrease) in the consumption of Y. Most consumers would view Coke and Pepsi as substitutes. If the price of Pepsi increased, most people would tend to consume more Coke. If goods X and Y are substitutes, a reduction in the price of X would lead the consumer to move from point A in Figure 4–9 to a point such as B, where less of Y is consumed than at point A.

Second, goods X and Y are called *complements* if an increase (decrease) in the price of good X leads to a decrease (increase) in the consumption of good Y. Beer and pretzels are an example of complementary goods. If the price of beer increased, most beer drinkers would decrease their consumption of pretzels. When goods X and Y are complements, a reduction in the price of X would lead the consumer to move from point A in Figure 4–10 to a point such as B, where more of Y is consumed than before.

From a managerial perspective, the key thing to note is that changes in prices affect the market rate at which a consumer can substitute among various goods. Therefore, changes in prices will change the behavior of consumers. Price changes might occur because of updated pricing strategies within your own firm. Or they might arise because of price changes made by rivals or firms in other industries. Ultimately, price changes alter consumer incentives to buy different goods, thereby changing the mix of goods they purchase in equilibrium. The primary advantage of indifference curve analysis is that it allows a manager to see how price changes affect the mix of goods that consumers purchase in equilibrium. As we will see below, indifference curve analysis also allows us to see how changes in *income* affect the mix of goods consumers purchase.

FIGURE 4–10 When the Price of Good X Falls, the Consumption of Complementary Good Y Rises

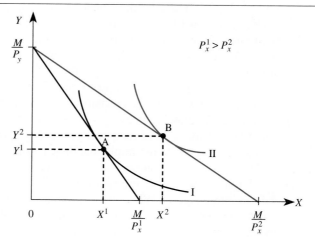

FIGURE 4–11   An Increase in Income Increases the Consumption of Normal Goods

FIGURE 4–11   An Increase in Income Increases the Consumption of Normal Goods

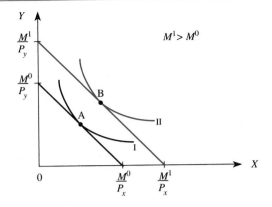

Income Changes and Consumer Behavior

A change in income also will lead to a change in the consumption patterns of consumers. The reason is that changes in income either expand or contract the consumer's budget constraint, and the consumer therefore finds it optimal to choose a new equilibrium bundle. For example, assume the consumer initially is at equilibrium at point A in Figure 4–11. Now suppose the consumer's income increases to M^1 so that his or her budget line shifts out. Clearly the consumer can now achieve a higher level of satisfaction than before. This particular consumer finds it in her or his interest to choose bundle *B* in Figure 4–11, where the indifference curve through point B is tangent to the new budget line.

As in the case of a price change, the exact location of the new equilibrium point will depend on consumer preferences. Let us now review our definitions of normal and inferior goods.

Recall that good *X* is a *normal good* if an increase (decrease) in income leads to an increase (decrease) in the consumption of good *X*. Normal goods include goods such as steak, airline travel, and designer jeans. As income goes up, consumers typically buy more of these goods. Note in Figure 4–11 that the consumption of both goods *X* and *Y* increased due to the increase in consumer income. Thus, the consumer views *X* and *Y* as normal goods.

Recall that good *X* is an *inferior good* if an increase (decrease) in income leads to a decrease (increase) in the consumption of good *X*. Bologna, bus travel, and generic jeans are examples of inferior goods. As income goes up, consumers typically consume less of these goods and services. It is important to repeat that by calling the goods *inferior,* we do not imply that they are of poor quality; it is simply a term used to define products consumers purchase less of when their incomes rise.

Figure 4–12 depicts the effect of an increase in income for the case when good *X* is an inferior good. When income increases, the consumer moves from point A to point B to maximize his or her satisfaction given the higher income. Since at point B the consumer consumes more of good *Y* than at point A, we know that good *Y* is a

FIGURE 4–12   An Increase in Income Decreases the Equilibrium Consumption of Good X—An Inferior Good

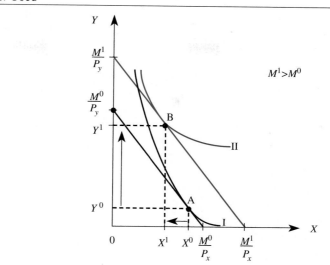

normal good. However, note that at point B less of good X is consumed than at point A, so we know this consumer views X as an inferior good.

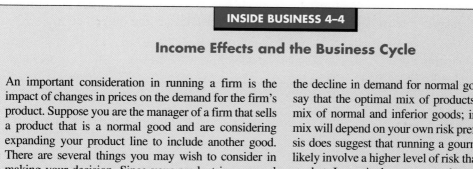

INSIDE BUSINESS 4–4

Income Effects and the Business Cycle

An important consideration in running a firm is the impact of changes in prices on the demand for the firm's product. Suppose you are the manager of a firm that sells a product that is a normal good and are considering expanding your product line to include another good. There are several things you may wish to consider in making your decision. Since your product is a normal good, you will sell more of it when the economy is booming (consumer incomes are high) than when times are tough (incomes are low). Your product is a cyclical product, that is, sales vary directly with the economy. This information may be useful to you when considering alternative products to include in your store. If you expand your offerings to include more normal goods, you will continue to have an operation that sells more during an economic boom than during a recession. But if you include in your operation some inferior goods, the demand for these products will increase during bad economic times (when incomes are low) and perhaps offset

the decline in demand for normal goods. This is not to say that the optimal mix of products involves a 50–50 mix of normal and inferior goods; indeed, the optimal mix will depend on your own risk preference. The analysis does suggest that running a gourmet food store will likely involve a higher level of risk than running a supermarket. In particular, gourmet shops sell almost exclusively normal goods, while supermarkets have a more "balanced portfolio" of normal and inferior goods. This explains why, during recessions, many gourmet shops go out of business while supermarkets do not.

It is also useful to know the magnitude of the income effect when designing a marketing campaign. If the product is a normal good, it is most likely in the firm's interest to target advertising campaigns toward individuals with higher incomes. These factors should be considered when determining which magazines and television shows are the best outlets for advertising messages.

Substitution and Income Effects

We can combine our analysis of price and income changes to gain a better understanding of the effect of a price change on consumer behavior. Suppose a consumer initially is in equilibrium at point A in Figure 4–13, along the budget line connecting points F and G. Suppose the price of good X increases so that the budget line rotates clockwise and becomes the budget line connecting points F and H. There are two things to notice about this change. First, since the budget set is smaller due to the price increase, the consumer will be worse off after the price increase. A lower "real income" will be achieved, as a lower indifference curve is all that can be reached after the price increase. Second, the increase in the price of good X leads to a budget line with a steeper slope, reflecting a higher market rate of substitution between the two goods. These two factors lead the consumer to move from the initial consumer equilibrium (point A) to a new equilibrium (point C) in Figure 4–13.

It is useful to isolate the two effects of a price change to see how each effect individually alters consumer choice. In particular, ignore for the moment the fact that the price increase leads to a lower indifference curve. Suppose that after the price increase, the consumer is given enough income to achieve the budget line connecting points J and I in Figure 4–13. This budget line has the same slope as budget line FH, but it implies a higher income than budget line FH. Given this budget line, the consumer will achieve equilibrium at point B, where less of good X is consumed than in the initial situation, point A. The movement from A to B is called the *substitution effect*; it reflects how a consumer will react to a different market rate of substitution. The substitution effect is the difference $X^0 - X^m$ in

substitution effect
The movement along a given indifference curve that results from a change in the relative prices of goods, holding real income constant.

FIGURE 4–13   An Increase in the Price of Good X Leads to a Substitution Effect (A to B) and an Income Effect (B to C)

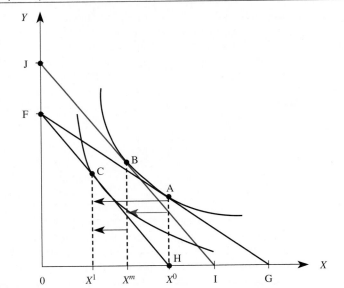

Figure 4–13. Importantly, the movement from A to B leaves the consumer on the same indifference curve, so the reduction in the consumption of good X implied by that movement reflects the higher market rate of substitution, not the reduced "real income," of the consumer.

The consumer does not actually face budget line JI when the price increases but instead faces budget line FH. Let us now take back the income we gave to the consumer to compensate for the price increase. When this income is taken back, the budget line shifts from JI to FH. This shift in the budget line reflects only a reduction in income; the slopes of budget lines JI and FH are identical. Thus, the movement from B to C is called the *income effect*. The income effect is the difference $X^m - X^1$ in Figure 4–13; it reflects the fact that when price increases, the consumer's "real income" falls. Since good X is a normal good in Figure 4–13, the reduction in income leads to a further reduction in the consumption of X.

The total effect of a price increase thus is composed of substitution and income effects. The substitution effect reflects a movement along an indifference curve, thus isolating the effect of a relative price change on consumption. The income effect results from a parallel shift in the budget line; thus, it isolates the effect of reduced "real income" on consumption and is represented by the movement from B to C. The total effect of a price increase, which is what we observe in the marketplace, is the movement from A to C. The total effect of a change in consumer behavior results not only from the effect of a higher relative price of good X (the movement from A to B) but also from the reduced real income of the consumer (the movement from B to C).

income effect
The movement from one indifference curve to another that results from the change in real income caused by a price change.

APPLICATIONS OF INDIFFERENCE CURVE ANALYSIS

Choices by Consumers

Buy One, Get One Free

A very popular sales technique at pizza restaurants is to offer the following deal:

Buy one large pizza, get one large pizza free (limit one free pizza per customer).

It is tempting to conclude that this is simply a 50 percent reduction in the price of pizza so that the budget line rotates as it does for any price decrease. This conclusion is invalid, however. A price reduction decreases the price of each unit purchased. The type of deal summarized above reduces only the price of the second unit purchased (in fact, it reduces the price of the second large pizza to zero). The offer does not change the price of units below one pizza and above two pizzas.

The *"buy one, get one free"* marketing scheme is quite easy to analyze in our framework. In Figure 4–14, a consumer initially faces a budget line connecting points A and B and is in equilibrium at point C. Point C represents one-half of a large pizza (say, a small pizza), so the consumer decides it is best to buy a small pizza instead of a large one. Point D represents the point at which she buys one large pizza, but, as we can see, the consumer prefers bundle C to bundle D, since it lies on a higher indifference curve.

FIGURE 4–14   A Buy One, Get One Free Pizza Deal

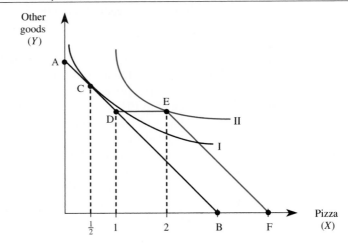

When the consumer is offered the "buy one, get one free" deal, her budget line becomes ADEF. The reason is as follows: If she buys less than one large pizza, she gets no deal, and her budget line to the left of one pizza remains as it was, namely AD. But if she buys one large pizza, she gets a second one free. In this instance, the budget line becomes DEF as soon as she buys one pizza. In other words, the price of pizza is zero for units between one and two large pizzas. This implies that the budget line for pizzas is horizontal between one and two units (recall that the slope of the budget line is $-(P_x/P_y)$, and for these units P_x is zero). If the consumer wants to consume more than two large pizzas, she must buy them at regular prices. But note that if she spent all of her income on pizza, she could buy one more than she could before (since one of the pizzas is free). Thus, for pizzas in excess of two units, the budget constraint is the line connecting points E and F. After the deal is offered, the opportunity set increases. In fact, bundle *E* is now an affordable bundle. Moreover, it is clear that bundle *E* is preferred to bundle *C,* and the consumer's optimal choice is to consume bundle *E,* as in Figure 4–14. The sales technique has induced the consumer to purchase more pizza than she would have otherwise.

Cash Gifts, In-Kind Gifts, and Gift Certificates

Along with death and taxes, lines in refund departments after Christmas appear to be an unpleasant but necessary aspect of life. To understand why, and to be able to pose a potential solution to the problem, consider the following story.

One Christmas morning, a consumer named Sam is in equilibrium, consuming bundle *A* as in Figure 4–15. He opens a package and, to his surprise, it contains a $10 fruitcake (good *X*). He smiles and tells Aunt Sarah that he always wanted a fruitcake. Graphically, when Sam receives the gift his opportunity set expands to include point B in Figure 4–15. Bundle *B* is just like bundle *A* except that it has one more fruitcake (good *X*) than bundle *A*. Given this new opportunity set, Sam moves to the higher indifference curve through point B after receiving the gift.

FIGURE 4–15 A Cash Gift Yields Higher Utility than an In-Kind Gift

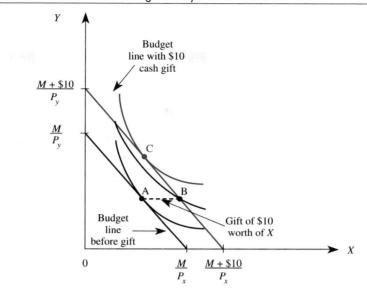

While Sam likes fruitcake and is better off after receiving it, the gift is not what he would have purchased had Aunt Sarah given him the cash she spent on the fruitcake. For concreteness, suppose the cost of the fruitcake was $10. Had Sam been given $10 in cash, his budget line would have shifted out, parallel to the old budget line but through point B, as in Figure 4–15. To see why, note that when Sam gets additional income, prices are not changed, so the slope of the budget line is unchanged. Note also that if Sam used the money to buy one more fruitcake, he would exactly exhaust his income. Thus, the budget line after the cash gift must go through point B—and, given the cash gift, Sam would achieve a higher level of satisfaction at point C compared to the gift of a fruitcake (point B).

Thus, a cash gift generally is preferred to an in-kind gift of equal value, unless the in-kind gift is exactly what the consumer would have purchased personally. This explains why refund departments are so busy after the Christmas holidays; individuals exchange gifts for cash so that they can purchase bundles they prefer.

One way stores attempt to reduce the number of gifts returned is to sell *gift certificates*. To see why, suppose Sam received a gift certificate, good for $10 worth of merchandise at store X, which sells good *X*, instead of the $10 fruitcake. Further, suppose the certificate is not good at store Y, which sells good *Y*. By receiving a gift certificate, Sam cannot purchase any more of good *Y* than he could before he received the certificate. But if he spends all his income on good *Y*, he can purchase $10 worth of good *X*, since he has a certificate worth $10 at store X. And if he spends all his income on good *X*, he can purchase $10 more than he could before because of the gift certificate. In effect, the gift certificate is like money that is good only at store X.

Graphically, the effect of receiving a gift certificate at store X is depicted in Figure 4–16. The straight black line is the budget line before Sam receives the gift

FIGURE 4–16   A Gift Certificate Valid at Store X

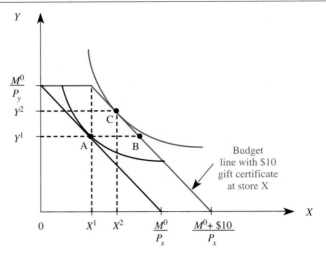

certificate. When he receives the $10 gift certificate, the budget constraint becomes the kinked blue line. In effect, the gift certificate allows the consumer up to $10 worth of good X without spending a dime of his own money.

    The effect of gift certificates on consumer behavior depends, among other things, on whether good X is a normal or inferior good. To examine what happens to behavior when a consumer receives a gift certificate, let us suppose a consumer initially is in equilibrium at point A in Figure 4–16, spending $10 on good X. What happens if the consumer is given a $10 gift certificate good only for items in store X? If both X and Y are normal goods, the consumer will desire to spend more on both goods as income increases. Thus, if both goods are normal goods, the consumer moves from A to C in Figure 4–16. In this instance, the consumer reacts to the gift certificate just as she or he would have reacted to a cash gift of equal value.

Demonstration Problem 4–2

How would the analysis of gift certificates just presented change if good X were an inferior good?

Answer:

In this instance, a gift of $10 in cash would result in a movement from point A in Figure 4–17 to a point like D, since X is an inferior good. However, when a $10 gift certificate is received, bundle D is not affordable, and the best the consumer can do is consume bundle E. In other words, had the consumer been given cash, his or her budget line would have extended up along the dotted line, and point D would have been an affordable bundle. If given cash, the consumer would have purchased less of good X than she or he did with the gift certificate. Also, note that the consumer would have achieved a higher indifference

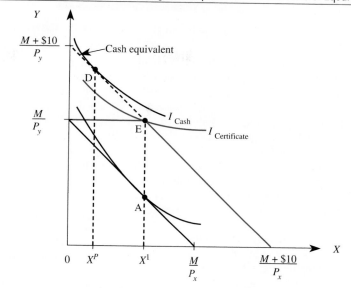

FIGURE 4–17 Here, a Cash Gift Yields Higher Utility than a Gift Certificate of Equal Dollar Value

curve with the cash than that achieved with the gift certificate. (An end-of-chapter problem asks you whether a gift certificate always leads to a lower indifference curve and higher sales than a cash gift when the good is inferior.)

This analysis reveals two important benefits to a firm that sells gift certificates. First, as a manager you can reduce the strain on your refund department by offering gift certificates to customers looking for gifts. This is true for both normal and inferior goods. Second, if you sell an inferior good, offering to sell gift certificates to those looking for gifts may result in a greater quantity sold than if customers resorted to giving cash gifts. (This assumes you do not permit individuals to redeem gift certificates for cash.)

Choices by Workers and Managers

Until now, our analysis of indifference curves has focused on the decisions of consumers of goods and services. Managers and workers also are individuals and therefore have preferences among the alternatives that confront them. In this section, we will see that the indifference curve analysis developed earlier for consumers can easily be modified to analyze the behavior of managers and other individuals employed by firms. In Chapter 6 we will show how these insights into the behavior of workers and managers can be used to construct efficient employment contracts.

A Simplified Model of Income–Leisure Choice
Most workers view both leisure and income as goods and substitute between them at a diminishing rate along an indifference curve. Thus, a typical worker's indifference

curve has the usual shape in Figure 4–18, where we measure the quantity of leisure consumed by an employee on the horizontal axis and worker income on the vertical axis. Note that while workers enjoy leisure, they also enjoy income.

FIGURE 4–18   Labor–Leisure Choice

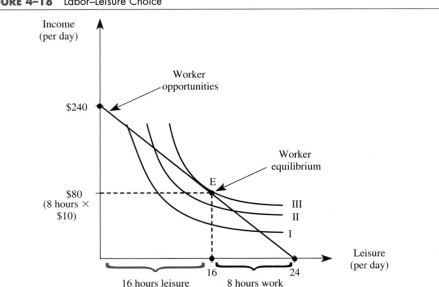

To induce workers to give up leisure, firms must compensate them. Suppose a firm offers to pay a worker $10 for each hour of leisure the worker gives up (i.e., spends working). In this instance, opportunities confronting the worker or manager are given by the straight line in Figure 4–18. If the worker chooses to work 24-hour days, he or she consumes no leisure but earns $10 × 24 = $240 per day, which is the vertical intercept of the line. If the worker chooses not to work, he or she consumes 24 hours of leisure but earns no income. This is the horizontal intercept of the line in Figure 4–18.

Worker behavior thus may be examined in much the same way we analyzed consumer behavior. The worker attempts to achieve a higher indifference curve until he or she achieves one that is tangent to the opportunity set at point E in Figure 4–18. In this instance, the worker consumes 16 hours of leisure and works 8 hours to earn a total of $80 per day.

For a video walkthrough of this problem, visit www.mhhe.com/baye8e

Demonstration Problem 4–3

Suppose a worker is offered a wage of $5 per hour, plus a fixed payment of $40. What is the equation for the worker's opportunity set in a given 24-hour day? What are the maximum total earnings the worker can earn in a day? The minimum? What is the price to the worker of consuming an additional hour of leisure?

Answer:

The total earnings (E) of a worker who consumes L hours of leisure in a 24-hour day is given by

$$E = \$40 + \$5(24 - L)$$

so the combinations of earnings (E) and leisure (L) satisfy

$$E = \$160 - \$5L$$

Thus, the most a worker can earn in a 24-hour day is $160 (by consuming no leisure); the least that can be earned is $40 (by not working at all). The price of a unit of leisure is $5, since the opportunity cost of an hour of leisure is one hour of work.

The Decisions of Managers

William Baumol[1] has argued that many managers derive satisfaction from the underlying output and profits of their firms. According to Baumol, higher profits and sales lead to a larger firm, and larger firms provide more "perks" like spacious offices, executive health clubs, corporate jets, and the like.

Suppose a manager's preferences are such that she or he views the "profits" and the "output" of the firm to be "goods" so that more of each is preferred to less.

---

[1] William J. Baumol, *Business Behavior, Value, and Growth,* rev. ed. (New York: Harcourt, Brace and World, 1967).

We are not suggesting that it is optimal for you, as a manager, to have these types of preferences, but there may be instances in which your preferences are so aligned. In many sales jobs, for example, individuals receive a bonus depending on the overall profitability of the firm. But the salesperson's ability to receive reimbursement for certain business-related expenses may depend on that individual's total output (e.g., number of cars sold). Additionally, perks such as a company plane, car, and so forth may be allocated to individuals based on the firm's output and profitability. In all of these scenarios, managerial preferences depend on the firm's output as well as profits.

Panels a, b, and c of Figure 4–19 show the relation between profits and the output of a firm on the curve labeled "firm's profits." This curve goes from the origin through points C, A, and B, and represents the profits of the firm as a function of output. When the firm sells no output, profits are zero. As the firm expands output, profits increase, reach a maximum at Q_m, and then begin to decline until, at point Q_0, they are again zero.

Given this relationship between output and profits, a manager who views output and profits as "goods" (the Baumol hypothesis) has indifference curves like those in Figure 4–19(a). She attempts to achieve higher and higher indifference curves until she eventually reaches equilibrium at point A. Note that this level of output, Q_u, is greater than the profit-maximizing level of output, Q_m. Thus, when the manager views both profits and output as "goods," she produces more than the profit-maximizing level of output.

In contrast, when the manager's preferences depend solely on output, the indifference curves look like those in Figure 4–19(b), which are vertical straight lines. One example of this situation occurs when the owner of a car dealership pays the manager based solely on the number of cars sold (the manager gets nothing if the company goes bankrupt). Since the manager does not care about profits, his or her indifference curves are vertical lines, and satisfaction increases as the lines move farther to the right. A manager with such preferences will attempt to obtain the

FIGURE 4–19 A Manager's Preferences Might Depend on:

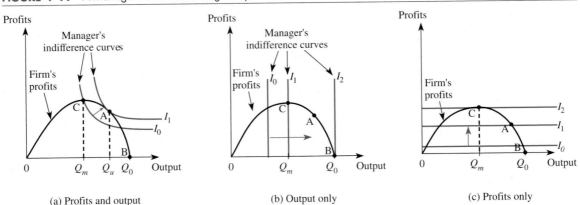

(a) Profits and output   (b) Output only   (c) Profits only

indifference curves farther and farther to the right until indifference curve I_2 is reached. Point B represents equilibrium for this manager, where Q_0 units of output are produced. Again, in this instance the manager produces more than the profit-maximizing level of output.

Finally, suppose the manager cares solely about the profits of the firm. In this instance, the manager's indifference curves are horizontal straight lines as shown in Figure 4–19(c). The manager maximizes satisfaction at point C, where the indifference curve I_2 is as high as possible given the opportunity set. In this instance, profits are greater and output is lower than in the other two cases.

An important issue for the firm's owners is to induce managers to care solely about profits so that the result is the maximization of the underlying value of the firm, as in Figure 4–19(c). We will examine this issue in more detail in Chapter 6.

THE RELATIONSHIP BETWEEN INDIFFERENCE CURVE ANALYSIS AND DEMAND CURVES

We have seen how the consumption patterns of an individual consumer depend on variables that include the prices of substitute goods, the prices of complementary goods, tastes (i.e., the shape of indifference curves), and income. The indifference curve approach developed in this chapter, in fact, is the basis for the demand functions we studied in Chapters 2 and 3. We conclude by examining the link between indifference curve analysis and demand curves.

INSIDE BUSINESS 4–6

Public Health Centers and Output Oriented Incentives

Unlike most private companies, government-run agencies and nonprofit organizations generally are not concerned with maximizing profits; instead they have other objectives, often output maximization. This is largely the case with public health centers, which seek to provide health care to as many citizens as possible. However, the employees at public health centers may not share the government's preference regarding output production.

Recently in Rwanda, the country's public health centers suffered several years of poor performance. In response, the Rwandan Ministry of Health along with HealthNet International decided to change their support strategy for Rwandan public health centers. Specifically, in addition to their salaries, employees were compensated via output-based bonuses. In short, as more services were provided, employees received more money.

This output-oriented incentive scheme helped to align employees' preferences with those of the government. In fact, the productivity of the public health centers that experienced this change in payment scheme showed productivity increases exceeding 50 percent!

Source: Meesen, B., Kashala, J.P., and Musango, L., "Output-based payment to boost staff productivity in public health centres: contracting in Kabutare district, Rwanda," *Bulletin of the World Health Organization*, 85, 2007, pp. 108–15.

FIGURE 4–20 Deriving an Individual's Demand Curve

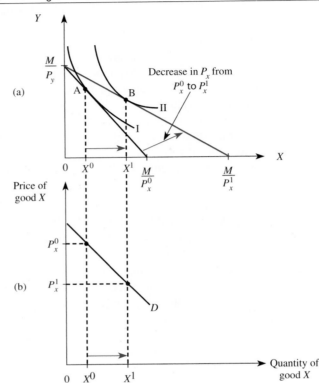

Individual Demand

To see where the demand curve for a normal good comes from, consider Figure 4–20(a). The consumer initially is in equilibrium at point A, where income is fixed at M and prices are P_x^0 and P_y. But when the price of good X falls to the lower level, indicated by P_x^1, the opportunity set expands and the consumer reaches a new equilibrium at point B. The important thing to notice is that the only change that caused the consumer to move from A to B was a change in the price of good X; income and the price of good Y are held constant in the diagram. When the price of good X is P_x^0, the consumer consumes X^0 units of good X; when the price falls to P_x^1, the consumption of X increases to X^1.

This relationship between the price of good X and the quantity consumed of good X is graphed in Figure 4–20(b) and is the individual consumer's demand curve for good X. This consumer's demand curve for good X indicates that, holding other things constant, when the price of good X is P_x^0, the consumer will purchase X^0 units of X; when the price of good X is P_x^1, the consumer will purchase X^1 units of X.

Market Demand

You will usually, in your role as a manager, be interested in determining the total demand by all consumers for your firm's product. This information is summarized in the market demand curve. The market demand curve is the horizontal summation of individual demand curves and indicates the total quantity all consumers in the market would purchase at each possible price.

This concept is illustrated graphically in Figures 4–21(a) and 4–21(b). The curves D_A and D_B represent the individual demand curves of two hypothetical consumers, Ms. A and Mr. B, respectively. When the price is $60, Ms. A buys 0 units and Mr. B buys 0 units. Thus, at the market level, 0 units are sold when the price is $60, and this is one point on the market demand curve (labeled D_M in Figure 4–21[b]). When the price is $40, Ms. A buys 10 units (point A) and Mr. B buys 20 units (point B). Thus, at the market level (Figure 4–21[b]), 30 units are sold when the price is $40, and this is another point (point A + B) on the market demand curve. When the price of good X is zero, Ms. A buys 30 units and Mr. B buys 60 units; thus, at the market level, 90 units are sold when the price is $0. If we repeat the analysis for all prices between $0 and $60, we get the curve labeled D_M in Figure 4–21(b).

Thus, the demand curves we studied in Chapters 2 and 3 are based on indifference curve analysis.

FIGURE 4–21 Deriving the Market Demand Curve

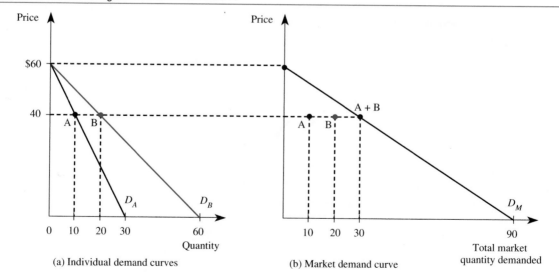

(a) Individual demand curves

(b) Market demand curve

ANSWERING THE HEADLINE

The question posed at the beginning of the chapter asked why Boxes Ltd. paid a higher overtime wage only on hours in excess of eight hours per day instead of offering workers a higher wage for every hour worked during a given day.

Figure 4–22 presents the analysis of income–leisure choice for a hypothetical worker. When the wage is $10 per hour, the worker's opportunity set is given by line DF. If the worker consumed no leisure, his earnings would be $10 × 24 = $240. However, given a $10 wage, this worker maximizes satisfaction at point A, where he consumes 16 hours of leisure (works 8 hours per day) to earn $80 in wage income.

With overtime pay of $15 for each hour worked in excess of 8 hours, the opportunity set becomes EAF. The reason is simple. If the worker works 8 hours or less, he does not earn overtime pay, and this part of his budget line (AF) remains the same. But if he consumes less than 16 hours of leisure, he gets $15 instead of $10 for these hours worked, so the budget line is steeper (EA). When no leisure is consumed (point E), the first 8 hours given up generate $10 × 8 = $80 in earnings, while the last 16 hours of leisure given up generate $15 × 16 = $240 in earnings. Thus, point E on the overtime budget line corresponds to earnings of $80 + $240 = $320. Given the overtime option, this worker maximizes satisfaction at point B, where he works 13 hours to earn $155. Overtime pay increases the amount of work from 8 hours to 13 hours.

Why doesn't the firm simply increase the wage to $15 instead of initiating the more complicated overtime system? If this worker were paid a wage of $15 for every hour worked, his budget line would be HF. This worker would obtain a higher indifference curve at point C, where 12 hours of leisure are consumed

FIGURE 4–22 An Overtime Wage Increases Hours Worked

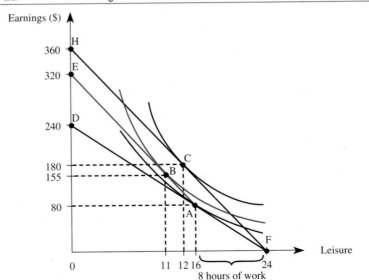

(12 hours of work). When leisure is a normal good, the $15 wage yields fewer hours of work from each worker than does the overtime system. In addition, labor costs are lower with overtime pay (point B) than a $15 wage (point C).

To summarize, we have shown that the manager could get workers who view leisure as a normal good to work longer hours with overtime pay than she could by simply offering a higher wage on all hours worked.

SUMMARY

In this chapter, we provided a basic model of individual behavior that enables the manager to understand the impact of various managerial decisions on the actions of consumers and workers.

After reading and working through the demonstration problems in this chapter, you should understand what a budget constraint is and how it changes when prices or income changes. You should also understand that when there is a change in the price of a good, consumers change their behavior because there is a change in the ratio of prices (which leads to a substitution effect) and a change in real income (which leads to the income effect). The model of consumer behavior also articulates the assumptions underlying the demand curve.

In equilibrium, consumers adjust their purchasing behavior so that the ratio of prices they pay just equals their marginal rate of substitution. This information, along with observations of consumer behavior, helps a manager determine when to use a "buy one, get one free" pricing strategy instead of a half-price offer. During holiday seasons, the same manager will have a sound basis for determining whether offering gift certificates is a wise strategy.

Effective managers also use the theory of consumer behavior to direct the behavior of employees. In this chapter, we examined the benefits to the firm of paying overtime wages; additional issues will be discussed in Chapter 6.

In conclusion, remember that the models of individual behavior developed in this chapter are basic tools for analyzing the behavior of your customers and employees. By taking the time to become familiar with the models and working through the demonstration and end-of-chapter problems, you will be better equipped to make decisions that will maximize the value of your firm.

KEY TERMS AND CONCEPTS

budget constraint	income effect
budget line	indifference curve
budget set	marginal rate of substitution (MRS)
"buy one, get one free" deals	market rate of substitution
completeness	more is better
consumer equilibrium	substitution effect
diminishing marginal rate of substitution	transitivity
gift certificates	

END-OF-CHAPTER PROBLEMS BY LEARNING OBJECTIVE

Every end-of-chapter problem addresses at least one learning objective. Below is a nonexhaustive sample of end-of-chapter problems for each learning objective.

LO1 Explain four basic properties of a consumer's preference ordering and their ramifications for a consumer's indifference curves.

Try these problems: 8, 11

LO2 Illustrate how changes in prices and income impact an individual's opportunities.

Try these problems: 1, 9

LO3 Illustrate a consumer's equilibrium choice and how it changes in response to changes in prices and income.

Try these problems: 2, 14

LO4 Separate the impact of a price change into substitution and income effects.

Try this problem: 24

LO5 Show how to derive an individual's demand curve from indifference curve analysis and market demand from a group of individuals' demands.

Try this problem: 25

LO6 Illustrate how "buy one, get one free" deals and gift certificates impact a consumer's purchase decisions.

Try these problems: 4, 13

LO7 Apply the income–leisure choice framework to illustrate the opportunities, incentives, and choices of workers and managers.

Try these problems: 10, 16

CONCEPTUAL AND COMPUTATIONAL QUESTIONS

1. A consumer has $300 to spend on goods X and Y. The market prices of these two goods are $P_x = \$15$ and $P_y = \$5$.
    a. What is the market rate of substitution between goods X and Y?
    b. Illustrate the consumer's opportunity set in a carefully labeled diagram.
    c. Show how the consumer's opportunity set changes if income increases by $300. How does the $300 increase in income alter the market rate of substitution between goods X and Y?

2. A consumer is in equilibrium at point A in the accompanying figure. The price of good X is $5.
    a. What is the price of good Y?
    b. What is the consumer's income?
    c. At point A, how many units of good X does the consumer purchase?
    d. Suppose the budget line changes so that the consumer achieves a new equilibrium at point B. What change in the economic environment led to this new equilibrium? Is the consumer better off or worse off as a result of the price change?

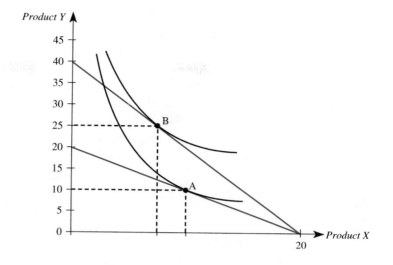

3. A consumer must divide $600 between the consumption of product X and product Y. The relevant market prices are $P_x = \$10$ and $P_y = \$40$.
   a. Write the equation for the consumer's budget line.
   b. Illustrate the consumer's opportunity set in a carefully labeled diagram.
   c. Show how the consumer's opportunity set changes when the price of good X increases to $20. How does this change alter the market rate of substitution between goods X and Y?

4. In the answer to Demonstration Problem 4–2 in the text, we showed a situation in which a gift certificate leads a consumer to purchase a greater quantity of an inferior good than he or she would consume if given a cash gift of equal value. Is this always the case? Explain.

5. Provide an intuitive explanation for why a "buy one, get one free" deal is not the same as a "half-price" sale.

6. In the following figure, a consumer is initially in equilibrium at point C. The consumer's income is $400, and the budget line through point C is given by $\$400 = \$100X + \$200Y$. When the consumer is given a $100 gift certificate that is good only at store X, she moves to a new equilibrium at point D.
   a. Determine the prices of goods X and Y.
   b. How many units of product Y could be purchased at point A?
   c. How many units of product X could be purchased at point E?
   d. How many units of product X could be purchased at point B?
   e. How many units of product X could be purchased at point F?
   f. Based on this consumer's preferences, rank bundles A, B, C, and D in order from most preferred to least preferred.
   g. Is product X a normal or an inferior good?

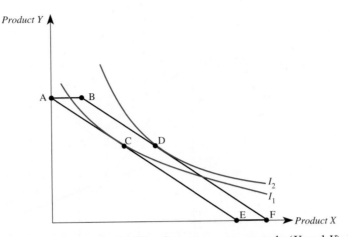

7. A consumer must spend all of her income on two goods (*X* and *Y*). In each of the following scenarios, indicate whether the equilibrium consumption of goods *X* and *Y* will increase or decrease. Assume good *X* is an normal good and good *Y* is a inferior good.
   a. Income doubles.
   b. Income quadruples and all prices double.
   c. Income and all prices quadruple.
   d. Income is halved and all prices double.

8. Determine which, if any, of Properties 4–1 through 4–4 are violated by the indifference curves shown in the following diagram.

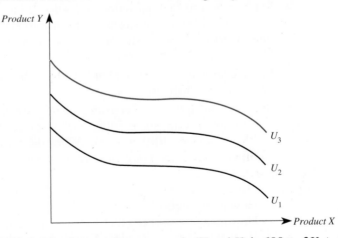

9. A consumer's budget set for two goods (*X* and *Y*) is $600 \geq 3X + 6Y$.
   a. Illustrate the budget set in a diagram.
   b. Does the budget set change if the prices of both goods double and the consumer's income also doubles? Explain.
   c. Given the equation for the budget set, can you determine the prices of the two goods? The consumer's income? Explain.

10. A worker views leisure and income as "goods" and has an opportunity to work at an hourly wage of $15 per hour.
    a. Illustrate the worker's opportunity set in a given 24-hour period.
    b. Suppose the worker is always willing to give up $11 of income for each hour of leisure. Do her preferences exhibit a diminishing marginal rate of substitution? How many hours per day will she choose to work?

PROBLEMS AND APPLICATIONS

11. It is common for supermarkets to carry both generic (store-label) and brand-name (producer-label) varieties of sugar and other products. Many consumers view these products as perfect substitutes, meaning that consumers are always willing to substitute a constant proportion of the store brand for the producer brand. Consider a consumer who is always willing to substitute four pounds of a generic store-brand sugar for two pounds of a brand-name sugar. Do these preferences exhibit a diminishing marginal rate of substitution between store-brand and producer-brand sugar? Assume that this consumer has $24 of income to spend on sugar, and the price of store-brand sugar is $1 per pound and the price of producer-brand sugar is $3 per pound. How much of each type of sugar will be purchased? How would your answer change if the price of store-brand sugar was $2 per pound and the price of producer-brand sugar was $3 per pound?

12. The U.S. government spends over $33 billion on its Food Stamp program to provide millions of Americans with the means to purchase food. These stamps are redeemable for food at over 160,000 store locations throughout the nation, and they cannot be sold for cash or used to purchase nonfood items. The average food stamp benefit is about $284 per month. Suppose that, in the absence of food stamps, the average consumer must divide $600 in monthly income between food and "all other goods" such that the following budget constraint holds: $600 = $12A + $4F, where A is the quantity of "all other goods" and F is the quantity of food purchased. Using the vertical axis for "all other goods," draw the consumer's budget line in the absence of the Food Stamp program. What is the market rate of substitution between food and "all other goods"? On the same graph, show how the Food Stamp program alters the average consumer's budget line. Would this consumer benefit from illegally exchanging food stamps for cash? Explain.

13. A recent newspaper circular advertised the following special on tires: "Buy three, get the fourth tire for free—limit one free tire per customer." If a consumer has $360 to spend on tires and other goods and each tire usually sells for $40, how does this deal impact the consumer's opportunity set?

14. Upscale hotels in the United States recently cut their prices by 25 percent in an effort to bolster dwindling occupancy rates among business travelers. A survey performed by a major research organization indicated that businesses are wary of current economic conditions and are now resorting to electronic

media, such as the Internet and the telephone, to transact business. Assume a company's budget permits it to spend $6,000 per month on either business travel or electronic media to transact business. Graphically illustrate how a 25 percent decline in the price of business travel would impact this company's budget set if the price of business travel was initially $1,200 per trip and the price of electronic media was $600 per hour. Suppose that, after the price of business travel drops, the company issues a report indicating that its marginal rate of substitution between electronic media and business travel is -1. Is the company allocating resources efficiently? Explain.

15. Consider an employee who does not receive employer-based health insurance and must divide her $1,000 per week in after-tax income between health insurance and "other goods." Draw this worker's opportunity set if the price of health insurance is $200 per week and the price of "other goods" is $100 per week. On the same graph, illustrate how the opportunity set would change if the employer agreed to give this employee $200 worth of health insurance per week (under current tax laws, this form of compensation is nontaxable). Would this employee be better or worse off if, instead of the health insurance, the employer gave her a $200 per week raise that was taxable at a rate of 25 percent? Explain.

16. An internal study at Mimeo Corporation—a manufacturer of low-end photocopiers—revealed that each of its workers assembles three photocopiers per hour and is paid $3 for each assembled copier. Although the company does not have the resources needed to supervise the workers, a full-time inspector verifies the quality of each unit produced before a worker is paid for his or her output. You have been asked by your superior to evaluate a new proposal designed to cut costs. Under the plan, workers would be paid a fixed wage of $8 per hour. Would you favor the plan? Explain.

17. The Einstein Bagel Corp. offers a frequent buyer program whereby a consumer receives a stamp each time she purchases one dozen bagels for $6. After a consumer accrues 10 stamps, she receives one dozen bagels free. This offer is an unlimited offer, valid throughout the year. The manager knows her products are normal goods. Given this information, construct the budget set for a consumer who has $200 to spend on bagels and other goods throughout the year. Does Einstein's frequent buyer program have the same effect on the consumption of its bagels that would occur if it simply lowered the price of one dozen bagels by 3 percent? Explain.

18. The average 15-year-old purchases 100 song downloads and buys 20 cheese pizzas in a typical year. If cheese pizzas are inferior goods, would the average 15-year-old be indifferent between receiving a $50 gift certificate at a local music store and $50 in cash? Explain.

19. A common marketing tactic among many liquor stores is to offer their clientele quantity (or volume) discounts. For instance, the second-leading brand of wine exported from Chile sells in the United States for $15 per bottle if the consumer purchases up to eight bottles. The price of each additional bottle is only $8. If a consumer has $200 to divide between purchasing this brand of

wine and other goods, graphically illustrate how this marketing tactic affects the consumer's budget set if the price of other goods is $1. Will a consumer ever purchase exactly eight bottles of wine? Explain.

20. Suppose that a CEO's goal is to increase profitability and output from her company by bolstering its sales force and that it is known that profits as a function of output are $\pi = 40q - 2q^2$ (in millions of U.S. dollars). Graph the company's profit function. Compare and contrast output and profits using the following compensation schemes based on the assumption that sales managers view output and profits as "goods": (a) the company compensates sales managers solely based on output: (b) the company compensates sales managers solely based on profits: (c) the company compensates sales managers based on a combination of output and profits.

21. Suppose that the owner of Boyer Construction is feeling the pinch of increased premiums associated with workers' compensation and has decided to cut the wages of its two employees (Albert and Sid) from $25 per hour to $22 per hour. Assume that Albert and Sid view income and leisure as "goods," that both experience a diminishing rate of marginal substitution between income and leisure, and that the workers have the same before- and after-tax budget constraints at each wage. Draw each worker's opportunity set for each hourly wage. At the wage of $25 per hour, both Albert and Sid are observed to consume 12 hours of leisure (and equivalently supply 12 hours of labor). After wages were cut to $22, Albert consumes 10 hours of leisure and Sid consumes 14 hours of leisure. Determine the number of hours of labor each worker supplies at a wage of $22 per hour. How can you explain the seemingly contradictory result that the workers supply a different number of labor hours?

22. A recent study by Web Mystery Shoppers International indicates that holiday gift cards are becoming increasingly popular at online retailers. Two years ago, online shoppers had to really hunt at most e-retailers' sites to purchase a gift certificate, but today it is easier to purchase gift cards online than at traditional retail outlets. Do you think online gift cards are merely a fad? Explain carefully.

23. Recently, an Internet service provider (ISP) in the UK implemented a "no-strings US-style flat-rate plan" whereby its commercial subscribers can send and receive unlimited volume (measured in gigabytes) up to a cap of 10,000 gigabytes (per month) via their broadband Internet service for a flat monthly fee of £399.99. Under the old "metered plan," Alistair Willoughby Cook sent and received a grand total of 3,500 gigabytes over their broadband connection and paid £399.99 in usage fees in a typical 30-day month. If all customers are exactly like Alistair, what is the impact of the flat-rate plan on consumer welfare and the company's profits? Explain.

24. A large Coca-Cola vendor recently hired some economic analysts to assess the effect of a price increase in its 16-ounce bottles from $1.00 to $2.00. The analysts determined that, on average, the vendor's customers spend about $15.00 on soda (Coke and all other brands) each week, and the average price for

other 16-ounce soda bottles is $1.00. The analysts also utilized some focus groups to determine the preferences of the vendor's customers. They used this analysis to build the following graph:

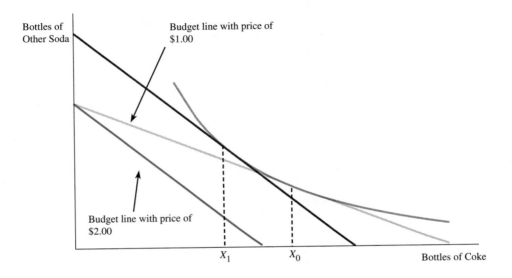

Suppose $X_0 = 9$ and $X_1 = 7$. Should the vendor expect to sell 7, more than 7, or less than 7 bottles of Coke after raising the price to $2.00 if Coke is a normal good?

25. When trying to assess differences in her customers, Claire—the owner of Claire's Rose Boutique—noticed a difference between the typical demand of her female versus her male customers. In particular, she found her female customers to be more price sensitive in general. After conducting some sales analysis, she determined that her female customers have the following demand curve for roses: $Q^F = 24 - 2P$. Here, Q^F is the quantity of roses demanded by a female customer, and P is the price charged per rose. She determined that her male customers have the following demand curve for roses: $Q^M = 27 - P$. Here, Q^M is the quantity of roses demanded by a male customer. If two unaffiliated customers walk into her boutique, one male and one female, determine the demand curve for these two customers combined (i.e., what is their aggregate demand?).

CONNECT EXERCISES

If your instructor has adopted Connect for the course and you are an active subscriber, you can practice with the questions presented above, along with many alternative versions of these questions. Your instructor may also assign a subset of these problems and/or their alternative versions as a homework assignment through Connect, allowing for immediate feedback of grades and correct answers.

CASE-BASED EXERCISES

Your instructor may assign additional problem-solving exercises (called *memos*) that require you to apply some of the tools you learned in this chapter to make a recommendation based on an actual business scenario. Some of these memos accompany the Time Warner case (pages 561–597 of your textbook). Additional memos, as well as data that may be useful for your analysis, are available online at www.mhhe.com/baye8e.

SELECTED READINGS

Baumol, William J., *Business Behavior, Value and Growth.* New York: Macmillan, 1959.

Battalio, Raymond C.; Kagel, John H.; and Kogut, Carl A., "Experimental Confirmation of the Existence of a Giffen Good." *American Economic Review* 81(4), September 1991, pp. 961–70.

Davis, J., "Transitivity of Preferences." *Behavioral Science,* Fall 1958, pp. 26–33.

Evans, William N., and Viscusi, W. Kip, "Income Effects and the Value of Health." *Journal of Human Resources* 28(3), Summer 1993, pp. 497–518.

Gilad, Benjamin; Kaish, Stanley; and Loeb, Peter D., "Cognitive Dissonance and Utility Maximization: A General Framework." *Journal of Economic Behavior and Organization* 8(1), March 1987, pp. 61–73.

Lancaster, Kelvin, *Consumer Demand: A New Approach.* New York: Columbia University Press, 1971.

MacKrimmon, Kenneth, and Toda, Maseo, "The Experimental Determination of Indifference Curves." *Review of Economic Studies* 37, October 1969, pp. 433–51.

Smart, Denise T., and Martin, Charles L., "Manufacturer Responsiveness to Consumer Correspondence: An Empirical Investigation of Consumer Perceptions." *Journal of Consumer Affairs* 26(1), Summer 1992, pp. 104–28.

Appendix
A Calculus Approach to Individual Behavior

The Utility Function

Suppose the preferences of a consumer are represented by a utility function $U(X, Y)$. Let $A = (X^A, Y^A)$ be the bundle with X^A units of good X and Y^A units of good Y, and let $B = (X^B, Y^B)$ be a different bundle of the two goods. If bundle A is preferred to bundle B, then $U(A) > U(B)$; the consumer receives a higher utility level from bundle A than from bundle B. Similarly, if $U(B) > U(A)$, the consumer views bundle B as "better" than bundle A. Finally, if $U(A) = U(B)$, the consumer views the two bundles to be equally satisfying; she or he is indifferent between bundles A and B.

Utility Maximization

Given prices of P_x and P_y and a level of income M, the consumer attempts to maximize utility subject to the budget constraint. Formally, this problem can be solved by forming the Lagrangian:

$$\mathcal{L} \equiv U(X, Y) + \lambda(M - P_x X - P_y Y)$$

where λ is the Lagrange multiplier. The first-order conditions for this problem are

$$\frac{\partial \mathcal{L}}{\partial X} = \frac{\partial U}{\partial X} - \lambda P_x = 0 \tag{A–1}$$

$$\frac{\partial \mathcal{L}}{\partial Y} = \frac{\partial U}{\partial Y} - \lambda P_y = 0 \tag{A–2}$$

$$\frac{\partial \mathcal{L}}{\partial \lambda} = M - P_x X - P_y Y = 0$$

Equations (A–1) and (A–2) imply that

$$\frac{\partial U / \partial X}{\partial U / \partial Y} = \frac{P_x}{P_y} \tag{A–3}$$

or in economic terms, the ratio of the marginal utilities equals the ratio of prices.

The Marginal Rate of Substitution

Along an indifference curve, utility is constant:

$$U(X, Y) = \text{constant}$$

Taking the total derivative of this relation yields

$$\frac{\partial U}{\partial X} dX + \frac{\partial U}{\partial Y} dY = 0$$

Solving for dY/dX along an indifference curve yields

$$\left. \frac{dY}{dX} \right|_{\text{utility constant}} = -\frac{\partial U / \partial X}{\partial U / \partial Y}$$

Thus, the slope of an indifference curve is

$$-\frac{\partial U / \partial X}{\partial U / \partial Y}$$

The absolute value of the slope of an indifference curve is the marginal rate of substitution (*MRS*). Thus,

$$MRS = \frac{\partial U / \partial X}{\partial U / \partial Y} \tag{A–4}$$

The *MRS* = P_x/P_y Rule

Substitution of Equation (A–4) into (A–3) reveals that to maximize utility, a consumer equates

$$MRS = \frac{P_x}{P_y}$$

CHAPTER FIVE

The Production Process and Costs

Boeing Loses the Battle but Wins the War

After nearly eight weeks, Boeing and its International Association of Machinists and Aerospace Workers Union (IAM) reached an agreement that ended a strike involving 27,000 workers. The strike followed several days of "last minute," around-the-clock talks that began when management and union negotiators failed to reach an agreement over compensation and job protection issues.

As a result of the agreement, IAM workers won benefits in areas that include healthcare, pensions, wages, and job security for 2,900 workers in inventory management and delivery categories. Boeing also agreed to retrain workers who are laid off or displaced. Despite these concessions, a spokesman for Boeing was quoted as saying that the agreement "gives us the flexibility we need to run the company." The four-year agreement allows Boeing to retain critical subcontracting provisions it won in past struggles with the union.

Commenting on all this, one analysis concluded that "the union probably won the battle and Boeing probably wins the war." Can you explain what this analyst means?

Sources: C. Isidore, "Union Strikes Boeing," *CNNMoney.com*, September 6, 2008; S. Freeman, "Boeing Contract Offers Pay Raise, Job Protections," *The Washington Post*, October 29, 2008.

Learning Objectives

After completing this chapter, you will be able to:

LO1 Explain alternative ways of measuring the productivity of inputs and the role of the manager in the production process.

LO2 Calculate input demand and the cost-minimizing combination of inputs and use isoquant analysis to illustrate optimal input substitution.

LO3 Calculate a cost function from a production function and explain how economic costs differ from accounting costs.

LO4 Explain the difference between and the economic relevance of fixed costs, sunk costs, variable costs, and marginal costs.

LO5 Calculate average and marginal costs from algebraic or tabular cost data and illustrate the relationship between average and marginal costs.

LO6 Distinguish between short-run and long-run production decisions and illustrate their impact on costs and economies of scale.

LO7 Conclude whether a multiple-output production process exhibits economies of scope or cost complementarities and explain their significance for managerial decisions.

163

INTRODUCTION

Companies as well as nonprofit organizations are in the business of producing goods or providing services, and their successful operation requires managers to optimally choose the quantity and types of inputs to use in the production process. The successful operation of a consulting business, for instance, requires getting the right quantity and mix of employees and optimally substituting among these and other inputs as wages and other input prices change.

This chapter provides the economic foundations needed to succeed in managerial positions such as production and pricing management. The concepts of production and costs presented below are also important in their own right, as they serve as the basic building blocks for business areas that include human resources, operations, managerial accounting, and strategic management.

THE PRODUCTION FUNCTION

We will begin by describing the technology available for producing output. Technology summarizes the feasible means of converting raw inputs, such as steel, labor, and machinery, into an output such as an automobile. The technology effectively summarizes engineering know-how. Managerial decisions, such as those concerning expenditures on research and development, can affect the available technology. In this chapter, we will see how a manager can exploit an existing technology to its greatest potential. In subsequent chapters, we will analyze the decision to improve a technology.

To begin our analysis, let us consider a production process that utilizes two inputs, *capital* and *labor,* to produce output. We will let K denote the quantity of capital, L the quantity of labor, and Q the level of output produced in the production process. Although we call the inputs capital and labor, the general ideas presented here are valid for any two inputs. However, most production processes involve machines of some sort (referred to by economists as *capital*) and people (*labor*), and this terminology will serve to solidify the basic ideas.

production function
A function that defines the maximum amount of output that can be produced with a given set of inputs.

The technology available for converting capital and labor into output is summarized in the production function. The *production function* is an engineering relation that defines the maximum amount of output that can be produced with a given set of inputs. Mathematically, the production function is denoted as

$$Q = F(K, L)$$

that is, the maximum amount of output that can be produced with K units of capital and L units of labor.

Short-Run versus Long-Run Decisions

As a manager, your job is to use the available production function efficiently; this means that you must determine how much of each input to use to produce output. In the short run, some factors of production are *fixed,* and this limits your choices in

**fixed and
variable factors
of production**
Fixed factors are
the inputs the
manager cannot
adjust in the short
run. Variable
factors are the
inputs a manager
can adjust to alter
production.

making input decisions. For example, it takes several years for automakers to develop and build new assembly lines for producing hybrids. The level of capital is generally fixed in the short run. However, in the short run automakers can adjust their use of inputs such as labor and steel; such inputs are called *variable* factors of production.

The *short run* is defined as the time frame in which there are fixed factors of production. To illustrate, suppose capital and labor are the only two inputs in production and that the level of capital is fixed in the short run. In this case the only short-run input decision to be made by a manager is how much labor to utilize. The short-run production function is essentially only a function of labor, since capital is fixed rather than variable. If K^* is the fixed level of capital, the short-run production function may be written as

$$Q = f(L) = F(K^*, L)$$

Columns 1, 2, and 4 in Table 5–1 give values of the components of a short-run production function where capital is fixed at $K^* = 2$. For this production function, 5 units of labor are needed to produce 1,100 units of output. Given the available technology and the fixed level of capital, if the manager wishes to produce 1,952 units of output, 8 units of labor must be utilized. In the short run, more labor is needed to produce more output, because increasing capital is not possible.

The *long run* is defined as the horizon over which the manager can adjust all factors of production. If it takes a company three years to acquire additional capital machines, the long run for its management is three years, and the short run is less than three years.

TABLE 5–1 The Production Function

(1)	(2)	(3)	(4)	(5)	(6)
K^*	L	ΔL	Q	$\dfrac{\Delta Q}{\Delta L} = MP_L$	$\dfrac{Q}{L} = AP_L$
Fixed Input (Capital) [Given]	Variable Input (Labor) [Given]	Change in Labor [$\Delta(2)$]	Output [Given]	Marginal Product of Labor [$\Delta(4)/\Delta(2)$]	Average Product of Labor [(4)/(2)]
2	0	—	0	—	—
2	1	1	76	76	76
2	2	1	248	172	124
2	3	1	492	244	164
2	4	1	784	292	196
2	5	1	1,100	316	220
2	6	1	1,416	316	236
2	7	1	1,708	292	244
2	8	1	1,952	244	244
2	9	1	2,124	172	236
2	10	1	2,200	76	220
2	11	1	2,156	−44	196

Measures of Productivity

An important component of managerial decision making is the determination of the productivity of inputs used in the production process. As we will see, these measures are useful for evaluating the effectiveness of a production process and for making input decisions that maximize profits. The three most important measures of productivity are total product, average product, and marginal product.

Total Product

total product
The maximum level of output that can be produced with a given amount of inputs.

Total product (TP) is simply the maximum level of output that can be produced with a given amount of inputs. For example, the total product of the production process described in Table 5–1 when 5 units of labor are employed is 1,100. Since the production function defines the maximum amount of output that can be produced with a given level of inputs, this is the amount that would be produced if the 5 units of labor put forth maximal effort. Of course, if workers did not put forth maximal effort, output would be lower. Five workers who drink coffee all day cannot produce any output, at least given this production function.

Average Product

average product
A measure of the output produced per unit of input.

In many instances, managerial decision makers are interested in the average productivity of an input. For example, a manager may wish to know, on average, how much each worker contributes to the total output of the firm. This information is summarized in the economic concept of average product. The *average product (AP)* of an input is defined as total product divided by the quantity used of the input. In particular, the average product of labor (AP_L) is

$$AP_L = \frac{Q}{L}$$

and the average product of capital (AP_K) is

$$AP_K = \frac{Q}{K}$$

Thus, average product is a measure of the output produced per unit of input. In Table 5–1, for example, five workers can produce 1,100 units of output; this amounts to 220 units of output per worker.

Marginal Product

marginal product
The change in total output attributable to the last unit of an input.

The *marginal product (MP)* of an input is the change in total output attributable to the last unit of an input. The marginal product of capital (MP_K) therefore is the change in total output divided by the change in capital:

$$MP_K = \frac{\Delta Q}{\Delta K}$$

The marginal product of labor (MP_L) is the change in total output divided by the change in labor:

$$MP_L = \frac{\Delta Q}{\Delta L}$$

For example, in Table 5–1 the second unit of labor increases output by 172 units, so the marginal product of the second unit of labor is 172.

Table 5–1 illustrates an important characteristic of the marginal product of an input. Notice that as the units of labor are increased from 0 to 5 in column 2, the marginal product of labor increases in column 5. This helps explain why assembly lines are used in so many production processes: By using several workers, each performing potentially different tasks, a manager can avoid inefficiencies associated with stopping one task and starting another. But note in Table 5–1 that after 5 units of labor, the marginal product of each additional unit of labor declines and eventually becomes negative. A negative marginal product means that the last unit of the input actually *reduced* the total product. This is consistent with common sense. If a manager continued to expand the number of workers on an assembly line, he or she would eventually reach a point where workers were packed like sardines along the line, getting in one another's way and resulting in less output than before.

Figure 5–1 shows graphically the relationship among total product, marginal product, and average product. The first thing to notice about the curves is that

FIGURE 5–1   Increasing, Decreasing, and Negative Marginal Returns

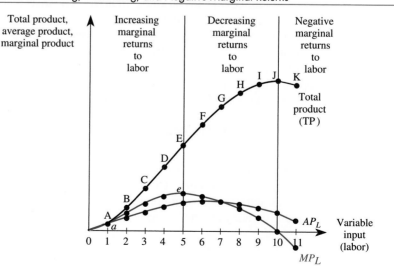

increasing marginal returns
Range of input usage over which marginal product increases.

decreasing (diminishing) marginal returns
Range of input usage over which marginal product declines.

negative marginal returns
Range of input usage over which marginal product is negative.

total product increases and its slope gets steeper as we move from point A to point E along the total product curve. As the use of labor increases between points A and E, the slope of the total product curve increases (becomes steeper); thus, marginal product increases as we move from point *a* to point *e*. The range over which marginal product increases is known as the range of *increasing marginal returns.*

In Figure 5–1, we see that marginal product reaches its maximum at point *e,* where 5 units of labor are employed. As the usage of labor increases from the 5th through the 10th unit, total output increases, but at a decreasing rate. This is why marginal product declines between 5 and 10 units of labor but is still positive. The range over which marginal product is positive but declining is known as the range of *decreasing* or *diminishing marginal returns* to the variable input.

In Figure 5–1, marginal product becomes negative when more than 10 units of labor are employed. After a point, using additional units of input actually reduces total product, which is what it means for marginal product to be negative. The range over which marginal product is negative is known as the range of *negative marginal returns.*

Principle	**Phases of Marginal Returns**
	As the usage of an input increases, marginal product initially increases (increasing marginal returns), then begins to decline (decreasing marginal returns), and eventually becomes negative (negative marginal returns).

In studying for an exam, you have very likely experienced various phases of marginal returns. The first few hours spent studying increase your grade much more than the last few hours. For example, suppose you will make a 0 if you do not study but will make a 75 if you study 10 hours. The marginal product of the first 10 hours thus is 75 points. If it takes 20 hours of studying to score 100 on the exam, the marginal product of the second 10 hours is only 25 points. Thus, the marginal improvement in your grade diminishes as you spend additional hours studying. If you have ever pulled an "all-nighter" and ended up sleeping through an exam or performing poorly due to a lack of sleep, you studied in the range of negative marginal returns. Clearly, neither students nor firms should ever employ resources in this range.

The Role of the Manager in the Production Process

The manager's role in guiding the production process described earlier is twofold: (1) to ensure that the firm operates on the production function and (2) to ensure that the firm uses the correct level of inputs. These two aspects ensure that the firm operates at the right point on the production function. These two aspects of production efficiency are discussed next.

Produce on the Production Function
The first managerial role is relatively simple to explain, but it is one of the most difficult for a manager to perform. The production function describes the maximum

possible output that can be produced with given inputs. For the case of labor, this means that workers must be putting forth maximal effort. To ensure that workers are in fact working at full potential, the manager must institute an incentive structure that induces them to put forth the desired level of effort. For example, the manager of a restaurant must institute an incentive scheme that ensures that food servers do a good job waiting on tables. Most restaurants pay workers low wages but allow them to collect tips, which effectively provides the workers with an incentive to perform well on the job. More generally, many firms institute profit-sharing plans to provide workers with an incentive to produce on the production function. A more detailed discussion of this role of the manager is presented in Chapter 6.

Use the Right Level of Inputs

The second role of the manager is to ensure that the firm operates at the right point on the production function. For a restaurant manager, this means hiring the "correct" number of servers. To see how this may be accomplished, let us assume that the output produced by a firm can be sold in a market at a price of $3. Furthermore, assume each unit of labor costs $400. How many units of labor should the manager hire to maximize profits? To answer this question, we must first determine the benefit of hiring an additional worker. Each worker increases the firm's output by his or her marginal product, and this increase in output can be sold in the market at a price of $3. Thus, the benefit to the firm from each unit of labor is $3 \times MP_L$. This number is called the *value marginal product* of labor. The value marginal product of an input thus is the value of the output produced by the last unit of that input. For example, if each unit of output can be sold at a price of P, the value marginal product of labor is

value marginal product
The value of the output produced by the last unit of an input.

$$VMP_L = P \times MP_L$$

and the value marginal product of capital is

$$VMP_K = P \times MP_K$$

In our example, the cost to the firm of an additional unit of labor is $400. As Table 5–2 shows, the first unit of labor generates $VMP_L = \$228$ and the VMP_L of the second unit is $516. If the manager were to look only at the first unit of labor and its corresponding VMP_L, no labor would be hired. However, careful inspection of the table shows that the second worker will add $116 in value above her or his cost. If the first worker is not hired, the second will not be hired.

In fact, each worker between the second and the ninth produces additional output whose value exceeds the cost of hiring the worker. It is profitable to hire units of labor so long as the VMP_L is greater than $400. Notice that the VMP_L of the 10th unit of labor is $228, which is less than the cost of the 10th unit of labor. It would not pay for the firm to hire this unit of labor, because the cost of hiring it would exceed the benefits. The same is true for additional units of labor. Thus, given the data in Table 5–2, the manager should hire nine workers to maximize profits.

TABLE 5–2   The Value Marginal Product of Labor

(1)	(2)	(3)	(4)	(5)
L	P	$\frac{\Delta Q}{\Delta L} = MP_L$	$VMP_L = P \times MP_L$	W
Variable Input (Labor) [Given]	Price of Output [Given]	Marginal Product of Labor [Column 5 of Table 5–1]	Value Marginal Product of Labor [(2) × (3)]	Unit Cost of Labor [Given]
0	$3	—	—	$400
1	3	76	$228	400
2	3	172	516	400
3	3	244	732	400
4	3	292	876	400
5	3	316	948	400
6	3	316	948	400
7	3	292	876	400
8	3	244	732	400
9	3	172	516	400
10	3	76	228	400
11	3	−44	−132	400

Principle	**Profit-Maximizing Input Usage**

Profit-Maximizing Input Usage

To maximize profits, a manager should use inputs at levels at which the marginal benefit equals the marginal cost. More specifically, when the cost of each additional unit of labor is w, the manager should continue to employ labor up to the point where $VMP_L = w$ in the range of diminishing marginal product.

The *profit-maximizing input usage* rule defines the demand for an input by a profit-maximizing firm. For example, in Figure 5–2 the value marginal product of labor is graphed as a function of the quantity of labor utilized. When the wage rate

FIGURE 5–2   The Demand for Labor

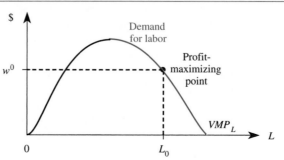

Where Does Technology Come From?

In this chapter, we simply assume that the manager knows the underlying technology available for producing goods. How do managers acquire information about technology? A study by Richard Levin suggests there are seven principal methods.

INDEPENDENT R&D

The most important means of acquiring product and process innovations is independent research and development (R&D). This essentially involves engineers employed by the firm who devise new production processes or products.

LICENSING TECHNOLOGY

The firm that was originally responsible for developing the technology and thus owns the rights to the technology often sells the production function to another firm for a licensing fee. The fee may be fixed, in which case the cost of acquiring the technology is a fixed cost of production. The fee may involve payments based on how much output is produced. In this instance, the cost of the technology is a variable cost of production.

PUBLICATIONS OR TECHNICAL MEETINGS

Trade publications and meetings provide a forum for the dissemination of information about production processes.

REVERSE ENGINEERING

As the term suggests, this involves working backward: taking a product produced by a competitor and devising a method of producing a similar product. The typical result is a product that differs slightly from the existing product and involves a slightly different production function from that used by the original developer.

HIRING EMPLOYEES OF INNOVATING FIRMS

Former employees of other firms often have information about the production process.

PATENT DISCLOSURES

A *patent* gives the holder the exclusive rights to an invention for a specified period of time—17 to 20 years in most countries. However, to obtain a patent an inventor must file detailed information about the invention, which becomes public information. Virtually anyone can look at the information filed, including competitors. In many instances, this information can enable a competitor to "clone" the product in a way that does not infringe on the patent. Interestingly, while a patent is pending, this information is not publicly available. For this reason, stretching out the time in which a patent is pending often provides more protection for an inventor than actually acquiring the patent.

CONVERSATIONS WITH EMPLOYEES OF INNOVATING FIRMS

Despite the obvious benefits of keeping trade secrets "secret," employees inadvertently relay information about the production process to competitors. This is especially common in industries where firms are concentrated in the same geographic region and employees from different firms intermingle in nonbusiness settings.

Source: Richard C. Levin, "Appropriability, R&D Spending, and Technological Performance," *American Economic Review* 78 (May 1988), pp. 424–28.

is w^0, the profit-maximizing quantity of labor is that quantity such that $VMP_L = w^0$ in the range of diminishing marginal returns. In the figure, we see that the profit-maximizing quantity of labor is L_0 units.

The downward-sloping portion of the VMP_L curve defines demand for labor by a profit-maximizing firm; it shows the relationship between the wage rate and the amount of labor a firm will want to hire at that rate. Thus, an important property of the demand for an input is that it slopes downward because of the law of diminishing marginal returns. Since the marginal product of an input declines as more of that input is used, the value of the marginal product also declines as more of the input is used. Since the demand for an input is the value marginal product of the input in the range of diminishing marginal returns, the demand for an input slopes downward. In effect, each additional unit of an input adds less profits than the previous unit. Profit-maximizing firms thus are willing to pay less for each additional unit of an input.

Algebraic Forms of Production Functions

Up until now, we have relied on tables and graphs to illustrate the concepts underlying production. The underlying notion of a production function can be expressed mathematically, and in fact it is possible to use statistical techniques like those discussed in Chapter 3 to estimate a particular functional form for a production function. In this section, we highlight some more commonly encountered algebraic forms of production functions. We begin with the most simple production function: a linear function of the inputs.

linear production function
A production function that assumes a perfect linear relationship between all inputs and total output.

The *linear production function* is

$$Q = F(K, L) = aK + bL$$

where a and b are constants. With a linear production function, inputs are perfect substitutes. There is a perfect linear relationship between all the inputs and total output. For instance, suppose it takes workers at a plant four hours to produce what a machine can make in one hour. In this case the production function is linear with $a = 4$ and $b = 1$:

$$Q = F(K, L) = 4K + L$$

This is the mathematical way of stating that capital is always 4 times as productive as labor. Furthermore, since $F(5,2) = 4(5) + 1(2) = 22$, we know that 5 units of capital and 2 units of labor will produce 22 units of output.

Leontief production function
A production function that assumes that inputs are used in fixed proportions.

The *Leontief production function* is given by

$$Q = F(K, L) = \min \{aK, bL\}$$

where a and b are constants. The Leontief production function is also called the *fixed-proportions production function,* because it implies that inputs are used in fixed proportions. To see this, suppose the production function for a word processing firm is Leontief, with $a = b = 1$; think of K as the number of keyboards and L as the number of keyboarders. The production function then implies that one keyboarder and one keyboard can produce one paper per hour, two keyboarders and two keyboards can produce two papers per hour, and so forth. But how many papers can one keyboarder and five keyboards produce per hour? The answer is only one paper. Additional keyboards are useful only to the extent that additional keyboarders are available to use them. In other words, keyboards and keyboarders must be used in the fixed proportion of one keyboarder for every keyboard.

Demonstration Problem 5–1

The engineers at Morris Industries obtained the following estimate of the firm's production function:

$$Q = F(K, L) = \min \{3K, 4L\}$$

How much output is produced when 2 units of labor and 5 units of capital are employed?

Answer:

We simply calculate $F(5, 2)$. But $F(5, 2) = \min\{3(5), 4(2)\} = \min\{15, 8\}$. Since the minimum of the numbers "15" and "8" is 8, we know that 5 units of capital and 2 units of labor produce 8 units of output.

Cobb-Douglas production function
A production function that assumes some degree of substitutability among inputs.

A production function that lies between the extremes of the linear production function and the Leontief production function is the Cobb-Douglas production function. The *Cobb-Douglas production function* is given by

$$Q = F(K, L) = K^a L^b$$

where a and b are constants.

Unlike in the case of the linear production function, the relationship between output and inputs is not linear. Unlike in the Leontief production function, inputs need not be used in fixed proportions. The Cobb-Douglas production function assumes some degree of substitutability between the inputs, albeit not perfect substitutability.

Algebraic Measures of Productivity

Given an algebraic form of a production function, we may calculate various measures of productivity. For example, we learned that the average product of an input is the output produced divided by the number of units used of the input. This concept can easily be extended to production processes that use more than one input.

To be concrete, suppose a consultant provides you with the following estimate of your firm's Cobb-Douglas production function:

$$Q = F(K, L) = K^{1/2} L^{1/2}$$

What is the average product of labor when 4 units of labor and 9 units of capital are employed? Since $F(9,4) = 9^{1/2} 4^{1/2} = (3)(2) = 6$, we know that 9 units of capital and 4 units of labor produce 6 units of output. Thus, the average product of 4 units of labor is $AP_L = 6/4 = 1.5$ units.

Notice that when output is produced with both capital and labor, the average product of labor will depend not only on how many units of labor are used but also on how much capital is used. Since total output (Q) is affected by the levels of both inputs, the corresponding measure of the average product depends on both capital and labor. Likewise, the average product of capital depends not only on the level of capital but also on the level of labor used to produce Q.

Recall that the marginal product of an input is the change in output that results from a given change in the input. When the production function is linear, the marginal product of an input has a very simple representation, as the following formula reveals.

Formula: Marginal Product for a Linear Production Function.   If the production function is linear and given by

$$Q = F(K, L) = aK + bL$$

then

$$MP_K = a$$

and

$$MP_L = b$$

A Calculus Alternative

The marginal product of an input is the derivative of the production function with respect to the input. Thus, the marginal product of labor is

$$MP_L = \frac{\partial Q}{\partial L}$$

and the marginal product of capital is

$$MP_K = \frac{\partial Q}{\partial K}$$

For the case of the linear production function, $Q = aK + bL$, so

$$MP_K = \frac{\partial Q}{\partial K} = a \quad \text{and} \quad MP_L = \frac{\partial Q}{\partial L} = b$$

Thus, for a linear production function, the marginal product of an input is simply the coefficient of the input in the production function. This implies that the marginal product of an input is independent of the quantity of the input used whenever the production function is linear; linear production functions do not obey the law of diminishing marginal product.

In contrast to the linear case, the marginal product of an input for a Cobb-Douglas production function does depend on the amount of the input used, as the following formula reveals.

Formula: Marginal Product for a Cobb-Douglas Production Function.   If the production function is Cobb-Douglas and given by

$$Q = F(K, L) = K^a L^b$$

then

$$MP_L = bK^aL^{b-1}$$

and

$$MP_K = aK^{a-1}L^b$$

A Calculus Alternative

The marginal product of an input is the derivative of the production function with respect to the input. Taking the derivative of the Cobb-Douglas production function yields

$$MP_K = \frac{\partial Q}{\partial K} = aK^{a-1}L^b$$

and

$$MP_L = \frac{\partial Q}{\partial L} = bK^aL^{b-1}$$

which correspond to the equations above.

Recall that the profit-maximizing use of an input occurs at the point where the value marginal product of an input equals the price of the input. As the next problem illustrates, we can apply the same principle to algebraic functional forms of production functions to attain the profit-maximizing use of an input.

Demonstration Problem 5–2

A firm produces output that can be sold at a price of $10. The production function is given by

$$Q = F(K, L) = K^{1/2}L^{1/2}$$

If capital is fixed at 1 unit in the short run, how much labor should the firm employ to maximize profits if the wage rate is $2?

Answer:

We simply set the value marginal product of labor equal to the wage rate and solve for L. Since the production function is Cobb-Douglas, we know that $MP_L = bK^aL^{b-1}$. Here $a = 1/2$, $b = 1/2$, and $K = 1$. Hence, $MP_L = .5L^{1/2-1}$. Now, since $P = \$10$, we know that $VMP_L = P \times MP_L = 5L^{-1/2} = 5/\sqrt{L}$. Setting this equal to the wage, which is $2, we get $5/\sqrt{L} = 2$. If we square both sides of this equation, we get $25/L = 4$. Thus the profit-maximizing quantity of labor is $L = 25/4 = 6.25$ units.

Isoquants

Our next task is to examine the optimal choice of capital and labor in the long run, when both inputs are free to vary. In the presence of multiple variables of production, various combinations of inputs enable the manager to produce the

FIGURE 5–3   A Family of Isoquants

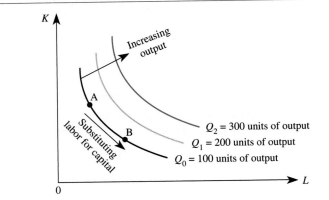

same level of output. For example, an automobile assembly line can produce 1,000 cars per hour by using 10 workers and one robot. It can also produce 1,000 cars by using only two workers and three robots. To minimize the costs of producing 1,000 cars, the manager must determine the efficient combination of inputs to use to produce them. The basic tool for understanding how alternative inputs can be used to produce output is an isoquant. An *isoquant* defines the combinations of inputs (*K* and *L*) that yield the producer the same level of output; that is, any combination of capital and labor along an isoquant produces the same level of output.

isoquant
Defines the combinations of inputs that yield the same level of output.

Figure 5–3 depicts a typical set of isoquants. Because input bundles *A* and *B* both lie on the same isoquant, each will produce the same level of output, namely, Q_0 units. Input mix *A* implies a more capital-intensive plant than does input mix *B*. As more of both inputs are used, a higher isoquant is obtained. Thus as we move in the northeast direction in the figure, each new isoquant is associated with higher and higher levels of output.

Notice that the isoquants in Figure 5–3 are convex. The reason isoquants are typically drawn with a convex shape is that inputs such as capital and labor typically are not perfectly substitutable. In Figure 5–3, for example, if we start at point A and begin substituting labor for capital, it takes increasing amounts of labor to replace each unit of capital that is taken away. The rate at which labor and capital can substitute for each other is called the *marginal rate of technical substitution (MRTS)*. The MRTS of capital and labor is the absolute value of the slope of the isoquant and is simply the ratio of the marginal products:

marginal rate of technical substitution (MRTS)
The rate at which a producer can substitute between two inputs and maintain the same level of output.

$$MRTS_{KL} = \frac{MP_L}{MP_K}$$

Different production functions will imply different marginal rates of technical substitution. For example, the linear production function implies isoquants that are *linear,* as in Figure 5–4(a). This is because the inputs are perfect substitutes for each other and the rate at which the producer can substitute between the inputs is

FIGURE 5–4 Linear and Leontief Isoquants

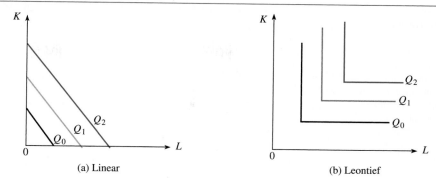

(a) Linear   (b) Leontief

independent of the level of input usage. Specifically, for the linear production function $Q = aK + bL$, the marginal rate of technical substitution is b/a, since $MP_L = b$ and $MP_K = a$. This is independent of the level of inputs utilized.

The Leontief production function, on the other hand, implies isoquants that are *L shaped,* as in Figure 5–4(b). In this case, inputs must be used in fixed proportions; the manager cannot substitute between capital and labor and maintain the same level of output. For the Leontief production function there is no MRTS, because there is no substitution among inputs along an isoquant.

For most production relations, the isoquants lie somewhere between the perfect-substitute and fixed-proportions cases. In these instances, the inputs are substitutable for one another, but not perfectly, and the rate at which a manager can substitute among inputs will change along an isoquant. For instance, by moving from point A to point B in Figure 5–5, the manager substitutes 1 unit of capital for 1 unit of labor and still produces 100 units of output. But in moving from point C to

FIGURE 5–5 The Marginal Rate of Technical Substitution

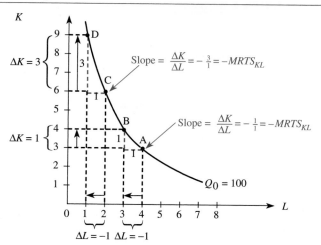

law of diminishing marginal rate of technical substitution
A property of a production function stating that as less of one input is used, increasing amounts of another input must be employed to produce the same level of output.

isocost line
A line that represents the combinations of inputs that will cost the producer the same amount of money.

point D, the manager would have to substitute 3 units of capital for 1 unit of labor to produce 100 units of output. Thus, the production function satisfies the *law of diminishing marginal rate of technical substitution:* As a producer uses less of an input, increasingly more of the other input must be employed to produce the same level of output. It can be shown that the Cobb-Douglas production function implies isoquants that have a diminishing marginal rate of technical substitution. Whenever an isoquant exhibits a diminishing marginal rate of technical substitution, the corresponding isoquants are convex from the origin; that is, they look like the isoquants in Figure 5–5.

Isocosts

Isoquants describe the combinations of inputs that produce a given level of output. Notice that different combinations of capital and labor end up costing the firm the same amount. The combinations of inputs that will cost the firm the same amount comprise an *isocost line.*

The relation for an isocost line is graphed in Figure 5–6. To understand this concept, suppose the firm spends exactly $\$C$ on inputs. Then the cost of labor plus the cost of capital exactly equals $\$C$:

$$wL + rK = C \qquad (5\text{–}1)$$

where w is the wage rate (the price of labor) and r is the rental rate (the price of capital). This equation represents the formula for an isocost line.

We may obtain a more convenient expression for the slope and intercept of an isocost line as follows. We multiply both sides of Equation 5–1 by $1/r$ and get

$$\frac{w}{r}L + K = \frac{C}{r}$$

or

FIGURE 5–6   Isocosts

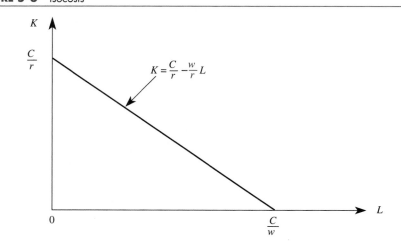

FIGURE 5-7 Changes in Isocosts

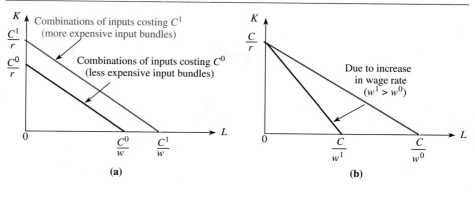

$$K = \frac{C}{r} - \frac{w}{r}L$$

Thus, along an isocost line, K is a linear function of L with a vertical intercept of C/r and a slope of $-w/r$.

Note that if the producer wishes to use more of both inputs, more money must be spent. Thus, isocosts associated with higher costs lie above those with lower costs. When input prices are constant, the isocost lines will be parallel to one another. Figure 5–7(a) illustrates the isocost lines for cost levels C^0 and C^1, where $C^0 < C^1$.

Similarly, changes in input prices affect the position of the isocost line. An increase in the price of labor makes the isocost curve steeper, while an increase in the price of capital makes it flatter. For instance, Figure 5–7(b) reveals that the isocost line rotates clockwise when the wage rate increases from w^0 to w^1.

Principle	**Changes in Isocosts** For given input prices, isocosts farther from the origin are associated with higher costs. Changes in input prices change the slopes of isocost lines.

Cost Minimization

The isocosts and isoquants just defined may be used to determine the input usage that minimizes production costs. If there were no scarcity, the producer would not care about production costs. But because scarcity is an economic reality, producers are interested in *cost minimization*—that is, producing output at the lowest possible cost. After all, to maximize profits, the firm must first produce its output in the least-cost manner. Even not-for-profit organizations can achieve their objectives by providing a given level of service at the lowest possible cost. Let us piece together the tools developed thus far to see how to choose the optimal mix of capital and labor.

cost minimization
Producing output at the lowest possible cost.

Consider an input bundle such as that at point A in Figure 5–8. This combination of L and K lies on the isoquant labeled Q_0 and thus produces Q_0 units of

FIGURE 5–8   Input Mix B Minimizes the Cost of Producing 100 Units of Output

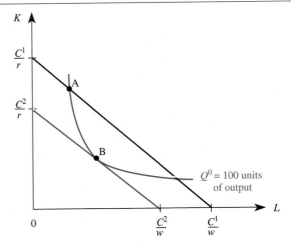

output. It also lies on the isocost line through point A. Thus, if the producer uses input mix A, he or she will produce Q_0 units of output at a total cost of C^1. Is this the cost-minimizing way to produce the given level of output? Clearly not, for by using input mix B instead of A, the producer could produce the same amount of output at a lower cost, namely C^2. In short, it is inefficient for the producer to use input mix A, because input mix B produces the same output and lies on a lower isocost line.

At the cost-minimizing input mix, the slope of the isoquant is equal to the slope of the isocost line. Recalling that the absolute value of the slope of the isoquant reflects the marginal rate of technical substitution and that the slope of the isocost line is given by $-w/r$, we see that at the cost-minimizing input mix,

$$MRTS_{KL} = w/r$$

If this condition did not hold, the technical rate at which the producer could substitute between L and K would differ from the market rate at which she or he could substitute between the inputs. For example, at point A in Figure 5–8, the slope of the isoquant is steeper than the slope of the isocost line. Consequently, capital is "too expensive"; the producer finds it in his or her interest to use less capital and more labor to produce the given level of output. This substitution continues until ultimately the producer is at a point such as B, where the MRTS is equal to the ratio of input prices. The condition for the cost-minimizing use of inputs also can be stated in terms of marginal products.

To see why this condition must hold to be able to minimize the cost of producing a given level of output, suppose $MP_L/w > MP_K/r$. Then, on a last-dollar-spent basis, labor is a better deal than capital, and the firm should use less capital and more labor to minimize costs. In particular, if the firm reduced its expenditures on capital by \$1, it could produce the same level of output if it increased its expenditures on labor by less than \$1. Thus, by substituting away from capital and toward

Principle	**Cost-Minimizing Input Rule**
	To minimize the cost of producing a given level of output, the marginal product per dollar spent should be equal for all inputs:
	$$\frac{MP_L}{w} = \frac{MP_K}{r}$$
	Equivalently, to minimize the cost of production, a firm should employ inputs such that the marginal rate of technical substitution is equal to the ratio of input prices:
	$$\frac{MP_L}{MP_K} = \frac{w}{r}$$

labor, the firm could reduce its costs while producing the same level of output. This substitution clearly would continue until the marginal product per dollar spent on capital exactly equaled the marginal product per dollar spent on labor.

For a video walkthrough of this problem, visit www.mhhe.com/baye8e

Demonstration Problem 5–3

Terry's Lawn Service rents five small push mowers and two large riding mowers to cut the lawns of neighborhood households. The marginal product of a small push mower is 3 lawns per day, and the marginal product of a large riding mower is 6 lawns per day. The rental price of a small push mower is $10 per day, whereas the rental price of a large riding mower is $25 per day. Is Terry's Lawn Service utilizing small push mowers and large riding mowers in a cost-minimizing manner?

Answer:

Let MP_S be the marginal product of a small push mower and MP_L be the marginal product of a large riding mower. If we let P_S and P_L be the rental prices of a small push mower and large riding mower, respectively, cost minimization requires that

$$\frac{MP_S}{P_S} = \frac{MP_L}{P_L}$$

Substituting in the appropriate values, we see that

$$\frac{3}{10} = \frac{MP_S}{P_S} > \frac{MP_L}{P_L} = \frac{6}{25}$$

Thus, the marginal product per dollar spent on small push mowers exceeds the marginal product per dollar spent on large riding mowers. Riding mowers are twice as productive as push mowers, but more than twice as expensive. The firm clearly is not minimizing costs and thus should use fewer riding mowers and more push mowers.

Optimal Input Substitution

A change in the price of an input will lead to a change in the cost-minimizing input bundle. To see this, suppose the initial isocost line in Figure 5–9 is FG and the

FIGURE 5–9 Substituting Capital for Labor, Due to Increase in the Wage Rate

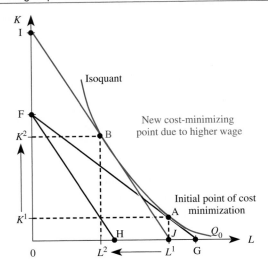

producer is cost-minimizing at input mix A, producing Q_0 units of output. Now suppose that the wage rate increases so that if the firm spent the same amount on inputs, its isocost line would rotate clockwise to FH in Figure 5–9. Clearly, if the firm spends the amount it spent prior to the increase in the wage rate, it cannot produce the same level of output.

Given the new slope of the isocost line, which reflects a higher relative price of labor, the cost-minimizing way to maintain the output implied by the initial isoquant is at point B, where isocost line IJ is tangent to the isoquant. Due to the increase in the price of labor relative to capital, the producer substitutes away from labor and toward capital and adopts a more capital-intensive mode of production. This suggests the following important result:

Principle **Optimal Input Substitution**
To minimize the cost of producing a given level of output, the firm should use less of an input and more of other inputs when that input's price rises.

Figure 5–10 shows the isocost line (AB) and isoquant for a firm that produces rugs using computers and labor. The initial point of cost minimization is at point M, where the manager has chosen to use 40 units of capital (computers) and 80 units of labor when the wage rate is $w = \$20$ and the rental rate of computers (capital) is $r^0 = \$20$. This implies that at point M, total costs are $C^0 = (\$20 \times 40) + (\$20 \times 80) = \$2,400$. Notice also at point M that the *MRTS* equals the ratio of the wage to the rental rate.

Now assume that due to a decrease in the supply of silicon chips, the rental rate of capital increases to $r^1 = \$40$. What will the manager do to minimize costs? Since the price of capital has increased, the isocost line will rotate counterclockwise from

FIGURE 5–10 Substituting Labor for Computers, Due to Higher Computer Prices

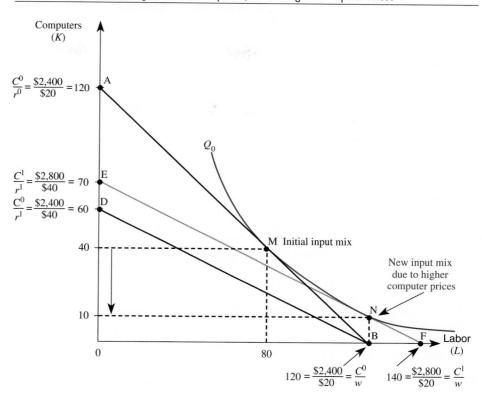

AB to DB. To produce the same amount of output, the manager will have to spend more than $C^0 = \$2,400$. The additional expenditures will shift the isocost line out to EF in Figure 5–10. The new point of cost minimization is at point N, where the firm now employs more labor (120 units) and less capital (10 units) to minimize the production costs of rugs. Costs are now $C^1 = (\$40 \times 10) + (\$20 \times 120) = \$2,800$, which are higher than C^0.

THE COST FUNCTION

For given input prices, different isoquants will entail different production costs, even allowing for optimal substitution between capital and labor. Each isoquant corresponds to a different level of output, and the isocost line tangent to higher isoquants will imply higher costs of production, even assuming the firm uses the cost-minimizing input mix. Since the cost of production increases as higher isoquants are reached, it is useful to let $C(Q)$ denote the cost to the firm of producing isoquant Q in the cost-minimizing fashion. The function, C, is called the *cost function*.

INSIDE BUSINESS 5–2

Fringe Benefits and Input Substitution

Government regulations often have unintended consequences. For instance, current federal tax law requires that firms provide fringe benefits in such a way as not to discriminate against lower-income workers. Presumably, the purpose of this regulation is to ensure that low-income workers will have access to health care, pension benefits, and other fringe benefits. Unfortunately, this policy often limits the employment opportunities of low-income workers.

To see why, consider a company that hires computer programmers and secretaries. Suppose the annual wage bill of a computer programmer is $50,000 and that of a secretary is $25,000. The company is considering offering a family health care plan worth $5,000 annually to its employees. Ignoring the fringe-benefit bill, the relative price of a secretary to a computer programmer is $25,000/$50,000 = .5. But when the cost of the health care plan is added in, the relative price of a secretary increases to a little over .55 of that of a computer programmer. Isoquant and isocost analysis suggests that firms should substitute away from the now higher-priced secretaries to minimize costs.

Seem far-fetched? Recently economists Frank Scott, Mark Berger, and Dan Black examined the relationship between health care costs and employment of low-wage workers. They found that industries that offered more generous health care plans employed significantly fewer bookkeepers, keypunch operators, receptionists, secretaries, clerk-typists, janitors, and food service workers than did industries with lower health care costs. Moreover, industries with higher levels of fringe benefits hired more part-time workers than did industries with lower fringe-benefit levels since the government does not require firms to offer pension, health care, and many other fringe benefits to part-time workers.

This law also creates an incentive to substitute away from older workers, for whom these mandated fringe benefits, particularly health care, are more expensive for firms. In a follow-up study, Frank Scott, Mark Berger, and John Garen found that the prohibition of discrimination in the provision of fringe benefits, along with prohibition against age discrimination, adversely affected older workers' employment opportunities.

Sources: Frank Scott, Mark Berger, and Dan Black, "Effects of Fringe Benefits on Labor Market Segmentation," *Industrial and Labor Relations Review* 42 (January 1989), pp. 216–29; Frank Scott, Mark Berger, and John Garen, "Do Health Insurance and Pension Costs Reduce the Job Opportunities of Older Workers?" *Industrial and Labor Relations Review* 48 (July 1995), pp. 775–91.

---

total cost
Sum of fixed and variable costs.

fixed costs
Costs that do not change with changes in output; include the costs of fixed inputs used in production.

variable costs
Costs that change with changes in output; include the costs of inputs that vary with output.

The cost function is extremely valuable because, as we will see in later chapters, it provides essential information a manager needs to determine the profit-maximizing level of output. In addition, the cost function summarizes information about the production process. The cost function thus reduces the amount of information the manager has to process to make optimal output decisions.

Short-Run Costs

Recall that the short run is defined as the period over which the amounts of some inputs are fixed. In the short run, the manager is free to alter the use of variable inputs but is "stuck" with existing levels of fixed inputs. Because inputs are costly whether fixed or variable, the *total cost* of producing output in the short run consists of (1) the cost of fixed inputs and (2) the cost of variable inputs. These two components of short-run total cost are called fixed costs and variable costs, respectively. *Fixed costs,* denoted *FC,* are costs that do not vary with output. Fixed costs include the costs of fixed inputs used in production. *Variable costs,* denoted *VC(Q),* are costs that change when output is changed. Variable costs include the costs of inputs that vary with output.

TABLE 5–3 The Cost Function

(1) K Fixed Input [Given]	(2) L Variable Input [Given]	(3) Q Output [Given]	(4) FC Fixed Cost [$1,000 × (1)]	(5) VC Variable Cost [$400 × (2)]	(6) TC Total Cost [(4) + (5)]
2	0	0	$2,000	$ 0	$2,000
2	1	76	2,000	400	2,400
2	2	248	2,000	800	2,800
2	3	492	2,000	1,200	3,200
2	4	784	2,000	1,600	3,600
2	5	1,100	2,000	2,000	4,000
2	6	1,416	2,000	2,400	4,400
2	7	1,708	2,000	2,800	4,800
2	8	1,952	2,000	3,200	5,200
2	9	2,124	2,000	3,600	5,600
2	10	2,200	2,000	4,000	6,000

short-run cost function
A function that defines the minimum possible cost of producing each output level when variable factors are employed in the cost-minimizing fashion.

Since all costs fall into one category or the other, the sum of fixed and variable costs is the firm's short-run cost function. In the presence of fixed factors of production, the *short-run cost function* summarizes the minimum possible cost of producing each level of output when variable factors are being used in the cost-minimizing way.

Table 5–3 illustrates the costs of producing with the technology used in Table 5–1. Notice that the first three columns comprise a short-run production function because they summarize the maximum amount of output that can be produced with two units of the fixed factor (capital) and alternative units of the variable factor (labor). Assuming capital costs $1,000 per unit and labor costs $400 per unit, we can calculate the fixed and variable costs of production, which are summarized in columns 4 and 5 of Table 5–3. Notice that irrespective of the amount of output produced, the cost of the capital equipment is $1,000 × 2 = $2,000. Thus, every entry in column 4 contains this number, illustrating the principle that fixed costs do not vary with output.

To produce more output, more of the variable factor must be employed. For example, to produce 1,100 units of output, 5 units of labor are needed; to produce 1,708 units of output, 7 units of labor are required. Since labor is the only variable input in this simple example, the variable cost of producing 1,100 units of output is the cost of 5 units of labor, or $400 × 5 = $2,000. Similarly, the variable cost of producing 1,708 units of output is $400 × 7 = $2,800. Total costs, summarized in the last column of Table 5–3, are simply the sum of fixed costs (column 4) and variable costs (column 5) at each level of output.

Figure 5–11 illustrates graphically the relations among total costs (TC), variable costs (VC), and fixed costs (FC). Because fixed costs do not change with output, they are constant for all output levels and must be paid even if zero units of output are produced. Variable costs, on the other hand, are zero if no output is produced but increase as output increases above zero. Total cost is the sum of fixed costs and variable costs. Thus, the distance between the TC and VC curves in

FIGURE 5-11 The Relationship among Costs

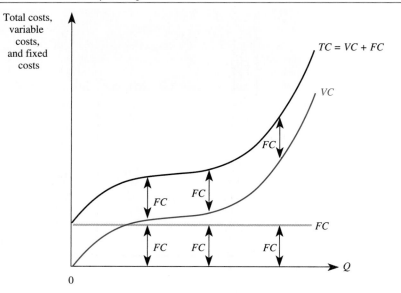

Figure 5–11 is simply fixed costs. Note that the curves look closer together as they get steeper; however, this is due to the fact that, with a fixed vertical difference in the curves, the horizontal difference will get smaller as the curves get steeper, making them look closer on that dimension.

Average and Marginal Costs

One common misconception about costs is that large firms have lower costs than smaller firms because they produce larger quantities of output. One fundamental implication of scarcity is that to produce more output, more must be spent. What individuals most likely have in mind when they consider the advantages of producing large quantities of output is that the overhead is spread out over a larger level of output. This idea is intricately related to the economic concept of average fixed cost. *Average fixed cost (AFC)* is defined as fixed costs (*FC*) divided by the number of units of output:

average fixed cost
Fixed costs divided by the number of units of output.

$$AFC = \frac{FC}{Q}$$

Since fixed costs do not vary with output, as more and more output is produced, the fixed costs are allocated over a greater quantity of output. As a consequence, average fixed costs decline continuously as output is expanded. This principle is revealed in column 5 of Table 5–4, where we see that average fixed costs decline as total output increases.

average variable cost
Variable costs divided by the number of units of output.

Average variable cost provides a measure of variable costs on a per-unit basis. *Average variable cost (AVC)* is defined as variable cost (*VC*) divided by the number of units of output:

$$AVC = \frac{VC(Q)}{Q}$$

TABLE 5–4   Derivation of Average Costs

(1) Q Output [Given]	(2) FC Fixed Cost [Given]	(3) VC Variable Cost [Given]	(4) TC Total Cost [(2) + (3)]	(5) AFC Average Fixed Cost [(2)/(1)]	(6) AVC Average Variable Cost [(3)/(1)]	(7) ATC Average Total Cost [(4)/(1)]
0	$2,000	$ 0	$2,000	—	—	—
76	2,000	400	2,400	$26.32	$5.26	$31.58
248	2,000	800	2,800	8.06	3.23	11.29
492	2,000	1,200	3,200	4.07	2.44	6.50
784	2,000	1,600	3,600	2.55	2.04	4.59
1,100	2,000	2,000	4,000	1.82	1.82	3.64
1,416	2,000	2,400	4,400	1.41	1.69	3.11
1,708	2,000	2,800	4,800	1.17	1.64	2.81
1,952	2,000	3,200	5,200	1.02	1.64	2.66
2,124	2,000	3,600	5,600	0.94	1.69	2.64
2,200	2,000	4,000	6,000	0.91	1.82	2.73

Column 6 of Table 5–4 provides the average variable cost for the production function in our example. Notice that as output increases, average variable cost initially declines, reaches a minimum between 1,708 and 1,952 units of output, and then begins to increase.

Average total cost is analogous to average variable cost, except that it provides a measure of total costs on a per-unit basis. *Average total cost (ATC)* is defined as total cost (*TC*) divided by the number of units of output:

$$ATC = \frac{C(Q)}{Q}$$

Column 7 of Table 5–4 provides the average total cost of various outputs in our example. Notice that average total cost declines as output expands to 2,124 units and then begins to rise. Furthermore, note that average total cost is the sum of average fixed costs and average variable costs (the sum of columns 5 and 6) in Table 5–4.

The most important cost concept is marginal (or incremental) cost. Conceptually, *marginal cost (MC)* is the cost of producing an additional unit of output, that is, the change in cost attributable to the last unit of output:

marginal (incremental) cost
The cost of producing an additional unit of output.

$$MC = \frac{\Delta C}{\Delta Q}$$

To understand this important concept, consider Table 5–5, which summarizes the short-run cost function with which we have been working. Marginal cost, depicted in column 7, is calculated as the change in costs arising from a given change in output. For example, increasing output from 248 to 492 units ($\Delta Q = 244$) increases costs from 2,800 to 3,200 ($\Delta C = 400). Thus, the marginal cost of increasing output to 492 units is $\Delta C/\Delta Q = 400/244 = 1.64.

TABLE 5–5 Derivation of Marginal Costs

(1) Q [Given]	(2) Δ Q [Δ(1)]	(3) VC [Given]	(4) Δ VC [Δ(3)]	(5) TC [Given]	(6) Δ TC [Δ(5)]	(7) MC [(6)/(2) or (4)/2)]
0	—	0	—	2,000	—	—
76	76	400	400	2,400	400	400/76 = 5.26
248	172	800	400	2,800	400	400/172 = 2.33
492	244	1,200	400	3,200	400	400/244 = 1.64
784	292	1,600	400	3,600	400	400/292 = 1.37
1,100	316	2,000	400	4,000	400	400/316 = 1.27
1,416	316	2,400	400	4,400	400	400/316 = 1.27
1,708	292	2,800	400	4,800	400	400/292 = 1.37
1,952	244	3,200	400	5,200	400	400/244 = 1.64
2,124	172	3,600	400	5,600	400	400/172 = 2.33
2,200	76	4,000	400	6,000	400	400/76 = 5.26

When only one input is variable, the marginal cost is the price of that input divided by its marginal product. Remember that marginal product increases initially, reaches a maximum, and then decreases. Since marginal cost is the reciprocal of marginal product times the input's price, it decreases as marginal product increases and increases when marginal product is decreasing.

Relations among Costs

Figure 5–12 graphically depicts average total, average variable, average fixed, and marginal costs under the assumption that output is infinitely divisible (the firm is not restricted to producing only the outputs listed in Tables 5–4 and 5–5 but can produce any outputs). The shapes of the curves indicate the relation between the marginal

FIGURE 5–12 The Relationship among Average and Marginal Costs

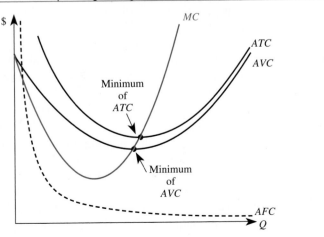

and average costs presented in those tables. These relations among the cost curves, also depicted in Figure 5–12, are very important. The first thing to notice is that the marginal cost curve intersects the *ATC* and *AVC* curves at their minimum points. This implies that when marginal cost is below an average cost curve, average cost is declining, and when marginal cost is above average cost, average cost is rising.

There is a simple explanation for this relationship among the various cost curves. Again consider your grade in this course. If your grade on an exam is below your average grade, the new grade lowers your average grade. If the grade you score on an exam is above your average grade, the new grade increases your average. In essence, the new grade is the marginal contribution to your total grade. When the marginal is above the average, the average increases; when the marginal is below the average, the average decreases. The same principle applies to marginal and average costs, and this is why the curves in Figure 5–12 look the way they do.

The second thing to notice in Figure 5–12 is that the *ATC* and *AVC* curves get closer together as output increases. This is because the only difference in *ATC* and *AVC* is *AFC*. To see why, note that total costs consist of variable costs and fixed costs:

$$C(Q) = VC(Q) + FC$$

If we divide both sides of this equation by total output (Q), we get

$$\frac{C(Q)}{Q} = \frac{VC(Q)}{Q} + \frac{FC}{Q}$$

But $C(Q)/Q = ATC$, $VC(Q)/Q = AVC$, and $FC/Q = AFC$. Thus,

$$ATC = AVC + AFC$$

The difference between average total costs and average variable costs is $ATC - AVC = AFC$. Since average fixed costs decline as output is expanded, as in Figure 5–12, this difference between average total and average variable costs diminishes as fixed costs are spread over increasing levels of output.

Fixed and Sunk Costs

sunk cost
A cost that is forever lost after it has been paid.

We now make an important distinction between fixed costs and sunk costs. Recall that a fixed cost is a cost that does not change when output changes. A related concept, called *sunk cost*, is a cost that is lost forever once it has been paid. To be concrete, imagine that you are the manager of a coal company and have just paid $10,000 to lease a railcar for one month. This expense reflects a fixed cost to your firm—the cost is $10,000 regardless of whether you use the railcar to transport 10 tons or 10,000 tons of coal. How much of this $10,000 is a sunk cost depends on the terms of your lease. If the lease does not permit you to recoup any of the $10,000 once it has been paid, the entire $10,000 is a sunk cost—you have already incurred the cost, and there is nothing you can do to change it. If the lease states that you will be refunded $6,000 in the event you do not need the railcar, then only $4,000 of the $10,000 in fixed costs are a sunk cost. Sunk costs are thus the amount of these fixed costs that cannot be recouped.

Since sunk costs are lost forever once they have been paid, they are irrelevant to decision making. To illustrate, suppose you paid a nonrefundable amount of $10,000 to lease a railcar for one month, but immediately after signing the lease, you realize that you do not need it—the demand for coal is significantly lower than you expected. A farmer approaches you and offers to sublease the railcar from you for $2,000. If the terms of your lease permit you to sublease the railcar, should you accept the farmer's offer?

You might reason that the answer is no; after all, your firm would appear to lose $8,000 by subleasing a $10,000 railcar for a measly $2,000. *This reasoning is wrong.* Your lease payment is nonrefundable, which means that the $10,000 is an unavoidable cost that has already been lost. Since there is nothing you can do to eliminate this $10,000 cost, the only relevant issue is whether you can do something to enhance your inflow of cash. In this case your optimal decision is to sublease the railcar because doing so provides you with $2,000 in revenues that you would not get otherwise. Notice that, while sunk costs are irrelevant in making your decision, they do affect your calculation of total profits. If you do not sublease the railcar, you lose $10,000; if you sublease it, you lose only $8,000.

Principle	**Irrelevance of Sunk Costs**
	A decision maker should ignore sunk costs to maximize profits or minimize losses.

Demonstration Problem 5–4

ACME Coal paid $5,000 to lease a railcar from the Reading Railroad. Under the terms of the lease, $1,000 of this payment is refundable if the railcar is returned within two days of signing the lease.

1. Upon signing the lease and paying $5,000, how large are ACME's fixed costs? Its sunk costs?
2. One day after signing the lease, ACME realizes that it has no use for the railcar. A farmer has a bumper crop of corn and has offered to sublease the railcar from ACME at a price of $4,500. Should ACME accept the farmer's offer?

Answer:

1. ACME's fixed costs are $5,000. For the first two days, its sunk costs are $4,000 (this is the amount that cannot be recouped). After two days, the entire $5,000 becomes a sunk cost.
2. Yes, ACME should sublease the railcar. Note that ACME's total loss is $500 if it accepts the farmer's offer. If it does not, its losses will equal $4,000 (assuming it returns the railcar by the end of the next business day).

cubic cost function
Costs are a cubic function of output; provides a reasonable approximation to virtually any cost function.

Algebraic Forms of Cost Functions

In practice, cost functions may take many forms, but the cubic cost function is frequently encountered and closely approximates any cost function. The *cubic cost function* is given by

$$C(Q) = f + aQ + bQ^2 + cQ^3$$

where a, b, c, and f are constants. Note that f represents fixed costs.

Given an algebraic form of the cubic cost function, we may directly calculate the marginal cost function.

Formula: Marginal Cost for Cubic Costs. For a cubic cost function,

$$C(Q) = f + aQ + bQ^2 + cQ^3$$

the marginal cost function is

$$MC(Q) = a + 2bQ + 3cQ^2$$

A Calculus Alternative

Marginal cost is simply the derivative of the cost function with respect to output:

$$MC(Q) = \frac{dC}{dQ}$$

For example, the derivative of the cubic cost function with respect to Q is

$$\frac{dC}{dQ} = a + 2bQ + 3cQ^2$$

which is the formula for marginal cost given above.

Demonstration Problem 5–5

The cost function for Managerial Enterprises is given by $C(Q) = 20 + 3Q^2$. Determine the marginal cost, average fixed cost, average variable cost, and average total cost when $Q = 10$.

Answer:
Using the formula for marginal cost (here $a = c = 0$), we know that $MC = 6Q$. Thus, the marginal cost when $Q = 10$ is $60.

To find the various average costs, we must first calculate total costs. The total cost of producing 10 units of output is

$$C(10) = 20 + 3(10)^2 = \$320$$

Fixed costs are those costs that do not vary with output; thus fixed costs are $20. Variable costs are the costs that vary with output, namely $VC(Q) = 3Q^2$. Thus, $VC(10) = 3(10)^2 = \$300$. It follows that the average fixed cost of producing 10 units is $2, the average variable cost is $30, and the average total cost is $32.

Long-Run Costs

In the long run all costs are variable, because the manager is free to adjust the levels of all inputs. In Figure 5–13, the short-run average cost curve ATC_0 is drawn under the assumption that there are some fixed factors of production. The average total cost of

---

INSIDE BUSINESS 5–3

Estimating Production Functions, Cost Functions, and Returns to Scale

While serving in the U.S. Army, Marc Nerlove conceived a research project to model the economic factors that impact the production of electricity. The primary innovation in Nerlove's model of electricity supply was the way it was rooted in the theory of production and costs. His approach was the first to empirically utilize the "dual" approach to production and costs—that is, to exploit the fact that a cost function summarizes all of the information contained in a production function, and vice versa.

Two primary findings emerged from Nerlove's empirical analysis. First, substantial economies of scale existed at the firm level in the market for electricity in the 1950s. The degree of the scale economies, however, varies inversely with output and is considerably lower than previously estimated for individual plant facilities. This was especially true for large firms. Second, though the size of an electricity company's operations impacted its economies of scale, it did not impact its marginal rate of substitution between factors of production.

Advances in the theory of duality between production and costs led Christensen and Greene to distinguish between scale economies and cost reductions that stem from technological change. Their analysis

suggests that technological change explains a large portion of the reductions in electricity costs that occurred between 1955 and 1970.

Today, these pioneering techniques—as well as more advanced econometric approaches—are used to estimate the production and cost functions needed to guide managerial decisions in industries ranging from electricity to health care as more recent work by economists Michael Maloney and James Thornton shows. The website for this book at www.mhhe.com/baye8e contains some spreadsheet files and data that give you an opportunity to use the econometric techniques introduced in Chapter 3 to estimate production and cost functions.

Sources: M. Nerlove, "Returns to Scale in Electricity Supply," *Measurement in Economics*, ed. C. Christ et al. (Palo Alto, CA: Stanford University Press, 1963), pp. 167–98; L.R. Christensen and W.H. Greene, "Economies of Scale in U.S. Electric Power Generation," *Journal of Political Economy*, Vol. 84(1976), pp. 655–76; M. Maloney, "Economies and Diseconomies: Estimating Electricity Cost Functions," *Review of Industrial Organization*, Vol. 19(2001), pp. 165–80; J. Thornton, "Estimating a Health Production Function for the US: Some New Evidence," *Applied Economics*, Vol. 34(2002), pp. 59–62.

---

long-run average cost curve
A curve that defines the minimum average cost of producing alternative levels of output, allowing for optimal selection of both fixed and variable factors of production.

producing output level Q_0, given the fixed factors of production, is $ATC_0(Q_0)$. In the short run, if the firm increases output to Q_1, it cannot adjust the fixed factors, and thus average costs rise to $ATC_0(Q_1)$. In the long run, however, the firm can adjust the fixed factors. Let ATC_1 be the average cost curve after the firm adjusts the fixed factors in the optimal manner. Now the firm can produce Q_1 with average cost curve ATC_1. If the firm produced Q_1 with average cost curve ATC_0, its average costs would be $ATC_0(Q_1)$. By adjusting the fixed factors in a way that optimizes the scale of operation, the firm economizes in production and can produce Q_1 units of output at a lower average cost, $ATC_1(Q_1)$. Notice that the curve labeled ATC_1 is itself a short-run average cost curve, based on the new levels of fixed inputs that have been selected to minimize the cost of producing Q_1. If the firm wishes to further expand output—say, to Q_2—it would follow curve ATC_1 in the short run to $ATC_1(Q_2)$ until it again changed its fixed factors to incur lower average costs of producing Q_2 units of output, namely $ATC_2(Q_2)$.

The *long-run average cost curve*, denoted *LRAC* in Figure 5–13, defines the minimum average cost of producing alternative levels of output, allowing for

FIGURE 5–13 Optimal Plant Size and Long-Run Average Cost

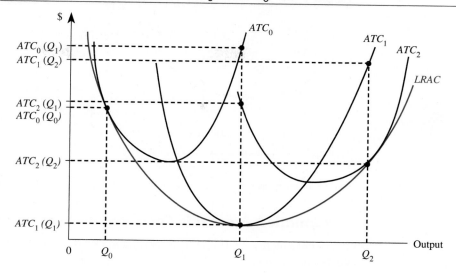

optimal selection of all variables of production (both fixed and variable factors). The long-run average cost curve is the lower envelope of all the short-run average cost curves. This means that the long-run average cost curve lies below every point on the short-run average cost curves, except that it equals each short-run average cost curve at the points where the short-run curve uses fixed factors optimally. In essence, we may think of each short-run average cost curve in Figure 5–13 as the average cost of producing in a plant of fixed size. Different short-run average cost curves are associated with different plant sizes. In the long run, the firm's manager is free to choose the optimal plant size for producing the desired level of output, and this determines the long-run average cost of producing that output level.

economies of scale
Exist when long-run average costs decline as output is increased.

diseconomies of scale
Exist when long-run average costs rise as output is increased.

constant returns to scale
Exist when long-run average costs remain constant as output is increased.

Economies of Scale

Notice that the long-run average cost curve in Figure 5–14(a) is U shaped. This implies that initially an expansion of output allows the firm to produce at lower long-run average cost, as is shown for outputs between 0 and Q^*. This condition is known as *economies of scale*. When there are economies of scale, increasing the size of the operation decreases the minimum average cost. After a point, such as Q^* in Figure 5–14(a), further increases in output lead to an increase in average costs. This condition is known as *diseconomies of scale*. Sometimes the technology in an industry allows a firm to produce different levels of output at the same minimum average cost, as in Figure 5–14(b). This condition is called *constant returns to scale*.

FIGURE 5–14   Scale Economies

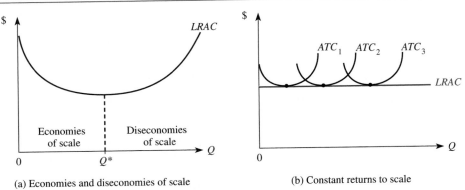

(a) Economies and diseconomies of scale   (b) Constant returns to scale

A Reminder: Economic Costs versus Accounting Costs

In concluding this section, it is important to recall the difference between economic costs and accounting costs. Accounting costs are the costs most often associated with the costs of producing. For example, accounting costs include direct payments to labor and capital to produce output. Accounting costs are the costs that appear on the income statements of firms.

These costs are not the only costs of producing a good, however. The firm could use the same resources to produce some other good. By choosing to produce one good, producers give up the opportunity for producing some other good. Thus,

---

INSIDE BUSINESS 5–4

International Companies Exploit Economies of Scale

In industries with economies of scale, firms that produce greater levels of output produce at lower average costs and thus gain a potential competitive advantage over rivals. Recently, two international businesses pursued such strategies to enhance their bottom line.

Japan's Matsushita Plasma Display Panel Company, Ltd., invested $835 million to build the world's largest plant for producing plasma display panels. The factory—a joint venture between Panasonic and Toray Industries—had the capacity to produce 250,000 panels per month by the late 2000s. This strategy was implemented in response to rising global demand for plasma display panels, and a desire on the part of the company to gain a competitive advantage over rivals in this increasingly competitive industry.

An automaker in India—Maruti Udyog Ltd.—produced tangible evidence that economies of scale are important in business decisions. It enjoyed a 271 percent increase in net profits in the mid-2000s, thanks to its ability to exploit these economies. The increase was spawned by a 30 percent increase in sales volume that permitted the firm to spread its sizable fixed costs over greater output. Importantly, the company's reduction in average costs due to economies of scale was more than enough to offset the higher costs stemming from increases in the price of steel.

Sources: "Matsushita Plans Big Expansion of PDP Manufacturing," *IDG News Service,* May 19, 2004; "MUL Gains from Cost-Saving Measures," *Sify India,* May 18, 2004.

the costs of production include not only the accounting costs but also the opportunities forgone by producing a given product.

MULTIPLE-OUTPUT COST FUNCTIONS

multiproduct cost function
A function that defines the cost of producing given levels of two or more types of outputs assuming all inputs are used efficiently.

Until now, our analysis of the production process has focused on situations where the firm produces a single output. There are also numerous examples of firms that produce multiple outputs. Toyota produces cars, trucks, and SUVs (and many varieties of each); Dell produces many different types of computers and printers. While our analysis for the case of a firm that produces a single output also applies to a multiproduct firm, the latter raises some additional issues. This section will highlight these concepts.

In this section, we will assume that the cost function for a multiproduct firm is given by $C(Q_1, Q_2)$, where Q_1 is the number of units produced of product 1 and Q_2 is the number of units produced of product 2. The *multiproduct cost function* thus defines the cost of producing Q_1 units of product 1 and Q_2 units of product 2 assuming all inputs are used efficiently.

Notice that the multiproduct cost function has the same basic interpretation as a single-output cost function. Unlike with a single-product cost function, however, the costs of production depend on how much of each type of output is produced. This gives rise to what economists call economies of scope and cost complementarities, discussed next.

Economies of Scope

economies of scope
When the total cost of producing two types of outputs together is less than the total cost of producing each type of output separately.

Economies of scope exist when the total cost of producing Q_1 and Q_2 together is less than the total cost of producing Q_1 and Q_2 separately, that is, when

$$C(Q_1, 0) + C(0, Q_2) > C(Q_1, Q_2)$$

In a restaurant, for example, to produce given quantities of steak and chicken dinners, it generally is cheaper to produce both products in the same restaurant than to have two restaurants, one that sells only chicken and one that sells only steak. The reason is, of course, that producing the dinners separately would require duplication of many common factors of production, such as ovens, refrigerators, tables, the building, and so forth.

Cost Complementarity

cost complementarity
When the marginal cost of producing one type of output decreases when the output of another good is increased.

Cost complementarities exist in a multiproduct cost function when the marginal cost of producing one output is reduced when the output of another product is increased. Let $C(Q_1, Q_2)$ be the cost function for a multiproduct firm, and let $MC_1(Q_1, Q_2)$ be the marginal cost of producing the first output. The cost function exhibits cost complementarity if

$$\frac{\Delta MC_1(Q_1, Q_2)}{\Delta Q_2} < 0$$

that is, if an increase in the output of product 2 decreases the marginal cost of producing product 1.

An example of cost complementarity is the production of doughnuts and doughnut holes. The firm can make these products separately or jointly. But the cost of making additional doughnut holes is lower when workers roll out the dough, punch the holes, and fry both the doughnuts and the holes instead of making the holes separately.

The concepts of economies of scope and cost complementarity can also be examined within the context of an algebraic functional form for a multiproduct cost function. For example, suppose the multiproduct cost function is quadratic:

$$C(Q_1, Q_2) = f + aQ_1Q_2 + (Q_1)^2 + (Q_2)^2$$

For this cost function,

$$MC_1 = aQ_2 + 2Q_1$$

Notice that when $a < 0$, an increase in Q_2 reduces the marginal cost of producing product 1. Thus, if $a < 0$, this cost function exhibits cost complementarity. If $a > 0$, there are no cost complementarities.

Formula: Quadratic Multiproduct Cost Function. The multiproduct cost function

$$C(Q_1, Q_2) = f + aQ_1Q_2 + (Q_1)^2 + (Q_2)^2$$

has corresponding marginal cost functions,

$$MC_1(Q_1, Q_2) = aQ_2 + 2Q_1$$

and

$$MC_2(Q_1, Q_2) = aQ_1 + 2Q_2$$

To examine whether economies of scope exist for a quadratic multiproduct cost function, recall that there are economies of scope if

$$C(Q_1, 0) + C(0, Q_2) > C(Q_1, Q_2)$$

or, rearranging,

$$C(Q_1, 0) + C(0, Q_2) - C(Q_1, Q_2) > 0$$

This condition may be rewritten as

$$f + (Q_1)^2 + f + (Q_2)^2 - [f + aQ_1Q_2 + (Q_1)^2 + (Q_2)^2] > 0$$

which may be simplified to

$$f - aQ_1Q_2 > 0$$

Thus, economies of scope are realized in producing output levels Q_1 and Q_2 if $f > aQ_1Q_2$.

Summary of the Properties of the Quadratic Multiproduct Cost Function. The multiproduct cost function $C(Q_1, Q_2) = f + aQ_1Q_2 + (Q_1)^2 + (Q_2)^2$

1. Exhibits cost complementarity whenever $a < 0$.
2. Exhibits economies of scope whenever $f - aQ_1Q_2 > 0$.

Demonstration Problem 5–6

Suppose the cost function of firm A, which produces two goods, is given by

$$C = 100 - .5Q_1Q_2 + (Q_1)^2 + (Q_2)^2$$

The firm wishes to produce 5 units of good 1 and 4 units of good 2.

1. Do cost complementarities exist? Do economies of scope exist?
2. Firm A is considering selling the subsidiary that produces good 2 to firm B, in which case it will produce only good 1. What will happen to firm A's costs if it continues to produce 5 units of good 1?

Answer:

1. For this cost function, $a = -1/2 < 0$, so indeed there are cost complementarities. To check for economies of scope, we must determine whether $f - aQ_1Q_2 > 0$. This is clearly true, since $a < 0$ in this problem. Thus, economies of scope exist in producing 5 units of good 1 and 4 units of good 2.
2. To determine what will happen to firm A's costs if it sells the subsidiary that produces good 2 to firm B, we must calculate costs under the alternative scenarios. By selling the subsidiary, firm A will reduce its production of good 2 from 4 to 0 units; since there are cost complementarities, this will increase the marginal cost of producing good 1. Notice that the total costs to firm A of producing the 5 units of good 1 fall from

$$C(5, 4) = 100 - 10 + 25 + 16 = 131$$

to

$$C(5, 0) = 100 + 25 = 125$$

But the costs to firm B of producing 4 units of good 2 will be

$$C(0, 4) = 100 + 16 = 116$$

Firm A's costs will fall by only $6 when it stops producing good 2, and the costs to firm B of producing 4 units of good 2 will be $116. The combined costs to the two firms of producing the output originally produced by a single firm will be $110 more than the cost of producing by a single firm.

The preceding problem illustrates some important aspects of mergers and sales of subsidiaries. First, when there are economies of scope, two firms producing distinct outputs could merge into a single firm and enjoy a reduction in costs. Second, selling off an unprofitable subsidiary could lead to only minor reductions in costs.

In effect, when economies of scope exist, it is difficult to "allocate costs" across product lines.

ANSWERING THE HEADLINE

In the opening headline, the phrase "wins the battle" refers to the short-run implications of the agreement between Boeing and the IAM, while "wins the war" refers to the agreement's long-run implications. The analyst recognizes that the agreement benefited union workers in the short run, but the agreement also increased Boeing's long-term value by giving it the *flexibility* to substitute away from more costly unionized inputs.

More specifically, Boeing's new union contract provided a number of "short-term" provisions (health and pension benefits, higher wages, and job security for some of the union's more senior workers) that were costly to Boeing but beneficial to the union. In the long run, however, the higher labor costs associated with the agreement provide Boeing with an incentive to substitute away from more expensive union labor, and the agreement provides Boeing the *flexibility* to do so. For instance, the subcontracting provisions Boeing won in the agreement may, in the long run, permit the company to substitute away from its costly and heavily unionized Pacific Northwest inputs toward assembly facilities in less costly areas. In short, the analyst concluded that the long-run flexibility imbedded in the agreement translates into cost-reducing substitution possibilities for Boeing that generate long-run benefits that probably more than offset the short-run costs.

SUMMARY

In this chapter, we introduced the production and cost functions, which summarize important information about converting inputs into outputs sold by a firm. For firms that use several inputs to produce output, isocosts and isoquants provide a convenient way to determine the optimal input mix.

We broke down the cost function into average total cost, average fixed cost, average variable cost, and marginal cost. These concepts help build a foundation for understanding the profit-maximizing input and output decisions that will be covered in greater detail in later chapters.

Given a desired level of output, isoquants and isocosts provide the information needed to determine the cost-minimizing level of inputs. The cost-minimizing level of inputs is determined by the point at which the ratio of input prices equals the ratio of marginal products for the various inputs.

Finally, we showed how economies of scale, economies of scope, and cost complementarities influence the level and mix of outputs produced by single- and multiproduct firms. In the next chapter we will look at the acquisition of inputs. We will see how managers can use spot markets, contracts, or vertical integration to efficiently obtain the inputs needed to produce their desired mix of outputs.

KEY TERMS AND CONCEPTS

average fixed cost (*AFC*)
average product (*AP*)
average total cost (*ATC*)
average variable cost (*AVC*)
capital
Cobb-Douglas production function
constant returns to scale
cost complementarity
cost function
cost minimization
cubic cost function
decreasing (or diminishing) marginal
  returns
diminishing marginal rate of technical
  substitution
diseconomies of scale
economies of scale
economies of scope
fixed costs
fixed factors of production
increasing marginal returns
isocost line
isoquant
labor

Leontief (or fixed proportions)
  production function
linear production function
long run
long-run average cost curve
marginal (incremental) cost (*MC*)
marginal product (*MP*)
marginal rate of technical substitution
  (*MRTS*)
multiproduct cost function
negative marginal returns
optimal input substitution
patent
production function
profit-maximizing input usage
short run
short-run cost function
sunk costs
total cost
total product (*TP*)
value marginal product
variable costs
variable factors of production

END-OF-CHAPTER PROBLEMS BY LEARNING OBJECTIVE

Every end-of-chapter problem addresses at least one learning objective. Below is a nonexhaustive sample of end-of-chapter problems for each learning objective.

LO1 Explain alternative ways of measuring the productivity of inputs and the role of the manager in the production process.

Try these problems: 1, 13

LO2 Calculate input demand and the cost-minimizing combination of inputs and use isoquant analysis to illustrate optimal input substitution.

Try these problems: 5, 10

LO3 Calculate a cost function from a production function and explain how economic costs differ from accounting costs.

Try these problems: 15, 22

LO4 Explain the difference between and the economic relevance of fixed costs, sunk costs, variable costs, and marginal costs.

Try these problems: 4, 17

LO5 Calculate average and marginal costs from algebraic or tabular cost data and illustrate the relationship between average and marginal costs.

Try these problems: 3, 6

LO6 Distinguish between short-run and long-run production decisions and illustrate their impact on costs and economies of scale.

Try these problems: 2, 18

LO7 Conclude whether a multiple-output production process exhibits economies of scope or cost complementarities and explain their significance for managerial decisions.

Try these problems: 7, 21

CONCEPTUAL AND COMPUTATIONAL QUESTIONS

connect
|ECONOMICS

1. A firm can manufacture a product according to the production function
    $$Q = F(K, L) = K^{3/4}L^{1/4}$$
    a. Calculate the average product of labor, AP_L, when the level of capital is fixed at 81 units and the firm uses 16 units of labor. How does the average product of labor change when the firm uses 256 units of labor?
    b. Find an expression for the marginal product of labor, MP_L, when the amount of capital is fixed at 81 units. Then, illustrate that the marginal product of labor depends on the amount of labor hired by calculating the marginal product of labor for 16 and 81 units of labor.
    c. Suppose capital is fixed at 81 units. If the firm can sell its output at a price of $200 per unit and can hire labor at $50 per unit, how many units of labor should the firm hire in order to maximize profits?

2. A firm's product sells for $4 per unit in a highly competitive market. The firm produces output using capital (which it rents at $25 per hour) and labor (which is paid a wage of $30 per hour under a contract for 20 hours of labor services). Complete the following table and use that information to answer these questions.
    a. Identify the fixed and variable inputs.
    b. What are the firm's fixed costs?
    c. What is the variable cost of producing 475 units of output?
    d. How many units of the variable input should be used to maximize profits?
    e. What are the maximum profits this firm can earn?
    f. Over what range of the variable input usage do increasing marginal returns exist?
    g. Over what range of the variable input usage do decreasing marginal returns exist?
    h. Over what range of input usage do negative marginal returns exist?

K	L	Q	MP$_K$	AP$_K$	AP$_L$	VMP$_K$
0	20	0				
1	20	50				
2	20	150				
3	20	300				
4	20	400				
5	20	450				
6	20	475				
7	20	475				
8	20	450				
9	20	400				
10	20	300				
11	20	150				

3. Explain the difference between the law of diminishing marginal returns and the law of diminishing marginal rate of technical substitution.

4. An economist estimated that the cost function of a single-product firm is

$$C(Q) = 100 + 20Q + 15Q^2 + 10Q^3$$

Based on this information, determine:

a. The fixed cost of producing 10 units of output.

b. The variable cost of producing 10 units of output.

c. The total cost of producing 10 units of output.

d. The average fixed cost of producing 10 units of output.

e. The average variable cost of producing 10 units of output.

f. The average total cost of producing 10 units of output.

g. The marginal cost when $Q = 10$.

5. A manager hires labor and rents capital equipment in a very competitive market. Currently the wage rate is $12 per hour and capital is rented at $8 per hour. If the marginal product of labor is 60 units of output per hour and the marginal product of capital is 45 units of output per hour, is the firm using the cost-minimizing combination of labor and capital? If not, should the firm increase or decrease the amount of capital used in its production process?

6. A firm's fixed costs for 0 units of output and its average total cost of producing different output levels are summarized in the table below. Complete the table to find the fixed cost, variable cost, total cost, average fixed cost, average variable cost, and marginal cost at all relevant levels of output.

Q	FC	VC	TC	AFC	AVC	ATC	MC
0	$15,000					–	
100						300	
200						200	
300						175	
400						225	
500						325	
600						400	

7. A multiproduct firm's cost function was recently estimated as
$$C(Q_1, Q_2) = 90 - 0.5Q_1Q_2 + 0.4Q_1^2 + 0.3Q_2^2$$

   a. Are there economies of scope in producing 10 units of product 1 and 10 units of product 2?

   b. Are there cost complementarities in producing products 1 and 2?

   c. Suppose the division selling product 2 is floundering and another company has made an offer to buy the exclusive rights to produce product 2. How would the sale of the rights to produce product 2 change the firm's marginal cost of producing product 1?

8. Explain the difference between fixed costs, sunk costs, and variable costs. Provide an example that illustrates that these costs are, in general, different.

9. A firm produces output according to a production function $Q = F(K,L) = $ min $\{4K, 8L\}$.

   a. How much output is produced when $K = 2$ and $L = 3$?

   b. If the wage rate is $60 per hour and the rental rate on capital is $20 per hour, what is the cost-minimizing input mix for producing 8 units of output?

   c. How does your answer to part b change if the wage rate decreases to $20 per hour but the rental rate on capital remains at $20 per hour?

10. A firm produces output according to the production function $Q = F(K,L) = 4K + 8L$.

   a. How much output is produced when $K = 2$ and $L = 3$?

   b. If the wage rate is $60 per hour and the rental rate on capital is $20 per hour, what is the cost-minimizing input mix for producing 32 units of output?

   c. How does your answer to part b change if the wage rate decreases to $20 per hour but the rental rate on capital remains at $20 per hour?

PROBLEMS AND APPLICATIONS

11. In an effort to stop the migration of many of the automobile manufacturing facilities from the Detroit area, Detroit's city council is considering passing a statute that would give investment tax credits to auto manufacturers. Effectively, this would reduce auto manufacturers' costs of using capital and high-tech equipment in their production processes. On the evening of the vote, local union officials voiced serious objections to this statute. Outline the basis of the argument most likely used by union officials. (*Hint:* Consider the impact that the statute would have on auto manufacturers' capital-to-labor ratio.) As a representative for one of the automakers, how would you counter the union officials' argument?

12. You were recently hired to replace the manager of the Roller Division at a major conveyor-manufacturing firm, despite the manager's strong external sales record. Roller manufacturing is relatively simple, requiring only labor and a machine that cuts and crimps rollers. As you begin reviewing the company's production information, you learn that labor is paid $12 per hour

and the last worker hired produced 80 rollers per hour. The company rents roller cutters and crimping machines for $15 per hour, and the marginal product of capital is 110 rollers per hour. What do you think the previous manager could have done to keep his job?

13. You are a manager for Herman Miller, a major manufacturer of office furniture. You recently hired an economist to work with engineering and operations experts to estimate the production function for a particular line of office chairs. The report from these experts indicates that the relevant production function is

$$Q = 2(K)^{1/2}(L)^{1/2}$$

where K represents capital equipment and L is labor. Your company has already spent a total of $8,000 on the 9 units of capital equipment it owns. Due to current economic conditions, the company does not have the flexibility needed to acquire additional equipment. If workers at the firm are paid a competitive wage of $120 per day and chairs can be sold for $400 each, what is your profit-maximizing level of output and labor usage? What is your maximum profit?

14. Recently, the Boeing Commercial Airline Group (BCAG) recorded orders for more than 15,000 jetliners and delivered more than 13,000 airplanes. To maintain its output volume, this Boeing division combines efforts of capital and more than 90,000 workers. Suppose the European company, Airbus, enjoys a similar production technology and produces a similar number of aircraft, but that labor costs (including fringe benefits) are higher in Europe than in the United States. Would you expect workers at Airbus to have the same marginal product as workers at Boeing? Explain carefully.

15. You are a manager at Glass Inc.—a mirror and window supplier. Recently, you conducted a study of the production process for your single-side encapsulated window. The results from the study are summarized below, and are based on the eight units of capital currently available at your plant. Workers are paid $60 per unit, per unit capital costs are $20, and your encapsulated windows sell for $12 each. Given this information, optimize your human resource and production decisions. Do you anticipate earning a profit or a loss? Explain carefully.

Labor	Output
0	0
1	10
2	30
3	60
4	80
5	90
6	95
7	95
8	90
9	80
10	60
11	30

16. The World of Videos operates a retail store that rents movie videos. For each of the last 10 years, World of Videos has consistently earned profits exceeding $30,000 per year. The store is located on prime real estate in a college town. World of Videos pays $2,400 per month in rent for its building, but it uses only 50 percent of the square footage rented for video rental purposes. The other portion of rented space is essentially vacant. Noticing that World of Videos only occupies a portion of the building, a real estate agent told the owner of World of Videos that she could add $1,500 per month to her firm's profits by renting out the unused portion of the store. While the prospect of adding an additional $1,500 to World of Videos's bottom line was enticing, the owner was also contemplating using the additional space to rent video games. What is the opportunity cost of using the unused portion of the building for video game rentals?

17. A local restaurateur who had been running a profitable business for many years recently purchased a three-way liquor license. This license gives the owner the legal right to sell beer, wine, and spirits in her restaurant. The cost of obtaining the three-way license was about $90,000, since only 300 such licenses are issued by the state. While the license is transferable, only $75,000 is refundable if the owner chooses not to use the license. After selling alcoholic beverages for about one year, the restaurateur came to the realization that she was losing dinner customers and that her profitable restaurant was turning into a noisy, unprofitable bar. Subsequently, she spent about $8,000 placing advertisements in various newspapers and restaurant magazines across the state offering to sell the license for $80,000. After a long wait, she finally received one offer to purchase her license for $77,000. What is your opinion of the restaurateur's decisions? Would you recommend that she accept the $77,000 offer?

18. In the wake of the energy crisis in California, many electricity generating facilities across the nation are reassessing their projections of future demand

Average Total Cost for Various Plant Sizes

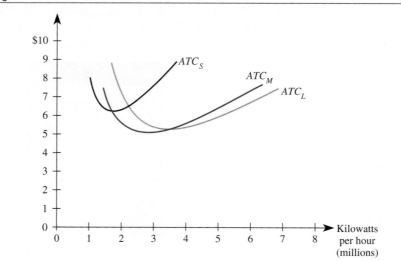

and capacity for electricity in their respective markets. As a manager at Florida Power & Light Company, you are in charge of determining the optimal size of two electricity generating facilities. The accompanying figure on the previous page illustrates the short-run average total cost curves associated with different facility sizes. Demand projections indicate that 6 million kilowatts must be produced at your South Florida facility, and 2 million kilowatts must be produced at your facility in the Panhandle. Determine the optimal facility size (S, M, or L) for these two regions, and indicate whether there will be economies of scale, diseconomies of scale, or constant returns to scale if the facilities are built optimally.

19. The A-1 Corporation supplies airplane manufacturers with preformed sheet metal panels that are used on the exterior of aircraft. Manufacturing these panels requires only five sheet metal–forming machines, which cost $500 each, and workers. These workers can be hired on an as-needed basis in the labor market at $9,000 each. Given the simplicity of the manufacturing process, the preformed sheet metal panel market is highly competitive. Therefore, the market price for one of A-1's panels is $80. Based on the production data in the accompanying table, how many workers should A-1 hire to maximize its profits?

Sheet Metal-Forming Machines	Workers	Number of Panels Produced
5	0	0
5	1	600
5	2	1,000
5	3	1,290
5	4	1,480
5	5	1,600
5	6	1,680

20. According to *The Wall Street Journal*, Mitsubishi Motors recently announced a major restructuring plan in an attempt to reverse declining global sales. Suppose that as part of the restructuring plan Mitsubishi conducts an analysis of how labor and capital are used in its production process. Prior to restructuring Mitsubishi's marginal rate of technical substitution is 0.12 (in absolute value). To hire workers, suppose that Mitsubishi must pay the competitive hourly wage of ¥1,800. In the study of its production process and markets where capital is procured, suppose that Mitsubishi determines that its marginal productivity of capital is 0.8 small cars per hour at its new targeted level of output and that capital is procured in a highly competitive market. The same study indicates that the average selling price of Mitsubishi's smallest car is ¥1,200,000. Determine the rate at which Mitsubishi can rent capital and the marginal productivity of labor at its new targeted level of output. To minimize costs Mitsubishi should hire capital and labor until the marginal rate of technical substitution reaches what proportion?

21. Hyundai Heavy Industries Co. is one of Korea's largest industrial producers. According to an article in *BusinessWeek Online,* the company is not only the world's largest shipbuilder but also manufactures other industrial goods ranging from construction equipment and marine engines to building power plants and oil refineries worldwide. Despite being a major industrial force in Korea, several of the company's divisions are unprofitable, or "bleeding red ink" in the words of the article. Indeed, last year the power plant and oil refineries building division recorded a $105 million loss, or 19 percent of its sales. Hyundai Heavy Industries recently hired a new CEO who is charged with the mission of bringing the un-profitable divisions back to profitability. According to *BusinessWeek,* Hyundai's profit-driven CEO has provided division heads with the following ultimatum: " . . . hive off money-losing businesses and deliver profits within a year—or else resign." Suppose you are the head of the marine engine division and that it has been unprofitable for 7 of the last 10 years. While you build and sell in the competitive marine engines industry, your primary customer is Hyundai's profitable ship-building division. This tight relationship is due, in large part, to the technical specifications of building ships around engines. Suppose that in your end-of-year report to the CEO you must disclose that while your division reduced costs by 10 percent, it still remains unprofitable. Make an argument to the CEO explaining why your division should not be shut down. What conditions must hold for your argument to withstand the CEO's criticism?

22. In the aftermath of a hurricane, an entrepreneur took a one-month leave of absence (without pay) from her $5,000 per month job in order to operate a kiosk that sold fresh drinking water. During the month she operated this venture, the entrepreneur paid the government $2,500 in kiosk rent and purchased water from a local wholesaler at a price of $1.34 per gallon. Write an equation that summarizes the cost function for her operation, as well as equations that summarize the marginal, average variable, average fixed, and average total costs of selling fresh drinking water at the kiosk. If consumers were willing to pay $2.25 to purchase each gallon of fresh drinking water, how many units did she have to sell in order to turn a profit? Explain carefully.

23. You are the manager of a large but privately held online retailer that currently uses 17 unskilled workers and 6 semiskilled workers at its warehouse to box and ship the products it sells online. Your company pays its unskilled workers the minimum wage but pays the semiskilled workers $9.75 per hour. Thanks to government legislation, the minimum wage in your state will increase from $7.25 per hour to $8.15 per hour on July 24, 2013. Discuss the implications of this legislation for your company's operations and in particular the implications for your optimal mix of inputs and long-run investment decisions.

CONNECT EXERCISES

If your instructor has adopted Connect for the course and you are an active subscriber, you can practice with the questions presented above, along with many alternative versions of these questions. Your instructor may also assign a subset of these problems and/or their alternative versions as a homework assignment through Connect, allowing for immediate feedback of grades and correct answers.

CASE-BASED EXERCISES

Your instructor may assign additional problem-solving exercises (called *memos*) that require you to apply some of the tools you learned in this chapter to make a recommendation based on an actual business scenario. Some of these memos accompany the Time Warner case (pages 561–597 of your textbook). Additional memos, as well as data that may be useful for your analysis, are available online at www.mhhe.com/baye8e.

SELECTED READINGS

Anderson, Evan E., and Chen, Yu Min, "Implicit Prices and Economies of Scale of Secondary Memory: The Case of Disk Drives." *Managerial and Decision Economics* 12(3), June 1991, pp. 241–48.

Carlsson, Bo; Audretsch, David B.; and Acs, Zoltan J., "Flexible Technology and Plant Size: U.S. Manufacturing and Metalworking Industries." *International Journal of Industrial Organization* 12(3), 1994, pp. 359–72.

Eaton, C., "The Geometry of Supply, Demand, and Competitive Market Structure with Economies of Scope." *American Economic Review* 81, September 1991, pp. 901–11.

Ferrier, Gary D., and Lovell, C. A. Knox, "Measuring Cost Efficiency in Banking: Econometric and Linear Programming Evidence." *Journal of Econometrics* 46(12), October–November 1990, pp. 229–45.

Gold, B., "Changing Perspectives on Size, Scale, and Returns: An Interpretive Survey." *Journal of Economic Literature* 19(1), March 1981, pp. 5–33.

Gropper, Daniel M., "An Empirical Investigation of Changes in Scale Economies for the Commercial Banking Firm, 1979–1986." *Journal of Money, Credit, and Banking* 23(4), November 1991, pp. 718–27.

Kohn, Robert E., and Levin, Stanford L., "Complementarity and Anticomplementarity with the Same Pair of Inputs." *Journal of Economic Education* 25(1), Winter 1994, pp. 67–73.

Mills, D., "Capacity Expansion and the Size of Plants." *Rand Journal of Economics* 21, Winter 1990, pp. 555–66.

Appendix
The Calculus of Production and Costs

The Profit-Maximizing Usage of Inputs

In this section we use calculus to show that the profit-maximizing level of an input is the level at which the value marginal product of the input equals the input's price. Let P denote the price of the output, Q, which is produced with the production function $F(K, L)$. The profits of the firm are

$$\pi = PQ - wL - rK$$

PQ is the revenue of the firm, and wL and rK are labor costs and capital costs, respectively. Since $Q = F(K,L)$, the objective of the manager is to choose K and L so as to maximize

$$\pi = PF(K, L) - wL - rK$$

The first-order condition for maximizing this function requires that we set the first derivatives equal to zero:

$$\frac{\partial \pi}{\partial K} = P\frac{\partial F(K, L)}{\partial K} - r = 0$$

and

$$\frac{\partial \pi}{\partial L} = P\frac{\partial F(K, L)}{\partial L} - w = 0$$

But since

$$\partial F(K, L)/\partial L = MP_L$$

and

$$\partial F(K, L)/\partial K = MP_K$$

this implies that to maximize profits, $P \times MP_L = w$ and $P \times MP_K = r$; that is, each input must be used up to the point where its value marginal product equals its price.

The Slope of an Isoquant

In this section, we use calculus to show that the slope of an isoquant is the negative of the ratio of the marginal products of two inputs.

Let the production function be $Q = F(K, L)$. If we take the total derivative of this relation, we have

$$dQ = \frac{\partial F(K, L)}{\partial K}dK + \frac{\partial F(K, L)}{\partial L}dL$$

Since output does not change along an isoquant, then $dQ = 0$. Thus,

$$0 = \frac{\partial F(K, L)}{\partial K}dK + \frac{\partial F(K, L)}{\partial L}dL$$

Solving this relation for dK/dL yields

$$\frac{dK}{dL} = -\frac{\partial F(K, L)/\partial L}{\partial F(K, L)/\partial K}$$

Since

$$\partial F(K, L)/\partial L = MP_L$$

and

$$\partial F(K, L)/\partial K = MP_K$$

we have shown that the slope of an isoquant (dK/dL) is

$$\frac{dK}{dL} = -\frac{MP_L}{MP_K}$$

The Optimal Mix of Inputs

In this section, we use calculus to show that to minimize the cost of production, the manager chooses inputs such that the slope of the isocost line equals the MRTS.

To choose K and L so as to minimize

$$wL + rK \text{ subject to } F(K, L) = Q$$

we form the Lagrangian

$$H = wL + rK + \mu[Q - F(K, L)]$$

where μ is the Lagrange multiplier. The first-order conditions for a minimum are

$$\frac{\partial H}{\partial L} = w - \mu \frac{\partial F(K, L)}{\partial L} = 0 \qquad\qquad \text{(A–1)}$$

$$\frac{\partial H}{\partial K} = r - \mu \frac{\partial F(K, L)}{\partial K} = 0 \qquad\qquad \text{(A–2)}$$

and

$$\frac{\partial H}{\partial \mu} = Q - F(K, L) = 0$$

Taking the ratio of Equations (A–1) and (A–2) gives us

$$\frac{w}{r} = \frac{\partial F(K, L)/\partial L}{\partial F(K, L)/\partial K}$$

which is

$$\frac{w}{r} = \frac{MP_L}{MP_K} = MRTS$$

The Relation between Average and Marginal Costs

Finally, we will use calculus to show that the relation between average and marginal costs in the diagrams in this chapter is indeed correct. If $C(Q)$ is the cost function (the analysis that follows is valid for both variable and total costs, so we do not distinguish between them here), average cost is $AC(Q) = C(Q)/Q$. The change in average cost due to a change in output is simply the derivative of average cost with respect to output. Taking the derivative of $AC(Q)$ with respect to Q and using the quotient rule, we see that

$$\frac{dAC(Q)}{dQ} = \frac{Q(dC/dQ) - C(Q)}{Q^2} = \frac{1}{Q}[MC(Q) - AC(Q)]$$

since $dC(Q)/dQ = MC(Q)$. Thus, when $MC(Q) < AC(Q)$, average cost declines as output increases. When $MC(Q) > AC(Q)$, average cost rises as output increases. Finally, when $MC(Q) = AC(Q)$, average cost is at its minimum.

CHAPTER SIX

The Organization of the Firm

HEADLINE

Google Buys Motorola Mobility to Vertically Integrate

Recently, Google purchased Motorola Mobility—the recently spun-off cellular arm of Motorola—for $12.5 billion. This move marks an attempt by Google to vertically integrate into the smartphone hardware market. Industry experts note that the purchase will allow Google to build prototypes and advanced hardware devices that will help to point its software business partners in the direction Google wants to go. Google is banking on the increased coordination between its software and Motorola's hardware and the reduction in risks associated with vertical integration outweighing the costs.

If you were a decision maker at Google, would you have recommended vertical integration?

Sources: "Google Looks for Vertical Integration," *New York Times Online*, August 15, 2011; "Google Buys Motorola Mobility . . . And So Begins the Dark Ages," *Forbes Online*, August 22, 2011.

INTRODUCTION

In Chapter 5 we saw how a manager can select the mix of inputs that minimizes the cost of production. However, our analysis in that chapter left unresolved two important questions. First, what is the optimal way to acquire this efficient mix of inputs? Second, how can the owners of a firm ensure that workers put forth the maximum effort consistent with their capabilities? In this chapter, we address these two issues.[1]

Figure 6–1 illustrates why it is important to resolve these two questions. The cost function defines the minimum possible cost of producing each level of output. Point A corresponds to the situation where a firm has costs in excess of the minimum costs necessary to produce a given level of output. At point A, 10 units of output are being produced for a total cost of $100. Notice that this cost is greater than $80, which is the minimum cost necessary to produce 10 units of output. Even if the firm has the right mix of inputs, if it did not obtain them efficiently, or if workers are not expending the maximum effort consistent with their capabilities, the firm's costs will be higher than the minimum possible costs.

In this chapter we consider techniques a firm can use to ensure that it is operating on the cost function (point B in Figure 6–1) and not above it (point A). We begin by discussing three methods managers can use to obtain inputs needed in production: spot exchange, contracts, and vertical integration. To minimize costs, a

FIGURE 6–1   Producing at Minimum Cost

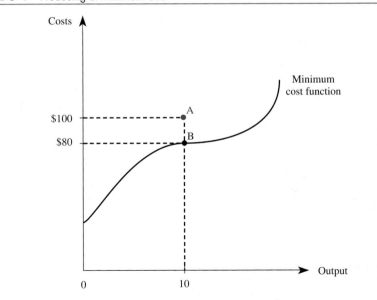

_____

[1]Other questions that remain include how much output to produce and how to price the product. These important questions will be answered in the remaining chapters of this book.

firm must not only use all inputs efficiently (the $MRTS_{KL} = w/r$ rule discussed in Chapter 5); it must use the least-cost method of obtaining the inputs. We will explain when it is optimal to acquire inputs (1) via spot exchange, (2) by writing contracts with input suppliers, or (3) by producing the inputs within the firm (vertical integration). Thus, the first part of this chapter provides managers with the information needed to acquire a given set of inputs in the optimal manner.

The second part of the chapter examines how a firm can ensure that labor inputs, including both managers and workers, put forth the maximum effort consistent with their capabilities. This is an important consideration because conflicts of interest often arise among workers, managers, and the firm's owners. For example, the manager may wish to spend the firm's resources on plush office carpeting or corporate jets, while the owners prefer that the funds be invested to increase profits, which accrue to them by virtue of their status as owners. Or workers may wish to spend most of their day gossiping in the lunchroom instead of working. When employees and owners have conflicting interests, a *principal–agent* problem is said to exist. We will see how manager and worker compensation plans can be constructed to ensure that all employees put forth their highest levels of effort.

METHODS OF PROCURING INPUTS

A manager can use several approaches to obtain the inputs needed to produce a final product. Consider the manager of a car rental company. One input needed to produce output (rental cars) is automobile servicing (tune-ups, oil changes, lube jobs, and the like). The manager has three options: (1) simply take the cars to a firm that services automobiles and pay the market price for the services; (2) sign a contract with a firm that services automobiles and, when service is needed, pay the price negotiated in the contract for that particular service; or (3) create within the firm a division that services automobiles. Each of these methods of servicing automobiles generally will imply different cost functions for producing car rental services. The manager's job is to choose the method that minimizes costs. Before we examine how to determine the best method of acquiring a given type of input, it is useful to provide a broad overview of these three methods of acquiring inputs.

Purchase the Inputs Using Spot Exchange

spot exchange
An informal relationship between a buyer and seller in which neither party is obligated to adhere to specific terms for exchange.

One method of acquiring inputs is to use spot exchange. *Spot exchange* occurs when the buyer and seller of an input meet, exchange, and then go their separate ways. If the manager of a car rental company simply takes a car to one of many firms that provide automobile servicing and pays for the services, the manager has used spot exchange to obtain automobile servicing. With the spot exchange, buyers and sellers essentially are "anonymous"; the parties may make an exchange without even knowing each other's names, and there is no formal (legal) relationship between buyer and seller.

A key advantage of acquiring inputs with spot exchange is that the firm gets to specialize in doing what it does best: converting the inputs into output. The input manufacturer specializes in what it does best: producing inputs. Spot exchange often is used when inputs are "standardized." In that case, one simply purchases the desired input from one of many suppliers that will sell the input.

Acquire Inputs Under a Contract

contract
A formal relationship between a buyer and seller that obligates the buyer and seller to exchange at terms specified in a legal document.

A *contract* is a legal document that creates an extended relationship between a particular buyer and seller of an input. It specifies the terms under which they agree to exchange over a given time horizon, say, three years. For example, the manager of a car rental firm might choose to formalize her relationship with a particular firm that services automobiles by signing a contract. Such a contract specifies the range of services covered, the price of each service, and the hours during which the cars will be serviced. As long as the service requirements for the automobiles are understood beforehand, the parties can address all the important issues in the written contract. However, if the number of services needed during the term of the contract is very large, or if some types of unanticipated breakdowns occur, the contract may be incomplete. A contract is incomplete if, for example, a car needs a new transmission and the contract does not specify the price at which the servicing firm will provide this service. Of course, this opens the door to a dispute between the two parties regarding the price of the service needed but not spelled out in the contract.

By acquiring inputs with contracts, the purchasing firm enjoys the benefits of specializing in what it does best because the other firm actually produces the inputs the purchasing firm needs. Contracts also allow the purchasing firm a greater ability to purchase "nonstandard" inputs for which there may not be many suppliers. This method of obtaining inputs works well when it is relatively easy to write a contract that describes the characteristics of the inputs needed. One key disadvantage of contracts is that they are costly to write; it takes time, and often legal fees, to draw up a contract that specifies precisely the obligations of both parties. Also, it can be extremely difficult to cover all the contingencies that could occur in the future. Thus, in complex contracting environments, contracts will necessarily be incomplete.

Produce the Inputs Internally

vertical integration
A situation where a firm produces the inputs required to make its final product.

Finally, a manager may choose to produce the inputs needed for production within the firm. In this situation the manager of the car rental company dispenses with outside service firms entirely. She sets up a facility to service the automobile fleet with her own employees as service personnel. The firm thus bypasses the service market completely and does the work itself. When a firm shuns other suppliers and chooses to produce an input internally, it has engaged in *vertical integration.*

With vertical integration, however, a firm loses the gains in specialization it would realize were the inputs purchased from an independent supplier. Moreover, the firm now has to manage the production of inputs as well as the production of the final product produced with those inputs. This leads to the bureaucratic costs associated with a larger organization. On the other hand, by producing the inputs it needs internally, the firm no longer has to rely on other firms to provide the desired inputs. This allows the firm to utilize highly "nonstandard" inputs, even those for which writing a contract with an outside supplier would be difficult.

Demonstration Problem 6–1

Determine whether the following transactions involve spot exchange, a contract, or vertical integration:

1. Clone 1 PC is legally obligated to purchase 300 computer chips each year for the next three years from AMI. The price paid in the first year is $200 per chip, and the price rises during the second and third years by the same percentage by which the wholesale price index rises during those years.
2. Clone 2 PC purchased 300 computer chips from a firm that ran an advertisement in the back of a computer magazine.
3. Clone 3 PC manufactures its own motherboards and computer chips for its personal computers.

Answer:

1. Clone 1 PC is using a contract to purchase its computer chips.
2. Clone 2 PC used spot exchange to acquire its chips.
3. Clone 3 PC uses vertical integration to obtain its chips and motherboards.

TRANSACTION COSTS

transaction costs
Costs associated with acquiring an input that are in excess of the amount paid to the input supplier.

When a firm acquires an input, it may incur costs in excess of the actual amount paid to the input supplier. These costs are known as *transaction costs* and play a crucial role in determining optimal input procurement.

The transaction costs of acquiring an input are the costs of locating a seller of the input, negotiating a price at which the input will be purchased, and putting the input to use. Transaction costs include:

1. The cost of searching for a supplier willing to sell a given input.
2. The costs of negotiating a price at which the input will be purchased. These costs may be in terms of the opportunity cost of time, legal fees, and so forth.
3. Other investments and expenditures required to facilitate exchange.

Many transaction costs are obvious. For example, if an input supplier charges a price of $10 per unit but requires you to furnish your own trucks and drivers to pick up the input, the transaction costs to your firm include the cost of the trucks and the personnel needed to "deliver" the input to your plant. Clearly, the relevant price of the input to your firm includes not only the $10 per unit but also the transaction costs of getting the input to your plant.

Some important transaction costs, however, are less obvious. To understand these "hidden" transaction costs, we must distinguish between transaction costs that are specific to a particular trading relationship and those that are general in nature. The key to this distinction is the notion of a specialized investment.

specialized investment
An expenditure that must be made to allow two parties to exchange but has little or no value in any alternative use.

A *specialized investment* is simply an investment in a particular exchange that cannot be recovered in another trading relationship. For example, suppose that to ascertain the quality of bolts, it is necessary to spend $100 on a machine that tests the bolts' strength. If the machine is useful only for testing a particular manufacturer's bolts and the investment in the machine is a sunk (and therefore nonrecoverable) cost, it is a specialized investment. In contrast, if the machine can be resold at its purchase price or used to test the quality of bolts produced by other firms, it does not represent a specialized investment.

relationship-specific exchange
A type of exchange that occurs when the parties to a transaction have made specialized investments.

When specialized investments are required to facilitate an exchange, the resulting relationship between the parties is known as a *relationship-specific exchange*. The distinguishing feature of relationship-specific exchange is that the two parties are "tied together" because of the specific investments made to facilitate exchange between them. As we will see, this feature often creates transaction costs due to the sunk nature of the specific investments.

Types of Specialized Investments

Before we examine how specialized investments affect transaction costs and the optimal method of acquiring inputs, it is important to recognize that specialized investments occur in many forms. Common examples of different types of specialized investments are provided next.

Site Specificity

Site specificity occurs when the buyer and the seller of an input must locate their plants close to each other to be able to engage in exchange. For example, electric power plants often locate close to a particular coal mine to minimize the transportation costs of obtaining coal; the output (electricity) is less expensive to ship than the input (coal). The cost of building the two plants close to each other represents a specialized investment that would have little value if the parties were not involved in exchange.

Physical-Asset Specificity

Physical-asset specificity refers to a situation where the capital equipment needed to produce an input is designed to meet the needs of a particular buyer and cannot be readily adapted to produce inputs needed by other buyers. For example, if producing a lawn mower engine requires a special machine that is useful only for producing engines for a particular buyer, the machine is a specific physical asset for producing the engines.

Dedicated Assets

Dedicated assets are general investments made by a firm that allow it to exchange with a particular buyer. For example, suppose a computer manufacturer opens a new assembly line to enable it to produce enough computers for a large government purchaser. If opening the new assembly line is profitable only if the government actually purchases the firm's computers, the investment represents a dedicated asset.

Human Capital

A fourth type of specialized investment is *human capital*. In many employment relationships, workers must learn specific skills to work for a particular firm. If these skills are not useful or transferable to other employers, they represent a specialized investment.

Implications of Specialized Investments

Now that you have a broad understanding of specialized investments and relationship-specific exchange, we will consider how the presence of specialized investments can affect the transaction costs of acquiring inputs. Specialized investments increase transaction costs because they lead to (1) costly bargaining, (2) underinvestment, and (3) opportunism.

Costly Bargaining

In situations where transaction costs are low and the desired input is of uniform quality and sold by many firms, the price of the input is determined by the forces of supply and demand. When specialized investments are not required to facilitate exchange, very little time is expended negotiating a price. The scenario differs, however, if specialized investments are required to obtain the input.

Specialized investments imply that only a few parties are prepared for a trading relationship. There is no other supplier capable of providing the desired input at a moment's notice; obtaining the input the buyer needs requires making a specialized investment before the input becomes available. Consequently, there generally is no "market price" for the input; the two parties in the relationship-specific exchange bargain with each other over a price at which the input will be bought and sold. The bargaining process generally is costly, as each side employs negotiators to obtain a more favorable price. The parties may also behave strategically to enhance their bargaining positions. For example, the buyer may refuse to accept delivery to force the seller to accept a lower price. Ultimatums may be given. The supplier may reduce the quality of the input and the buyer may complain about the input's quality through company attorneys. All of these factors generate transaction costs as the two firms negotiate a price for the input.

Underinvestment

When specialized investments are required to facilitate exchange, the level of the specialized investment often is lower than the optimal level. To see this, suppose the specialized investment is human capital. To work for a particular firm, a worker must first invest his own time in learning how to perform some task. If the worker perceives that he may not work at the firm for very long (due to being laid off or accepting another job), he will not invest as heavily in learning the task as he otherwise would. For example, if you plan to transfer to another university at the end of the semester, you will not invest very heavily in learning how to use the library facilities at your present university. The investment in learning about the library facilities is an investment in human capital specific to your present university and will have little value at another university with a completely different library setup.

Similar problems exist with other types of specialized investments. For example, if an input supplier must invest in a specific machine to produce an input used by a particular buyer (physical-asset specificity), the supplier may invest in a cheaper machine that produces an input of inferior quality. This is because the supplier recognizes that the machine will not be useful if the buyer decides to purchase from another firm, in which case the supplier will be "stuck" with an expensive machine it cannot use. Thus, specialized investments may be lower than optimal, resulting in higher transaction costs because the input produced is of inferior quality.

Opportunism and the "Hold-Up Problem"

When a specialized investment must be made to acquire an input, the buyer or seller may attempt to capitalize on the "sunk" nature of the investment by engaging in *opportunism*. To be concrete, suppose the buyer of an input must make a specific investment of $10—say, the cost of verifying the quality of a particular supplier's input. The manager knows there are many firms willing to sell the input at a price of $100, so she goes to one of them at random and spends $10 inspecting the input. Once she has paid this $10, the supplier attempts to take advantage of the specialized investment and behave in an opportunistic manner: It attempts to "hold up" the manager by asking for a price of $109—$9 more than the price charged by all other suppliers. Since the manager has already spent $10 inspecting this firm's input, she is better off paying the $109 than spending an additional $10 inspecting another supplier's input. After all, even if the other supplier did not engage in opportunistic behavior, it would cost the firm $10 + $100 = $110 to inspect and purchase another supplier's input. This is the "hold-up problem": Once a firm makes a specialized investment, the other party may attempt to "rob" it of its investment by taking advantage of the investment's sunk nature. This behavior, of course, would make firms reluctant to engage in relationship-specific investments in the first place unless they can structure contracts to mitigate the hold-up problem.

In many instances, both sides in a trading relationship are required to make specialized investments, in which case both parties may engage in opportunism. For example, suppose an automaker needs crankshafts as an input for making engines. The crankshafts are a specialized input designed for use by that particular automobile manufacturer and require an investment by the producer in highly specialized capital equipment to produce them. If the crankshaft manufacturer does not sell the crankshafts to the automaker, the automaker's investment in continuing production of the engine will be effectively worthless. Similarly, if the automobile manufacturer does not buy the crankshafts, the supplier's investment in the capital equipment is likely to be wasted as well, since the equipment is not designed to serve the needs of other automobile makers. The investments made by both parties have tied them together in a relationship-specific exchange, giving each firm a potential incentive to engage in opportunistic behavior. Once the supplier has invested in the equipment to make crankshafts, the automaker may attempt to capitalize on the sunk nature of the investment by asking for a lower

---

price. On the other hand, once the automaker reaches the stage of production where it must have crankshafts to finish the cars, the crankshaft supplier may ask for a higher price to capitalize on the sunk investment made by the automaker. The result is that the two parties spend considerable time negotiating over precisely how much will be paid for the crankshafts, thus increasing the transaction costs of acquiring the input.

OPTIMAL INPUT PROCUREMENT

Now we will examine how the manager should acquire inputs in such a way as to minimize costs. The cost-minimizing method will depend on the extent to which there is relationship-specific exchange.

Spot Exchange

The most straightforward way for a firm to obtain inputs for a production process is to use spot exchange. If there are no transaction costs and there are many buyers and sellers in the input market, the market price (say, p^*) is determined by the intersection of the supply and demand curves for the input. The manager can easily obtain the input from a supplier chosen at random by paying a price of p^* per unit of input. If any supplier attempted to charge a price greater than p^*, the manager could simply decline and purchase the input from another supplier at a price of p^*.

Why, then, would a manager ever wish to bear the expense of drafting a contract or have the firm expend resources to integrate vertically and manufacture the inputs itself? The reason is that in the presence of specialized investments, spot exchange does not insulate a buyer from opportunism, and the parties may end up spending considerable time bargaining over the price and incur substantial costs if negotiations break down. These problems will occur each time the buyer attempts to obtain additional units of the input. Also, as we noted earlier, the input purchased may be of inferior quality due to underinvestment in specialized investments needed to facilitate the exchange.

Demonstration Problem 6–2

Jiffyburger, a fast-food outlet, sells approximately 8,000 quarter-pound hamburgers in a given week. To meet that demand, Jiffyburger needs 2,000 pounds of ground beef delivered to its premises every Monday morning by 8:00 AM sharp.

1. As the manager of a Jiffyburger franchise, what problems would you anticipate if you acquired ground beef using spot exchange?
2. As the manager of a firm that sells ground beef, what problems would you anticipate if you were to supply meat to Jiffyburger through spot exchange?

Answer:

1. While ground beef for hamburgers is a relatively standardized product, the delivery of one ton of meat to a particular store involves specialized investments (in the form of dedicated assets) on the part of both Jiffyburger and the supplier. In particular, Jiffyburger would face a hold-up problem if the supplier showed up at 8:00 AM and threatened not to unload the meat unless Jiffyburger paid it "ransom"; it would be difficult to find another supplier that could supply the desired quantity of meat on such short notice. The supplier may even attempt to unload meat of inferior quality. Thus, Jiffyburger is not protected from opportunism, bargaining, and underinvestment in quality when it uses spot exchange to acquire such a large quantity of ground beef.

2. By showing up at Jiffyburger at 8:00 AM with one ton of meat, the supplier makes a specific investment in selling to Jiffyburger. Consequently, the supplier also is subject to a potential hold-up problem. Suppose Jiffyburger behaves opportunistically by asking 10 other suppliers to show up with a ton of meat at 8:00 AM too. Since each supplier would rather unload its meat at a low price than let it spoil, Jiffyburger can bargain with the suppliers to get a great deal on the meat. In this case, each supplier risks selling meat at a low price or not at all, since it is not protected from opportunism by using spot exchange.

When the acquisition of an input requires substantial specialized investments, spot exchange is likely to result in high transaction costs due to opportunism, bargaining costs, and underinvestment. Clearly, managers must consider alternatives to spot exchange when inputs require substantial specialized investments.

Contracts

Given the prospect of the hold-up problem and a need to bargain over price each time an input is to be purchased, an alternative strategy is to acquire an input from a particular supplier under an appropriately structured contract. While a contract often requires substantial up-front expenditures in terms of negotiations, attorneys' fees, and the like, it offers several advantages. First, a contract can specify prices of the input before the parties make specialized investments. This feature reduces the magnitude of costly opportunism down the road. For example, if the managers in Demonstration Problem 6–2 had written a contract that specified a price and a quantity of ground beef before the specialized investments were made, they would not have been subject to the hold-up problem. Both parties would have been legally obligated to honor the contracted price and quantity.

Second, by guaranteeing an acceptable price for both parties for an extended time horizon, a contract reduces the incentive for either the buyer or the seller to skimp on the specialized investments required for the exchange. For example, a worker who has a contract that guarantees employment with a particular firm for three years will have a greater incentive to invest in human capital specific to that firm. Similarly, if the firm knows the worker will be around for three years, it will be willing to invest in more training for the worker.

Demonstration Problem 6–3

In the real world, virtually all purchases involve some type of specialized investment. For instance, by driving to a particular supermarket, you invest time (and gasoline) that is valuable to you only if you purchase groceries at that supermarket. Why, then, don't consumers sign contracts with supermarkets to prevent the supermarkets from engaging in opportunism once they are inside the store?

Answer:

The cost of driving to another supermarket if you are "held up" is relatively low: The cashier may be able to extract an extra few cents on a can of beans, but not much more. Thus, when specialized investments involve only small sums of money, the potential cost of being held up is very low compared to the cost of writing a contract to protect against such opportunism. It doesn't make sense to pay an attorney $200 to write a contract that would potentially save you only a few cents. Moreover, when only a small gain can be realized by engaging in opportunistic behavior, the supermarket will likely not find it in its interest to hold up customers. If a supermarket attempts to take advantage of a customer's minuscule specialized investment, the customer can threaten to tell others not to ever shop at that store. In this instance, the extra few cents extracted from the customer would not be worth the lost future business. In essence, there is an implicit agreement between the two parties—not an agreement that is enforceable in a court of law, but one that is enforceable by consumers' future actions. Thus, when the gains from opportunistic behavior are small compared to the costs of writing contracts, formal contracts will not emerge. However, when the gains from opportunism are sufficiently large, formal contracts are needed to prevent opportunistic behavior.

FIGURE 6–2 Optimal Contract Length

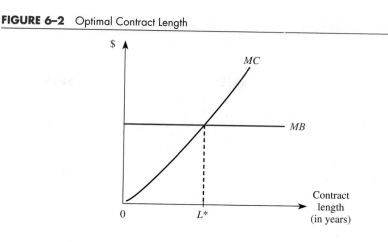

Once the decision is made to use a contract to acquire an input, how long should the contract last? The "optimal" contract length reflects a fundamental economic trade-off between the marginal costs and marginal benefits of extending the length of a contract. The marginal cost (*MC*) of extending contract length increases as contracts become longer, as illustrated in Figure 6–2. This is because as a contract gets longer, more time and money must be spent writing into the contract a larger number of increasingly hypothetical contingencies (for example, "If an Ice Age begins, the price will be . . . "). It may be easy to specify a mutually acceptable price for a contract that is to be executed tomorrow, but with a 10-year agreement it is difficult (and expensive) to write clauses that include contingencies and prices for each year of the contract. Furthermore, the longer the contract, the more locked in the buyer is to a particular seller and the greater the likelihood that some other supplier can provide the input at a lower cost in the future. In other words, the longer the contract, the less flexibility the firm has in choosing an input supplier. For these reasons, the marginal cost of contract length in Figure 6–2 is upward sloping.

The marginal benefit (*MB*) of extending a contract for another year is the avoided transaction costs of opportunism and bargaining. These benefits may vary with the length of the contract, but for simplicity we have drawn a flat *MB* curve in Figure 6–2. The optimal contract length, L^*, is the point at which the marginal costs and marginal benefits of longer contracts are equal.

The optimal contract length will increase when the level of specialized investment required to facilitate an exchange increases. To see this, note that as specialized investments become more important, the parties face higher transaction costs once the contract expires. Since these costs can be avoided by writing longer contracts, higher levels of specialized investments increase the marginal benefit of writing longer contracts from MB^0 to MB^1 in Figure 6–3. The result is an increase in the length of the optimal contract from L_0 to L_1.

The optimal contract length also depends on factors that affect the marginal cost of writing longer contracts. As an input becomes more standardized and the

FIGURE 6–3 Specialized Investments and Contract Length

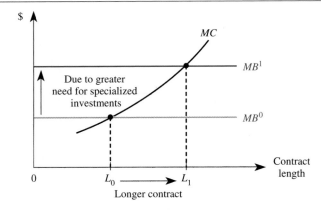

INSIDE BUSINESS 6–2

Factors Affecting the Length of Coal and Natural-Gas Contracts

Two studies have examined how specialized investments and the contracting environment affect the length of contracts. Paul Joskow studied the effect of specialized investments on the length of contracts between coal mines and electric utilities. As the importance of specialized investments increases, transaction costs due to opportunism and bargaining rise, and longer contracts are desirable. Joskow found that site specificity (the need for the utilities to locate close to the coal mine) increased the length of the contracts by an average of 12 years. Joskow also found that the degree of physical-asset specificity affected contract length. Since each generation facility uses equipment designed to burn a specific type of coal, plants designed to burn low-energy, low-sulfur western coal were tightly tied to their suppliers because there were few transportation alternatives. Plants designed to use high-energy, high-sulfur eastern coal, on the other hand, could purchase from numerous sources. Because physical-asset specificity is more pronounced in transactions involving western coal, the average contract for western coal was 11 years longer than contracts for eastern coal.

Keith Crocker and Scott Masten examined how changes in the contracting environment affected the length of contracts between owners of natural-gas wells and owners of natural-gas pipelines. Historically, these contracts were long in duration due to the specialized investments involved in laying pipes and drilling wells. During the early 1970s, however, two factors affected the cost of writing contracts. First, price controls placed on natural-gas sales by the government induced pipelines to try to compensate well owners in nonprice terms of the contracts, such as agreeing to accept delivery of the gas when they preferred not to. These nonprice agreements made contracts less efficient and increased the costs of being bound by a contract. The result was that price controls reduced contract length by an average of 14 years. Second, the increased uncertainty in the natural-gas market caused by the Arab oil embargo raised the cost of writing contracts and reduced contract length by an additional three years.

Sources: Paul Joskow, "Contract Duration and Relationship-Specific Investments: Empirical Evidence from Coal Markets," *American Economic Review* 77 (March 1987), pp. 168–85; Keith Crocker and Scott Masten, "Mitigating Contractual Hazards: Unilateral Options and Contract Length," *Rand Journal of Economics* 19 (Autumn 1988), pp. 327–43.

FIGURE 6-4 Contracting Environment and Contract Length

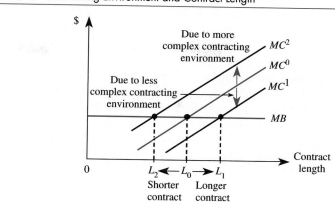

future economic environment becomes more certain, the marginal cost of writing longer contracts in Figure 6–4 decreases from MC^0 to MC^1. This decrease in the complexity of the contracting environment leads to longer optimal contracts (from L_0 to L_1). In contrast, as the input becomes more complex and the future economic environment becomes more uncertain, contracts must be made more detailed. This increase in the complexity of the contracting environment increases the marginal cost of writing longer contracts from MC^0 to MC^2 in Figure 6–4. Optimal contracts, in this case, will be shorter in duration.

As the contract length shortens due to the complexity of the contracting environment, firms must continually write new contracts as existing ones expire. Considerable resources are spent on attorneys' fees and bargaining over contract terms, and because of the complex contracting environment it is not efficient to write longer contracts to reduce these costs. Faced with such a prospect, a manager may wish to use yet another method to procure a necessary input: have the firm integrate vertically and make the input itself.

Vertical Integration

When specialized investments generate transaction costs (due to opportunism, bargaining costs, or underinvestment), and when the product being purchased is extremely complex or the economic environment is plagued by uncertainty, complete contracts will be extremely costly or even impossible to write. The only choice left is for the firm to set up a facility to produce the input internally. This process is referred to as *vertical integration* because it entails the firm moving farther up the production stream toward increasingly basic inputs. For example, most automobile manufacturers make their own fenders from sheet steel and plastics, having vertically integrated up the production stream from automobile assembly to the fabrication of body parts.

The advantage of vertical integration is that the firm "skips the middleman" by producing its own inputs. This reduces opportunism by uniting previously distinct firms into divisions of a single, integrated firm. While this strategy might seem desirable in general because it mitigates transaction costs by eliminating the market, this approach has some disadvantages as well. Managers must replace the discipline of the market with an internal regulatory mechanism, a formidable task to anyone familiar with the failure of central planning often encountered in nonmarket economies. In addition, the firm must bear the cost of setting up production facilities for producing a product that, at best, may be tangentially related to the firm's main line of business; the firm no longer specializes in doing what it does best. Because of these difficulties, vertical integration should be viewed as a last resort, undertaken only when spot exchange or contracts have failed.

The Economic Trade-Off

The cost-minimizing method of acquiring an input depends on the characteristics of the input. Whether a manager chooses spot exchange or an alternative method such as a contract or vertical integration depends on the importance of the specialized investments that lead to relationship-specific exchange. The basic questions involved are illustrated in Figure 6–5.

FIGURE 6–5   Optimal Procurement of Inputs

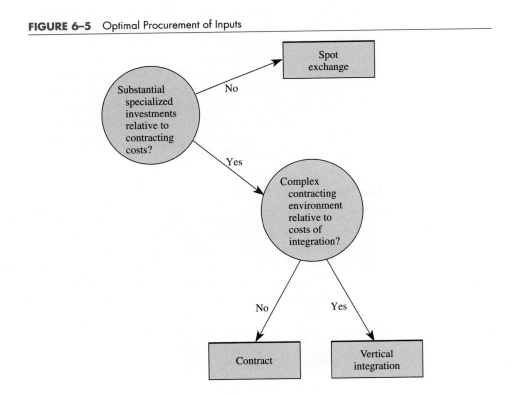

INSIDE BUSINESS 6–3

The Evolution of Input Decisions in the Automobile Industry

An interesting account of a firm moving from spot exchange to a long-term contractual relationship and finally to vertical integration is provided by the General Motors–Fisher Body relationship, which has been extensively documented by Benjamin Klein. In the early part of the 20th century, car bodies were primarily open, wooden structures built by craftspeople with fairly general skills. Thus specialized investments were relatively unimportant, and General Motors bought the bodies for its cars using spot exchange.

As the automobile industry developed, it became apparent that closed metal bodies would be a superior method of manufacturing cars. This finding, however, introduced a high degree of physical-asset specificity because it required investment in very specialized machines to stamp out the body parts. To constrain opportunism, General Motors and Fisher Body signed a 10-year contract that set the price of the car bodies and obligated General Motors to purchase all of its closed metal car bodies from Fisher Body.

Initially this agreement worked well enough to permit the parties to make the necessary specialized investments. But as time went on, it became clear that the original agreement was not nearly complete, leaving numerous opportunities for the parties to engage in opportunism. For example, the pricing formula contained in the contract permitted Fisher Body to receive a 17.6 percent profit on labor and transportation costs. This encouraged Fisher to produce with inefficient labor-intensive technologies in remotely located plants and pass on the costs of inefficiency to General Motors.

In retrospect, it appears that both General Motors and Fisher Body underestimated the difficulty of writing a contract to govern their relationship. Rather than spend time and money writing a more detailed contract, the problem was solved in 1926 when General Motors vertically integrated by purchasing Fisher Body.

Source: Benjamin Klein, "Vertical Integration as Organizational Ownership: The Fisher Body–General Motors Relationship Revisited," *Journal of Law, Economics and Organization* 4 (Spring 1988), pp. 199–213. For an alternative view suggesting that the merger was motivated out of a desire to improve coordination of production and inventories, to assure GM of adequate supplies of auto bodies, and to provide GM with access to the executive talents of the Fisher brothers, see Ramon Casadesus-Masanell and Daniel F. Spulber, "The Fable of Fisher Body," *Journal of Law and Economics* 43 (April 2000), pp. 67–104.

When the desired input does not involve specialized investments, the firm can use spot exchange to obtain the input without concern for opportunism and bargaining costs. By purchasing the input from a supplier, the firm can specialize in doing what it does best rather than spending money writing contracts or engaging in vertical integration.

When substantial specialized investments are required to facilitate exchange, managers should think twice about using spot exchange to purchase inputs. Specialized investments lead to opportunism, bargaining costs, and underinvestment, and these transaction costs of using spot exchange often can be reduced by using some other method to acquire an input. When the contracting environment is simple and the cost of writing a contract is less than the transaction costs associated with spot exchange, it is optimal to acquire the input through a contract. In this case, the optimal contract length is determined by the intersection of the marginal cost and marginal benefits of writing a longer contract, as we illustrated previously in Figure 6–2.

Finally, when substantial specialized investments are required and the desired input has complex characteristics that are difficult to specify in a contract, or when it is very costly to write into the contract all the clauses needed to protect the parties from changes in future conditions, the manager should integrate vertically to minimize the cost of acquiring inputs needed for production—provided the costs of integration are not too high. In this instance, the firm produces the input internally. The firm no longer specializes in doing what it does best, but the elimination of opportunism, bargaining, and underinvestment more than makes up for lack of specialization.

Demonstration Problem 6–4

Big Bird Air is legally obligated to purchase 50 jet engines from ERUS at the end of two years at a price of $200,000 per engine. Confident that it is protected from opportunism with this contract, Big Bird begins making aircraft bodies designed to fit ERUS's engines. Due to unforeseen events in the aerospace industry, in the second year of the contract ERUS is on the brink of bankruptcy. It tells Big Bird that unless it increases the engine price to $300,000, it will go bankrupt.

1. What should the manager of Big Bird Air do?
2. How could this problem have been avoided?
3. Did the manager of Big Bird Air use the wrong method of acquiring inputs?

Answer:

1. Big Bird is experiencing a hold-up problem because of an incomplete contract; the contract did not specify what would happen if ERUS went belly-up. ERUS claims it will go bankrupt if Big Bird does not pay a price of $300,000 for the engines, in which case Big Bird will lose its specialized investment in aircraft bodies. The manager should verify that ERUS is indeed on the brink of bankruptcy. If not, Big Bird can take ERUS to court if ERUS does not honor the contract price. If ERUS is on the verge of bankruptcy, the manager should determine how much it would cost to obtain engines from another supplier versus making them within the firm. Once the manager knows the cost of each alternative, Big Bird may wish to bargain with ERUS over how much more it will pay for the engines. This could be risky, however; the lower the price negotiated, the greater the chance ERUS will go bankrupt. New clauses must be put into the contract to protect Big Bird against ERUS's bankruptcy. The manager should especially guard against attempts by ERUS to reduce the quality of the engines in an attempt to save money. In any event, Big Bird should not spend more money drawing up a new contract and paying for ERUS's engines than it would cost to obtain them from the best alternative source.

2. This problem illustrates that when contracts are incomplete, unanticipated events can occur that lead to costly bargaining and opportunism. The problem could have been avoided had Big Bird written clauses into the contract that protected it against ERUS's going bankrupt. If this was not possible, it could have vertically integrated and produced its own engines.

3. Big Bird's manager did not necessarily choose the wrong method of acquiring engines. If it was not possible (or would have been extremely costly) to write into the

initial contract protection against ERUS's going bankrupt, and if the costs of vertically integrating would exceed the likely costs of opportunism due to an incomplete contract, the manager made the correct decision at the time. Sometimes bad things happen even when managers make good decisions. If this was not the case, either a more complete contract should have been written or Big Bird should have decided to make its own engines.

MANAGERIAL COMPENSATION AND THE PRINCIPAL–AGENT PROBLEM

You now know the principal factors in selecting the best method of acquiring inputs. Our remaining task in this chapter is to explain how to compensate labor inputs to ensure that they put forth their "best" effort. After completing this section you will better understand why restaurants rely on tips to compensate employees, why secretaries usually are paid an hourly wage, and even why textbook authors are paid royalties. We will begin, however, by examining managerial compensation.

One characteristic of many large firms is the separation of ownership and control: The owners of the firm often are distantly located stockholders, and the firm is run on a day-to-day basis by a manager. The fact that the firm's owners are not physically present to monitor the manager creates a fundamental incentive problem. Suppose the owners pay the manager a salary of $50,000 per year to manage the firm. Since the owners cannot monitor the manager's effort, if the firm has lost $1 million by year's end, they will not know whether the fault lies with the manager or with bad luck. Uncertainty regarding whether low profits are due to low demand or to low effort by the manager makes it difficult for the owners to determine precisely why profits are low. Even if the fault lies with the manager—perhaps he or she never showed up at the plant but instead took an extended fishing trip—the manager can claim it was just a "bad year." The manager might say, "You should be very glad you hired me as your manager. Had I not worked 18-hour days, your company would have lost twice the amount it did. I was lucky to keep our loss to its current level, but I am confident things will improve next year when our new product line hits the market." Since the owners are not present at the firm, they will not know the true reason for the low profits.

By creating a firm, an owner enjoys the benefits of reduced transaction costs. But when ownership is separated from control, the *principal–agent problem* emerges: If the owner is not present to monitor the manager, how can she get the manager to do what is in her best interest?

The essence of the problem is that the manager likes to earn income, but he also likes to consume leisure. Clearly, if the manager spent every waking hour on the job, he would be unable to consume any leisure. But the less time he spends on the job, the more time he has for ball games, fishing trips, and other activities that he values. The job description indicates that the manager is supposed to spend eight hours per day on the job. The important question, from the owner's point of view, is how much leisure (shirking) the manager will consume while on the job. Shirking may take the form of excessive coffee breaks, long lunch hours, leaving work early,

TABLE 6–1   Managerial Earnings and Firm Profits under a Fixed Salary

Manager's Earnings	Hours Worked by Manager	Hours Shirked by Manager	Profits of Firm
$50,000	8	0	$3,000,000
50,000	7	1	2,950,000
50,000	6	2	2,800,000
50,000	5	3	2,500,000
50,000	4	4	2,000,000
50,000	3	5	1,800,000
50,000	2	6	1,300,000
50,000	1	7	700,000
50,000	0	8	0

or, in the extreme case, not showing up on the job at all. Note that while the manager enjoys shirking, the owner wants the manager to work hard to enhance profits.

When the manager is offered a fixed salary of $50,000 and the owner is not physically present at the workplace, he will receive the same $50,000 regardless of whether he works a full eight hours (hence, doesn't shirk) or spends the entire day at home (shirks eight hours). This situation is illustrated in Table 6–1. From the point of view of the owner, the fixed salary does not give the manager a strong incentive to monitor the other employees, and this has an adverse effect on the firm's profits. For example, as Table 6–1 shows, if the manager spends the entire day on the job monitoring the other employees (i.e., making sure that they put out maximum effort), shirking is zero and the firm's profits are $3 million. If the manager spends the entire day shirking, profits are zero. If the manager shirks two hours and thus works six hours, the firm's profits are $2.8 million. Since the fixed salary of $50,000 provides the manager with the same income regardless of his effort level, he has a strong incentive to shirk eight hours. In this case the profits of the firm are zero but the manager still earns $50,000.

How can the owner of the firm get the manager to spend time monitoring the production process? You might think if she paid the manager a higher salary, the manager would work harder. But this will not work when the owner cannot observe the manager's effort; the employment contract is such that there is absolutely no cost to the manager of shirking. Many managers would prefer to earn money without having to work for it, and such a contract allows this manager to do just that.

Suppose the owner of the firm offers the manager the following *incentive contract:* The manager is to receive 10 percent of profits (gross of managerial compensation) earned by the firm. Table 6–2 summarizes the implications of such a contract. Note that if the manager spends eight hours shirking, profits are zero and the manager earns nothing. But if the manager does not shirk at all, the firm earns $3 million in gross profits and the manager receives compensation equal to 10 percent of those profits: $300,000.

Exactly what the manager does under the profit-sharing compensation scheme depends on his preferences for leisure and money. But one thing is clear: If the manager wants to earn income, he cannot shirk the entire day. The manager faces a trade-off: He can consume more leisure on the job, but at a cost of lower compensation.

TABLE 6–2 Managerial Earnings and Firm Profits with Profit Sharing

Hours Worked by Manager	Hours Shirked by Manager	Gross Profits for Firm (π)	Manager's Share of Profits (.10 × π)
8	0	$3,000,000	$300,000
7	1	2,950,000	295,000
6	2	2,800,000	280,000
5	3	2,500,000	250,000
4	4	2,000,000	200,000
3	5	1,800,000	180,000
2	6	1,300,000	130,000
1	7	700,000	70,000
0	8	0	0

For example, suppose the manager has carefully evaluated the trade-off between leisure on the job and income in Table 6–2 and wishes to earn $250,000. He can achieve this by working five hours instead of shirking all day. What is the impact of the profit-sharing plan on the owner of the firm? The manager has decided to work five hours to earn $250,000 in compensation. The five hours of managerial effort generate $2.5 million in gross profits for the firm. Thus, by making managerial compensation dependent on performance, the gross profits for the owner rise from zero (under the fixed-salary arrangement) to $2.5 million. Note that even after deducting the manager's compensation, the owner ends up with a hefty $2,500,000 – $250,000 = $2.25 million in profits. The performance bonus has increased not only the manager's earnings, but also the owner's net profits.

FORCES THAT DISCIPLINE MANAGERS

Incentive Contracts

Typically the chief executive officer of a corporation receives stock options and other bonuses directly related to profits. It may be tempting to argue that a CEO who earns over $1 million per year is receiving excessive compensation. What is important, however, is *how* the executive earns the $1 million. If the earnings are due largely to a performance bonus, it could be a big mistake to reduce the executive's compensation. This point is important, because the media often imply that it is unfair to heavily reward CEOs of major corporations. Remember, however, that performance-based rewards benefit stockholders as well as CEOs, and reducing such rewards may result in declining profits for the firm.

Demonstration Problem 6–5

You are attending the annual stockholders' meeting of PIC Company. A fellow shareholder points out that the manager of PIC earned $100,000 last year, while the manager of a rival firm, CUP Enterprises, earned only $50,000. A motion is made to lower the salary of PIC's manager. Given only this information, what should you do?

Answer:

There is not enough information to make an informed decision about the appropriate way to vote; you should ask for additional information. If none is forthcoming, you should move to table the motion until shareholders can obtain additional information about such things as the profits and sales of the two firms, how much of each manager's earnings is due to profit sharing and performance bonuses, and the like. Explain to the other shareholders that the optimal contract will reward the manager for high profits; if PIC's manager's high earnings are due to a huge performance bonus paid because of high profits, eliminating the bonus would not be prudent. On the other hand, if CUP's manager has generated larger profits for that firm than your manager has for PIC, you may wish to adjust your manager's contract to reflect incentives similar to those of the rival firm or even attempt to hire CUP's manager to work for PIC.

External Incentives

The preceding analysis focused on factors within the firm that provide the manager with an incentive to maximize profits. In addition, forces outside the firm often provide managers with an incentive to maximize profits.

Reputation

Managers have increased job mobility when they can demonstrate to other firms that they have the managerial skills needed to maximize profits. It is costly to be an effective manager; many hours must be spent supervising workers and planning production outlays. These costs represent an investment by the manager in a reputation for being an excellent manager. In the long run, this reputation can be sold at a premium in the market for managers, where other firms compete for the right to hire the best managers. Thus, even when the employment contract does not explicitly include a performance bonus, a manager may choose to do a good job of running the firm if he or she wishes to work for another firm at some future date.

Takeovers

Another external force that provides managers with an incentive to maximize profits is the threat of a takeover. If a manager is not operating the firm in a profit-maximizing manner, investors will attempt to buy the firm and replace management with new managers who will. By installing a better manager, the firm's profits will rise and the value of the firm's stock will increase. Thus, one cost to a manager of doing a poor job of running the firm is the increased likelihood of a takeover. To avoid paying this cost, managers will work harder than they otherwise would, even if they are paid only a fixed salary.

THE MANAGER–WORKER PRINCIPAL–AGENT PROBLEM

When we introduced the principal–agent problem, the owner of the firm was viewed as having different objectives from the manager. There is nothing special about the owner–manager relationship that gives rise to the principal–agent problem; indeed, there is a similar problem between the manager and the employees she or he supervises.

To see this, suppose the manager is being paid a fraction of profits and thus has an incentive to increase the firm's profits. The manager cannot be in several places at the same time and thus cannot monitor every worker even if he or she wanted to. The workers, on the other hand, would just as soon gossip and drink coffee as work. How can the manager (the principal) induce the workers (the agents) not to shirk?

Solutions to the Manager–Worker Principal–Agent Problem

Profit Sharing

profit sharing
Mechanism used to enhance workers' efforts that involves tying compensation to the underlying profitability of the firm.

One mechanism the manager can use to enhance workers' efforts is *profit sharing*—making the workers' compensation dependent on the underlying profitability of the firm. Offering workers compensation that is tied to underlying profitability provides an incentive for workers to put forth more effort.

Revenue Sharing

revenue sharing
Mechanism used to enhance workers' efforts that involves linking compensation to the underlying revenues of the firm.

Another mechanism for inducing greater effort by workers is *revenue sharing*—linking compensation to the underlying revenues of the firm. Examples of this type of incentive scheme include tips and sales commissions. Food servers usually receive a very low wage, plus tips. Tips are simply a commission paid by the person being served. If the server does a terrible job, the tip is low; if the server does an excellent job, the tip usually is higher. Similarly, car salespeople and insurance agents usually receive a percentage of the sales they generate. The idea behind all these compensation schemes is that it is difficult, if not impossible, for the manager to monitor these people's efforts, and there is uncertainty regarding what final sales will be. By making these workers' incomes dependent on their performance, the manager gives workers an incentive to work harder than they otherwise would. By working harder, they benefit both the firm and themselves.

Revenue sharing is particularly effective when worker productivity is related to revenues rather than costs. For example, a restaurant manager can design a contract whereby servers get some fraction of a tip; the tip is presumed to be an increasing function of the servers' quality (productivity). The manager of a sales firm can provide incentives to employees by paying them a percentage of the sales they generate. In contrast, a retail store that hires a security guard to prevent shoplifting will likely find revenue sharing with the security guard to be ineffective; his productivity is much more strongly related to the store's costs compared to its revenues.

One problem with revenue-based incentive schemes is that they do not provide an incentive for workers to minimize costs. For example, a food server may attempt to collect a big tip by offering the customer larger portions, free drinks, and the like, which will enhance the tip at the expense of the restaurant's costs.

Piece Rates

An alternative compensation method is to pay workers based on a *piece rate* rather than on a fixed hourly wage. For example, by paying a typist a fixed amount per page typed, the payment to the typist depends on the output produced. To earn more money, the typist must type more pages during a given time period.

A potential problem with paying workers based on a piece rate is that effort must be expended in quality control; otherwise, workers may attempt to produce quantity at the expense of quality. One advantage of revenue or profit sharing is that it reduces the incentive to produce low-quality products. Lower quality reduces sales, thus reducing compensation to those receiving revenue- or profit-sharing incentives.

For a video
walkthrough of
this problem, visit
www.mhhe.com/
baye8e

Demonstration Problem 6–6

Your boss, who just earned an MBA, finished reading Chapter 6 of a noted economics text-book. She asks you why the firm pays its secretaries an hourly wage instead of piece rates or a percentage of the firm's profits. How do you answer her?

Answer:

Incentive contracts such as piece rates and profit sharing are designed to solve principal–agent problems when effort is not observable. There is little need to provide "incentive contracts" to secretaries given the presence of bosses in the workplace. In particular, it is very easy to monitor the secretaries' effort; they usually are within the boss's eyesight, and there are numerous opportunities to observe the quality of their work (e.g., letters for the boss's signature). Thus, there is no real separation between the "principal" (the boss) and the "agent" (the secretary); the secretary's "boss" knows when the secretary "messes up" and can fire him or her if performance is consistently low. In most instances, this provides secretaries with a stronger incentive to work hard than would paying them a fraction of the profits generated by the effort of all employees in the firm.

Paying secretaries piece rates would be an administrative nightmare; it would be extremely costly to keep track of all of the pages typed and tasks performed during the course of a week. Piece rates may also encourage secretaries to worry more about the quantity instead of the quality of the work done. All things considered, hourly wages are a reasonable way to compensate most secretaries—provided their bosses are given an incentive to monitor them.

Time Clocks and Spot Checks

Many firms use time clocks to assist managers in monitoring workers. However, time clocks are generally not useful in addressing the principal–agent problem. Time clocks essentially are designed to verify when an employee arrives and departs from the job. They do not monitor effort; rather, they simply measure presence at the workplace at the beginning and end of the workday.

A more useful mechanism for monitoring workers is for a manager to engage in spot checks of the workplace. In this case, the manager enters the workplace from

INSIDE BUSINESS 6–4

Paying for Performance

An interesting study by Edward Lazear on the employment practices of the Safelite Glass Corporation documents the importance of properly structuring incentives. The company's average output per worker increased by almost 50 percent when it changed compensation from an hourly wage to a piece-rate system. Moreover, the average worker's pay increased by about 10 percent under piece-rate compensation. By more closely aligning the incentives of workers and the firm, both the firm and its employees benefited from the change.

Pay-for-performance contracts are most effective in environments where a worker's responsibilities are clearly identified and each worker's output is objectively measured. They are least effective when the measurement of individual effort is garbled or when it is not possible to write a contract to control important aspects of worker behavior. For instance, the usual benefits of pay-for-performance are mitigated when the production process requires a team of workers. In this case, workers may "shirk" in anticipation of being able to "piggyback" on other employees' hard work (this behavior is called "free riding" in the economics literature). Likewise, when contracts are incomplete, high-powered contracts may lead to dysfunctional behavior. For example, workers may focus exclusively on those aspects of their jobs where performance is rewarded.

For these reasons, the optimality and prevalence of high-powered incentive schemes like piece-rate systems vary across different types of occupations. As the accompanying table shows, piece-rate pay is more common in occupations where output is clearly measurable and quality is relatively unimportant (such as farm labor). It is much less common when quality is important or difficult to objectively measure.

The Percentage of Young Workers Paid a Piece Rate in Selected Occupations

Occupation	Percentage Paid a Piece Rate
Farm labor	16.7
Craftsmen	3.6
Clerical	1.3
Managers	0.9

Sources: Edward P. Lazear, "Performance Pay and Productivity," *American Economic Review* (December 2000), pp. 1346–61; Canice Prendergast, "The Provision of Incentives in Firms," *Journal of Economic Literature* (March 1999), pp. 7–63.

time to time to monitor workers. Spot checks allow the manager to verify not only that workers are physically present but also that worker effort and the quality of the work are satisfactory.

The advantage of spot checks is that they reduce the cost of monitoring workers. With spot checks, the manager needn't be in several places at the same time. Because workers do not know when the manager will show up, they will put forth more effort than they would otherwise, since getting caught "goofing off" may lead to dismissal or a reduction in pay. Thus, to be effective, spot checks need to be random; that is, workers should not be able to predict when the manager will be monitoring the workplace.

A disadvantage of spot checks is that they must occur frequently enough to induce workers not to risk getting caught shirking and they must entail some penalty for workers caught shirking. Spot checks work, in effect, through threat.

Performance bonuses, on the other hand, work through a promise of reward. These characteristics can have different psychological effects on workers.

ANSWERING THE HEADLINE

Smartphone software and hardware require a great deal of interoperability to work well together. This means that both the software producers and hardware manufacturers often must make substantial specialized investments. Google's purchase of Motorola Mobility gives it direct control of the specialized hardware investments made by Motorola Mobility, ensuring they will be tailored for Google's software products and avoiding any risk of hold-up. The high-tech nature of the smartphone market also makes for significant uncertainty about future products and market conditions, resulting in a complex contracting environment. Consequently, there is sound economic rationale for vertical integration, but before making such a recommendation you should verify that the expected benefits of avoided hold-up problems and quality improvements justify the costs of vertical integration.

SUMMARY

In this chapter, we examined the optimal institutional choice for input procurement and the principal–agent problem as it relates to managerial compensation and worker incentives. The manager must decide which inputs will be purchased from other firms and which inputs the firm will manufacture itself. Spot exchange generally is the most desirable alternative when there are many buyers and sellers and low transaction costs. It becomes less attractive when substantial specialized investments generate opportunism, resulting in transaction costs associated with using a market.

When market transaction costs are high, the manager may wish to purchase inputs from a specific supplier using a contract or, alternatively, forgo the market entirely and have the firm set up a subsidiary to produce the required input internally. In a fairly simple contracting environment, a contract may be the most effective solution. But as the contracting environment becomes more complex and uncertain, internal production through vertical integration becomes an attractive managerial strategy.

The chapter also demonstrated a solution to the principal–agent problem: Rewards must be constructed so as to induce the activities desired of workers. For example, if all a manager wants from a worker is for the worker to show up at the workplace, an hourly wage rate and a time clock form an excellent incentive scheme. If it is desirable to produce a high level of output with very little emphasis on quality, piece-rate pay schemes work well. However, if both quantity and quality of output are concerns, profit sharing is an excellent motivator.

KEY TERMS AND CONCEPTS

contract
dedicated assets

human capital
incentive contracts

opportunism
physical-asset specificity
piece-rate system
principal–agent problem
profit sharing
relationship-specific exchange

revenue sharing
site specificity
specialized investments
spot exchange
transaction costs
vertical integration

END-OF-CHAPTER PROBLEMS BY LEARNING OBJECTIVE

Every end-of-chapter problem addresses at least one learning objective. Below is a nonexhaustive sample of end-of-chapter problems for each learning objective.

LO1 Discuss the economic trade-offs associated with obtaining inputs through spot exchange, contract, or vertical integration.
Try these problems: 2, 12

LO2 Identify four types of specialized investments, and explain how each can lead to costly bargaining, underinvestment, and/or a "hold-up problem."
Try these problems: 4, 24

LO3 Explain the optimal manner of procuring different types of inputs.
Try these problems: 1, 9

LO4 Describe the principal–agent problem as it relates to owners and managers.
Try these problems: 6, 13

LO5 Discuss three forces that owners can use to discipline managers.
Try these problems: 15, 27

LO6 Describe the principal–agent problem as it relates to managers and workers.
Try these problems: 7, 20

LO7 Discuss four tools the manager can use to mitigate incentive problems in the workplace.
Try these problems: 7, 17

CONCEPTUAL AND COMPUTATIONAL QUESTIONS

connect
|ECONOMICS

1. Discuss the optimal method for procuring inputs that have well-defined and measurable quality specifications and require highly specialized investments. What are the primary advantages and disadvantages of acquiring inputs through this means? Give an example not used in the textbook that uses this method of procurement.

2. Discuss the optimal method for procuring a modest number of standardized inputs that are sold by many firms in the marketplace. What are the primary advantages and disadvantages of using this method to acquire inputs? Give an example not used in the textbook that uses this method of procurement.

3. Identify whether each of the following transactions involves spot exchange, contract, or vertical integration.

   a. Barnacle, Inc., has a legal obligation to purchase 2 tons of structural steel per week to manufacture conveyor frames.
   b. Exxon-Mobil uses the oil extracted from its wells to produce raw polypropylene, a type of plastic.
   c. Boat Lifts R Us purchases generic AC motors from a local distributor.
   d. Kaspar Construction—a home-building contractor—purchases 50 pounds of nails from the local Home Depot.

4. Explain why automobile manufacturers produce their own engines but purchase mirrors from independent suppliers.

5. Identify the type of specialized investment that each of the following situations requires.

   a. You hire an employee to operate a machine that only your company uses.
   b. An aerosol canning company designs a filling line that can be used only for a particular firm's product.
   c. A company builds a manufacturing facility across the street from its primary buyer.

6. Describe how a manager who derives satisfaction from both income and shirking allocates a 10-hour day between these activities when paid an annual, fixed salary of $100,000. When this same manager is given an annual, fixed salary of $100,000 and 4 percent of the firm's profits—amounting to $130,000 per year—the manager chooses to work eight hours and shirks for two hours. Explain which of the compensation schemes the manager prefers.

7. Compare the advantages and disadvantages of using spot checks/hidden video cameras in the workplace and pay-for-performance pay schemes as means to influence worker performance.

8. Discuss the impact of the following factors on the optimal method of procuring an input.

   a. Benefits from specialization.
   b. Bureaucracy costs.
   c. Opportunism on either side of the transaction.
   d. Specialized investments.
   e. Unspecifiable events.
   f. Bargaining costs.

9. Suppose the marginal benefit of writing a contract is $100, independent of its length. Find the optimal contract length when the marginal cost of writing a contract of length L is:

   a. $MC(L) = 30 + 4L$.
   b. $MC(L) = 40 + 5L$.
   c. What happens to the optimal contract length when the marginal cost of writing a contract declines?

10. Suppose the marginal cost of writing a contract of length L is $MC(L) = 20 + 5L$. Find the optimal contract length when the marginal benefit of writing a contract is:
    a. $MB(L) = 120$.
    b. $MB(L) = 180$.
    c. What happens to the optimal contract length when the marginal benefit of writing a contract increases?

PROBLEMS AND APPLICATIONS

11. During the beginning of the 21st century, the growth in computer sales declined for the first time in almost two decades. As a result, PC makers dramatically reduced their orders of computer chips from Intel and other vendors. Explain why computer manufacturers such as Dell are likely to write relatively short contracts for computer chips.

12. DonutVille caters to its retirement population by selling over 10,000 donuts each week. To produce that many donuts weekly, DonutVille uses 1,000 pounds of flour, which must be delivered by 5:00 AM every Friday morning. How should the manager of DonutVille acquire flour? Explain.

13. The manager of your company's pension fund is compensated based entirely on fund performance; he earned over $1.2 million last year. As a result, the fund is contemplating a proposal to cap the compensation of fund managers at $100,000. Provide an argument against the proposal.

14. The division of a large office services company that makes high-end copiers recently signed a five-year, $25 million contract for IT services from CGI Group, a Canadian information technology company. If you were the manager of the division, how would you justify the long-term nature of your contract with CGI Group?

15. *The Wall Street Journal* reported that Juniper Networks, Inc.—a maker of company network equipment—plans to offer its more than 1,000 employees the opportunity to reprice their stock options. Juniper's announcement comes at a time when its stock price is down 90 percent, leaving many employees' stock options worthless. How do you think Juniper's CEO justified repricing the employees' stock options to the shareholders?

16. Suppose that Honda is on the verge of signing a 15-year contract with TRW to supply airbags. The terms of the contract include providing Honda with 85 percent of the airbags used in new automobiles. Just prior to signing the contract, a manager reads that one of TRW's competitors has introduced a comparable airbag using a new technology that reduces the cost by 30 percent. How would this information affect Honda's optimal contract length with TRW?

17. *EFI*—a material handling company—pays each of its salespersons a base salary plus a percentage of revenues generated. To reduce overhead, *EFI* has switched from giving each salesperson a company car to reimbursing them

$0.35 for each business-related mile driven. Accounting records show that, on average, each salesperson drives 100 business-related miles per day, 240 days per year. Can you think of an alternative way to restructure the compensation of *EFI*'s sales force that could potentially enhance profits? Explain.

18. Teletronics reported record profits of $100,000 last year and is on track to exceed those profits this year. Teletronics competes in a very competitive market where many of the firms are merging in an attempt to gain competitive advantages. Currently, the company's top manager is compensated with a fixed salary that does not include any performance bonuses. Explain why this manager might nonetheless have a strong incentive to maximize the firm's profits.

19. Recently, a 10-year contract between Boeing Commercial Airplane Group (BCAG) and Thyssen Inc.—a distributor of raw aluminum—expired. The contract, valued at $300 million when initially signed, stemmed from Boeing's desire in the late 1990s to reduce production bottlenecks resulting from supply shortages. Declines in the demand for commercial aircraft during the past decade led some analysts to challenge BCAG's wisdom in signing such a long-term contract. Do you share this view? Explain.

20. A few years ago, the *Boston Globe* reported that the city of Boston planned to spend $14 million to convert the FleetCenter sports arena and entertainment center into an appropriate venue for the Democratic National Convention (DNC). The city engaged Shawmut Design and Construction in a contractual relationship to complete the work, which was supposed to start 48 days prior to the commencement of the DNC on July 26. However, when negotiations between Boston's mayor and the police union broke down, the Boston Police Patrolmen's Association took to the picket lines surrounding the FleetCenter and prevented construction crews from beginning the work. The *Globe* reported that "a truck attempting to deliver steel turned around after a crowd of union members stood at a chain-link gate in front of the arena, shouting 'back it up,' and 'respect the line, buddy.'" Moreover, the *Globe* reported that "On-duty police officers, who had been instructed to prevent pickets from restricting access, did not intervene." Given the tight construction schedule, construction delays reportedly cost about $100,000 per day. Identify the principal–agent problem in this situation. Did the mayor and the city of Boston face the classical "hold-up problem" or another problem? Explain.

21. According to *BusinessWeek Online,* worldwide spending on IT services and outsourcing are expected to modestly grow through the end of this decade. Growth in business-process outsourcing (BPO)—the practice of hiring a third party to administer and manage functions ranging from human resources and management training to sales, marketing, finance, and accounting—is projected to be particularly strong, reaching $200 million by the end of the decade. Competition among firms in the BPO market is already strong. Companies based in the United States include Electronic Data Services (EDS), Affiliated Computer Services, and Automated Data Processing (ADP). A

number of Indian companies, however, also provide worldwide BPO services, such as Infosys, Wipro, and Satyam Computer Services. The *BusinessWeek* article suggests that BPO can save end users anywhere from 15 to 85 percent. This contrasts with traditional IT services, which alone offer a savings range of 10 to 15 percent. International BPO service providers are particularly attractive since offshore labor offers an additional 25 to 30 percent cost savings. Furthermore, approximately 25 percent of the cost savings results from BPO firms' proprietary products. The remaining 10 to 30 percent in cost reduction accrues from consolidated operations. Suppose you are the manager of a U.S.-based company and must decide whether to outsource your human resources department. Outline arguments supporting and opposing a decision to outsource this function of your business. From a purely business standpoint, do any issues arise from contracting with an international-based versus U.S.-based BPO service firm? Explain.

22. You are a management consultant for a 30-year-old partner in a large law firm. In a meeting, your client says: "According to an article in *The New York Times,* 57 percent of large law firms have a mandatory retirement age for partners in the firm. Before they retire, partners are paid directly for the work that they do, and, as an owners, they are entitled to a share of the profits of the firm. Once they retire, partners do not receive either form of compensation. In light of this, I think we should eliminate mandatory retirement in order to gain a 'competitive advantage' in attracting high-quality lawyers to work for our firm. Of course, you are the expert." What do you recommend? Explain.

23. Automated Data Processing (ADP) provides computer software and services to a host of companies, including automobile dealerships. ADP charges dealerships a monthly lease for hardware, software, and support services, but does not charge for training the dealerships' employees. Dealerships need only pay for their employees' time and travel to ADP headquarters, where they attend "Software U" at no additional charge. Discuss the specialized investments (if any) made by an automobile dealership, its employees, and ADP—and identify two potential vulnerabilities that a dealership faces under this arrangement.

24. Andrew has decided to open an online store that sells home and garden products. After searching around, he chooses the software company Initech to provide the software for his website, since their product required the least amount of specialized investments for him to use it. They agreed upon a price of $3,000. To use Initech's software, Andrew makes $1,000 in sunk capital investments, and spends 40 hours learning how to use Initech's software, which is very different from other software packages. Both Andrew and Initech view Andrew's time as worth $25 per hour, and Initech is fully aware of the investments Andrew must make to use their product. After Andrew's investments were made, Initech came to Andrew and asked for more money. How much do you think they asked for?

25. HomeGrown is a small restaurant that specializes in serving local fruits, vegetables, and meats. The company has chosen to enter into a long-term relationship with Family Farms, a local farming operation. The two parties have decided to enter into a long-term contract, where Family Farms will supply produce to HomeGrown at specified prices and volume each year. Before signing a contract, HomeGrown is trying to decide how long the contract should be. It estimates that each year the contract covers saves the restaurant $1,000 in bargaining and opportunism costs. However, each year the contract covers also requires more legal fees. HomeGrown estimates that the number of hours required from lawyers, L, has a quadratic relationship with the number of years on the contract, so that $L = Y^2$, where Y is the number of years for the contract. If HomeGrown's lawyers charge $100 per hour, how long should the contract be?

26. Jim's diner is just about to open in Memphis, Tennessee. However, Jim is trying to decide whether he wants to offer Coke or Pepsi soda products. He determines that, to offer either product, he will have to spend $1,800 in sunk costs to purchase and install the appropriate paraphernalia, e.g., a large Coca-Cola or Pepsi sign out front. Ultimately, he chooses to offer Coke products, and agrees to pay Coke 5 cents per ounce of Coke sold for the right to use its product. After Jim makes the investments specific to his soda choice, Coke returns and asks for a fixed (one-time) fee in addition to the 5 cents per ounce. What is the most Jim should be willing to pay?

27. Recently, the owner of a Trader Joe's franchise decided to change how she compensated her top manager. Last year, she paid him a fixed salary of $65,000, and her store made $120,000 in profits (not counting payment to her top manager). She suspected the store could do much better and feared the fixed salary was causing her top manager to shirk on the job. Therefore, this year she decided to offer him a fixed salary of $30,000 plus 15% of the store's profits. Since the change, the store is performing much better, and she forecasts profits this year to be $280,000 (again, not counting the payment to her top manager). Assuming the change in compensation is the reason for the increased profits, and that the forecast is accurate, how much more money will the owner make (net of payment to her top manager) because of this change? Does the manager make more money under the new payment scheme?

CONNECT EXERCISES

If your instructor has adopted Connect for the course and you are an active subscriber, you can practice with the questions presented above, along with many alternative versions of these questions. Your instructor may also assign a subset of these problems and/or their alternative versions as a homework assignment through Connect, allowing for immediate feedback of grades and correct answers.

CASE-BASED EXERCISES

Your instructor may assign additional problem-solving exercises (called *memos*) that require you to apply some of the tools you learned in this chapter to make a recommendation based on an actual business scenario. Some of these memos accompany the Time Warner case (pages 561–597 of your textbook). Additional memos, as well as data that may be useful for your analysis, are available online at www.mhhe.com/baye8e.

SELECTED READINGS

Alchian, Armen A., and Demsetz, Harold, "Production, Information Costs, and Economic Organization." *American Economic Review* 62, December 1972, pp. 777–95.

Antle, Rick, and Smith, Abbie, "An Empirical Investigation of the Relative Performance Evaluation of Corporate Executives." *Journal of Accounting Research* 24(1), Spring 1986, pp. 1–39.

Coase, R. H., "The Nature of the Firm." *Economica,* November 1937, pp. 366–405.

Gibbons, Robert, and Murphy, Kevin J., "Relative Performance Evaluation for Chief Executive Officers." *Industrial and Labor Relations Review* 43, February 1990, pp. 30–51.

Jensen, Michael C., "Takeovers: Their Causes and Consequences." *Journal of Economic Perspectives* 1, Winter 1988, pp. 21–48.

Jensen, Michael C., and Murphy, Kevin J., "Performance Pay and Top Management Incentives." *Journal of Political Economy* 98(2), April 1990, pp. 225–64.

Klein, Benjamin; Crawford, Robert G.; and Alchian, Armen A., "Vertical Integration, Appropriable Rents, and the Competitive Contracting Process." *Journal of Law and Economics* 21(2), October 1978, pp. 297–326.

Lewis, Tracy R., and Sappington, David E. M., "Incentives for Monitoring Quality." *Rand Journal of Economics* 22(3), Autumn 1991, pp. 370–84.

Williamson, Oliver E., "Markets and Hierarchies: Some Elementary Considerations." *American Economic Review* 63, May 1973, pp. 316–25.

Winn, Daryl N., and Shoenhair, John D., "Compensation Based (Dis)incentives for Revenue Maximizing Behavior: A Test of the 'Revised' Baumol Hypothesis." *Review of Economics and Statistics* 70(1), February 1988, pp. 154–58.

Appendix
An Indifference Curve Approach to Managerial Incentives

The essence of the problem with compensation payments that are not tied to performance is depicted graphically in Figure 6–6. The manager views both leisure and income to be goods. Moreover, the manager is willing to substitute between leisure on the job (shirking) and income. This is why his indifference curve has the usual shape in Figure 6–6, where we measure the quantity of leisure consumed at the workplace on the horizontal axis and income on the vertical axis. Note that while the manager enjoys shirking, the owner does not want the manager to shirk.

When the manager is offered a fixed salary of $50,000, his opportunity set becomes the shaded area in Figure 6–6. The reason is simple: Since the owner is not physically present at the workplace, the manager will receive the same $50,000 regardless of whether he works a

FIGURE 6–6   Impact of a Fixed Salary on Managerial Behavior

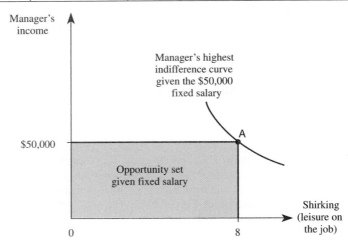

full eight hours (and hence doesn't shirk) or spends the entire day at home (and shirks eight hours). If profits are low, the owner will not know whether this is due to poor managerial effort or simply bad luck. The manager can take advantage of the separation of ownership from control by pushing his indifference curve as far to the northeast as possible until he is in equilibrium at point A, where he shirks the entire day every day of the year but still collects the $50,000.

From the viewpoint of the firm's owner, the fixed salary has an adverse effect on profits because it does not provide the manager with an incentive to monitor other employees. To see this, suppose the profits of the firm are a simple linear function of the amount of shirking done by the manager during each eight-hour period. Such a relationship is graphed in Figure 6–7. The line through point C defines the level of firm profits, which depends on the manager's degree of shirking. For example, if the manager spends the entire day on the job monitoring other employees, shirking is zero and firm profits are $3 million. If the manager spends the entire day shirking, profits are zero. If the manager shirks two hours and thus works six hours, the profits of the firm are $2.25 million. Since the fixed salary of $50,000 provides the manager with an incentive to shirk eight hours, the profits of the firm will be zero if it uses that compensation plan.

How can the owner get the manager to spend time monitoring the production process? You might think that if she paid the manager a bigger salary, the manager would work harder. But this is not correct; a larger salary would simply shift the vertical intercept of the opportunity set in Figure 6–6 above $50,000, but the equilibrium would still imply eight hours of shirking. In essence, the employment contract is such that there is absolutely no cost to the manager of shirking.

Suppose the owner offers the manager the following type of employment contract: a fixed salary of $50,000, plus a bonus of 10 percent of the profits. In this instance, if the manager spends eight hours shirking, profits are zero and the manager gets only $50,000. If the manager does not shirk at all, the firm earns $3 million in profits and the manager gets a bonus equal to 10 percent of those profits. In this instance, the bonus is $300,000. The bonus to the manager, as a function of his level of shirking, is depicted in Figure 6–7 as the line

FIGURE 6-7 A Profit-Sharing Incentive Bonus

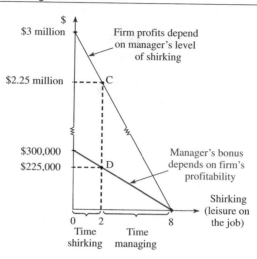

through point D. Note that when the manager shirks for two hours each day, the firm earns $2.25 million in gross profits and the manager's bonus is $225,000.

The effect of a salary-plus-bonus compensation plan on managerial behavior is illustrated in Figure 6–8. The manager's opportunity set is now given by the line through points A and B. For example, if the manager shirks eight hours, profits are zero and he receives no bonus; therefore, his income is $50,000. If the manager does not shirk at all, a bonus of $300,000 is added to his fixed salary; thus, the manager can earn $350,000 if he does not shirk.

Exactly what the manager does under the salary-plus-bonus plan depends on his preferences. But as we see in Figure 6–8, this manager can attain a higher indifference curve by

FIGURE 6-8 A Profit-Sharing Incentive Scheme Increases Managerial Effort

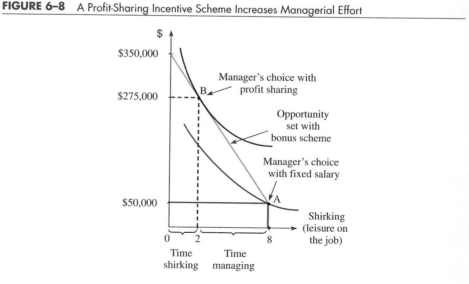

shirking less and moving from point A to point B. At point B, the manager earns $275,000 in income—$225,000 in the form of a bonus payment and $50,000 as a fixed salary. The manager clearly prefers this compensation scheme. Note also that the manager still shirks two hours each day, but this is considerably less than under the fixed-salary/no-bonus plan.

What is the impact of the bonus on the owner of the firm? In Figure 6–7, we see that when the manager shirks two hours each day, the firm earns $2.25 million in gross profits. Thus, the salary plus bonus increases the owner's gross profits from zero (under the fixed salary) to $2.25 million. The bonus has increased the welfare not only of the manager but of the owner; profits, net of managerial compensation, are

$$\$2,250,000 - \$275,000 = \$1,975,000$$

CHAPTER SEVEN

The Nature of Industry

LINE

Microsoft Puts Halt to Intuit Merger

Several years ago, the U.S. Justice Department filed suit to block software giant Microsoft's planned acquisition of financial software maker Intuit. Estimated reports placed Microsoft's share of the personal finance software market at about 20 percent, compared with Intuit's 70 percent share. After spending over $4 million on merger plans, Microsoft announced one month later that it had decided to call off the deal. In addition to the lost $4 million, Microsoft paid Intuit over $40 million for backing out of the deal.

Do you think Microsoft should have spent $4 million on merger plans in the first place? Explain.

Learning Objectives

After completing this chapter, you will be able to:

LO1 Calculate alternative measures of industry structure, conduct, and performance, and discuss their limitations.

LO2 Describe examples of vertical, horizontal, and conglomerate mergers, and explain the economic basis for each type of merger.

LO3 Explain the relevance of the Herfindahl-Hirschman index for antitrust policy under the horizontal merger guidelines.

LO4 Describe the structure-conduct-performance paradigm, the feedback critique, and their relation to the five forces framework.

LO5 Identify whether an industry is best described as perfectly competitive, a monopoly, monopolistically competitive, or an oligopoly.

INTRODUCTION

Managers of firms do not make decisions in a vacuum. Numerous factors affect decisions such as how much output to produce, what price to charge, and how much to spend on research and development, advertising, and so on. Unfortunately, no single theory or methodology provides managers with the answers to these questions. The optimal pricing strategy for an automobile manufacturer generally will differ from that of a computer firm; the level of research and development will differ for food manufacturers and defense contractors. In this chapter we highlight important differences that exist among industries. In subsequent chapters, we will see why these differences arise and examine how they affect managerial decisions.

Much of the material in this chapter is factual and is intended to acquaint you with aspects of the "real world" that are relevant for managers. You will be exposed to statistics for numerous industries. Some of these statistics summarize how many firms exist in various industries; others indicate which firms and industries are the largest and which industries tend to charge the highest markups.

The numbers presented in this chapter will change over time; the largest firm today is unlikely to be the largest firm in 40 years. Consequently, the most important thing for you to grasp in this chapter is that industries differ substantially in nature; not all industries are created equal. Our task in the remaining chapters of this book is to determine what it is about firms and industries that gives rise to systematic differences in price–cost margins, advertising expenditures, and other managerial decision variables. This will be particularly valuable to you as a manager, since you do not know in which industry you will work during the next 40 years of your career. An effective manager is able to adapt to the nature of the industry in which his or her firm competes. As the nature of the industry changes, so will the manager's optimal decisions.

MARKET STRUCTURE

market structure
Factors that affect managerial decisions, including the number of firms competing in a market, the relative size of firms, technological and cost considerations, demand conditions, and the ease with which firms can enter or exit the industry.

Market structure refers to factors such as the number of firms that compete in a market, the relative size of the firms (concentration), technological and cost conditions, demand conditions, and the ease with which firms can enter or exit the industry. Different industries have different structures, and these structures affect the decisions the prudent manager will make. The following subsections provide an overview of the major structural variables that affect managerial decisions.

Firm Size

It will come as no surprise to you that some firms are larger than others. Consider Table 7–1, which provides a snapshot of the sales of companies in a variety of different industries. Notice that there are considerable differences in the size of the largest firm in each industry. In 2012, for instance, Wal-Mart was the largest general merchandiser with sales of approximately $447 billion. In contrast, Crown Holdings was the largest producer of packaging and containers, but it had sales of only $8.6 billion.

Industries are also dynamic. Over time, changes in competitors' strategies or changes in market conditions can change a firm's relative position within an

TABLE 7–1 Largest Firms in Selected Industries

Industry	Largest Company	Sales (millions)
Advertising/Marketing	Omnicon Group	$13,873
Aerospace and Defense	Boeing	68,735
Airlines	United Continental Holdings	37,110
Apparel	Nike	20,862
Beverages	Coca-Cola	46,542
Chemicals	Dow Chemical	59,985
Computer Software	Microsoft	69,943
Computers, Office Equipment	Hewlett-Packard	127,245
Electronics, Electrical Equipment	Emerson Electric	24,234
Entertainment	Walt Disney	40,893
General Merchandisers	Wal-Mart Stores	446,950
Household and Personal Products	Procter & Gamble	82,559
Industrial Machinery	Illinois Tool Works	18,257
Information Technology Services	International Business Machines	106,916
Internet Services and Retailing	Amazon.com	48,077
Motor Vehicles and Parts	General Motors	150,276
Packaging, Containers	Crown Holdings	8,644
Real Estate	CBRE Group	5,912
Telecommunications	AT&T	126,723
Tobacco	Philip Morris International	31,097
Transportation and Logistics	C.H. Robinson Worldwide	10,336

Source: *Fortune 500* List, May 21, 2012; author's calculations.

industry—or potentially change the viability of the industry itself. For instance, Verizon Communications had the largest sales of any telecommunications firm in 2006, but in 2012, AT&T was the industry leader with sales of $127 billion. Also, in 2008 Google was the leader in Internet services and retailing, but it had been overtaken by Amazon.com by 2012.

What drives these differences in sales across industries, and why do firms' relative positions tend to change over time? Are they driven by differences or changes in market structure? Did firms become "large" by combining activities through mergers? To what extent do they stem from differences (or changes) in research and development (R&D) or advertising expenditures? The remainder of this chapter, and indeed the remainder of this book, takes a deeper look at these and other questions.

Industry Concentration

The data in Table 7–1 reveal considerable variation in the size of the largest firm in various industries. Another factor that affects managerial decisions is the size distribution of firms within an industry; that is, are there many small firms within an industry or only a few large firms? This question is important because, as we will see in later chapters, the optimal decisions of a manager who faces little competition from other firms in the industry will differ from those of a manager who works in an industry in which there are many firms.

Some industries are dominated by a few large firms, while others are composed of many small firms. Before presenting concentration data for various U.S. industries, we examine two measures that economists use to gauge the degree of concentration in an industry.

Measures of Industry Concentration

Concentration ratios measure how much of the total output in an industry is produced by the largest firms in that industry. The most common concentration ratio is the four-firm concentration ratio (C_4). The *four-firm concentration ratio* is the fraction of total industry sales produced by the four largest firms in the industry.

Let S_1, S_2, S_3, and S_4 denote the sales of the four largest firms in an industry, and let S_T denote the total sales of all firms in the industry. The four-firm concentration ratio is given by

four-firm concentration ratio
The fraction of total industry sales generated by the four largest firms in the industry.

$$C_4 = \frac{S_1 + S_2 + S_3 + S_4}{S_T}$$

Equivalently, the four-firm concentration ratio is the sum of the market shares of the top four firms:

$$C_4 = w_1 + w_2 + w_3 + w_4$$

where

$w_1 = S_1/S_T$,
$w_2 = S_2/S_T$,
$w_3 = S_3/S_T$, and
$w_4 = S_4/S_T$

When an industry is composed of a very large number of firms, each of which is very small, the four-firm concentration ratio is close to zero. When four or fewer firms produce all of an industry's output, the four-firm concentration ratio is 1. The closer the four-firm concentration ratio is to zero, the less concentrated is the industry; the closer the ratio is to 1, the more concentrated is the industry.

Demonstration Problem 7–1

Suppose an industry is composed of six firms. Four firms have sales of $10 each, and two firms have sales of $5 each. What is the four-firm concentration ratio for this industry?

Answer:
Total industry sales are $S_T = \$50$. The sales of the four largest firms are

$$S_1 + S_2 + S_3 + S_4 = \$40$$

Therefore, the four-firm concentration ratio is

$$C_4 = \frac{40}{50} = .80$$

This means that the four largest firms in the industry account for 80 percent of total industry output.

Concentration ratios provide a very crude measure of the size structure of an industry. Four-firm concentration ratios that are close to zero indicate markets in which there are many sellers, giving rise to much competition among producers for the right to sell to consumers. Industries with four-firm concentration ratios close to 1 indicate markets in which there is little competition among producers for sales to consumers.

Another measure of concentration is the Herfindahl-Hirschman index. The *Herfindahl-Hirschman index (HHI)* is the sum of the squared market shares of firms in a given industry, multiplied by 10,000 to eliminate the need for decimals. By squaring the market shares before adding them up, the index weights firms with high market shares more heavily.

Suppose firm i's share of the total market output is $w_i = S_i/S_T$, where S_i is firm i's sales and S_T is total sales in the industry. Then the Herfindahl-Hirschman index is

$$HHI = 10,000 \, \Sigma w_i^2$$

The value of the Herfindahl-Hirschman index lies between 0 and 10,000. A value of 10,000 arises when a single firm (with a market share of $w_1 = 1$) exists in the industry. A value of zero results when there are numerous infinitesimally small firms.

Herfindahl-Hirschman index (HHI)
The sum of the squared market shares of firms in a given industry multiplied by 10,000.

Demonstration Problem 7–2

Suppose an industry consists of three firms. Two firms have sales of $10 each, and one firm has sales of $30. What is the Herfindahl-Hirschman index for this industry? What is the four-firm concentration ratio?

Answer:

Since total industry sales are $S_T = \$50$, the largest firm has a market share of $w_1 = 30/50$ and the other two firms have a market share of 10/50 each. Thus, the Herfindahl-Hirschman index for this industry is

$$HHI = 10,000 \left[\left(\frac{30}{50} \right)^2 + \left(\frac{10}{50} \right)^2 + \left(\frac{10}{50} \right)^2 \right] = 4,400$$

The four-firm concentration ratio is 1, since the top three firms account for all industry sales.

The Concentration of U.S. Industry

Now that you understand the algebra of industry concentration and Herfindahl-Hirschman indexes, we may use these indexes to examine the concentration of representative industries within the United States. Table 7–2 provides concentration

TABLE 7–2 Four-Firm Concentration Ratios and Herfindahl-Hirschman Indexes for Selected U.S. Manufacturing Industries

Industry	C_4 (percentage)	HHI
Breweries	90	NA
Distilleries	70	1,519
Electronic computers	87	NA
Fluid milk	46	1,075
Furniture and related products	11	62
Jewelry (excluding costume)	29	347
Men's and boys' cut and sew apparel	27	324
Motor vehicles	68	1,744
Ready-mix concrete	23	313
Semiconductor and other electronic components	34	476
Snack foods	53	1,984
Soap and cleaning compound	47	848
Soft drinks	52	891
Women's and girls' cut and sew apparel	20	174

Source: *Concentrations Ratios: 2007*, U.S. Bureau of the Census, 2012.

Note: The U.S. Bureau of the Census approximates the HHI by using only data on the top 50 firms in the industry

ratios (in percentages) and Herfindahl-Hirschman indexes for selected U.S. industries. Notice that there is considerable variation among industries in the degree of concentration. The top four producers of electronic computers account for 87 percent of the industry's total output, suggesting considerable concentration. Distilleries, as well as the industry that makes motor vehicles, also have high four-firm concentration ratios. In contrast, the four-firm concentration ratios for the jewelry, ready-mix concrete, and women's and girls' apparel industries are low, suggesting greater competition among sellers. For example, the four largest producers of ready-mix concrete account for only 23 percent of the total market.

On balance, the Herfindahl-Hirschman indexes reported in Table 7–2 reveal a similar pattern: The industries with high four-firm concentration ratios tend to have higher Herfindahl-Hirschman indexes. There are exceptions, however. Notice that according to the four-firm concentration ratio, the motor vehicle industry is more concentrated than the snack food industry. However, the Herfindahl-Hirschman index for the snack food industry is higher than that for the motor vehicle industry.

There are several reasons that inferences drawn about an industry's level of concentration may differ, depending on whether one uses the four-firm concentration or Herfindahl-Hirschman index. First, the four-firm concentration ratio is based on the market shares of only the four largest firms in an industry, while the Herfindahl-Hirschman index is based on the market shares of all firms in an industry. In other words, the four-firm concentration ratio does not take into account the fifth largest firm, whereas the Herfindahl-Hirschman index does. Second, the HHI is based on squared market shares, while the four-firm concentration ratio is not. Consequently, the Herfindahl-Hirschman index places a greater weight on firms with large market shares than does the four-firm concentration ratio. These two factors can lead to differences in the ranking of firms by the C_4 and the HHI.

Limitations of Concentration Measures

Statistics and other data should always be interpreted with caution, and the preceding measures of concentration are no exception. For instance, the HHI indexes reported in Table 7–2 are only approximations, because the Census Bureau uses data on only the top 50 firms in the industry rather than data on all firms in the industry. In concluding our discussion of the concentration of U.S. industries, it is important to point out three additional limitations of the numbers reported in Table 7–2.

Global Markets.   The four-firm concentration ratios and Herfindahl-Hirschman indexes reported in Table 7–2 are based on a definition of the product market that excludes foreign imports. That is, in calculating C_4 and HHI, the Bureau of the Census does not take into account the penetration by foreign firms into U.S. markets. This tends to overstate the true level of concentration in industries in which a significant number of foreign producers serve the market.

For example, consider the four-firm concentration ratio for the brewery industry. Based on Table 7–2, the top four U.S. firms account for 90 percent of industry sales. However, this figure ignores beer produced by the many well-known breweries in Mexico, Canada, Europe, Australia, and Asia. The four-firm concentration ratio based on both domestic and imported beer would be considerably lower.

National, Regional, and Local Markets.   A second deficiency in the numbers reported in Table 7–2 is that they are based on figures for the entire United States. In many industries, the relevant markets are local and may be composed of only a few firms. When the relevant markets are local, the use of national data tends to understate the actual level of concentration in the local markets.

For example, suppose that each of the 50 states had only one gasoline station. If all gasoline stations were the same size, each firm would have a market share of only 1/50. The four-firm concentration ratio, based on national data, would be 4/50, or 8 percent. This would suggest that the market for gasoline services is not very concentrated. However, it does a consumer in central Texas little good to have gas stations in 49 other states, since the relevant market for buying gasoline for this consumer is his or her local market. Thus, geographical differences among markets can lead to biases in concentration measures.

In summary, indexes of market structure based on national data tend to understate the degree of concentration when the relevant markets are local.

Industry Definitions and Product Classes.   We already emphasized that the geographic definition of the relevant market (local or national) can lead to a bias in concentration ratios. Similarly, the definition of product classes used to define an industry also affects indexes.

Specifically, in constructing indexes of market structure, there is considerable aggregation across product classes. Consider the four-firm concentration ratio for soft drinks, which is 52 percent in Table 7–2. This number may seem surprisingly

The 2012 North American Industry Classification System (NAICS)

Industry classification systems provide information about different businesses in the U.S. economy. For instance, if you were interested in starting a business that sells tablets, you might want to know how many companies were already in that business. Or, you might want to know about the number of people employed in the industry and the total value of shipments. The answers to these and other questions can be found by using classification systems such as the North American Industry Classification System (NAICS).

The NAICS is a standardized classification system for the three partners of the North American Free Trade Agreement (NAFTA): Canada, Mexico, and the United States. It uses a six-digit code to classify industries into 20 different sectors. Since the first five digits of the NAICS code are the same for Canada, Mexico, and the United States, you can compare industry trends among NAFTA partners. The sixth digit of the NAICS code is country-specific; it varies to accommodate special identification needs in different countries.

The six-digit NAICS code contains varying levels of specificity about a classification. The first two digits comprise the economic sector code, the third digit comprises the subsector, the fourth the industry group, the fifth the NAICS industry, and the sixth digit designates

the national industry. The broadest classification is the two-digit code, which simply classifies firms into one of 20 possible sectors. The six-digit code provides the most specific information about a firm's classification: It places firms into a country-specific industry.

To illustrate, suppose a U.S. firm is assigned an NAICS code of 512131. As shown in the accompanying table, the first two digits *(51)* of this code tell us that the firm belongs to the sector called *Information (51)*. This is a very broad classification that includes publishing industries (newspapers, periodicals, books, and software); motion pictures and sound recording industries; TV and radio broadcasting; telecommunications; and data processing, hosting, and related services. The first three digits provide a more specific classification: The firm belongs to a subsector called *Motion Picture and Sound Recording (512)*. Looking at the first four digits further refines the nature of the firm's product: The firm belongs to an industry group called *Motion Picture and Video Industries (5121)*. Moving to the five-digit code, we see that the firm belongs to the NAICS industry called *Motion Picture and Video Exhibition (51213)*. All digits together tell us that the firm belongs to the national industry that the United States calls *Motion Picture Theaters except Drive-Ins (512131)*.

Interpreting NAICS Code

NAICS Level	NAICS Code	Description
Sector	51	Information
Subsector	512	Motion Picture and Sound Recording
Industry Group	5121	Motion Picture and Video Industries
NAICS Industry	51213	Motion Picture and Video Exhibition
National Industry	512131	Motion Picture Theaters (except Drive-Ins)

low when one considers how Coca-Cola and Pepsi dominate the market for cola. However, the concentration ratio of 52 percent is based on a much more broadly defined notion of soft drinks. In fact, the product classes the Bureau of the Census uses to define the industry include many more types of bottled and canned drinks, including birch beer, root beer, fruit drinks, ginger ale, iced tea, and lemonade.

How does one determine which products belong in which industry? As a general rule, products that are close substitutes (have large, positive cross-price elasticities) are considered to belong to a given industry class. Indeed, one might view the above-mentioned soft drinks to be close substitutes for cola drinks, thus justifying their inclusion into the industry before calculating concentration ratios.

Technology

Industries also differ with regard to the technologies used to produce goods and services. Some industries are very labor intensive, requiring much labor to produce goods and services. Other industries are very capital intensive, requiring large investments in plant, equipment, and machines to be able to produce goods or services. These differences in technology give rise to differences in production techniques across industries. In the petroleum-refining industry, for example, firms utilize approximately one employee for each $5 million in sales. In contrast, the beverage industry utilizes roughly 15 workers for each $5 million in sales.

Technology is also important within a given industry. In some industries, firms have access to identical technologies and therefore have similar cost structures. In other industries, one or two firms have access to a technology that is not available to other firms. In these instances, the firms with superior technology will have an advantage over other firms. When this technological advantage is significant, the technologically superior firm (or firms) will completely dominate the industry. In the remaining chapters, we will see how such differences in technologies affect managerial decisions.

Demand and Market Conditions

Industries also differ with regard to the underlying demand and market conditions. In industries with relatively low demand, the market may be able to sustain only a few firms. In industries where demand is great, the market may require many firms to produce the quantity demanded. One of our tasks in the remaining chapters is to explain how the degree of market demand affects the decisions of managers.

The information accessible to consumers also tends to vary across markets. It is very easy for a consumer to find the lowest airfare on a flight from Washington to Los Angeles; all one has to do is call a travel agent or surf the Internet to obtain price quotes. In contrast, it is much more difficult for consumers to obtain information about the best deal on a used car. The consumer not only has to bargain with potential sellers over the price but also must attempt to ascertain the quality of the used car. As we will learn in subsequent chapters, the optimal decisions of managers will vary depending on the amount of information available in the market.

Finally, the elasticity of demand for products tends to vary from industry to industry. Moreover, the elasticity of demand for an individual firm's product generally will differ from the market elasticity of demand for the product. In some industries, there is a large discrepancy between an individual firm's elasticity of demand and the market elasticity. The reason for this can be easily explained.

In Chapter 3 we learned that the demand for a specific product depends on the number of close substitutes available for the product. As a consequence, the demand for a particular brand of product (e.g., 7Up) will be more elastic than the demand for the product group in general (soft drinks). In markets where there are no close substitutes for a given firm's product, the elasticity of demand for that product will coincide with the market elasticity of demand for the product group (since there is only one product in the market). In industries where many firms produce substitutes for a given firm's product, the demand for the individual firm's product will be more elastic than the overall industry demand.

One measure of the elasticity of industry demand for a product relative to that of an individual firm is the Rothschild index. The *Rothschild index* provides a measure of the sensitivity to price of the product group as a whole relative to the sensitivity of the quantity demanded of a single firm to a change in its price.

Rothschild index
A measure of the sensitivity to price of a product group as a whole relative to the sensitivity of the quantity demanded of a single firm to a change in its price.

The Rothschild index is given by

$$R = \frac{E_T}{E_F}$$

where E_T is the elasticity of demand for the total market and E_F is the elasticity of demand for the product of an individual firm.

The Rothschild index takes on a value between 0 and 1. When the index is 1, the individual firm faces a demand curve that has the same sensitivity to price as the market demand curve. In contrast, when the elasticity of demand for an individual firm's product is much greater (in absolute value) than the elasticity of the market demand, the Rothschild index is close to zero. In this instance, an individual firm's quantity demanded is more sensitive to a price increase than is the industry as a whole. In other words, when the Rothschild index is less than 1, a 10 percent increase in one firm's price will decrease that firm's quantity demanded by more than the total industry quantity would fall if all firms in the industry increased their prices by 10 percent. The Rothschild index therefore provides a measure of how price sensitive an individual firm's demand is relative to the entire market. When an industry is composed of many firms, each producing similar products, the Rothschild index will be close to zero.

Table 7–3 provides estimates of the firm and market elasticities of demand and the Rothschild indexes for 10 U.S. industries. The table reveals that firms in some industries are more sensitive to price increases than firms in other industries. Notice that the Rothschild indexes for tobacco and for chemicals are unity. This means that the representative firm in the industry faces a demand curve that has exactly the same elasticity of demand as the total industry demand. In contrast, the Rothschild index for food is .26, which means that the demand for an individual food producer's product is roughly four times more elastic than that of the industry as a whole. Firms in the food industry face a demand curve that is much more sensitive to price than the industry as a whole.

TABLE 7–3 Market and Representative Firm Demand Elasticities and Corresponding Rothschild Indexes for Selected U.S. Industries

Industry	Own Price Elasticity of Market Demand	Own Price Elasticity of Demand for Representative Firm's Product	Rothschild Index
Food	−1.0	−3.8	0.26
Tobacco	−1.3	−1.3	1.00
Textiles	−1.5	−4.7	0.32
Apparel	−1.1	−4.1	0.27
Paper	−1.5	−1.7	0.88
Printing and publishing	−1.8	−3.2	0.56
Chemicals	−1.5	−1.5	1.00
Petroleum	−1.5	−1.7	0.88
Rubber	−1.8	−2.3	0.78
Leather	−1.2	−2.3	0.52

Source: Matthew D. Shapiro, "Measuring Market Power in U.S. Industry," National Bureau of Economic Research, Working Paper No. 2212, 1987.

Demonstration Problem 7–3

The industry elasticity of demand for airline travel is −3, and the elasticity of demand for an individual carrier is −4. What is the Rothschild index for this industry?

Answer:

The Rothschild index is

$$R = \frac{-3}{-4} = .75$$

Potential for Entry

The final structure variable we discuss in this chapter is the potential for entry into an industry. In some industries, it is relatively easy for new firms to enter the market; in others, it is more difficult. The optimal decisions by firms in an industry will depend on the ease with which new firms can enter the market.

Numerous factors can create a *barrier to entry*, making it difficult for other firms to enter an industry. One potential barrier to entry is the explicit cost of entering an industry, such as capital requirements. Another is patents, which give owners of patents the exclusive right to sell their products for a specified period of time.

Economies of scale also can create a barrier to entry. In some markets, only one or two firms exist because of economies of scale. If additional firms attempted to enter, they would be unable to generate the volume necessary to enjoy the reduced average costs associated with economies of scale. As we will learn in subsequent chapters, barriers to entry have important implications for the long-run profits a firm will earn in a market.

The Elasticity of Demand at the Firm and Market Levels

In general, the demand for an individual firm's product is more elastic than that for the industry as a whole. The exception is the case of monopoly where a single firm comprises the market (the demand for a monopolist's product is the same as the industry demand). How much more elastic is the demand for an individual firm's product compared to that for the market?

Table 7–4 provides an answer to this question. The second column gives the own price elasticity of the market demand for a given industry. This elasticity measures how responsive total industry quantity demanded is to an industrywide price increase. The third column provides the elasticity of demand for an individual firm's product. Thus, that column measures how responsive the quantity demanded of an individual firm's product is to a change in that firm's price.

Notice in Table 7–4 that the market elasticity of demand in the agriculture industry is −1.8. This means that a 1 percent increase in the industrywide price would lead to a 1.8 percent reduction in the total quantity demanded of agricultural products. In contrast, the elasticity of demand for a representative firm's product is −96.2. If an individual firm raised its price by 1 percent, the quantity demanded of the firm's product would fall by a whopping 96.2 percent. The demand for an individual agricultural firm's product is very elastic indeed, because there are numerous firms in the industry selling close substitutes. The more competition among producers in an industry, the more elastic will be the demand for an individual firm's product.

TABLE 7–4 Market and Representative Firm Demand Elasticities for Selected U.S. Industries

Industry	Own Price Elasticity of Market Demand	Own Price Elasticity of Demand for Representative Firm's Product
Agriculture	−1.8	−96.2
Construction	−1.0	−5.2
Durable manufacturing	−1.4	−3.5
Nondurable manufacturing	−1.3	−3.4
Transportation	−1.0	−1.9
Communication and utilities	−1.2	−1.8
Wholesale trade	−1.5	−1.6
Retail trade	−1.2	−1.8
Finance	−0.1	−5.5
Services	−1.2	−26.4

Source: Matthew D. Shapiro, "Measuring Market Power in U.S. Industry," National Bureau of Economic Research, Working Paper No. 2212, 1987.

CONDUCT

In addition to structural differences across industries, the *conduct*, or behavior, of firms also tends to differ across industries. Some industries charge higher markups than other industries. Some industries are more susceptible to mergers or takeovers than others. In addition, the amount spent on advertising and research and development tends to vary across industries. The following subsections describe important differences in conduct that exist across industries.

Pricing Behavior

Firms in some industries charge higher markups than firms in other industries. To illustrate this fact, we introduce what economists refer to as the Lerner index. The *Lerner index* is given by

Lerner index
A measure of the difference between price and marginal cost as a fraction of the product's price.

$$L = \frac{P - MC}{P}$$

where P is price and MC is marginal cost. Thus, the Lerner index measures the difference between price and marginal cost as a fraction of the price of the product.

When a firm sets its price equal to the marginal cost of production, the Lerner index is zero; consumers pay a price for the product that exactly equals the cost to the firm of producing another unit of the good. When a firm charges a price that is higher than marginal cost, the Lerner index takes on a value greater than zero, with the maximum possible value being unity. The Lerner index therefore provides a measure of how much firms in an industry mark up their prices over marginal cost. The higher the Lerner index, the greater the firm's markup. In industries in which firms rigorously compete for consumer sales by attempting to charge the lowest price in the market, the Lerner index is close to zero. When firms do not rigorously compete for consumers through price competition, the Lerner index is closer to 1.

The Lerner index is related to the markup charged by a firm. In particular, we can rearrange the formula for the Lerner index to obtain

$$P = \left(\frac{1}{1 - L}\right)MC$$

In this equation, $1/(1 - L)$ is the markup factor. It defines the factor by which marginal cost is multiplied to obtain the price of the good. When the Lerner index is zero, the markup factor is 1, and thus the price is exactly equal to marginal cost. If the Lerner index is 1/2, the markup factor is 2. In this case, the price charged by a firm is two times the marginal cost of production.

Table 7–5 provides estimates of the Lerner index and markup factor for 10 U.S. industries. Notice that there are considerable differences in Lerner indexes and markup factors across industries. The industry with the highest Lerner index and markup factor is the tobacco industry. In this industry, the Lerner index is 76 percent. This means that for each $1 paid to the firm by consumers, $.76 is markup. Alternatively, the price is 4.17 times the actual marginal cost of production.

In contrast, the Lerner index and markup factor for apparel are much lower. Based on the Lerner index for apparel, we see that for each $1 a clothing manufacturer receives, only $.24 is markup. Alternatively, the price of an apparel product is only 1.32 times the actual marginal cost of production. Again, the message for managers is that the markup charged for a product will vary depending on the nature of the market in which the product is sold. An important goal in the remaining chapters is to help managers determine the optimal markup for a product.

TABLE 7–5 Lerner Indexes and Markup Factors for Selected U.S. Industries

Industry	Lerner Index	Markup Factor
Food	0.26	1.35
Tobacco	0.76	4.17
Textiles	0.21	1.27
Apparel	0.24	1.32
Paper	0.58	2.38
Printing and publishing	0.31	1.45
Chemicals	0.67	3.03
Petroleum	0.59	2.44
Rubber	0.43	1.75
Leather	0.43	1.75

Source: Michael R. Baye and Jae-Woo Lee, "Ranking Industries by Performance: A Synthesis," Texas A&M University, Working Paper No. 90-20, March 1990; Matthew D. Shapiro, "Measuring Market Power in U.S. Industry," National Bureau of Economic Research, Working Paper No. 2212, 1987.

For a video walkthrough of this problem, visit www.mhhe.com/baye8e

Demonstration Problem 7–4

A firm in the airline industry has a marginal cost of $200 and charges a price of $300. What are the Lerner index and markup factor?

Answer:
The Lerner index is

$$L = \frac{P - MC}{P} = \frac{300 - 200}{300} = \frac{1}{3}$$

The markup factor is

$$\frac{1}{1 - L} = \frac{1}{1 - 1/3} = 1.5$$

Integration and Merger Activity

Integration and merger activity also differ across industries. *Integration* refers to uniting productive resources. Integration can occur through a merger, in which two or more existing firms "unite," or merge, into a single firm. Alternatively (and as discussed in Chapter 6), integration can occur during the formation of a firm. By its very nature, integration results in larger firms than would exist in the absence of integration.

Mergers can result from an attempt by firms to reduce transaction costs, reap the benefits of economies of scale and scope, increase market power, or gain better access to capital markets. Some mergers are "friendly" in that both firms desire to merge into a single firm. Others are "hostile," meaning that one of the firms does not desire the merger to take place.

In some instances, mergers or takeovers occur because it is perceived that the management of one of the firms is doing an inadequate job of managing the firm. In this instance, the benefit of the takeover is the increased profits that result from "cleaning house," that is, firing the incompetent managers. Many managers fear mergers and acquisitions because they are uncertain about the impact of a merger on their positions.

Economists distinguish among three types of integration, or mergers: vertical, horizontal, and conglomerate.

Vertical Integration

Vertical integration refers to a situation where various stages in the production of a single product are carried out in a single firm. For instance, an automobile manufacturer that produces its own steel, uses the steel to make car bodies and engines, and finally sells an automobile is vertically integrated. This is in contrast to a firm that buys car bodies and engines from other firms and then assembles all the parts supplied by the different suppliers. A *vertical merger* is the integration of two or more firms that produce components for a single product. We learned in Chapter 6 that firms vertically integrate to reduce the transaction costs associated with acquiring inputs.

Horizontal Integration

Horizontal integration refers to the merging of the production of similar products into a single firm. For example, if two computer firms merged into a single firm, horizontal integration would occur. Horizontal integration involves merging two or more final products into a single firm, whereas vertical integration involves merging two or more phases of production into a single firm.

In contrast to vertical integration, which occurs because this strategy reduces transaction costs, the primary reasons firms engage in horizontal integration are (1) to enjoy the cost savings of economies of scale or scope and (2) to enhance their market power. In some instances, horizontal integration allows firms to enjoy economies of scale and scope, thus leading to cost savings in producing the good. As a general rule, these types of horizontal mergers are socially beneficial. On the other hand, a *horizontal merger*, by its very definition, reduces the number of firms that compete in the product market. This tends to increase both the four-firm concentration ratio and the Herfindahl-Hirschman index for the industry, which reflects an increase in the market power of firms in the industry. The social benefits of the reduced costs due to a horizontal merger must be weighed against the social costs associated with a more concentrated industry.

When the benefits of cost reductions are small relative to the gain in market power enjoyed by the horizontally integrated firm, the government may challenge the merger. Specifically, the Federal Trade Commission (FTC) and the Antitrust Division of the U.S. Department of Justice (DOJ) are empowered to file a lawsuit to prevent firms from merging into a single firm. Under their current *Horizontal Merger Guidelines*, these antitrust authorities view industries with Herfindahl-Hirschman indexes in excess of 2,500 to be "highly concentrated" and may attempt to block a horizontal merger if it will increase the Herfindahl-Hirschman index by more than 200. It is important to stress, however, that these are merely guidelines. In the absence of evidence that a merger is likely to harm consumers, the FTC and DOJ may decide not to challenge a merger even though the HHI (and its change) exceed these thresholds. In addition, antitrust authorities sometimes permit mergers in industries that have high Herfindahl-Hirschman indexes when there is evidence of significant foreign competition, an emerging new technology, increased efficiency, or when one of the firms has financial problems.

Industries with Herfindahl-Hirschman indexes below 1500 after a merger generally are considered "unconcentrated" by the FTC and DOJ, and horizontal mergers usually are not challenged. Also, if a merger changes the Herfindahl-Hirschman index by less than 100, it usually goes unchallenged. If the Herfindahl-Hirschman index is between 1,500 and 2,500 after a merger, and the merger increases the Herfindahl-Hirschman index by more than 100, the FTC and DOJ may potentially challenge the merger. A challenge is also possible if the Herfindahl-Hirschman index exceeds 2,500 and the merger increases the Herfindahl-Hirschman index by 100 to 200. However, in these last two cases, the agencies generally rely more heavily on other factors, such as economies of scale and ease of entry into an industry, in determining whether to attempt to block a horizontal merger. In Chapter 14, we will discuss these and other government actions designed to reduce market power.

Conglomerate Mergers

Finally, a *conglomerate merger* involves the integration of different product lines into a single firm. For example, if a cigarette maker and a cookie manufacturer merged into a single firm, a conglomerate merger would result. A conglomerate merger is similar to a horizontal merger in that it involves merging final products into a single firm. It differs from a horizontal merger because the final products are not related.

The economic rationale for conglomerates is far from clear; merging completely different business lines is often counterproductive because doing so leads to a loss of specialization without offsetting beneficial synergies. Some have argued that conglomerate mergers can create synergies through improved cash flows for products with cyclical demands. Revenues derived from one product line can be used to generate working capital when the demand for another product is low. While this is a potential rationale when imperfections in capital markets prevent a firm from using financial markets to obtain working capital, engaging in a conglomerate merger for this purpose should be viewed as a last resort. Others have argued that, when the supply of superior managerial talent is tight, the overall profits of a conglomerate managed by a superior CEO can exceed the combined profits of several independent (but highly focused) firms that are managed by different CEOs with only average managerial talent.

Research and Development

Earlier we noted that firms and industries differ with respect to the underlying technologies used to produce goods and services. One way firms gain a technological advantage is by engaging in research and development (R&D) and then obtaining a patent for the technology developed through the R&D. Table 7–6 provides R&D spending as a percentage of sales for selected firms. Notice the variation in R&D spending across industries. In the pharmaceutical industry, for example, Bristol-Myers

TABLE 7–6   R&D, Advertising, and Profits as a Percentage of Sales for Selected Firms

Company	Industry	R&D as Percentage of Sales	Advertising as Percentage of Sales	Profit as Percentage of Sales
Bristol-Myers Squibb	Pharmaceuticals	19.7	4.9	15.9
Ford	Motor vehicle and parts	4.1	3.2	5.1
Goodyear Tire and Rubber	Rubber and plastic parts	2.0	2.5	Negative
Kellogg	Food	1.5	9.2	10.1
Procter & Gamble	Soaps and cosmetics	2.5	11.7	16.0

Source: Annual reports of the companies; author's calculation.

Squibb reinvested 19.7 percent of sales revenue in R&D; in the food industry, Kellogg reinvested only 1.5 percent of sales revenue in R&D.

The message for managers is clear: The optimal amount to spend on R&D will depend on the characteristics of the industry in which the firm operates. One goal in the remaining chapters is to examine the major determinants of R&D spending.

Advertising

As Table 7–6 reveals, there is also considerable variation across firms in the level of advertising utilized. Firms in the food industry, such as Kellogg, spend about 9 percent of their sales revenue on advertising. In contrast, firms in the rubber and plastic parts industry, such as Goodyear, spend about 2 percent of their sales revenue on advertising. Another goal of the remaining chapters is to examine why advertising intensities vary across firms in different industries. We will also see how firms determine the optimal amount and type of advertising to utilize.

PERFORMANCE

Performance refers to the profits and social welfare that result in a given industry. It is important for future managers to recognize that profits and social welfare vary considerably across industries.

Profits

Table 7–6 highlights differences in profits across firms in different industries. Ford's sales were among the highest in the group, yet its profits as a percentage of sales were second lowest in the group. One task in the next several chapters is to examine why "big" firms do not always earn big profits. As a manager, it would be a mistake to believe that just because your firm is large, it will automatically earn profits.

Social Welfare

Another gauge of industry performance is the amount of consumer and producer surplus generated in a market. While this type of performance is difficult to measure,

TABLE 7–7 Dansby-Willig Performance Indexes for Selected U.S. Industries

Industry	Dansby-Willig Index
Food	0.51
Textiles	0.38
Apparel	0.47
Paper	0.63
Printing and publishing	0.56
Chemicals	0.67
Petroleum	0.63
Rubber	0.49
Leather	0.60

Source: Michael R. Baye and Jae-Woo Lee, "Ranking Industries by Performance: A Synthesis," Texas A & M Working Paper No. 90–20, March 1990.

Dansby-Willig performance index
Ranks industries according to how much social welfare would improve if the output in an industry were increased by a small amount.

R. E. Dansby and R. D. Willig have proposed a useful index. The *Dansby-Willig (DW) performance index* measures how much social welfare (defined as the sum of consumer and producer surplus) would improve if firms in an industry expanded output in a socially efficient manner. If the Dansby-Willig index for an industry is zero, there are no gains to be obtained by inducing firms in the industry to alter their outputs; consumer and producer surplus are maximized given industry demand and cost conditions. When the index is greater than zero, social welfare would improve if industry output were expanded.

The Dansby-Willig index thus allows one to rank industries according to how much social welfare would rise if the industry altered its output. Industries with large index values have poorer performance than industries with lower values. In Table 7–7, for instance, we see that the chemical industry has the highest DW index. This suggests that a slight change in output in the chemical industry would increase social welfare more than would a slight change in the output in any of the other industries. The textile industry has the lowest DW index, which reveals the best performance.

Demonstration Problem 7–5

Suppose you are the manager of a firm in the textile industry. You have just learned that the government has placed the textile industry at the top of its list of industries it plans to regulate and intends to force the industry to expand output and lower the price of textile products. How should you respond?

Answer:

You should point out to government's counsel that the textile industry has the lowest Lerner index out of the 10 major industries listed in Table 7–5; only $.21 of each $1 paid by consumers is markup. Furthermore, the Dansby-Willig index for the textile industry is the lowest of nine industries listed in Table 7–7. The efficient way for government to improve social welfare is to alter output in the other industries first.

THE STRUCTURE–CONDUCT–PERFORMANCE PARADIGM

You now have a broad overview of the structure, conduct, and performance of U.S. industry. The *structure* of an industry refers to factors such as technology, concentration, and market conditions. *Conduct* refers to how individual firms behave in the market; it involves pricing decisions, advertising decisions, and decisions to invest in research and development, among other factors. *Performance* refers to the resulting profits and social welfare that arise in the market. The *structure–conduct–performance paradigm* views these three aspects of industry as being integrally related.

The Causal View

The *causal view* of industry asserts that market structure "causes" firms to behave in a certain way. In turn, this behavior, or conduct, "causes" resources to be allocated in certain ways, leading to either "good" or "poor" market performance. To better understand the causal view, consider a highly concentrated industry in which only a few firms compete for the right to sell products to consumers. According to the causal view, this structure gives firms market power, enabling them to charge high prices for their products. The behavior (charging high prices) is caused by market structure (the presence of few competitors). The high prices, in turn, "cause" high profits and poor performance (low social welfare). Thus, according to the causal view, a concentrated market "causes" high prices and poor performance.

The Feedback Critique

Today most economists recognize that the causal view provides, at best, an incomplete view of the relation among structure, conduct, and performance. According to the *feedback critique*, there is no one-way causal link among structure, conduct, and performance. The conduct of firms can affect market structure; market performance can affect conduct as well as market structure. To illustrate the feedback critique, let us apply it to the previous analysis, which stated that concentration causes high prices and poor performance.

According to the feedback critique, the conduct of firms in an industry may itself lead to a concentrated market. If the (few) existing firms are charging low prices and earning low economic profits, there will be no incentive for additional firms to enter the market. If this is the case, it could actually be low prices that "cause" the presence of few firms in the industry. In summary, then, it is a simplification of reality to assert that concentrated markets cause high prices. Indeed, the pricing behavior of firms can affect the number of firms. As we will see in subsequent chapters, low prices and good performance can occur even if only one or two firms are operating in an industry. A detailed explanation of this possibility will have to wait until we develop models for various market structures.

FIGURE 7–1   The Five Forces Framework with Feedback Effects

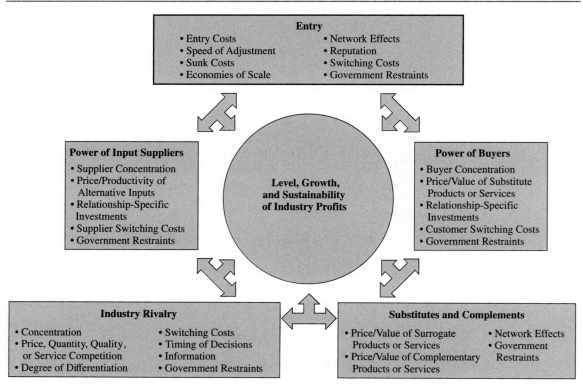

Relation to the Five Forces Framework

The structure–conduct–performance paradigm and the feedback critique are closely related to the *five forces framework* discussed in Chapter 1. Recall that the five forces framework suggests that five interrelated "forces" affect the level, growth, and sustainability of industry profits: (1) entry, (2) power of input suppliers, (3) power of buyers, (4) industry rivalry, and (5) substitutes and complements. These five forces capture elements of the structure and conduct of firms in the industry, while the level, growth, and sustainability of industry profits are elements of performance. In light of the feedback critique, the five forces framework can be modified as shown in Figure 7–1 to illustrate that these forces are interconnected.

OVERVIEW OF THE REMAINDER OF THE BOOK

In the remaining chapters of this book, we examine the optimal managerial conduct under a variety of market structures. To have some terminology that will enable us to distinguish among various types of market structures, it is useful to introduce the four basic models we will use to accomplish this goal. Recognize, however, that our discussion of these four models provides only an overview; indeed, entire chapters will be devoted to making managerial decisions in each of these situations.

Perfect Competition

In markets characterized by *perfect competition*, there are many firms, each of which is small relative to the entire market. The firms have access to the same technologies and produce similar products, so no firm has any real advantage over other firms in the industry. Firms in perfectly competitive markets do not have market power; that is, no individual firm has a perceptible impact on the market price, quantity, or quality of the product produced in the market. In perfectly competitive markets, both concentration ratios and Rothschild indexes tend to be close to zero. We will study perfectly competitive markets in detail in the next chapter.

Monopoly

A *monopoly* is a firm that is the sole producer of a good or service in the relevant market. For instance, most local utility companies are the sole providers of electricity and natural gas in a given city. Some towns have a single gasoline station or movie theater that serves the entire local market. All of these constitute local monopolies.

When there is a single provider of a good or service in a market, there is a tendency for the seller to capitalize on the monopoly position by restricting output and charging a price above marginal cost. Because there are no other firms in the market, consumers cannot switch to another producer in the face of higher prices. Consequently, consumers either buy some of the product at the higher price or go without it. In monopolistic markets, there is extreme concentration and the Rothschild index is unity.

Monopolistic Competition

In a market characterized by *monopolistic competition*, there are many firms and consumers, just as in perfect competition. Thus, concentration measures are close to zero. Unlike in perfect competition, however, each firm produces a product that is slightly different from the products produced by other firms; Rothschild indexes are greater than zero. Those who manage restaurants in a city containing numerous food establishments operate in a monopolistically competitive industry.

A firm in a monopolistically competitive market has some control over the price charged for the product. By raising the price, some consumers will remain loyal to the firm due to a preference for the particular characteristics of its product. But some consumers will switch to other brands. For this reason, firms in monopolistically competitive industries often spend considerable sums on advertising in an attempt to convince consumers that their brands are "better" than other brands. This reduces the number of customers who switch to other brands when a firm raises the price for its product.

Oligopoly

In an *oligopolistic* market, a few large firms tend to dominate the market. Firms in highly concentrated industries such as the airline, automobile, and aerospace industries operate in an oligopolistic market.

When one firm in an oligopolistic market changes its price or marketing strategy, not only its own profits but the profits of the other firms in the industry are affected. Consequently, when one firm in an oligopoly changes its conduct, other

INSIDE BUSINESS 7–3

The Evolution of Market Structure in the Computer Industry

Industries can change dramatically over time. During the course of its evolution, a given industry may go through phases that include monopoly, oligopoly, monopolistic competition, and perfect competition. For this reason, it is important to understand how to make decisions in all four environments, even if you "know" you will work for a monopoly when you graduate. The following description of the evolution in the computer industry should convince you of this fact.

In the 1960s, a few large firms produced mainframe computers for universities, scientific think tanks, and large business applications. Each computer was designed almost exclusively for a specific user, and its cost often was over $100,000. Because each computer kept its own standards, a customer whose computer needed repair was forced to go to the original manufacturer or write off the original purchase. This allowed the few companies that produced computers to act as virtual monopolists once they had a customer base. The early computer firms enjoyed high profit margins, some as high as 50 to 60 percent. These large profits induced several new firms to enter the computer market.

With entry came innovations in technology that reduced the size of mainframes, lowered the cost of production, and, because of increased competition, reduced the price to the customer. This influx of new competitors and products brought the market for computers into an oligopolistic-type structure. As a result, each firm became acutely aware of competitors and their actions. However, each firm held on to the specialized hardware and software for each user. Because of the specialized nature of the smaller machines, customers were still subject to their original purchases when it came to upgrades. However, since the price of the original machines was lower in the new environment, it was less costly to write off the original purchase and shift from one company to another. Of course, suppliers recognized this fact, which led to more vigorous competition. In the 1970s, the combination of lower prices and more competition decreased the returns in the market to 20 to 40 percent for the industry.

The 1980s brought the personal computer into many medium-size businesses that previously could not afford a computer. Along with the PC came workstations and minicomputers. Although profit margins had dropped in the 1970s, they were still high enough in the 1980s to entice new entry. The computer market of the 1980s was moving toward monopolistic competition, with a few large firms and many small firms, each producing slightly different styles of computers. Computers became affordable to many households and smaller businesses. As more firms entered the market, profit margins dropped drastically and copycat firms began opening the systems; thus, many parts became interchangeable among machines. Economic profits still were being earned, but profit margins had dropped to around 10 to 20 percent.

During the 1990s, computer makers attempted to maintain margins by differentiating their products. This tactic was of limited success, as the open systems of the 1990s led to standardized technology at virtually all levels of the computer industry. By the early 2000s, many components of PCs had become "commodities" that were bought and sold in markets resembling those with perfect competition. As a consequence, there were few dimensions other than price for PC makers to use in differentiating their products. This heightened price competition in the 2000s significantly reduced the profits of computer manufacturers, including key players such as Dell and Gateway. By the end of the first decade of the twenty-first century, competitive strains have led some firms to abandon their "direct sales" approach in favor of distributing computers through popular retailers. The strain on profits is being translated into exit and consolidation within the industry. Further changes in industry structure are almost certain over the next decade. The computer industry thus provides an enlightening look at the dynamics of industry.

Sources: Simon Forge, "Why the Computer Industry Is Restructuring Now," *Futures* 23 (November 1991), pp. 960–77; "Gateway CEO Out after Profit Miss," *Ecommerce Times,* November 26, 2006; annual reports of the companies.

firms in the industry have an incentive to react to the change by altering their own conduct. Thus, the distinguishing feature of an oligopolistic market is *mutual inter-dependence* among firms in the industry.

The interdependence of profits in an oligopoly gives rise to strategic interaction among firms. For example, suppose the manager of an oligopoly is considering increasing the price charged for the firm's product. To determine the impact of the price increase on profits, the manager must consider how rival firms in the industry will respond to the price increase. Thus, the strategic plans of one firm in an oligopoly depend on how that firm expects other firms in the industry to respond to the plans, if they are adopted. For this reason, it is very difficult to manage a firm that operates in an oligopoly. Because large rewards are paid to managers who know how to operate in oligopolistic markets, we will devote two chapters to an analysis of managerial decisions in such markets.

ANSWERING THE HEADLINE

Given that Microsoft was unwilling to fight the battle in court, the safe strategy would have been not to spend $4 million on the merger plans in the first place. Since Microsoft's share of the financial software market was 20 percent and Intuit's was 70 percent, Microsoft should have realized that the merger would be heavily scrutinized by antitrust authorities and that strong justifications would be needed to overcome the presumption that the merger would harm consumers. As we learned in this chapter, the FTC and DOJ *Horizontal Merger Guidelines* suggest that U.S. antitrust authorities are likely to challenge a merger when the relevant Herfindahl-Hirschman index is greater than 2,500 and the resulting increase in the index as a result of the merger is more than 200. Based on the reported market shares of Microsoft and Intuit, the Herfindahl-Hirschman index for the personal finance software market was at least 5,300 before the proposed merger and would have increased to at least 8,100 after the merger. Thus, it seems that Microsoft should have realized that the Justice Department would attempt to block the merger. Spending $4 million attempting to justify the merger on technological or efficiency grounds was a gamble that did not pay off for Microsoft.

SUMMARY

This chapter reveals that different industries have different market structures and require different types of managerial decisions. The structure of an industry, and therefore the job of the manager, is dependent on the number of firms in the industry, the structure of demand and costs, the availability of information, and the behavior of other firms in the industry.

The four-firm concentration ratio is one measure of market structure. If the ratio equals one, the industry is a monopoly or oligopoly; if it is zero, the industry is competitive. Another measure of market structure is the Herfindahl-Hirschman index (HHI), which can range from 10,000 for a monopoly to zero for a perfectly competitive industry. Of course, these indexes must be used in conjunction with other information, including whether the market is local and whether the firm competes with foreign firms.

Other summary statistics include the Lerner index, the Rothschild index, and the Dansby-Willig index. These indexes provide a manager information about industry cost and demand conditions. For instance, the greater the Lerner index in an industry, the greater the ability of a firm in the industry to charge a high markup on its product.

The data presented in this chapter reveal industrywide differences in activities such as advertising and research and development. The remainder of the book will explain why these differences exist and the optimal managerial decisions for alternative market structures. The next chapter begins with a study of managerial decisions under perfect competition, monopoly, and monopolistic competition.

KEY TERMS AND CONCEPTS

barrier to entry
conduct
conglomerate merger
Dansby-Willig performance index
feedback critique
five forces framework
four-firm concentration ratio
Herfindahl-Hirschman index (HHI)
horizontal merger
integration
Lerner index

market structure
monopolistic competition
monopoly
oligopoly
perfect competition
performance
Rothschild index
structure
structure–conduct–performance paradigm
vertical merger

END-OF-CHAPTER PROBLEMS BY LEARNING OBJECTIVE

Every end-of-chapter problem addresses at least one learning objective. Following is a nonexhaustive sample of end-of-chapter problems for each learning objective.

LO1 Calculate alternative measures of industry structure, conduct, and performance, and discuss their limitations.

Try these problems: 1, 12

LO2 Describe examples of vertical, horizontal, and conglomerate mergers, and explain the economic basis for each type of merger.

Try these problems: 14, 21

LO3 Explain the relevance of the Herfindahl-Hirschman index for antitrust policy under the horizontal merger guidelines.

Try these problems: 2, 15

LO4 Describe the structure-conduct-performance paradigm, the feedback critique, and their relation to the five forces framework.

Try these problems: 6, 13

LO5 Identify whether an industry is best described as perfectly competitive, a monopoly, monopolistically competitive, or an oligopoly.

Try these problems: 5, 17

CONCEPTUAL AND COMPUTATIONAL QUESTIONS

1. Ten firms compete in a market to sell product X. The total sales of all firms selling the product are $2 million. Ranking the firms' sales from highest to lowest, we find the top four firms' sales to be $260,000, $220,000, $150,000, and $130,000, respectively. Calculate the four-firm concentration ratio in the market for product X.

2. An industry consists of three firms with sales of $300,000, $700,000, and $250,000.
   a. Calculate the Herfindahl-Hirschman index (HHI).
   b. Calculate the four-firm concentration ratio (C_4).
   c. Based on the FTC and DOJ *Horizontal Merger Guidelines* described in the text, do you think the Department of Justice would attempt to block a horizontal merger between two firms with sales of $300,000 and $250,000? Explain.

3. Suppose the own price elasticity of market demand for retail gasoline is -0.8, the Rothschild index is 0.5, and a typical gasoline retailer enjoys sales of $1.5 million annually. What is the price elasticity of demand for a representative gasoline retailer's product?

4. A firm has $1.5 million in sales, a Lerner index of 0.57, and a marginal cost of $50, and competes against 800 other firms in its relevant market.
   a. What price does this firm charge its customers?
   b. By what factor does this firm mark up its price over marginal cost?
   c. Do you think this firm enjoys much market power? Explain.

5. Evaluate the following statement: "Managers should specialize by acquiring only the tools needed to operate in a particular market structure. That is, managers should specialize in managing either a perfectly competitive, monopoly, monopolistically competitive, or oligopoly firm."

6. Under what conditions might the Justice Department approve a merger between two companies that operate in an industry with a premerger Herfindahl-Hirschman index of 2,900 if the postmerger index is expected to increase by 225?

7. Based only on the knowledge that the premerger market share of two firms proposing to merge was 30 percent each, an economist working for the Justice Department was able to determine that, if approved, the postmerger HHI would increase by 1,800. How was the economist able to draw this conclusion without knowledge of the other firms' market shares? From this information, can you devise a general rule explaining how the Herfindahl-Hirschman index is affected when exactly two firms in the market merge? (*Hint:* Compare $a^2 + b^2$ with $[a + b]^2$.)

8. Consider a firm that operates in a market that competes aggressively in prices. Due to the high fixed cost of obtaining the technology associated with entering this market, only a limited number of other firms exist. Furthermore, over 70 percent of the products sold in this market are protected by patents for the

next eight years. Does this industry conform to an economist's definition of a perfectly competitive market?

9. Based on the information given, indicate whether the following industry is best characterized by the model of perfect competition, monopoly, monopolistic competition, or oligopoly.

   a. Industry A has a four-firm concentration ratio of 0.005 percent and a Herfindahl-Hirschman index of 75. A representative firm has a Lerner index of 0.45 and a Rothschild index of 0.34.

   b. Industry B has a four-firm concentration ratio of 0.0001 percent and Herfindahl-Hirschman index of 55. A representative firm has a Lerner index of 0.0034 and Rothschild index of 0.00023.

   c. Industry C has a four-firm concentration ratio of 100 percent and Herfindahl-Hirschman index of 10,000. A representative firm has a Lerner index of 0.4 and Rothschild index of 1.0.

   d. Industry D has a four-firm concentration ratio of 100 percent and Herfindahl-Hirschman index of 5,573. A representative firm has a Lerner index equal to 0.43 and Rothschild index of 0.76.

10. The four-firm concentration ratios for industries X and Y are 81 percent and 74 percent, respectively, while the corresponding Herfindahl-Hirschman indexes are 3,100 and 1,600. The Dansby-Willig performance index for industry X is 0.7, while that for industry Y is 0.55. Based on this information, which would lead to the greater increase in social welfare: A slight increase in industry X's output, or a slight increase in industry Y's output?

PROBLEMS AND APPLICATIONS

11. You work at a firm on Wall Street that specializes in mergers, and you are the team leader in charge of getting approval for a merger between two major beer manufacturers in the United States. While Table 7–2 in the text indicates that the four-firm concentration ratio for all of the breweries operating in the United States is 90 percent, your team has put together a report suggesting that the merger does not present antitrust concerns even though the two firms each enjoy a 15 percent share of the U.S. market. Provide an outline of your report.

12. Forey, Inc., competes against many other firms in a highly competitive industry. Over the last decade, several firms have entered this industry and, as a consequence, Forey is earning a return on investment that roughly equals the interest rate. Furthermore, the four-firm concentration ratio and the Herfindahl-Hirschman index are both quite small, but the Rothschild index is significantly greater than zero. Based on this information, which market structure best characterizes the industry in which Forey competes? Explain.

13. Firms like Papa John's, Domino's, and Pizza Hut sell pizza and other products that are differentiated in nature. While numerous pizza chains exist in most locations, the differentiated nature of these firms' products permits them to charge prices above marginal cost. Given these observations, is the pizza

industry most likely a monopoly, perfectly competitive, monopolistically competitive, or an oligopoly industry? Use the causal view of structure, conduct, and performance to explain the role of differentiation in the market for pizza. Then apply the feedback critique to the role of differentiation in the industry.

14. Which of the following would most likely be scrutinized under the FTC and DOJ *Horizontal Merger Guidelines*?
    a. Two major players in Internet services and retailing—Amazon.com and eBay—merge.
    b. Cigarette maker Philip Morris merges with the Miller Brewing Company.
    c. Lockheed Martin, a large firm that manufactures aircraft, merges with United States Steel.

15. Nationwide Bank has approached Hometown Bank with a proposal to merge. The following table lists the sales of the banks in the area. Use this information to calculate the four-firm concentration ratio and the Herfindahl-Hirschman index. Based on the FTC and DOJ *Horizontal Merger Guidelines,* do you think the Justice Department is likely to challenge the proposed merger?

Bank Name	Sales (in millions)
MegaBank	$1,100
City Bank	950
Nationwide Bank	845
Atlantic Savings	785
Bulk Bank	665
Metropolitan Bank	480
American Bank	310
Hometown Bank	260
Urban Bank	140

16. Suppose Fiat recently entered into an Agreement and Plan of Merger with Case for $4.3 billion. Prior to the merger, the market for four-wheel-drive tractors consisted of five firms. The market was highly concentrated, with a Herfindahl-Hirschman index of 2,765. Case's share of that market was 22 percent, while Fiat comprised just 12 percent of the market. If approved, by how much would the postmerger Herfindahl-Hirschman index increase? Based only on this information, do you think the Justice Department would challenge the merger? Explain.

17. Use the estimated elasticities in Table 7–4 to calculate the Rothschild index for each industry. Based on these calculations, which industry most closely resembles perfect competition? Which industry most closely resembles monopoly?

18. Several years ago, Pfizer and Warner-Lambert agreed to a $90 billion merger, thus creating one of the world's largest pharmaceutical companies. Pharmaceutical companies tend to spend a greater percentage of sales on R&D activities than other industries. The government encourages these R&D activities by granting companies patents for drugs approved by the Food and Drug

Administration. For instance, Pfizer-Warner-Lambert spent large sums of money developing its popular cholesterol-lowering drug, Lipitor, which is currently protected under a patent. Lipitor sells for about $3 per pill. Calculate the Lerner index if the marginal cost of producing Lipitor is $0.30 per pill. Does the Lerner index make sense in this situation? Explain.

19. Many MBAs who ventured into the "dot-com" world of the late 1990s found themselves unemployed by 2001 as many firms in that industry ceased to exist. However, during their tenure with these companies, these managers gained valuable skills in how to operate within a highly competitive environment. Based on the numbers in Table 7–3 in this chapter, which industries represent the best match for these managers' expertise? Looking at the industries listed in Table 7–3, what factors give rise to the varying levels of market power?

20. In the 1990s five firms supplied amateur color film in the United States: Kodak, Fuji, Konica, Agfa, and 3M. From a technical viewpoint, there was little difference in the quality of color film produced by these firms, yet Kodak's market share was 67 percent. The own price elasticity of demand for Kodak film was -2.0 and the market elasticity of demand was -1.75. Suppose that in the 1990s, the average retail price of a roll of Kodak film was $6.95 and that Kodak's marginal cost was $3.475 per roll. Based on this information, discuss industry concentration, demand and market conditions, and the pricing behavior of Kodak in the 1990s. Do you think the industry environment is significantly different today? Explain.

21. Del Monte has a long and rich tradition in the American food processing industry. It is perhaps best known for packaging canned fruits and vegetables. Part of its success has involved acquiring other brands of canned fruits and vegetables. Suppose that Del Monte is continuing its business plan of expansion by acquisition and that the following table summarizes potential acquisition targets. As the CEO's horizontal merger and acquisition advisor, it is your task to guide the decision-making process. Based only on the information contained in the table, is a horizontal merger with one of these companies likely to pass the U.S. government's scrutiny and enhance Del Monte's performance? Justify your conclusion.

Company	Product Line	Profit as % of Sales	C_4	HHI	Rothschild Index	Lerner Index	Dansby-Willig Index
Unilever	Dove—personal care	5.2	24.1%	874	0.11	0.94	0.01
TricorBraun	Food-grade cans	6.8	32.7%	1,065	0.64	0.67	0.40
Goya	Canned tomatoes	7.1	86.3%	3,297	0.74	0.32	0.66
Dole	Canned pineapple	8.7	94.2%	5,457	0.76	0.14	0.72

22. In January 2007, XM enjoyed about 58 percent of satellite radio subscribers, and Sirius had the remaining 42 percent. Both firms were suffering losses, despite their dominance in the satellite radio market. In 2008, the DOJ decided not to challenge a merger, and these two firms united to become Sirius XM. If you

were an economic consultant for Sirius, what economic arguments would you have presented to the DOJ to persuade it not to challenge the merger? Explain.

23. Recently, the Federal Communications Commission (FCC) implemented "local number portability" rules allowing cellular phone consumers to switch cellular providers within the same geographic area and maintain the same phone number. How would you expect this change to affect the Rothschild index for the cellular service industry?

CONNECT EXERCISES

If your instructor has adopted Connect for the course and you are an active subscriber, you can practice with the questions presented above, along with many alternative versions of these questions. Your instructor may also assign a subset of these problems and/or their alternative versions as a homework assignment through Connect, allowing for immediate feedback of grades and correct answers.

CASE-BASED EXERCISES

Your instructor may assign additional problem-solving exercises (called *memos*) that require you to apply some of the tools you learned in this chapter to make a recommendation based on an actual business scenario. Some of these memos accompany the Time Warner case (pages 561–597 of your textbook). Additional memos, as well as data that may be useful for your analysis, are available online at www.mhhe.com/baye8e.

SELECTED READINGS

Conant, John L., "The Role of Managerial Discretion in Union Mergers." *Journal of Economic Behavior and Organization* 20(1), January 1993, pp. 49–62.

Dansby, R. E., and Willig, R. D., "Industry Performance Gradient Indexes." *American Economic Review* 69, 1979, pp. 249–60.

Davis, Douglas D., and Holt, Charles A., "Market Power and Mergers in Laboratory Markets with Posted Prices." *Rand Journal of Economics* 25(3), Autumn 1994, pp. 467–87.

Golbe, Devra L., and White, Lawrence J., "Catch a Wave: The Time Series Behavior of Mergers." *Review of Economics and Statistics* 75(3), August 1993, pp. 493–99.

Hirschman, Albert O., "The Paternity of an Index." *American Economic Review* 54(5), September 1964, p. 761.

Johnson, Ronald N., and Parkman, Allen M., "Premerger Notification and the Incentive to Merge and Litigate." *Journal of Law, Economics and Organization* 7(1), Spring 1991, pp. 145–62.

Kim, E. Han, and Singal, Vijay, "Mergers and Market Power: Evidence from the Airline Industry." *American Economic Review* 83(3), June 1993, pp. 549–69.

Lerner, A. P., "The Concept of Monopoly and the Measurement of Monopoly Power." *Review of Economic Studies,* October 1933, pp. 157–75.

O'Neill, Patrick B., "Concentration Trends and Profitability in U.S. Manufacturing: A Further Comment and Some New (and Improved) Evidence." *Applied Economics* 25(10), October 1993, pp. 1285–86.

Rothschild, K. W., "The Degree of Monopoly." *Economica* 9, 1942, pp. 24–39.

"Symposia: Horizontal Mergers and Antitrust." *Journal of Economic Perspectives* 1(2), Fall 1987.

CHAPTER EIGHT

Managing in Competitive, Monopolistic, and Monopolistically Competitive Markets

Learning Objectives

After completing this chapter, you will be able to:

LO1 Identify the conditions under which a firm operates as perfectly competitive, monopolistically competitive, or a monopoly.

LO2 Identify sources of (and strategies for obtaining) monopoly power.

LO3 Apply the marginal principle to determine the profit-maximizing price and output.

LO4 Show the relationship between the elasticity of demand for a firm's product and its marginal revenue.

LO5 Explain how long-run adjustments impact perfectly competitive, monopoly, and monopolistically competitive firms; discuss the ramifications of each of these market structures on social welfare.

LO6 Decide whether a firm making short-run losses should continue to operate or shut down its operations.

LO7 Illustrate the relationship between marginal cost, a competitive firm's short-run supply curve, and the competitive industry supply; explain why supply curves do not exist for firms that have market power.

LO8 Calculate the optimal output of a firm that operates two plants and the optimal level of advertising for a firm that enjoys market power.

McDonald's New Buzz: Specialty Coffee

Recently, McDonald's unveiled plans to roll out McCafé in the United States, a premium line of coffee that includes cappuccino, latte, and iced mocha. The recession during the late 2000s in the United States left some analysts questioning whether it was the right time for McDonald's to roll out its line of new specialty drinks. However, McDonald's quickly saw a tripling of its share of U.S. coffee sales.

Why do you think McDonald's embarked on the program, and related, what do you think was the source of its success? Do you think this new product line will have a sustainable impact on the company's bottom line? Explain.

Sources: J. Adamy, "McDonald's Coffee Strategy is a Tough Sell," *The Wall Street Journal*, October 27, 2008; M. Brandau, "McDonald's McCafé: An Evolution," *Nation's Restaurant News*, August 16, 2011; www.mymccafe.com

INTRODUCTION

In Chapter 7, we examined the nature of industries and saw that industries differ with respect to their underlying structures, conduct, and performances. In this chapter, we characterize the optimal price, output, and advertising decisions of managers operating in environments of (1) perfect competition, (2) monopoly, and (3) monopolistic competition. We will analyze oligopoly decisions in Chapters 9 and 10 and examine more sophisticated pricing strategies in Chapter 11. With an understanding of the concepts presented in these chapters, you will be prepared to manage a firm that operates in virtually any environment.

Because this is the beginning of our analysis of output decisions of managers operating in an industry, it is logical to start with the simplest case: a situation where managerial decisions have no perceptible impact on the market price. Thus, in the first section of this chapter we will analyze output decisions of managers operating in perfectly competitive markets. In subsequent sections, we will examine output decisions by firms that have market power: monopoly and monopolistic competition. The analysis in this chapter will serve as a building block for the analyses in the remainder of the book.

PERFECT COMPETITION

perfectly competitive market
A market in which (1) there are many buyers and sellers; (2) each firm produces a homogeneous product; (3) buyers and sellers have perfect information; (4) there are no transaction costs; and (5) there is free entry and exit.

We begin our analysis by examining the output decisions of managers operating in perfectly competitive markets. The key conditions for *perfect competition* are as follows:

1. There are many buyers and sellers in the market, each of which is "small" relative to the market.
2. Each firm in the market produces a homogeneous (identical) product.
3. Buyers and sellers have perfect information.
4. There are no transaction costs.
5. There is free entry into and exit from the market.

Taken together, the first four assumptions imply that no single firm can influence the price of the product. The fact that there are many small firms, each selling an identical product, means that consumers view the products of all firms in the market as perfect substitutes. Because there is perfect information, consumers know the quality and price of each firm's product. There are no transaction costs (such as the cost of traveling to a store); if one firm charged a slightly higher price than the other firms, consumers would not shop at that firm but instead would purchase from a firm charging a lower price. Thus, in a perfectly competitive market all firms charge the same price for the good, and this price is determined by the interaction of all buyers and sellers in the market.

The assumption of *free entry* and *exit* simply implies that additional firms can enter the market if economic profits are being earned, and firms are free to leave the market if they are sustaining losses. As we will show later in this chapter, this assumption implies that in the long run, firms operating in a perfectly competitive market earn zero economic profits.

One classic example of a perfectly competitive market is agriculture. There are many farmers and ranchers, and each is so small relative to the market that he or she has no perceptible impact on the prices of corn, wheat, pork, or beef. Agricultural products tend to be homogeneous; there is little difference between corn produced by farmer Jones and corn produced by farmer Smith. The retail mail-order market for computer software and computer memory chips also is close to perfect competition. A quick look at the back of a computer magazine reveals that there are hundreds of mail-order computer product retailers, each selling identical brands of software packages and memory chips and charging the same price for a given product. The reason there is so little price variation is that if one mail-order firm charged a higher price than a competitor, consumers would purchase from another retailer.

Demand at the Market and Firm Levels

No single firm operating in a perfectly competitive market exerts any influence on price; price is determined by the interaction of all buyers and sellers in the market. The firm manager must charge this "market price" or consumers will purchase from a firm charging a lower price. Before we characterize the profit-maximizing output decisions of managers operating in perfectly competitive markets, it is important to explain more precisely the relation between the market demand for a product and the demand for a product produced by an individual perfectly competitive firm.

In a competitive market, price is determined by the intersection of the market supply and demand curves. Because the market supply and demand curves depend on all buyers and sellers, the market price is outside the control of a single perfectly competitive firm. In other words, because the individual firm is "small" relative to the market, it has no perceptible influence on the market price.

firm demand curve
The demand curve for an individual firm's product; in a perfectly competitive market, it is simply the market price.

Figure 8–1 illustrates the distinction between the market demand curve and the *demand curve* facing a perfectly competitive firm. The left-hand panel depicts the market, where the equilibrium price, P^e, is determined by the intersection of the market supply and demand curves. From the individual firm's point of view, the firm can sell as much as it wishes at a price of P^e; thus, the demand curve facing an individual perfectly competitive firm is given by the horizontal line in the right-hand panel, labeled D^f. The fact that the individual firm's demand curve is perfectly elastic reflects the fact that if the firm charged a price even slightly above the market price, it would sell nothing. Thus, in a perfectly competitive market, the demand curve for an individual firm's product is simply the market price.

Since the demand curve for an individual perfectly competitive firm's product is perfectly elastic, the pricing decision of the individual firm is trivial: Charge the price that every other firm in the industry charges. All that remains is to determine how much output should be produced to maximize profits.

FIGURE 8–1   Demand at the Market and Firm Levels under Perfect Competition

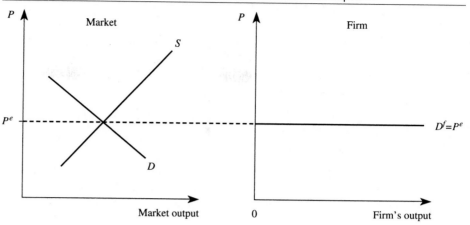

Short-Run Output Decisions

Recall that the short run is the period of time in which there are some fixed factors of production. For example, suppose a building is leased at a cost of $10,000 for a one-year period. In the short run (for one year) these costs are fixed, and they are paid regardless of whether the firm produces zero or one million units of output. In the long run (after the lease is up), this cost is variable; the firm can decide whether or not to renew the lease. To maximize profits in the short run, the manager must take as given the fixed inputs (and thus the fixed costs) and determine how much output to produce given the variable inputs that are within his or her control. The next subsection characterizes the profit-maximizing output decision of the manager of a perfectly competitive firm.

Maximizing Profits

marginal revenue
The change in revenue attributable to the last unit of output; for a competitive firm, *MR* is the market price.

Under perfect competition, the demand for an individual firm's product is the market price of output, which we denote P. If we let Q represent the output of the firm, the total revenue to the firm of producing Q units is $R = PQ$. Since each unit of output can be sold at the market price of P, each unit adds exactly P dollars to revenues. As Figure 8–2 illustrates, there is a linear relation between revenues and the output of a competitive firm. *Marginal revenue* is the change in revenue attributable to the last unit of output. Geometrically, it is the slope of the revenue curve. Expressed in economic terms, the marginal revenue for a competitive firm is the market price.

A Calculus Alternative

Marginal revenue is the derivative of the revenue function. If revenues are a function of output,

$$R = R(Q)$$

then

$$MR = \frac{dR}{dQ}$$

FIGURE 8–2   Revenue, Costs, and Profits for a Perfectly Competitive Firm

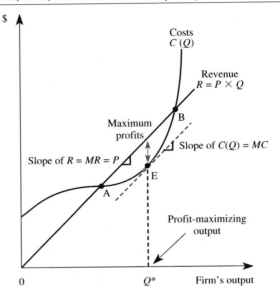

Principle   **Competitive Firm's Demand**
The demand curve for a competitive firm's product is a horizontal line at the market price. This price is the competitive firm's marginal revenue.
$$D^f = P = MR$$

A Calculus Alternative

Marginal revenue is the derivative of the revenue function. For a perfectly competitive firm, revenue is
$$R = PQ$$
where P is the market equilibrium price. Thus,
$$MR = \frac{dR}{dQ} = P$$

The profits of a perfectly competitive firm are simply the difference between revenues and costs:
$$\pi = PQ - C(Q)$$

Geometrically, profits are given by the vertical distance between the cost function, labeled $C(Q)$ in Figure 8–2, and the revenue line. Note that for output levels to the left of point A, the cost curve lies above the revenue line, which implies that the firm would incur losses if it produced any output to the left of point A. The same is true of output levels to the right of point B.

For output levels between points A and B, the revenue line lies above the cost curve. This implies that these outputs generate positive levels of profit. The profit-maximizing level of output is the level at which the vertical distance between the revenue line and the cost curve is greatest. This is given by the output level Q^* in Figure 8–2.

There is a very important geometric property at the profit-maximizing level of output. As we see in Figure 8–2, the slope of the cost curve at the profit-maximizing level of output (point E) exactly equals the slope of the revenue line. Recall that the slope of the cost curve is marginal cost and the slope of the revenue line is marginal revenue. Therefore, the profit-maximizing output is the output at which marginal revenue equals marginal cost. Since marginal revenue is equal to the market price for a perfectly competitive firm, the manager must equate the market price with marginal cost to maximize profits.

An alternative way to express the competitive output rule is depicted in Figure 8–3, where standard average and marginal cost curves have been drawn. If the market price is given by P^e, this price intersects the marginal cost curve at an output of Q^*. Thus, Q^* represents the profit-maximizing level of output. For outputs below Q^*, price exceeds marginal cost. This implies that by expanding output, the firm can sell additional units at a price that exceeds the cost of producing the additional units. Thus, a profit-maximizing firm will not choose to produce output levels below Q^*. Similarly, output levels above Q^* correspond to the situation in which marginal cost exceeds price. In this instance, a reduction in output would reduce costs by more than it would reduce revenue. Thus, Q^* is the profit-maximizing level of output.

The shaded rectangle in Figure 8–3 represents the maximum profits of the firm. To see this, note that the area of the shaded rectangle is given by its base (Q^*) times

FIGURE 8–3 Profit Maximization under Perfect Competition

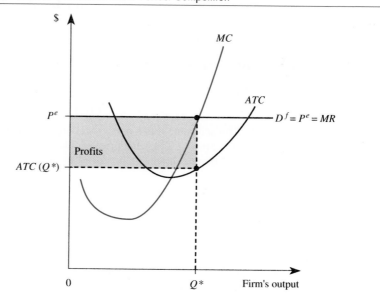

the height $[P^e - ATC(Q^*)]$. Recall that $ATC(Q^*) = C(Q^*)/Q^*$; that is, average total cost is total cost divided by output. The area of the shaded rectangle is

$$Q^*\left[P^e - \frac{C(Q^*)}{Q^*}\right] = P^e Q^* - C(Q^*)$$

which is the definition of profits. Intuitively, $[P^e - ATC(Q^*)]$ represents the profits per unit produced. When this is multiplied by the profit-maximizing level of output (Q^*), the result is the amount of total profits earned by the firm.

Principle

Competitive Output Rule
To maximize profits, a perfectly competitive firm produces the output at which price equals marginal cost in the range over which marginal cost is increasing:
$$P = MC(Q)$$

A Calculus Alternative

The profits of a perfectly competitive firm are
$$\pi = PQ - C(Q)$$
The first-order condition for maximizing profits requires that the marginal profits be zero:
$$\frac{d\pi}{dQ} = P - \frac{dC(Q)}{dQ} = 0$$
Thus, we obtain the profit-maximizing rule for a firm in perfect competition:
$$P = \frac{dC}{dQ}$$
or
$$P = MC$$

Demonstration Problem 8–1

The cost function for a firm is given by
$$C(Q) = 5 + Q^2$$

If the firm sells output in a perfectly competitive market and other firms in the industry sell output at a price of $20, what price should the manager of this firm put on the product? What level of output should be produced to maximize profits? How much profit will be earned?

(*Hint:* Recall that for a cubic cost function
$$C(Q) = f + aQ + bQ^2 + cQ^3$$
the marginal cost function is
$$MC(Q) = a + 2bQ + 3cQ^2$$

Since $a = 0$, $b = 1$, and $c = 0$ for the cost function in this problem, we see that the marginal cost function for the firm is $MC(Q) = 2Q$.)

Answer:

Since the firm competes in a perfectly competitive market, it must charge the same price other firms charge; thus, the manager should price the product at $20. To find the profit-maximizing output, we must equate price with marginal cost. This firm's marginal costs are $MC = 2Q$. Equating this with price yields

$$20 = 2Q$$

so the profit-maximizing level of output is 10 units. The maximum profits are thus

$$\pi = (20)(10) - (5 + 10^2) = 200 - 5 - 100 = \$95$$

Minimizing Losses

In the previous section, we demonstrated the optimal level of output to maximize profits. In some instances, short-run losses are inevitable. Here we analyze procedures for minimizing losses in the short run. If losses are sustained in the long run, the best thing for the firm to do is exit the industry.

Short-Run Operating Losses. Consider first a situation where there are some fixed costs of production. Suppose the market price, P^e, lies below the average total cost curve but above the average variable cost curve, as in Figure 8–4. In this instance, if the firm produces the output Q^*, where $P^e = MC$, a loss of the shaded area will result. However, since the price exceeds the average variable cost, each unit sold generates more revenue than the cost per unit of the variable inputs. Thus, the firm should continue to produce in the short run, even though it is incurring losses.

Expressed differently, notice that the firm in Figure 8–4 has fixed costs that would have to be paid even if the firm decided to shut down its operation. Therefore,

FIGURE 8–4 Loss Minimization

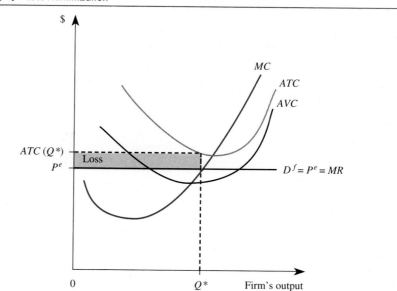

the firm would *not* earn zero economic profits if it shut down but would instead realize a loss equal to these fixed costs. Since the price in Figure 8–4 exceeds the average variable cost of producing Q^* units of output, the firm earns revenues on each unit sold that are more than enough to cover the variable cost of producing each unit. By producing Q^* units of output, the firm is able to put an amount of money into its cash drawer that exceeds the variable costs of producing these units and thus contributes toward the firm's payment of fixed costs. In short, while the firm in Figure 8–4 suffers a short-run loss by operating, this loss is less than the loss that would result if the firm completely shut down its operation.

The Decision to Shut Down.   Now suppose the market price is so low that it lies below the average variable cost, as in Figure 8–5. If the firm produced Q^*, where $P^e = MC$ in the range of increasing marginal cost, it would incur a loss equal to the sum of the two shaded rectangles in Figure 8–5. In other words, for each unit sold, the firm would lose

$$ATC(Q^*) - P^e$$

When this per-unit loss is multiplied by Q^*, negative profits result that correspond to the sum of the two shaded rectangles in Figure 8–5.

Now suppose that instead of producing Q^* units of output this firm decided to shut down its operation. In this instance, its losses would equal its fixed costs; that is, those costs that must be paid even if no output is produced. Geometrically, fixed costs are represented by the top rectangle in Figure 8–5, since the area of this rectangle is

$$[ATC(Q^*) - AVC(Q^*)]Q^*$$

FIGURE 8–5   The Shut-Down Case

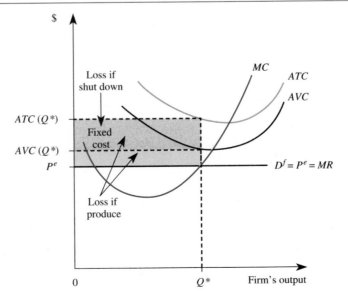

INSIDE BUSINESS 8–1

Peugeot-Citroën of France: A Price-Taker in China's Auto Market

Competition in international markets is often more keen than in domestic markets. This is especially true in developing economies, where price rather than product differentiation is the main driver of consumer purchase decisions.

Consider, for instance, the French automaker PSA Peugeot-Citroën. Its Citroën division has a minuscule share of China's auto market—especially compared to the market share it enjoys in France and Europe. In an interview regarding the Chinese market, one of its managers remarked, "If prices fall, we will also follow suit, but not by more than the decrease in the market." Another manager added, "This is a very competitive market . . . we have to think about the capacity at the factory . . ."

These remarks suggest that, in China, Citroën has very little control over price; in essence, it operates as a "price taker" in the Chinese market for auto-

mobiles. As a price taker, it has no incentive to price below the market price. Furthermore, Citroën would lose customers to other automakers if it attempted to charge a price premium in the developing Chinese market.

As a price taker, Citroën's main decision is how many cars to produce at the market price. Managers in China must ensure that the capacity at factories is sufficient for producing the optimal volume of cars. In light of the large capacities of GM and other automakers with operations in China, Peugeot-Citroën is likely to continue to have limited power over its price for many years to come.

Sources: "Citroën Forecasts Slowdown in Sales Growth in China this Year," *Channel News Asia,* June 9, 2004; "General Motors' China Success," *BusinessWeek,* January 8, 2006.

---

which equals fixed costs. Thus, when price is less than the average variable cost of production, the firm loses less by shutting down its operation (and producing zero units) than it does by producing Q^* units. To summarize, we have demonstrated the following principle:

Principle	**Short-Run Output Decision under Perfect Competition** To maximize short-run profits, a perfectly competitive firm should produce in the range of increasing marginal cost where $P = MC$, provided that $P \geq AVC$. If $P < AVC$, the firm should shut down its plant to minimize its losses.

Demonstration Problem 8–2

Suppose the cost function for a firm is given by $C(Q) = 100 + Q^2$. If the firm sells output in a perfectly competitive market and other firms in the industry sell output at a price of $10, what level of output should the firm produce to maximize profits or minimize losses? What will be the level of profits or losses if the firm makes the optimal decision?

Answer:

First, note that there are fixed costs of 100 and variable costs of Q^2, so the question deals with a short-run scenario. If the firm produces a positive level of output, it will produce where price equals marginal cost. The firm's marginal costs are $MC = 2Q$. Equating this with price yields $10 = 2Q$, or $Q = 5$ units. The average variable cost of producing 5 units of output is $AVC = 5^2/5 = 25/5 = 5$. Since $P \geq AVC$, the firm should produce 5 units in the short run. By producing 5 units of output, the firm incurs a loss of

$$\pi = (10)(5) - (100 + 5^2) = 50 - 100 - 25 = -\$75$$

which is less than the loss of \$100 (fixed costs) that would result if the firm shut down its plant in the short run.

The Short-Run Firm and Industry Supply Curves

Now that you understand how perfectly competitive firms determine their output, we will examine how to derive firm and industry short-run supply curves.

Recall that the profit-maximizing perfectly competitive firm produces the output at which price equals marginal cost. For example, when the price is given by P_0 as in Figure 8–6, the firm produces Q_0 units of output (the point where $P = MC$ in the range of increasing marginal cost). When the price is P_1, the firm produces Q_1 units of output. For prices between P_0 and P_1, output is determined by the intersection of price and marginal cost.

When the price falls below the AVC curve, however, the firm produces zero units, because it does not cover the variable costs of production. Thus, to determine how much a perfectly competitive firm will produce at each price, we simply determine the output at which marginal cost equals that price. To ensure that the firm will produce a positive level of output, price must be above the average variable cost curve.

Principle	**The Firm's Short-Run Supply Curve**

The short-run supply curve for a perfectly competitive firm is its marginal cost curve above the minimum point on the AVC curve, as illustrated in Figure 8–6.

FIGURE 8–6 The Short-Run Supply Curve for a Competitive Firm

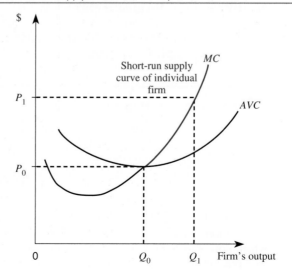

FIGURE 8–7 The Market Supply Curve

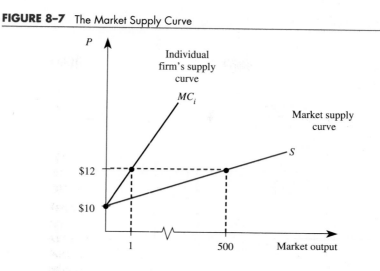

The market (or industry) supply curve is closely related to the supply curve of individual firms in a perfectly competitive industry. Recall that the market supply curve reveals the total quantity that will be produced in the market at each possible price. Since the amount an individual firm will produce at a given price is determined by its marginal cost curve, the horizontal sum of the marginal costs of all firms determines how much total output will be produced at each price. More specifically, since each firm's supply curve is the firm's marginal cost curve above the minimum AVC, the market supply curve for a perfectly competitive industry is the horizontal sum of the individual marginal costs above their respective AVC curves.

Figure 8–7 illustrates the relation between an individual firm's supply curve (MC_i) and the market supply curve (S) for a perfectly competitive industry composed of 500 firms. When the price is $10, each firm produces zero units, and thus total industry output also is zero. When the price is $12, each firm produces 1 unit, so the total output produced by all 500 firms is 500 units. Notice that the industry supply curve is flatter than the supply curve of an individual firm and that the more firms in the industry, the farther to the right is the market supply curve.

Long-Run Decisions

One important assumption underlying the theory of perfect competition is that of free entry and exit. If firms earn short-run economic profits, in the long run additional firms will enter the industry in an attempt to reap some of those profits. As more firms enter the industry, the industry supply curve shifts to the right. This is illustrated in Figure 8–8 as the shift from S^0 to S^1, which lowers the equilibrium market price from P^0 to P^1. This shifts down the demand curve for an individual firm's product, which in turn lowers its profits.

FIGURE 8–8 Entry and Exit: The Market and Firm's Demand

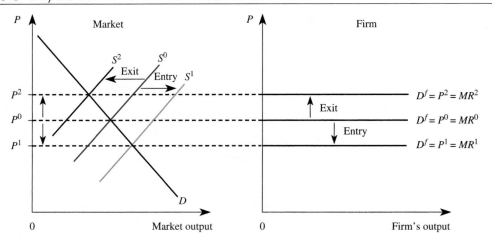

If firms in a competitive industry sustain short-run losses, in the long run they will exit the industry since they are not covering their opportunity costs. As firms exit the industry, the market supply curve decreases from S^0 in Figure 8–8 to S^2, thus increasing the market price from P^0 to P^2. This, in turn, shifts up the demand curve for an individual firm's product, which increases the profits of the firms remaining in the industry.

The process just described continues until ultimately the market price is such that all firms in the market earn zero economic profits. This is the case in Figure 8–9. At the price of P^e, each firm receives just enough to cover the average costs of production (AC is used because in the long run there is no distinction between fixed and variable costs), and economic profits are zero. If economic profits were positive, entry would occur and the market price would fall until the demand curve for an individual firm's product was

FIGURE 8–9 Long-Run Competitive Equilibrium

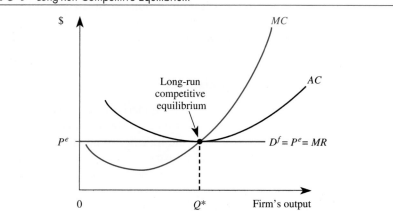

just tangent to the AC curve. If economic profits were negative, exit would occur, increasing the market price until the firm demand curve was tangent to the AC curve.

Principle	**Long-Run Competitive Equilibrium**
	In the long run, perfectly competitive firms produce a level of output such that
	1. $P = MC$
	2. $P =$ minimum of AC

These long-run properties of perfectly competitive markets have two important welfare implications. First, note that the market price is equal to the marginal cost of production. The market price reflects the value to society of an additional unit of output. This valuation is based on the preferences of all consumers in the market. Marginal cost reflects the cost to society of producing another unit of output. These costs represent the resources that would have to be taken from some other sector of the economy to produce more output in this industry.

To see why it is important, from a social perspective, that price equal marginal cost, suppose price exceeded marginal cost in equilibrium. This would imply that society would value another unit of output more than it would cost to produce another unit of output. If the industry produced at a level such that price exceeded the marginal cost of the last unit produced, it would thus be inefficient; social welfare would be improved by expanding output. Since in a competitive industry price equals marginal cost, the industry produces the socially efficient level of output.

The second thing to note about long-run competitive equilibrium is that price equals the minimum point on the average cost curve. This implies not only that firms are earning zero economic profits (that is, just covering their opportunity costs) but also that all economies of scale have been exhausted. There is no way to produce the output at a lower average cost of production.

It is important to remember the distinction we made in Chapters 1 and 5 between economic profits and accounting profits. The fact that a firm in a perfectly competitive industry earns zero economic profits in the long run does not mean that accounting profits are zero; rather, zero economic profits implies that accounting profits are just high enough to offset any implicit costs of production. The firm earns no more, and no less, than it could earn by using the resources in some other capacity. This is why firms continue to produce in the long run even though their economic profits are zero.

MONOPOLY

In the previous section we characterized the optimal output decisions of firms that are small relative to the total market. In this context, *small* means the firms have

monopoly
A market structure in which a single firm serves an entire market for a good that has no close substitutes.

no control whatsoever over the prices they charge for the product. In this section, we will consider the opposite extreme: monopoly. *Monopoly* refers to a situation where a single firm serves an entire market for a good for which there are no close substitutes.

Monopoly Power

In determining whether a market is characterized by monopoly, it is important to specify the relevant market for the product. For example, some utilities, such as electric or water companies, are local monopolies in that only one utility offers service to a given neighborhood. Even though there may be similar companies serving other towns, they do not directly compete against one another for customers. The substitutes for electric services in a given city are poor and, short of moving to a different city, consumers must pay the price for local utility services or go without electricity. It is in this sense that a utility company may be a monopoly in the local market for utility services.

When one thinks of a monopoly, one usually envisions a very large firm. This needn't be the case, however; the relevant consideration is whether there are other firms selling close substitutes for the good in a given market. For example, a gas station located in a small town that is several hundred miles from another gas station is a monopolist in that town. In a large town there typically are many gas stations, and the market for gasoline is not characterized by monopoly.

The fact that a firm is the sole seller of a good in a market clearly gives that firm greater market power than it would have if it competed against other firms for consumers. Since there is only one producer in the market, the market demand curve is the demand curve for the monopolist's product. This is in contrast to the case of perfect competition, where the demand curve for an individual firm is perfectly elastic. A monopolist does not have unlimited power, however.

Figure 8–10 depicts the demand curve for a monopolist. Since all consumers in the market demand the good from the monopolist, the market demand curve, D^M, is the same as the demand for the firm's product, D^f. In the absence of legal restrictions, the monopolist is free to charge any price for the product. But this does not mean the firm can sell as much as it wants to at that price. Given the price set by the monopolist, consumers decide how much to purchase. For example, if the monopolist sets the relatively low price of P^1, the quantity demanded by consumers is Q^1. The monopolist can set a higher price of P^0, but there will be a lower quantity demanded of Q^0 at that price.

In summary, the monopolist is restricted by consumers to choose only those price–quantity combinations along the market demand curve. The monopolist can choose a price or a quantity, but not both. The monopolist can sell higher quantities only by lowering the price. If the price is too high, consumers may choose to buy nothing at all.

FIGURE 8–10 The Monopolist's Demand

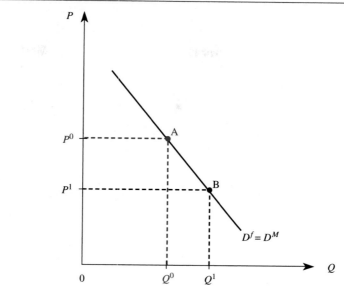

Sources of Monopoly Power

The next issue we will address is how a firm obtains monopoly power, that is, why a monopolist has no competitors. There are four primary sources of monopoly power. One or more of these sources create a barrier to entry that prevents other firms from entering the market to compete against the monopolist.

Economies of Scale

economies of scale
Exist whenever long-run average costs decline as output increases.

diseconomies of scale
Exist whenever long-run average costs increase as output increases.

The first source of monopoly power we will discuss is technological in nature. First, however, it is useful to recall some important terminology. *Economies of scale* exist whenever long-run average costs decline as output increases. *Diseconomies of scale* exist whenever long-run average costs increase as output increases. For many technologies, there is a range over which economies of scale exist and a range over which diseconomies exist. For example, in Figure 8–11 there are economies of scale for output levels below Q^* (since *ATC* is declining in this range) and diseconomies of scale for output levels above Q^* (since *ATC* is increasing in this range).

Notice in Figure 8–11 that if the market were composed of a single firm that produced Q^M units, consumers would be willing to pay a price of P^M per unit for the Q^M units. Since $P^M > ATC(Q^M)$, the firm sells the goods at a price that is higher than the average cost of production and thus earns positive profits. Now suppose another firm entered the market and the two firms ended up sharing the market (each firm producing $Q^M/2$). The total quantity produced would be the same, and thus the price would remain at P^M. But with two firms, each producing only $Q^M/2$ units, each firm has an

FIGURE 8–11   Economies of Scale and Minimum Prices

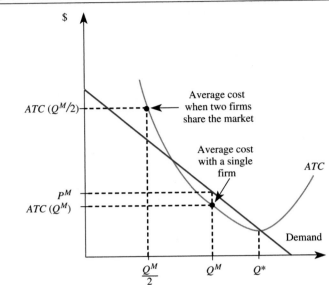

average total cost of $ATC(Q^M/2)$—a higher average total cost than when a single firm produced all the output. For example, in a market with overhead costs and two firms, each firm must incur these costs of production, and each can only spread the costs over half as much output as a monopolist. Also notice in Figure 8–11 that each firm's average cost is greater than P^M, which is the price consumers are willing to pay for the total Q^M units produced in the market. Having two firms in the industry leads to losses, but a single firm can earn positive profits because it has higher volume and enjoys reduced average costs due to economies of scale. Thus, we see that economies of scale can lead to a situation where a single firm services the entire market for a good.

This analysis of economies of scale also reveals why it is so important to define the relevant market when determining whether or not a firm is a monopolist. As we noted earlier, a gas station may be a monopolist in a small town located several hundred miles from another gas station, whereas a gas station situated in a large city is unlikely to be a monopolist. In terms of Figure 8–11, the demand for gasoline in a small town typically is low relative to Q^*, which gives rise to economies of scale in the relevant range (outputs below Q^*). In large cities the demand for gasoline is large relative to Q^*, which makes it possible for several gas stations to coexist in the market.

economies of scope
Exist when the total cost of producing two products within the same firm is lower than when the products are produced by separate firms.

Economies of Scope

Recall that *economies of scope* exist when the total cost of producing two products within the same firm is lower than when the products are produced by separate firms, that is, when it is cheaper to produce outputs Q_1 and Q_2 jointly. Pharmaceutical companies often enjoy economies of scope in their development of new drugs; breakthroughs in developing a product that cures one disease may reduce the cost of developing additional products that cure other illnesses.

In the presence of economies of scope, efficient production requires that a firm produce several products jointly. While multiproduct firms do not necessarily have more market power than firms producing a single product, economies of scope tend to encourage "larger" firms. In turn, this may provide greater access to capital markets, where working capital and funds for investment are obtained. To the extent that smaller firms have more difficulty obtaining funds than do larger firms, the higher cost of capital may serve as a barrier to entry. In extreme cases, economies of scope can lead to monopoly power.

cost complementarities
Exist when the marginal cost of producing one output is reduced when the output of another product is increased.

Cost Complementarity

Cost complementarities exist in a multiproduct cost function when the marginal cost of producing one output is reduced when the output of another product is increased; that is, when an increase in the output of product 2 decreases the marginal cost of producing output 1. A simple example of a multiproduct cost function with cost complementarities involves the production of doughnuts and doughnut holes.

Multiproduct firms that enjoy cost complementarities tend to have lower marginal costs than firms producing a single product. This gives multiproduct firms a cost advantage over single-product firms. Thus, in the presence of cost complementarities, firms must produce several products to be able to compete against the firm with lower marginal costs. To the extent that greater capital requirements exist for multiproduct firms than for single-product firms, this requirement can limit the ability of small firms to enter the market. In extreme cases, monopoly power can result.

Patents and Other Legal Barriers

The sources of monopoly power just described are technological in nature. In some instances, government may grant an individual or a firm a monopoly right. For example, a city may prevent another utility company from competing against the local utility company. Another example is the potential monopoly power generated by the *patent* system.

The patent system gives the inventor of a new product the exclusive right to sell the product for a given period of time (see Inside Business 8–2). The rationale behind granting monopoly power to a new inventor is based on the following argument: Inventions take many years and considerable sums of money to develop. Once an invention becomes public information, in the absence of a patent system, other firms could produce the product and compete against the individual or firm that developed it. Since these firms do not have to expend resources developing the product, they would make higher profits than the original developer. In the absence of a patent system, there would be a reduced incentive on the part of firms to develop new technologies and products.

It is important to stress that patents rarely lead to absolute monopoly because competitors are often quick to develop similar products or technologies in order to get a piece of the action. Furthermore, several firms taking different R&D paths may each obtain a patent for a product that is a close substitute for other patented products. For example, the two best-selling erectile dysfunction medications—Pfizer's Viagra and Eli Lilly's Cialis—are competitors even though both have "enjoyed" patents. For these reasons, managers enjoying patent protection are by no means immune from competitive pressures.

FIGURE 8–12   Elasticity of Demand and Total Revenues

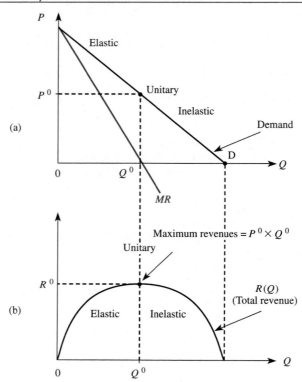

Maximizing Profits

Now that you know what monopoly power is and the factors that lead to monopoly power, we will see how the manager of a monopoly may exploit this power to maximize profits. In particular, in this section we presume that the manager is in charge of a firm that is a monopoly. Our goal is to characterize the price and output decisions that maximize the monopolist's profits.

Marginal Revenue

Suppose the monopolist faces a demand curve for its product such as the one in Figure 8–12(a). In Chapter 3, we learned that a linear demand curve is elastic at high prices and inelastic at low prices. If the monopolist produces zero units of output, its revenues are zero. As output is increased above zero, demand is elastic and the increase in output (which implies a lower price) leads to an increase in total revenue, as shown in Figure 8–12(b). This follows from the total revenue test. As output is increased beyond Q^0 into the inelastic region of demand, further increases in output actually decrease total revenue, until at point D the price is zero and revenues are again zero. This is depicted in Figure 8–12(b). Thus, total

---

INSIDE BUSINESS 8–2

Patent, Trademark, and Copyright Protection

The United States grants inventors three types of patent protection: utility, design, and plant patents. A "utility patent" protects the way an invention is used and works, while a "design patent" protects the way an invention looks. A "plant patent" protects an inventor who has discovered and asexually reproduced a distinct and new variety of plant (excluding tuber propagated plants or plants found in uncultivated states). Utility and plant patents provide 20 years of protection, while design patents last 14 years.

Trademarks are different from patents in that they protect words, names, symbols, or images that are used in connection with goods or services. Similarly, a copyright protects a creator's form of expression (including literary, dramatic, musical, and artistic works). Patents and trademarks are administered through the U.S. Patent and Trademark Office, while the U.S. Copyright Office handles copyrights.

Sources: United States Patent and Trademark Office; United States Copyright Office.

---

revenue is maximized at an output of Q^0 in Figure 8–12(b). This corresponds to the price of P^0 in Figure 8–12(a), where demand is unitary elastic.

The line labeled MR in Figure 8–12(a) is the marginal revenue schedule for the monopolist. Recall that marginal revenue is the change in total revenue attributable to the last unit of output; geometrically, it is the slope of the total revenue curve. As Figure 8–12(a) shows, the marginal revenue schedule for a monopolist lies below the demand curve; in fact, for a linear demand curve, the marginal revenue schedule lies exactly halfway between the demand curve and the vertical axis. This means that for a monopolist, marginal revenue is less than the price charged for the good.

There are two ways to understand why the marginal revenue schedule lies below the monopolist's demand curve. Consider first a geometric explanation. Marginal revenue is the slope of the total revenue curve [$R(Q)$] in Figure 8–12(b). As output increases from zero to Q^0, the slope of the total revenue curve decreases until it becomes zero at Q^0. Over this range, marginal revenue decreases until it reaches zero when output is Q^0. As output expands beyond Q^0, the slope of the total revenue curve becomes negative and gets increasingly negative as output continues to expand. This means that marginal revenue is negative for outputs in excess of Q^0.

Formula: Monopolist's Marginal Revenue. The marginal revenue of a monopolist is given by the formula

$$MR = P\left[\frac{1+E}{E}\right]$$

where E is the elasticity of demand for the monopolist's product and P is the price charged for the product.

A Calculus
Alternative

The monopolist's revenue is

$$R(Q) = P(Q)Q$$

Taking the derivative with respect to Q yields

$$\frac{dR}{dQ} = \frac{dP}{dQ}Q + P$$

$$= P\left[\left(\frac{dP}{dQ}\right)\left(\frac{Q}{P}\right) + 1\right]$$

$$= P\left[\frac{1}{E} + 1\right]$$

$$= P\left[\frac{1+E}{E}\right]$$

where E is the elasticity of demand. Since $dR/dQ = MR$, this means that

$$MR = P\left[\frac{1+E}{E}\right]$$

Demonstration Problem 8–3

Show that if demand is elastic (say, $E = -2$), marginal revenue is positive but less than price. Show that if demand is unitary elastic ($E = -1$), marginal revenue is zero. Finally, show that if demand is inelastic (say, $E = -0.5$), marginal revenue is negative.

Answer:
Setting $E = -2$ in the marginal revenue formula yields

$$MR = P\left[\frac{1-2}{-2}\right] = \frac{-1}{-2}P$$

so $MR = 0.5P$. Thus, when demand is elastic, marginal revenue is positive but less than price (in this example, marginal revenue is one-half of the price).
    Setting $E = -1$ in the marginal revenue formula yields

$$MR = P\left[\frac{1-1}{-1}\right] = 0$$

so $MR = 0$. Thus, when demand is unitary elastic, marginal revenue is zero.
    Finally, setting $E = -0.5$ in the marginal revenue formula yields

$$MR = P\left[\frac{1-5}{-.5}\right] = P\left[\frac{.5}{-.5}\right] = -P$$

so $MR = -P$. Thus, when demand is inelastic, marginal revenue is negative and less than price (in this example, marginal revenue is the negative of the price).

An alternative explanation for why marginal revenue is less than price for a monopolist is as follows: Suppose a monopolist sells one unit of output at a price of $4 per unit, for a total revenue of $4. What happens to revenue if the monopolist produces one more unit of output? Revenue increases by less than $4. To see why, note that the monopolist can sell one more unit of output only by lowering price, say, from $4 to $3 per unit. But the price reduction necessary to sell one more unit lowers the price received on the first unit from $4 to $3. The total revenue associated with two units of output thus is $6. The change in revenue due to producing one more unit is therefore $2, which is less than the price charged for the product.

Since the price a monopolist can charge for the product depends on how much is produced, let $P(Q)$ represent the price per unit paid by consumers for Q units of output. This relation summarizes the same information as a demand curve, but because price is expressed as a function of quantity instead of the other way around, it is called an *inverse demand function*. The inverse demand function, denoted $P(Q)$, indicates the price per unit as a function of the firm's output. The most common inverse demand function is the linear inverse demand function. The *linear inverse demand function* is given by

$$P(Q) = a + bQ$$

where a is a number greater than zero and b is a number less than zero.

In addition to the general formula for marginal revenue that is valid for all demand functions, it is useful to have the following formula for marginal revenue, which is valid for the special case of a linear inverse demand function.

Formula: MR for Linear Inverse Demand.   For the linear inverse demand function, $P(Q) = a + bQ$, marginal revenue is given by

$$MR = a + 2bQ$$

A Calculus Alternative

With a linear inverse demand function, the revenue function is
$$R(Q) = (a + bQ)Q$$

Marginal revenue is

$$MR = \frac{dR}{dQ} = a + 2bQ$$

Demonstration Problem 8–4

Suppose the inverse demand function for a monopolist's product is given by

$$P = 10 - 2Q$$

What is the maximum price per unit a monopolist can charge to be able to sell 3 units? What is marginal revenue when $Q = 3$?

Answer:

First, we set $Q = 3$ in the inverse demand function (here $a = 10$ and $b = -2$) to get

$$P = 10 - 2(3) = 4$$

Thus, the maximum price per unit the monopolist can charge to be able to sell 3 units is $4. To find marginal revenue when $Q = 3$, we set $Q = 3$ in the marginal revenue formula for linear inverse demand to get

$$MR = 10 - [(2)(2)(3)] = -2$$

The Output Decision

Revenues are one determinant of profits; costs are the other. Since the revenue a monopolist receives from selling Q units is $R(Q) = Q[P(Q)]$, the profits of a monopolist with a cost function of $C(Q)$ are

$$\pi = R(Q) - C(Q)$$

Typical revenue and cost functions are graphed in Figure 8–13(a). The vertical distance between the revenue and cost functions in panel (a) reflects the profits to the monopolist of alternative levels of output. Output levels below point A and above point B imply losses, since the cost curve lies above the revenue curve. For output levels between points A and B, the revenue function lies above the cost function, and profits are positive for those output levels.

Figure 8–13(b) depicts the profit function, which is the difference between R and C in panel (a). As Figure 8–13(a) shows, profits are greatest at an output of Q^M, where the vertical distance between the revenue and cost functions is the greatest. This corresponds to the maximum profit point in panel (b). A very important property of the profit-maximizing level of output (Q^M) is that the slope of the revenue function in panel (a) equals the slope of the cost function. In economic terms, marginal revenue equals marginal cost at an output of Q^M.

Principle   **Monopoly Output Rule**

A profit-maximizing monopolist should produce the output, Q^M, such that marginal revenue equals marginal cost:

$$MR(Q^M) = MC(Q^M)$$

A Calculus Alternative

The profits for a monopolist are

$$\pi = R(Q) - C(Q)$$

where $R(Q)$ is total revenue. To maximize profits, marginal profits must be zero:

$$\frac{d\pi}{dQ} = \frac{dR(Q)}{dQ} - \frac{dC(Q)}{dQ} = 0$$

or

$$MR = MC$$

FIGURE 8–13 Costs, Revenues, and Profits under Monopoly

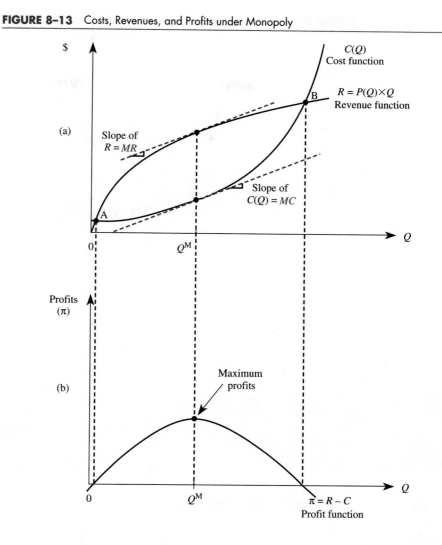

The economic intuition behind this important rule is as follows: If marginal revenue was greater than marginal cost, an increase in output would increase revenues more than it would increase costs. Thus, a profit-maximizing manager of a monopoly should continue to expand output when $MR > MC$. On the other hand, if marginal cost exceeded marginal revenue, a reduction in output would reduce costs by more than it would reduce revenue. A profit-maximizing manager thus is motivated to produce where marginal revenue equals marginal cost.

An alternative characterization of the profit-maximizing output decision of a monopoly is presented in Figure 8–14. The marginal revenue curve intersects the marginal cost curve when Q^M units are produced, so the profit-maximizing level of output is Q^M. The maximum price per unit that consumers are willing to pay for Q^M units is

FIGURE 8–14   Profit Maximization under Monopoly

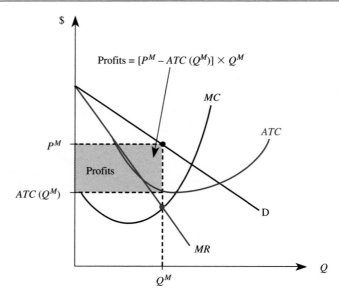

P^M, so the profit-maximizing price is P^M. Monopoly profits are given by the shaded rectangle in the figure, which is the base (Q^M) times the height [$P^M - ATC(Q^M)$].

Principle	**Monopoly Pricing Rule** Given the level of output, Q^M, that maximizes profits, the monopoly price is the price on the demand curve corresponding to the Q^M units produced: $$P^M = P(Q^M)$$

For a video walkthrough of this problem, visit www.mhhe.com/baye8e

Demonstration Problem 8–5

Suppose the inverse demand function for a monopolist's product is given by

$$P = 100 - 2Q$$

and the cost function is given by

$$C(Q) = 10 + 2Q$$

Determine the profit-maximizing price and quantity and the maximum profits.

Answer:

Using the marginal revenue formula for linear inverse demand and the formula for marginal cost, we see that

$$MR = 100 - (2)(2)(Q) = 100 - 4Q$$
$$MC = 2$$

Next, we set $MR = MC$ to find the profit-maximizing level of output:

$$100 - 4Q = 2$$

or

$$4Q = 98$$

Solving for Q yields the profit-maximizing output of $Q^M = 24.5$ units. We find the profit-maximizing price by setting $Q = Q^M$ in the inverse demand function:

$$P = 100 - 2(24.5) = 51$$

Thus, the profit-maximizing price is \$51 per unit. Finally, profits are given by the difference between revenues and costs:

$$\pi = P^M Q^M - C(Q^M)$$

$$= (51)(24.5) - [10 + 2(24.5)]$$

$$= \$1,190.50$$

The Absence of a Supply Curve

Recall that a supply curve determines how much will be produced at a given price. Since perfectly competitive firms determine how much output to produce based on price ($P = MC$), supply curves exist in perfectly competitive markets. In contrast, a monopolist determines how much to produce based on marginal revenue, which is less than price ($P > MR = MC$). This is because a change in quantity by a monopolist actually changes the market price. Consequently, there is no way to express how a monopolist's quantity choice would change for different given prices, so there is no supply curve for a monopolist. In fact there is no supply curve in markets served by firms with market power, such as monopolistic competition, which we discuss in the next section.

Multiplant Decisions

Up until this point, we have assumed that the monopolist produces output at a single location. In many instances, however, a monopolist has different plants at different locations. An important issue for the manager of such a *multiplant monopoly* is the determination of how much output to produce at each plant.

Suppose the monopolist produces output at two plants. The cost of producing Q_1 units at plant 1 is $C_1(Q_1)$, and the cost of producing Q_2 units at plant 2 is $C_2(Q_2)$. Further, suppose the products produced at the two plants are identical, so the price per unit consumers are willing to pay for the total output produced at the two plants is $P(Q)$, where

$$Q = Q_1 + Q_2$$

Profit maximization implies that the two-plant monopolist should produce output in each plant such that the marginal cost of producing in each plant equals the marginal revenue of total output.

Principle	**Multiplant Output Rule**
	Let $MR(Q)$ be the marginal revenue of producing a total of $Q = Q_1 + Q_2$ units of output. Suppose the marginal cost of producing Q_1 units of output in plant 1 is $MC_1(Q_1)$ and that of producing Q_2 units in plant 2 is $MC_2(Q_2)$. The profit maximization rule for the two-plant monopolist is to allocate output among the two plants such that

$$MR(Q) = MC_1(Q_1)$$
$$MR(Q) = MC_2(Q_2)$$

A Calculus Alternative

If profits are

$$\pi = R(Q_1 + Q_2) - C_1(Q_1) - C_2(Q_2)$$

the first-order conditions for maximizing profits are

$$\frac{d\pi}{dQ_1} = \frac{dR(Q_1 + Q_2)}{dQ_1} - \frac{dC_1(Q_1)}{dQ_1} = 0$$

$$\frac{d\pi}{dQ_2} = \frac{dR(Q_1 + Q_2)}{dQ_2} - \frac{dC_2(Q_2)}{dQ_2} = 0$$

The economic intuition underlying the multiplant output rule is precisely the same as all of the profit maximization principles. If the marginal revenue of producing output in a plant exceeds the marginal cost, the firm will add more to revenue than to cost by expanding output in the plant. As output is expanded, marginal revenue declines until it ultimately equals the marginal cost of producing in the plant. The conditions for maximizing profits in a multiplant setting imply that

$$MC_1(Q_1) = MC_2(Q_2)$$

This too has a simple economic explanation. If the marginal cost of producing in plant 1 is lower than that of producing in plant 2, the monopolist could reduce costs by producing more output in plant 1 and less in plant 2. As more output is produced in plant 1, the marginal cost of producing in the plant increases until it ultimately equals the marginal cost of producing in plant 2.

Demonstration Problem 8–6

Suppose the inverse demand for a monopolist's product is given by

$$P(Q) = 70 - .5Q$$

The monopolist can produce output in two plants. The marginal cost of producing in plant 1 is $MC_1 = 3Q_1$, and the marginal cost of producing in plant 2 is $MC_2 = Q_2$. How much output should be produced in each plant to maximize profits, and what price should be charged for the product?

Answer:

To maximize profits, the firm should produce output in the two plants such that

$$MR(Q) = MC_1(Q_1)$$

$$MR(Q) = MC_2(Q_2)$$

In this instance, marginal revenue is given by

$$MR(Q) = 70 - Q$$

where $Q = Q_1 + Q_2$. Substituting these values into the formula for the multiplant output rule, we get

$$70 - (Q_1 + Q_2) = 3Q_1$$

$$70 - (Q_1 + Q_2) = Q_2$$

Thus, we have two equations and two unknowns, and we must solve for the two unknowns. The first equation implies that

$$Q_2 = 70 - 4Q_1$$

Substituting this into the second equation yields

$$70 - (Q_1 + 70 - 4Q_1) = 70 - 4Q_1$$

Solving this equation, we find that $Q_1 = 10$. Next, we substitute this value of Q_1 into the first equation:

$$70 - (10 + Q_2) = 3(10)$$

Solving this equation, we find that $Q_2 = 30$. Thus, the firm should produce 10 units in plant 1 and 30 units in plant 2 for a total output of $Q = 40$ units.

To find the profit-maximizing price, we must find the maximum price per unit that consumers will pay for 40 units of output. To do this, we set $Q = 40$ in the inverse demand function:

$$P = 70 - .5(40) = 50$$

Thus, the profit-maximizing price is $50.

Implications of Entry Barriers

Our analysis of monopoly reveals that a monopolist may earn positive economic profits. If a monopolist is earning positive economic profits, the presence of barriers to entry prevents other firms from entering the market to reap a portion of those profits. Thus, monopoly profits, if they exist, will continue over time so long as the firm maintains its monopoly power. It is important to note, however, that the presence of monopoly power does not imply positive profits; it depends solely on where the demand curve lies in relation to the average total cost curve. For example, the monopolist depicted in Figure 8–15 earns zero economic profits, because the optimal price exactly equals the average total cost of production. Moreover, in the short run a monopolist may even experience losses.

FIGURE 8–15   A Monopolist Earning Zero Profits

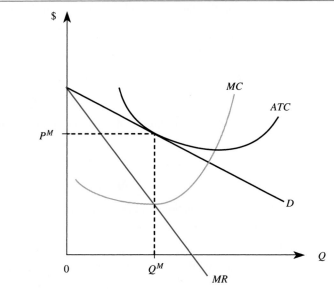

The monopoly power a monopolist enjoys often implies some social costs to society. Consider, for example, the monopolist's demand, marginal revenue, and marginal cost curves graphed in Figure 8–16. For simplicity, these curves are graphed as linear functions of output, and the position of the average cost curve is

FIGURE 8–16   Deadweight Loss of Monopoly

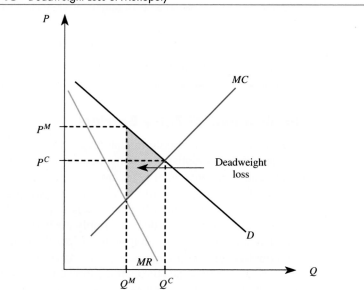

suppressed for now. The profit-maximizing monopolist produces Q^M units of output and charges a price of P^M.

The first thing to notice about monopoly is that price exceeds the marginal cost of production: $P^M > MC$. The price in a market reflects the value to society of another unit of output. Marginal cost reflects the cost to society of the resources needed to produce an additional unit of output. Since price exceeds marginal cost, the monopolist produces less output than is socially desirable. In effect, society would be willing to pay more for one more unit of output than it would cost to produce the unit. Yet the monopolist refuses to do so because it would reduce the firm's profits. This is because marginal revenue for a monopolist lies below the demand curve, and thus $MR < MC$ at this level of output.

deadweight loss of monopoly
The consumer and producer surplus that is lost due to the monopolist charging a price in excess of marginal cost.

In contrast, given the same demand and cost conditions, a firm in a perfectly competitive industry would continue to produce output up to the point where price equals marginal cost; this corresponds to an industry output and price of Q^C and P^C under perfect competition. Thus, the monopolist produces less output and charges a higher price than would a perfectly competitive industry. The shaded area in Figure 8–16 represents the *deadweight loss of monopoly*, that is, the welfare loss to society due to the monopolist producing output below the competitive level. To see this, recall from Chapter 2 that the vertical difference between demand and marginal cost (competitive supply) at each quantity represents the change in social welfare associated with each incremental unit of output. Summing these vertical distances for all units between the monopoly (Q^M) and competitive (Q^C) outputs yields the shaded triangle in Figure 8–16 and thus represents the welfare loss to society (in dollars) due to the monopolization of the market.

MONOPOLISTIC COMPETITION

monopolistically competitive market
A market in which (1) there are many buyers and sellers; (2) each firm produces a differentiated product; and (3) there is free entry and exit.

A market structure that lies between the extremes of monopoly and perfect competition is *monopolistic competition*. This market structure exhibits some characteristics present in both perfect competition and monopoly.

Conditions for Monopolistic Competition

An industry is monopolistically competitive if:

1. There are many buyers and sellers.
2. Each firm in the industry produces a differentiated product.
3. There is free entry into and exit from the industry.

There are numerous industries in which firms produce products that are close substitutes, and the market for hamburgers is a prime example. Many fast-food restaurants produce hamburgers, but the hamburgers produced by one firm differ from those produced by other firms. Moreover, it is relatively easy for new firms to enter the market for hamburgers.

The key difference between the models of monopolistic competition and perfect competition is that in a market with monopolistic competition, each firm produces a product that differs slightly from other firms' products. The products are close, but not perfect, substitutes. For example, other things being equal, some consumers prefer McDonald's hamburgers, whereas others prefer to eat at Wendy's, Burger King, or one of the many other restaurants that serve hamburgers. As the price of a McDonald's hamburger increases, some consumers will substitute toward hamburgers produced by another firm. But some consumers may continue to eat at McDonald's even if the price is higher than at other restaurants. The fact that the products are not perfect substitutes in a monopolistically competitive industry thus implies that each firm faces a downward-sloping demand curve for its product. To sell more of its product, the firm must lower the price. In this sense, the demand curve facing a monopolistically competitive firm looks more like the demand for a monopolist's product than like the demand for a competitive firm's product.

There are two important differences between a monopolistically competitive market and a market serviced by a monopolist. First, while a monopolistically competitive firm faces a downward-sloping demand for its product, there are other firms in the industry that sell similar products. Second, in a monopolistically competitive industry, there are no barriers to entry. As we will see later, this implies that firms will enter the market if existing firms earn positive economic profits.

Profit Maximization

The determination of the profit-maximizing price and output under monopolistic competition is precisely the same as for a firm operating under monopoly. To see this, consider the demand curve for a monopolistically competitive firm presented in Figure 8–17. Since the demand curve slopes downward, the marginal revenue curve lies below it, just as under monopoly. To maximize profits, the monopolistically

FIGURE 8–17   Profit Maximization under Monopolistic Competition

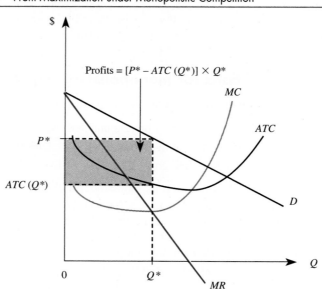

competitive firm produces where marginal revenue equals marginal cost. This output is given by Q^* in Figure 8–17. The profit-maximizing price is the maximum price consumers are willing to pay for Q^* units of the firm's output. The firm's profits are given by the shaded region.

Now that you understand that the basic principles of profit maximization are the same under monopolistic competition and monopoly, it is important to highlight one important difference in the interpretation of our analysis. The demand and marginal revenue curves used to determine the monopolistically competitive firm's profit-maximizing output and price are based not on the market demand for the product but on the demand for the individual firm's product. The demand curve facing a monopolist, in contrast, is the market demand curve.

In fact, because the firms in a monopolistically competitive industry produce differentiated products, the notion of an industry or market demand curve is not well defined. To find market demand, one must add up the total quantities purchased from all firms in the market at each price. But in monopolistically competitive markets, each firm produces a product that differs from other firms' products. Adding up these different products would be like adding up apples and oranges.

Principle	**Profit Maximization Rule for Monopolistic Competition**

Profit Maximization Rule for Monopolistic Competition

To maximize profits, a monopolistically competitive firm produces where its marginal revenue equals marginal cost. The profit-maximizing price is the maximum price per unit that consumers are willing to pay for the profit-maximizing level of output. In other words, the profit-maximizing output, Q^*, is such that

$$MR(Q^*) = MC(Q^*)$$

and the profit-maximizing price is

$$P^* = P(Q^*)$$

Demonstration Problem 8–7

Suppose the inverse demand function for a monopolistically competitive firm's product is given by

$$P = 100 - 2Q$$

and the cost function is given by

$$C(Q) = 5 + 2Q$$

Determine the profit-maximizing price and quantity and the maximum profits.

Answer:

Using the marginal revenue formula for linear inverse demand and the formula for marginal cost, we see that

$$MR = 100 - (2)(2)(Q) = 100 - 4Q$$
$$MC = 2$$

Next, we set $MR = MC$ to find the profit-maximizing level of output:

$$100 - 4Q = 2$$

or

$$4Q = 98$$

Solving for Q yields the profit-maximizing output of $Q^* = 24.5$ units. The profit-maximizing price is found by setting $Q = Q^*$ in the inverse demand function:

$$P^* = 100 - 2 \times 24.5 = 51$$

Thus, the profit-maximizing price is $51 per unit. Finally, profits are given by the difference between revenues and costs:

$$\pi = P^*Q^* - C(Q^*)$$

$$= (51)(24.5) - [5 + 2(24.5)]$$

$$= \$1,195.50$$

Long-Run Equilibrium

Because there is free entry into monopolistically competitive markets, if firms earn short-run profits in a monopolistically competitive industry, additional firms will enter the industry in the long run to capture some of those profits. Similarly, if existing firms incur losses, in the long run some firms will exit the industry.

INSIDE BUSINESS 8–3

Product Differentiation, Cannibalization, and Colgate's Smile

In 1896, Colgate dental cream was introduced in tubes similar to those we use now. Today, the Colgate-Palmolive Company's brand of toothpaste is the best-selling toothpaste in the world (ahead of the Crest brand marketed by Procter & Gamble, which was introduced in 1955).

While Colgate and Crest enjoy the lion's share of the toothpaste market, if you view the oral care shelf at your local drugstore or supermarket you will find over a hundred different varieties of toothpaste. Colgate alone sells over 40 different varieties that are marketed under names ranging from *Shrek Bubble Fruit* to *Colgate Total Advanced Whitening*.

Why would a dominant company like Colgate choose to sell so many different varieties of toothpaste—varieties that compete against each other for consumers' dollars?

The high level of product differentiation in the toothpaste market stems from firms introducing new varieties in an attempt to boost their economic profits. In environments where makers of other brands (such as Crest) can easily enter profitable segments of the market, a profitable strategy is to attempt to quickly cover that segment (introducing *Shrek Bubble Fruit* toothpaste, for instance) in order to earn short-run profits until other firms enter to steal a share of that segment. While introducing new varieties may cannibalize sales of your existing products, cannibalizing your own sales is better than having them stolen by a hungry competitor.

Sources: Corporate websites of the Colgate-Palmolive Company and Procter & Gamble and *Hoover's Online*.

To explain the impact of entry and exit in monopolistically competitive markets, suppose a monopolistically competitive firm is earning positive economic profits. The potential for profits induces other firms to enter the market and produce slight variations of the existing firm's product. As additional firms enter the market, some consumers who were buying the firm's product will begin to consume one of the new firms' products. Thus, one would expect the existing firms to lose a share of the market when new firms enter.

To make this notion more precise, suppose a monopolistically competitive firm that sells brand X faces an initial demand curve of D^0 in Figure 8–18. Since this demand curve lies above the ATC curve, the firm is earning positive economic profits. This, of course, lures more firms into the industry. As additional firms enter, the demand for this firm's product will decrease because some consumers will substitute toward the new products offered by the entering firms. Entry continues until the demand curve decreases to D^1, where it is just tangential to the firm's average cost curve. At this point, firms in the industry are earning zero economic profits, and there is no incentive for additional firms to enter the industry.

The story is similar if firms in the industry initially are incurring losses. However, in this instance firms will exit the industry, and the demand for the products offered by the firms that remain will increase. This process leads to increased profits (or, more accurately, reduced losses) for the remaining firms. Ultimately, firms stop leaving the industry when the remaining firms earn zero economic profits.

FIGURE 8–18 Effect of Entry on a Monopolistically Competitive Firm's Demand

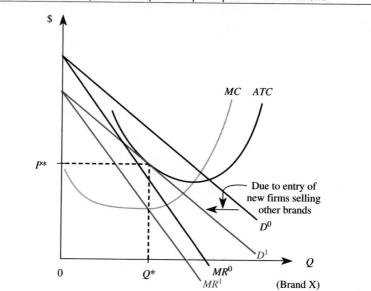

FIGURE 8-19   Long-Run Equilibrium under Monopolistic Competition

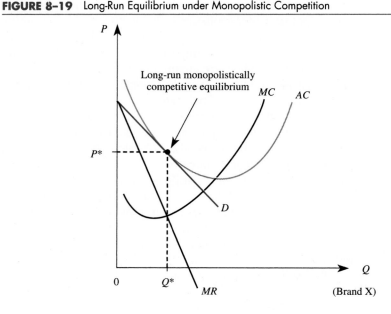

Thus, the long-run equilibrium in a monopolistically competitive industry is characterized by the situation in Figure 8–19. Each firm earns zero economic profits but charges a price that exceeds the marginal cost of producing the good.

Principle	**The Long Run and Monopolistic Competition** In the long run, monopolistically competitive firms produce a level of output such that 1. $P > MC$. 2. $P = ATC >$ minimum of average costs.

As in the case of monopoly, the fact that price exceeds marginal cost implies that monopolistically competitive firms produce less output than is socially desirable. In essence, consumers are willing to pay more for another unit than it would cost the firm to produce another unit; yet the firm will not produce more output because of its concern with profits.

Because price equals average costs, firms earn zero economic profits just as firms in perfectly competitive markets do. Even though the firms have some control over price, competition among them leads to a situation where no firm earns more than its opportunity cost of producing.

Finally, note that the price of output exceeds the minimum point on the average cost curve. This implies that firms do not take full advantage of economies of scale in production. In a sense there are too many firms in the industry to enable any individual firm to take full advantage of economies of scale in production. On the other hand, some argue that this is simply the cost to society of having product variety. If there were fewer firms, economies of scale could be fully exploited, but there would be less product variety in the market.

Implications of Product Differentiation

The key difference between perfect competition and monopolistic competition is the assumption that firms produce *differentiated products.* Since there are many products in a monopolistically competitive industry, the only reason firms have any control over their price is that consumers view the products as differentiated. The demand for a firm's product is less elastic when consumers view other firms' products as poor substitutes for it. The less elastic the demand for a firm's product, the greater the potential for earning profits.

comparative advertising
A form of advertising where a firm attempts to increase the demand for its brand by differentiating its product from competing brands.

For this reason, many firms in monopolistically competitive industries continually attempt to convince consumers that their products are better than those offered by other firms. A number of examples of such industries come readily to mind: fast-food restaurants, toothpaste, mouthwash, gasoline, aspirin, car wax—undoubtedly you can add other industries to the list. Each of these industries consists of many firms, and the different brands offered by firms in each industry are very close substitutes. In some instances, firms introduce several varieties of products; each soft-drink producer, for example, produces a variety of cola and noncola drinks.

brand equity
The additional value added to a product because of its brand.

Firms in monopolistically competitive industries employ two strategies to persuade consumers that their products are better than those offered by competitors. First, monopolistically competitive firms spend considerable amounts on advertising campaigns. Very typically, these campaigns involve *comparative advertising* designed to differentiate a given firm's brand from brands sold by competing firms. Comparative advertising is common in the fast-food industry. For example, Subway attempts to stimulate demand for its food by differentiating itself as the healthy fast-food alternative. To the extent that comparative advertising is effective, it may induce consumers to pay a premium for a particular brand. The additional value that a brand adds to the product is known as *brand equity.*

niche marketing
A marketing strategy where goods and services are tailored to meet the needs of a particular segment of the market.

green marketing
A form of niche marketing where firms target products toward consumers who are concerned about environmental issues.

Second, firms in monopolistically competitive industries frequently introduce new products into the market to further differentiate their products from other firms. These include not only "new, improved" products, such as an "improved" version of laundry detergent, but completely different product lines. Monopolistically competitive firms may also attempt to create and advertise new products that fill special needs in the market. This strategy—called *niche marketing*—involves products or services targeted to a specific group of consumers. Through *green marketing*, for instance, firms create and advertise "environmentally friendly" products in an attempt to capture the segment of the market that is concerned with environmental issues. Examples of green marketing include package labels that prominently indicate that a toy is made from recycled plastic or a particular brand of laundry detergent is biodegradable.

brand myopic
A manager or company that rests on a brand's past laurels instead of focusing on emerging industry trends or changes in consumer preferences.

Unfortunately, successful differentiation and branding strategies sometimes make managers myopic. A *brand myopic* manager is satisfied with an existing brand, is slow to launch new products, and is not aware of emerging industry trends or changes in consumer preferences. Essentially, a brand myopic company rests on its past laurels and, in so doing, misses opportunities to enhance (and hence protect) its brand. A few decades ago, for instance, Crest became the best-selling toothpaste through advertising campaigns that touted Crest as the brand that helps fight cavities. In recent years, however, fresh breath, white teeth, and gum sensitivity emerged as issues that consumers care about. Colgate capitalized on Crest's brand myopia by exploiting these new trends in consumer preferences and recently surpassed Crest as the leading toothpaste in the market.

As the manager of a firm in a monopolistically competitive industry, it is important for you to remember that, in the long run, additional firms will enter the market if your firm earns short-run profits with its product. Thus, while you may make short-run profits by introducing a new product line, in the long run other firms will mimic your product and/or introduce new product lines, and your economic profits will decrease to zero.

OPTIMAL ADVERTISING DECISIONS

How much should a firm spend on advertising in order to maximize profits? The answer depends, in part, on the nature of the industry in which the firm operates. Firms that operate in perfectly competitive markets generally do not find it profitable to advertise because consumers already have perfect information about the large number of substitutes that exist for any given firm's product. A wheat farmer who operates a small family farm, for instance, is unlikely to profit by spending family funds on an advertising campaign designed to increase the demand for the family's wheat. In contrast, firms that have market power—such as monopolists and monopolistically competitive firms—will generally find it profitable to spend a fraction of their revenues on advertising.

As with any economic decision, the optimal amount of advertising balances marginal benefits and marginal costs: To maximize these profits, managers should advertise up to the point where the incremental revenue from advertising equals the incremental cost. The incremental cost of advertising is simply the dollar cost of the resources needed to increase the level of advertising. These costs include fees paid for additional advertising space and the opportunity cost of the human resources needed to put together the advertising campaign. The incremental revenue is the extra revenue the firm gets as a result of the advertising campaign. These extra revenues depend on the number of additional units that will be sold as a result of an advertising campaign and how much is earned on each of these units. Fortunately, a simple formula is available that permits managers to easily determine the optimal level of advertising.

Formula: The Profit-Maximizing Advertising-to-Sales Ratio. The profit-maximizing advertising-to-sales ratio (*A/R*) is given by

$$\frac{A}{R} = \frac{E_{Q,A}}{-E_{Q,P}}$$

where $E_{Q,P}$ represents the own-price elasticity of demand for the firm's product, $E_{Q,A}$ is the advertising elasticity of demand for the firm's product, A represents the firm's expenditures on advertising, and $R = PQ$ denotes the dollar value of the firm's sales (that is, the firm's revenues).

A Calculus Alternative

A firm's profits are revenues minus production costs and advertising expenditures. If we let A represent advertising expenditures, $Q = Q(P, A)$ denote the demand for the firm's product, and $C(Q)$ denote production costs, firm profit is a function of P and A:

$$\pi(P, A) = Q(P, A)P - C[Q(P, A)] - A$$

The first-order conditions for maximizing profits require

$$\frac{\partial \pi}{\partial P} = \frac{\partial Q}{\partial P}P + Q - \frac{\partial C}{\partial Q}\frac{\partial Q}{\partial P} = 0 \tag{8–1}$$

and

$$\frac{\partial \pi}{\partial A} = \frac{\partial Q}{\partial A}P - \frac{\partial C}{\partial Q}\frac{\partial Q}{\partial A} - 1 = 0 \tag{8–2}$$

Noting that $\partial C/\partial Q = MC$ and $E_{Q,P} = (\partial Q/\partial P)(P/Q)$, we may write Equation 8–1 as

$$\frac{P - MC}{P} = \frac{-1}{E_{Q,P}} \tag{8–3}$$

Similarly, using the fact that $E_{Q,A} = (\partial Q/\partial A)(A/Q)$, Equation 8–2 implies

$$\frac{A}{R} = \left(\frac{P - MC}{P}\right)E_{Q,A} \tag{8–4}$$

Substituting Equation 8–3 into Equation 8–4 yields the above formula.

Two aspects of this formula are worth noting. First, the more elastic the demand for a firm's product, the lower the optimal advertising-to-sales ratio. In the extreme case where $E_{Q,P} = -\infty$ (perfect competition), the formula indicates that the optimal advertising-to-sales ratio is zero. Second, the greater the advertising elasticity, the greater the optimal advertising-to-sales ratio. Firms that have market power (such as monopolists and monopolistically competitive firms) face a demand curve that is not perfectly elastic. As a consequence, these firms will generally find it optimal to engage in some degree of advertising. Exactly how much such firms should spend on advertising, however, depends on the quantitative impact of advertising on demand. The more sensitive demand is to advertising (that is, the greater the advertising elasticity), the greater the number of additional units sold because of a given increase in advertising expenditures, and thus the greater the optimal advertising-to-sales ratio.

Demonstration Problem 8–8

Corpus Industries produces a product at constant marginal cost that it sells in a monopolistically competitive market. In an attempt to bolster profits, the manager hired an economist to estimate the demand for its product. She found that the demand for the firm's product is log-linear, with an own price elasticity of demand of -10 and an advertising elasticity of demand of 0.2. To maximize profits, what fraction of revenues should the firm spend on advertising?

Answer:

To find the profit-maximizing advertising-to-sales ratio, we simply plug $E_{Q,P} = -10$ and $E_{Q,A} = 0.2$ into the formula for the optimal advertising-to-sales ratio:

$$\frac{A}{R} = \frac{E_{Q,A}}{-E_{Q,P}} = \frac{0.2}{10} = 0.02$$

Thus, Corpus Industries' optimal advertising-to-sales ratio is 2 percent—to maximize profits, the firm should spend 2 percent of its revenues on advertising.

ANSWERING THE HEADLINE

As noted earlier in this chapter, the fast-food restaurant business has many features of monopolistic competition. Indeed, the owner of a typical McDonald's franchise competes not only against Burger King and Wendy's but against a host of other establishments. While each of these restaurants offers quick meals at reasonable prices, the products offered are clearly differentiated. Product differentiation gives these businesses some market power.

The McCafé program discussed in the opening headline was designed to further differentiate McDonald's from the competition. In so doing, McDonald's hoped to increase its own demand by attracting customers away from traditional coffee shops and other fast-food restaurants. In fact, this is exactly what happened, as McDonald's saw a large increase in its coffee sales over a short period of time. While a monopolistically competitive business like McDonald's might benefit in the short run by introducing new products more quickly than its rivals, in the long run its competitors will attempt to mimic the strategies that are profitable. For example, Starbucks recently acquired the La Boulange bakery brand, allowing it to offer more food options along with its coffee—an apparent response to McDonald's invading its turf. This type of entry by rival firms would likely reduce the demand for meals (and coffee) at McDonald's and ultimately result in long-run economic profits of zero. It is worth noting that a similar chain of events occurred in 1978 when McDonald's successfully launched its Egg McMuffin. Other fast-food restaurants eventually responded by launching their own breakfast items, which ultimately reduced McDonald's share of the breakfast market and its economic profits. For these reasons, it is unlikely that McDonald's McCafé program will have a sustainable impact on its bottom line.

SUMMARY

In this chapter, we examined managerial decisions in three market environments: perfect competition, monopoly, and monopolistic competition. Each of these market structures provides a manager with a different set of variables that can influence the firm's profits. A manager may need to pay particularly close attention to different decision parameters because different market structures allow control of only certain variables. Managers who recognize which variables are relevant for a particular industry will make more profits for their firms.

Managers in perfectly competitive markets should concentrate on producing the proper quantity and keeping costs low. Because perfectly competitive markets contain a very large number of firms that produce perfect substitutes, a manager in this market has no control over price. A manager in a monopoly, in contrast, needs to recognize the relation between price and quantity. By setting a quantity at which marginal cost equals marginal revenue, the manager of a monopoly will maximize profits. This is also true for the manager of a firm in a monopolistically competitive market, who also must evaluate the firm's product periodically to ensure that it is differentiated from other products in the market. In many instances, the manager of a monopolistically competitive firm will find it advantageous to slightly change the product from time to time to enhance product differentiation.

KEY TERMS AND CONCEPTS

brand equity
brand myopic
comparative advertising
cost complementarities
deadweight loss of monopoly
diseconomies of scale
economies of scale
economies of scope
firm demand curve
free entry
free exit

green marketing
inverse demand function
linear inverse demand function
marginal revenue
monopolistic competition
monopoly
multiplant monopoly
niche marketing
patents
perfectly competitive market
product differentiation

END-OF-CHAPTER PROBLEMS BY LEARNING OBJECTIVE

Every end-of-chapter problem addresses at least one learning objective. Following is a nonexhaustive sample of end-of-chapter problems for each learning objective.

LO1 Identify the conditions under which a firm operates as perfectly competitive, monopolistically competitive, or a monopoly.
    Try these problems: 6, 15

LO2 Identify sources of (and strategies for obtaining) monopoly power.
    Try these problems: 13, 23

LO3 Apply the marginal principle to determine the profit-maximizing price and output.
    Try these problems: 2, 21

LO4 Show the relationship between the elasticity of demand for a firm's product and its marginal revenue.

Try these problems: 4, 14

LO5 Explain how long-run adjustments impact perfectly competitive, monopoly, and monopolistically competitive firms; discuss the ramifications of each of these market structures on social welfare.

Try these problems: 3, 16

LO6 Decide whether a firm making short-run losses should continue to operate or shut down its operations.

Try these problems: 1, 17

LO7 Illustrate the relationship between marginal cost, a competitive firm's short-run supply curve, and the competitive industry supply; explain why supply curves do not exist for firms that have market power.

Try these problems: 5, 20

LO8 Calculate the optimal output of a firm that operates two plants and the optimal level of advertising for a firm that enjoys market power.

Try these problems: 8, 19

CONCEPTUAL AND COMPUTATIONAL QUESTIONS

■ connect
|ECONOMICS

1. The top graph on page 315 summarizes the demand and costs for a firm that operates in a perfectly competitive market.
   a. What level of output should this firm produce in the short run?
   b. What price should this firm charge in the short run?
   c. What is the firm's total cost at this level of output?
   d. What is the firm's total variable cost at this level of output?
   e. What is the firm's fixed cost at this level of output?
   f. What is the firm's profit if it produces this level of output?
   g. What is the firm's profit if it shuts down?
   h. In the long run, should this firm continue to operate or shut down?

2. A firm sells its product in a perfectly competitive market where other firms charge a price of $90 per unit. The firm's total costs are $C(Q) = 50 + 10Q + 2Q^2$.
   a. How much output should the firm produce in the short run?
   b. What price should the firm charge in the short run?
   c. What are the firm's short-run profits?
   d. What adjustments should be anticipated in the long run?

3. The bottom graph on page 315 summarizes the demand and costs for a firm that operates in a monopolistically competitive market.
   a. What is the firm's optimal output?
   b. What is the firm's optimal price?
   c. What are the firm's maximum profits?
   d. What adjustments should the manager be anticipating?

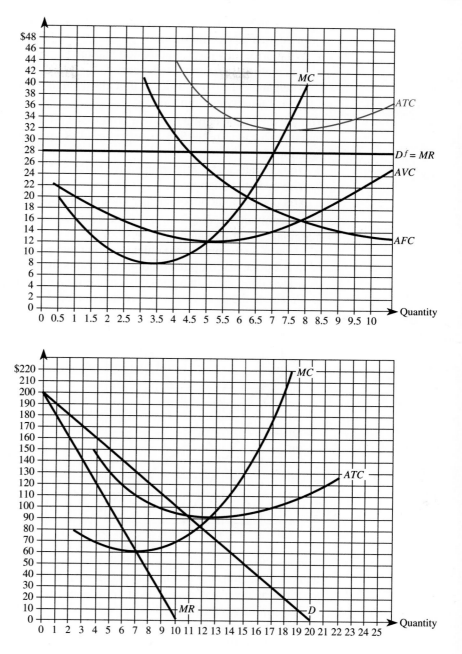

4. You are the manager of a monopoly, and your demand and cost functions are given by $P = 300 - 3Q$ and $C(Q) = 1,500 + 2Q^2$, respectively.
   a. What price–quantity combination maximizes your firm's profits?
   b. Calculate the maximum profits.

    c. Is demand elastic, inelastic, or unit elastic at the profit-maximizing
price–quantity combination?

    d. What price–quantity combination maximizes revenue?

    e. Calculate the maximum revenues.

    f. Is demand elastic, inelastic, or unit elastic at the revenue-maximizing
price–quantity combination?

5. You are the manager of a firm that produces a product according to the cost
function $C(q_i) = 160 + 58q_i - 6q_i^2 + q_i^3$. Determine the short-run supply
function if:

    a. You operate a perfectly competitive business.

    b. You operate a monopoly.

    c. You operate a monopolistically competitive business.

6. The accompanying diagram shows the demand, marginal revenue, and
marginal cost of a monopolist.

    a. Determine the profit-maximizing output and price.

    b. What price and output would prevail if this firm's product were sold by
price-taking firms in a perfectly competitive market?

    c. Calculate the deadweight loss of this monopoly.

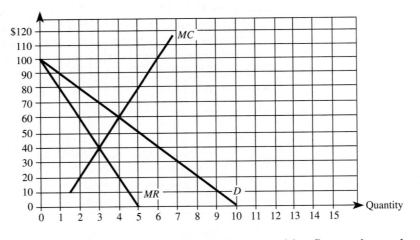

7. You are the manager of a monopolistically competitive firm, and your demand
and cost functions are given by $Q = 36 - 4P$ and $C(Q) = 124 - 16Q + Q^2$.

    a. Find the inverse demand function for your firm's product.

    b. Determine the profit-maximizing price and level of production.

    c. Calculate your firm's maximum profits.

    d. What long-run adjustments should you expect? Explain.

8. The elasticity of demand for a firm's product is -2.5 and its advertising
elasticity of demand is 0.2.

    a. Determine the firm's optimal advertising-to-sales ratio.

    b. If the firm's revenues are $40,000, what is its profit-maximizing level of
advertising?

9. A monopolist's inverse demand function is $P = 150 - 3Q$. The company produces output at two facilities; the marginal cost of producing at facility 1 is $MC_1(Q_1) = 6Q_1$, and the marginal cost of producing at facility 2 is $MC_2(Q_2) = 2Q_2$.
   a. Provide the equation for the monopolist's marginal revenue function. (*Hint:* Recall that $Q_1 + Q_2 = Q$.)
   b. Determine the profit-maximizing level of output for each facility.
   c. Determine the profit-maximizing price.

10. The manager of a local monopoly estimates that the elasticity of demand for its product is constant and equal to -3. The firm's marginal cost is constant at $20 per unit.
   a. Express the firm's marginal revenue as a function of its price.
   b. Determine the profit-maximizing price.

PROBLEMS AND APPLICATIONS

11. The CEO of a major automaker overheard one of its division managers make the following statement regarding the firm's production plans: "In order to maximize profits, it is essential that we operate at the minimum point of our average total cost curve." If you were the CEO of the automaker, would you praise or chastise the manager? Explain.

12. You are the manager of a small U.S. firm that sells nails in a competitive U.S. market (the nails you sell are a standardized commodity; stores view your nails as identical to those available from hundreds of other firms). You are concerned about two events you recently learned about through trade publications: (1) the overall market supply of nails will decrease by 2 percent, due to exit by foreign competitors; and (2) due to a growing U.S. economy, the overall market demand for nails will increase by 2 percent. Based on this information, should you plan to increase or decrease your production of nails? Explain.

13. When the first Pizza Hut opened its doors back in 1958, it offered consumers one style of pizza: its Original Thin Crust Pizza. Since its modest beginnings, Pizza Hut has established itself as the leader of the $25 billion pizza industry. Today, Pizza Hut offers six styles of pizza, including Pan Pizza, Stuffed Crust Pizza, and its Hand-Tossed Style. Explain why Pizza Hut has expanded its offerings of pizza over the past five decades, and discuss the long-run profitability of such a strategy.

14. You are the manager of a small pharmaceutical company that received a patent on a new drug three years ago. Despite strong sales ($150 million last year) and a low marginal cost of producing the product ($0.50 per pill), your company has yet to show a profit from selling the drug. This is, in part, due to the fact that the company spent $1.7 billion developing the drug and obtaining FDA approval. An economist has estimated that, at the current price of $1.50 per pill, the own price elasticity of demand for the drug is -2. Based on this information, what can you do to boost profits? Explain.

15. The second-largest public utility in the nation is the sole provider of electricity in 32 counties of southern Florida. To meet the monthly demand for electricity in these counties, which is given by the inverse demand function $P = 1,200 - 4Q$, the utility company has set up two electric generating facilities: Q_1 kilowatts are produced at facility 1, and Q_2 kilowatts are produced at facility 2 (so $Q = Q_1 + Q_2$). The costs of producing electricity at each facility are given by $C_1(Q_1) = 8,000 + 6Q_1^2$ and $C_2(Q_2) = 6,000 + 3Q_2^2$, respectively. Determine the profit-maximizing amounts of electricity to produce at the two facilities, the optimal price, and the utility company's profits.

16. You are the manager of College Computers, a manufacturer of customized computers that meet the specifications required by the local university. Over 90 percent of your clientele consists of college students. College Computers is not the only firm that builds computers to meet this university's specifications; indeed, it competes with many manufacturers online and through traditional retail outlets. To attract its large student clientele, College Computers runs a weekly ad in the student paper advertising its "free service after the sale" policy in an attempt to differentiate itself from the competition. The weekly demand for computers produced by College Computers is given by $Q = 800 - 2P$, and its weekly cost of producing computers is $C(Q) = 1,200 + 2Q^2$. If other firms in the industry sell PCs at $300, what price and quantity of computers should you produce to maximize your firm's profits? What long-run adjustments should you anticipate? Explain.

17. You are the general manager of a firm that manufactures personal computers. Due to a soft economy, demand for PCs has dropped 50 percent from the previous year. The sales manager of your company has identified only one potential client, who has received several quotes for 10,000 new PCs. According to the sales manager, the client is willing to pay $800 each for 10,000 new PCs. Your production line is currently idle, so you can easily produce the 10,000 units. The accounting department has provided you with the following information about the unit (or average) cost of producing three potential quantities of PCs:

	10,000 PCs	15,000 PCs	20,000 PCs
Materials (PC components)	$600	$600	$600
Depreciation	300	225	150
Labor	150	150	150
Total unit cost	$1,050	$975	$900

Based on this information, should you accept the offer to produce 10,000 PCs at $800 each? Explain.

18. You are a manager at Spacely Sprockets—a small firm that manufactures Type A and Type B bolts. The accounting and marketing departments have provided you with the following information about the per-unit costs and demand for Type A bolts:

Accounting Data for Type A Bolts		Marketing Data for Type A Bolts	
Item	Unit Cost	Quantity	Price
Materials and labor	$2.75	0	$10
Overhead	5.00	1	9
		2	8
Total cost per unit	$7.75	3	7
		4	6
		5	5

Materials and labor are obtained in a competitive market on an as-needed basis, and the reported costs per unit for materials and labor are constant over the relevant range of output. The reported unit overhead costs reflect the $10 spent last month on machines, divided by the projected output of 2 units that was planned when the machines were purchased. In addition to the above information, you know that the firm's assembly line can produce no more than five bolts. Since the firm also makes Type B bolts, this means that each Type A bolt produced reduces the number of Type B bolts that can be produced by one unit; the total number of Type A and B bolts produced cannot exceed 5 units. A call to a reputable source has revealed that unit costs for producing Type B bolts are identical to those for producing Type A bolts, and that Type B bolts can be sold at a constant price of $4.75 per unit. Determine your relevant marginal cost of producing Type A bolts and your profit-maximizing production of Type A bolts.

19. In a statement to Gillette's shareholders, Chairman and CEO James Kilts indicated, "Despite several new product launches, Gillette's advertising-to-sales declined dramatically . . . to 7.5 percent last year. Gillette's advertising spending, in fact, is one of the lowest in our peer group of consumer product companies." If the elasticity of demand for Gillette's consumer products is similar to other firms in its peer group (which averages -4), what is Gillette's advertising elasticity? Is Gillette's demand more or less responsive to advertising than other firms in its peer group? Explain.

20. According to the American Metal Markets Magazine, the spot market price of U.S. hot rolled steel recently reached $600 per ton. Less than a year ago this same ton of steel was only $300. A number of factors are cited to explain the large price increase. The combination of China's increased demand for

raw steel—due to expansion of its manufacturing base and infrastructure changes when preparing for the 2008 Beijing Olympics—and the weakening U.S. dollar against the euro and yuan partially explain the upward spiral in raw steel prices. Supply-side changes have also dramatically affected the price of raw steel. In the last 20 years there has been a rapid movement away from large integrated steel mills to mini-mills. The mini-mill production process replaces raw iron ore as its primary raw input with scrap steel. Today, mini-mills account for approximately 52 percent of all U.S. steel production. However, the worldwide movement to the mini-mill production model has bid up the price of scrap steel. In December, the per-ton price of scrap was around $140, and it soared to $285 just two months later. Suppose that, as a result of this increase in the price of scrap, the supply of raw steel changed from $Q^s_{raw} = 4,400 + 4P$ to $Q^s_{raw} = 800 + 4P$. Assuming the market for raw steel is competitive and that the current worldwide demand for steel is $Q^d_{raw} = 4,400 - 8P$, compute the equilibrium price and quantity when the per-ton price of scrap steel was $140, and the equilibrium price–quantity combination when the price of scrap steel reached $285 per ton. Suppose the cost function of a representative mini-mill producer is $C(Q) = 1,200 + 15Q^2$. Compare the change in the quantity of raw steel exchanged at the market level with the change in raw steel produced by a representative firm. How do you explain this difference?

21. The French government announced plans to convert state-owned power firms EDF and GDF into separate limited companies that operate in geographically distinct markets. BBC News reported that France's CFT union responded by organizing a mass strike, which triggered power outages in some Paris suburbs. Union workers are concerned that privatizing power utilities would lead to large-scale job losses and power outages similar to those experienced in parts of the eastern coast of the United States and parts of Italy in 2003. Suppose that prior to privatization, the price per kilowatt-hour of electricity was €0.13 and that the inverse demand for electricity in each of these two regions of France is $P = 1.35 - 0.002Q$ (in euros). Furthermore, to supply electricity to its particular region of France, it costs each firm $C(Q) = 120 + 0.13Q$ (in euros). Once privatized, each firm will have incentive to maximize profits. Determine the number of kilowatt-hours of electricity each firm will produce and supply to the market, and the per–kilowatt-hour price. Compute the price elasticity of demand at the profit-maximizing price–quantity combination. Explain why the price elasticity makes sense at the profit-maximizing price–quantity combination. Compare the price–quantity combination before and after privatization. How much more profit will each firm earn as a result of privatization?

22. The owner of an Italian restaurant has just been notified by her landlord that the monthly lease on the building in which the restaurant operates will increase by 20 percent at the beginning of the year. Her current prices are competitive with nearby restaurants of similar quality. However, she is now

considering raising her prices by 20 percent to offset the increase in her monthly rent. Would you recommend that she raise prices? Explain.

23. Last month you assumed the position of manager for a large car dealership. The distinguishing feature of this dealership is its "no hassle" pricing strategy; prices (usually well below the sticker price) are posted on the windows, and your sales staff has a reputation for not negotiating with customers. Last year, your company spent $2 million on advertisements to inform customers about its "no hassle" policy, and had overall sales revenue of $40 million. A recent study from an agency on Madison Avenue indicates that, for each 3 percent increase in TV advertising expenditures, a car dealer can expect to sell 12 percent more cars—but that it would take a 4 percent decrease in price to generate the same 12 percent increase in units sold. Assuming the information from Madison Avenue is correct, should you increase or decrease your firm's level of advertising? Explain.

CONNECT EXERCISES

If your instructor has adopted Connect for the course and you are an active subscriber, you can practice with the questions presented above, along with many alternative versions of these questions. Your instructor may also assign a subset of these problems and/or their alternative versions as a homework assignment through Connect, allowing for immediate feedback of grades and correct answers.

CASE-BASED EXERCISES

Your instructor may assign additional problem-solving exercises (called *memos*) that require you to apply some of the tools you learned in this chapter to make a recommendation based on an actual business scenario. Some of these memos accompany the Time Warner case (pages 561–597 of your textbook). Additional memos, as well as data that may be useful for your analysis, are available online at www.mhhe.com/baye8e.

SELECTED READINGS

Gal-Or, Esther, and Spiro, Michael H., "Regulatory Regimes in the Electric Power Industry: Implications for Capacity." *Journal of Regulatory Economics* 4(3), September 1992, pp. 263–78.

Gius, Mark Paul, "The Extent of the Market in the Liquor Industry: An Empirical Test of Localized Brand Rivalry, 1970–1988." *Review of Industrial Organization* 8(5), October 1993, pp. 599–608.

Lamdin, Douglas J., "The Welfare Effects of Monopoly versus Competition: A Clarification of Textbook Presentations." *Journal of Economic Education* 23(3), Summer 1992, pp. 247–53.

Malueg, David A., "Monopoly Output and Welfare: The Role of Curvature of the Demand Function." *Journal of Economic Education* 25(3), Summer 1994, pp. 235–50.

Nguyen, Dung, "Advertising, Random Sales Response, and Brand Competition: Some The-oretical and Econometric Implications." *Journal of Business* 60(2), April 1987, pp. 259–79.

Simon, Herbert A., "Organizations and Markets." *Journal of Economic Perspectives* 5(2), Spring 1991, pp. 25–44.

Stegeman, Mark, "Advertising in Competitive Markets." *American Economic Review* 81(1), March 1991, pp. 210–23.

Zupan, Mark A., "On Cream Skimming, Coase, and the Sustainability of Natural Monopolies." *Applied Economics* 22(4), April 1990, pp. 487–92.

APPENDIX
The Calculus of Profit Maximization

Perfect Competition

The profits of a perfectly competitive firm are

$$\pi = PQ - C(Q)$$

The first-order conditions for maximizing profits require that marginal profits be zero:

$$\frac{d\pi}{dQ} = P - \frac{dC(Q)}{dQ} = 0$$

Thus, we obtain the profit-maximizing rule for a firm in perfect competition:

$$P = \frac{dC}{dQ}$$

or

$$P = MC$$

The second-order condition for maximizing profits requires that

$$\frac{d^2\pi}{dQ^2} = -\frac{d^2C}{dQ^2} = -\frac{dMC}{dQ} < 0$$

This means that $d(MC)/dQ > 0$, or that marginal cost must be increasing in output.

Monopoly and Monopolistic Competition

MR = MC Rule

The profits for a firm with market power are

$$\pi = R(Q) - C(Q)$$

where $R(Q) = P(Q)Q$ is total revenue. To maximize profits, marginal profits must be zero:

$$\frac{d\pi}{dQ} = \frac{dR(Q)}{dQ} - \frac{dC(Q)}{dQ} = 0$$

or

$$MR = MC$$

The second-order condition requires that

$$\frac{d^2\pi}{dQ^2} = \frac{d^2R(Q)}{dQ^2} - \frac{d^2C(Q)}{dQ^2} < 0$$

which means that

$$\frac{dMR}{dQ} < \frac{dMC}{dQ}$$

But this simply means that the slope of the marginal revenue curve must be less than the slope of the marginal cost curve.

APPENDIX
The Algebra of Perfectly Competitive Supply Functions

This appendix shows how to obtain the short-run firm and industry supply functions from cost data. Suppose there are 500 firms in a perfectly competitive industry, with each firm having a cost function of

$$C(q_i) = 50 + 2q_i + 4q_i^2$$

The corresponding average total cost (*ATC*), average variable cost (*AVC*), and marginal cost (*MC*) functions are

$$ATC_i = \frac{50}{q_i} + 2 + 4q_i$$

$$AVC_i = 2 + 4q_i$$

and

$$MC_i = 2 + 8q_i$$

Recall that a firm's supply curve is the firm's marginal cost curve above the minimum of average variable cost. Since *AVC* is at its minimum where it equals marginal cost, to find the quantity where average variable cost equals marginal cost, we must set the two functions equal to each other and solve for q_i. When we do this for the above equations, we find that the quantity at which marginal cost equals average variable cost is $q_i = 0$.

Next, we recognize that an individual firm maximizes profits by equating $P = MC_i$, so

$$P = 2 + 8q_i$$

Solving for q_i gives us the individual firm's supply function:

$$q_i = -\frac{2}{8} + \frac{1}{8}P$$

To find the supply curve for the industry, we simply sum the above equation over all 500 firms in the market:

$$Q = \sum_{i=1}^{500} q_i = 500\left(-\frac{2}{8} + \frac{1}{8}P\right) = -\frac{1,000}{8} + \frac{500}{8}P$$

or

$$Q = -125 + 62.5P$$

CHAPTER NINE

Basic Oligopoly Models

Crude Oil Prices Fall, but Consumers in Some Areas See No Relief at the Pump

Thanks to a recent decline in crude oil prices, consumers in most locations recently enjoyed lower gasoline prices. In a few isolated areas, however, consumers cried foul because gasoline retailers did not pass on the price reductions to those who pay at the pump. Consumer groups argued that this corroborated their claim that gasoline retailers in these areas were colluding in order to earn monopoly profits. For obvious reasons, the gasoline retailers involved denied the allegations.

Based on the evidence, do you think that gasoline stations in these areas were colluding in order to earn monopoly profits? Explain.

Learning Objectives

After completing this chapter, you will be able to:

LO1 Explain how beliefs and strategic interaction shape optimal decisions in oligopoly environments.

LO2 Identify the conditions under which a firm operates in a Sweezy, Cournot, Stackelberg, or Bertrand oligopoly, and the ramifications of each type of oligopoly for optimal pricing decisions, output decisions, and firm profits.

LO3 Apply reaction (or best-response) functions to identify optimal decisions and likely competitor responses in oligopoly settings.

LO4 Identify the conditions for a contestable market, and explain the ramifications for market power and the sustainability of long-run profits.

INTRODUCTION

Up until now, our analysis of markets has not considered the impact of strategic behavior on managerial decision making. At one extreme, we examined profit maximization in perfectly competitive and monopolistically competitive markets. In these types of markets, so many firms are competing with one another that no individual firm has any effect on other firms in the market. At the other extreme, we examined profit maximization in a monopoly market. In this instance there is only one firm in the market, and strategic interactions among firms thus are irrelevant.

This chapter is the first of two chapters in which we examine managerial decisions in oligopoly markets. Here we focus on basic output and pricing decisions in four specific types of oligopolies: Sweezy, Cournot, Stackelberg, and Bertrand. In the next chapter, we will develop a more general framework for analyzing other decisions, such as advertising, research and development, entry into an industry, and so forth. First, let us briefly review what is meant by the term *oligopoly*.

CONDITIONS FOR OLIGOPOLY

oligopoly
A market structure in which there are only a few firms, each of which is large relative to the total industry.

Oligopoly refers to a situation where there are relatively few large firms in an industry. No explicit number of firms is required for oligopoly, but the number usually is somewhere between 2 and 10. The products the firms offer may be either identical (as in a perfectly competitive market) or differentiated (as in a monopolistically competitive market). An oligopoly composed of only two firms is called a *duopoly*.

Oligopoly is perhaps the most interesting of all market structures; in fact, the next chapter is devoted entirely to the analysis of situations that arise under oligopoly. But from the viewpoint of the manager, a firm operating in an oligopoly setting is the most difficult to manage. The key reason is that there are few firms in an oligopolistic market and the manager must consider the likely impact of her or his decisions on the decisions of other firms in the industry. Moreover, the actions of other firms will have a profound impact on the manager's optimal decisions. It should be noted that due to the complexity of oligopoly, there is no single model that is relevant for all oligopolies.

THE ROLE OF BELIEFS AND STRATEGIC INTERACTION

To gain an understanding of oligopoly interdependence, consider a situation where several firms selling differentiated products compete in an oligopoly. In determining what price to charge, the manager must consider the impact of his or her decisions on other firms in the industry. For example, if the price for the product is lowered, will other firms lower their prices or maintain their existing prices? If the price is increased, will other firms do likewise or maintain their current prices? The optimal decision of whether to raise or lower price will depend on how the manager believes other managers will respond. If other firms lower their prices when the firm lowers its price, it will not sell as much as it would if the other firms maintained their existing prices.

FIGURE 9-1 A Firm's Demand Depends on Actions of Rivals

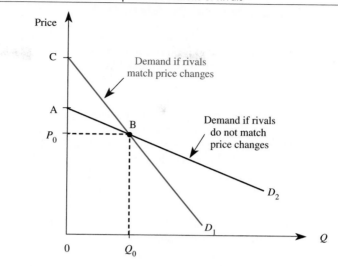

As a point of reference, suppose the firm initially is at point B in Figure 9–1, charging a price of P_0. Demand curve D_1 is based on the assumption that rivals will match any price change, while D_2 is based on the assumption that they will not match a price change. Note that demand is more inelastic when rivals match a price change than when they do not. The reason for this is simple. For a given price reduction, a firm will sell more if rivals do not cut their prices (D_2) than it will if they lower their prices (D_1). In effect, a price reduction increases quantity demanded only slightly when rivals respond by lowering their prices. Similarly, for a given price increase, a firm will sell more when rivals also raise their prices (D_1) than it will when they maintain their existing prices (D_2).

Demonstration Problem 9–1

Suppose the manager is at point B in Figure 9–1, charging a price of P_0. If the manager believes rivals will not match price reductions but will match price increases, what does the demand for the firm's product look like?

Answer:

If rivals do not match price reductions, prices below P_0 will induce quantities demanded along curve D_2. If rivals do match price increases, prices above P_0 will generate quantities demanded along D_1. Thus, if the manager believes rivals will not match price reductions but will match price increases, the demand curve for the firm's product is given by CBD_2.

Demonstration Problem 9–2

Suppose the manager is at point B in Figure 9–1, charging a price of P_0. If the manager believes rivals will match price reductions but will not match price increases, what does the demand for the firm's product look like?

Answer:

If rivals match price reductions, prices below P_0 will induce quantities demanded along curve D_1. If rivals do not match price increases, prices above P_0 will induce quantities demanded along D_2. Thus, if the manager believes rivals will match price reductions but will not match price increases, the demand curve for the firm's product is given by ABD_1.

The preceding analysis reveals that the demand for a firm's product in oligopoly depends critically on how rivals respond to the firm's pricing decisions. If rivals will match any price change, the demand curve for the firm's product is given by D_1. In this instance, the manager will maximize profits where the marginal revenue associated with demand curve D_1 equals marginal cost. If rivals will not match any price change, the demand curve for the firm's product is given by D_2. In this instance, the manager will maximize profits where the marginal revenue associated with demand curve D_2 equals marginal cost. In each case, the profit-maximizing rule is the same as that under monopoly; the only difficulty for the firm manager is determining whether or not rivals will match price changes.

PROFIT MAXIMIZATION IN FOUR OLIGOPOLY SETTINGS

In the following subsections, we will examine profit maximization based on alternative assumptions regarding how rivals will respond to price or output changes. Each of the four models has different implications for the manager's optimal decisions, and these differences arise because of differences in the ways rivals respond to the firm's actions.

Sweezy Oligopoly

Sweezy oligopoly
An industry in which (1) there are few firms serving many consumers; (2) firms produce differentiated products; (3) each firm believes rivals will respond to a price reduction but will not follow a price increase; and (4) barriers to entry exist.

The Sweezy model is based on a very specific assumption regarding how other firms will respond to price increases and price cuts. An industry is characterized as a *Sweezy oligopoly* if

1. There are few firms in the market serving many consumers.
2. The firms produce differentiated products.
3. Each firm believes rivals will cut their prices in response to a price reduction but will not raise their prices in response to a price increase.
4. Barriers to entry exist.

Because the manager of a firm competing in a Sweezy oligopoly believes other firms will match any price decrease but not match price increases, the demand curve for the firm's product is given by ABD_1 in Figure 9–2. For prices above P_0,

FIGURE 9–2 Sweezy Oligopoly

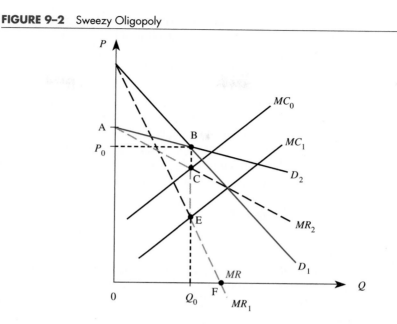

the relevant demand curve is D_2; thus, marginal revenue corresponds to this demand curve. For prices below P_0, the relevant demand curve is D_1, and marginal revenue corresponds to D_1. Thus, the marginal revenue curve (MR) the firm faces is initially the marginal revenue curve associated with D_2; at Q_0, it jumps down to the marginal revenue curve corresponding to D_1. In other words, the Sweezy oligopolist's marginal revenue curve, denoted MR, is ACEF in Figure 9–2.

The profit-maximizing level of output occurs where marginal revenue equals marginal cost, and the profit-maximizing price is the maximum price consumers will pay for that level of output. For example, if marginal cost is given by MC_0 in Figure 9–2, marginal revenue equals marginal cost at point C. In this case the profit-maximizing output is Q_0 and the optimal price is P_0. Since price exceeds marginal cost ($P_0 > MC_0$), output is below the socially efficient level. This situation translates into a deadweight loss (lost consumer and producer surplus) that does not arise in a perfectly competitive market.

An important implication of the Sweezy model of oligopoly is that there will be a range (CE) over which changes in marginal cost do not affect the profit-maximizing level of output. This is in contrast to competitive, monopolistically competitive, and monopolistic firms, all of which increase output when marginal costs decline.

To see why firms competing in a Sweezy oligopoly may not increase output when marginal cost declines, suppose marginal cost decreases from MC_0 to MC_1 in Figure 9–2. Marginal revenue now equals marginal cost at point E, but the output corresponding to this point is still Q_0. Thus the firm continues to maximize profits by producing Q_0 units at a price of P_0.

In a Sweezy oligopoly, firms have an incentive not to change their pricing behavior provided marginal costs remain in a given range. The reason for this stems purely from the assumption that rivals will match price cuts but not price increases.

Firms in a Sweezy oligopoly do not want to change their prices because of the effect of price changes on the behavior of other firms in the market.

The Sweezy model has been criticized because it offers no explanation of how the industry settles on the initial price P_0 that generates the kink in each firm's demand curve. Nonetheless, the Sweezy model does show us that strategic interactions among firms and a manager's beliefs about rivals' reactions can have a profound impact on pricing decisions. In practice, the initial price and a manager's beliefs may be based on a manager's experience with the pricing patterns of rivals in a given market. If your experience suggests that rivals will match price reductions but will not match price increases, the Sweezy model is probably the best tool to use in formulating your pricing decisions.

Cournot Oligopoly

Imagine that a few large oil producers must decide how much oil to pump out of the ground. The total amount of oil produced will certainly affect the market price of oil, but the underlying decision of each firm is not a pricing decision but rather the *quantity* of oil to produce. If each firm must determine its output level at the same time other firms determine their output levels, or more generally, if each firm expects its own output decision to have no impact on rivals' output decisions, then this scenario describes a Cournot oligopoly.

Cournot oligopoly
An industry in which (1) there are few firms serving many consumers; (2) firms produce either differentiated or homogeneous products; (3) each firm believes rivals will hold their output constant if it changes its output; and (4) barriers to entry exist.

More formally, an industry is a *Cournot oligopoly* if

1. There are few firms in the market serving many consumers.
2. The firms produce either differentiated or homogeneous products.
3. Each firm believes rivals will hold their output constant if it changes its output.
4. Barriers to entry exist.

Thus, in contrast to the Sweezy model of oligopoly, the Cournot model is relevant for decision making when managers make output decisions and believe that their decisions do not affect the output decisions of rival firms. Furthermore, the Cournot model applies to situations in which the products are either identical or differentiated.

Reaction Functions and Equilibrium

To highlight the implications of Cournot oligopoly, suppose there are only two firms competing in a Cournot duopoly: Each firm must make an output decision, and each firm believes that its rival will hold output constant as it changes its own output. To determine its optimal output level, firm 1 will equate marginal revenue with marginal cost. Notice that since this is a duopoly, firm 1's marginal revenue is affected by firm 2's output level. In particular, the greater the output of firm 2, the lower the market price and thus the lower is firm 1's marginal revenue. This means that the profit-maximizing level of output for firm 1 depends on firm 2's output level: A greater output by firm 2 leads to a lower profit-maximizing output for firm 1. This relationship between firm 1's profit-maximizing output and firm 2's output is called a best-response or reaction function.

best-response (or reaction) function
A function that defines the profit-maximizing level of output for a firm for given output levels of another firm.

A *best-response function* (also called a *reaction function*) defines the profit-maximizing level of output for a firm for given output levels of the other firm. More formally, the profit-maximizing level of output for firm 1 given that firm 2 produces Q_2 units of output is

$$Q_1 = r_1(Q_2)$$

Similarly, the profit-maximizing level of output for firm 2 given that firm 1 produces Q_1 units of output is given by

$$Q_2 = r_2(Q_1)$$

Cournot reaction (best-response) functions for a duopoly are illustrated in Figure 9–3, where firm 1's output is measured on the horizontal axis and firm 2's output is measured on the vertical axis.

To understand why reaction functions are shaped as they are, let us highlight a few important points in the diagram. First, if firm 2 produced zero units of output, the profit-maximizing level of output for firm 1 would be Q_1^M, since this is the point on firm 1's reaction function (r_1) that corresponds to zero units of Q_2. This combination of outputs corresponds to the situation where only firm 1 is producing a positive level of output; thus, Q_1^M corresponds to the situation where firm 1 is a monopolist. If instead of producing zero units of output firm 2 produced Q_2^* units, the profit-maximizing level of output for firm 1 would be Q_1^*, since this is the point on r_1 that corresponds to an output of Q_2^* by firm 2.

The reason the profit-maximizing level of output for firm 1 decreases as firm 2's output increases is as follows: The demand for firm 1's product depends on the

FIGURE 9–3 Cournot Reaction Functions

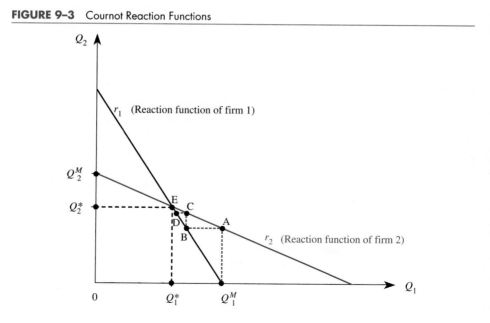

output produced by other firms in the market. When firm 2 increases its level of output, the demand and marginal revenue for firm 1 decline. The profit-maximizing response by firm 1 is to reduce its level of output.

Demonstration Problem 9–3

In Figure 9–3, what is the profit-maximizing level of output for firm 2 when firm 1 produces zero units of output? What is it when firm 1 produces Q_1^* units?

Answer:

If firm 1 produces zero units of output, the profit-maximizing level of output for firm 2 will be Q_2^M, since this is the point on firm 2's reaction function that corresponds to zero units of Q_1. The output of Q_2^M corresponds to the situation where firm 2 is a monopolist. If firm 1 produces Q_1^* units, the profit-maximizing level of output for firm 2 will be Q_2^*, since this is the point on r_2 that corresponds to an output of Q_1^* by firm 1.

To examine equilibrium in a Cournot duopoly, suppose firm 1 produces Q_1^M units of output. Given this output, the profit-maximizing level of output for firm 2 will correspond to point A on r_2 in Figure 9–3. Given this positive level of output by firm 2, the profit-maximizing level of output for firm 1 will no longer be Q_1^M, but will correspond to point B on r_1. Given this reduced level of output by firm 1, point C will be the point on firm 2's reaction function that maximizes profits. Given this new output by firm 2, firm 1 will again reduce output to point D on its reaction function.

How long will these changes in output continue? Until point E in Figure 9–3 is reached. At point E, firm 1 produces Q_1^* and firm 2 produces Q_2^* units. Neither firm has an incentive to change its output given that it believes the other firm will hold its output constant at that level. Point E thus corresponds to the Cournot equilibrium. *Cournot equilibrium* is the situation where neither firm has an incentive to change its output given the output of the other firm. Graphically, this condition corresponds to the intersection of the reaction curves.

Thus far, our analysis of Cournot oligopoly has been graphical rather than algebraic. However, given estimates of the demand and costs within a Cournot oligopoly, we can explicitly solve for the Cournot equilibrium. How do we do this? To maximize profits, a manager in a Cournot oligopoly produces where marginal revenue equals marginal cost. The calculation of marginal cost is straightforward; it is done just as in the other market structures we have analyzed. The calculation of marginal revenues is a little more subtle. Consider the following formula:

Cournot equilibrium
A situation in which neither firm has an incentive to change its output given the other firm's output.

Formula: Marginal Revenue for Cournot Duopoly. If the (inverse) market demand in a homogeneous-product Cournot duopoly is

$$P = a - b(Q_1 + Q_2)$$

where a and b are positive constants, then the marginal revenues of firms 1 and 2 are

$$MR_1(Q_1, Q_2) = a - bQ_2 - 2bQ_1$$
$$MR_2(Q_1, Q_2) = a - bQ_1 - 2bQ_2$$

A Calculus Alternative

Firm 1's revenues are

$$R_1 = PQ_1 = [a - b(Q_1 + Q_2)]Q_1$$

Thus,

$$MR_1(Q_1, Q_2) = \frac{\partial R_1}{\partial Q_1} = a - bQ_2 - 2bQ_1$$

A similar analysis yields the marginal revenue for firm 2.

Notice that the marginal revenue for each Cournot oligopolist depends not only on the firm's own output but also on the other firm's output. In particular, when firm 2 increases its output, firm 1's marginal revenue falls. This is because the increase in output by firm 2 lowers the market price, resulting in lower marginal revenue for firm 1.

Since each firm's marginal revenue depends on its own output *and* that of the rival, the output where a firm's marginal revenue equals marginal cost depends on the other firm's output level. If we equate firm 1's marginal revenue with its marginal cost and then solve for firm 1's output as a function of firm 2's output, we obtain an algebraic expression for firm 1's reaction function. Similarly, by equating firm 2's marginal revenue with marginal cost and performing some algebra, we obtain firm 2's reaction function. The results of these computations are summarized below.

Formula: Reaction Functions for Cournot Duopoly. For the linear (inverse) demand function

$$P = a - b(Q_1 + Q_2)$$

and cost functions,

$$C_1(Q_1) = c_1 Q_1$$
$$C_2(Q_2) = c_2 Q_2$$

the reaction functions are

$$Q_1 = r_1(Q_2) = \frac{a - c_1}{2b} - \frac{1}{2}Q_2$$

$$Q_2 = r_2(Q_1) = \frac{a - c_2}{2b} - \frac{1}{2}Q_1$$

To see how the preceding formulas are derived, note that firm 1 sets output such that

$$MR_1(Q_1, Q_2) = MC_1$$

For the linear (inverse) demand and cost functions, this means that

$$a - bQ_2 - 2bQ_1 = c_1$$

Solving this equation for Q_1 in terms of Q_2 yields

$$Q_1 = r_1(Q_2) = \frac{a - c_1}{2b} - \frac{1}{2}Q_2$$

The reaction function for firm 2 is computed similarly.

For a video walkthrough of this problem, visit www.mhhe.com/ baye8e

Demonstration Problem 9–4

Suppose the inverse demand function for two Cournot duopolists is given by

$$P = 10 - (Q_1 + Q_2)$$

and their costs are zero.

1. What is each firm's marginal revenue?
2. What are the reaction functions for the two firms?
3. What are the Cournot equilibrium outputs?
4. What is the equilibrium price?

Answer:

1. Using the formula for marginal revenue under Cournot duopoly, we find that

$$MR_1(Q_1, Q_2) = 10 - Q_2 - 2Q_1$$
$$MR_2(Q_1, Q_2) = 10 - Q_1 - 2Q_2$$

2. Similarly, the reaction functions are

$$Q_1 = r_1(Q_2) = \frac{10}{2} - \frac{1}{2}Q_2$$
$$= 5 - \frac{1}{2}Q_2$$
$$Q_2 = r_2(Q_1) = \frac{10}{2} - \frac{1}{2}Q_1$$
$$= 5 - \frac{1}{2}Q_1$$

3. To find the Cournot equilibrium, we must solve the two reaction functions for the two unknowns:

$$Q_1 = 5 - \frac{1}{2}Q_2$$

$$Q_2 = 5 - \frac{1}{2}Q_1$$

Inserting Q_2 into the first reaction function yields

$$Q_1 = 5 - \frac{1}{2}\left[5 - \frac{1}{2}Q_1\right]$$

Solving for Q_1 yields

$$Q_1 = \frac{10}{3}$$

To find Q_2, we plug $Q_1 = 10/3$ into firm 2's reaction function to get

$$Q_2 = 5 - \frac{1}{2}\left(\frac{10}{3}\right)$$

$$= \frac{10}{3}$$

4. Total industry output is

$$Q = Q_1 + Q_2 = \frac{10}{3} + \frac{10}{3} = \frac{20}{3}$$

The price in the market is determined by the (inverse) demand for this quantity:

$$P = 10 - (Q_1 + Q_2)$$

$$= 10 - \frac{20}{3}$$

$$= \frac{10}{3}$$

Regardless of whether Cournot oligopolists produce homogeneous or differentiated products, industry output is lower than the socially efficient level. This inefficiency arises because the equilibrium price exceeds marginal cost. The amount by which price exceeds marginal cost depends on the number of firms in the industry as well as the degree of product differentiation. The equilibrium price declines toward marginal cost as the number of firms rises. When the number of firms is arbitrarily large, the equilibrium price in a homogeneous product Cournot market is arbitrarily close to marginal cost, and industry output approximates that under perfect competition (there is no deadweight loss).

FIGURE 9–4 Isoprofit Curves for Firm 1

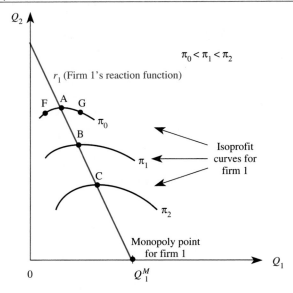

Isoprofit Curves

Now that you have a basic understanding of Cournot oligopoly, we will examine how to graphically determine the firm's profits. Recall that the profits of a firm in an oligopoly depend not only on the output it chooses to produce but also on the output produced by other firms in the oligopoly. In a duopoly, for instance, increases in firm 2's output will reduce the price of the output. This is due to the law of demand: As more output is sold in the market, the price consumers are willing and able to pay for the good declines. This will, of course, alter the profits of firm 1.

The basic tool used to summarize the profits of a firm in Cournot oligopoly is an *isoprofit curve,* which defines the combinations of outputs of all firms that yield a given firm the same level of profits.

Figure 9–4 presents the reaction function for firm 1 (r_1), along with three isoprofit curves (labeled π_0, π_1, and π_2). Four aspects of Figure 9–4 are important to understand:

isoprofit curve
A function that defines the combinations of outputs produced by all firms that yield a given firm the same level of profits.

1. Every point on a given isoprofit curve yields firm 1 the same level of profits. For instance, points F, A, and G all lie on the isoprofit curve labeled π_0; thus, each of these points yields profits of exactly π_0 for firm 1.
2. Isoprofit curves that lie closer to firm 1's monopoly output Q_1^M are associated with higher profits for that firm. For instance, isoprofit curve π_2 implies higher profits than does π_1, and π_1 is associated with higher profits than π_0. In other words, as we move down firm 1's reaction function from point A to point C, firm 1's profits increase.
3. The isoprofit curves for firm 1 reach their peak where they intersect firm 1's reaction function. For instance, isoprofit curve π_0 peaks at point A, where it intersects r_1; π_1 peaks at point B, where it intersects r_1, and so on.
4. The isoprofit curves do not intersect one another.

FIGURE 9–5 Firm 1's Best Response to Firm 2's Output

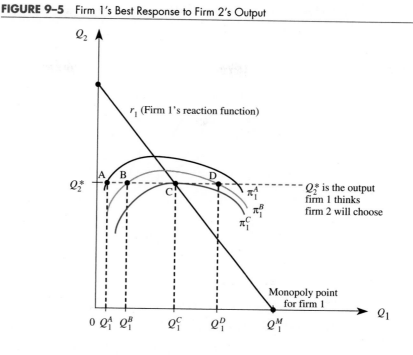

With an understanding of these four aspects of isoprofit curves, we now provide further insights into managerial decisions in a Cournot oligopoly. Recall that one assumption of Cournot oligopoly is that each firm takes as given the output decisions of rival firms and simply chooses its output to maximize profits given other firms' output. This is illustrated in Figure 9–5, where we assume firm 2's output is given by Q_2^*. Since firm 1 believes firm 2 will produce this output regardless of what firm 1 does, it chooses its output level to maximize profits when firm 2 produces Q_2^*. One possibility is for firm 1 to produce Q_1^A units of output, which would correspond to point A on isoprofit curve π_1^A. However, this decision does not maximize profits, because by expanding output to Q_1^B, firm 1 moves to a higher isoprofit curve (π_1^B, which corresponds to point B). Notice that profits can be further increased if firm 1 expands output to Q_1^C, which is associated with isoprofit curve π_1^C.

It is not profitable for firm 1 to increase output beyond Q_1^C, given that firm 2 produces Q_2^*. To see this, suppose firm 1 expanded output to, say, Q_1^D. This would result in a combination of outputs that corresponds to point D, which lies on an isoprofit curve that yields lower profits. We conclude that the profit-maximizing output for firm 1 is Q_1^C whenever firm 2 produces Q_2^* units. This should not surprise you: This is exactly the output that corresponds to firm 1's reaction function.

To maximize profits, firm 1 pushes its isoprofit curve as far down as possible (as close as possible to the monopoly point), until it is just tangential to the given output of firm 2. This tangency occurs at point C in Figure 9–5.

FIGURE 9–6   Firm 2's Reaction Function and Isoprofit Curves

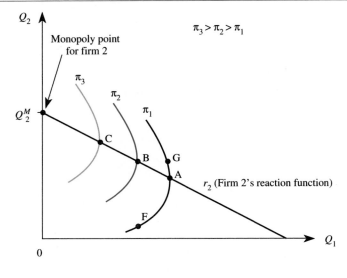

Demonstration Problem 9–5

Graphically depict isoprofit curves for firm 2, and explain the relation between points on the isoprofit curves and firm 2's reaction function.

Answer:

Isoprofit curves for firm 2 are the mirror image of those for firm 1. Representative isoprofit curves are depicted in Figure 9–6. Points G, A, and F lie on the same isoprofit curve and thus yield the same level of profits for firm 2. These profits are π_1, which are less than those of curves π_2 and π_3. As the isoprofit curves get closer to the monopoly point, the level of profits for firm 2 increases. The isoprofit curves begin to bend backward at the point where they intersect the reaction function.

We can use isoprofit curves to illustrate the profits of each firm in a Cournot equilibrium. Recall that Cournot equilibrium is determined by the intersection of the two firms' reaction functions, such as point C in Figure 9–7. Firm 1's isoprofit curve through point C is given by π_1^C, and firm 2's isoprofit curve is given by π_2^C.

Changes in Marginal Costs

In a Cournot oligopoly, the effect of a change in marginal cost is very different than in a Sweezy oligopoly. To see why, suppose the firms initially are in equilibrium at point E in Figure 9–8, where firm 1 produces Q_1^* units and firm 2 produces Q_2^* units. Now suppose firm 2's marginal cost declines. At the given level of output, marginal revenue remains unchanged but marginal cost is reduced. This means that for firm 2, marginal revenue exceeds the lower marginal cost, and it is optimal to produce

FIGURE 9–7 Cournot Equilibrium

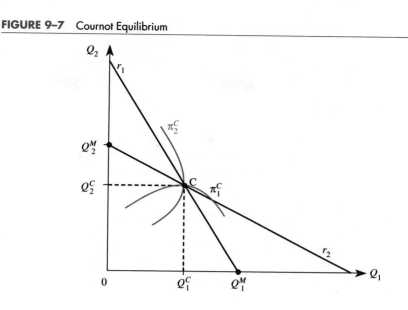

FIGURE 9–8 Effect of Decline in Firm 2's Marginal Cost on Cournot Equilibrium

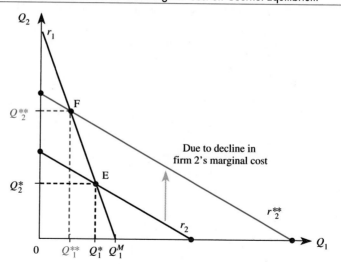

more output for any given level of Q_1. Graphically, this shifts firm 2's reaction function up from r_2 to r_2^{**}, leading to a new Cournot equilibrium at point F. Thus, the reduction in firm 2's marginal cost leads to an increase in firm 2's output, from Q_2^* to Q_2^{**}, and a decline in firm 1's output from Q_1^* to Q_1^{**}. Firm 2 enjoys a larger market share due to its improved cost situation.

The reason for the difference between the preceding analysis and the analysis of Sweezy oligopoly is the difference in the way a firm perceives how other firms will respond to a change in its decisions. These differences lead to differences in the way a manager should optimally respond to a reduction in the firm's marginal cost. If the manager believes other firms will follow price reductions but not price increases, the Sweezy model applies. In this instance, we learned that it may be optimal to continue to produce the same level of output even if marginal cost declines. If the manager believes other firms will maintain their existing output levels if the firm expands output, the Cournot model applies. In this case, it is optimal to expand output if marginal cost declines. The most important ingredient in making managerial decisions in markets characterized by interdependence is obtaining an accurate grasp of how other firms in the market will respond to the manager's decisions.

Collusion

Whenever a market is dominated by only a few firms, firms can benefit at the expense of consumers by "agreeing" to restrict output or, equivalently, to charge higher prices. Such an act by firms is known as *collusion*. In the next chapter, we will devote considerable attention to collusion; for now, it is useful to use the model of Cournot oligopoly to show why such an incentive exists.

In Figure 9–9, point C corresponds to a Cournot equilibrium; it is the intersection of the reaction functions of the two firms in the market. The equilibrium profits of firm 1 are given by isoprofit curve π_1^C and those of firm 2 by π_2^C. Notice that the shaded lens-shaped area in Figure 9–9 contains output levels for the two firms that yield higher profits for both firms than they earn in a Cournot equilibrium. For example, at point D each firm produces less output and enjoys greater profits, since

FIGURE 9–9   The Incentive to Collude in a Cournot Oligopoly

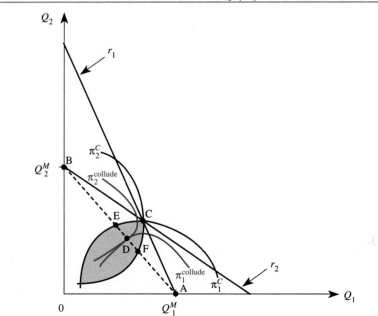

each of the firms' isoprofit curves at point D are closer to the respective monopoly point. In effect, if each firm agreed to restrict output, the firms could charge higher prices and earn higher profits. The reason is easy to see. Firm 1's profits would be highest at point A, where it is a monopolist. Firm 2's profits would be highest at point B, where it is a monopolist. If each firm "agreed" to produce an output that in total equaled the monopoly output, the firms would end up somewhere on the line connecting points A and B. In other words, any combination of outputs along line AB would maximize total industry profits.

The outputs on the line segment containing points E and F in Figure 9–9 thus maximize total industry profits, and since they are inside the lens-shaped area, they also yield both firms higher profits than would be earned if the firms produced at point C (the Cournot equilibrium). If the firms colluded by restricting output and splitting the monopoly profits, they would end up at a point like D, earning higher profits of $\pi_1^{collude}$ and $\pi_2^{collude}$. At this point, the corresponding market price and output are identical to those arising under monopoly: Collusion leads to a price that exceeds marginal cost, an output below the socially optimal level, and a deadweight loss. However, the colluding firms enjoy higher profits than they would earn if they competed as Cournot oligopolists.

It is not easy for firms to reach such a collusive agreement, however. We will analyze this point in greater detail in the next chapter, but we can use our existing framework to see why collusion is sometimes difficult. Suppose firms agree to collude, with each firm producing the collusive output associated with point D in Figure 9–10 to earn collusive profits. Given that firm 2 produces $Q_2^{collusive}$, firm 1 has an incentive

FIGURE 9–10   The Incentive to Renege on Collusive Agreements in Cournot Oligopoly

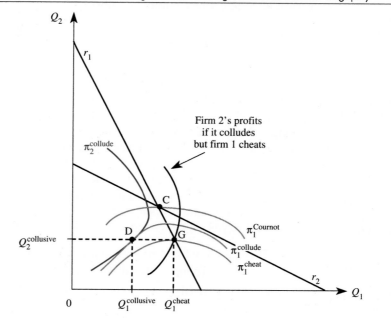

to "cheat" on the collusive agreement by expanding output to point G. At this point, firm 1 earns even higher profits than it would by colluding, since $\pi_1^{cheat} > \pi_1^{collude}$. This suggests that a firm can gain by inducing other firms to restrict output and then expanding its own output to earn higher profits at the expense of its collusion partners. Because firms know this incentive exists, it is often difficult for them to reach collusive agreements in the first place. This problem is amplified by the fact that firm 2 in Figure 9–10 earns less at point G (where firm 1 cheats) than it would have earned at point C (the Cournot equilibrium).

Stackelberg oligopoly
An industry in which (1) there are few firms serving many consumers; (2) firms produce either differentiated or homogeneous products; (3) a single firm (the leader) chooses an output before rivals select their outputs; (4) all other firms (the followers) take the leader's output as given and select outputs that maximize profits given the leader's output; and (5) barriers to entry exist.

Stackelberg Oligopoly

Up until this point, we have analyzed oligopoly situations that are symmetric in that firm 2 is the "mirror image" of firm 1. In many oligopoly markets, however, firms differ from one another. In a *Stackelberg oligopoly,* firms differ with respect to when they make decisions. Specifically, one firm (the leader) is assumed to make an output decision before the other firms. Given knowledge of the leader's output, all other firms (the followers) take as given the leader's output and choose outputs that maximize profits. Thus, in a Stackelberg oligopoly, each follower behaves just like a Cournot oligopolist. In fact, the leader does not take the followers' outputs as given but instead chooses an output that maximizes profits given that each follower will react to this output decision according to a Cournot reaction function.

An industry is characterized as a Stackelberg oligopoly if

1. There are few firms serving many consumers.
2. The firms produce either differentiated or homogeneous products.
3. A single firm (the leader) chooses an output before all other firms choose their outputs.

4. All other firms (the followers) take as given the output of the leader and choose outputs that maximize profits given the leader's output.
5. Barriers to entry exist.

To illustrate how a Stackelberg oligopoly works, let us consider a situation where there are only two firms. Firm 1 is the *leader* and thus has a "first-mover" advantage; that is, firm 1 produces before firm 2. Firm 2 is the *follower* and maximizes profit given the output produced by the leader.

Because the follower produces after the leader, the follower's profit-maximizing level of output is determined by its reaction function. This is denoted by r_2 in Figure 9–11. However, the leader knows the follower will react according to r_2. Consequently, the leader must choose the level of output that will maximize its profits given that the follower reacts to whatever the leader does.

How does the leader choose the output level to produce? Since it knows the follower will produce along r_2, the leader simply chooses the point on the follower's reaction curve that corresponds to the highest level of profits. Because the leader's profits increase as the isoprofit curves get closer to the monopoly output, the resulting choice by the leader will be at point S in Figure 9–11. This isoprofit curve, denoted π_1^S, yields the highest profits consistent with the follower's reaction function. It is tangential to firm 2's reaction function. Thus, the leader produces Q_1^S. The follower observes this output and produces Q_2^S, which is the profit-maximizing response to Q_1^S. The corresponding profits of the leader are given by π_1^S, and those of the follower by π_2^S. Notice that the leader's profits are higher than they would be in Cournot equilibrium (point C), and the follower's profits are lower than in Cournot equilibrium. By getting to move first, the leader earns higher profits than would otherwise be the case.

The algebraic solution for a Stackelberg oligopoly can also be obtained, provided firms have information about market demand and costs. In particular, recall

FIGURE 9–11 Stackelberg Equilibrium

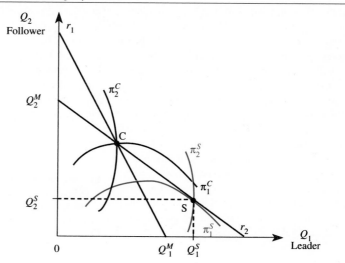

that the follower's decision is identical to that of a Cournot model. For instance, with homogeneous products, linear demand, and constant marginal cost, the output of the follower is given by the reaction function

$$Q_2 = r_2(Q_1) = \frac{a - c_2}{2b} - \frac{1}{2}Q_1$$

which is simply the follower's Cournot reaction function. However, the leader in the Stackelberg oligopoly takes into account this reaction function when it selects Q_1. With a linear inverse demand function and constant marginal costs, the leader's profits are

$$\pi_1 = \left\{a - b\left[Q_1 + \left(\frac{a - c_2}{2b} - \frac{1}{2}Q_1\right)\right]\right\}Q_1 - c_1 Q_1$$

The leader chooses Q_1 to maximize this profit expression. It turns out that the value of Q_1 that maximizes the leader's profits is

$$Q_1 = \frac{a + c_2 - 2c_1}{2b}$$

Formula: Equilibrium Outputs in Stackelberg Oligopoly. For the linear (inverse) demand function

$$P = a - b(Q_1 + Q_2)$$

INSIDE BUSINESS 9–2

Commitment in Stackelberg Oligopoly

In the Stackelberg oligopoly model, the leader obtains a first-mover advantage by committing to produce a large quantity of output. The follower's best response, upon observing the leader's choice, is to produce less output. Thus, the leader gains market share and profit at the expense of his rival. Evidence from the real world as well as experimental laboratories suggests that the benefits of commitment in Stackelberg oligopolies can be sizeable—provided it is not too costly for the follower to observe the leader's output.

For example, the South African communications company, Telkom, once enjoyed a 177 percent increase in its net profits, thanks to a first-mover advantage it obtained by getting the jump on its rival. Telkom committed to the Stackelberg output by signing long-term contracts with 90 percent of South Africa's companies. By committing to this high output, Telkom ensured that its rival's best response was a low level of output.

The classic Stackelberg model assumes that the follower costlessly observes the leader's quantity. In practice, however, it is sometimes costly for the follower to gather information about the quantity of output produced by the leader. Professors Morgan and Várdy have conducted a variety of laboratory experiments to investigate whether these "observation costs" reduce the leader's ability to secure a first-mover advantage. The results of their experiments indicate that when the observation costs are small, the leader captures the bulk of the profits and maintains a first-mover advantage. As the second-mover's observation costs increase, the profits of the leader and follower become more equal.

Sources: Neels Blom, "Telkom Makes Life Difficult for Any Potential Rival," *Business Day* (Johannesburg), June 9, 2004; J. Morgan, and F. Várdy, "An Experimental Study of Commitment in Stackelberg Games with Observation Costs," *Games and Economic Behavior* 20(2), November 2004, pp. 401–23.

and cost functions

$$C_1(Q_1) = c_1Q_1$$
$$C_2(Q_2) = c_2Q_2$$

the follower sets output according to the Cournot reaction function

$$Q_2 = r_2(Q_1) = \frac{a - c_2}{2b} - \frac{1}{2}Q_1$$

The leader's output is

$$Q_1 = \frac{a + c_2 - 2c_1}{2b}$$

A Calculus Alternative

To maximize profits, firm 1 sets output so as to maximize

$$\pi_1 = \left\{ a - b\left[Q_1 + \left(\frac{a - c_2}{2b} - \frac{1}{2}Q_1 \right) \right] \right\} Q_1 - c_1Q_1$$

The first-order condition for maximizing profits is

$$\frac{d\pi_1}{dQ_1} = a - 2bQ_1 - \left(\frac{a - c_2}{2} \right) + bQ_1 - c_1 = 0$$

Solving for Q_1 yields the profit-maximizing level of output for the leader:

$$Q_1 = \frac{a + c_2 - 2c_1}{2b}$$

The formula for the follower's reaction function is derived in the same way as that for a Cournot oligopolist.

Demonstration Problem 9–6

Suppose the inverse demand function for two firms in a homogeneous-product Stackelberg oligopoly is given by

$$P = 50 - (Q_1 + Q_2)$$

and cost functions for the two firms are

$$C_1(Q_1) = 2Q_1$$
$$C_2(Q_2) = 2Q_2$$

Firm 1 is the leader, and firm 2 is the follower.

1. What is firm 2's reaction function?
2. What is firm 1's output?
3. What is firm 2's output?
4. What is the market price?

Answer:

1. Using the formula for the follower's reaction function, we find

$$Q_2 = r_2(Q_1) = 24 - \frac{1}{2}Q_1$$

2. Using the formula given for the Stackelberg leader, we find

$$Q_1 = \frac{50 + 2 - 4}{2} = 24$$

3. By plugging the answer to part 2 into the reaction function in part 1, we find the follower's output to be

$$Q_2 = 24 - \frac{1}{2}(24) = 12$$

4. The market price can be found by adding the two firms' outputs together and plugging the answer into the inverse demand function:

$$P = 50 - (12 + 24) = 14$$

In general, price exceeds marginal cost in a Stackelberg oligopoly, meaning industry output is below the socially efficient level. This translates into a deadweight loss, but the deadweight loss is lower than that arising under pure monopoly.

Bertrand Oligopoly

To further highlight the fact that there is no single model of oligopoly a manager can use in all circumstances and to illustrate that oligopoly power does not always imply firms will make positive profits, we will next examine Bertrand oligopoly. The treatment here assumes the firms sell identical products and that consumers are willing to pay the (finite) monopoly price for the good.

An industry is characterized as a *Bertrand oligopoly* if

1. There are few firms in the market serving many consumers.
2. The firms produce identical products at a constant marginal cost.
3. Firms engage in price competition and react optimally to prices charged by competitors.
4. Consumers have perfect information and there are no transaction costs.
5. Barriers to entry exist.

From the viewpoint of the manager, Bertrand oligopoly is undesirable: It leads to zero economic profits even if there are only two firms in the market. From the viewpoint of consumers, Bertrand oligopoly is desirable: It leads to precisely the same outcome as a perfectly competitive market.

To explain more precisely the preceding assertions, consider a Bertrand duopoly. Because consumers have perfect information, and zero transaction costs, and because the products are identical, all consumers will purchase from the firm charging the

Bertrand oligopoly
An industry in which (1) there are few firms serving many consumers; (2) firms produce identical products at a constant marginal cost; (3) firms compete in price and react optimally to competitors' prices; (4) consumers have perfect information and there are no transaction costs; and (5) barriers to entry exist.

INSIDE BUSINESS 9–3

Price Competition and the Number of Sellers: Evidence from Online and Laboratory Markets

Does competition really force homogeneous product Bertrand oligopolists to price at marginal cost? Two recent studies suggest that the answer critically depends on the number of sellers in the market.

Professors Baye, Morgan, and Scholten examined 4 million daily price observations for thousands of products sold at a leading price comparison site. Price comparison sites, such as Shopper.com, Nextag.com and Kelkoo.com, permit online shoppers to obtain a list of prices that different firms charge for homogeneous products. Theory would suggest that—in online markets where firms sell identical products and consumers have excellent information about firms' prices—firms will fall victim to the "Bertrand trap." Contrary to this expectation, the authors found that the "gap" between the two lowest prices charged for identical products sold online averaged 22 percent when only two firms sold the product, but declined to less than 3 percent when more than 20 firms listed prices for the homogeneous products. Expressed differently, real-world firms appear to be able to escape from the Bertrand trap when there are relatively few sellers, but fall victim to the trap when there are more competitors.

Professors Dufwenberg and Gneezy provide experimental evidence that corroborates this finding. These authors conducted a sequence of experiments with subjects who competed in a homogeneous product pricing game in which marginal cost was $2 and the monopoly (collusive) price was $100. In the experiments, sellers offering the lowest price "win" and earned real cash. As the accompanying figure shows, theory predicts that a monopolist would price at $100 and that prices would fall to $2 in markets with two, three, or four sellers. In reality, the average market price (the winning price) was about $27 when there were only two sellers, and declined to about $9 in sessions with three or four sellers. In practice, prices (and profits) rapidly decline as the number of sellers increases—but not nearly as sharply as predicted by theory.

Sources: Martin Dufwenberg and Uri Gneezy, "Price Competition and Market Concentration: An Experimental Study," *International Journal of Industrial Organization* 18 (2000), pp. 7–22; Michael R. Baye, John Morgan, and Patrick Scholten, "Price Dispersion in the Small and in the Large: Evidence from an Internet Price Comparison Site," *Journal of Industrial Economics* 52(2004), pp. 463–96.

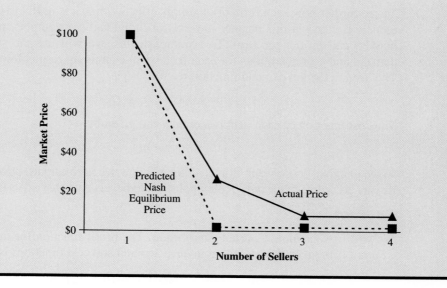

lowest price. For concreteness, suppose firm 1 charges the monopoly price. By slightly undercutting this price, firm 2 would capture the entire market and make positive profits, while firm 1 would sell nothing. Therefore, firm 1 would retaliate by undercutting firm 2's lower price, thus recapturing the entire market.

When would this "price war" end? When each firm charged a price that equaled marginal cost: $P_1 = P_2 = MC$. Given the price of the other firm, neither firm would choose to lower its price, for then its price would be below marginal cost and it would make a loss. Also, no firm would want to raise its price, for then it would sell nothing. In short, Bertrand oligopoly and homogeneous products lead to a situation where each firm charges marginal cost and economic profits are zero. Since $P = MC$, homogeneous product Bertrand oligopoly results in a socially efficient level of output. Indeed, total market output corresponds to that in a perfectly competitive industry, and there is no deadweight loss.

Chapters 10 and 11 provide strategies that managers can use to mitigate the "Bertrand trap"—the cut-throat competition that ensues in homogeneous-product Bertrand oligopoly. As we will see, the key is to either raise switching costs or eliminate the perception that the firms' products are identical. The product differentiation induced by these strategies permits firms to price above marginal cost without losing customers to rivals. The appendix to this chapter illustrates that, under differentiated-product price competition, reaction functions are upward sloping and equilibrium occurs at a point where prices exceed marginal cost. This explains, in part, why firms such as Kellogg's and General Mills spend millions of dollars on advertisements designed to persuade consumers that their competing brands of corn flakes are not identical. If consumers did not view the brands as differentiated products, these two makers of breakfast cereal would have to price at marginal cost.

COMPARING OLIGOPOLY MODELS

To see further how each form of oligopoly affects firms, it is useful to compare the models covered in this chapter in terms of individual firm outputs, prices in the market, and profits per firm. To accomplish this, we will use the same market demand and cost conditions for each firm when examining results for each model. The inverse market demand function we will use is

$$P = 1,000 - (Q_1 + Q_2)$$

The cost function of each firm is identical and given by

$$C_i(Q_i) = 4Q_i$$

so the marginal cost of each firm is 4. We will now see how outputs, prices, and profits vary according to the type of oligopolistic interdependence that exists in the market.

Cournot

We will first examine Cournot equilibrium. The profit function for the individual Cournot firm given the preceding inverse demand and cost functions is

$$\pi_i = [1,000 - (Q_1 + Q_2)]Q_i - 4Q_i$$

The reaction functions of the Cournot oligopolists are

$$Q_1 = r_1(Q_2) = 498 - \frac{1}{2}Q_2$$

$$Q_2 = r_2(Q_1) = 498 - \frac{1}{2}Q_1$$

Solving these two reaction functions for Q_1 and Q_2 yields the Cournot equilibrium outputs, which are $Q_1 = Q_2 = 332$. Total output in the market thus is 664, which leads to a price of \$336. Plugging these values into the profit function reveals that each firm earns profits of \$110,224.

Stackelberg

With these demand and cost functions, the output of the Stackelberg leader is

$$Q_1 = \frac{a + c_2 - 2c_1}{2b} = \frac{1{,}000 + 4 - 2(4)}{2} = 498$$

The follower takes this level of output as given and produces according to its reaction function:

$$Q_2 = r_2(Q_1) = \frac{a - c_2}{2b} - \frac{1}{2}Q_1 = \frac{1{,}000 - 4}{2} - \frac{1}{2}(498) = 249$$

Total output in the market thus is 747 units. Given the inverse demand function, this output yields a price of \$253. Total market output is higher in a Stackelberg oligopoly than in a Cournot oligopoly. This leads to a lower price in the Stackelberg oligopoly than in the Cournot oligopoly. The profits for the leader are \$124,002, while the follower earns only \$62,001 in profits. The leader does better in a Stackelberg oligopoly than in a Cournot oligopoly due to its first-mover advantage. However, the follower earns lower profits in a Stackelberg oligopoly than in a Cournot oligopoly.

Bertrand

The Bertrand equilibrium is simple to calculate. Recall that firms that engage in Bertrand competition end up setting price equal to marginal cost. Therefore, with the given inverse demand and cost functions, price equals marginal cost (\$4) and profits are zero for each firm. Total market output is 996 units. Given symmetric firms, each firm gets half of the market.

Collusion

Finally, we will determine the collusive outcome, which results when the firms choose output to maximize total industry profits. When firms collude, total industry output is the monopoly level, based on the market inverse demand curve. Since the market inverse demand curve is

$$P = 1{,}000 - Q$$

Using a Spreadsheet to Calculate Cournot, Stackelberg, and Collusive Outcomes

The website for this eighth edition of the text at www.mhhe.com/baye8e contains three files named CournotSolver.xls, StackelbergSolver.xls, and CollusionSolver.xls. With a few clicks of a mouse, you can use these files to calculate the profit-maximizing price and quantity and the maximum profits for the following oligopoly situations.

COURNOT DUOPOLY

In a Cournot duopoly, each firm believes the other will hold its output constant as it changes its own output. Therefore, the profit-maximizing output level for firm 1 depends on firm 2's output. Each firm will adjust its profit-maximizing output level until the point where the two firms' reaction functions are equal. This point corresponds to the Cournot equilibrium. At the Cournot equilibrium, neither firm has an incentive to change its output, given the output of the other firm. Step-by-step instructions for computing the Cournot equilibrium outputs, price, and profits are included in the file named CournotSolver.xls.

STACKELBERG DUOPOLY

The Stackelberg duopoly model assumes that one firm is the leader while the other is a follower. The leader has a first-mover advantage and selects its profit-maximizing output level, knowing that the follower will move second and thus react to this decision according to a Cournot reaction function. Given the leader's output decision, the follower takes the leader's output as given and chooses its profit-maximizing level of output. Step-by-step instructions for computing the Stackelberg equilibrium outputs, price, and profits are included in the file named StackelbergSolver.xls.

COLLUSIVE DUOPOLY (THE MONOPOLY SOLUTION)

Under collusion, duopolists produce a total output that corresponds to the monopoly output. In a symmetric situation, the two firms share the market equally, each producing one-half of the monopoly output. Step-by-step instructions for computing the collusive (monopoly) output, price, and profits are included in the file named CollusionSolver.xls.

the associated marginal revenue is

$$MR = 1,000 - 2Q$$

Notice that this marginal revenue function assumes the firms act as a single profit-maximizing firm, which is what collusion is all about. Setting marginal revenue equal to marginal cost (which is $4) yields

$$1,000 - 2Q = 4$$

or $Q = 498$. Thus, total industry output under collusion is 498 units, with each firm producing half. The price under collusion is

$$P = 1,000 - 498 = \$502$$

Each firm earns profits of $124,002.

Comparison of the outcomes in these different oligopoly situations reveals the following: The highest market output is produced in a Bertrand oligopoly, followed by Stackelberg, then Cournot, and finally collusion. Profits are highest for the Stackelberg leader and the colluding firms, followed by Cournot, then the Stackelberg follower. The Bertrand oligopolists earn the lowest level of profits. If you become a manager in an oligopolistic market, it is important to recognize that your optimal decisions and profits will vary depending on the type of oligopolistic interaction that exists in the market.

CONTESTABLE MARKETS

Thus far, we have emphasized strategic interaction among existing firms in an oligopoly. Strategic interaction can also exist between existing firms and potential entrants into a market. To illustrate the importance of this interaction and its similarity to Bertrand oligopoly, let us suppose a market is served by a single firm but there is another firm (a potential entrant) free to enter the market whenever it chooses.

contestable market
A market in which (1) all firms have access to the same technology; (2) consumers respond quickly to price changes; (3) existing firms cannot respond quickly to entry by lowering their prices; and (4) there are no sunk costs.

Before we continue our analysis, let us make more precise what we mean by *free entry*. What we have in mind here is what economists refer to as a *contestable market*. A market is contestable if

1. All producers have access to the same technology.
2. Consumers respond quickly to price changes.
3. Existing firms cannot respond quickly to entry by lowering price.
4. There are no sunk costs.

If these four conditions hold, incumbent firms (existing firms in the market) have no market power over consumers. That is, the equilibrium price corresponds to marginal cost, and firms earn zero economic profits. This is true even if there is only one existing firm in the market.

The reason for this result follows. If existing firms charged a price in excess of what they required to cover costs, a new firm could immediately enter the market with the same technology and charge a price slightly below the existing firms' prices. Since the incumbents cannot quickly respond by lowering their prices, the entrant would get all the incumbents' customers by charging the lower price. Because the incumbents know this, they have no alternative but to charge a low price equal to the cost of production to keep out the entrant. Thus, if a market is perfectly contestable, incumbents are disciplined by the threat of entry by new firms.

An important condition for a contestable market is the absence of sunk costs. In this context, *sunk costs* are defined as costs a new entrant must bear that cannot be recouped upon exiting the market. For example, if an entrant pays $100,000 for a truck to enter the market for moving services, but receives $80,000 for the truck upon exiting the market, $20,000 represents the sunk costs of entering the market. Similarly, if a firm pays a nonrefundable fee of $20,000 for the nontransferable right to lease a truck for a year to enter the market, this reflects a sunk cost associated with entry. Or if a small firm must incur a loss of $2,000 per month for six months while waiting for customers to "switch" to that company, it incurs $12,000 of sunk costs.

Sunk costs are important for the following reason: Suppose incumbent firms are charging high prices, and a new entrant calculates that it could earn $70,000 by entering the market and charging a lower price than the existing firms. This calculation is, of course, conditional upon the existing firms continuing to charge their present prices. Suppose that to enter, the firm must pay sunk costs of $20,000. If it enters the market and the incumbent firms keep charging the high price, entry is profitable; indeed, the firm will make $70,000. However, if the incumbents do not continue charging the high price but instead lower their prices, the entrant can be left with no customers. The incumbents cannot lower their prices quickly, so the entrant may earn some profits early on; however, it likely will not earn enough profit to offset its sunk costs before the incumbents lower their prices. In this instance, the entrant would need to earn enough profit immediately after entering to cover its sunk cost of $20,000. In short, if a potential entrant must pay sunk costs to enter a market and has reason to believe incumbents will respond to entry by lowering their prices, it may find it unprofitable to enter even though prices are high. The end result is that with sunk costs, incumbents may not be disciplined by potential entry, and higher prices may prevail. Chapters 10 and 13 provide more detailed coverage of strategic interactions between incumbents and potential entrants.

ANSWERING THE HEADLINE

Although the price of crude oil fell, in a few areas there were no declines in the price of gasoline. The headline asks whether this is evidence of collusion by gasoline stations in those areas. To answer this question, notice that oil is an input in producing gasoline. A reduction in the price of oil leads to a reduction in the marginal cost of producing gasoline—say, from MC_0 to MC_1. If gasoline stations were colluding, a reduction in marginal cost would lead the firms to lower the price of gasoline. To see this, recall that under collusion, both the industry output and the price are set at the monopoly level and price. Thus, if firms were colluding when marginal cost was MC_0, the output that would maximize collusive profits would occur where $MR = MC_0$ in Figure 9–12. Thus, Q^* and P^* in Figure 9–12 denote the collusive output and

FIGURE 9–12   Reduction in Marginal Cost Lowers the Collusive Price

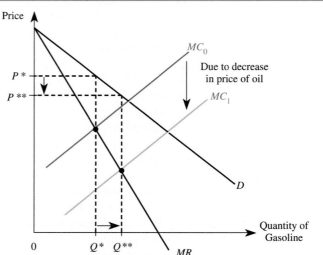

FIGURE 9–13 Price Rigidity in Sweezy Oligopoly

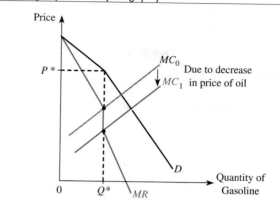

price when marginal cost is MC_0. A reduction in the marginal cost of producing gasoline would shift down the marginal cost curve to MC_1, leading to a greater collusive output (Q^{**}) and a lower price (P^{**}). Thus, collusion cannot explain why some gasoline firms failed to lower their prices. Had these firms been colluding, they would have found it profitable to lower gasoline prices when the price of oil fell.

Since collusion is not the reason gasoline prices in some areas did not fall when the marginal cost of gasoline declined, one may wonder what could explain the pricing behavior in these markets. One explanation is that these gasoline producers are Sweezy oligopolists. The Sweezy oligopolist operates on the assumption that if she raises her price, her competitors will ignore the change. However, if she lowers her price, all will follow suit and lower their prices. Figure 9–13 reveals that Sweezy oligopolists will not decrease gasoline prices when marginal cost falls from MC_0 to MC_1. They know they cannot increase their profits or market share by lowering their price, because all of their competitors will lower prices if they do.

SUMMARY

In this chapter, we examined several models of markets that consist of a small number of strategically interdependent firms. These models help explain several possible types of behavior when a market is characterized by oligopoly. You should now be familiar with the Sweezy, Cournot, Stackelberg, and Bertrand models.

In the Cournot model, a firm chooses quantity based on its competitors' given levels of output. Each firm earns some economic profits. Bertrand competitors, on the other hand, set prices given their rivals' prices. They end up charging a price equal to their marginal cost and earn zero economic profits. Sweezy oligopolists believe their competitors will follow price decreases but will ignore price increases, leading to extremely stable prices even when costs change in the industry. Finally, Stackelberg oligopolies have a follower and a leader. The leader knows how the follower will behave, and the follower simply maximizes profits given what the leader has chosen. This leads to profits for each firm but much higher profits for the leader than for the follower.

The next chapter will explain in more detail how managers go about reaching equilibrium in oligopoly. For now, it should be clear that your decisions will affect others in your market and their decisions will affect you as well.

KEY TERMS AND CONCEPTS

Bertrand oligopoly
best-response function
collusion
contestable markets
Cournot equilibrium
Cournot oligopoly
duopoly
follower

isoprofit curve
leader
oligopoly
reaction function
Stackelberg oligopoly
sunk costs
Sweezy oligopoly

END-OF-CHAPTER PROBLEMS BY LEARNING OBJECTIVE

Every end-of-chapter problem addresses at least one learning objective. Following is a nonexhaustive sample of end-of-chapter problems for each learning objective.

LO1 Explain how beliefs and strategic interaction shape optimal decisions in oligopoly environments.

Try these problems: 1, 15

LO2 Identify the conditions under which a firm operates in a Sweezy, Cournot, Stackelberg, or Bertrand oligopoly, and the ramifications of each type of oligopoly for optimal pricing decisions, output decisions, and firm profits.

Try these problems: 6, 19

LO3 Apply reaction (or best-response) functions to identify optimal decisions and likely competitor responses in oligopoly settings.

Try these problems: 2, 12

LO4 Identify the conditions for a contestable market, and explain the ramifications for market power and the sustainability of long-run profits.

Try these problems: 10, 16

CONCEPTUAL AND COMPUTATIONAL QUESTIONS

connect
|ECONOMICS

1. The graph that accompanies this question illustrates two demand curves for a firm operating in a differentiated product oligopoly. Initially, the firm charges a price of $60 and produces 10 units of output. One of the demand curves is relevant when rivals match the firm's price changes; the other demand curve is relevant when rivals do not match price changes.

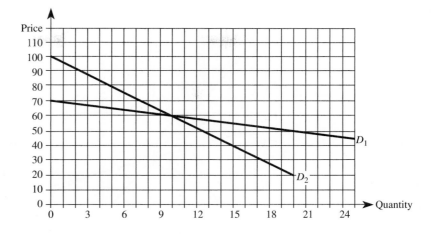

   a. Which demand curve is relevant when rivals will match any price change?

   b. Which demand curve is relevant when rivals will *not* match any price change?

   c. Suppose the manager believes that rivals will match price cuts but will not match price increases.

     (1) What price will the firm be able to charge if it produces 20 units?

     (2) How many units will the firm sell if it charges a price of $70?

     (3) For what range in marginal cost will the firm continue to charge a price of $60?

2. The inverse market demand in a homogeneous-product Cournot duopoly is $P = 200 - 3(Q_1 + Q_2)$ and costs are $C_1(Q_1) = 26Q_1$ and $C_2(Q_2) = 32Q_2$.

   a. Determine the reaction function for each firm.

   b. Calculate each firm's equilibrium output.

   c. Calculate the equilibrium market price.

   d. Calculate the profit each firm earns in equilibrium.

3. The following diagram illustrates the reaction functions and isoprofit curves for a homogeneous-product duopoly in which each firm produces at constant marginal cost.

   a. If your rival produces 50 units of output, what is your optimal level of output?

   b. In equilibrium, how much will each firm produce in a Cournot oligopoly?

   c. In equilibrium, what is the output of the leader and follower in a Stackelberg oligopoly?

   d. How much output would be produced if the market were monopolized?

   e. Suppose you and your rival agree to a collusive arrangement in which each firm produces half of the monopoly output.

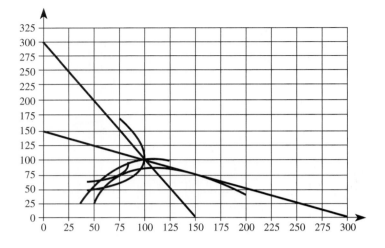

(1) What is your output under the collusive arrangement?

(2) What is your optimal output if you believe your rival will live up to the agreement?

4. The inverse demand for a homogeneous-product Stackelberg duopoly is $P = 16{,}000 - 4Q$. The cost structures for the leader and the follower, respectively, are $C_L(Q_L) = 4{,}000Q_L$ and $C_F(Q_F) = 6{,}000Q_F$.

    a. What is the follower's reaction function?

    b. Determine the equilibrium output level for both the leader and the follower.

    c. Determine the equilibrium market price.

    d. Determine the profits of the leader and the follower.

5. Consider a Bertrand oligopoly consisting of four firms that produce an identical product at a marginal cost of $260. The inverse market demand for this product is $P = 800 - 4Q$.

    a. Determine the equilibrium level of output in the market.

    b. Determine the equilibrium market price.

    c. Determine the profits of each firm.

6. Provide a real-world example of a market that approximates each oligopoly setting, and explain your reasoning.

    a. Cournot oligopoly.

    b. Stackelberg oligopoly.

    c. Bertrand oligopoly.

7. Two firms compete in a market to sell a homogeneous product with inverse demand function $P = 600 - 3Q$. Each firm produces at a constant marginal cost of $300 and has no fixed costs. Use this information to compare the output levels and profits in settings characterized by Cournot, Stackelberg, Bertrand, and collusive behavior.

8. Consider a homogeneous-product duopoly where each firm initially produces at a constant marginal cost of $200 and there are no fixed costs. Determine what would happen to each firm's equilibrium output and profits if firm 2's marginal cost increased to $210 but firm 1's marginal cost remained constant at $200 in each of the following settings:

   a. Cournot duopoly.
   b. Sweezy oligopoly.

9. Determine whether each of the following scenarios best reflects features of Sweezy, Cournot, Stackelberg, or Bertrand duopoly:

   a. Neither manager expects her own output decision to impact the other manager's output decision.
   b. Each manager charges a price that is a best response to the price charged by the rival.
   c. The manager of one firm gets to observe the output of the rival firm before making its own output decision.
   d. The managers perceive that rivals will match price reductions but not price increases.

10. Suppose a single firm produces all of the output in a contestable market. The market inverse demand function is $P = 150 - 2Q$, and the firm's cost function is $C(Q) = 4Q$. Determine the firm's equilibrium price and corresponding profits.

PROBLEMS AND APPLICATIONS

11. Ford executives announced that the company would extend its most dramatic consumer incentive program in the company's long history—the Ford Drive America Program. The program provides consumers with either cash back or zero percent financing for new Ford vehicles. As the manager of a Ford franchise, how would you expect this program to impact your firm's bottom line? Explain.

12. You are the manager of BlackSpot Computers, which competes directly with Condensed Computers to sell high-powered computers to businesses. From the two businesses' perspectives, the two products are indistinguishable. The large investment required to build production facilities prohibits other firms from entering this market, and existing firms operate under the assumption that the rival will hold output constant. The inverse market demand for computers is $P = 5,900 - Q$, and both firms produce at a marginal cost of $800 per computer. Currently, BlackSpot earns revenues of $4.25 million and profits (net of investment, R&D, and other fixed costs) of $890,000. The engineering department at BlackSpot has been steadily working on developing an assembly method that would dramatically reduce the marginal cost of producing these high-powered computers and has found a process that allows it to

manufacture each computer at a marginal cost of $500. How will this techno-logical advance impact your production and pricing plans? How will it impact BlackSpot's bottom line?

13. The Hull Petroleum Company and Inverted V are retail gasoline franchises that compete in a local market to sell gasoline to consumers. Hull and Inverted V are located across the street from each other and can observe the prices posted on each other's marquees. Demand for gasoline in this market is $Q = 80 - 6P$, and both franchises obtain gasoline from their supplier at $2.20 per gallon. On the day that both franchises opened for business, each owner was observed changing the price of gasoline advertised on its marquee more than 10 times; the owner of Hull lowered its price to slightly undercut Inverted V's price, and the owner of Inverted V lowered its advertised price to beat Hull's price. Since then, prices appear to have stabilized. Under current conditions, how many gallons of gasoline are sold in the market, and at what price? Would your answer differ if Hull had service attendants available to fill consumers' tanks but Inverted V was only a self-service station? Explain.

14. You are the manager of the only firm worldwide that specializes in exporting fish products to Japan. Your firm competes against a handful of Japanese firms that enjoy a significant first-mover advantage. Recently, one of your Japanese customers has called to inform you that the Japanese legislature is considering imposing a quota that would reduce the number of pounds of fish products you are permitted to ship to Japan each year. Your first instinct is to call the trade representative of your country to lobby against the import quota. Is following through with your first instinct necessarily the best decision? Explain.

15. The opening statement on the website of the Organization of Petroleum Exporting Countries (OPEC) says its members seek " . . . to secure an efficient, economic and regular supply of petroleum to consumers, a steady income to producers and a fair return on capital for those investing in the petroleum industry." To achieve this goal, OPEC attempts to coordinate and unify petroleum policies by raising or lowering its members' collective oil production. However, increased production by Russia, Oman, Mexico, Norway, and other non-OPEC countries has placed downward pressure on the price of crude oil. To achieve its goal of stable and fair oil prices, what must OPEC do to maintain the price of oil at its desired level? Do you think this will be easy for OPEC to do? Explain.

16. Semi-Salt Industries began its operation in 1975 and remains the only firm in the world that produces and sells commercial-grade polyglutamate. While virtually anyone with a degree in college chemistry could replicate the firm's formula, due to the relatively high cost, Semi-Salt has decided not to apply for a patent. Despite the absence of patent protection, Semi-Salt has averaged

accounting profits of 5.5 percent on investment since it began producing polyglutamate—a rate comparable to the average rate of interest that large banks paid on deposits over this period. Do you think Semi-Salt is earning monopoly profits? Why?

17. You are the manager of a firm that competes against four other firms by bidding for government contracts. While you believe your product is better than the competition, the government purchasing agent views the products as identical and purchases from the firm offering the best price. Total government demand is $Q = 1,000 - 5P$, and all five firms produce at a constant marginal cost of $60. For security reasons, the government has imposed restrictions that permit a maximum of five firms to compete in this market; thus entry by new firms is prohibited. A member of Congress is concerned because no restrictions have been placed on the price that the government pays for this product. In response, she has proposed legislation that would award each existing firm 20 percent of a contract for 625 units at a contracted price of $75 per unit. Would you support or oppose this legislation? Explain.

18. The market for a standard-sized cardboard container consists of two firms: CompositeBox and Fiberboard. As the manager of CompositeBox, you enjoy a patented technology that permits your company to produce boxes faster and at a lower cost than Fiberboard. You use this advantage to be the first to choose its profit-maximizing output level in the market. The inverse demand function for boxes is $P = 1,200 - 6Q$, CompositeBox's costs are $C_C(Q_C) = 60Q_C$, and Fiberboard's costs are $C_F(Q_F) = 120Q_F$. Ignoring antitrust considerations, would it be profitable for your firm to merge with Fiberboard? If not, explain why not; if so, put together an offer that would permit you to profitably complete the merger.

19. You are the manager of Taurus Technologies, and your sole competitor is Spyder Technologies. The two firms' products are viewed as identical by most consumers. The relevant cost functions are $C(Q_i) = 4Q_i$, and the inverse market demand curve for this unique product is given by $P = 160 - 2Q$. Currently, you and your rival simultaneously (but independently) make production decisions, and the price you fetch for the product depends on the total amount produced by each firm. However, by making an unrecoverable fixed investment of $200, Taurus Technologies can bring its product to market before Spyder finalizes production plans. Should you invest the $200? Explain.

20. During the 1980s, most of the world's supply of lysine was produced by a Japanese company named Ajinomoto. Lysine is an essential amino acid that is an important livestock feed component. At this time, the United States imported most of the world's supply of lysine—more than 30,000 tons—to use in livestock feed at a price of $1.65 per pound. The worldwide market for lysine, however, fundamentally changed in 1991 when U.S.-based Archer

Daniels Midland (ADM) began producing lysine—a move that doubled worldwide production capacity. Experts conjectured that Ajinomoto and ADM had similar cost structures and that the marginal cost of producing and distributing lysine was approximately $0.70 per pound. Despite ADM's entry into the lysine market, suppose demand remained constant at $Q = 208 - 80P$ (in millions of pounds). Shortly after ADM began producing lysine, the worldwide price dropped to $0.70. By 1993, however, the price of lysine shot back up to $1.65. Use the theories discussed in this chapter to provide a potential explanation for what happened in the lysine market. Support your answer with appropriate calculations.

21. PC Connection and CDW are two online retailers that compete in an Internet market for digital cameras. While the products they sell are similar, the firms attempt to differentiate themselves through their service policies. Over the last couple of months, PC Connection has matched CDW's price cuts, but has not matched its price increases. Suppose that when PC Connection matches CDW's price changes, the inverse demand curve for CDW's cameras is given by $P = 1,500 - 3Q$. When it does not match price changes, CDW's inverse demand curve is $P = 900 - 0.50Q$. Based on this information, determine CDW's inverse demand and marginal revenue functions over the last couple of months. Over what range will changes in marginal cost have no effect on CDW's profit-maximizing level of output?

22. Jones is the manager of an upscale clothing store in a shopping mall that contains only two such stores. While these two competitors do not carry the same brands of clothes, they serve a similar clientele. Jones was recently notified that the mall is going to implement a 10 percent across-the-board increase in rents to all stores in the mall, effective next month. Should Jones raise her prices 10 percent to offset the increase in monthly rent? Explain carefully.

23. In an attempt to increase tax revenues, legislators in several states have introduced legislation that would increase state excise taxes. Examine the impact of such an increase on the equilibrium prices paid and quantities consumed by consumers in markets characterized by (1) Sweezy oligopoly, (b) Cournot oligopoly, and (c) Bertrand oligopoly, and determine which of these market settings is likely to generate the greatest increase in tax revenues.

CONNECT EXERCISES

If your instructor has adopted Connect for the course and you are an active subscriber, you can practice with the questions presented above, along with many alternative versions of these questions. Your instructor may also assign a subset of these problems and/or their alternative versions as a homework assignment through Connect, allowing for immediate feedback of grades and correct answers.

CASE-BASED EXERCISES

Your instructor may assign additional problem-solving exercises (called *memos*) that require you to apply some of the tools you learned in this chapter to make a recommendation based on an actual business scenario. Some of these memos accompany the Time Warner case (pages 561–597 of your textbook). Additional memos, as well as data that may be useful for your analysis, are available online at www.mhhe.com/baye8e.

SELECTED READINGS

Alberts, William W., "Do Oligopolists Earn 'Noncompetitive' Rates of Return?" *American Economic Review* 74(4), September 1984, pp. 624–32.

Becker, Klaus G., "Natural Monopoly Equilibria: Nash and von Stackelberg Solutions." *Journal of Economics and Business* 46(2), May 1994, pp. 135–39.

Brander, James A., and Lewis, Tracy R., "Oligopoly and Financial Structure: The Limited Liability Effect." *American Economic Review* 76(5), December 1986, pp. 956–70.

Caudill, Steven B., and Mixon, Franklin G., Jr., "Cartels and the Incentive to Cheat: Evidence from the Classroom." *Journal of Economic Education* 25(3), Summer 1994, pp. 267–69.

Friedman, J. W., *Oligopoly Theory*. Amsterdam: North Holland, 1983.

Gal-Or, E., "Excessive Retailing at the Bertrand Equilibria." *Canadian Journal of Economics* 23(2), May 1990, pp. 294–304.

Levy, David T., and Reitzes, James D., "Product Differentiation and the Ability to Collude: Where Being Different Can Be an Advantage." *Antitrust Bulletin* 38(2), Summer 1993, pp. 349–68.

Plott, C. R., "Industrial Organization Theory and Experimental Economics." *Journal of Economic Literature* 20, 1982, pp. 1485–1527.

Ross, Howard N., "Oligopoly Theory and Price Rigidity." *Antitrust Bulletin* 32(2), Summer 1987, pp. 451–69.

Showalter, Dean M., "Oligopoly and Financial Structure: Comment." *American Economic Review* 85(3), June 1995, pp. 647–53.

Appendix
Differentiated-Product Bertrand Oligopoly

The model of Bertrand oligopoly presented in the text is based on Bertrand's classic treatment of the subject, which assumes oligopolists produce identical products. Because oligopolists that produce differentiated products may engage in price competition, this appendix presents a model of differentiated-product Bertrand oligopoly.

Suppose two oligopolists produce slightly differentiated products and compete by setting prices. In this case, one firm cannot capture all of its rival's customers by undercutting the rival's price; some consumers will have a preference for a firm's product even if the rival is charging a lower price. Thus, even if firm 2 were to "give its products away for free" (charge a zero price), firm 1 generally would find it profitable to charge a positive price. Moreover, as firm 2 raised its price, some of its customers would defect to firm 1, and thus the demand for firm 1's product would increase. This would raise firm 1's marginal revenue, making it profitable for the firm to increase its price.

In a differentiated-product price-setting oligopoly, the reaction function of firm 1 defines firm 1's profit-maximizing price given the price charged by firm 2. Based on the above reasoning, firm 1's reaction function is upward sloping, as illustrated in Figure 9–14. To see this, note that if firm 2 sets its price at zero, firm 1 will find it profitable to set its price at $P_1^{min} > 0$, since some consumers will prefer its product to the rival's. Effectively, P_1^{min} is the price that maximizes firm 1's profits when it sells only to its brand-loyal customers (customers who do not want the other product, even for free). If the rival raises its price to, say, P_2^* some of firm 2's customers will decide to switch to firm 1's product. Consequently, when firm 2 raises its price to P_2^* firm 1 will raise its price to P_1^* to maximize profits given the higher demand. In fact, each point along firm 1's reaction function defines the profit-maximizing price charged by firm 1 for each price charged by firm 2. Notice that firm 1's reaction function is upward sloping, unlike in the case of Cournot oligopoly.

Firm 2's reaction function, which defines the profit-maximizing price for firm 2 given the price charged by firm 1, also is illustrated in Figure 9–14. It is upward sloping for the same reason firm 1's reaction function is upward sloping; in fact, firm 2's reaction function is the mirror image of firm 1's.

FIGURE 9–14 Reaction Functions in a Differentiated-Product Bertrand Oligopoly

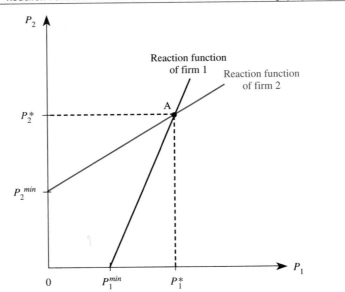

In a differentiated-product Bertrand oligopoly, equilibrium is determined by the intersection of the two firms' reaction functions, which corresponds to point A in Figure 9–14. To see that point A is indeed an equilibrium, note that the profit-maximizing price for firm 1 when firm 2 sets price at P_2^* is P_1^*. Similarly, the profit-maximizing price for firm 2 when firm 1 sets price at P_1^* is P_2^*.

In a differentiated-product Bertrand oligopoly, firms charge prices that exceed marginal cost. The reason they are able to do so is that the products are not perfect substitutes. As a firm raises its price, it loses some customers to the rival firm, but not all of them. Thus, the demand function for an individual firm's product is downward sloping, similar to the case in monopolistic competition. But unlike in monopolistic competition, the existence of entry barriers prevents other firms from entering the market. This allows the firms in a differentiated-product Bertrand oligopoly to potentially earn positive economic profits in the long run.

CHAPTER TEN

Game Theory: Inside Oligopoly

Learning Objectives

After completing this chapter, you will be able to:

LO1 Apply normal form and extensive form representations of games to formulate decisions in strategic environments that include pricing, advertising, coordination, bargaining, innovation, product quality, monitoring employees, and entry.

LO2 Distinguish among dominant, secure, Nash, mixed, and subgame perfect equilibrium strategies, and identify such strategies in various games.

LO3 Identify whether cooperative (collusive) outcomes may be supported as a Nash equilibrium in a repeated game, and explain the roles of trigger strategies, the interest rate, and the presence of an indefinite or uncertain final period in achieving such outcomes.

HEADLINE

US Airways Brings Back Complimentary Drinks

Less than one year after US Airways began charging domestic coach class passengers $2 for soft drinks, the company abandoned the strategy. Sources in the industry attribute the company's decision to return to the "industry standard of complementary drinks" to a variety of factors, including the depressed economy and the fact that US Airways was the only large network carrier to charge passengers for soft drinks.

Why do you think US Airways abandoned its $2 drink strategy?

Sources: Harry R. Weber, "US Airways Won't Charge for Sodas After All," *AP Newswire*, February 25, 2009; Michael R. Baye from US Airways, personal communication. February 23, 2009.

INTRODUCTION

In this chapter we continue our analysis of strategic interaction. As we saw in Chapter 9, when only a few firms compete in a market, the actions of one firm will have a drastic impact on its rivals. For example, the pricing and output decisions of one firm in an oligopoly generally will affect the profits of other firms in the industry. Consequently, to maximize profits a manager must take into account the likely impact of his or her decisions on the behavior of other managers in the industry.

In this chapter we will delve more deeply into managerial decisions that arise in the presence of interdependence. We will develop general tools that will assist you in making a host of decisions in oligopolistic markets, including what prices to charge, how much advertising to use, whether to introduce new products, and whether to enter a new market. The basic tool we will use to examine these issues is *game theory*. Game theory is a very useful tool for managers. In fact, we will see that game theory can be used to analyze decisions within a firm, such as those related to monitoring and bargaining with workers.

OVERVIEW OF GAMES AND STRATEGIC THINKING

Perhaps when you think of a game, a trivial game like tic-tac-toe, checkers, or Wheel of Fortune comes to mind. Game theory is actually a much more general framework to aid in decision making when your payoff depends on the actions taken by other players.

In a game, the players are individuals who make decisions. For example, in an oligopolistic market consisting of two firms, each of which must make a pricing decision, the firms (or, more precisely, the firms' managers) are the players. The planned decisions of the players are called *strategies*. The payoffs to the players are the profits or losses that result from the strategies. Due to interdependence, the payoff to a player depends not only on that player's strategy but also on the strategies employed by other players.

simultaneous-move game
Game in which each player makes decisions without knowledge of the other players' decisions.

sequential-move game
Game in which one player makes a move after observing the other player's move.

In the analysis of games, the order in which players make decisions is important. In a *simultaneous-move game,* each player makes decisions without knowledge of the other players' decisions. In a *sequential-move game,* one player makes a move after observing the other player's move. Tic-tac-toe, chess, and checkers are examples of sequential-move games (since players alternate moves), whereas matching pennies, dueling, and scissors-rock-paper are examples of simultaneous-move games. In the context of oligopoly games, if two firms must set prices without knowledge of each other's decisions, it is a simultaneous-move game; if one firm sets its price after observing its rival's price, it is a sequential-move game.

It is also important to distinguish between one-shot games and repeated games. In a *one-shot game,* the underlying game is played only once. In a *repeated game,* the underlying game is played more than once. For example, if you agree to play one, and only one, game of chess with a "rival," you are playing a one-shot game. If you agree to play chess two times with a rival, you are playing a repeated game.

Before we formally show how game theory can help managers solve business decisions, it is instructive to provide an example. Imagine that two gasoline stations are located side by side on the same block so that neither firm has a location advantage over the other. Consumers view the gasoline at each station as perfect substitutes and will purchase from the station that offers the lower price. The first thing in the morning, the manager of a gas station must phone the attendant to tell him what price to put on the sign. Since she must do so without knowledge of the rival's price, this "pricing game" is a simultaneous-move game. This type of game often is called the *Bertrand duopoly game.*

Given the structure of the game, if the manager of station A calls in a higher price than the manager of station B, consumers will not buy any gas from station A. The manager of station A, therefore, is likely to reason, "I think I'll charge $9.50 per gallon. But if station B thinks I will charge $9.50, they will charge $9.49, so I'd better charge $9.48. But if manager B thinks I think she'll charge $9.49, she will try to 'trick' me by charging $9.47. So I'd better charge $9.46. But if she thinks I think she thinks . . . " Perhaps you have gone through a similar thought process in trying to decide what to study for an exam ("The professor won't test us on this, but if he thinks we think he won't, he'll ask it to get us . . . ").

Game theory is a powerful tool for analyzing situations such as these. First, however, we must examine the foundations of game theory. We will begin with the study of simultaneous-move, one-shot games.

SIMULTANEOUS-MOVE, ONE-SHOT GAMES

This section presents the basic tools used to analyze simultaneous-move, one-shot games. Recall that in a simultaneous-move game, players must make decisions without knowledge of the decisions made by other players. The fact that a game is "one-shot" simply means that the players will play the game only once.

Knowledge of simultaneous-move, one-shot games is important to managers making decisions in an environment of interdependence. For example, it can be used to analyze situations where the profits of a firm depend not only on the firm's action but on the actions of rival firms as well. Before we look at specific applications of simultaneous-move, one-shot games, let us examine the general theory used to analyze such decisions.

strategy
In game theory, a decision rule that describes the actions a player will take at each decision point.

normal-form game
A representation of a game indicating the players, their possible strategies, and the payoffs resulting from alternative strategies.

Theory

We begin with two key definitions. First, a *strategy* is a decision rule that describes the actions a player will take at each decision point. Second, the *normal-form* representation of a game indicates the players in the game, the possible strategies of the players, and the payoffs to the players that will result from alternative strategies.

Perhaps the best way to understand precisely what is meant by *strategy* and *normal-form game* is to examine a simple example. The normal form of a simultaneous-move game is presented in Table 10–1. There are two players, whom

TABLE 10–1 A Normal-Form Game

		Player B	
	Strategy	**Left**	**Right**
Player A	**Up**	10, 20	15, 8
	Down	−10, 7	10, 10

we will call A and B to emphasize that the theory is completely general; that is, the players can be any two entities that are engaged in a situation of strategic interaction. If you wish, you may think of the players as the managers of two firms competing in a duopoly.

Player A has two possible strategies: He can choose *up* or *down*. Similarly, the feasible strategies for player B are *left* or *right*. This illustrates that the players may have different strategic options. Again, by calling the strategies *up, down,* and so on, we emphasize that these actions can represent virtually any decisions. For instance, *up* might represent raising the price and *down* lowering price, or *up* a high level of advertising and *down* a low level of advertising.

Finally, the payoffs to the two players are given by the entries in each cell of the matrix. The first entry refers to the payoff to player A, and the second entry denotes the payoff to player B. An important thing to notice about the description of the game is that the payoff to player A crucially depends on the strategy player B chooses. For example, if A chooses *up* and B chooses *left,* the resulting payoffs are 10 for A and 20 for B. Similarly, if player A's strategy is *up* while B's strategy is *right,* A's payoff is 15 while B's payoff is 8.

Since the game in Table 10–1 is a simultaneous-move, one-shot game, the players get to make one, and only one, decision and must make their decisions at the same time. For player A, the decision is simply *up* or *down*. Moreover, the players cannot make conditional decisions; for example, A can't choose *up* if B chooses *right* or *down* if B chooses *left.* The fact that the players make decisions at the same time precludes each player from basing his or her decisions on what the other player does.

What is the optimal strategy for a player in a simultaneous-move, one-shot game? As it turns out, this is a very complex question and depends on the nature of the game being played. There is one instance, however, in which it is easy to characterize the optimal decision—a situation that involves a dominant strategy. A strategy is a *dominant strategy* if it results in the highest payoff regardless of the action of the opponent.

In Table 10–1, the dominant strategy for player A is *up*. To see this, note that if player B chooses *left,* the best choice by player A is *up* since 10 units of profits are better than the −10 he would earn by choosing *down*. If B chose *right,* the best choice by A would be *up* since 15 units of profits are better than the 10 he would earn by choosing *down*. In short, regardless of whether player B's strategy is *left* or *right,* the best choice by player A is *up*. *Up* is a dominant strategy for player A.

dominant strategy
A strategy that results in the highest payoff to a player regardless of the opponent's action.

Principle	**Play Your Dominant Strategy**
	Check to see if you have a dominant strategy. If you have one, play it.

In simultaneous-move, one-shot games where a player has a dominant strategy, the optimal decision is to choose the dominant strategy. By doing so, you will maximize your payoff regardless of what your opponent does. In some games a player may not have a dominant strategy.

Demonstration Problem 10–1

In the game presented in Table 10–1, does player B have a dominant strategy?

Answer:

Player B does not have a dominant strategy. To see this, note that if player A chose *up,* the best choice by player B would be *left,* since 20 is better than the payoff of 8 she would earn by choosing *right.* But if A chose *down,* the best choice by B would be *right,* since 10 is better than the payoff of 7 she would realize by choosing *left.* Thus, there is no dominant strategy for player B; the best choice by B depends on what A does.

secure strategy
A strategy that guarantees the highest payoff given the worst possible scenario.

What should a player do in the absence of a dominant strategy? One possibility would be to play a *secure strategy*—a strategy that guarantees the highest payoff given the worst possible scenario. As we will see in a moment, this approach is not generally the optimal way to play a game, but it is useful to explain the reasoning that underlies this strategy. By using a secure strategy, a player maximizes the payoff that would result in the "worst-case scenario." In other words, to find a secure strategy, a player examines the worst payoff that could arise for each of his or her actions and chooses the action that has the highest of these worst payoffs.

Demonstration Problem 10–2

What is the secure strategy for player B in the game presented in Table 10–1?

Answer:

The secure strategy for player B is *right.* By choosing *left* B can guarantee a payoff of only 7, but by choosing *right* she can guarantee a payoff of 8. Thus, the secure strategy by player B is *right.*

While useful, the notion of a secure strategy suffers from two shortcomings. First, it is a very conservative strategy and should be considered only if you have a good reason to be extremely averse to risk. Second, it does not take into account the optimal decisions of your rival and thus may prevent you from earning a significantly higher payoff. In particular, player B in Table 10–1 should recognize that a dominant strategy for player A is to play *up*. Thus, player B should reason as follows: "Player A will surely choose *up*, since *up* is a dominant strategy. Therefore, I should not choose my secure strategy (*right*) but instead choose *left*." Assuming player A indeed chooses the dominant strategy (*up*), player B will earn 20 by choosing *left*, but only 8 by choosing the secure strategy (*right*).

Principle	**Put Yourself in Your Rival's Shoes**
	If you do not have a dominant strategy, look at the game from your rival's perspective. If your rival has a dominant strategy, anticipate that he or she will play it.

Nash equilibrium
A condition describing a set of strategies in which no player can improve her payoff by unilaterally changing her own strategy, given the other players' strategies.

A very natural way of formalizing the "end result" of such a thought process is captured in the definition of Nash equilibrium. A set of strategies constitute a *Nash equilibrium* if, given the strategies of the other players, no player can improve her payoff by unilaterally changing her own strategy. The concept of Nash equilibrium is very important because it represents a situation where every player is doing the best he or she can given what other players are doing.

Demonstration Problem 10–3

In the game presented in Table 10–1, what are the Nash equilibrium strategies for players A and B?

Answer:

The Nash equilibrium strategy for player A is *up*, and for player B it is *left*. To see this, suppose A chooses *up* and B chooses *left*. Would either player have an incentive to change his or her strategy? No. Given that player A's strategy is *up*, the best player B can do is choose *left*. Given that B's strategy is *left*, the best A can do is choose *up*. Hence, given the strategies (*up*, *left*), each player is doing the best he or she can given the other player's decision.

Applications of One-Shot Games

Pricing Decisions

Let us now see how game theory can help formalize the optimal managerial decisions in a Bertrand duopoly. Consider the game presented in Table 10–2, where two firms face a situation where they must decide whether to charge low or high prices. The first number in each cell represents firm A's profits, and the second number

INSIDE BUSINESS 10–1

Hollywood's (not so) Beautiful Mind: Nash or "Opie" Equilibrium?

Director Ron Howard scored a home run by strategically releasing *A Beautiful Mind* just in time to win four Golden Globe Awards in 2002. The film—based loosely on the life of Nobel Laureate John Forbes Nash, Jr., whose "Nash equilibrium" revolutionized economics and game theory—won best dramatic picture and best screenplay. Actor Russell Crowe also won a Golden Globe for his portrayal of the brilliant man whose battle with delusions, mental illness, and paranoid schizophrenia almost kept him from winning the 1994 Nobel Prize in Economics. While some know Ron Howard for his accomplishments as a director, he is best known as the kid who played Opie Taylor and Richie Cunningham in the popular *Andy Griffith* and *Happy Days* TV shows. For this reason, Eddie Murphy once dubbed him "Little Opie Cunningham" in a *Saturday Night Live* skit.

While *A Beautiful Mind* is an enjoyable film, its portrait of Nash's life is at odds with Sylvia Nasar's carefully documented and best-selling book with the same title. More relevant to students of game theory, the film does not accurately illustrate the concept for which Nash is renowned. Translation: Don't rent the movie as a substitute for learning how to use Nash's equilibrium concept to make business decisions.

Hollywood attempts to illustrate Nash's insight into game theory in a bar scene in which Nash and his buddies are eyeing one absolutely stunning blonde and several of her brunette friends. All of the men prefer the blonde. Nash ponders the situation and says, "If we all go for the blonde, we block each other. Not a single one of us is going to get her. So then we go for her friends. But they will all give us the cold shoulder because nobody likes to be second choice. But what if no one goes for the blonde? We don't get in each other's way, and we don't insult the other girls. That's the only way we win." The camera shows a shot of the blonde sitting all alone at the bar while the men dance happily with the brunettes. The scene concludes with Nash rushing off to write a paper on his new concept of equilibrium.

What's wrong with this scene? Recall that a Nash equilibrium is a situation where *no player* can gain by changing his decision, given the decisions of the other players. In Hollywood's game, the men are players and their decisions are which of the women to pursue. If the other men opt for the brunettes, the blonde is all alone just waiting to dance. This means that the remaining man's best response, given the decisions of the others, is to pursue the lonely blonde! Hollywood's dance scene does not illustrate a Nash equilibrium, but the exact opposite: a situation where any one of the men could unilaterally gain by switching to the blonde, given that the other men are dancing with brunettes! What is the correct term for Hollywood's dance scene in which the blonde is left all alone? Personally, I like the term "Opie equilibrium" because it honors the director of the film and sounds much more upbeat than "disequilibrium."

Hollywood also uses the dance scene to spin its view that "Adam Smith was wrong." In particular, since the men are better off dancing with the brunettes than all pursuing the blonde, viewers are to conclude that it is never socially efficient for individuals to pursue their own selfish desires. While Chapter 14 of this book shows a number of situations where markets may fail, Hollywood's illustration is not one of them. Its "Opie equilibrium" outcome is actually *socially inefficient* because none of the men get to enjoy the company of the stunning blonde. In contrast, a real Nash equilibrium to the game entails one man dancing with the blonde and the others dancing with brunettes. Any Nash equilibrium to Hollywood's game not only has the property that each man is selfishly maximizing his own satisfaction, given the strategies of the others, but the outcome is also *socially efficient* because it doesn't squander a dance with the blonde.

represents firm B's profits. For example, if firm A charges a high price while firm B charges a low price, A loses 10 units of profits while B earns 50 units of profits.

While the numbers in Table 10–2 are arbitrary, their relative magnitude is consistent with the nature of Bertrand competition. In particular, note that the profits of

TABLE 10–2 A Pricing Game

		Firm B	
	Strategy	**Low Price**	**High Price**
Firm A	**Low price**	0, 0	50, −10
	High price	−10, 50	10, 10

both firms are higher when both charge high prices than when they both charge low prices because in each instance consumers have no incentive to switch to the other firm. On the other hand, if one firm charges a high price and the other firm under-cuts that price, the lower-priced firm will gain all the other firm's customers and thus earn higher profits at the expense of the competitor.

We are considering a one-shot play of the game in Table 10–2, that is, a situation where the firms meet once, and only once, in the market. Moreover, the game is a simultaneous-move game in that each firm makes a pricing decision without knowl-edge of the decision made by the other firm. In a one-shot play of the game, the Nash equilibrium strategies are for each firm to charge the low price. The reason is simple. If firm B charges a high price, firm A's best choice is to charge a low price, since 50 units of profits are better than the 10 units it would earn if A charged the high price. Similarly, if firm B charges the low price, firm A's best choice is to charge the low price, since 0 units of profits are preferred to the 10 units of losses that would result if A charged the high price. Similar arguments hold from firm B's perspective. Firm A is always better off charging the low price regardless of what firm B does, and B is always better off charging the low price regardless of what A does. Hence, charging a low price is a dominant strategy for both firms. To summarize, in the one-shot version of the above game, each firm's best strategy is to charge a low price regardless of the other firm's action. The outcome of the game is that both firms charge low prices and earn profits of zero.

Clearly, profits are less than the firms would earn if they colluded and "agreed" to both charge high prices. For example, in Table 10–2 we see that each firm would earn profits of 10 units if both charged high prices. This is a classic result in eco-nomics and is called a *dilemma* because the Nash equilibrium outcome is inferior (from the viewpoint of the firms) to the situation where they both "agree" to charge high prices.

Why can't firms collude and agree to charge high prices? One answer is that collusion is illegal in the United States; firms are not allowed to meet and "con-spire" to set high prices. There are other reasons, however. Suppose the managers did secretly meet and agree to charge high prices. Would they have an incentive to live up to their promises? Consider firm A's point of view. If it "cheated" on the col-lusive agreement by lowering its price, it would increase its profits from 10 to 50. Thus, firm A has an incentive to induce firm B to charge a high price so that it can "cheat" to earn higher profits. Of course, firm B recognizes this incentive, which precludes the agreement from being reached in the first place.

INSIDE BUSINESS 10–2

Cola Wars in India

One of the most well-known examples of duopoly price competition is Coca-Cola versus PepsiCo. Although there are many firms competing in the cola industry, the dominance in market share by Coke and Pepsi results in each firm's profits being heavily influenced by the pricing decision of the other. The pricing "game" between Coke and Pepsi is not unlike the one illustrated in Table 10-2. Each firm has a strong incentive to charge low prices regardless of its opponent's pricing decision, often leading to low prices and low profits, as compared to the outcome when both charge high prices.

Recently, Coke announced it was lowering its price for a 200 ml bottle in India to a uniform 8 rupees across the entire country. This price drop was made in anticipation of the summer spike in demand for cola. If Coke views the summer market as a one-shot game with Pepsi, charging this low price is likely its dominant

strategy. In fact, Pepsi was expected to quickly follow suit by cutting its prices, again consistent with the prediction for a one-shot game.

While the one-shot game in Table 10-2 is quite effective in explaining the recent price war between Coke and Pepsi in India, we know that these two firms actually face each other many times in many markets. In 2003, both firms engaged in a similar price war in India, only to later jointly raise prices after seeing significant damage to their profits. Later in this chapter, you will see how the repeated nature of the price war between Coke and Pepsi can allow them to keep prices high over extended periods of time, despite the temptation to cut prices in any given period.

Sources: Sharma, S., "Coca-Cola Cuts Prices, Pepsi May Follow Suit," *The Economic Times*, February 15, 2012. Srivastava, S., "Why Coke May Have Triggered a New Price War This Season," *Forbes India*, June 30, 2012.

However, suppose the manager of firm A is "honest" and would never cheat on a promise to charge a high price. (She is "honest" enough to keep her word to the other manager, but not so honest as to obey the law against collusion.) What happens to firm A if the manager of firm B cheats on the collusive agreement? If B cheats, A experiences losses of $10. When firm A's stockholders ask the manager why they lost $10 when the rival firm earned profits of $50, how can the manager answer? She cannot admit she was cheated on in a collusive agreement, for doing so might send her to jail for having violated the law. Whatever her answer, she risks being fired or sent to prison.

Advertising and Quality Decisions

Our framework for analyzing simultaneous-move, one-shot games can also be used to analyze advertising and quality decisions. In oligopolistic markets, firms advertise and/or increase their product quality in an attempt to increase the demand for their products. While both quality and advertising can be used to increase the demand for a product, our discussion will use advertising as a placeholder for both quality and advertising.

An important issue in evaluating the consequences of advertising is to recognize where the increase in demand comes from. In most oligopolistic markets, advertising increases the demand for a firm's product by taking customers away from other firms in the industry. An increase in one firm's advertising increases its profits at the expense of other firms in the market; there is interdependency among the advertising decisions of firms.

A classic example of such a situation is the breakfast cereal industry, which is highly concentrated. By advertising its brand of cereal, a particular firm does not induce many consumers to eat cereal for lunch and dinner; instead, it induces customers to switch to its brand from another brand. This can lead to a situation where each firm advertises just to "cancel out" the effects of other firms' advertising, resulting in high levels of advertising, no change in industry or firm demand, and low profits.

Demonstration Problem 10–4

For a video walkthrough of this problem, visit www.mhhe.com/baye8e

Suppose your firm competes against another firm for customers. You and your rival know your products will be obsolete at the end of the year and must simultaneously determine whether or not to advertise. In your industry, advertising does not increase total industry demand but instead induces consumers to switch among the products of different firms. Thus, if both you and your rival advertise, the two advertising campaigns will simply offset each other, and you will each earn $4 million in profits. If neither of you advertises, you will each earn $10 million in profits. However, if one of you advertises and the other one does not, the firm that advertises will earn $20 million and the firm that does not advertise will earn $1 million in profits. Is your profit-maximizing choice to advertise or not to advertise? How much money do you expect to earn?

Answer:

The description of the game corresponds to the matrix presented in Table 10–3. The game is a one-shot game. Note that the dominant strategy for each firm is to advertise, and thus the unique Nash equilibrium for the game is for each firm to advertise. The profit-maximizing choice by your firm, therefore, is to advertise. You can expect to earn $4 million. Collusion would not work because this is a one-shot game; if you and your rival "agreed" not to advertise (in the hope of making $10 million each), each of you would have an incentive to cheat on the agreement.

Coordination Decisions

Thus far, our analysis of oligopoly has focused on situations where firms have competing objectives: One firm can gain only at the expense of other firms. Not all games have this structure, however.

Imagine a world where producers of electrical appliances have a choice of which type of electrical outlets to put on appliances: 90-volt, four-prong outlets or 120-volt, two-prong outlets. In an environment where different appliances require different outlets, a consumer who desires several appliances would have to spend a

TABLE 10–3 An Advertising Game

		Firm B	
Firm A	Strategy	Advertise	Don't Advertise
	Advertise	$4, $4	$20, $1
	Don't Advertise	$1, $20	$10, $10

considerable sum wiring the house to accommodate all the appliances. This would reduce the amount the consumer has available for buying appliances and therefore would adversely affect the profits of appliance manufacturers. In contrast, if the appliance manufacturers can "coordinate" their decisions (that is, produce appliances that require the same types of wiring), they will earn higher profits.

Table 10–4 presents a hypothetical example of what is called a *coordination game*. Two firms must decide whether to produce appliances requiring 120-volt or 90-volt outlets. If each firm produces appliances requiring 120-volt outlets, each firm will earn profits of $100. Similarly, if each firm produces appliances requiring 90-volt outlets, each firm will earn $100. However, if the two firms produce appliances requiring different types of outlets, each firm will earn zero profits due to the lower demand that will result from consumers' need to spend more money wiring their houses.

What would you do if you were the manager of firm A in this example? If you do not know what firm B is going to do, you have a very tough decision. All you can do is "guess" what B will do. If you think B will produce 120-volt appliances, you should produce 120-volt appliances as well. If you think B will produce 90-volt appliances, you should do likewise. You will thus maximize profits by doing what firm B does. Effectively, both you and firm B will do better by "coordinating" your decisions.

The game in Table 10–4 has two Nash equilibria. One Nash equilibrium is for each firm to produce 120-volt appliances; the other is for each firm to produce 90-volt appliances. The question is how the firms will get to one of these equilibria. If the firms could "talk" to each other, they could agree to produce 120-volt systems. Alternatively, the government could set a standard that electrical outlets be required to operate on 120-volt, two-prong outlets. In effect, this would allow the firms to "coordinate" their decisions. Notice that once they agree to produce 120-volt appliances, there is no incentive to cheat on this agreement. The game in Table 10–4 is not analogous to the pricing or advertising games analyzed earlier; it is a game of coordination rather than a game of conflicting interests.

Monitoring Employees

Game theory can also be used to analyze interactions between workers and the manager. In Chapter 6, we discussed the principal–agent problem and argued that there can be conflicting goals between workers and managers. Managers desire workers to work hard, while workers enjoy leisure.

In our discussion of manager–worker principal–agent problems in Chapter 6, we noted that one way a manager can reduce workers' incentives to shirk is to

TABLE 10–4   A Coordination Game

	Strategy	Firm B 120-Volt Outlets	Firm B 90-Volt Outlets
Firm A 120-Volt Outlets		$100, $100	$0, $0
Firm A 90-Volt Outlets		$0, $0	$100, $100

engage in "random" spot checks of the workplace. Game theory provides a way of seeing why this can work. Consider a game between a worker and a manager. The manager has two possible actions: (1) monitor the worker or (2) don't monitor the worker. The worker has two choices: (1) work or (2) shirk. These possible actions and resulting payoffs are depicted in Table 10–5.

The interpretation of this normal-form game is as follows: If the manager monitors while the worker works, the worker "wins" and the manager "loses." The manager has spent time monitoring a worker who was already working. In this case, suppose the manager's payoff is -1 and the worker's payoff is 1. The payoffs are the same if the manager does not monitor the worker and the worker shirks; the worker wins because she gets away with shirking.

In contrast, if the manager monitors while the worker shirks, the manager wins 1 and the worker who gets caught loses 1. Similarly, if the worker works and the manager does not monitor, the manager wins 1 and the worker loses 1. The numbers in Table 10–5 are, of course, purely hypothetical, but they are consistent with the relative payoffs that arise in such situations.

Notice that the game in Table 10–5 does not have a Nash equilibrium, at least in the usual sense of the term. To see this, suppose the manager's strategy is to monitor the worker. Then the best choice of the worker is to work. But if the worker works, the manager does better by changing his strategy: choosing not to monitor. Thus, "monitoring" is not part of a Nash equilibrium strategy. The paradox, however, is that "not monitoring" isn't part of a Nash equilibrium either. To see why, suppose the manager's strategy is "don't monitor." Then the worker will maximize her payoff by shirking. Given that the worker shirks, the manager does better by changing the strategy to "monitor" to increase his payoff from -1 to 1. Thus, we see that "don't monitor" is not part of a Nash equilibrium strategy either.

The thing to notice in this example is that both the worker and the manager want to keep their actions "secret"; if the manager knows what the worker is doing, it will be curtains for the worker, and vice versa. In such situations, players find it in their interest to engage in a *mixed (randomized) strategy*. What this means is that players "randomize" over their available strategies; for instance, the manager flips a coin to determine whether or not to monitor. By doing so, the worker cannot predict whether the manager will be present to monitor her and, consequently, cannot outguess the manager.

Those of you who have taken multiple-choice tests have had firsthand experience with randomized strategies. If your professor made *a* the correct answer more often than *b*, *c*, or *d*, you could gain by answering *a* in those instances when you did

mixed (randomized) strategy
A strategy whereby a player randomizes over two or more available actions in order to keep rivals from being able to predict his or her action.

TABLE 10–5   A Game with No Nash Equilibrium

		Worker	
	Strategy	**Work**	**Shirk**
	Monitor	$-1, 1$	$1, -1$
Manager	**Don't Monitor**	$1, -1$	$-1, 1$

not know the correct answer. This would enable you to earn a higher grade than you deserved based on your knowledge of subject matter. To prevent this strategy from working for you, professors randomize which option is the correct answer so that you cannot systematically guess the correct answer on an exam.

Nash Bargaining

The final application of simultaneous-move, one-shot games we will consider is a simple bargaining game. In a *Nash bargaining* game, two players "bargain" over some object of value. In a simultaneous-move, one-shot bargaining game, the players have only one chance to reach an agreement, and the offers made in bargaining are made simultaneously.

To be concrete, suppose management and a labor union are bargaining over how much of a $100 surplus to give to the union. Suppose, for simplicity, that the $100 can be split only into $50 increments. The players have one shot to reach an agreement. The parties simultaneously write the amount they desire on a piece of paper (0, 50, or 100). If the sum of the amounts each party asks for does not exceed $100, the players get the specified amounts. But if the sum of the amounts requested exceeds $100, bargaining ends in a stalemate. Let's suppose that the delays caused by this stalemate cost both the union and management $1.

Table 10–6 presents the normal form of this hypothetical bargaining game. If you were management, what amount would you ask for? Suppose you wrote down $100. Then the only way you would get any money is if the union asked for zero. Notice that if management asked for $100 and the union asked for $0, neither party would have an incentive to change its amounts; we would be in Nash equilibrium.

Before concluding that you should ask for $100, think again. Suppose the union wrote down $50. Management's best response to this move would be to ask for $50. And given that management asked for $50, the union would have no incentive to change its amount. Thus, a 50–50 split of the $100 also would be a Nash equilibrium.

Finally, suppose management asked for $0 and the union asked for the entire $100. This too would constitute a Nash equilibrium. Neither party could improve its payoff by changing its strategy given the strategy of the other.

Thus, there are three Nash equilibrium outcomes to this bargaining game. One outcome splits the money evenly among the parties, while the other two outcomes give all the money to either the union or management.

This example illustrates that the outcomes of simultaneous-move bargaining games are difficult to predict because there are generally multiple Nash equilibria.

TABLE 10–6 A Bargaining Game

		Union		
	Strategy	0	50	100
	0	0, 0	0, 50	0, 100
Management	50	50, 0	50, 50	−1, −1
	100	100, 0	−1,−1	−1, −1

This multiplicity of equilibria leads to inefficiencies when the parties fail to "coordinate" on an equilibrium. In Table 10–6, for instance, six of the nine potential outcomes are inefficient in that they result in total payoffs that are less than the amount to be divided. Three of these outcomes entail negative payoffs due to stalemate. Unfortunately, stalemate is common in labor disputes: Agreements often fail or are delayed because the two sides ask for more (in total) than there is to split.

Experimental evidence suggests that bargainers often perceive a 50–50 split to be "fair." Consequently, many players in real-world settings tend to choose strategies that result in such a split even though there are other Nash equilibria. Clearly, for the game in Table 10–6, if you expect the union to ask for $50, you, as management, should ask for $50.

Demonstration Problem 10–5

Suppose a $1 bill is to be divided between two players according to a simultaneous-move, one-shot bargaining game. Is there a Nash equilibrium to the bargaining game if the smallest unit in which the money can be divided is $.01? Assume that if the players ask for more in total than is available, they go home empty-handed.

Answer:

Yes, in fact there are many Nash equilibria. Any amount the players ask for that sums to exactly 100 cents constitutes a Nash equilibrium. As examples, one player asks for $.01 and the other asks for $.99; one player asks for $.02 and the other asks for $.98; and so on. In each case, neither party can gain by asking for more, given what the other player has asked for.

INFINITELY REPEATED GAMES

infinitely repeated game
A game that is played over and over again forever and in which players receive payoffs during each play of the game.

Based on our analysis of one-shot pricing and advertising games, one might be led to believe that collusion is impossible in an industry. This conclusion is erroneous, however, and stems from the fact that firms in some industries do not play a one-shot game. Instead, they compete week after week, year after year. In these instances, the appropriate mode of analysis is to consider a situation where a game is repeated over time. In this section, we analyze a situation where players perpetually interact.

An *infinitely repeated game* is a game that is played over and over again forever. Players receive payoffs during each repetition of the game.

Theory

When a game is played again and again, players receive payoffs during each repetition of the game. Due to the time value of money, a dollar earned during the first repetition of the game is worth more than a dollar earned in later repetitions; players must appropriately discount future payoffs when they make current decisions. For this reason, we will review the key aspects of present value analysis before we begin examining repeated games.

Review of Present Value

The value of a firm is the present value of all future profits earned by the firm. If the interest rate is i, π_0 represents profits today, π_1 profits one year from today, π_2 profits two years from today, and so on, the value of a firm that will be in business for T years is

$$PV_{Firm} = \pi_0 + \frac{\pi_1}{1+i} + \frac{\pi_2}{(1+i)^2} + \cdots + \frac{\pi_T}{(1+i)^T} = \sum_{t=0}^{T} \frac{\pi_t}{(1+i)^t}$$

If the profits earned by the firm are the same in each period ($\pi_t = \pi$ for each period, t) and the horizon is infinite ($T = \infty$), this formula simplifies to

$$PV_{Firm} = \left(\frac{1+i}{i}\right)\pi$$

As we will see, this formula is very useful in analyzing decisions in infinitely repeated games.

Supporting Collusion with Trigger Strategies

Now consider the simultaneous-move Bertrand pricing game presented in Table 10–7. The Nash equilibrium in a one-shot play of this game is for each firm to charge low prices and earn zero profits. Let us suppose the firms play the game in Table 10–7 day after day, week after week, for all eternity. Thus, we are considering an infinitely repeated Bertrand pricing game, not a one-shot game. In this section, we will examine the impact of repeated play on the equilibrium outcome of the game.

When firms repeatedly face a payoff matrix such as that in Table 10–7, it is possible for them to "collude" without fear of being cheated on. They do this by using trigger strategies. A *trigger strategy* is a strategy that is contingent on the past plays of players in a game. A player who adopts a trigger strategy continues to choose the same action until some other player takes an action that "triggers" a different action by the first player.

trigger strategy
A strategy that is contingent on the past play of a game and in which some particular past action "triggers" a different action by a player.

To see how trigger strategies can be used to support collusive outcomes, suppose firm A and firm B secretly meet and agree to the following arrangement: "We will each charge the high price, provided neither of us has ever 'cheated' in the past (i.e., charged the low price in any previous period). If one of us cheats and charges the low price, the other player will 'punish' the deviator by charging the low price

TABLE 10–7   A Pricing Game That Is Repeated

		Firm B	Firm B
	Price	Low	High
Firm A	Low	0, 0	50, −40
	High	−40, 50	10, 10

in every period thereafter." Thus, if firm A cheats, it pulls a "trigger" that leads firm B to charge the low price forever after, and vice versa. It turns out that if both firms adopt such a trigger strategy, there are conditions under which neither firm has an incentive to cheat on the collusive agreement. Before we show this formally, let us examine the basic intuition.

If neither firm in Table 10–7 cheats on the collusive agreement, each firm will earn $10 each period forever. But if one firm plays according to the agreement, the other firm could cheat and earn an immediate profit of $50 instead of $10. Thus, there is still the immediate benefit to a firm of cheating on the agreement. However, because the firms compete repeatedly over time, there is a future cost of cheating. According to the agreement, if a firm ever cheats, the other firm will charge a low price in all future periods. Thus, the best the firm that cheated can do is earn $0 in the periods after cheating instead of the $10 it would have earned had it not broken the agreement.

In short, the benefit of cheating today on the collusive agreement is earning $50 instead of $10 today. The cost of cheating today is earning $0 instead of $10 in each future period. If the present value of the cost of cheating exceeds the one-time benefit of cheating, it does not pay for a firm to cheat, and high prices can be sustained.

Now let us formalize this idea. Suppose the firms agree to the collusive plan just outlined, and firm A believes firm B will live up to the agreement. Does firm A have an incentive to cheat and charge a low price? If firm A cheats by charging a low price, its profits will be $50 today but $0 in all subsequent periods, since cheating today will lead firm B to charge a low price in all future periods. The best choice of firm A when firm B charges the low price in these future periods is to charge the low price to earn $0. Thus, if firm A cheats today, the present value of its profits are

$$PV^{Cheat}_{Firm\,A} = \$50 + 0 + 0 + 0 + 0 + \cdots$$

If firm A does not cheat, it earns $10 each period forever. Thus, the present value of the profits of firm A if it "cooperates" (does not cheat) are

$$PV^{Coop}_{Firm\,A} = 10 + \frac{10}{1+i} + \frac{10}{(1+i)^2} + \frac{10}{(1+i)^3} + \cdots = \frac{10(1+i)}{i}$$

where i is the interest rate. Firm A has no incentive to cheat if the present value of its earnings from cheating is less than the present value of its earnings from not cheating. For the numbers in this example, there is no incentive to cheat if

$$PV^{Cheat}_{Firm\,A} = 50 \leq \frac{10(1+i)}{i} = PV^{Coop}_{Firm\,A}$$

which is true if $i \leq 1/4$. In other words, if the interest rate is less than 25 percent, firm A will lose more (in present value) by cheating than it will gain. Since firm B's incentives are symmetric, the same is true for firm B. Thus, when oligopolistic firms compete repeatedly over time, it is possible for them to collude and charge high prices to earn $10 each period. This benefits firms at the expense of consumers and also leads to a deadweight loss. This explains why there are laws against collusion.

More generally, we may state the following principle:

Principle	**Sustaining Cooperative Outcomes with Trigger Strategies**
	Suppose a one-shot game is infinitely repeated and the interest rate is i. Further, suppose the "cooperative" one-shot payoff to a player is π^{Coop}, the maximum one-shot payoff if the player cheats on the collusive outcome is π^{Cheat}, the one-shot Nash equilibrium payoff is π^N, and $$\frac{\pi^{Cheat} - \pi^{Coop}}{\pi^{Coop} - \pi^N} \le \frac{1}{i}$$ Then the cooperative (collusive) outcome can be sustained in the infinitely repeated game with the following trigger strategy: "Cooperate provided no player has ever cheated in the past. If any player cheats, 'punish' the player by choosing the one-shot Nash equilibrium strategy forever after."

The condition written in the preceding principle has a very intuitive interpretation. It can be rewritten as

$$\pi^{Cheat} - \pi^{Coop} \le \frac{1}{i}(\pi^{Coop} - \pi^N)$$

The left-hand side of this equation represents the one-time gain of breaking the collusive agreement today. The right-hand side represents the present value of what is given up in the future by cheating today. Provided the one-time gain is less than the present value of what would be given up by cheating, players find it in their interest to live up to the agreement.

Demonstration Problem 10–6

Suppose firm A and firm B repeatedly face the situation presented in Table 10–7 on page 378, and the interest rate is 40 percent. The firms agree to charge a high price each period, provided neither firm has cheated on this agreement in the past.

1.   What are firm A's profits if it cheats on the collusive agreement?
2.   What are firm A's profits if it does not cheat on the collusive agreement?
3.   Does an equilibrium result where the firms charge the high price each period?

Answer:

1.   If firm B lives up to the collusive agreement but firm A cheats, firm A will earn $50 today and zero forever after.

2.   If firm B lives up to the collusive agreement and firm A does not cheat, the present value of firm A's profits is

$$10 + \frac{10}{1 + .4} + \frac{10}{(1 + .4)^2} + \frac{10}{(1 + .4)^3} + \cdots = \frac{10(1 + .4)}{.4} = 35$$

3.   Since $50 > 35$, the present value of firm A's profits is higher if A cheats on the collusive agreement than if it does not cheat. Since the payoff matrix is symmetric,

each firm has an incentive to cheat on the collusive agreement, even if it believes the other firm will not cheat. In equilibrium, each firm will charge the low price each period to earn profits of $0 each period.

In summary, in a one-shot game there is no tomorrow; any gains must be had today or not at all. In an infinitely repeated game there is always a tomorrow, and firms must weigh the benefits of current actions against the future costs of those actions. The principal result of infinitely repeated games is that when the interest rate is low, firms may find it in their interest to collude and charge high prices, unlike in the case of a one-shot game. The basic reason for this important result is this: If a player deviates from the "collusive strategy," he or she is punished in future periods long enough to wipe out the gains from having deviated from the collusive outcome. The threat of punishment makes cooperation work in repeated games. In one-shot games there is no tomorrow, and threats have no bite.

Factors Affecting Collusion in Pricing Games

It is easier to sustain collusive arrangements via the punishment strategies outlined earlier when firms know (1) who their rivals are, so they know whom to punish should the need arise; (2) who their rivals' customers are, so that if punishment is necessary they can take away those customers by charging lower prices; and (3) when their rivals deviate from the collusive arrangement, so they know when to begin the punishments. Furthermore, they must (4) be able to successfully punish rivals for deviating from the collusive agreement, for otherwise the threat of punishment would not work. These factors are related to several variables reflected in the structure and conduct of the industry.

Number of Firms

Collusion is easier when there are few firms rather than many. If there are n firms in the industry, the total amount of monitoring that must go on to sustain the collusive arrangement is $n \times (n - 1)$. For example, let the firms be indexed by A, B, C, ... If there are only two firms in the industry, then to punish a firm for deviating, each firm must know whether its rival has deviated and, if so, where its customers are so it can punish the rival by getting some of its customers. To do this, each must keep an eye on its rival. With two firms, this information may be obtained if A monitors B and B monitors A.

The total number of monitors needed in the market grows very rapidly as the number of firms increases. For example, if there are five firms, each firm must monitor four other firms, so the total number of monitors needed in the market is $5 \times 4 = 20$. The cost of monitoring rivals reduces the gains to colluding. If the number of firms is "large enough," the monitoring costs become so high relative to collusive profits that it does not pay to monitor the actions of other firms. Under these circumstances, the "threat" used to sustain the collusive outcome is not credible, and the collusion fails. This is one reason why it is easier for two firms to collude than it is for, say, four firms to do so.

INSIDE BUSINESS 10–3

Trigger Strategies in the Waste Industry

For trigger strategies to work, players must be able to monitor their rivals' actions, so that they know whether to take punitive actions. For punishments to deter cheating, players do not actually have to punish cheaters forever. As long as they punish cheaters long enough to take away the profits earned by cheating, no player will find it profitable to cheat. In this case, players can achieve collusive outcomes. Real-world firms recognize these points.

Firms that pick up trash in Dade County, Florida, devised a mechanism to use trigger strategies to enforce high prices in a Bertrand market. To ensure that competitors did not undercut their high prices, firms monitored one another quite closely.

One company hired several people to follow the trucks of rival firms to make sure they did not steal its customers by undercutting its price. What did the firm do if it found a competitor servicing one of its clients? It took away 5 or 10 of the competitor's customers for every one that had been lost to punish the rival for stealing its customers. It accomplished this by offering these customers a more favorable price than the competitor offered. After a while, its competitors learned that it did not pay to steal this firm's customers. In the end there was little cheating, and firms in the market charged collusive prices.

Before you decide to adopt similar methods, be aware that this example was taken from court transcripts in the U.S. District Court of Southern Florida, where those involved in the conspiracy were tried. In situations with repeated interaction, trigger strategies can be used to enhance profits—but it is illegal to conspire to engage in such practices.

Source: Docket No. 84-6107-Cr-KING (MISHLER), March 17, 1986. U.S. District Court of Southern Florida, Miami Division.

Firm Size

Economies of scale exist in monitoring. Monitoring and policing costs constitute a much greater share of total costs for small firms than for larger firms. Thus, it may be easier for a large firm to monitor a small firm than for a small firm to monitor a large firm. For example, a large firm (with, say, 20 outlets) can monitor the prices charged by a small competitor (with 1 outlet) by simply checking prices at the one store. But to check the prices of its rival, the smaller firm must hire individuals to monitor 20 outlets.

History of the Market

One key issue not addressed thus far is how firms reach an understanding to collude. One way is for the firms to explicitly meet and verbally warn their rivals not to steal their customers, or else they will be punished. Alternatively, firms might not meet at all but instead gain an understanding over time of the way the game is played and thus achieve "tacit collusion." *Tacit collusion* occurs when the firms do not explicitly conspire to collude but accomplish collusion indirectly. For example, in many instances firms learn from experience how other firms will behave in a market. If a firm observes over time that it is "punished" each time it charges a low price or attempts to steal customers from a rival, it eventually will learn that it does not pay to charge low prices. In these instances, tacit collusion will be the likely outcome.

In contrast, if a firm learns over time that its opponents are unable to successfully punish it for undercutting prices, tacit collusion will be unlikely to result. If firms never carry out their threats, the history of the industry will be such that collusion by threat of reprisal is not an equilibrium. But if firms observe that rivals indeed carry out their threats, this "history" ultimately will result in collusion.

Punishment Mechanisms

The pricing mechanisms firms use also affect their ability to punish rivals that do not cooperate. For example, in a posted-price market, where a single price is posted and charged to all of a firm's customers, the cost of punishing an opponent is higher than in markets in which different customers are quoted different prices. The reason is as follows: If a single price is charged to all customers, a firm that wishes to punish a rival by stealing its customers not only has to charge a low price to the rival's customers but also must lower its price to its own customers. This is essentially what a retailer must do to get customers away from another retailer. In contrast, in an industry in which different prices are quoted to different customers, a firm can punish its rival by charging the rival's customers a low price while continuing to charge its own customers a higher price. This, of course, substantially reduces the cost of engaging in punishment.

An Application of Infinitely Repeated Games to Product Quality

The theory of infinitely repeated games can be used to analyze the desirability of firm policies such as warranties and guarantees. Effectively, a game occurs between consumers and firms: Consumers desire durable, high-quality products at a low price, while firms wish to maximize profits. In a one-shot game, any profits made by the firm must be made today; there is no prospect for repeat business. Thus, in a one-shot game, a firm may have an incentive to sell shoddy products. This is particularly true if consumers cannot determine the quality of the products prior to purchase.

To see this, consider the normal-form game in Table 10–8. Here the game is between a consumer and a firm. The consumer has two strategies: buy the product or don't buy it. The firm can produce a low-quality product or a high-quality product. In a one-shot play of the game, the Nash equilibrium strategy is for the firm to produce a low-quality product and for consumers to shun the product. To see this, note that if the consumer decided to buy the product, the firm would benefit by selling a low-quality product, since profits of 10 are better than the 1 it would earn by producing a high-quality product. Given a low-quality product, the consumer

TABLE 10–8 A Product Quality Game

		Firm	
	Strategy	Low-Quality Product	High-Quality Product
Consumer	Don't Buy	0, 0	0, −10
	Buy	−10, 10	1, 1

chooses not to buy, since 0 is better than losing 10 by purchasing a shoddy product. But since the consumer chooses not to buy, it does not pay for the firm to produce a high-quality product. In a one-shot game, the consumer chooses not to buy the product because he or she knows the firm will "take the money and run."

The story differs if the game is infinitely repeated. Suppose the consumer tells the firm, "I'll buy your product and will continue to buy it if it is of good quality. But if it turns out to be shoddy, I'll tell all my friends never to purchase anything from you again." Given this strategy by the consumer, what is the best thing for the firm to do? If the interest rate is not too high, the best alternative is to sell a high-quality product. The reason is simple. By selling a shoddy product, the firm earns 10 instead of 1 that period. This is, in effect, "the gain to cheating" (selling a poor-quality product). The cost of selling a shoddy product, however, is to earn zero forever after, as the firm's reputation is ruined by having sold such a product. When the interest rate is low, the one-time gain will be more than offset by the lost future sales. It will not pay for the firm to "cheat" by selling shoddy merchandise.

The lesson to be drawn from this example is twofold. First, if your firm desires to be a "going concern," that is, infinitely lived, it does not pay to "cheat" customers if the one-time gain is more than offset by lost future sales. Notice that this is true even if your firm cannot be sued or if there are no government regulations against selling shoddy merchandise.

Second, you should recognize that any production process is likely to have "bad runs," in which some low-quality products are produced out of honest error. Notice in this example that even if the firm "tried" to produce high-quality merchandise but, due to an inadvertent error, one unit was defective, that error could ruin the firm. To guard against this, many firms offer guarantees that the product will be of high quality. That way, if an error occurs in production, the consumer can obtain a new item, be satisfied, and not "punish" the firm by spreading the news that it sells shoddy merchandise.

FINITELY REPEATED GAMES

So far we have considered two extremes: games that are played only once and games that are played infinitely many times. This section summarizes important implications of games that are repeated a finite number of times, that is, games that eventually end. We will consider two classes of *finitely repeated games:* (1) games in which players do not know when the game will end and (2) games in which players know when it will end.

Games with an Uncertain Final Period

Suppose two duopolists repeatedly play the pricing game in Table 10–9 until their products become obsolete, at which point the game ends. Thus, we are considering a finitely repeated game. Suppose the firms do not know the exact date at which their products will become obsolete. Thus, there is uncertainty regarding the final period in which the game will be played.

TABLE 10–9 A Pricing Game That Is Finitely Repeated

		Firm B	
	Price	**Low**	**High**
Firm A	**Low**	0, 0	50, −40
	High	−40, 50	10, 10

Suppose the probability that the game will end after a given play is θ, where $0 < \theta < 1$. Thus, when a firm makes today's pricing decision, there is a chance that the game will be played again tomorrow; if the game is played again tomorrow, there is a chance that it will be played again the next day; and so on. For example, if $\theta = 1/2$, there is a 50–50 chance the game will end after one play, a 1/4 chance it will end after two plays, a 1/8 chance that it will end after three plays, or, more generally, a $(\frac{1}{2})^t$ chance that the game will end after t plays of the game. It is as if a coin is flipped at the end of every play of the game, and if the coin comes up heads, the game terminates. The game terminates after t plays if the first heads occurs after t consecutive tosses of the coin.

It turns out that when there is uncertainty regarding precisely when the game will end, the finitely repeated game in Table 10–9 exactly mirrors our analysis of infinitely repeated games. To see why, suppose the firms adopt trigger strategies, whereby each agrees to charge a high price provided the other has not charged a low price in any previous period. If a firm deviates by charging a low price, the other firm will "punish" it by charging a low price until the game ends. For simplicity, let us assume the interest rate is zero so that the firms do not discount future profits.

Given such trigger strategies, does firm A have an incentive to cheat by charging a low price? If A cheats by charging a low price when B charges a high price, A's profits are $50 today but zero in all remaining periods of the game. This is because cheating today "triggers" firm B to charge a low price in all future periods, and the best A can do in these periods is to earn $0. Thus, if firm A cheats today, it earns

$$\Pi_{Firm\,A}^{Cheat} = \$50$$

regardless of whether the game ends after one play, two plays, or whenever.

If firm A does not cheat, it earns $10 today. In addition, there is a probability of $1 - \theta$ that the game will be played again, in which case the firm will earn another $10. There is also a probability of $(1 - \theta)^2$ that the game will not terminate after two plays, in which case A will earn yet another $10. Carrying out this reasoning for all possible dates at which the game terminates, we see that firm A can expect to earn

$$\Pi_{Firm\,A}^{Coop} = 10 + (1 - \theta)10 + (1 - \theta)^2 10 + (1 - \theta)^3 10 + \cdots = \frac{10}{\theta}$$

if it does not cheat. In this equation, θ is the probability the game will terminate after one play. Notice that when $\theta = 1$, firm A is certain the game will end after one play; in this case, A's profits if it cooperates are $10. But if $\theta < 1$, the probability the game will end after one play is less than 1 (there is a chance they will play again), and the profits of cooperating are greater than $10.

The important thing to notice is that when the game is repeated a finite but uncertain number of times, the benefits of cooperating look exactly like the benefits of cooperating in an infinitely repeated game, which are

$$PV_{Firm\,A}^{Coop} = 10 + \frac{10}{1+i} + \frac{10}{(1+i)^2} + \frac{10}{(1+i)^3} + \cdots = \frac{10(1+i)}{i}$$

where i is the interest rate. In a repeated game with an uncertain end point, $1 - \theta$ plays the role of $1/(1 + i)$; players discount the future not because of the interest rate but because they are not certain future plays will occur.

In a finitely repeated game with an unknown end point, firm A has no incentive to cheat if it expects to earn less from cheating than from not cheating. For the numbers in our example, firm A has no incentive to cheat if

$$\Pi_{Firm\,A}^{Cheat} = 50 \leq \frac{10}{\theta} = \Pi_{Firm\,A}^{Coop}$$

which is true if $\theta \leq 1/5$. In other words, if after each play of the game the probability the game will end is less than 20 percent, firm A will lose more by cheating than it will gain. Since firm B's incentives are symmetric, the same is true for B. Thus, when oligopolistic firms compete a finite but uncertain number of times, it is possible for them to collude and charge high prices—to earn $10 each period—just as they can when they know the game will be played forever. The key is that there must be a sufficiently high probability that the game will be played in subsequent periods. In the extreme case where $\theta = 1$, players are certain they will play the game only once. In this case, the profits of cheating ($50) are much greater than the profits of cooperating ($10), and collusion cannot work. This should come as no surprise to you; when $\theta = 1$, the game is really a one-shot game, and the dominant strategy for each firm is to charge the low price.

Demonstration Problem 10–7

Two cigarette manufacturers repeatedly play the following simultaneous-move billboard advertising game. If both advertise, each earns profits of $0 million. If neither advertises, each earns profits of $10 million. If one advertises and the other does not, the firm that advertises earns $20 million and the other firm loses $1 million. If there is a 10 percent chance that the government will ban cigarette sales in any given year, can the firms "collude" by agreeing not to advertise?

Answer:

The normal form of the one-shot game that is to be repeated an uncertain number of times is presented in Table 10–10. Suppose the players have adopted a trigger strategy, whereby each agrees not to advertise provided the other firm has not advertised in any previous

TABLE 10–10 A Billboard Advertising Game

		Firm B	
	Strategy	Advertise	Don't Advertise
Firm A	Advertise	0, 0	20, −1
	Don't Advertise	−1, 20	10, 10

period. If a firm deviates by advertising, the other firm will "punish" the offender by advertising until the game ends. If firm A cheats on the agreement, its profits are $20 today but $0 in all subsequent periods until the game terminates. If firm A does not cheat, it can expect to earn

$$\Pi_{Firm\ A}^{Coop} = 10 + (.90)10 + (.90)^2 10 + (.90)^3 10 + \cdots = \frac{10}{.10} = 100$$

(this assumes the interest rate is 0). Since $20 < $100, firm A has no incentive to cheat. The incentives for firm B are symmetric. Thus, the firms can collude by using this type of trigger strategy.

Repeated Games with a Known Final Period: The End-of-Period Problem

Now suppose a game is repeated some known finite number of times. For simplicity, we will suppose the game in Table 10–11 is repeated two times. However, the arguments that follow apply even when a game is repeated a larger number of times (e.g., 1,000 times), provided the players know precisely when the game will end and the game has only one Nash equilibrium.

The important thing about repeating the game in Table 10–11 two times is that in the second play of the game there is no tomorrow, and thus each firm has an incentive to use the same strategy during that period that it would use in a one-shot version of the game. Since there is no possibility of playing the game in the third period, the players cannot punish their rival for actions it takes in the second period. For this

TABLE 10–11 A Pricing Game

		Firm B	
	Price	Low	High
Firm A	Low	0, 0	50, −40
	High	−40, 50	10, 10

game, this implies that each player will charge a low price in period 2; even if firm B thought firm A would "cooperate" by charging a high price during the second period, A would maximize its profits by charging a low price during the last period. There is nothing B could do in the future to "punish" A for doing so. In fact, A would be very happy if B charged a high price in the second period; if it did, A could charge a low price and earn profits of $50.

Of course, firm B knows firm A has an incentive to charge a low price in period 2 (the last period) and will likewise want to charge a low price in this period. Since both players know their opponent will charge a low price in the second period, the first period is essentially the last period. There is a tomorrow, but it is the last period, and each player knows what the opponent will do in the last period. Thus, in period 1, each player has an incentive to choose the same strategy as in a one-shot version of the game, (i.e., charge a low price), since they cannot be punished in period 2 for their actions in period 1. In short, the Nash equilibrium for the two-shot version of the game in Table 10–11 is to charge a low price each period. Each player earns zero profits during each of the two periods.

In fact, collusion cannot work even if the game is played for 3 periods, 4 periods, or even 1,000 periods, provided the firms know precisely when the game will end. The key reason firms cannot collude in a finitely repeated known end point version of the game in Table 10–11 is that eventually a point will come when both players are certain there is no tomorrow. At that point, any promises to "cooperate" made during previous periods will be broken, because there is no way a player can be punished tomorrow for having broken the promise. Effectively, a player has an incentive to break a promise in the second to the last period, since there is no effective punishment during the last period. Because all the players know this, there is effectively no tomorrow in the third period from the last. This type of "backward unraveling" continues until the players realize no effective punishment can be used during any period. The players charge low prices in every period, right up to the known last period.

Demonstration Problem 10–8

You and a rival will play the game in Table 10–11 two times. Suppose your strategy is to charge a high price each period provided your opponent never charged a low price in any previous period. How much will you earn? Assume the interest rate is zero.

Answer:
Given your strategy, your opponent's best strategy is to charge a high price the first period and a low price the second period. To see why, note that if she charges a high price each period, she will earn 10 the first period and 10 the second period, for a total of 20 units of profit. She does better by charging a high price the first period (earning 10 units) and a low price the second period (earning 50 units), for a total of 60 units of profit. You will earn 10 units the first period but lose 40 units the second period, for a total loss of 30 units. Since each of you knows exactly when the game will end, trigger strategies will not enhance your profits.

Applications of the End-of-Period Problem

When players know precisely when a repeated game will end, what is known as the *end-of-period problem* arises. In the final period there is no tomorrow, and there is no way to "punish" a player for doing something "wrong" in the last period. Consequently, in the last period, players will behave just as they would in a one-shot game. In this section, we will examine some implications of the end-of-period problem for managerial decisions.

Resignations and Quits

As we discussed in Chapter 6, one reason workers find it in their interest to work hard is that they are implicitly threatened with the prospect of being fired if they get caught not working. As long as the benefits of shirking are less than the cost to workers of getting fired, workers will find it in their interest to work hard.

When a worker announces that she or he plans to quit, say, tomorrow, the cost of shirking to the worker is considerably reduced. Specifically, since the worker does not plan to work tomorrow anyway, the benefits of shirking on the last day generally will exceed the expected costs. In other words, since the worker does not plan to show up tomorrow, the "threat" of being fired has no bite.

What can the manager do to overcome this problem? One possibility is to "fire" the worker as soon as he or she announces the plan to quit. While in some instances there are legal restrictions against this practice, there is a more fundamental reason why a firm should not adopt such a policy. If you, as a manager, adopt a strategy of firing workers as soon as they notify you they plan to quit, how will workers respond? The best strategy for a worker would be to wait and tell you at the end of the day he or she plans to quit! By keeping the plan to quit a secret, the worker gets to work longer than he or she would otherwise. Notice that the worker's incentive to shirk is just as strong as it would be if you did not adopt this policy. Consequently, you will not solve the end-of-period problem, but instead will be continually "surprised" by worker resignations, with no lead time to find new workers to replace them.

A better managerial strategy is to provide some rewards for good work that extend beyond the termination of employment with your firm. For instance, you can emphasize to workers that you are very well connected and will be pleased to write a letter of recommendation should a worker need one in the future. By doing this, you send a signal to workers that quitting is not really the end of the game. If a worker takes advantage of the end-of-period problem, you, being well connected, can "punish" the worker by informing other potential employers of this fact.

The "Snake-Oil" Salesman

In old TV westerns, "snake-oil" salesmen move from town to town, selling bottles of an elixir that is promised to cure every disease known to humankind. Unfortunately, buyers of the "medicine" soon learn that it is worthless and that they have been had. Nonetheless, these salesmen make a livelihood selling the worthless substance because they continue moving from town to town. By moving about, they ensure that buyers cannot "punish" them for selling worthless bottles of fluid.

In contrast, if a local merchant were to sell worthless medicine, customers could have punished him or her by refusing to buy from the merchant in the future. As we saw earlier, this threat can be used to induce firms to sell products of good quality. But in the days of the snake-oil salesman, no such threat was possible.

For punishments to work, there must be some way to link the past, present, and future as it relates to the seller. The inadequate communication networks of the Old West precluded consumers from spreading the word about the snake-oil salesman to future customers; thus, the loss of his "reputation" was not a threat to him. However, over time consumers learned from past experience not to trust such salesmen, and when a new salesman came to town, they would "run him out."

Perhaps you have learned from experience that "sidewalk vendors" sell inferior merchandise. The reason, as you should now recognize, is that consumers have no way of tracking such vendors down in the event the merchandise is inferior. These salespeople indeed take advantage of the end-of-period problem.

MULTISTAGE GAMES

An alternative class of games is called *multistage games*. Multistage games differ from the class of games examined earlier in that timing is very important. In particular, the multistage framework permits players to make sequential rather than simultaneous decisions.

Theory

extensive-form game
A representation of a game that summarizes the players, the information available to them at each stage, the strategies available to them, the sequence of moves, and the payoffs resulting from alternative strategies.

To understand how multistage games differ from one-shot and infinitely repeated games, it is useful to introduce the extensive form of a game. An *extensive-form game* summarizes who the players are, the information available to the players at each stage of the game, the strategies available to the players, the order of the moves of the game, and the payoffs that result from the alternative strategies.

Once again, the best way to understand the extensive-form representation of a game is by way of example. Figure 10–1 depicts the extensive form of a game. The circles are called *decision nodes,* and each circle indicates that at that stage of the

FIGURE 10–1 A Sequential-Move Game in Extensive Form

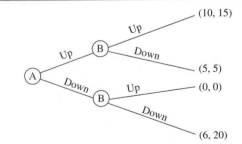

game the particular player must choose a move. The single point (denoted A) at which all of the lines originate is the beginning of the game, and the numbers at the ends of the branches represent the payoffs at the end of the game. For example, in this game player A moves first. A's feasible strategies are *up* or *down*. Once player A moves, it is player B's turn. Player B must then decide whether to move *up* or *down*. If both players move *up*, player A receives a payoff of 10 and player B receives a payoff of 15. If player A moves *up* and player B moves *down*, both players receive a payoff of 5. Thus, the first number in parentheses reflects the payoff to player A (the first mover in the game), while the second number refers to the payoff of player B (the second mover).

As in simultaneous-move games, each player's payoff depends not only on his or her action but on the action of the other player as well. For example, if player A moves *down* and player B moves *up*, the resulting payoff to A is 0. But if player B moves *down* when player A moves *down*, A receives 6.

There is, however, an important difference between the sequential-move game depicted in Figure 10–1 and the simultaneous-move games examined in the previous sections. Since player A must make a decision before player B, A cannot make actions conditional on what B does. Thus, A can choose only *up* or *down*. In contrast, B gets to make a decision after A. Consequently, a strategy for player B will specify an action for both of his decision nodes. If player A chooses *up*, player B can choose either *up* or *down*. If A chooses *down*, B can choose either *up* or *down*. Thus, one example of a strategy for B is to choose *up* if A chooses *up*, and *down* if A chooses *down*. Notice that player B's strategy is allowed to depend on what player A has done, since this is a sequential-move game and B moves second. In contrast, there is no conditional "if " in player A's strategy.

To illustrate how strategies work in sequential-move games, suppose player B's strategy is: "Choose *down* if player A chooses *up*, and *down* if player A chooses *down*." Given this strategy, what is the best choice by player A? If A chooses *up*, she earns 5, since B will choose *down*. If A chooses *down*, she earns 6, since B will choose *down*. Given a choice between earning 5 and 6, player A prefers 6 and therefore will choose *down*.

Given that player A chooses *down*, does player B have an incentive to change his strategy? B's strategy specifies that he chooses *down* if A chooses *down*. By choosing down B earns 20, whereas he earns 0 by choosing *up*. We thus see that player B has no incentive to change his strategy given that player A chose *down*.

Since neither player has an incentive to change his or her strategies, we have found a Nash equilibrium to the game in Figure 10–1. These strategies are:

Player A: *down.*

Player B: *down* if player A chooses *up*, and *down* if player A chooses *down*.

The payoffs that result in this equilibrium are 6 for player A and 20 for player B.

You should ask yourself whether this is a reasonable outcome for the game. In particular, notice that the highest payoff for player A results when A chooses *up* and B chooses *up* as well. Why didn't player A choose *up?* Because player B "threatened" to choose *down* if A chose *up*. Should player A believe this threat? If she chooses *up*, player B's best choice is *up*, since the payoff of 15 is better for B than the payoff of 5 that results from choosing *down*. But if B chooses *up*, A earns 10. This is higher than the payoff that resulted in the Nash equilibrium we examined earlier.

What do we make of all this? There is, in fact, another Nash equilibrium to this game. In particular, suppose player B's strategy is "Choose *up* if player A chooses *up*, choose *down* if player A chooses *down*." Given this strategy by player B, player A earns 10 by choosing *up* and 6 by choosing *down*. Clearly the best response by A to this strategy by B is *up*. Given that player A chooses *up*, player B has no incentive to change his strategy, and thus we have another Nash equilibrium. In this Nash equilibrium, player A earns 10 and player B earns 15.

Which of these two Nash equilibrium outcomes is the more reasonable? The answer is the second one. The reason is as follows: In the first Nash equilibrium, player A chooses *down* because player B threatened to play *down* if A chooses *up*. But player A should recognize that this threat is really not credible. If this stage of the game (decision node) were in fact reached, player B would have an incentive to renege on his threat to choose *down*. Choosing *down* at this stage of the game would result in lower profits for B than he would earn by choosing *up*. Player B therefore has no incentive to do what he said he would do. In the jargon of game theory, the Nash equilibrium in which player A earns 6 and player B earns 20 is not

subgame perfect equilibrium
A condition describing a set of strategies that constitutes a Nash equilibrium and allows no player to improve his own payoff at any stage of the game by changing strategies.

a subgame perfect equilibrium. A set of strategies constitutes a *subgame perfect equilibrium* if (1) it is a Nash equilibrium and (2) at each stage of the game (decision node) neither player can improve her payoff by changing her own strategy. Thus, a subgame perfect equilibrium is a Nash equilibrium that involves only credible threats. For the game in Figure 10–1, the only subgame perfect equilibrium involves player A choosing *up* and player B choosing *up* when player A chooses *up*.

The analysis in this section typically is difficult for students to grasp on the first or second reading, so I encourage you to review this section if you are not clear on the concepts presented. Before you do so, or move on to the next section, let me provide a fable that may help you understand the notion of a subgame perfect equilibrium.

A teenager is given the following instructions by her father: "If you're not home by midnight, I'll burn down the house and you will lose everything you own." If the teenager believes her father, it will certainly be in her best interest to return before midnight, since she does not want to lose everything she owns. And if the teenager returns before midnight, the father never has to burn down the house; there is no cost to the father of threatening to do so. The threat of the father and the return of the daughter before midnight are Nash equilibrium strategies. However, they are not subgame perfect equilibrium strategies. The father's threat to burn down the house, which is what led the teenager to choose to return before midnight, is not credible. The father will not find it in his interest to burn down his own house if his daughter returns late. If the daughter knows this, she knows that the threat is not credible and will not let it affect whether or not she returns home before midnight. Thus, since the Nash equilibrium is obtained by a threat that is not credible, it is not a subgame perfect equilibrium.

FIGURE 10–2 An Entry Game

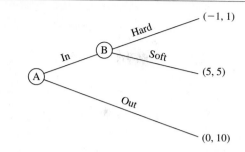

Applications of Multistage Games

The Entry Game

To illustrate the use of the theory of multistage games in a market setting, consider the extensive-form game presented in Figure 10–2. Here, firm B is an existing firm in the market and firm A is a potential entrant. Firm A must decide whether to enter the market (*in*) or stay out (*out*). If A decides to stay out of the market, firm B continues its existing behavior and earns profits of $10 million, while A earns $0. But if A decides to enter the market, B must decide whether to engage in a price war (*hard*) or to simply share the market (*soft*). By choosing *hard,* firm B ensures that firm A incurs a loss of $1 million, but B makes only $1 million in profits. On the other hand, if firm B chooses *soft* after A enters, A takes half of the market and each firm earns profits of $5 million.

It turns out that there are two Nash equilibria for this game. The first occurs where firm B threatens to choose *hard* if A enters the market, and thus A stays *out* of the market. To see that these strategies indeed comprise a Nash equilibrium, note the following: Given that firm B's strategy is to choose *hard* if firm A enters, A's best choice is not to enter. Given that A doesn't enter, B may as well threaten to choose *hard* if A enters. Thus, neither firm has an incentive to change its strategy; firm A earns $0, and firm B earns profits of $10 million.

However, this Nash equilibrium involves a threat that is not credible. The reason firm A chooses not to enter is that firm B threatens to choose *hard* if A enters. Does B have an incentive to carry through its threat of choosing *hard* if firm A enters? The answer is no. Given that firm A enters the market, firm B will earn $5 million by choosing *soft* but only $1 million by choosing *hard.* If firm A enters, it is not in firm B's best interest to play *hard.* Thus, the outcome in which firm A stays out of the market because firm B threatens to choose *hard* if it enters is a Nash equilibrium, but it is not a subgame perfect equilibrium. It involves a threat that is not credible, namely, the threat by firm B to engage in a price war if firm A enters.

The other Nash equilibrium for this game is for firm A to choose *in* and firm B to follow this move by playing *soft.* In particular, if firm A enters, firm B's best choice is to play *soft* (by playing *soft,* B earns $5 million instead of the $1 million it would earn by playing *hard*). Given that firm B plays *soft* if firm A enters,

A's best choice is to enter (by choosing *in,* A earns $5 million instead of the $0 it would earn by staying out). This is a subgame perfect equilibrium, because it is clearly in firm B's self-interest to play *soft* whenever A chooses to enter. Thus, while there are two Nash equilibria for the entry game, there is a unique subgame perfect equilibrium in which firm A chooses *in* and firm B plays *soft.*

Innovation

Our analysis of the entry game reveals an important lesson for future managers: It does not pay to heed threats made by rivals when the threats are not credible. We can also use the theory of sequential, or multistage, games to analyze innovation decisions, as the next problem illustrates.

Demonstration Problem 10–9

Your firm must decide whether or not to introduce a new product. If you introduce the new product, your rival will have to decide whether or not to clone the new product. If you don't introduce the new product, you and your rival will earn $1 million each. If you introduce the new product and your rival clones it, you will lose $5 million and your rival will earn $20 million (you have spent a lot on research and development, and your rival doesn't have to make this investment to compete with its clone). If you introduce the new product and your rival does not clone, you will make $100 million and your rival will make $0.

FIGURE 10–3   An Innovation Game

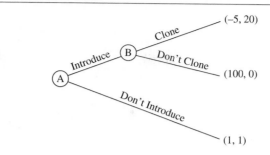

1.   Set up the extensive form of this game.
2.   Should you introduce the new product?
3.   How would your answer change if your rival has "promised" not to clone your product?
4.   What would you do if patent law prevented your rival from cloning your product?

Answer:

1.   The new-product game is depicted in Figure 10–3. Note that this is a multistage game in which your firm (A) moves first, followed by your rival (B).
2.   If you introduce the product, B's best choice is to clone, in which case your firm loses $5 million. If you don't introduce the product, you earn $1 million. Thus, your profit-maximizing decision is not to introduce the new product.
3.   If you believe your rival's "promise" not to clone, you will earn $100 million by introducing the new product and only $1 million if you do not introduce it. However, B's promise is not credible; B would love you to spend money developing the product so that B could clone it and earn profits of $20 million. In this case, you stand to lose $5 million. Since the promise is not credible, you had better think twice about letting it affect your behavior.
4.   If you can obtain a patent on your new product, B will be forced by law to refrain from cloning. In this case, you should introduce the product to earn $100 million. This illustrates that the ability to patent a new product often induces firms to introduce products that they would not introduce in the absence of a patent system.

Sequential Bargaining

The final application of multistage games that we will consider is a *sequential-move bargaining game*. Specifically, suppose a firm and a labor union are engaged in negotiations over how much of a $100 surplus will go to the union and how much will go to management. Suppose management (M) moves first by offering an amount to the union (U). Given the offer, the union gets to decide to accept or reject the offer. If the offer is rejected, neither party receives anything. If the offer is accepted, the union gets the amount specified and management gets the residual.

FIGURE 10–4 A Sequential-Move Bargaining Game

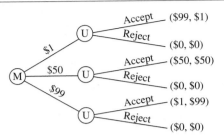

To simplify matters, suppose management can offer the union one of three amounts: $1, $50, or $99.

The extensive form of this game is depicted in Figure 10–4. Notice that the union gets to make its decision after it learns of management's offer. For instance, if management offers the union $1 and the union accepts the offer, management gets $99 and the union gets $1. If the union rejects the offer, both parties get $0.

Suppose you are management and the union makes the following statement to you before you make an offer: "Give us $99 or else we will reject the offer." What should you do? If you believe the union, then if you offered it a lower amount, it would reject the offer and you would get nothing. Given the union's strategy, your best choice is to give the union $99, since that action gives you a payoff of $1 instead of $0. And given that you offer the union $99, its best choice is to accept the offer. Thus, one Nash equilibrium outcome of this sequential bargaining process yields $1 for management and $99 for the union.

Does this mean that the optimal action for management is to give the union $99? The answer is no. Notice that this equilibrium is supported by a union threat that is not credible. According to the union, if management offered the union $1, the union would reject the offer. But by rejecting such an offer, the union would earn $0 instead of the $1 it could earn by accepting it. Thus, it is not in the union's best interest to reject the offer.

In fact, the unique subgame perfect equilibrium for this sequential bargaining game is for management to offer the union $1 and for the union to accept the offer. To see this, notice that if management offered the union $1, the union's best choice would be to accept, since $1 is preferred to the $0 it would earn by rejecting the offer. In this sequential-move bargaining game, the unique subgame perfect equilibrium results in management getting $99 and the union getting $1.

Demonstration Problem 10–10

Consider the bargaining game just described, but suppose the order of play is reversed: The union gets to make an offer, and then management decides whether to accept or reject it. What is the subgame perfect equilibrium outcome of this bargaining process?

Answer:

The profit-maximizing choice by management to any offer is to accept it if that yields more than the $0 management would earn by rejecting the offer. Therefore, the subgame perfect equilibrium is for the union to offer management $1 and keep $99 for itself. Given this offer, management's best choice is to accept it. Any threat by management to refuse an offer of $1 or $50 would not be credible.

This section has illustrated a remarkable feature of two-stage sequential bargaining games. Effectively, the first mover in the bargaining game makes a take-it-or-leave-it offer. The second mover can accept the offer or reject it and receive nothing. The player making the take-it-or-leave-it offer extracts virtually all the amount bargained over. The following example illustrates this principle.

Suppose a consumer wishes to buy a car that the dealer values at $10,000. The consumer values the car at $12,000. Effectively, the bargaining game is over the $2,000 difference between the consumer's valuation and the dealer's cost. Suppose the consumer makes the following take-it-or-leave-it offer to the dealer: "I'll pay you $10,001 for the car. If you don't accept it, I will buy a car from the dealer down the road." If the dealer believes the consumer's threat to terminate the bargaining process if the offer is rejected, he will accept the offer; the dealer prefers earning $1 to earning $0 by not selling the car. The consumer buys the car at $1 over the dealer's cost.

In contrast, suppose the order of the bargaining process is reversed, and the dealer tells the consumer: "Another buyer wants the car. Pay me $11,999, or I'll sell it to the other customer." In this case, if the buyer believes the dealer's threat to sell to another buyer is credible and has no other options, her best choice is to buy the car, since it costs $1 less than her valuation. In this case, the dealer makes a handsome profit.

In concluding this section, we note that several aspects of reality often complicate sequential-bargaining processes. First, the players do not always know the true payoffs to other players. For instance, if a car buyer does not know the dealer's cost of a car, he or she cannot make a take-it-or-leave-it offer and be assured of getting the car. Similarly, if a dealer does not know the maximum price a consumer will pay for a car, she or he cannot be assured of making a sale by making a take-it-or-leave-it offer. In bargaining processes, it is worthwhile to invest some time in learning about your opponent. This explains why there is a market for publications that specialize in providing information to consumers about the dealer cost of automobiles.

Second, an important assumption in the bargaining process analyzed in this section is that bargaining terminates as soon as the second player rejects or accepts an offer. If this were not the case, the person making the decision to accept or reject the offer might reason as follows: "If I reject the offer, perhaps the other party will make a new, more attractive offer." Effectively, this changes the game and can change the players' underlying decisions. On the other hand, a player who can credibly commit to making a take-it-or-leave-it offer will do very well in the bargaining game. But if the commitment is not credible, he or she may end up "eating crow" when the other party makes a counteroffer that the first player would prefer over walking away from the bargaining table.

TABLE 10–12　The Complimentary Drink Game

		Rivals	
US Airways	**Strategy**	**Complimentary Drinks**	**$2 Drinks**
	Complimentary Drinks	0, 0	5, −5
	$2 Drinks	−5, 5	4, 4

ANSWERING THE HEADLINE

While a number of factors contributed to US Airways' decision to stop charging $2 for soft drinks, the strategy failed primarily because the airline was the only major carrier to charge passengers for soft drinks. This damaged the US Airways' image and led some of its customers to switch to more friendly carriers. These negative effects of the company's unilateral strategy to charge passengers $2 for drinks swamped any revenues (or cost savings) it gained by collecting cash from passengers. US Airways learned the hard way that offering complimentary drinks is the dominant strategy in the brutal game it plays with other carriers.

The payoff matrix in Table 10–12 contains some hypothetical numbers that illustrate these points. Notice that if US Airways and its rivals all offer complementary drinks, each of the airlines earns a zero payoff. If US Airways and its rivals all charge $2 for drinks, US Airways and its rivals earn an extra $4 million. But when US Airways charges $2 for drinks and the other carriers offer complimentary drinks, US Airways gives up $5 million and its rivals gain $5 million. Looking at the payoff matrix in Table 10–12, it is clear that US Airways' dominant strategy is to offer complimentary drinks. While US Airways probably hoped that other carriers would follow if it started charging $2 for drinks, it was not in its rivals' interests to do so. If pricing managers at US Airways had put themselves in their rivals' shoes, perhaps they would have realized that the dominant strategy of the other carriers in this game is to offer complimentary drinks and never have traveled along this unprofitable path in the first place.

SUMMARY

This chapter opened with the study of Nash equilibrium in one-shot, simultaneous-move games. We learned that the resulting payoffs are sometimes lower than would arise if players colluded. The reason higher payoffs cannot be achieved in one-shot games is that each participant has an incentive to cheat on a collusive agreement. In many games, what primarily motivates firms to cheat is the fact that cheating is a dominant strategy. Dominant strategies, when they exist, determine the optimal decision in a one-shot game.

We also examined solutions to games that are infinitely repeated. The use of trigger strategies in these games enables players to enter and enforce collusive agreements when the interest rate is low. By adopting strategies that punish cheaters over long periods of time, collusive agreements can be self-enforcing when the game is infinitely repeated. Other factors that affect collusion are the number of firms, the history in the market, the ability of firms to monitor one another's behavior, and the ability to punish cheaters. Similar features of repeated interaction also help consumers and businesses continue trading with each other and keep product quality high.

Finally, we covered finitely repeated games with both uncertain and known terminal periods, as well as sequential-move entry and bargaining games. When the interaction among parties is for a known time period, problems with cheating in the last period can unravel cooperative agreements that would have been supported by trigger strategies in infinitely repeated games or games with an uncertain end point. In sequential-move games, one must determine whether the threats to induce a particular outcome in the game are credible.

KEY TERMS AND CONCEPTS

coordination game
dominant strategy
end-of-period problem
extensive-form game
finitely repeated game
game theory
infinitely repeated game
mixed (randomized) strategy
multistage game
Nash bargaining
Nash equilibrium

normal-form game
one-shot game
repeated game
secure strategy
sequential bargaining
sequential-move game
simultaneous-move game
strategy
subgame perfect equilibrium
trigger strategy

END-OF-CHAPTER PROBLEMS BY LEARNING OBJECTIVE

Every end-of-chapter problem addresses at least one learning objective. Following is a nonexhaustive sample of end-of-chapter problems for each learning objective.

LO1 Apply normal form and extensive form representations of games to formulate decisions in strategic environments that include pricing, advertising, coordination, bargaining, innovation, product quality, monitoring employees, and entry.
Try these problems: 11, 17

LO2 Distinguish among dominant, secure, Nash, mixed, and subgame perfect equilibrium strategies, and identify such strategies in various games.
Try these problems: 1, 12

LO3 Identify whether cooperative (collusive) outcomes may be supported as a Nash equilibrium in a repeated game, and explain the roles of trigger strategies, the interest rate, and the presence of an indefinite or uncertain final period in achieving such outcomes.
Try these problems: 3, 16

CONCEPTUAL AND COMPUTATIONAL QUESTIONS

connect
|ECONOMICS

1. Use the following one-shot, normal-form game to answer the questions below.

		Player 2		
	Strategy	D	E	F
Player 1	A	−200, 150	350, 100	−50, 600
	B	200, −300	400, 400	300, 100
	C	−150, 200	−250, 550	750, −350

   a. Find each player's dominant strategy, if it exists.
   b. Find each player's secure strategy.
   c. Find the Nash equilibrium.

2. In a two-player, one-shot, simultaneous-move game, each player can choose strategy A or strategy B. If both players choose strategy A, each earns a payoff of $400. If both players choose strategy B, each earns a payoff of $200. If player 1 chooses strategy A and player 2 chooses strategy B, then player 1 earns $100 and player 2 earns $600. If player 1 chooses strategy B and player 2 chooses strategy A, then player 1 earns $600 and player 2 earns $100.
   a. Write the above game in normal form.
   b. Find each player's dominant strategy, if it exists.
   c. Find the Nash equilibrium (or equilibria) of this game.
   d. Rank strategy pairs by aggregate payoff (highest to lowest).
   e. Can the outcome with the highest aggregate payoff be sustained in equilibrium? Why or why not?

3. Use the following payoff matrix for a simultaneous-move one-shot game to answer the accompanying questions.

		Player 2		
	Strategy	C	D	E	F
Player 1	A	6, 14	7, 11	18, 20	10, 19
	B	12, 5	15, 1	7, 25	16, 17

   a. What is player 1's optimal strategy? Why?
   b. Determine player 1's equilibrium payoff.

4. Use the following normal-form game to answer the questions below.

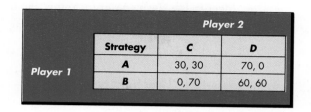

	Strategy	C	D
Player 1	A	30, 30	70, 0
	B	0, 70	60, 60

(Player 2 heads columns C and D)

   a. Identify the one-shot Nash equilibrium.

   b. Suppose the players know this game will be repeated exactly three times. Can they achieve payoffs that are better than the one-shot Nash equilibrium? Explain.

   c. Suppose this game is infinitely repeated and the interest rate is 6 percent. Can the players achieve payoffs that are better than the one-shot Nash equilibrium? Explain.

   d. Suppose the players do not know exactly how many times this game will be repeated, but they do know that the probability the game will end after a given play is θ. If θ is sufficiently low, can players earn more than they could in the one-shot Nash equilibrium?

5. Use the following normal-form game to answer the questions below.

	Strategy	C	D
Player 1	A	3, 7 − x	2, 3
	B	4, 4	7 − x, 5

(Player 2 heads columns C and D)

   a. For what values of x is strategy D (strictly) dominant for player 2?

   b. For what values of x is strategy B (strictly) dominant for player 1?

   c. For what values of x is (B, D) the only Nash equilibrium of the game?

6. Consider a two-player, sequential-move game where each player can choose to play *right* or *left*. Player 1 moves first. Player 2 observes player 1's actual move and then decides to move *right* or *left*. If player 1 moves *right,* player 1 receives $0 and player 2 receives $25. If both players move *left,* player 1 receives −$5 and player 2 receives $10. If player 1 moves *left* and player 2 moves *right,* player 1 receives $20 and player 2 receives $20.

   a. Write the above game in extensive form.

   b. Find the Nash equilibrium outcomes to this game.

   c. Which of the equilibrium outcomes is most reasonable? Explain.

7. Use the following extensive-form game to answer the questions below.
   a. List the feasible strategies for player 1 and player 2.
   b. Identify the Nash equilibria to this game.
   c. Find the subgame perfect equilibrium.

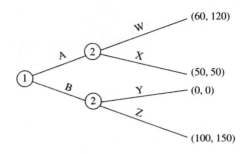

8. Use the following payoff matrix for a one-shot game to answer the accompanying questions.

		Player 2	
	Strategy	X	Y
Player 1	A	25, 25	−100, 5
	B	5, −100	15, 15

   a. Determine the Nash equilibrium outcomes that arise if the players make decisions independently, simultaneously, and without any communication. Which of these outcomes would you consider most likely? Explain.
   b. Suppose player 1 is permitted to "communicate" by uttering one syllable before the players simultaneously and independently make their decisions. What should player 1 utter, and what outcome do you think would occur as a result?
   c. Suppose player 2 can choose its strategy before player 1, that player 1 observes player 2's choice before making her decision, and that this move structure is known by both players. What outcome would you expect? Explain.

9. Use the following payoff matrix to answer the following questions.

		Player 2	
	Strategies	C	D
Player 1	A	−10, −10	200, −100
	B	−100, 220	140, 180

Suppose this is a one-shot game:

    a. Determine the dominant strategy for each player. If such strategies do not exist, explain why not.

    b. Determine the secure strategy for each player. If such strategies do not exist, explain why not.

    c. Determine the Nash equilibrium of this game. If such an equilibrium does not exist, explain why not.

10. Using the same payoff matrix as in question 9, suppose this game is infinitely repeated and that the interest rate is sufficiently "low." Identify trigger strategies that permit players 1 and 2 to earn equilibrium payoffs of 140 and 180, respectively, in each period.

PROBLEMS AND APPLICATIONS

11. While there is a degree of differentiation among general merchandise retailers like Target and Kmart, weekly newspaper circulars announcing sales provide evidence that these firms engage in price competition. This suggests that Target and Kmart simultaneously choose to announce one of two prices for a given product: a regular price or a sale price. Suppose that when one firm announces the sale price and the other announces the regular price for a particular product, the firm announcing the sale price attracts 50 million extra customers to earn a profit of $7 billion, compared to the $4 billion earned by the firm announcing the regular price. When both firms announce the sale price, the two firms split the market equally (each getting an extra 25 million customers) to earn profits of $2 billion each. When both firms announce the regular price, each company attracts only its 50 million loyal customers and the firms each earn $4 billion in profits. If you were in charge of pricing at one of these firms, would you have a clear-cut pricing strategy? If so, explain why. If not, explain why not and propose a mechanism that might solve your dilemma. (*Hint:* Unlike Walmart, neither of these two firms guarantees "Everyday low prices.")

12. Suppose Toyota and Honda must decide whether to make a new breed of side-impact airbags standard equipment on all models. Side-impact airbags raise the price of each automobile by $1,000. If both firms make side-impact airbags standard equipment, each company will earn profits of $2.5 billion. If neither company adopts the side-impact airbag technology, each company will earn $1 billion (due to lost sales to other automakers). If one company adopts the technology as standard equipment and the other does not, the adopting company will earn a profit of $3 billion and the other company will lose $1.5 billion. If you were a decision maker at Honda, would you make side-impact airbags standard equipment? Explain.

13. Coca-Cola and PepsiCo are the leading competitors in the market for cola products. In 1960 Coca-Cola introduced Sprite, which today is the worldwide leader in the lemon-lime soft drink market and ranks fourth among all soft

drinks worldwide. Prior to 1999, PepsiCo did not have a product that competed directly against Sprite and had to decide whether to introduce such a soft drink. By not introducing a lemon-lime soft drink, PepsiCo would continue to earn a $200 million profit, and Coca-Cola would continue to earn a $300 million profit. Suppose that by introducing a new lemon-lime soft drink, one of two possible strategies could be pursued: (1) PepsiCo could trigger a price war with Coca-Cola in both the lemon-lime and cola markets, or (2) Coca-Cola could acquiesce and each firm maintain its current 50/50 split of the cola market and split the lemon-lime market 30/70 (PepsiCo/Coca-Cola). If PepsiCo introduced a lemon-lime soft drink and a price war resulted, both companies would earn profits of $100 million. Alternatively, Coca-Cola and PepsiCo would earn $275 million and $227 million, respectively, if PepsiCo introduced a lemon-lime soft drink and Coca-Cola acquiesced and split the markets as listed above. If you were a manager at PepsiCo, would you try to convince your colleagues that introducing the new soft drink is the most profitable strategy? Why or why not?

14. Suppose a UAW labor contract with General Dynamics is being renegotiated. Some of the many issues on the table include job security, health benefits, and wages. If you are an executive in charge of human resource issues at General Dynamics, would you be better off (*a*) letting the union bear the expense of crafting a document summarizing its desired compensation, or (*b*) making the union a take-it-or-leave-it offer? Explain.

15. Price comparison services on the Internet (as well as "shopbots") are a popular way for retailers to advertise their products and a convenient way for consumers to simultaneously obtain price quotes from several firms selling an identical product. Suppose that you are the manager of Digital Camera, Inc., a firm that specializes in selling digital cameras to consumers that advertises with an Internet price comparison service. In the market for one particular high-end camera, you have only one rival firm—The Camera Shop—with which you've competed for the last four years by setting prices day after day. Being savvy entrepreneurs, the ease of using the Internet to monitor rival firms' prices has enabled you and your rival to charge extremely high prices for this particular camera. In a recent newspaper article, you read that The Camera Shop has exhausted its venture capital and that no new investors are willing to sink money into the company. As a result, The Camera Shop will discontinue its operations next month. Will this information alter your pricing decisions today? Explain.

16. You are the manager of a firm that manufactures front and rear windshields for the automobile industry. Due to economies of scale in the industry, entry by new firms is not profitable. Toyota has asked your company and your only rival to simultaneously submit a price quote for supplying 100,000 front and rear windshields for its new Highlander. If both you and your rival submit a low price, each firm supplies 50,000 front and rear windshields and earns a zero profit. If one firm quotes a low price and the other a high price, the low-price firm supplies 100,000 front and rear windshields and earns a profit

of $11 million and the high-price firm supplies no windshields and loses $2 million. If both firms quote a high price, each firm supplies 50,000 front and rear windshields and earns a $6 million profit. Determine your optimal pricing strategy if you and your rival believe that the new Highlander is a "special edition" that will be sold only for one year. Would your answer differ if you and your rival were required to resubmit price quotes year after year and if, in any given year, there was a 60 percent chance that Toyota would discontinue the Highlander? Explain.

17. At a time when demand for ready-to-eat cereal was stagnant, a spokesperson for the cereal maker Kellogg's was quoted as saying, " . . . for the past several years, our individual company growth has come out of the other fellow's hide." Kellogg's has been producing cereal since 1906 and continues to implement strategies that make it a leader in the cereal industry. Suppose that when Kellogg's and its largest rival advertise, each company earns $0 in profits. When neither company advertises, each company earns profits of $12 billion. If one company advertises and the other does not, the company that advertises earns $52 billion and the company that does not advertise loses $4 billion. Under what conditions could these firms use trigger strategies to support the collusive level of advertising?

18. You are a pricing manager at Argyle Inc.—a medium-sized firm that recently introduced a new product into the market. Argyle's only competitor is Baker Company, which is significantly smaller than Argyle. The management of Argyle has decided to pursue a short-term strategy of maximizing this quarter's revenues, and you are in charge of formulating a strategy that will permit the firm to do so. After talking with an employee who was recently hired from the Baker Company, you are confident that (*a*) Baker is constrained to charge $10 or $20 for its product, (*b*) Baker's goal is to maximize this quarter's profits, and (*c*) Baker's relevant unit costs are identical to yours. You have been authorized to price the product at two possible levels ($5 or $10) and know that your relevant costs are $2 per unit. The marketing department has provided the following information about the expected number of units sold (in millions) this quarter at various prices to help you formulate your decision:

Argyle Price	Baker Price	Argyle Quantity (millions of units)	Baker Quantity (millions of units)
$ 5	$10	3	2
5	20	3	1
10	10	1	2
10	20	1	1

Argyle and Baker currently set prices at the same time. However, Argyle can become the first-mover by spending $2 million on computer equipment that would permit it to set its price before Baker. Determine Argyle's optimal price and whether you should invest the $2 million.

19. You are the manager of GearNet and must decide how many Internet hubs to produce to maximize your firm's profit. GearNet and its only rival (NetWorks) sell dual-speed Internet hubs that are identical from consumers' perspectives. The market price for hubs depends on the total quantity produced by the two firms. A survey reveals that the market price of hubs depends on total market output as follows:

Combined Hub Production of GearNet and NetWorks	Market Price of Hubs (per unit)
500 units	$140
750 units	110
1,000 units	95

GearNet and NetWorks each use labor, materials, and machines to produce output. GearNet purchases labor and materials on an as-needed basis; its machines were purchased three years ago and are being depreciated according to the straight-line method. GearNet's accounting department has provided the following data about its unit production costs:

Item	GearNet's Unit Cost for an Output of:	
	250 units	500 units
Direct labor	$35	$35
Direct materials	25	25
Depreciation charge	120	60

Reports from industry experts suggest that NetWorks' cost structure is similar to GearNet's cost structure and that technological constraints require each firm to produce either 250 hubs or 500 hubs. Identify the costs that are relevant for your decision, and then determine whether GearNet should produce 250 hubs or 500 hubs.

20. Suppose that U.S.-based Qualcomm and European-based T-Mobile are contemplating infrastructure investments in a developing mobile telephone market. Qualcomm currently uses a code-division multiple access (CDMA) technology, which almost 67 million users in the United States utilize. In contrast, T-Mobile uses a global systems for mobile communication (GSM) technology that has become the standard in Europe and Asia. Each company must (simultaneously and independently) decide which of these two technologies to introduce in the new market. Qualcomm estimates that it will cost $1.2 billion to install its CDMA technology and $2.0 billion to install GSM technology.

T-Mobile's projected cost of installing GSM technology is $1.1 billion, while the cost of installing the CDMA technology is $2.7 billion. As shown in the accompanying table, each company's projected revenues depend not only on the technology it adopts, but also on that adopted by its rival.

Projected Revenues for Different Combinations of Mobile
Technology Standards (in billions)

Standards (Qualcomm–T-Mobile)	Qualcomm's Revenues	T-Mobile's Revenues
CDMA–GSM	$13.5	$ 9.7
CDMA–CDMA	$17.2	$15.6
GSM–CDMA	$16.7	$10.1
GSM–GSM	$15.5	$19.8

Construct the normal form of this game. Then, explain the economic forces that give rise to the structure of the payoffs and any difficulties the companies might have in achieving Nash equilibrium in the new market.

21. Japanese officials are considering a new tariff on imported pork products from the United States in an attempt to reduce Japan's reliance on U.S. pork. Due to political pressure, the U. S. International Trade Representative's (ITR) office is also considering a new tariff on imported steel from Japan. Officials in both Japan and the United States must assess the social welfare ramifications of their tariff decisions. Reports from a reliable think tank indicate the following: If neither country imposes a new tariff, social welfare in Japan's economy will remain at $10 billion and social welfare in the United States will remain at $50 billion. If both countries impose a new tariff, welfare in the United States declines $49.1 billion and welfare in Japan declines by $9.5 billion. If Japan does not impose a tariff but the United States does, projected welfare in Japan is $8.9 billion while welfare in the United States is $52.5 billion. Finally, if the United States does not impose a tariff but Japan does, welfare is projected at $48.2 billion in the United States and $11.4 billion in Japan. Determine the Nash equilibrium outcome when policy makers in the two countries simultaneously but independently make tariff decisions in a myopic (one-shot) setting. Is it possible for the two countries to improve their social welfare by "agreeing" to different strategies? Explain.

22. An office manager is concerned with declining productivity. Despite the fact that she regularly monitors her clerical staff four times each day—at 9:00 AM, 11:00 AM, 1:00 PM, and again at 3:00 PM—office productivity has declined 30 percent since she assumed the helm one year ago. Would you recommend that the office manager invest more time monitoring the productivity of her clerical staff? Explain.

23. You manage a company that competes in an industry that is comprised of five equal-sized firms. A recent industry report indicates that a tariff on foreign

imports would boost industry profits by $30 million—and that it would only take $5 million in expenditures on (legal) lobbying activities to induce Congress to implement such a tariff. Discuss your strategy for improving your company's profits.

CONNECT EXERCISES

If your instructor has adopted Connect for the course and you are an active subscriber, you can practice with the questions presented above, along with many alternative versions of these questions. Your instructor may also assign a subset of these problems and/or their alternative versions as a homework assignment through Connect, allowing for immediate feedback of grades and correct answers.

CASE-BASED EXERCISES

Your instructor may assign additional problem-solving exercises (called memos) that require you to apply some of the tools you learned in this chapter to make a recommendation based on an actual business scenario. Some of these memos accompany the Time Warner case (pages 561–597 of your textbook). Additional memos, as well as data that may be useful for your analysis, are available online at www.mhhe.com/baye8e.

SELECTED READINGS

Bolton, Gary E., "A Comparative Model of Bargaining: Theory and Evidence." *American Economic Review* 81(5), December 1991, pp. 1096–136.

Friedman, James W., ed., *Problems of Coordination in Economic Activity.* Boston: Kluwer Academic, 1994.

Gardner, Roy, and Ostrom, Elinor, "Rules and Games." *Public Choice* 70(2), May 1991, pp. 121–49.

Gilbert, Richard J., "The Role of Potential Competition in Industrial Organization." *Journal of Economic Perspectives* 3(3), Summer 1989, pp. 107–28.

Hansen, Robert G., and Samuelson, William F., "Evolution in Economic Games." *Journal of Economic Behavior and Organization* 10(3), October 1988, pp. 315–38.

Morrison, C. C., and Kamarei, H., "Some Experimental Testing of the Cournot-Nash Hypothesis in Small Group Rivalry Situations." *Journal of Economic Behavior and Organization* 13(2), March 1990, pp. 213–31.

Rasmusen, Eric, *Games and Information: An Introduction to Game Theory.* New York: Basil Blackwell, 1989.

Rosenthal, Robert W., "Rules of Thumb in Games." *Journal of Economic Behavior and Organization* 22(1), September 1993, pp. 1–13.

CHAPTER ELEVEN

Pricing Strategies for Firms with Market Power

Mickey Mouse Lets You Ride "for Free" at Disney World

Walt Disney World Theme Parks offer visitors a wide variety of ticket choices. The one thing these ticket options have in common is that they entail a fixed entrance fee and allow customers to take as many rides as they want at no additional charge. For instance, by purchasing a 1-Day ticket for about $95, a customer gains unlimited access to the park of her choice for one day.

Wouldn't Disney earn higher profits if it charged visitors, say, $9.50, each time they went on a ride?

Learning Objectives

After completing this chapter, you will be able to:

LO1 Apply simple elasticity-based markup formulas to determine profit-maximizing prices in environments where a business enjoys market power, including monopoly, monopolistic competition, and Cournot oligopoly.

LO2 Formulate pricing strategies that permit firms to extract additional surplus from consumers—including price discrimination, two-part pricing, block pricing, and commodity bundling—and explain the conditions needed for each of these strategies to yield higher profits than standard pricing.

LO3 Formulate pricing strategies that enhance profits for special cost and demand structures— such as peak-load pricing, cross-subsidies, and transfer pricing—and explain the conditions needed for each strategy to work.

LO4 Explain how price-matching guarantees, brand loyalty programs, and randomized pricing strategies can be used to enhance profits in markets with intense price competition.

INTRODUCTION

In this chapter, we deal with pricing decisions by firms that have some market power: firms in monopoly, monopolistic competition, and oligopoly. As we learned in Chapter 8, firms in perfect competition have no control over the prices they charge for their products; prices are determined by market forces. Therefore, the pricing decision in perfect competition is simple: Charge the same price other firms in the market charge for their products.

In contrast, firms with market power have some influence over the prices they charge. Therefore, it is important for you, as a manager, to learn some basic pricing strategies for maximizing a firm's profits. This chapter provides practical advice that you can use to implement such pricing strategies, typically using information that is readily available to managers. For instance, we will see how a manager can use publicly available information about demand elasticities to determine the profit-maximizing markup used to set product price.

The optimal pricing decisions will vary from firm to firm depending on the underlying market structure of the industry and the instruments (such as advertising) available. Thus, we will begin with basic pricing strategies firms use in monopoly, monopolistic competition, and oligopoly to set the price that maximizes profits. Then we will develop more sophisticated pricing strategies that enable a firm to extract even greater profits. As you work through this chapter, remember that some of these more advanced pricing strategies would work in some situations but will not be viable in others. You should familiarize yourself not only with how to implement the strategies but also with the conditions under which each type of strategy is feasible.

BASIC PRICING STRATEGIES

In this section we will examine the most basic pricing strategy used by firms with market power: Charge a single price to all customers such that marginal revenue equals marginal cost. We will begin with a review of the economic basis for such a pricing strategy and then discuss how it can be easily implemented in monopoly, monopolistic competition, and Cournot oligopoly.

Review of the Basic Rule of Profit Maximization

Firms with market power face a downward-sloping demand for their products. This means that by charging a higher price, the firm reduces the amount it will sell. Thus, there is a trade-off between selling many units at a low price and selling only a few units at a high price.

In Chapter 8 we learned how the manager of a firm with market power balances off these two forces: Output is set at the point where marginal revenue (MR) equals marginal cost (MC). The profit-maximizing price is the maximum price per unit that consumers will pay for this level of output. The following problem summarizes what we learned in Chapter 8 about the profit-maximizing pricing decision of a firm with market power.

Demonstration Problem 11–1

Suppose the (inverse) demand for a firm's product is given by

$$P = 10 - 2Q$$

and the cost function is

$$C(Q) = 2Q$$

What is the profit-maximizing level of output and price for this firm?

Answer:

For this (inverse) demand function, marginal revenue is

$$MR = 10 - 4Q$$

and marginal cost is

$$MC = 2$$

Setting $MR = MC$ yields

$$10 - 4Q = 2$$

Thus, the profit-maximizing level of output is $Q = 2$. Substituting this into the inverse demand function yields the profit-maximizing price

$$P = 10 - 2(2) = \$6$$

A Simple Pricing Rule for Monopoly and Monopolistic Competition

As we saw in the previous section, in instances where a manager has estimates of the demand and cost functions for the firm's product, calculation of the profit-maximizing price is straightforward. In some cases, a manager lacks access to an estimated form of demand or cost functions. This is particularly true of managers of small firms that do not have research departments or funds to hire economists to estimate demand and cost functions.

Fortunately, all is not lost in these instances. It turns out that given minimal information about demand and costs, a manager can do a reasonably good job of determining what price to charge for a product. Specifically, most retailers have a rough estimate of the marginal cost of each item sold. For instance, the manager of a clothing store knows how much the store pays the supplier for each pair of jeans and thus has crude information about the marginal cost of selling jeans. (This information is "crude" because the cost to the firm of buying jeans will slightly understate the true marginal cost of selling jeans, since it does not include the cost of the sales force, etc.)

The clothing store manager also has some crude information about the elasticity of demand for jeans at its store. Chapter 7 provided tables with estimates of the elasticity of demand for a "representative firm" in broadly defined industries. For instance, Table 7–3 presented a study that estimated the own-price elasticity of demand for a representative apparel firm's product to be -4.1. In the absence of better information, the manager of a clothing store can use this estimate to approximate the elasticity of demand for jeans sold at his or her store.

Thus, even small firms can obtain some information about demand and costs from publicly available information. All that remains is to show how this information can be used to make pricing decisions. The key is to recall the relation between the elasticity of demand for a firm's product and marginal revenue, which we derived in Chapter 8. This relation is summarized in the following formula.

Formula: Marginal Revenue for a Firm with Market Power.   The marginal revenue for a firm with market power is given by

$$MR = P\left[\frac{1 + E_F}{E_F}\right]$$

where E_F is the own-price elasticity of demand for the firm's product and P is the price charged.

Since the profit-maximizing level of output is where marginal revenue equals marginal cost, this formula implies that

$$P\left[\frac{1 + E_F}{E_F}\right] = MC$$

at the profit-maximizing level of output. If we solve this equation for P, we obtain the profit-maximizing price for a firm with market power:

$$P = \left[\frac{E_F}{1 + E_F}\right]MC$$

In other words, the price that maximizes profits is a number K times marginal cost:

$$P = K \times MC$$

where $K = E_F/(1 + E_F)$. The number K can be viewed as the profit-maximizing markup factor. For the case of the clothing store, the manager's best estimate of the elasticity of demand is -4.1, so $K = -4.1/(1 - 4.1) = 1.32$. In this instance, the profit-maximizing price is 1.32 times marginal cost:

$$P = 1.32\,MC$$

Principle	**Profit-Maximizing Markup for Monopoly and Monopolistic Competition**

The price that maximizes profit is given by

$$P = \left[\frac{E_F}{1 + E_F}\right]MC$$

where E_F is the own-price elasticity of demand for the firm's product and MC is the firm's marginal cost. The term in brackets is the optimal markup factor.

A manager should note two important things about this pricing rule. First, the more elastic the demand for the firm's product, the lower the profit-maximizing markup. Since demand is more elastic when there are many available substitutes for a product, managers that sell such products should have a relatively low markup. In the extreme case when the elasticity of demand is perfectly elastic ($E_F = -\infty$), this markup rule reveals that price should be set equal to marginal cost. This should come as no surprise, since we learned in Chapter 8 that a perfectly competitive firm that faces a perfectly elastic demand curve charges a price equal to marginal cost.

The second thing to notice is that the higher the marginal cost, the higher the profit-maximizing price. Firms with higher marginal costs will charge higher prices than firms with lower marginal costs, other things being the same.

One caveat that you should keep in mind when applying the markup formula is that the elasticity of demand may change when you alter the price of a good or service. For instance, in Chapter 3 we learned that when the demand function is linear, demand is more elastic at higher prices than at lower prices. In this case, a slight increase in price will lead to a slight increase in the elasticity of demand, which in turn makes the optimal markup slightly lower than that calculated based on the original estimate of the elasticity of demand. For this reason, if you have an estimate of the demand function, you may more accurately determine the profit-maximizing price by computing marginal revenue directly from the demand function, equating it with marginal cost, and then determining the profit-maximizing price.

In managerial practice, however, many pricing decisions must be made without estimates of demand functions. If the only information available is a numerical estimate of the elasticity of demand, the profit-maximizing markup formula may be used to approximate the optimal markup and price. Under certain conditions, this approach exactly yields the optimal markup. More specifically, we learned in Chapter 3 that the elasticity of demand is constant for a log-linear demand function. Thus, when demand is log-linear, you needn't worry about this caveat because the elasticity does not change when the price changes. In this case, all you need to determine the profit-maximizing markup is a numerical estimate of the elasticity of demand.

Demonstration Problem 11–2

The manager of a convenience store competes in a monopolistically competitive market and buys cola from a supplier at a price of $1.25 per liter. The manager thinks that because there are several supermarkets nearby, the demand for cola sold at her store is slightly more elastic than the elasticity for the representative food store reported in Table 7–3 in Chapter 7 (which is -3.8). Based on this information, she perceives that the elasticity of demand for cola sold by her store is -4. What price should the manager charge for a liter of cola to maximize profits?

Answer:

The marginal cost of cola to the firm is $1.25, or 5/4 per liter, and $K = 4/3$. Using the pricing rule for a monopolistically competitive firm, the profit-maximizing price is

$$P = \left[\frac{4}{3}\right]\left[\frac{5}{4}\right] = \frac{5}{3}$$

or about $1.67 per liter.

A Simple Pricing Rule for Cournot Oligopoly

Recall that in Cournot oligopoly, there are few firms in the market servicing many consumers. The firms produce either differentiated or homogeneous products, and each firm believes rivals will hold their output constant if it changes its own output.

In Chapter 9 we saw that to maximize profits, a manager of a firm in Cournot oligopoly produces where marginal revenue equals marginal cost. We also saw how to calculate the profit-maximizing price and quantity given information about demand and cost curves. Recall that this procedure requires full information about the demand and costs of all firms in the industry and is complicated by the fact that the marginal revenue of a Cournot oligopolist depends on the outputs produced by all firms in the market. Ultimately, the solution is based on the intersection of reaction functions.

Fortunately, we can also provide a simple pricing rule that managers can use in Cournot oligopoly. Suppose an industry consists of N Cournot oligopolists, each having identical cost structures and producing similar products. In this instance, the profit-maximizing price in Cournot equilibrium is given by a simple formula.

Principle	**Profit-Maximizing Markup for Cournot Oligopoly**

If there are N identical firms in a Cournot oligopoly, the profit-maximizing price for a firm in this market is

$$P = \left[\frac{NE_M}{1 + NE_M}\right]MC$$

where N is the number of firms in the industry, E_M is the market elasticity of demand, and MC is marginal cost.

A Calculus Alternative

Instead of having to memorize this formula, we can simply substitute the relation between a Cournot oligopolist's own-price elasticity of demand and that of the market into the formula for the markup rule for monopoly and monopolistic competition. In particular, for a homogeneous-product Cournot oligopoly with N firms, we will show that the elasticity of demand for an individual firm's product is N times that of the market elasticity of demand:

$$E_F = NE_M$$

When we substitute this for E_F in the pricing formula for monopoly and monopolistic competition, the result is the pricing formula for Cournot oligopoly.

To see that $E_F = NE_M$, we need a little calculus. Specifically, if

$$Q = \sum_{i=1}^{N} Q_i$$

is total industry output and industry demand is $Q = f(P)$, the own-price elasticity of market demand is

$$E_M = \frac{dQ}{dP} \frac{P}{Q} = \frac{df(P)}{dP} \frac{P}{Q}$$

The demand facing an individual firm (say, firm 1) is

$$Q_1 = f(P) - Q_2 - Q_3 - \cdots - Q_N$$

Thus, since the firm views the output of other firms as fixed, the elasticity of demand for an individual firm is

$$E_F = \frac{\partial Q_1}{\partial P} \frac{P}{Q_1} = \frac{df(P)}{dP} \frac{P}{Q_1}$$

But with identical firms $Q_1 = Q/N$, so

$$E_F = \frac{df(P)}{dP} \frac{PN}{Q} = NE_M$$

which is what we needed to establish.

The pricing rule given for a firm in Cournot oligopoly has a very simple justification. When firms in a Cournot oligopoly sell identical products, the elasticity of demand for an individual firm's product is N times the market elasticity of demand:

$$E_F = NE_M$$

If $N = 1$ (monopoly), there is only one firm in the industry, and the elasticity of demand for that firm's product is the same as the market elasticity of demand ($E_F = E_M$). When $N = 2$ (Cournot duopoly), there are two firms in the market, and each firm's elasticity of demand is twice as elastic as that for the market ($E_F = 2E_M$). Thus, the markup formula for Cournot oligopoly is really identical to that presented in the previous section, except that we are using the relation between elasticity of demand for an individual firm's product and that of the market.

Three aspects of this pricing rule for Cournot oligopoly are worth noting. First, the more elastic the market demand, the closer the profit-maximizing price is to marginal cost. In the extreme case where the absolute value of the market elasticity of demand is infinite, the profit-maximizing price is marginal cost, regardless of how many firms are in the industry. Second, notice that as the number of firms increases, the profit-maximizing price gets closer to marginal cost. Notice that in the limiting case where there are infinitely many firms ($N = \infty$), the profit-maximizing price is exactly equal to marginal cost. This is consistent with our analysis of perfect competition: When many firms produce a homogeneous product, price equals marginal cost. Thus, perfect competition can be viewed as the limiting case of Cournot oligopoly, as the number of firms approaches infinity. Finally, notice that the higher the marginal cost, the higher the profit-maximizing price in Cournot oligopoly.

Demonstration Problem 11–3

Suppose three firms compete in a homogeneous-product Cournot industry. The market elasticity of demand for the product is -2, and each firm's marginal cost of production is $50. What is the profit-maximizing equilibrium price?

Answer:
Simply set $N = 3$, $E_M = -2$, and $MC = \$50$ in the markup formula for Cournot oligopoly to obtain

$$P = \left[\frac{(3)(-2)}{1 + (3)(-2)}\right]\$50 = \$60$$

STRATEGIES THAT YIELD EVEN GREATER PROFITS

The analysis in the previous section demonstrated how a manager can implement the familiar $MR = MC$ rule for setting the profit-maximizing price. Given estimates of demand and cost functions, such a price can be computed directly. Alternatively, given publicly available estimates of demand elasticities, a manager can implement the rule by using the appropriate markup formula.

In some markets, managers can enhance profits above those they would earn by simply charging a single per-unit price to all consumers. As we will see in this section, several pricing strategies can be used to yield profits above those earned by simply charging a single price where marginal revenue equals marginal cost.

Extracting Surplus from Consumers

The first four strategies we will discuss—price discrimination, two-part pricing, block pricing, and commodity bundling—are strategies appropriate for firms with various cost structures and degrees of market interdependence. Thus, these strategies can enhance profits of firms in industries with monopolistic, monopolistically competitive, or oligopolistic structures. The pricing strategies discussed in this section enhance profits by enabling a firm to extract additional surplus from consumers.

Price Discrimination

Up until this point, our analysis of pricing decisions presumes the firm must charge the same price for each unit that consumers purchase in the market. Sometimes, how-

price discrimination
The practice of charging different prices to consumers for the same good or service.

ever, firms can earn higher profits by charging different prices for the same product or service, a strategy referred to as *price discrimination*. The three basic types of price discrimination—first-, second-, and third-degree price discrimination—are examined next. As we will see, each type requires that the manager have different types of information about consumers.

Ideally, a firm would like to engage in *first-degree price discrimination*—that is, charge each consumer the maximum price he or she would be willing to pay for each unit of the good purchased. By adopting this strategy, a firm extracts all surplus from consumers and thus earns the highest possible profits. Unfortunately for managers, first-degree price discrimination (also called perfect price discrimination) is extremely difficult to implement because it requires the firm to know precisely the maximum price each consumer is willing and able to pay for alternative quantities of the firm's product.

Nonetheless, some service-related businesses, including car dealers, mechanics, doctors, and lawyers, successfully practice a form of first-degree price discrimination. For instance, most car dealers post sticker prices on cars that are well above the dealer's actual marginal cost, but offer "discounts" to customers on a case-by-case basis. The best salespersons are able to size up customers to determine the minimum discount necessary to get them to drive away with the car. In this way they are able to charge different prices to different consumers depending on each consumer's willingness and ability to pay. This practice permits them to sell more cars and to earn higher profits than they would if they charged the same price to all consumers. Similarly, most professionals also charge rates for their services that vary, depending on their assessment of customers' willingness and ability to pay.

Panel (a) of Figure 11–1 shows how first-degree price discrimination works. Each point on the market demand curve reflects the maximum price that consumers would be willing to pay for each incremental unit of the output. Consumers start out with 0 units of the good, and the firm can sell the first incremental unit for $10.

INSIDE BUSINESS 11–2

Is Price Discrimination Bad for Consumers?

The practice of price discrimination may seem unfair from consumers' perspectives. Why should one consumer pay a different price than another for the same product? Further, the concept of "discrimination" can conjure notions of *exclusion* from other contexts such as racial or gender discrimination. However, in many circumstances, price discrimination can actually serve as a means of *inclusion*, allowing groups of consumers to enjoy a product that would not be accessible if producers could only charge one price to everyone.

For example, many amusement parks, such as Kings Island and Cedar Point in Ohio, charge one price for regular admission and a different, lower price for senior citizens. This pricing scheme is a simple example of third degree price discrimination, where different demographic groups face different prices for the same product. Without the ability to price discriminate, it is likely the parks would charge everyone the (higher) regular admission fee, since senior citizens comprise only a small fraction of the parks' customer base. This higher price would drive many senior citizens out of the market, given they are often a more price-sensitive group. However, by charging seniors a lower price, the parks induce many more seniors to participate in this market, and make greater profits in the process.

FIGURE 11–1   First- and Second-Degree Price Discrimination

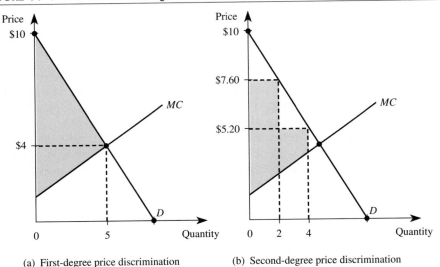

(a) First-degree price discrimination   (b) Second-degree price discrimination

Since the demand curve slopes downward, the maximum price the firm can charge for each additional unit declines, ultimately to $4 at an output of 5 units. The difference between each point on the demand curve and the firm's marginal cost represents the profits earned on each incremental unit sold. Thus, the shaded area between the demand curve and the firm's marginal cost curve reflects the total contribution to the firm's profit when it charges each consumer the maximum price he or she will pay for small increments of output between 0 and 5 units. This strategy allows the firm to earn the maximum possible profits. Notice that consumers receive no consumer surplus on the 5 units they purchase: The firm extracts all surplus under first-degree price discrimination. As noted earlier, however, this favorable outcome (from the firm's perspective) can occur only if the manager has perfect information about the price that each consumer is willing and able to pay for each incremental unit of output.

In situations where the firm does not know the maximum price that each consumer will pay for a good, or when it is not practical to post a continuous schedule of prices for each incremental unit purchased, a firm might be able to employ second-degree price discrimination to extract part of the surplus from consumers. *Second-degree price discrimination* is the practice of posting a discrete schedule of declining prices for different ranges of quantities. This practice is very common in the electric utility industry, where firms typically charge a higher rate on the first hundred kilowatt-hours of electricity used than on subsequent units. The primary advantage of this strategy is that the firm can extract some consumer surplus from consumers without needing to know beforehand the identity of the consumers who will choose to purchase small amounts (and thus are willing and able to pay a higher price per unit). Given the posted schedule of prices, consumers sort themselves according to their willingness to pay for alternative quantities of the good. Thus, the firm charges different prices to different consumers, but does not need to know specific characteristics of individual consumers.

To illustrate how second-degree price discrimination works, suppose the Acme Beverage Company charges consumers $7.60 per case for the first two cases purchased and $5.20 for each additional case. The shaded region in panel (b) of Figure 11–1 shows Acme's contributions to profits with this strategy. The first two cases are sold at a price of $7.60 each, and the shaded region between this price and the marginal cost curve reflects the firm's contribution to profits on sales of these two cases. The second two cases are priced at $5.20 each, so the shaded region between that price and the marginal cost curve between 2 and 4 units of output reflects Acme's profit contributions from selling the second two cases. Notice that consumers end up with some consumer surplus, which means that second-degree price discrimination yields lower profits for the firm than it would have earned if it were able to perfectly price discriminate. Nonetheless, profits are still higher than they would have been if the firm had used the simple strategy of charging the same price for all units sold. In effect, consumers purchasing small quantities (or alternatively, those having higher marginal valuations) pay higher prices than those who purchase in bulk.

The final type of price discrimination is commonly practiced by firms that recognize that the demand for their product differs systematically across consumers in different demographic groups. In these instances firms can profit by charging different groups of consumers different prices for the same product, a strategy referred to as *third-degree price discrimination*. For example, it is common for stores to offer "student discounts" and for hotels and restaurants to offer "senior citizen discounts." These practices effectively mean that students and senior citizens pay less for some goods than do other consumers. One might think that these pricing strategies are instituted to benefit students and senior citizens, but there is a more compelling reason: to increase the firm's profits.

To see why third-degree price discrimination enhances profits, suppose a firm with market power can charge two different prices to two groups of consumers and the marginal revenues of selling to group 1 and group 2 are MR_1 and MR_2, respectively. The basic profit-maximizing rule is to produce output such that marginal revenue is equal to marginal cost. This principle is still valid, but the presence of two marginal revenue functions introduces some ambiguity.

It turns out that to maximize profits, the firm should equate the marginal revenue from selling output to each group to marginal cost: $MR_1 = MC$ and $MR_2 = MC$. To see why, suppose $MR_1 > MC$. If the firm produced one more unit and sold it to group 1, it would increase revenue by more than costs would increase. As additional output is sold to group 1, marginal revenue declines until it ultimately equals marginal cost.

Since $MR_1 = MC$ and $MR_2 = MC$, it follows that the firm will allocate output between the two groups such that $MR_1 = MR_2$. To see why, suppose the marginal revenue for group 1 is 10 and the marginal revenue for group 2 is 5. If one less unit were sold to group 2, revenue from that group would fall by 5. If the extra unit of output were sold to group 1, revenue would increase by 10. Thus, it pays for the firm to allocate output to the group with the greater marginal revenue. As additional output is allocated to the group, its marginal revenue falls until, in equilibrium, the marginal revenues to the two groups are exactly equal.

To understand the basis for third-degree price discrimination, suppose two groups of consumers have elasticities of demand of E_1 and E_2, and the firm can charge group 1 a price of P_1 and group 2 a price of P_2. Using the formula for the marginal revenue of a firm with market power, it follows that the marginal revenue of selling the product to group 1 at a price of P_1 is

$$MR_1 = P_1\left[\frac{1 + E_1}{E_1}\right]$$

while the marginal revenue of selling to group 2 at a price of P_2 is

$$MR_2 = P_2\left[\frac{1 + E_2}{E_2}\right]$$

As mentioned, a profit-maximizing firm should equate the marginal revenue of each group to marginal cost, which implies that $MR_1 = MR_2$. Using the formula for marginal revenue, this condition may be rewritten as

$$P_1\left[\frac{1 + E_1}{E_1}\right] = P_2\left[\frac{1 + E_2}{E_2}\right]$$

If $E_1 = E_2$, the terms in brackets are equal, and thus the firm will maximize profits by charging each group the same price. If the demand by group 1 is more elastic than that by group 2, $E_1 < E_2 < 0$. In this instance, the firm should charge a lower price to group 1, since it has a more elastic demand than group 2.

Thus, in order for third-degree price discrimination to enhance profits, differences must exist in the elasticity of demand of various consumers. In the examples cited earlier, there is reason to believe that senior citizens have a more elastic demand for a hotel room or a restaurant meal than other consumers. Most retired individuals are on fixed incomes and thus are much more sensitive to price than people who still work. The fact that they are charged lower prices for a hotel room is a simple implication of third-degree price discrimination, namely, charging a lower price to people with more elastic demands.

Another condition that must exist for third-degree price discrimination to be effective is that the firm must have some means of identifying the elasticity of demand by different groups of consumers; otherwise, the firm has no way of knowing to which group of consumers it should charge the higher price. In practice, this is not difficult to do. Hotels require individuals seeking a senior citizens' discount to present evidence of their age, such as a driver's license. This effectively identifies an individual as likely to have a more elastic demand for a hotel room.

Finally, note that no type of price discrimination will work if the consumers purchasing at lower prices can resell their purchases to individuals being charged higher prices. In this instance, consumers who purchase the good at a low price could buy extra quantities and resell them to those who face the higher prices. The firm would sell nothing to the group being charged the higher price, because those consumers would save money by buying from consumers who purchased at the low price. In essence, the possibility of resale makes the goods purchased by the consumers charged the low price a perfect substitute for the firm's product. Those consumers can undercut the price the firm is charging the other group, thus reducing the firm's profits.

Formula: Third-Degree Price Discrimination Rule. To maximize profits, a firm with market power produces the output at which the marginal revenue to each group equals marginal cost:

$$\underbrace{P_1\left[\frac{1 + E_1}{E_1}\right]}_{MR_1} = MC$$

$$\underbrace{P_2\left[\frac{1 + E_2}{E_2}\right]}_{MR_2} = MC$$

Demonstration Problem 11–4

You are the manager of a pizzeria that produces at a marginal cost of $6 per pizza. The pizzeria is a local monopoly near campus (there are no other restaurants or food stores within 500 miles). During the day, only students eat at your restaurant. In the evening, while students are studying, faculty members eat there. If students have an elasticity of demand for pizzas of −4 and the faculty has an elasticity of demand of −2, what should your pricing policy be to maximize profits?

Answer:

Assuming faculty would be unwilling to purchase cold pizzas from students, the conditions for effective price discrimination hold. It will be profitable to charge one price—say, P_L—on the "lunch menu" (effectively a student price) and another price, such as P_D, on the "dinner menu" (effectively a faculty price). To determine precisely what price to put on each menu, note that the people buying pizza off the lunch menu have an elasticity of demand of −4, while those buying off the dinner menu have an elasticity of demand of −2. The conditions for profit maximization require that the marginal revenue of selling a pizza to each group equal marginal cost. Using the third-degree price discrimination rule, this means that

$$P_L\left[\frac{1 + E_L}{E_L}\right] = MC$$

and

$$P_D\left[\frac{1 + E_D}{E_D}\right] = MC$$

Setting $E_D = -2$, $E_L = -4$, and $MC = 6$ yields

$$P_L\left[\frac{1-4}{-4}\right] = 6$$

$$P_D\left[\frac{1-2}{-2}\right] = 6$$

which simplifies to

$$P_L\left[\frac{3}{4}\right] = 6$$

$$P_D\left[\frac{1}{2}\right] = 6$$

Solving these two equations yields $P_L = \$8$ and $P_D = \$12$. Thus, to maximize profits, you should price a pizza on the lunch menu at \$8 and a pizza on the dinner menu at \$12. Since students have a more elastic demand for pizza than do faculty members, they should be charged a lower price to maximize profits.

---

two-part pricing
Pricing strategy in which consumers are charged a fixed fee for the right to purchase a product, plus a per-unit charge for each unit purchased.

Two-Part Pricing

Another strategy that firms with market power can use to enhance profits is *two-part pricing*. With two-part pricing, a firm charges a fixed fee for the right to purchase its goods, plus a per-unit charge for each unit purchased. This pricing strategy is commonly used by athletic clubs to enhance profits. Golf courses and health clubs, for instance, typically charge a fixed "initiation fee" plus a charge (either per month or per visit) to use the facilities. In this section, we will see how such a pricing strategy can enhance the profits of a firm.

Figure 11–2(a) provides a diagram of the demand, marginal revenue, and marginal cost for a firm with market power. Here the demand function is $Q = 10 - P$ and the cost function is $C(Q) = 2Q$. If the firm adopted a pricing strategy of simply charging a single price to all consumers, the profit-maximizing level of output would be $Q = 4$ and the profit-maximizing price would be $P = 6$. This price–quantity combination corresponds to the point where marginal revenue equals marginal cost. Notice that the firm's profits are given by the shaded rectangle, which is

$$(\$6 - \$2)4 = \$16$$

Notice that the consumer surplus received by all consumers in the market—the value received but not paid for—corresponds to the upper triangle in Figure 11–2(a), which is

$$\frac{1}{2}[(\$10 - \$6)4] = \$8$$

In other words, consumers receive a total of \$8 in value from the four units purchased that is not extracted through the price they paid.

FIGURE 11–2 Comparisons of Standard Monopoly Pricing and Two-Part Pricing

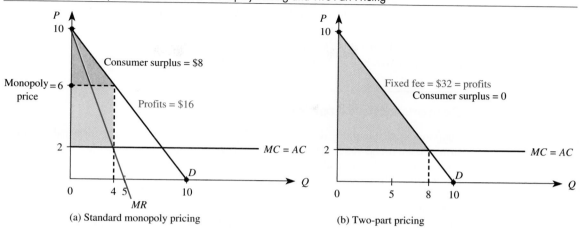

(a) Standard monopoly pricing   (b) Two-part pricing

Like first-degree price discrimination, two-part pricing allows a firm to extract all consumer surplus from consumers. In particular, suppose the demand function in Figure 11–2(a) is that of a single individual and the firm uses the following pricing scheme: a fixed fee of $32 that gives the consumer the right to buy the product at a per-unit charge of $2. This situation is depicted in Figure 11–2(b) for the same demand and cost functions as in Figure 11–2(a). With a per-unit charge of $2, the consumer will purchase eight units and receive a consumer surplus of

$$\frac{1}{2}[(\$10 - \$2)8] = \$32$$

By charging a fixed fee of $32, the firm extracts all of this consumer's surplus. The firm sells each unit at its marginal cost of $2, and thus makes no profit on each unit sold at this price. But the firm also receives the fixed payment of $32, which is pure profit. The $32 in profits earned using the two-part pricing scheme is larger than the $16 the firm would earn by using a simple pricing strategy.

Principle

Two-Part Pricing
A firm can enhance profits by engaging in two-part pricing: charge a per-unit price that equals marginal cost, plus a fixed fee equal to the consumer surplus each consumer receives at this per-unit price.

We mentioned that athletic clubs often engage in two-part pricing. They charge an initiation fee, plus a per-unit fee for each visit to the facility. Notice that if the marginal cost is low, the optimal per-unit fee will be low as well. In the extreme case where marginal cost is zero, an athletic facility's profit-maximizing two-part pricing strategy will be to charge $0 for each visit but a fixed initiation fee equal to a consumer's surplus. With two-part pricing, all profits are derived from the fixed fee. Setting the per-unit fee equal to marginal cost ensures that the surplus is as large as possible, thus allowing the largest fixed fee consistent with maximizing profits.

There are numerous other examples of two-part pricing strategies. Buying clubs are an excellent example. By paying a membership fee in a buying club, members get to buy products at "cost." Notice that if the membership fee is set equal to each consumer's surplus, the owner of a buying club actually makes higher profits than would be earned by simply setting the monopoly price.

Demonstration Problem 11–5

Suppose the total monthly demand for golf services is $Q = 20 - P$. The marginal cost to the firm of each round is $1. If this demand function is based on the individual demands of 10 golfers, what is the optimal two-part pricing strategy for this golf services firm? How much profit will the firm earn?

Answer:

The optimal per-unit charge is marginal cost. At this price, $20 - 1 = 19$ rounds of golf will be played each month. The total consumer surplus received by all 10 golfers at this price is thus

$$\frac{1}{2}[(20 - 1)19] = \$180.50$$

Since this is the total consumer surplus enjoyed by all 10 consumers, the optimal fixed fee is the consumer surplus enjoyed by an individual golfer ($180.50/10 = $18.05 per month). Thus, the optimal two-part pricing strategy is for the firm to charge a monthly fee to each golfer of $18.05, plus greens fees of $1 per round. The total profits of the firm thus are $180.50 per month, minus the firm's fixed costs.

Two-part pricing allows a firm to earn higher profits than it would earn by simply charging a price for each unit sold. By charging a fixed fee, the firm is able to extract consumer surplus, thus enhancing its profits. Unlike price discrimination, two-part pricing does not require that consumers have different elasticities of demand for the firm's product. By charging a per-unit fee for each unit purchased, consumers can vary the amounts they purchase according to their individual demands for the product.

Block Pricing

block pricing
Pricing strategy in which identical products are packaged together in order to enhance profits by forcing customers to make an all-or-none decision to purchase.

Another way a firm with market power can enhance profits is to engage in *block pricing*. If you have purchased toilet paper in packages of four rolls or cans of soda in a six-pack, you have had firsthand experience with block pricing.

Let us see how block pricing can enhance a firm's profits. Suppose an individual consumer's demand function is $Q = 10 - P$ and the firm's costs are $C(Q) = 2Q$. Figure 11–3 graphs the relevant curves. We see that if a firm charges a price of $2 per unit, it will sell eight units to the consumer. Notice, however, that the consumer receives a surplus of the upper triangle, which is

$$\frac{1}{2}[(\$10 - \$2)8] = \$32$$

FIGURE 11-3   Block Pricing

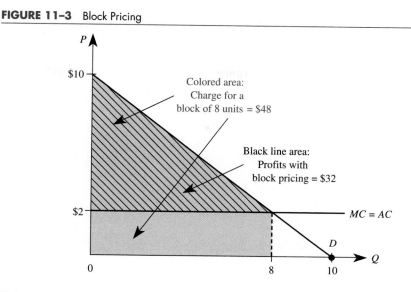

This consumer's surplus reflects the value the consumer receives over and above the cost of buying eight units. In fact, in this case the consumer pays $2 × 8 = $16 to the firm for the eight units, but receives additional surplus of $32. The total value to the consumer of the eight units is $16 + $32 = $48.

Block pricing provides a means by which the firm can get the consumer to pay the full value of the eight units. It works very simply. Suppose the firm packaged eight units of its product and charged a price for the package. In this case, the consumer has to make an all-or-none decision between buying eight units and buying nothing. We just saw that the total value to the consumer of eight units is $48. Thus, so long as the price of the package of eight units is not greater than $48, this consumer will find it in her or his interest to buy the package.

Principle	**Block Pricing** By packaging units of a product and selling them as one package, the firm earns more than by posting a simple per-unit price. The profit-maximizing price on a package is the total value the consumer receives for the package.

Thus, the profit-maximizing price for the firm to charge for the package of eight units is $48. By charging this price for a package of eight instead of pricing each unit separately and letting the consumer choose how many units to buy, the firm earns $32 in profits—the value of the would-be consumer's surplus when the price is $2.

Demonstration Problem 11–6

Suppose a consumer's (inverse) demand function for gum produced by a firm with market power is given by $P = .2 - .04Q$ and the marginal cost is zero. What price should the firm charge for a package containing five pieces of gum?

FIGURE 11–4 Optimal Block Pricing with Zero Marginal Cost

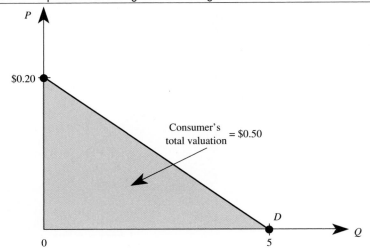

Answer:

When $Q = 5$, $P = 0$; when $Q = 0$, $P = .2$. This linear demand is graphed in Figure 11–4. Thus, the total value to the consumer of five pieces of gum is

$$\frac{1}{2}[(\$.2 - \$0)5] = \$.50$$

which corresponds to the shaded area in Figure 11–4. The firm extracts all this surplus by charging a price of $.50 for a package of five pieces of gum.

Block pricing enhances profits by forcing consumers to make an all-or-none decision to purchase units of a good. Notice that block pricing can enhance profits even in situations where consumers have identical demands for a firm's product.

Commodity Bundling

commodity bundling
The practice of bundling several different products together and selling them at a single "bundle price."

Another strategy managers can use to enhance profits is *commodity bundling*. Commodity bundling refers to the practice of bundling two or more different products together and selling them at a single "bundle price." For instance, travel companies often sell "package deals" that include airfare, hotel, and meals at a bundled price instead of pricing each component of a vacation separately. Computer firms bundle computers, monitors, and software and sell them at a bundled price. Many car dealers bundle options such as air-conditioning, power steering, and automatic transmission and sell them at a "special package price." Let us see how these practices can enhance profits.

TABLE 11-1 Commodity Bundling

Consumer	Valuation of Computer	Valuation of Monitor
1	$2,000	$200
2	1,500	300

Suppose the manager of a computer firm knows there are two consumers who value its computers and monitors differently. Table 11–1 shows the maximum amount the two consumers would pay for a computer and a monitor. The first consumer is willing to pay $2,000 for a computer and $200 for a monitor. The second consumer is willing to pay $1,500 for a computer and $300 for a monitor. However, the manager does not know the identity of each consumer; thus, she cannot price discriminate by charging each consumer a different price.

Suppose the manager priced each component separately: one price for a computer, P_C, and another price for a monitor, P_M. (To simplify profit computations, suppose the cost to the firm of computers and monitors is zero.) If the firm charged $2,000 for a computer, it would sell a computer only to consumer 1 and earn $2,000, because consumer 2 is willing to pay only $1,500 for a computer. If the firm charged $1,500 for a computer, both consumers would buy a computer, netting the firm $3,000. Clearly the profit-maximizing price to charge for a computer is $1,500.

Similarly, if the firm priced monitors at $300, only consumer 2 would purchase a monitor, because consumer 1 would pay only $200 for a monitor. By pricing monitors at $200, it would sell two monitors and earn $400. The profit-maximizing price to charge for a monitor thus is $200.

On the surface, it appears that the most the firm can earn is $3,400 by pricing computers at $1,500 and monitors at $200. In this case, the firm sells two computers and two monitors. However, the firm can earn higher profits by bundling computers and monitors and selling the bundle at a price of $1,800. To see why, notice that the total value to the first consumer of a computer and a monitor is $2,000 + $200 = $2,200, and the total value to the second consumer of a computer and a monitor is $1,500 + $300 = $1,800. By bundling a computer and a monitor and selling the bundle for $1,800, the firm will sell a bundle to both consumers and earn $3,600—a full $200 more than it would earn if it did not engage in commodity bundling.

This example illustrates that commodity bundling can enhance profits when consumers differ with respect to the amounts they are willing to pay for multiple products sold by a firm. It is important to emphasize that commodity bundling can enhance profits even when the manager cannot distinguish among the amounts different consumers are willing to pay for the firm's products. If the manager did know precisely how much each consumer was willing to pay for each product, the firm could earn even higher profits by engaging in price discrimination: charging higher prices to those consumers willing to pay more for its products.

INSIDE BUSINESS 11–3

Bundling and "Price Frames" in Online Markets

Consumers who purchase from online and mail order firms that do not have a brick-and-mortar presence are, in essence, purchasing a "bundle" that includes both the product and home delivery. Does the manner in which a seller displays the price of such a bundle affect its sales? Companies that run TV advertisements for products "not sold in stores" seem to think so. For instance, an offer for a 10-piece Ginsu knife set is framed as costing "only" $39.95 plus $9.95 shipping and handling. If consumers were perfectly rational, sales of Ginsu knives would depend only on the effective (total) price of the "bundle"—the product price plus the shipping charge ($49.90)—and not the prices of each component.

To test the effects of different price "frames," economists Tanjim Hossain and John Morgan auctioned off pairs of popular music CDs and Xbox video game discs on eBay. For each product, one of the auctions started at a $4 opening price and shipping was free. The other auction had an opening price of 1 cent but had a shipping charge of $3.99. Thus, the effective

starting price in both auctions was $4. Item descriptions of both auctions clearly stated that the goods would be shipped via first-class mail.

Hossain and Morgan found that the auctions with an opening price of 1 cent consistently attracted more bidders and yielded significantly higher revenues than auctions with an opening price of $4—even though the effective prices taking into account shipping charges were the same in all of these auctions. Similar results also held for auctions of Xbox game discs when $2 was added to the opening bid and the shipping charge. Thus, it appears that real-world consumers use some sort of mental accounting system that favors bundles with lower product prices—even when these lower prices are associated with higher shipping charges.

Source: Tanjim Hossain and John Morgan, " . . . Plus Shipping and Handling: Revenue (Non) Equivalence in Field Experiments on eBay," *Advances in Economic Analysis & Policy* 6, no. 2 (2006).

For a video walkthrough of this problem, visit www.mhhe.com/ baye8e

Demonstration Problem 11–7

Suppose three purchasers of a new car have the following valuations for options:

Consumer	Air Conditioner	Power Brakes
1	$1,000	$500
2	800	300
3	100	800

The firm's costs are zero.

1. If the manager knows the valuations and identity of each consumer, what is the optimal pricing strategy?
2. Suppose the manager does not know the identities of the buyers. How much will the firm make if the manager sells brakes and air conditioners for $800 each but offers a special options package (power brakes and an air conditioner) for $1,100?

Answer:

1. If the manager knows the buyers' identities, he will maximize profits through price discrimination, since resale for these products is unlikely; charge consumer 1 $1,500 for an air conditioner and power brakes; charge consumer 2 $1,100 for an air conditioner and power brakes; and charge consumer 3 $900 for an air conditioner and power brakes. The firm's profits will be $3,500. It makes no difference whether the manager charges the consumers a bundled price equal to their total

valuation of an air conditioner and power brakes or charges a separate price for each component that equals the consumers' valuation.

2. The total value of a bundle containing an air conditioner and power brakes is $1,500 for consumer 1, $1,100 for consumer 2, and $900 for consumer 3. Thus, consumers 1 and 2 will buy the option package because a bundle with an air conditioner and power brakes is worth at least $1,100 to them. The firm earns $2,200 on these consumers. Consumer 3 will not buy the bundle because its total cost is greater than the consumer's valuation ($900). However, consumer 3 will buy power brakes at the price of $800. Thus, the firm earns $3,000 with this pricing strategy—$2,200 comes from consumers 1 and 2, who each purchase the special options package for $1,100, and $800 comes from consumer 3, who chooses to buy only power brakes.

Pricing Strategies for Special Cost and Demand Structures

The pricing strategies we will discuss in this section—peak-load pricing and cross-subsidization—enhance profits for firms that have special cost and demand structures.

Peak-Load Pricing

Many markets have periods in which demand is high and periods in which demand is low. Toll roads tend to have more traffic during rush hour than at other times of the day; utility companies tend to have higher demand during the day than during the late-night hours; and airlines tend to have heavier traffic during the week than during weekends. When the demand during peak times is so high that the capacity of the firm cannot serve all customers at the same price, the profitable thing for the firm to do is engage in *peak-load pricing*.

peak-load pricing
Pricing strategy in which higher prices are charged during peak hours than during off-peak hours.

Figure 11–5 illustrates a classic case of such a situation. Notice that marginal cost is constant up to Q_H, where it becomes vertical. At this point, the firm is operating at full capacity and cannot provide additional units at any price.

The two demand curves in Figure 11–5 correspond to peak and off-peak demand for the product: D_{Low} is the off-peak demand, which is lower than D_{High}, the peak demand. In general, where there are two types of demand, a firm will maximize profits by charging different prices to the different groups of demanders. In the case of peak-load pricing, the "groups" refer to those who purchase at different times during the day.

In Figure 11–5, for instance, demand during low-peak times is such that marginal revenue equals marginal cost at point Q_L. Thus, the profit-maximizing price during low-peak times is P_L. In contrast, during high-peak times, marginal revenue equals marginal cost at point Q_H, which corresponds to the firm's full capacity. The profit-maximizing price during high-peak times is P_H. Thus, as is the case in price discrimination, the firm charges two different prices: a low price during low-peak demand and a high price during high-peak demand.

Notice in Figure 11–5 that if the firm charged a high price of P_H at all times of the day, no one would purchase during low-peak periods. By lowering the price during low-peak times but charging a high price during high-peak times, the firm increases its profits by selling to some consumers during low-peak times. Similarly, if the firm charged a low price during all times of the day, it would lose money during high-peak times, when consumers are willing to pay a higher price for services.

FIGURE 11-5   Peak-Load Pricing

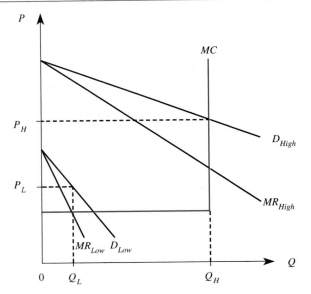

Peak-Load Pricing

When demand is higher at some times of the day than at other times, a firm may enhance profits by peak-load pricing: charging a higher price during peak times than is charged during off-peak times.

Demonstration Problem 11–8

Airports typically charge a higher price for parking during holidays than they do during other times of the year. Why?

Answer:

It pays for airports to engage in peak-load pricing. Since the demand for parking is much higher during holidays, when travelers spend extended periods with families, parking lots tend to fill up during that time. If airports charged a high price year round, they would have empty spaces most of the time. If they charged low prices year round, they would lose out on the additional amount consumers are willing to pay during holidays. Thus, with peak-load pricing, airports earn higher profits.

cross-subsidy
Pricing strategy in which profits gained from the sale of one product are used to subsidize sales of a related product.

Cross-Subsidies

The next pricing strategy we will discuss—cross-subsidies—is relevant in situations where a firm has cost complementarities and the demand by consumers for a group of products is interdependent. A firm that engages in a strategy of *cross-subsidies* uses profits made with one product to subsidize sales of another product.

For example, Adobe charges dramatically different prices for two of its products. One product—its *Adobe Reader*—may be obtained "for free" by anyone willing to download the software from Adobe's Internet site. This software permits users to view documents created in portable document format (pdf). In contrast, individuals wishing to create pdf documents must *pay* for a software product called *Adobe Acrobat.*

Adobe engages in this cross-subsidization because complementaries in demand and costs make doing so profitable. More specifically, Adobe enjoys economies of scope and cost complementarities in making these two products jointly (it is cheaper to design and distribute both types of software within one firm). Furthermore these two products are complementary: The greater the number of people who use *Adobe Reader* to view documents, the greater the amount they will be willing to pay to use *Adobe Acrobat* for document creation. In short, Adobe finds it profitable to price *Adobe Reader* at or below cost because doing so stimulates demand for its complementary software product, thus permitting it to charge a significantly higher price for *Adobe Acrobat* than it would otherwise be able to charge. As we will see in Chapter 13, a number of similar pricing strategies (such as penetration pricing) can be used to enhance profits in strategic environments (including online auctions) where network effects are present.

Principle	**Cross-Subsidization**
	Whenever the demands for two products produced by a firm are interrelated through costs or demand, the firm may enhance profits by cross-subsidization: selling one product at or below cost and the other product above cost.

Transfer Pricing

Thus far, our analysis of pricing decisions has presumed that a single manager is in charge of pricing and output decisions. However, most large firms have upstream and downstream managers who must make price and output decisions for their own divisions. For example, automakers like Toyota have upstream managers who control the production of inputs (like car engines) produced in *upstream divisions.* These inputs are "transferred" to *downstream divisions,* where downstream managers operate plants that use the inputs to produce the final output (automobiles). An important issue in this setting is optimal *transfer pricing*—the internal price at which an upstream division should sell inputs to the firm's downstream division to maximize the overall profits of the firm.

transfer pricing
Pricing strategy in which a firm optimally sets the internal price at which an upstream division sells an input to a downstream division.

Transfer pricing is important because most division managers are provided an incentive to maximize their own division's profits. As we will see, if the owners of a firm do not set optimal transfer prices, but instead let division managers set the prices of internally manufactured inputs so as to maximize their division's profits, the result might be lower overall profits for the firm.

To illustrate, suppose there is no outside market for the input produced by the upstream division, and that divisional managers are instructed to maximize the profits of their divisions. In this case the upstream division manager has market power and maximizes the profits of the upstream division by producing where the marginal revenue derived from selling to the downstream division equals the upstream division's marginal cost of producing the input. Because of the monopoly power enjoyed by the upstream division, the input is sold to the downstream division at a price that exceeds the firm's actual marginal cost. Given this input price, the downstream manager would then maximize divisional profits by producing where the marginal revenue it earns in the final product market (MR_d) equals its marginal cost. This implies that it, too, prices above marginal cost. Moreover, because the price the downstream division pays the upstream division for the input is higher than the true marginal cost of the input, the downstream division ends up charging a price for the final product that is actually higher than the price that maximizes overall firm profits. In short, when both divisions mark up prices in excess of marginal cost, *double marginalization* occurs and the result is less than optimal overall firm profits.

To circumvent the problem of double marginalization, transfer prices must be set that maximize the overall value of the firm rather than the profits of the upstream division. To see how this can be accomplished, suppose the downstream division requires one unit of the input (one engine, say) to produce one unit of the final output (one car). Assume that the downstream division has a marginal cost of assembling the final output, denoted MC_d, that is in addition to the cost of acquiring the input from the upstream division. In this case the overall profits of the firm are maximized when the upstream division produces engines such that its marginal cost, MC_u, equals the net marginal revenue to the downstream division (NMR_d):

$$NMR_d = MR_d - MC_d = MC_u$$

To see why, notice that it costs the firm MC_u to produce another unit of the input. This input can be converted into another unit of output and sold to generate additional revenues of MR_d in the final product market only after the downstream division expends an additional MC_d to convert the input into the final output. Thus, the actual marginal benefit to the firm of producing another unit of the input is NMR_d. Setting this equal to the marginal cost of producing the input maximizes overall firm profits.

Now that we know the necessary conditions for maximizing overall firm profits, we show how a firm can institute an incentive system that induces the divisional managers to indeed maximize overall firm profits. Suppose higher authorities within the firm determine that the level of final output that maximizes overall firm profits is Q^*. They set the transfer price, P_T, equal to the upstream division's marginal cost of producing the amount of input required by the downstream division to produce Q^* units of final output. According to this internal pricing scheme, the downstream manager can now purchase as many units of the input as it desires from the upstream division at a fixed price of P_T per unit. The upstream and downstream managers are instructed to maximize divisional profits, taking as given the transfer price set by higher authorities within the firm.

Since the upstream division now must sell the input internally at a fixed price of P_T per unit, it behaves like a perfectly competitive firm and maximizes profits by producing where price equals marginal cost: $P_T = MC_u$. Since one unit of input is required for each unit of output, the downstream division's marginal cost of producing final output is now $MC = MC_d + P_T$. The downstream divisional manager maximizes divisional profits by producing where marginal revenue equals marginal cost: $MR_d = MC_d + P_T$. Since $P_T = MC_u$, we may rewrite this as $MR_d - MC_d = MC_u$, which is exactly our condition for maximizing overall firm profits. Thus, we see that by setting the transfer price at the upstream division's marginal cost of producing the firm's profit-maximizing quantity of the input, the problem of double marginalization is avoided even though divisional managers operate independently to maximize their division's profits.

A concrete example will help illustrate how a firm can implement optimal transfer pricing. Suppose that the (inverse) demand for Aviation General's single-engine planes is given by $P = 15{,}000 - Q$. Its upstream division produces engines at a cost of $C_u(Q_e) = 2.5Q_e^2$, and the downstream division's cost of assembling planes is $C_d(Q) = 1{,}000Q$. Let us derive the optimal transfer price when there is no external market for engines.

The optimal transfer price is set where the firm's net marginal revenue from engine production equals the upstream division's marginal cost of producing the engines. Downstream marginal revenue and marginal cost is $MR_d = 15{,}000 - 2Q$ and $MC_d = 1{,}000$, respectively, while the upstream division's marginal cost of producing engines is $MC_u = 5Q_e$. Since it takes one engine to produce one plane ($Q = Q_e$), equating NMR_d and MC_u implies

$$NMR_d = 15{,}000 - 2Q_e - 1{,}000 = 5Q_e$$

Solving for Q_e, we see that to maximize overall firm profits, the upstream division should produce 2,000 engines. Since $Q_e = Q$, the downstream division should produce 2,000 planes to maximize overall firm profits. The optimal transfer price is the upstream division's marginal cost evaluated at 2,000 engines, or $P_T = \$10{,}000$. Thus, the firm maximizes its overall profits when its accountants set the (internal) transfer price of engines at \$10,000 per unit, and divisional managers are provided an incentive to maximize divisional profits given this price.

Pricing Strategies in Markets with Intense Price Competition

The final pricing strategies we will examine—price matching, inducing brand loyalty, and randomized pricing—are valuable for firms competing in Bertrand oligopoly. Recall that firms in Bertrand oligopoly compete in price and sell similar products. As we learned in Chapters 9 and 10, in these instances price wars will likely result, leading to prices that are close to marginal cost and profits that are near zero. While the pricing strategies discussed in this section can be used in situations other than Bertrand oligopoly, they are particularly useful for mitigating the price wars that frequently occur in such a market.

Price Matching

In Chapters 9 and 10, we showed that when two or more firms compete in a homogeneous-product Bertrand oligopoly, the Nash equilibrium is for each firm to charge marginal cost and earn zero profits. However, in Chapter 10 we showed that if the game is infinitely repeated, firms can maintain collusive outcomes by adopting trigger strategies, which punish rivals that deviate from the high price. In an infinitely repeated game, punishments are threatened in the future if a firm cheats on a collusive agreement, and this can lead to a situation where firms end up charging high prices. However, recall that this strategy can work only if the interest rate is low and firms can effectively monitor the behavior of other firms in the market.

In cases where trigger strategies do not work (because the game is not infinitely repeated or the firms cannot monitor other firms' behavior), there is another way firms can attain higher profits: by advertising a price-matching strategy. A firm that uses a *price-matching strategy* advertises a price and a promise to "match" any lower price offered by a competitor.

price matching
A strategy in which a firm advertises a price and a promise to match any lower price offered by a competitor.

To illustrate how such a strategy can enhance profits, suppose the firms in a market play a one-shot Bertrand pricing game. However, in addition to advertising a price, the firms advertise a commitment to match any lower price found in the market. Such an advertisement would look something like the following:

> Our price is *P*. If you find a better price in the market, we will match that price. We will not be undersold!

This sounds like a good deal for consumers; indeed, simply announcing this strategy may induce some consumers to buy from the firm to be "assured" of a great deal.

It turns out, however, that if all firms in the market announce such a policy, they can set the price (*P*) to the high monopoly price and earn large profits instead of the zero profits they would earn in the usual one-shot Bertrand oligopoly. How does this work?

Suppose all firms advertised the high monopoly price but promised to match any lower price found by consumers. Since all firms are charging the same high price, consumers can't find a better price in the market. The result is that firms share the market, charge the monopoly price, and earn high profits. Furthermore, notice that no firm has an incentive to charge a lower price in an attempt to steal customers from rivals. If a firm lowered its price, the rivals would match that price and gain back their share of the market. By lowering its price, a firm effectively triggers a price war, which results in no greater share of the market and lower profits. Thus, if all firms adopt price-matching strategies, the result is that each firm charges the monopoly price and shares the market to earn high profits.

An important aspect of price-matching policies is that the firms need not monitor the prices charged by rivals. This is in contrast to trigger strategies, in which firms must monitor rivals' prices to know whether to punish a rival that has charged a low price. With a price-matching strategy, it is up to a consumer to show the firm that some rival is offering a better deal. At that point, the firm can match the price for that consumer. The consumers who have not found a better deal continue to pay the higher price. Thus, even if some other firm happened to charge a low price, a

---

INSIDE BUSINESS 11–4

The Prevalence of Price-Matching Policies and Other Low-Price Guarantees

Competition in the market for online travel services has heightened to the point that some companies run advertisements like this one by Orbitz:

> If you find a lower rate for the same hotel, room type, and check-in and check-out dates on Orbitz or any other website within 24 hours following your confirmed reservation on Orbitz.com, Orbitz will refund you the difference upon verification you have qualified for a refund.[1]

This advertisement is an example of what economists call a *low-price guarantee* (LPG).

As noted in the text, LPGs permit firms to charge higher prices because the guarantees weaken the incentive for rivals to undercut any given store's price. If you page through almost any Sunday newspaper, you will see that LPGs are becoming increasingly popular among car dealers, office supply stores, electronics stores, supermarkets, and a variety of other retailers. Maria Arbatskaya, Morten Hviid, and Greg Shaffer, for instance, examined the frequency with which tire retailers use LPGs in their newspaper advertisements. Based on samples of over 500 tire advertisements across the country, over half contained LPGs.

[1] An excerpt from Orbitz.com at www.orbitz.com/pagedef/content/legal/bestPriceGuarantee.jsp (viewed on February 28, 2009).

Sources: Maria Arbatskaya, Morten Hviid, and Greg Shaffer, "The Effects of Low-Price Guarantees on Tire Prices," *Advances in Applied Microeconomics* 8 (1999), pp. 123–38.

---

firm using a price-matching strategy would get to price discriminate between those consumers who found such a price and those who did not.

Before you choose to adopt a price-matching strategy, there are two things to consider. First, you must devise a mechanism that precludes consumers from claiming to have found a lower price when in fact they have not. Otherwise, consumers will have an incentive to tell you that another firm is "giving goods away" and ask you to match the lower price. One way firms avoid such deception is by promising to match prices that are advertised in some widely circulated newspaper. In this case, the consumer must bring in the advertisement before the price will be matched.

Second, you can get into trouble with a price-matching strategy if a competitor has lower costs than your firm. For instance, if your competitor's marginal cost is $300 for a television set and yours is $400, the profit-maximizing (monopoly) price set by your firm will be higher than that set by the rival. In such an instance, the monopoly price set by your rival may be lower than your cost. In this case, if you have to match your rival's price, you will incur losses on each unit sold.

Inducing Brand Loyalty

Another strategy a firm can use to reduce the tension of Bertrand competition is to adopt strategies that induce *brand loyalty*. Brand-loyal customers will continue to buy a firm's product even if another firm offers a (slightly) better price. By inducing brand loyalty, a firm reduces the number of consumers who will "switch" to another firm if it undercuts its price.

Firms can use several methods to induce brand loyalty. One of the more common methods is to engage in advertising campaigns that promote a firm's product as being better than those of competitors. If advertisements make consumers believe that other products in the market are not perfect substitutes, firms engaging in price competition can earn higher profits. When a rival undercuts a firm's price, some customers will remain loyal to the firm, allowing it to charge a higher price and make positive profits.

Notice, however, that such an advertising strategy will not work if consumers believe products to be homogeneous. A self-service gasoline station would be hard-pressed to convince consumers that its product is really "different" from the identical brand sold across the street. In these instances, firms can resort to alternative strategies to promote brand loyalty.

Some gasoline stations now have "frequent-filler" programs, modeled after the frequent-flyer programs initiated by the airlines. Frequent-filler programs provide consumers with a cash rebate after a specified number of fill-ups. With this strategy, even though the products are identical, the consumer has an incentive to remain loyal to the same station to maximize the number of times he or she obtains a rebate. For example, suppose a station offers a $5 rebate after 10 fill-ups. If the consumer fills up at 10 different stations, he or she does not get the rebate, but if all 10 fill-ups are at the same station, the consumer gets $5. Thus, a frequent-filler strategy provides the consumer with an incentive to remain loyal to a particular station even though it offers products identical to its rivals.

Randomized Pricing

randomized pricing
Pricing strategy in which a firm intentionally varies its price in an attempt to "hide" price information from consumers and rivals.

The final strategy firms can use to enhance profits in markets with intense price competition is to engage in randomized pricing. With a *randomized-pricing strategy*, a firm varies its price from hour to hour or day to day. Such a strategy can benefit a firm for two reasons.

First, when firms adopt randomized pricing strategies, consumers cannot learn from experience which firm charges the lowest price in the market. On some days, one firm charges the lowest price; on another day, some other firm offers the best deal. By increasing the uncertainty about where the best deal exists, firms reduce consumers' incentive to shop for price information. Because one store offers the best deal today does not mean it will also offer the best deal tomorrow. To continually find the best price in the market, a consumer must constantly shop for a new deal. In effect, there is only a one-shot gain to a consumer of becoming informed; the information is worthless when new prices are set. This reduces consumers' incentive to invest in information about prices. As consumers have less information about the prices offered by competitors, firms are less vulnerable to rivals stealing customers by setting lower prices.

The second advantage of randomized prices is that they reduce the ability of rival firms to undercut a firm's price. Recall that in Bertrand oligopoly, a firm wishes to slightly undercut the rival's price. If another firm offers a slightly better deal, informed consumers will switch to that firm. Randomized pricing not only reduces the information available to consumers but it precludes rivals from knowing precisely what price to charge to undercut a given firm's price. Randomized-pricing strategies tend to reduce rivals' incentive to engage in price wars and thus can enhance profits.

We should point out that it is not always profitable to engage in randomized-pricing strategies. In many instances, other strategies, such as price-matching

---

INSIDE BUSINESS 11–5

Randomized Pricing in the Airline Industry

Airlines compete in a Bertrand market in which rivals continually attempt to learn rivals' prices so that they can undercut them. Despite some brand loyalty created by frequent-flyer programs, a large number of airline customers search online to identify the carrier charging the lowest price on a given route. To get these price-conscious customers, an airline must succeed in charging the lowest price in the market.

Given the structure of the airline market, airlines sometimes find it profitable to "randomize" their prices so that rivals and consumers cannot learn from experience exactly what the price of a particular route is. By frequently changing its prices, an airline prevents rivals from learning the price they have to

undercut to steal customers. With prices that vary randomly over time, an airline may be charging the highest price or lowest price in the market at a given instant. When it charges the lowest price, it sells tickets to both its price-conscious and loyal customers. When it charges high prices, it sells tickets only to its loyal customers, as the price-conscious flyers buy tickets from another airline.

Sources: Michael R. Baye and Casper G. de Vries, "Mixed Strategy Trade Equilibrium," *Canadian Journal of Economics* 25 (May 1992), pp. 281–93; Susan Chen, "Differences in Average Prices on the Internet: Evidence from the Online Market for Air Travel," *Economic Inquiry*, 44, 2007, pp. 666–70.

---

strategies, can be a more effective means of enhancing profits. Moreover, in some instances it may not be feasible to change prices as frequently as randomized-pricing strategies require. The cost of hiring personnel to continually change price tags can be prohibitive. Randomized pricing can work, however, when prices are entered in a computer and not directly on the products. It can also work when firms advertise "sales" in a weekly newspaper. In these instances, the prices advertised in the sales circular can be varied from week to week so the competition will not know what price to advertise to undercut the firm's price.

ANSWERING THE HEADLINE

Why does Disney World charge a cover fee for entering the park and then let everyone who enters ride for free? The answer lies in the ability to extract consumer surplus by engaging in two-part pricing. In particular, the marginal cost of an individual ride at an amusement park is close to zero, as in Figure 11–6. If the average consumer has a demand curve like the one in Figure 11–6, setting the monopoly price would result in a price of $9.50 per ride. Since each customer would go on five rides, the amusement park would earn $47.50 per customer. (This ignores fixed costs, which must be paid regardless of the pricing strategy.) But this would leave the average consumer with $23.75 in consumer surplus. By charging an entry fee of $95 but pricing each ride at $0, each consumer rides an average of 10 rides and the park extracts all consumer surplus and earns higher profits.[1]

---

[1]Walter Oi, "A Disneyland Dilemma: Two-Part Tariffs for a Mickey Mouse Monopoly," *Quarterly Journal of Economics* 85 (February 1971), pp. 77–96.

FIGURE 11-6 The Disneyland Dilemma

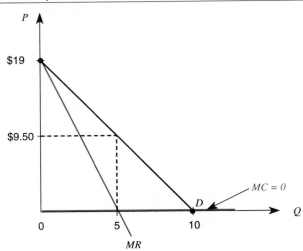

SUMMARY

This chapter presented pricing strategies used by firms with some market power. Unlike firms in a perfectly competitive market, when there are a small number of firms and products are slightly differentiated, a manager can use pricing strategies that will foster positive economic profits. These strategies range from simple markup rules to more complex two-part pricing strategies that enable a firm to extract all consumer surplus.

This chapter showed how markup rules come into existence. If a firm is monopolistic or monopolistically competitive, the elasticity from the firm's demand function can be used to find the markup factor that will maximize the firm's profits. If a manager operates in a Cournot oligopoly, the firm's own price elasticity is simply the number of firms in the market times the market elasticity. Knowing this, a manager in this kind of market can easily calculate the appropriate markup rule for his or her pricing strategies.

In some markets, the manager can actually do better than the single monopoly price. This can be accomplished through price discrimination or two-part pricing. Other pricing strategies that enhance profits include peak-load pricing, block pricing, commodity bundling, cross-subsidization, and optimal transfer pricing. The chapter concluded with descriptions of strategies that can help managers in a Bertrand oligopoly avoid the tendency toward zero economic profits.

KEY TERMS AND CONCEPTS

block pricing	price discrimination
brand loyalty	price matching
commodity bundling	randomized pricing
cross-subsidies	second-degree price discrimination
double marginalization	third-degree price discrimination
downstream division	transfer pricing
first-degree price discrimination	two-part pricing
peak-load pricing	upstream division

END-OF-CHAPTER PROBLEMS BY LEARNING OBJECTIVE

Every end-of-chapter problem addresses at least one learning objective. Following is a nonexhaustive sample of end-of-chapter problems for each learning objective.

LO1 Apply simple elasticity-based markup formulas to determine profit-maximizing prices in environments where a business enjoys market power, including monopoly, monopolistic competition, and Cournot oligopoly.

Try these problems: 1, 21

LO2 Formulate pricing strategies that permit firms to extract additional surplus from consumers—including price discrimination, two-part pricing, block pricing, and commodity bundling – and explain the conditions needed for each of these strategies to yield higher profits than standard pricing.

Try these problems: 2, 13

LO3 Formulate pricing strategies that enhance profits for special cost and demand structures—such as peak-load pricing, cross-subsidies, and transfer pricing—and explain the conditions needed for each strategy to work.

Try these problems: 8, 16

LO4 Explain how price-matching guarantees, brand loyalty programs, and randomized pricing strategies can be used to enhance profits in markets with intense price competition.

Try these problems: 9, 19

CONCEPTUAL AND COMPUTATIONAL QUESTIONS

connect
|ECONOMICS

1. Based on the best available econometric estimates, the market elasticity of demand for your firm's product is -2. The marginal cost of producing the product is constant at \$150, while average total cost at current production levels is \$225. Determine your optimal per unit price if:

   a. You are a monopolist.

   b. You compete against one other firm in a Cournot oligopoly.

   c. You compete against 19 other firms in a Cournot oligopoly.

2. Based on the following graph (which summarizes the demand, marginal revenue, and relevant costs for your product), determine your firm's optimal price, output, and the resulting profits for each of the following scenarios:
   a. You charge the same unit price to all consumers.
   b. You engage in first-degree price discrimination.
   c. You engage in two-part pricing.
   d. You engage in block pricing.

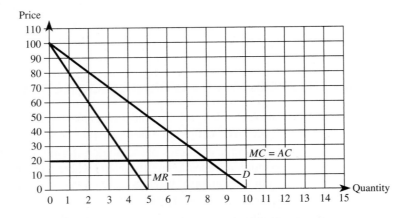

3. You are the manager of a firm that charges customers $16 per unit for the first unit purchased, and $12 per unit for each additional unit purchased in excess of one unit. The accompanying graph summarizes your relevant demand and costs.
   a. What is the economic term for your firm's pricing strategy?
   b. Determine the profits you earn from this strategy.
   c. How much additional profit would you earn if you were able to perfectly price discriminate?

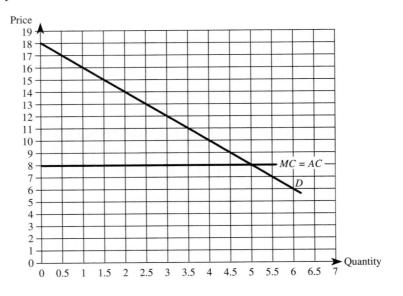

4. You are the manager of a monopoly that sells a product to two groups of consumers in different parts of the country. Group 1's elasticity of demand is -3, while group 2's is -5. Your marginal cost of producing the product is $40.
   a. Determine your optimal markups and prices under third-degree price discrimination.
   b. Identify the conditions under which third-degree price discrimination enhances profits.

5. You are the manager of a monopoly. A typical consumer's inverse demand function for your firm's product is $P = 250 - 40Q$, and your cost function is $C(Q) = 10Q$.
   a. Determine the optimal two-part pricing strategy.
   b. How much additional profit do you earn using a two-part pricing strategy compared with charging this consumer a per-unit price?

6. A monopoly is considering selling several units of a homogeneous product as a single package. A typical consumer's demand for the product is $Q^d = 80 - .5P$, and the marginal cost of production is $100.
   a. Determine the optimal number of units to put in a package.
   b. How much should the firm charge for this package?

7. You are the manager of a firm that produces products X and Y at zero cost. You know that different types of consumers value your two products differently, but you are unable to identify these consumers individually at the time of the sale. In particular, you know there are three types of consumers (1,000 of each type) with the following valuations for the two products:

Consumer Type	Product X	Product Y
1	$90	$60
2	70	140
3	40	160

   a. What are your firm's profits if you charge $40 for product X and $60 for product Y?
   b. What are your profits if you charge $90 for product X and $160 for product Y?
   c. What are your profits if you charge $150 for a bundle containing one unit of product X and one unit of product Y?
   d. What are your firm's profits if you charge $210 for a bundle containing one unit of X and one unit of Y, but also sell the products individually at a price of $90 for product X and $160 for product Y?

8. A large firm has two divisions: an upstream division that is a monopoly supplier of an input whose only market is the downstream division that produces the final output. To produce one unit of the final output, the downstream division requires one unit of the input. If the inverse demand for the final output is $P = 1,000 - 80Q$, would the company's value be maximized by paying upstream and downstream divisional managers a percentage of their divisional profits? Explain.

9. According to some translations, Nobel Laureate Albert Einstein once said, "God does not play dice with the universe." Does this mean that a profit-maximizing firm would never use something like dice or a roulette wheel to help shape its pricing decisions? Explain.

10. Does the presence of online auction sites, such as eBay, make it easier or harder for traditional retailers and wholesalers to engage in profitable price discrimination? Explain.

PROBLEMS AND APPLICATIONS

11. You are the owner of a local Honda dealership. Unlike other dealerships in the area, you take pride in your "no-haggle" sales policy. Last year, your dealership earned record profits of $1.5 million. In your market, you compete against two other dealers, and the market-level price elasticity of demand for midsized Honda automobiles is –1.3. In each of the last five years, your dealership has sold more midsized automobiles than any other Honda dealership in the nation. This entitled your dealership to an additional 30 percent off the manufacturer's suggested retail price (MSRP) in each year. Taking this into account, your marginal cost of a midsized automobile is $12,000. What price should you charge for a midsized automobile if you expect to maintain your record profits?

12. You are a pricing analyst for QuantCrunch Corporation, a company that recently spent $15,000 to develop a statistical software package. To date, you only have one client. A recent internal study revealed that this client's demand for your software is $Q^d = 300 - 0.2P$ and that it would cost you $1,000 per unit to install and maintain software at this client's site. The CEO of your company recently asked you to construct a report that compares (1) the profit that results from charging this client a single per-unit price with (2) the profit that results from charging $1,450 for the first 10 units and $1,225 for each additional unit of software purchased. Construct this report, including in it a recommendation that would result in even higher profits.

13. You are the manager of a local sporting goods store and recently purchased a shipment of 60 sets of skis and ski bindings at a total cost of $25,000 (your wholesale supplier would not let you purchase the skis and bindings separately, nor would it let you purchase fewer than 60 sets). The community in which your store is located consists of many different types of skiers, ranging from advanced to beginners. From experience, you know that different skiers value skis and bindings differently. However, you cannot profitably price discriminate because you cannot prevent resale. There are about 20 advanced skiers who value skis at $400 and ski bindings at $275; 20 intermediate skiers who value skis at $300 and ski bindings at $400; and 20 beginning skiers who value skis at $200 and ski bindings at $350. Determine your optimal pricing strategy.

14. According to the Cahner's In-Stat Group, the number of worldwide wireless phone subscribers will soon reach the 1 billion mark. In the United States alone, the number of wireless subscribers is projected to grow by almost 17 million subscribers per year for the next five years. Contributing to the extensive growth are lower prices, larger geographic coverage, prepaid services, and Internet enabled phones. While the actual cost of a basic wireless phone is about $150, most wireless carriers offer their customers a "free" phone with a one-year wireless service agreement. Is this pricing strategy rational? Explain.

15. The American Baker's Association reports that annual sales of bakery goods last year rose 15 percent, driven by a 50 percent increase in the demand for bran muffins. Most of the increase was attributed to a report that diets rich in bran help prevent certain types of cancer. You are the manager of a bakery that produces and packages gourmet bran muffins, and you currently sell bran muffins in packages of three. However, as a result of this new report, a typical consumer's inverse demand for your bran muffins is now $P = 8 - 1.5Q$. If your cost of producing bran muffins is $C(Q) = 0.5Q$, determine the optimal number of bran muffins to sell in a single package and the optimal package price.

16. You own a franchise of rental car agencies in Florida. You recently read a report indicating that about 80 percent of all tourists visit Florida during the winter months in any given year, and that 60 percent of all tourists traveling to Florida by air rent automobiles. Travelers not planning ahead often have great difficulty finding rental cars due to high demand. However, during nonwinter months tourism drops dramatically, and travelers have no problem securing rental car reservations. Determine the optimal pricing strategy, and explain why it is the best pricing strategy.

17. Blue Skies Aviation is a manufacturer of small single-engine airplanes. The company is relatively small and prides itself on being the only manufacturer of customized airplanes. The company's high standard of quality is attributed to its refusal to purchase engines from outside vendors, and it preserves its competitive advantage by refusing to sell engines to competitors. To achieve maximum efficiencies, the company has organized itself into two divisions: a division that manufactures engines and a division that manufactures airplane bodies and assembles airplanes. Demand for Blue Skies' customized planes is given by $P = 812,000 - 3,000Q$. The cost of producing engines is $C_e(Q_e) = 5,000Q_e^2$, and the cost of assembling airplanes is $C_a(Q) = 12,000Q$. What problems would occur if the managers of each division were given incentives to maximize each division's profit separately? What price should the owners of Blue Skies set for engines in order to avoid this problem and maximize overall profits?

18. As a manager of a chain of movie theaters that are monopolies in their respective markets, you have noticed much higher demand on weekends than during the week. You therefore conducted a study that has revealed two different demand curves at your movie theaters. On weekends, the inverse demand function is $P = 20 - 0.001Q$; on weekdays, it is $P = 15 - 0.002Q$. You

acquire legal rights from movie producers to show their films at a cost of $25,000 per movie, plus a $2.50 "royalty" for each moviegoer entering your theaters (the average moviegoer in your market watches a movie only once). Devise a pricing strategy to maximize your firm's profits.

19. Many home improvement retailers like Home Depot and Lowe's have low-price guarantee policies. At a minimum, these guarantees promise to match a rival's price, and some promise to beat the lowest advertised price by a given percentage. Do these types of pricing strategies result in cutthroat Bertrand competition and zero economic profits? If not, why not? If so, suggest an alternative pricing strategy that will permit these firms to earn positive economic profits.

20. BAA is a private company that operates some of the largest airports in the United Kingdom, including Heathrow and Gatwick. Suppose that BAA recently commissioned your consulting team to prepare a report on traffic congestion at Heathrow. Your report indicates that Heathrow is more likely to experience significant congestion between July and September than at other time of the year. Based on your estimates, demand is $Q_1^d = 600 - 0.25P$, where Q_1^d is quantity demanded for runway time slots between July and September. Demand during the remaining nine months of the year is $Q_2^d = 220 - 0.1P$, where Q_2^d is quantity demanded for runway time slots. The additional cost BAA incurs each time one of the 80 different airlines utilizes the runway is £1,100 provided 80 or fewer airplanes use the runway on a given day. When more than 80 airplanes use Heathrow's runways, the additional cost incurred by BAA is £6 billion (the cost of building an additional runway and terminal). BAA currently charges airlines a uniform fee of £1,712.50 each time the runway is utilized. As a consultant to BAA, devise a pricing plan that would enhance Heathrow's profitability.

21. Suppose the European Union (EU) is investigating a proposed merger between two of the largest distillers of premium Scotch liquor. Based on some economists' definition of the relevant market, the two firms proposing to merge enjoyed a combined market share of about two-thirds, while another firm essentially controlled the remaining share of the market. Additionally, suppose that the (wholesale) market elasticity of demand for Scotch liquor is -1.3 and that it costs $16.20 to produce and distribute each liter of Scotch. Based only on these data, provide quantitative estimates of the likely pre- and postmerger prices in the wholesale market for premium Scotch liquor. In light of your estimates, are you surprised that the EU might raise concerns about potential anticompetitive effects of the proposed merger? Explain carefully.

22. An analyst for FoodMax estimates that the demand for its Brand X potato chips is given by $\ln Q_X^d = 12.14 - 2.8\ln P_X + 3.4P_Y + 0.7 \ln A_X$, where Q_X and P_X are the respective quantity and price of a four-ounce bag of Brand X potato

chips, P_Y is the price of a six-ounce bag sold by its only competitor, and A_X is FoodMax's level of advertising on Brand X potato chips. Last year, FoodMax sold 7 million bags of Brand X chips and spent $0.42 million on advertising. Its plant lease is $2.1 million (this annual contract includes utilities) and its depreciation charge for capital equipment was $2.8 million; payments to employees (all of whom earn annual salaries) were $0.8 million. The only other costs associated with manufacturing and distributing Brand X chips are the costs of raw potatoes, peanut oil, and bags; last year FoodMax spent $2.8 million on these items, which were purchased in competitive input markets. Based on this information, what is the profit-maximizing price for a bag of Brand X potato chips?

23. You manage a company that competes in an industry that is comprised of four equal-sized firms that produce similar products. A recent industry report indicates that the market is fairly saturated, in that a 10 percent industrywide price increase would lead to an 18 percent decline in units sold by all firms in the industry. Currently, Congress is considering legislation that would impose a tariff on a key input used by the industry. Your best estimate is that, if the legislation passes, your marginal cost will increase by $2. Based on this information, what price increase would you recommend if the tariff legislation is passed by Congress? Explain.

CONNECT EXERCISES

If your instructor has adopted Connect for the course and you are an active subscriber, you can practice with the questions presented above, along with many alternative versions of these questions. Your instructor may also assign a subset of these problems and/or their alternative versions as a homework assignment through Connect, allowing for immediate feedback of grades and correct answers.

CASE-BASED EXERCISES

Your instructor may assign additional problem-solving exercises (called *memos*) that require you to apply some of the tools you learned in this chapter to make a recommendation based on an actual business scenario. Some of these memos accompany the Time Warner case (pages 561–597 of your textbook). Additional memos, as well as data that may be useful for your analysis, are available online at www.mhhe.com/baye8e.

SELECTED READINGS

Adams, William J., and Yellen, Janet I., "Commodity Bundling and the Burden of Monopoly." *Quarterly Journal of Economics* 90, August 1976, pp. 475–98.

Baum, T., and Mudambi, R., "An Empirical-Analysis of Oligopolistic Hotel Pricing." *Annals of Tourism Research* 22, 1995, pp. 501–16.

Cain, Paul, and Macdonald, James M., "Telephone Pricing Structures: The Effects on Universal Service." *Journal of Regulatory Economics* 3(4), December 1991, pp. 293–308.

Carroll, K., and Coates, D., "Teaching Price Discrimination: Some Clarification." *Southern Economic Journal* 66, October 1999, pp. 466–80.

Jeitschko, T. D., "Issues in Price Discrimination: A Comment on and Addendum to 'Teaching Price Discrimination' by Carroll and Coates." *Southern Economic Journal* 68, July 2001, pp. 178–86.

Karni, Edi, and Levin, Dan, "Social Attributes and Strategic Equilibrium: A Restaurant Pricing Game." *Journal of Political Economy* 102(4), August 1994, pp. 822–40.

Masson, Robert, and Shaanan, Joseph, "Optimal Oligopoly Pricing and the Threat of Entry: Canadian Evidence." *International Journal of Industrial Organization* 5(3), September 1987, pp. 323–39.

McAfee, R. Preston, McMillan, John, and Whinston, Michael D., "Multiproduct Monopoly, Commodity Bundling, and Correlation of Values." *Quarterly Journal of Economics* 104(2), May 1989, pp. 371–83.

Oi, Walter Y., "A Disneyland Dilemma: Two-Part Tariffs for a Mickey Mouse Monopoly." *Quarterly Journal of Economics* 85, February 1971, pp. 77–96.

Romano, Richard E., "Double Moral Hazard and Resale Price Maintenance." *Rand Journal of Economics* 25(3), Autumn 1994, pp. 455–66.

Scitovsky, T., "The Benefits of Asymmetric Markets." *Journal of Economics Perspectives* 4(1), Winter 1990, pp. 135–48.

CHAPTER TWELVE

The Economics of Information

Firm Chickens Out in the FCC Spectrum Auction

The U.S. Congress passed legislation requiring the FCC to abandon its "public hearing" format for awarding radio spectrum licenses. As a result of the legislation, the FCC now auctions off spectrum rights; the high bidder in the auction obtains exclusive rights to the spectrum for a period of 10 years. In its first auction, the FCC auctioned off 10 licenses, netting the U.S. Treasury $600 million in revenues from the winning bidders.

To individual bidders like Bell South and McCaw (now part of AT&T), the auction format involved considerable uncertainty. While the value of a given license was virtually identical to all of the bidders, no single firm knew for sure what their profits would be if they won the auction. Each firm had its own private estimates of the value of a license, but these estimates differed across bidders.

One firm's private estimate of the value of a license was $85 million. This means that the firm estimated that it would earn $85 million over and above all costs (in present value terms) if it were awarded a license. Yet, this firm dropped out of the bidding when the auction price reached $80 million.

Why do you think the firm dropped out of the bidding when the price was below its private estimate of the value of a license?

Learning Objectives

After completing this chapter, you will be able to:

LO1 Identify strategies to manage risk and uncertainty, including diversification and optimal search strategies.

LO2 Calculate the profit-maximizing output and price in an environment of uncertainty.

LO3 Explain why asymmetric information about "hidden actions" or "hidden characteristics" can lead to moral hazard and adverse selection, and identify strategies for mitigating these potential problems.

LO4 Explain how differing auction rules and information structures impact the incentives in auctions, and determine the optimal bidding strategies in a variety of auctions with independent or correlated values.

INTRODUCTION

Throughout most of this book, we have assumed that participants in the market process—both consumers and firms—enjoy the benefits of perfect information. One need not look very hard at the real world to notice that this assumption is more fiction than fact. Nevertheless, our analyses in the preceding chapters can help us understand the market process. In fact, they are the basis for more complicated analysis that incorporates the effects of uncertainty and imperfect information.

More advanced courses in economics build on the foundations set forth in earlier chapters of this book by relaxing the assumption that people enjoy perfect information. While formal theoretical models of decision making in the presence of imperfect information are well beyond the scope and purpose of this book, it is useful to present an overview of some of the more important aspects of decision making under uncertainty. First, we will describe more formally what we mean by *uncertainty* and examine the impact of uncertainty on consumer behavior. Then we will briefly demonstrate means by which the manager can cope with risk. Finally, we will look at several important implications of uncertainty on the market process, including auction markets.

THE MEAN AND THE VARIANCE

The easiest way to summarize information about uncertain outcomes is to use the statistical concepts of the mean and the variance of a random variable. More specifically, suppose there is some uncertainty regarding the value of some variable. The random variable, x, might represent profits, the price of output, or consumer income. Since x is a random variable, we cannot be sure what its actual value is. All we know is that with given probabilities, different values of the random variable will occur. For example, suppose someone promises to pay you (in dollars) whatever number comes up when a fair die is tossed. If x represents the payment to you, it is clear that you cannot be sure how much you will be paid. If you are lucky, you will roll a 6 and be paid $6. If you are unlucky, you will roll a 1 and receive $1. The probability that any number between 1 and 6 is rolled is 1/6, because there are six sides on the die. The expected value (or mean) of x is given by

$$E[x] = \frac{1}{6}(\$1) + \frac{1}{6}(\$2) + \frac{1}{6}(\$3) + \frac{1}{6}(\$4) + \frac{1}{6}(\$5) + \frac{1}{6}(\$6) = \$3.50$$

In other words, even though you do not know for certain how much you will be paid when you roll the die, on average you will earn $3.50.

mean (expected value)
The sum of the probabilities that different outcomes will occur multiplied by the resulting payoffs.

The *mean* or *expected value* of a random variable, x, is defined as the sum of the probabilities that different outcomes will occur times the resulting payoffs. Formally, if the possible outcomes of the random variable are $x_1, x_2, \ldots, x_n$ and the corresponding probabilities of the outcomes are $q_1, q_2, \ldots, q_n$, the expected value of x is given by

$$E[x] = q_1 x_1 + q_2 x_2 + \cdots + q_n x_n$$

where $q_1 + q_2 + \cdots + q_n = 1$.

The mean of a random variable thus collapses information about the likelihood of different outcomes into a single statistic. This is a very convenient way of economizing on the amount of information needed to make decisions.

The mean provides information about the average value of a random variable but it yields no information about the degree of risk associated with the random variable. To illustrate the importance of considering risk in making decisions, consider the following two options:

Option 1: Flip a coin. If it comes up heads, you receive $1; if it comes up tails, you pay $1.

Option 2: Flip a coin. If it comes up heads, you receive $10; if it comes up tails, you pay $10.

Even though the stakes are much higher under option 2 than under option 1, each option has an expected value of zero. On average, you will neither make nor lose money with either option. To see this, note that there is a 50–50 chance the coin will land on heads. Thus, the expected value of option 1 is

$$E_{Option\ 1}[x] = \frac{1}{2}(\$1) + \frac{1}{2}(-\$1) = 0$$

and the expected value of option 2 is

$$E_{Option\ 2}[x] = \frac{1}{2}(\$10) + \frac{1}{2}(-\$10) = 0$$

The two options have the same expected value but are inherently different in nature. By summarizing information about the options using the mean, we have lost some information about the risk associated with the two options. Regardless of which option you choose, you will either gain money or lose money by flipping the coin. Under option 1, half the time you will make $1 more than the average and half the time you will make $1 less than the average. Under option 2, the deviation from the mean of the actual gain or loss is much greater: Half the time you will make $10 more than the average, and half the time you will lose $10 more than the average. Since these deviations from the mean are much larger under option 2 than under option 1, it is natural to think of option 2 as being more risky than option 1.

While the preceding discussion provides a rationale for calling option 2 more risky than option 1, it is often convenient for the manager to have a number that summarizes the risk associated with random outcomes. The most common measure of *risk* is the variance, which depends in a special way on the deviations of possible outcomes from the mean. The *variance* of a random variable is the sum of the probabilities that different outcomes will occur times the squared deviations from the mean of the random variable. Formally, if the possible outcomes of the random variable are $x_1, x_2, \ldots, x_n$, their corresponding probabilities are $q_1, q_2, \ldots, q_n$, and the expected value of x is given by $E[x]$, then the variance of x is given by

variance
The sum of the probabilities that different outcomes will occur multiplied by the squared deviations from the mean of the resulting payoffs.

$$\sigma^2 = q_1(x_1 - E[x])^2 + q_2(x_2 - E[x])^2 + \cdots + q_n(x_n - E[x])^2$$

The *standard deviation* is simply the square root of the variance:

$$\sigma = \sqrt{\sigma^2} = \sqrt{q_1(x_1 - E[x])^2 + q_2(x_2 - E[x])^2 + \cdots + q_n(x_n - E[x])^2}$$

Since a larger variance implies a larger standard deviation (and vice versa), it may seem that the standard deviation provides no useful information beyond that contained in the variance. However, the standard deviation does have some very practical applications. In particular, the outcomes for any random variable always will fall within two standard deviations of its mean at least 75 percent of the time. For example, if a random variable, x, has mean of 5 and standard deviation of 1, you can be sure x will take on a value between 3 $[= 5 - 2(1)]$ and 7 $[= 5 + 2(1)]$ at least 75 percent of the time.

Let us apply these formulas to our coin tossing examples to see how the variance can be used to obtain a number that summarizes the risk associated with the options. In each case, only two possible outcomes occur with equal probabilities, so $q_1 = q_2 = 1/2$. The mean of each option is zero. Thus, the variance of option 1 is

$$\sigma^2_{Option\ 1} = \frac{1}{2}(1 - 0)^2 + \frac{1}{2}(-1 - 0)^2 = \frac{1}{2}(1) + \frac{1}{2}(1) = 1$$

The variance of option 2 is

$$\sigma^2_{Option\ 2} = \frac{1}{2}(10 - 0)^2 + \frac{1}{2}(-10 - 0)^2 = \frac{1}{2}(100) + \frac{1}{2}(100) = 100$$

Since

$$\sigma^2_{Option\ 1} = 1 < \sigma^2_{Option\ 2} = 100$$

option 2 is more risky than option 1. Since the standard deviation is the square root of the variance, the standard deviation of option 1 is 1 and the standard deviation of option 2 is 10.

Demonstration Problem 12–1

The manager of XYZ Company is introducing a new product that will yield $1,000 in profits if the economy does not go into a recession. However, if a recession occurs, demand for the normal good will fall so sharply that the company will lose $4,000. If economists project that there is a 10 percent chance the economy will go into a recession, what are the expected profits to XYZ Company of introducing the new product? How risky is the introduction of the new product?

Answer:
If there is a 10 percent chance of a recession, there is a 90 percent chance that there will not be a recession. Using the formula for the expected value of a random variable, the expected profits of introducing the new product are found to be

$$E[x] = q_1 x_1 + q_2 x_2 = .1(-\$4,000) + .9(\$1,000) = \$500$$

Thus, the expected profits of introducing the new product are $500. Using variance as a measure of risk,

$$\sigma^2 = .1(-4,000 - 500)^2 + .9(1,000 - 500)^2 = 2,250,000$$

UNCERTAINTY AND CONSUMER BEHAVIOR

Now that you understand how to calculate the mean and variance of an uncertain outcome, we will see how the presence of *uncertainty* affects economic decisions of both consumers and managers.

Risk Aversion

In Chapter 4 we assumed consumers have preferences for bundles of goods, which were assumed to be known with certainty. We now will extend our analysis to preferences over uncertain outcomes.

Let F and G represent two uncertain prospects. F might represent the prospects associated with buying 100 shares of stock in company F and G the prospects associated with buying 100 shares of stock in company G. When you purchase a stock, you are uncertain what your actual profits or losses will be; all you know is that there is some mean and variance in return associated with each stock. Different people exhibit different preferences for the same set of prospects. You may prefer F to G, while a friend prefers G to F. It simply is a matter of taste for risky prospects.

Because attitudes toward risk will differ among consumers, we must introduce some additional terminology to differentiate among these attitudes. First, a *risk-averse* person prefers a sure amount of $M to a risky prospect with an expected value of $M. A *risk-loving* individual prefers a risky prospect with an expected value of $M to a sure amount of $M. Finally, a *risk-neutral* individual is indifferent between a risky prospect with an expected value of $M and a sure amount of $M.

It is possible that for some prospects individuals will be risk loving, while for others they will be risk averse. For small gambles people typically are risk loving, whereas for larger gambles they are risk averse. You may be willing to bet a quarter that you can guess whether a flipped coin will come up heads or tails. The expected value of this gamble is zero. In this instance, you are behaving as a risk lover: You prefer the gamble with an expected payoff of zero to not playing (receiving zero for certain). If the stakes are raised to, say, $25,000, you will most likely choose not to bet. In this instance, you will prefer not betting (zero for certain) to the gamble with an expected value of zero.

Managerial Decisions with Risk-Averse Consumers

For gambles with nontrivial outcomes, most individuals are risk averse. Here we will point out some implications of risk-averse consumers for optimal managerial decisions.

Product Quality. The analysis of risk can be used to analyze situations where consumers are uncertain about product quality. For instance, suppose a consumer regularly purchases a particular brand of car wax and thus is relatively certain about the underlying quality and characteristics of the product. If the consumer is risk averse, when will she be willing to purchase a car wax newly introduced to the market?

risk averse
Preferring a sure amount of $M to a risky prospect with an expected value of $M.

risk loving
Preferring a risky prospect with an expected value of $M to a sure amount of $M.

risk neutral
Indifferent between a risky prospect with an expected value of $M and a sure amount of $M.

Risk Aversion and the Value of Selling the Firm: The St. Petersburg Paradox

Corporations often are sold at a price that seems much lower than the expected value of future profits. Before you conclude the market is not rational, ask yourself how much you would be willing to pay for the right to toss a coin when

- You receive 2 cents if the first heads is on the first flip.
- You receive 4 cents if the first heads is on the second flip.
- You receive 8 cents if the first heads is on the third flip.
- More generally, you receive 2^n cents if the first heads is on the nth toss.

Since coin flips are independent events, the expected value of participating in this coin toss gamble is

$$E[x] = \left(\frac{1}{2}\right)2 + \left(\frac{1}{2}\right)^2 2^2 + \left(\frac{1}{2}\right)^3 2^3 + \left(\frac{1}{2}\right)^4 2^4 + \cdots$$
$$= 1 + 1 + 1 + 1 + \cdots$$
$$= \infty \text{ cents}$$

Thus, the expected value of this gamble is infinity: On average, you will make an infinite amount of money if you play this game. Of course, we know of no person willing to give up the world to play this particular game. We have found that in a class of 200 students, the most people will pay is about $2, which is considerably lower than the infinite expected value of the gamble. This outcome is known as the *St. Petersburg paradox*.

The answer to this paradox is that it is the utility individuals receive from winning a gamble, not the money itself, that is important. The satisfaction you derive from winning your first $1 million is much greater than that derived from winning your second $1 million, and so on. This diminishing marginal utility of income gives rise to risk aversion, meaning that individuals are willing to pay less than the expected value. For the case of the coin flip above, the difference between the expected value and the amount an individual is willing to pay is substantial. The same can be true when corporations are up for sale.

A risk-averse consumer prefers a sure thing to an uncertain prospect of equal expected value. Thus, if the consumer expects the new car wax to work just as well as the one she regularly purchases, then, other things equal, she will not buy the new product. The reason is that there is risk associated with using a new product; the new wax may make a car look much better than the old wax, or it may damage the paint on the car. When the consumer weighs these possibilities and concludes that the new wax is expected to be just as good as the wax she now uses, she decides not to buy the new product. The consumer prefers the sure thing (the current brand) to the risky prospect (the new product).

Firms use two primary tactics to induce risk-averse consumers to try a new product. First, the firm's manager may lower the price of the new product below that of the existing product to compensate the consumer for the risk associated with trying the new product. When firms send out free samples, they essentially use this technique because to the consumer the price of the new product is zero.

Alternatively, the manager can attempt to make the consumer think that the expected quality of the new product is higher than the certain quality of the old product. Typically firms do this using comparison advertising. For example, an advertisement might show 50 cars being waxed with a new wax and 50 cars being waxed with competitors' products; then the cars are repeatedly washed until only the 50 cars waxed with the new product still shine. If consumers are convinced by such an advertisement, they may go ahead and purchase the new product because its higher expected quality offsets the risk associated with trying a new product.

Chain Stores. Risk aversion also explains why it may be in a firm's interest to become part of a chain store instead of remaining independent. For example, suppose a consumer drives through Smalltown, USA, and decides to eat lunch. There are two restaurants in the town: a local diner and a national hamburger chain. While the consumer knows nothing about this particular diner, his experience suggests that local diners typically are either very good or very bad. On the other hand, national hamburger chains have standardized menus and ingredients; the type and quality of product offered are relatively certain, albeit of average quality. Because the consumer is risk averse, he will choose to eat at the national chain unless he expects the product of the local diner to be sufficiently better than the chain restaurant.

There is nothing special about the restaurant example; similar examples apply to retailing outlets, transmission shops, and other types of stores. While there are exceptions, out-of-town visitors typically prefer to make purchases at chain stores. Local customers are in a better position to know for certain the type and quality of products offered at stores in their town and may shop at the local store instead of the national chain. The key thing to notice is that even if the local store offers a better product than the national chain, the national chain can remain in business if the number of out-of-town customers is large enough.

Insurance. The fact that consumers are risk averse implies that they are willing to pay to avoid risk. This is precisely why individuals choose to buy insurance on their homes and automobiles. By buying insurance, individuals give up a small (relative to potential losses) amount of money to eliminate the risk associated with a catastrophic loss. For example, if a $100,000 house burns down, an uninsured homeowner loses $100,000; if it does not burn down, the homeowner loses nothing. Most homeowners are willing to pay several hundred dollars to avoid this risk. If the house burns down, the insurance company reimburses the homeowner for the loss. Thus, to a consumer, insurance represents a purchase of a "sure thing"—a house that is worth $100,000 regardless of whether or not it burns down.

Some firms give insurance to customers through "money-back guarantees." Other firms sell a form of insurance to customers. For example, many car manufacturers sell extended-warranty plans to customers whereby the company agrees to pay repair costs. This eliminates the risk associated with owning a car, thus making car ownership more attractive to risk-averse consumers.

Consumer Search

Up until now, we have assumed consumers know the prices of goods with certainty. The analysis is more complicated in situations where consumers do not know the prices charged by different firms for the same product.

Suppose consumers do not know the prices charged by different stores for some homogeneous commodity. Suppose there are numerous stores charging different prices for the same brand of watch. A consumer would like to purchase the product from the store charging the lowest price, but she does not know the prices being charged by individual stores. Let c denote the cost of obtaining information about the price charged by an individual store. For example, c might represent the cost of making a phone call, the cost of traveling to a store to find out what price it charges for a watch, or the cost of looking up a price in a catalog or on the Internet.

Suppose that three-quarters of the stores in the market charge $100 for a particular brand of watch and one-quarter charge $40. If the consumer locates a store that sells a watch for $40, she clearly should stop searching; no store charges a price below $40.

What should a risk-neutral consumer do if she visits a store that charges $100? For simplicity, suppose the consumer searches with *free recall* and with *replacement*. By free recall we mean that the consumer is free to return to the store at any time to purchase the watch for $100. The fact that a consumer searches with replacement means that the distribution of prices charged by other firms does not change just because the consumer has learned that the one store charges $100 for a watch. Under these assumptions, if the consumer searches again, one-quarter of the time she will find a price of $40 and thus will save $100 − $40 = $60. But three-quarters of the time the consumer will find a price of $100, and the gains from having searched will be zero. Thus, the expected benefit of an additional search is

$$EB = \frac{1}{4}(\$100 - \$40) + \frac{3}{4}(0) = \$15$$

In other words, if the consumer searches for a price lower than $100, one-quarter of the time she will save $60, and three-quarters of the time she will save nothing. The expected benefit of searching for a lower price thus is $15.

The consumer should search for a lower price so long as the expected benefits are greater than the cost of an additional search. For example, if the cost of each search is $5, the consumer will find it in her interest to continue to search for a lower price. But if the cost of searching once more for a lower price is $20, it does not pay to continue searching for a better price.

This example reveals that the expected benefits of searching depend on the lowest price found during previous searches. If the lowest known price is p, the expected benefits (EB) from searching for a price lower than p slopes upward, as in Figure 12–1. Intuitively, as lower prices are found, the savings associated with finding even lower prices diminish.

reservation price
The price at which a consumer is indifferent between purchasing at that price and searching for a lower price.

Figure 12–1 also illustrates the optimal search strategy for a consumer. The cost of each search is the horizontal line labeled c. If the consumer finds a price higher than R, the expected benefits of searching are greater than the cost, and the consumer should reject this price (continue to search for a lower price). On the other hand, if the consumer locates a price below R, it is best to accept this price (stop searching and purchase the product). This is because the expected benefits of searching for an even lower price are less than the cost of searching. If the con-

FIGURE 12–1 The Optimal Search Strategy

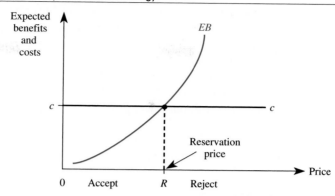

sumer located a price of R, she would be indifferent between purchasing at that price and continuing to search for a lower price.

The *reservation price, R,* is the price at which the consumer is indifferent between purchasing at that price and searching for a lower price. Formally, if $EB(p)$ is the expected benefit of searching for a price lower than p, and c represents the cost per search, the reservation price satisfies the condition

$$EB(R) = c$$

Principle	**The Consumer's Search Rule**
	The optimal search rule is such that the consumer rejects prices above the reservation price (R) and accepts prices below the reservation price. Stated differently, the optimal search strategy is to search for a better price when the price charged by a firm is above the reservation price and stop searching when a price below the reservation price is found.

What happens if the cost of searching increases? As Figure 12–2 shows, an increase in search costs shifts up the horizontal line to c^*, resulting in a higher reservation price, R^*. This means the consumer will now find more prices acceptable and

FIGURE 12–2 An Increase in Search Costs Raises the Reservation Price

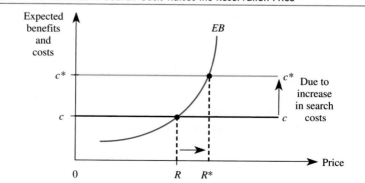

will search less intensively. Similarly, if the cost of searching for lower prices falls, the consumer will search more heavily for lower prices.

Our analysis of a consumer's decision to shop for lower prices can be used to aid managers in setting prices. In particular, when consumers have imperfect information about prices and search costs are low, the optimal prices set by a manager will be lower than when search costs are high. Moreover, managers must be careful not to price their products above consumers' reservation price; doing so will induce consumers to seek out lower prices at other firms. If you observe a large number of consumers "browsing" in your store but not making purchases, it may be a sign that your prices are set above their reservation price and that they have decided to continue to search for a lower price.

UNCERTAINTY AND THE FIRM

We have seen that the presence of uncertainty has a direct impact on consumer behavior and that the firm manager must take these effects into account to fully understand the nature of consumer demand. Uncertainty also affects the manager's input and output decisions. In this section, we will examine the implications of uncertainty for production and output decisions. It is important to point out that all our analysis of the impact of uncertainty on consumer behavior is directly applicable to the firm's manager. We will briefly discuss extensions of the analysis of uncertainty to highlight its direct influence on managerial decisions.

Risk Aversion

Just as consumers have preferences regarding risky prospects, so does the manager of the firm. A manager who is risk neutral is interested in maximizing expected profits; the variance of profits does not affect a risk-neutral manager's decisions. If the manager is risk averse, he or she may prefer a risky project with a lower expected value if it has lower risk than one with a higher expected value. Alternatively, if given a choice between a risky project with an expected return of $1 million and a certain return of $1 million, a risk-averse manager will prefer the sure thing. For the manager to be willing to undertake a risky project, the project must offer a higher expected return than a comparable "safe" project. Just how much higher depends on the manager's particular risk preferences.

Whenever a manager faces a decision to choose among risky projects, it is important to carefully evaluate the risks and expected returns of the projects and then to document this evaluation. The reason is simple. Risky prospects may result in bad outcomes. A manager is less likely to get fired over a bad outcome if she or he provides evidence that, based on the information available at the time the decision was made, the decision was sound. A convenient way to do this is to use mean-variance analysis, as the next demonstration problem illustrates.

INSIDE BUSINESS 12–2

The Value of Information in Online Markets

Shoppers who use price comparison sites such as Shopper.com, Nextag.com, or Kelkoo.com gain information about the prices that different online retailers charge for a given product. This permits them to easily click through to the firm charging the lowest price to purchase the item. Consumers on the wrong side of the so-called "digital divide" are not privy to this information, and on average pay higher prices than "informed" consumers who are able to purchase at the lowest possible price. The value of information is the average savings that an informed consumer enjoys as a result of being able to purchase at the lowest price.

If you visit *Nash-equilibrium.com* you can track the value of information and a variety of other measures related to online retail markets. This site is based on ongoing academic research by professors at Indiana University's Kelley School of Business, Berkeley's Haas Business School, and the Business School at Bentley University. The charts are based on millions of prices for thousands of products sold online.

The screenshot below shows historical data for the value of information. As you can see from the graph, the value of information fluctuated between 16 and 19 percent between 2006 and 2007. This means that during this period, consumers using price comparison sites to gather price information saved an average of 16 to 19 percent on purchases compared to those not using such sites.

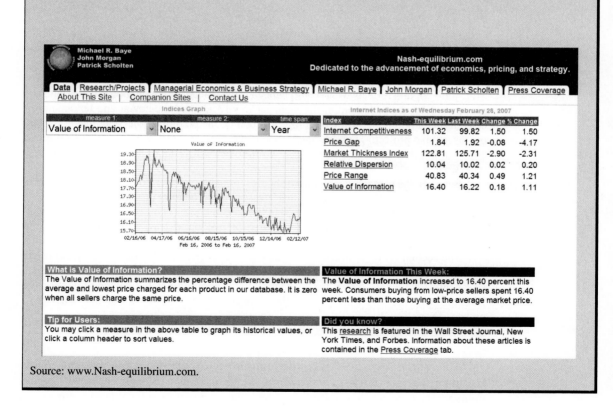

Source: www.Nash-equilibrium.com.

Demonstration Problem 12–2

A risk-averse manager is considering two projects. The first project involves expanding the market for bologna; the second involves expanding the market for caviar. There is a 10 percent chance of a recession and a 90 percent chance of an economic boom. During a boom, the bologna project will lose $10,000 whereas the caviar project will earn $20,000. During a recession, the bologna project will earn $12,000 and the caviar project will lose $8,000. If the alternative is earning $3,000 on a safe asset (say, a Treasury bill), what should the manager do? Why?

Answer:

The first thing the manager should do is summarize the available information to document the relevant alternatives:

Project	Boom (90%)	Recession (10%)	Mean	Standard Deviation
Bologna	−$10,000	$12,000	−$ 7,800	6,600
Caviar	20,000	−8,000	17,200	8,400
Joint	10,000	4,000	9,400	1,800
T-bill	3,000	3,000	3,000	0

The "joint" option reflects what would happen if the manager adopted both the bologna and caviar projects. For example, if the manager jointly adopted the caviar and bologna projects, during a boom the firm would lose $10,000 on the bologna project but make $20,000 on the caviar project. Thus, during a boom the joint project will result in a return of $10,000. Similar calculations reveal the joint project will yield a return of $4,000 during a recession.

Based on the preceding table, what should a prudent manager do? The first thing to note is that the manager should not invest in a Treasury bill. The joint project will generate profits of $4,000 during a recession and $10,000 during a boom. Thus, regardless of what happens to the economy, the manager is assured of making at least $4,000 under the joint project, which is greater than the return of $3,000 on the Treasury bill.

The second thing to notice is that the expected (mean) profits of the bologna project are negative. A risk-averse manager would never choose this project (neither would a risk-neutral manager). Thus, the manager should adopt either the caviar project or the joint project. Precisely which choice the manager makes will depend on his or her preferences for risk.

The returns associated with the joint project in the preceding problem reveal the important notion of *diversification,* which is taught in basic business finance courses. By investing in multiple projects, the manager may be able to reduce risk.

This is merely a technical version of the old adage, "Don't put all your eggs in one basket." As the example reveals, there are benefits to diversification, but whether it is optimal to diversify depends on a manager's risk preference and the incentives provided to the manager to avoid risk.

While many managers are risk averse, generally the owners of the firm (the stockholders) want the manager to behave in a risk-neutral manner. A manager who is risk neutral cares only about the expected value of a risky project, not the underlying risk. More specifically, a risk-neutral manager's objective is to take actions that maximize the expected present value of the firm, that is, actions that maximize expected profits. A risk-neutral manager would choose a risky action over a sure thing provided the expected profits of the risky prospect exceeded those of the sure thing.

Why would shareholders want managers to take actions that maximize expected profits even when doing so might involve considerable risk? Shareholders can pool and diversify risks by purchasing shares of many different firms to eliminate the systematic risk associated with the firm's operation. It therefore is inefficient for managers to spend time and money attempting to diversify against risk when doing so will reduce the firm's expected profits. Thus, while the owners of a firm may be risk averse, they prefer managers who make risk-neutral decisions.

A simple example will illustrate why shareholders desire managers to behave in a risk-neutral manner. Suppose a manager must decide which of two projects to undertake. The first project is risky, with a 50–50 chance of yielding profits of $2 million or zero. The second project will yield a certain return of $900,000. The expected profits earned by the risky project are $1 million, which is greater than those of the project yielding a certain return. But the variance of the risky project is greater than that of the certain one; half the time profits will be zero, half the time they will be $2 million. Why would shareholders want the manager to undertake the risky project even though it has greater risk? The answer is that shareholders can purchase shares of many firms in the economy. If the managers of each of these firms choose the risky project, the projects will not pay off for some firms but will pay off for others. If the profits earned by one firm are independent of those earned by other firms, then, on average, the unfavorable outcomes experienced by some firms will be more than offset by the favorable outcomes at other firms. This situation is similar to flipping a coin: Flip a coin once, and you cannot be sure it will turn up heads; flip a coin many times, and you can rest assured that half the flips will be heads. Similarly, when shareholders own shares of many different firms, each of which takes on risky projects, they can rest assured that half of the firms will earn $2 million.

For these reasons, as a manager you are likely to be given an incentive to maximize the expected profits of your firm. If you are provided with such incentives, you will behave in a risk-neutral manner even if you and the owners of the firm are risk averse.

Producer Search

Just as consumers search for stores charging low prices, producers search for low prices of inputs. When there is uncertainty regarding the prices of inputs, optimizing firms employ optimal search strategies. The search strategy for a risk-neutral manager will be precisely the same as that of a risk-neutral consumer. Rather than repeat the basic theory, it is more useful to illustrate these concepts with an example.

Demonstration Problem 12–3

A risk-neutral manager is attempting to hire a worker. All workers in the market are of identical quality but differ with respect to the wage at which they are willing to work. Suppose half of the workers in the labor market are willing to work for a salary of $40,000 and half will accept a salary of $38,000. The manager spends three hours interviewing a given worker and values this time at $300. The first worker the manager interviews says he will work only if paid $40,000. Should the firm manager make him an offer, or interview another worker?

Answer:

This is an optimal search problem with a search cost of $300. If the manager searches for another worker, half of the time she will find one willing to work for $38,000 and thus will save $2,000. But half of the time the manager will find a worker just like the one she chose not to hire, and the effort will have been for nothing. Thus, the expected benefit of interviewing another worker is

$$EB = \frac{1}{2}(\$2,000) + \frac{1}{2}(0) = \$1,000$$

Since this is greater than the cost of $300, the manager should not hire the worker but instead search for a worker willing to work for $38,000.

Profit Maximization

The basic principles of profit maximization can also be modified to deal with uncertainty. To illustrate how the basic principles of profit maximization are affected by the presence of uncertainty, let us suppose the manager is risk neutral and demand is uncertain. Recall that the goal of a risk-neutral manager is to maximize expected profits.

The risk-neutral manager must determine what output to produce before she is certain of the demand for the product. Because demand is uncertain, revenues are uncertain. This means that to maximize expected profits, the manager should equate expected marginal revenue with marginal cost in setting output:

$$E[MR] = MC$$

The reason is simple. If expected marginal revenue exceeded marginal cost, the manager could increase expected profits by expanding output. The production of another unit of output would, on average, add more to revenue than it would to costs. Similarly, if expected marginal revenue were less than marginal cost, the manager should reduce output. This is because by reducing output, the firm would reduce costs by more than it would reduce expected revenue.

Thus we see that when the manager is risk neutral, profit maximization under uncertain demand is very similar to profit maximization under certainty. All the manager needs to do is adjust the corresponding formula to represent the expected marginal revenue.

For a video walkthrough of this problem, visit www.mhhe.com/baye8e

Demonstration Problem 12–4

Appleway Industries produces apple juice and sells it in a competitive market. The firm's manager must determine how much juice to produce before he knows what the market (competitive) price will be. Economists estimate that there is a 30 percent chance the market price will be \$2 per gallon and a 70 percent chance it will be \$1 when the juice hits the market. If the firm's cost function is $C = 200 + .0005Q^2$, how much juice should be produced to maximize expected profits? What are the expected profits of Appleway Industries?

Answer:

The profits of Appleway Industries are given by

$$\pi = pQ - 200 - .0005Q^2$$

Since price is uncertain, the firm's revenues and profits are uncertain. For a competitive firm, $MR = p$; thus, marginal revenue also is uncertain. Marginal cost is given by $MC = .001Q$. To maximize expected profits, the manager equates expected price with marginal cost:

$$E[p] = .001Q$$

The expected price is given by

$$E[p] = .3(2) + .7(1) = .60 + .70 = \$1.30$$

Equating this with marginal cost, we obtain

$$1.30 = .001Q$$

Solving for Q, we find that the output that maximizes expected profits is $Q = 1,300$ gallons. Expected profits for Appleway Industries are

$$E[\pi] = E[p]Q - 200 - .0005Q^2$$

$$= 1.30(1,300) - 200 - .0005(1,300)^2$$

$$= 1,690 - 200 - 845 = \$645$$

Thus, Appleway Industries can expect to make \$645 in profits.

While our analysis of profit maximization under uncertainty is far from exhaustive, it points out that much of our previous analysis can be easily extended to deal with uncertainty. In fact, these extensions are important topics in more advanced courses in economics.

UNCERTAINTY AND THE MARKET

The presence of uncertainty can have a profound impact on the ability of markets to efficiently allocate resources. In this section, we examine some problems created in markets when there is uncertainty. We also show how managers and other market participants can overcome some of these problems.

Asymmetric Information

When some people in the market have better information than others, the people with the least information may choose not to participate in a market. To see why this is so, suppose someone offers to sell you a box full of money. You do not know how much money is in the box, but she does. Should you choose to buy the box?

The answer is no. Since she knows how much money is in the box, she will never sell you the box unless you offer her more for the box than is in it. Suppose she knows the box contains $10. If you offered her $6 for the box, she would have no incentive to engage in the transaction. If you offered her $12, she would gladly sell you the box, and you would lose $2.

asymmetric information
A situation that exists when some people have better information than others.

As the preceding example reveals, *asymmetric information* can result in a situation where people with the least information rationally refuse to participate in the market. If you think of the box in the example as being a company whose stock is traded on the NASDAQ or the New York Stock Exchange, it should be clear why there is so much concern over insider trading—the buying and selling of stocks by persons who have privileged information about a firm. If some people know for certain what a stock will sell for tomorrow (say, due to a takeover) and others do not, asymmetric information exists. The only time insiders will purchase stock is when they know it is selling at a price below what it is worth; the only time insiders will sell stock is when they know it is selling at a premium over what it is worth. If people know that insiders regularly trade in the stock market, people who are not insiders may rationally choose to stay out of the stock market to avoid paying too much for a stock or selling it for too little. In extreme cases, this situation can completely destroy the stock market, as no one is willing to buy or sell shares of firms' stock. For this reason, and as discussed in Chapter 14, there are laws that restrict persons with privileged information about a firm from buying shares of that firm's stock.

Asymmetric information between consumers and the firm can affect firm profits. For example, suppose a firm invests in developing a new product that it knows to be superior to existing products in the market. Consumers, on the other hand, are unlikely to know whether the new product is truly superior to existing products or whether the firm is falsely claiming the product to be superior. If the degree of asymmetric information is severe enough, consumers may refuse to buy a new product even if it really is better than existing products. The reason is that they do not know the product is indeed superior.

Asymmetric information affects many other managerial decisions, including hiring workers and issuing credit to customers. In particular, job applicants have much better information about their own capabilities than does the person in charge of hiring new workers. A job applicant who claims to have excellent skills may be lying or telling the truth; the personnel manager has less information than the applicant. This is why firms spend considerable sums designing tests to evaluate job applicants, doing background checks, and the like. The basic reason for these types of expenditures is to provide the firm with better information about the capabilities and tendencies of job applicants. Similarly, a consumer who wishes to make a purchase on credit has much better information about his own ability to pay off the debt than does the creditor. Of course, every consumer seeking to purchase on credit will claim that he or she will pay off the debt. Asymmetric information makes it difficult for the firm to know whether a person actually will pay off the debt. In fact, firms pay sizable sums to credit bureaus to obtain better information about their credit customers. These expenditures reduce asymmetric information and make it more difficult for customers to take advantage of it.

With this overview of some problems that can arise in the presence of asymmetric information, we turn now to two specific manifestations of asymmetric information: adverse selection and moral hazard. These two concepts are often difficult to distinguish, so it is useful first to distinguish between the types of asymmetric information that generally lead to adverse selection and moral hazard.

hidden characteristics
Things one party to a transaction knows about itself but which are unknown by the other party.

hidden action
Action taken by one party in a relationship that cannot be observed by the other party.

adverse selection
Situation where individuals have hidden characteristics and in which a selection process results in a pool of individuals with undesirable characteristics.

Adverse selection generally arises when an individual has *hidden characteristics* —characteristics that she knows but that are unknown by the other party in an economic transaction. In our example of the job applicant, for instance, the worker knows his own abilities but the employer does not. The worker's ability thus reflects a hidden characteristic. In contrast, moral hazard generally occurs when one party takes *hidden actions*—actions that it knows another party cannot observe. For example, if the manager of a firm cannot monitor a worker's effort, then the worker's effort represents a hidden action. Just as it is often difficult to distinguish between ability (a characteristic) and effort (an action), it is sometimes difficult to distinguish between adverse selection and moral hazard.

Adverse Selection

Adverse selection refers to a situation where a selection process results in a pool of individuals with economically undesirable characteristics. A simple example highlights the basic issues involved in adverse selection.

Consider an industry in which all firms allow their employees five days of paid sick leave. Suppose one firm decides to increase the number of paid sick leave days from 5 to 10 to attract more workers. If the workers have hidden characteristics— that is, if the firm cannot distinguish between healthy and unhealthy workers—the plan will probably lure many workers away from other firms. But what type of workers is the firm most likely to attract? Workers who know they are frequently ill and thus who value sick leave the most. Workers who know they never get sick will have little incentive to leave their current employers, but those who are frequently sick will. From the firm's point of view, the policy attracts undesirable workers. In economic terms, the policy results in adverse selection.

Adverse selection explains why people with poor driving records find it difficult to buy automobile insurance. Suppose there are two types of people with bad

INSIDE BUSINESS 12–3

Groucho Marx the Economist?

One of the most famous American comedians of all time, Groucho Marx, was renowned for his witty one-liners. One of his best-known one-liners goes like this: "Please accept my resignation. I don't care to belong to any club that will have me as a member." On its surface, the statement sounds absurd. However, it is also a very subtle and clever example of adverse selection at work.

To illustrate, first note that the asymmetric information in this case concerns the quality of a club. Groucho does not know the quality level of a given club, but each club knows its own quality level. Further, each club can observe the type of person Groucho is, and decide whether to let him join. To see

why Groucho may choose to reject every club that offers him membership, consider the following simple scenario. Suppose there are two clubs—a high-quality club and a low-quality club. Groucho cannot tell which is which, but only is willing to join the high-quality club. However, knowing the type of person Groucho is, only the low-quality club will offer him membership. The process of deciding whether to admit Groucho has generated adverse selection—by limiting Groucho to the set of clubs willing to admit him, he is left with only the low-quality club. Hence, even though Groucho cannot tell either club's quality by looking at it, he knows only the low-quality club will allow him to join, and so rejects the offer.

driving records: (1) those who are poor drivers and frequently have accidents and (2) those who are good drivers but, due purely to bad luck, have been involved in numerous accidents in the past. Past accidents by bad drivers are a result of their driving habits and are good indicators of the number of expected future accidents. Past accidents by good drivers, on the other hand, are not a good indicator of the expected number of future accidents; they merely reflect an unusual string of bad luck.

An insurance company has asymmetric information; it does not know whether a person with a bad driving record is truly a poor driver or whether past accidents were unusual events due to bad luck. Assuming that those who have poor driving records know their own type, we have a situation where one side of the insurance market has hidden characteristics. Suppose an insurance company decides to insure drivers with poor driving records, but at a very high premium to cover the anticipated future claims due to bad driving. The insurance company must charge all drivers with bad records the same insurance rate, since it cannot distinguish between those who are good drivers and those who are bad drivers. By charging the same price to both types of drivers, adverse selection results. As the insurance company raises insurance rates to cover the losses of bad drivers, the only people who will be willing to pay the higher price are those drivers who know they are most likely to have accidents. The good drivers, who know that their past accidents were unusual events, will not be willing to pay the high rate. Thus, the insurance company will end up selling policies only to the drivers most likely to wreck their cars. Since insurance works only when there are some drivers who pay premiums and do not wreck their automobiles, insurance companies typically find it in their interest to charge lower prices for insurance and refuse to insure any driver with a bad driving record. Doing otherwise would lead to adverse selection within the pool of drivers with poor records.

Moral Hazard

Sometimes when two parties engage in a contract, one party agrees to insulate the other party from economic loss. If the contract induces the party that is insulated from loss to take a hidden action that harms the other party, we say that *moral hazard* exists.

moral hazard
Situation where one party to a contract takes a hidden action that benefits him or her at the expense of another party.

Consider, for instance, the principal–agent problem we first examined in Chapter 6. In this setting the owner hires a manager to operate the firm, which earns profits that vary randomly with economic conditions. Unfortunately, profits also depend on the manager's effort, which is unobservable to the owner. Thus, the effort of the manager represents a hidden action. Notice that if the owner agrees to pay the manager a fixed salary of $50,000 (the contract), then the manager is completely insulated from any economic loss that might arise due to random fluctuations in the firm's profits. The manager now has an incentive to spend less time at the office (the hidden action), and the reduced effort of the manager results in lower firm profits (and thus harms the owner). In other words, the fixed salary contract, coupled with the hidden action of the manager, results in moral hazard. As we learned in Chapter 6, the owner can overcome this problem by either monitoring the manager (taking away the hidden action) or by making the manager's pay contingent on the firm's profits (taking away the manager's insurance against economic loss).

As you might suspect, the nature of insurance markets makes insurance companies particularly vulnerable to the moral hazard problem. As we discussed earlier in this chapter, the fact that individuals are risk averse provides an incentive for them to purchase insurance against large losses. Most people have insurance on their homes and automobiles and some form of health insurance. Usually the probability of a loss depends on the hidden effort expended by the insured to avoid the loss. Thus, a moral hazard exists: When individuals are fully insured, they have a reduced incentive to put forth effort to avoid a loss.

For example, suppose a company rents cars and fully insures renters against damage to the cars. Obviously, the company cannot observe the effort put forth by renters to avoid damages to rented vehicles. Since renters are fully insured and can take hidden actions that may result in damages to cars, they are indifferent between returning the car with a stolen radio and returning the car in perfect condition. If a radio is stolen, the replacement cost is paid for out of the company's pocket. Thus, when the car is fully insured, the driver has no incentive to take the time to lock the car or to avoid parking the car in areas where theft is likely. If the car were uninsured, the driver would have to replace stolen items with his or her own money and therefore would be much more careful with the car. Thus, if the company insures renters against damage, drivers will be less careful with cars than if they were not insured against damage. In economic terms a moral hazard exists.

One way car insurance companies attempt to reduce moral hazard is by requiring a deductible on all insurance claims. If the deductible is $200, the first $200 in losses is paid by the insured. This effectively means that the person buying insurance must pay something in the event of a loss and thus has an incentive to take actions to reduce the likelihood of a loss.

Moral hazard is one factor that has contributed to rising medical costs during the past decade. When individuals have health insurance or belong to a health maintenance organization (HMO), they do not pay for the full marginal cost of medical services. As a consequence, individuals are more likely to visit a doctor when they have a minor illness (say, a cold) than they would if they had to pay the full marginal cost of going to a doctor.

The effect of this is twofold. First, the moral hazard results in an increase in the demand for medical services, leading to a higher equilibrium price of medical services. This is because individuals do not pay the full cost of a visit to a doctor and thus use physicians' services more frequently than they would if they were required to pay the full cost of each visit. Second, insurance companies must increase the rates they charge for medical insurance to cover the higher costs of insurance claims due to more frequent visits. This might lead those who know they are in good health to decide against insurance coverage, which means that the higher medical insurance premiums also lead to adverse selection. In this case the insurance company is left to insure a pool of less healthy individuals, which exacerbates the problem. Thus, moral hazard and adverse selection may be partially responsible for the recent increases in the cost of medical insurance.

Signaling and Screening

We learned that incentive contracts can be used to mitigate moral hazard problems that stem from hidden actions. We now show how managers and other market participants can use signaling and screening to mitigate some of the problems that arise when one party to a transaction has hidden characteristics.

Signaling occurs when an informed party sends a signal (or indicator) of his or her hidden characteristics to an uninformed party in an attempt to provide information about these hidden characteristics. In product markets, firms use a host of devices to signal product quality to consumers: money-back guarantees, free trial periods, and packaging labels that indicate the product has won a "special award" or that the manufacturer has been in business since 1933. In labor markets, job applicants attempt to signal their ability through résumés that tout their "pedigree" (the school at which they earned an undergraduate degree) or the fact that they earned an advanced degree such as an MBA or PhD.

For a signal to provide useful information to an otherwise uninformed party, the signal must be observable by the uninformed party. Moreover, the signal must be a reliable indicator of the underlying unobservable characteristic and difficult for parties with other characteristics to easily mimic. To be concrete, consider a manager who wishes to hire a worker from an employment pool that consists of two types of individuals: (1) unproductive workers, who produce nothing; and (2) productive workers, who each have a value marginal product of $80,000 per year. Obviously, if the labor market is perfectly competitive and the manager can observe the productivity of workers before hiring them, unproductive workers will earn a salary of zero and productive workers will earn a salary that equals their value marginal product—$80,000 per year.

The situation is dramatically different when managers cannot observe the productivity of a worker by simply looking at the worker. Suppose that at the time of the hiring decision, workers know whether or not they are productive, but managers do not. From the manager's perspective, there is a 50–50 chance that a given worker is productive or unproductive. Since the expected value marginal product of a worker is

.5(0) + .5($80,000) = $40,000, a risk-neutral manager will only be willing to pay a salary of $40,000 to hire a worker with unobservable characteristics. Notice that the unproductive worker earns more than he would have earned if his characteristic were observable to the manager, and the productive worker earns less than he would have earned if the manager knew he was productive. The manager's lack of information, in this case, benefits unproductive workers at the expense of productive ones.

Since productive workers are harmed by the manager's lack of information, it is in their best interest to attempt to provide information to the manager that reveals that they are indeed productive; doing so will boost their salary from $40,000 to $80,000. How can they signal their productivity to the manager? You might think that it would be enough for productive workers to simply tell the manager that they are productive. The problem with this approach is that talk is cheap; if productive workers could boost their earnings by $40,000 by simply declaring "I'm productive," then unproductive workers could easily mimic this strategy to earn an extra $40,000. For this reason, a rational manager would ignore this idle chatter—everyone has an incentive to claim to be productive, so this message does not reveal anything about the true characteristics of workers.

For signaling to enhance the salaries of productive workers, they must send a signal that cannot be mimicked easily by unproductive workers. For instance, suppose productive workers have innate abilities that make it easy for them to earn a college degree, and unproductive workers have lower innate abilities that preclude them (or more generally, make it very costly for them) from earning a college degree. In this case, those individuals who know they are productive can earn a college degree to "signal" to managers that they are indeed productive. Since unproductive types cannot mimic this signal, managers can infer that workers with college degrees are the productive types. As a consequence, competitive pressures will result in college graduates earning $80,000. Signaling works because unproductive workers are unable (or more generally, unwilling to bear the cost required) to mimic this signal; managers know that anyone with a college degree is indeed a productive worker.

Screening occurs when an uninformed party attempts to sort individuals according to their characteristics. This sorting may be achieved through a *self-selection device:* Individuals who have information about their own characteristics are presented with a set of options, and the options they choose reveal their characteristics to the uninformed party.

A simple example will illustrate how an uninformed manager can use a self-selection device to gain information about the hidden characteristics of workers. Suppose two workers—Fred and Mitchell—have different characteristics: Fred is the better administrator, and Mitchell is the better salesperson. Fred and Mitchell know what they do better, but their personnel director does not. Specifically, Fred knows the firm's profits would increase by $20,000 if he were employed as an administrator and that he would be unable to generate any sales if he were employed as a salesperson. Mitchell knows the firm's profits would increase by $15,000 if he were employed as an administrator and that he could generate $1 million in sales if he were employed as a salesman. The personnel director, Natalie, wants to place each worker in the position that adds the most value to the firm, but she lacks the information needed to make these assignments.

screening
An attempt by an uninformed party to sort individuals according to their characteristics.

self-selection device
A mechanism in which informed parties are presented with a set of options, and the options they choose reveal their hidden characteristics to an uninformed party.

Natalie can overcome her lack of information by offering Fred and Mitchell different employment options and letting them self-select into the job that is best for them as well as for the firm. In particular, suppose Natalie uses a self-selection device whereby she announces the following compensation for administrators and salespeople: Administrators earn a fixed salary of $20,000; salespeople receive a 10 percent sales commission. Confronted with these options, Fred realizes that he would earn $0 as a salesperson and thus will self-select into his best-paying option: the administrative position. Mitchell will opt for the sales position, since the $100,000 he earns as a salesperson (10 percent of the $1 million he generates in sales) exceeds the $20,000 he would earn as an administrator. Thus, even though Natalie does not know which of the two individuals would be the better administrator and the better salesperson, the self-selection device sorts workers into the jobs she would have assigned if she had known Fred's and Mitchell's characteristics.

Demonstration Problem 12–5

One-Jet Airlines has 100 customers and is the only airline servicing two small cities in the Midwest. Half of One-Jet's customers are leisure travelers, and half are business travelers. Business travelers are willing to pay $600 for a ticket that does not require a Saturday stayover and $100 for a ticket that requires a Saturday stayover. Leisure travelers are flexible, willing to pay $300 for a ticket regardless of whether it requires a Saturday stayover. One-Jet is unable to determine whether a particular customer is a business or leisure traveler. Consequently, the airline's current pricing policy is to charge $300 for all tickets. As a pricing consultant for One-Jet Airlines, can you devise a self-selection mechanism that will permit One-Jet to increase revenues and continue to serve all its customers? Explain.

Answer:

Yes. One-Jet can offer two types of tickets: a $300 "supersaver" ticket that requires a Saturday stayover and a $600 "full-fare" ticket that does not require a Saturday stayover. Given the options, leisure travelers will select the supersaver ticket and business travelers will select the full-fare ticket. This screening device not only sorts travelers by their characteristics but increases One-Jet's revenues from $30,000 (computed as 100 × $300) to $45,000 (computed as 50 × $300 + 50 × $600).

AUCTIONS

In an *auction*, potential buyers compete for the right to own a good, service, or, more generally, anything of value. Auctions are used to sell a variety of things, including art, Treasury bills, furniture, real estate, oil leases, corporations, electricity, and numerous consumer goods at auction sites on the Internet. When the auctioneer is a seller, as in an art auction, she or he wishes to obtain the highest possible price for the item. Buyers, on the other hand, seek to obtain the item at the lowest possible price. In some instances, the auctioneer is the person seeking bids from potential suppliers. For instance, a firm that needs new capital equipment may hold an auction in which potential suppliers bid prices that reflect what they would charge for the equipment. In auctions with multiple bidders, competition among bidders leads to more favorable terms for the auctioneer.

Auctions are important for managers to understand because in many instances, firms participate either as the auctioneer or as a bidder in the auction process. In other words, a firm may wish to sell a good in an auction or buy a good (or input) in an auction. For this reason it is important for managers to understand the implications of auctions for managerial decisions.

While the bidders' risk preferences can affect bidding strategies and the expected revenue the auctioneer receives, we will assume throughout this section that bidders are risk neutral. This assumption is satisfied in many auction settings, since bidders can mitigate their overall risk by participating in a large number of auctions. Before we explain how much a risk-neutral bidder should bid in an auction, we first describe the rules of some different types of auctions and the nature of the information bidders can have about the item for which they are competing.

Types of Auctions

There are four basic types of auction: English (ascending-bid); first-price, sealed-bid; second-price, sealed-bid; and Dutch (descending-bid) auctions. These auctions differ with respect to (1) the timing of bidder decisions (whether bids are made simultaneously or sequentially) and (2) the amount the winner is required to pay. Keep these two sources of differences in auctions in mind as we discuss each type of auction.

English auction
An ascending sequential-bid auction in which bidders observe the bids of others and decide whether or not to increase the bid. The auction ends when a single bidder remains; this bidder obtains the item and pays the auctioneer the amount of the bid.

English Auction

The auction you probably are most familiar with is the English auction. In an *English auction,* a single item is to be sold to the highest bidder. The auction begins with an opening bid. Given knowledge of the opening bid, the auctioneer asks if anyone is willing to pay a higher price. The bids continue to rise in a sequential fashion until no other participants wish to increase the bid. The highest bidder—the only bidder left—pays the auctioneer his or her bid and takes possession of the item.

Notice that in an English auction, the bidders continually obtain information about one another's bids. Given this information, if they think the item is worth more than the current high bid, they will increase their bids. The auction ends when no other bidder is willing to pay more for the item than the highest bid. For this reason, in an English auction the person who ends up with the item is the one who values the item the most.

To illustrate, suppose three firms are competing for the right to purchase a machine in an English auction at a bankruptcy sale. Firm A values the machine at $1 million, firm B values it at $2 million, and firm C values it at $1.5 million. Which firm will acquire the machine, and at what price?

All three firms will bid up to $1 million for the machine. Once the bid is slightly above this amount, firm A will drop out, since it values the machine at $1 million. When the bid reaches $1.5 million, firm C will drop out, which means firm B will acquire the machine for $1.5 million (or perhaps $1.5 million plus $.01). Effectively, the winner of the auction simply has to top the second-highest valuation of the machine.

first-price, sealed-bid auction
A simultaneous-move auction in which bidders simultaneously submit bids on pieces of paper. The auctioneer awards the item to the high bidder, who pays the amount bid.

First-Price, Sealed-Bid Auction

In a *first-price, sealed-bid auction,* the bidders write their bids on pieces of paper without knowledge of bids made by other players. The auctioneer collects the bids

---

INSIDE BUSINESS 12–4

Second-Price Auctions on eBay

In a second-price auction, the dominant strategy is to bid your true valuation of the item. If you have ever participated in an auction on eBay, chances are you have participated in a second-price auction.

eBay's proxy bidding mechanism permits a bidder to submit his reservation price or "maximum bid." This amount is kept secret by eBay's system. The system automatically updates the bid, using the smallest increment required above the previous high bid. This process continues until the bid required exceeds the reservation price.

This environment is essentially a second-price auction, and the optimal reservation price to submit early in the auction is your true valuation of the item. As eBay explains on its website:

eBay always recommends bidding the absolute maximum that one is willing to pay for an item early in the auction. eBay uses

a proxy bidding system, you may bid as high as you wish, but the current bid that is registered will only be a small increment above the next lowest bid. The remainder of your Maximum Bid is held, by the system, to be used in the event someone bids against you. . . . Thus, if one is outbid, one should be at worst, ambivalent toward being outbid. After all, someone else was simply willing to pay more than you wanted to pay for it. If someone does outbid you toward the last minutes of an auction, it may feel unfair, but if you had bid your maximum amount up front and let the Proxy Bidding system work for you, the outcome would not be based on time.

Sources: http://pages.ebay.co.uk/help/community/notabuse.html, June 8, 2004; Alvin E. Roth and Axel Ockenfels, "Last-Minute Bidding and the Rules for Ending Second-Price Auctions: Evidence from eBay and Amazon Auctions on the Internet," *American Economic Review,* September 2002, pp. 1093–1103.

---

second-price, sealed-bid auction
A simultaneous-move auction in which bidders simultaneously submit bids. The auctioneer awards the item to the high bidder, who pays the amount bid by the second-highest bidder.

Dutch auction
A descending sequential-bid auction in which the auctioneer begins with a high asking price and gradually reduces the asking price until one bidder announces a willingness to pay that price for the item.

and awards the item to the high bidder. The high bidder pays the auctioneer the amount he or she has written on the piece of paper.

Thus, in a first-price, sealed-bid auction, the highest bidder wins the item just as in an English auction. However, unlike in an English auction, the bidders do not know the bids of other players. As we will see, this characteristic can affect bidding behavior and, consequently, the price collected by the auctioneer.

Second-Price, Sealed-Bid Auction

A *second-price, sealed-bid auction* is similar to a first-price, sealed-bid auction in that bidders submit bids without knowledge of the bids submitted by others. The person submitting the highest bid wins but has to pay only the amount bid by the second highest bidder. Consider, for instance, the situation where a machine is auctioned off to one of three firms in a second-price, sealed-bid auction. If Firm A bids $1 million, Firm B bids $2 million, and Firm C bids $1.5 million, then the high bidder—Firm B—wins the item. But it pays only the second highest bid, which is $1.5 million.

Dutch Auction

In a *Dutch auction,* the seller begins by asking for a very high price for the item (a price so high that she or he is certain no one will be willing to buy). The auctioneer gradually lowers the price until one buyer indicates a willingness to buy the item at that price. At this point, the auction is over: The bidder buys the item at the last announced price. Dutch auctions are used extensively in the Netherlands to auction flowers such as tulips. Car dealers sometimes use a Dutch auction to sell cars; a price for a particular car is posted each day on a marquee, and the price is lowered each day until someone purchases the car.

The information available to bidders in a Dutch auction is identical to that in a first-price, sealed-bid auction. In particular, no information is available about the bids of other players until the auction is over, that is, when the first bidder speaks up. Consequently, a Dutch auction is strategically equivalent to a first-price, sealed-bid auction. The reason is that in both types of auctions, bidders do not know the bids of other players. Furthermore, in each case the bidder pays what he or she bid for the item. In terms of optimal bidding behavior and the profits earned by the auctioneer, the Dutch auction and first-price, sealed-bid auctions are identical.

Principle	**Strategic Equivalence of Dutch and First-Price Auctions**
	The Dutch and first-price, sealed-bid auctions are strategically equivalent; that is, the optimal bids by participants are identical for both types of auctions.

Information Structures

The four basic types of auctions differ with respect to the information bidders have about the bids of other players. In the English auction, players know the current bid and can choose to raise it if they so desire. In the other three types of auctions, players make bids without knowledge of other players' bids; they cannot decide to increase their own bids based on bids made by others.

In analyzing an auction, it is also important to consider the information players have about their valuations of the item being auctioned. One possibility is that each bidder in an auction knows for certain what the item is worth, and furthermore, all players know the valuations of other players in an auction. For example, if a $5 bill were being auctioned off, every bidder would know that the item is worth $5 to each bidder. This is the case of *perfect information.*

Rarely do bidders in an auction enjoy perfect information. Even in situations in which each bidder knows how much he or she values the item, it is unlikely that other bidders are privy to this information. Moreover, individuals may be unsure of an item's true value and must rely on whatever information they have to form an estimate of its worth. These circumstances reflect situations of asymmetric information: Each bidder has information about his or her valuation or value estimate that is unknown by other bidders. These information structures are discussed next.

independent private values
Auction environment in which each bidder knows his own valuation of the item but does not know other bidders' valuations, and in which each bidder's valuation does not depend on other bidders' valuations of the object.

Independent Private Values

Consider an antique auction in which the bidders are consumers who wish to acquire an antique for personal use. Thus, the bidders' valuations of the item are determined by their individual tastes. While a bidder knows his or her own tastes, he or she does not know the preferences of the other bidders. Thus, there is asymmetric information.

The auction just described is one in which bidders have *independent private values.* The term *private value* refers to the fact that the item's worth to an individual bidder is determined by personal tastes that are known only to that bidder. The fact that these private values are *independent* means that they do not depend on the valuations of others: Even if a player could obtain information about other bidders' valuations, his or her valuation of the object would not change. This information might, however, induce him or her to bid differently in the auction.

To be concrete, imagine that the item is an antique desk, which you value at $200 because you know it would make studying managerial economics even more enjoyable (if that's possible). You face another bidder who, unbeknown to you, values the desk at $50. (He only wants the desk for scrap lumber.) Notice the asymmetric information that is present regarding these private values—you each know how much you value the desk but do not know how much the other values it. These valuations are also independent: Even if you knew the other bidder valued the desk at $50, it would not affect your own valuation of the desk. Of course, information about the other bidder's valuation might induce you to bid less aggressively for the antique desk.

Correlated Value Estimates

affiliated (or correlated) value estimates
Auction environment in which bidders do not know their own valuation of the item or the valuations of others. Each bidder uses his or her own information to estimate their valuation, and these value estimates are affiliated: The higher a bidder's value estimate, the more likely it is that other bidders also have high value estimates.

In many auction settings, bidders are unsure of an item's true valuation. Bidders may have access to different information about an item's actual worth and thus may form different estimates of the item's value. Consider an art auction, where the authenticity of the artist is uncertain. In this case, bidders will likely have different estimates of a painting's value for two reasons. First, individual tastes might lead some individuals to value the painting more than others. Second, bidders might have different estimates of the painting's authenticity. Furthermore, the bidders' estimates of the painting's value are likely to be interdependent. Your estimate of the painting's value would likely be higher if you knew others valued the painting, since you value owning a painting that is admired by others. Likewise, your valuation of the painting would likely be higher if you knew others valued the painting because of information they have about the painting's authenticity.

This example illustrates an environment in which bidders have *affiliated* (or *correlated*) *value estimates*. Each bidder must base his or her decision on an estimate (or guess) of his or her valuation of the item. Furthermore, the bidders' value estimates are correlated, or, more precisely, *affiliated:* The higher one bidder's value estimate, the more likely it is that other bidders also have high value estimates.

A special case of this environment, the *common-value* auction, arises when the true underlying value of the item is the same for all bidders. In this case, individual tastes play no role in shaping the bidders' value estimates. The uncertainty stems purely from the fact that different bidders use different information to form their estimates of the common value of the item.

common value
Auction environment in which the true value of the item is the same for all bidders, but this common value is unknown. Bidders each use their own (private) information to form an estimate of the item's true common value.

A good example of a common-value auction is the government's use of auctions to sell oil, gas, and mineral rights to prospective firms. The true value of these rights (the amount of oil, gas, or ore underneath the earth) is unknown to the bidders, but whatever the amount, the value is the same for all bidders. Each bidder forms an estimate of the true common value by taking seismic readings and performing other tests. Even though the true value is the same for all bidders, each bidder will likely obtain different estimates through their own tests.

Optimal Bidding Strategies for Risk-Neutral Bidders

This section presents the optimal bidding strategies for risk-neutral bidders, that is, strategies that maximize a bidder's expected profits. As we will see, a player's optimal bidding strategy depends not only on the type of auction but on the information available to the bidders when they make their bids.

Strategies for Independent Private Values Auctions

It is easiest to characterize optimal bidding strategies for environments in which the bidders have independent private valuations. In this case, each bidder already knows how much he or she values the item before the auction starts, so bidders learn nothing useful about their own valuations during the auction process.

Consider first an English auction, in which the auctioneer starts with a low price and gradually raises it until only one bidder remains. A bidder who remains in the auction after the price exceeds his valuation risks having to pay more for the item than it is worth to him. A bidder who drops out of the auction before the price reaches her valuation misses an opportunity to obtain the item at a price below her value. Thus, the optimal bidding strategy in an English auction is for each bidder to remain active until the price exceeds his or her own valuation of the object. Thus, the bidder with the highest valuation will win the object and pay an amount to the auctioneer that equals the second-highest valuation (the price at which the last competitor drops out).

Principle	**The Optimal Bidding Strategy for an English Auction**
	A player's optimal bidding strategy in an English auction with independent, private valuations is to remain active until the price exceeds his or her own valuation of the object.

Next, consider a second-price, sealed-bid auction: The highest bidder wins and pays the amount bid by the second-highest bidder. In this case something remarkable happens: Each player has an incentive to bid precisely his or her own valuation of the item. Since each player bids his or her own valuation, the amount actually paid by the highest bidder is the valuation of the second-highest bidder, just as in the English auction.

Why should players bid their true valuation in a second-price auction? The reason is quite simple. Since the winner pays the bid of the second-highest bidder, not his or her own bid, it does not pay for players to bid more or less than their own valuations. To see this, suppose a player bid more than the item was worth to him to increase the likelihood of being the high bidder. If the second-highest bid is less than his valuation, this strategy yields no additional returns; he also would have won had he bid his true valuation. If the second-highest bid is above his valuation, then by bidding more than his valuation he may indeed win. But if he does win, he pays the second-highest bid, which we assumed is above his own valuation! In this case, he pays more for the item than the item is worth to him. Thus, it does not pay for a player to bid more than his or her valuation in a second-price auction. Will a player ever bid less than his valuation? No. A player who bids less merely reduces the chance of winning, since the player never pays his or her own bid! For this reason, the dominant strategy for bidders in a second-price, sealed-bid auction is to bid their valuations.

Finally, consider a first-price auction (which as we have seen is strategically equivalent to a Dutch auction). In this case, the high bidder wins and pays his or her own bid. Since players do not know the valuations or bids of others and must pay their own bid if they win, players have an incentive to bid less than their own valuation of the item. By bidding less than his or her own valuation of the item, a player reduces the probability of submitting the highest bid. But the profit the bidder earns if he or she does win more than offsets the reduced probability of winning. The amount by which a bidder shades down his bid depends on how many other bidders are competing for the item. The more competitive the auction (that is, the greater the number of other bidders), the closer a player should bid to his or her true valuation. The following principle includes a formula you can use to explicitly compute your optimal bid in situations in which you and other bidders perceive that the lowest possible valuation of other bidders is L and the highest possible valuation is H.

In the above formula, notice that the greater the number of bidders (n) or the closer the bidder's valuation is to the lowest possible valuation of the other bidders (that is, the closer $v - L$ is to zero), then the closer the optimal bid (b) is to the player's actual valuation of the item (v). The following demonstration problem shows how you can use this formula to determine your optimal bid in both first-price and Dutch auctions.

Demonstration Problem 12–6

Consider an auction where bidders have independent private values. Each bidder perceives that valuations are evenly distributed between $1 and $10. Sam knows his own valuation is $2. Determine Sam's optimal bidding strategy in (1) a first-price, sealed-bid auction with two bidders, (2) a Dutch auction with three bidders, and (3) a second-price, sealed-bid auction with 20 bidders.

Answer:

1. With only two bidders, $n = 2$. The lowest possible valuation is $L = \$1$, and Sam's own valuation is $v = \$2$. Thus, Sam's optimal sealed bid is

$$b = v - \frac{v - L}{n} = 2 - \frac{2 - 1}{2} = \$1.50$$

2. Since a Dutch auction is strategically equivalent to a first-price, sealed-bid auction, we can use that formula to determine the price at which Sam should declare his willingness to buy the item. Here, $n = 3$, the lowest possible valuation is $L = \$1$, and Sam's own valuation is $v = \$2$. Thus,

$$b = v - \frac{v - L}{n} = 2 - \frac{2 - 1}{3} = \$1.67$$

Sam's optimal strategy is to let the auctioneer continue to lower the price until it reaches \$1.67 and then yell "Mine!"

3. Sam should bid his true valuation, which is \$2.

Strategies for Correlated Values Auctions

Optimal bidding strategies with affiliated (or correlated) values are more difficult to describe, for two main reasons. First, the bidders do not know their own valuations of the item, let alone the valuations of others. This not only makes it difficult for players to determine how much to bid, but as we will see, it makes them vulnerable to what is called the *winner's curse*. Second, the auction process itself may reveal information about how much the other bidders value the object. When players' value estimates are affiliated, optimal bidding requires that players use this information to update their own value estimates during the auction process.

To illustrate, suppose 100 firms bid for the rights to an oil lease in a first-price, sealed-bid common-values auction. Thus, each bidder is uncertain about the true amount of oil underneath the earth, but nevertheless it is worth the same to each bidder. Before participating in the bidding process, each firm runs an independent test to obtain an estimate of the amount of oil in the ground. Naturally, these estimates vary randomly from firm to firm.

winner's curse
The "bad news" conveyed to the winner that his or her estimate of the item's value exceeds the estimates of all other bidders.

Suppose the differences in their estimates of the amount of oil in the ground are due purely to random variations in test procedures. Some firms think there is more oil in the ground than others, not because they are better informed but due purely to random chance. In this case, the firm that submits the winning bid is the firm with the most optimistic estimate of the amount of oil in the ground. Expressed differently, one of the spoils of victory in a common-values auction is the *winner's curse:* Winning conveys news to the victor that all the other firms think the lease is worth less than he or she paid for it. The chance that the other 99 firms are wrong and the winner is right is slim indeed. Notice that if the bidders could "pool" their information and average it, they would have a more precise estimate of the true amount of oil in the ground.

The winner's curse presents a danger that prudent managers must avoid. To illustrate, suppose a geologist for one of the above firms estimated that the lease is worth $50 million. The manager of this firm, being naïve, ignores the fact that $50 million is only an estimate of the common value. In fact, he calculates his firm's bid by using the formula described earlier for a first-price, sealed-bid auction with independent private valuations. He knows the number of bidders ($n = 100$), recognizes that some firms might think there is no oil underneath the earth ($L = 0$), and sets $v = \$50,000,000$ in the formula to arrive at a bid of $49.5 million. He submits this bid and wins but then learns that the second-highest bid was only $40 million. By the rules of the auction, his firm must pay $49.5 million for a lease that his firm's geologist thinks is worth $50 million. Chances are, the lease is worth millions of dollars less than this estimate of $50 million since the other 99 firms were not willing to pay more than $40 million for the lease. He should have realized that the only way he could win with a bid of $49.5 million is if the other 99 firms obtained more pessimistic value estimates. For this reason, a player who submits a bid based purely on his or her initial value estimate will, on average, pay more for the item than it is worth. To avoid the winner's curse, a bidder must revise downward his or her value estimate to account for this fact.

Principle	**Avoiding the Winner's Curse**
	In a common-values auction, the winner is the bidder who is the most optimistic about the true value of the item. To avoid the winner's curse, a bidder should revise downward his or her private estimate of the value to account for this fact.

The winner's curse is most pronounced in sealed-bid auctions because players do not learn anything about other players' value estimates until it is too late to act on it. In contrast, in an English auction the auction process provides information to the bidders. Each bidder shows up at the auction with an initial estimate of the item's value. During the auction process, each bidder gains information about the item's worth and can revise his or her value estimate accordingly. Specifically, as the price gets higher and higher and the other bidders continue to remain active, you should realize that the other bidders also estimate the object to be of high value—if their private information suggested the object was of low value, they would have already dropped out of the auction. By affiliation, you should revise upward your estimate of the item's worth, since higher-value estimates by other bidders make it more likely that the value to you is also high. Conversely, if you observe that many bidders dropped out at a low price, you should revise downward your private estimate. The optimal strategy in an English auction with affiliated value estimates is to continue to bid so long as the price does not exceed the value estimate you obtain based not only on your private information but on information gleaned through the auction process.

Expected Revenues in Alternative Types of Auctions

Now that you have a basic understanding of bidding strategies in auctions, we can compare the prices that result, on average, in each type of auction. In particular, suppose an auctioneer is interested in maximizing her expected profits. Which type of auction will generate the highest profits: English, second-price, first-price, or Dutch? As Table 12–1 shows, the "best" auction from the auctioneer's viewpoint depends on the nature of the information the bidders hold.

The first row in Table 12–1 indicates that, with independent private values, the auctioneer's expected revenues are the same for all four auction types. The reason for this result, known as *revenue equivalence,* is as follows:

With independent private values, players already know their own valuations and therefore learn nothing useful about the item's worth during the auction process. As we saw in the previous section, the price ultimately paid by the winner in an English auction is the second-highest valuation—the price at which the last competitor drops out. This is also the case in a second-price auction. In particular, each player bids his or her own value, and thus the price paid by the winner (the second-highest price) is the second-highest valuation. It follows that, with independent private values, the expected revenue earned by the auctioneer is the same in an English auction as a second-price auction.

In a first-price auction, each bidder has an incentive to shade his bid. In effect, each bidder estimates how far below his own valuation the next highest valuation is and then shrinks his or her bid by that amount. The player who wins the auction is the one with the highest valuation, and therefore he pays an amount to the auctioneer that is, on average, equal to the second-highest valuation. Thus, with independent private values, the expected revenue earned by the auctioneer in a first-price auction is identical to that in English and second-price auctions. Since the Dutch auction is strategically equivalent to a first-price auction, the expected revenues under the two auctions are the same. For these reasons, all four of these auctions generate the same expected revenues for the auctioneer when bidders have independent private values.

Table 12–1 shows that revenue equivalence does not hold for affiliated values. Players shrink their bids below what they would have bid based purely on their private value estimates in order to avoid the winner's curse. In an English auction, players gain the most information about the value estimates of others, and this additional information mitigates the winner's curse to some extent. Thus, bidders shrink their bids less in an English auction than in sealed-bid or Dutch auctions. In contrast, in first-price and Dutch auctions, players learn nothing about other players' value estimates during the auction process. Bidders thus shrink their bids most in first-price and

TABLE 12–1 Comparison of Expected Revenues in Auctions with Risk-Neutral Bidders

Information Structure	Expected Revenues
Independent private values	English = Second-price = First-price = Dutch
Affiliated value estimates	English > Second-price > First-price = Dutch

INSIDE BUSINESS 12–5

Auctions with Risk-Averse Bidders

Risk aversion affects bidder behavior in some types of auctions but not in others. Consider the independent private values case. In an English auction, players know their own valuation and get to observe the bids of others. Therefore, risk aversion plays no real role in the analysis of bidding strategies: Risk-averse bidders will remain active until the price exceeds their valuation and then drop out. The winner will pay an amount that equals the second-highest valuation. Likewise, in a second-price auction, it is a dominant strategy for a risk-averse bidder to bid his or her true valuation, so this type of auction also results in a price that equals the second-highest valuation.

In contrast, risk aversion induces players to bid more aggressively in a first-price auction with independent private values. To see why, recall that risk-neutral bidders shade down their bids in a first-price auction. This increases the chance that some other player outbids them, but risk-neutral bidders are willing to accept this risk because of the greater profits they get if they win.

Risk-averse bidders are less willing to accept this risk and therefore shrink their bids by a lower amount. Consequently, with risk-averse bidders and independent private values, the expected revenue of the auctioneer is greatest in first-price and Dutch auctions and lowest in English and second-price auctions:

First-price = Dutch > Second-price = English

What happens when risk-averse bidders have affiliated value estimates? Recall that the information revealed in an English auction lessens the winner's curse. This reduction in risk induces risk-averse bidders to bid more aggressively, on average, in an English auction than in a second-price auction. Consequently, the English auction always generates greater expected revenues than a second-price auction. It may, in fact, even generate higher revenues than a first-price or Dutch auction:

English > Second-price ≥ First-price = Dutch

Dutch auctions. In a second-price auction, bidders also learn nothing about the value estimates of others. However, the winner does not have to pay his or her own bid but rather the amount bid by the second-highest bidder. The fact that the second-highest bid is linked to information another bidder has about the item's valuation mitigates to some extent the winner's curse, thus inducing players to shrink their bids by less than they would in a first-price auction. As a result, with affiliated value estimates, the auctioneer earns greater expected revenues in an English auction than a second-price auction, and the lowest expected revenues in a first-price or Dutch auction.

Demonstration Problem 12–7

Suppose your firm is in need of cash and plans to auction off a subsidiary to the highest bidder. Which type of auction will maximize your firm's revenues from the sale if: (1) The bidders are risk neutral and have independent private valuations? (2) The bidders are risk neutral and have affiliated value estimates?

Answer:
1. With independent private valuations, all four auction types will lead to identical expected revenues under these conditions.
2. With affiliated value estimates and risk-neutral bidders, the English auction will yield the highest expected revenues.

ANSWERING THE HEADLINE

The opening headline asked why one of the firms in the FCC auction dropped out of the bidding before the price reached its estimate of $85 million for a license. Since the spectrum rights auction was a common-values auction, or more generally, an auction with affiliated value estimates, the firm that has the highest private estimate is the firm with the most optimistic estimate of the true value of the license. If firms as a whole form correct expectations of the value, this means that the winner's estimated value is likely to overestimate the true value of a license. In this case a firm that bids its private estimate would expect to lose money over the 10-year life of the license. To circumvent this winner's curse, the firm correctly dropped out of the bidding before the price reached its private estimate of $85 million.

SUMMARY

In this chapter, we examined some of the complications uncertainty and asymmetric information add to managerial decision making. It should be clear that in many instances, consumers and firms' managers have imperfect information about demand functions, costs, sources of products, and product quality. Decisions are harder to make because the outcomes are uncertain. If your information is probabilistic in nature, you should take the time to find the mean, variance, and standard deviation of outcomes that will result from alternative actions. By doing this, you can use marginal analysis to make optimal decisions.

Consumers and producers have different risk preferences. Some people like to go to the mountains to ski treacherous slopes, while others prefer to sit in the lodge and take in the scenery outside. Similarly, some individuals have a preference for risky prospects, while others are risk averse. If you or the firm you work for has a preference for not taking risks (i.e., is risk averse), you will accept projects with low expected returns, provided the corresponding risk is lower than projects with higher expected returns. However, if risk taking excites you, you will be willing to take on riskier projects.

Risk structures and the use of the mean, variance, and standard deviation also help identify how customers will respond to uncertain prospects. For example, those individuals who most actively seek insurance and are willing to pay the most for it frequently are bad risks. This results in adverse selection. Moreover, once individuals obtain insurance, they will tend to take fewer precautions to avoid losses than they would otherwise. This creates a moral hazard. Incentive contracts, signaling, and screening can be used to reduce some of the problems associated with asymmetric information.

We also examined how consumers will react to uncertainty about prices or quality through search behavior. Consumers will change their search for quality and "good" prices based on both their perceptions of the probability of finding a better deal and the value of their time. Putting this information to work can help you keep more of your customers. When your customers have a low value of time, you know you will need to lower prices to keep them, because their opportunity cost of searching is low.

Finally, we examined auctions, which play a central role in capitalistic economies. We covered four types of auctions: the English auction; the Dutch auction; the first-price, sealed-bid auction; and the second-price, sealed-bid auction. Bidding strategies and expected revenues vary across auction types depending on the type of auction and whether bidders have independent private values or affiliated value estimates.

KEY TERMS AND CONCEPTS

adverse selection	replacement
affiliated (or correlated) value estimates	reservation price
asymmetric information	revenue equivalence
common value	risk
diversification	risk averse
Dutch auction	risk loving
English auction	risk neutral
first-price, sealed-bid auction	screening
free recall	second-price, sealed-bid auction
hidden action	self-selection device
hidden characteristics	signaling
independent private values	standard deviation
mean (expected) value	uncertainty
moral hazard	variance
perfect information	winner's curse

END-OF-CHAPTER PROBLEMS BY LEARNING OBJECTIVE

Every end-of-chapter problem addresses at least one learning objective. Following is a nonexhaustive sample of end-of-chapter problems for each learning objective.

LO1 Identify strategies to manage risk and uncertainty, including diversification and optimal search strategies.

Try these problems: 1, 14

LO2 Calculate the profit-maximizing output and price in an environment of uncertainty.

Try these problems: 4, 12

LO3 Explain why asymmetric information about "hidden actions" or "hidden characteristics" can lead to moral hazard and adverse selection, and identify strategies for mitigating these potential problems.

Try these problems: 5, 16

LO4 Explain how differing auction rules and information structures impact the incentives in auctions, and determine the optimal bidding strategies in a variety of auctions with independent or correlated values.

Try these problems: 6, 19

CONCEPTUAL AND COMPUTATIONAL QUESTIONS

connect
|ECONOMICS

1. Consider the two options in the following table, both of which have random outcomes:

Option 1		Option 2	
Probability of Outcome	Possible Outcomes ($)	Probability of Outcome	Possible Outcomes ($)
1/16	150	1/5	120
4/16	300	1/5	255
6/16	750	1/5	1,500
4/16	300	1/5	255
1/16	150	1/5	120

    a. Determine the expected value of each option.
    b. Determine the variance and standard deviation of each option.
    c. Which option is most risky?

2. For each of the following scenarios, determine whether the decision maker is risk neutral, risk averse, or risk loving.
    a. A manager prefers a 20 percent chance of receiving $1,400 and an 80 percent chance of receiving $500 to receiving $680 for sure.
    b. A shareholder prefers receiving $920 with certainty to an 80 percent chance of receiving $1,100 and a 20 percent chance of receiving $200.
    c. A consumer is indifferent between receiving $1,360 for sure and a lottery that pays $2,000 with a 60 percent probability and $400 with a 40 percent probability.

3. Your store sells an item desired by a consumer. The consumer is using an optimal search strategy; the accompanying graph shows the consumer's expected benefits and costs of searching for a lower price.
    a. What is the consumer's reservation price?
    b. If your price is $3 and the consumer visits your store, will she purchase the item or continue to search? Explain.

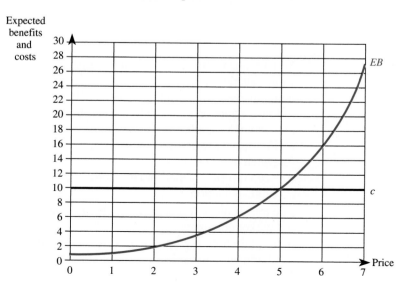

    c. Suppose the consumer's cost of each search rises to $16. What is the highest price you can charge and still sell the item to the consumer if she visits your store?

    d. Suppose the consumer's cost of each search falls to $2. If the consumer finds a store charging $3, will she purchase at that price or continue to search?

4. You are the manager of a firm that sells a "commodity" in a market that resembles perfect competition, and your cost function is $C(Q) = 2Q + 3Q^2$. Unfortunately, due to production lags, you must make your output decision prior to knowing for certain the price that will prevail in the market. You believe that there is a 70 percent chance the market price will be $200 and a 30 percent chance it will be $600.

    a. Calculate the expected market price.

    b. What output should you produce in order to maximize expected profits?

    c. What are your expected profits?

5. A risk-neutral consumer is deciding whether to purchase a homogeneous product from one of two firms. One firm produces an unreliable product and the other a reliable product. At the time of the sale, the consumer is unable to distinguish between the two firms' products. From the consumer's perspective, there is an equal chance that a given firm's product is reliable or unreliable. The maximum amount this consumer will pay for an unreliable product is $0, while she will pay $100 for a reliable product.

    a. Given this uncertainty, what is the most this consumer will pay to purchase one unit of this product?

    b. How much will this consumer be willing to pay for the product if the firm offering the reliable product includes a warranty that will protect the consumer? Explain.

6. You are a bidder in an independent private values auction, and you value the object at $4,000. Each bidder perceives that valuations are uniformly distributed between $1,500 and $9,000. Determine your optimal bidding strategy in a first-price, sealed-bid auction when the total number of bidders (including you) is:

    a. 2.

    b. 10.

    c. 100.

7. You are one of five risk-neutral bidders participating in an independent private values auction. Each bidder perceives that all other bidders' valuations for the item are evenly distributed between $10,000 and $30,000. For each of the following auction types, determine your optimal bidding strategy if you value the item at $22,000.

    a. First-price, sealed-bid auction.

    b. Dutch auction.

    c. Second-price, sealed-bid auction.

    d. English auction.

8. The text points out that asymmetric information can have deleterious effects on market outcomes.

    a. Explain how asymmetric information about a hidden action or a hidden characteristic can lead to moral hazard or adverse selection.

    b. Discuss a few tactics that managers can use to overcome these problems.

9. An advertisement in the local paper offers a "fully loaded" car that is only six months old and has only been driven 5,000 miles at a price that is 20 percent lower than the average selling price of a brand new car with the same options. Use precise economic terminology to explain whether this discount most likely reflects a "fantastic deal" or something else.

10. Life insurance policies typically have clauses stipulating the insurance company will not pay claims arising from suicide for a specified term—typically two years from the date the policy was issued. Use precise economic terminology to explain the likely impact on an insurance company's bottom line if it were to eliminate such a clause.

PROBLEMS AND APPLICATIONS

11. The FCC has hired you as a consultant to design an auction to sell wireless spectrum rights. The FCC indicates that its goal of using auctions to sell these spectrum rights is to generate revenue. Since most bidders are large telecommunications companies, you rationally surmise that all participants in the auction are risk neutral. Which auction type—first-price, second-price, English, or Dutch—would you recommend if all bidders value spectrum rights identically but have different estimates of the true underlying value of spectrum rights? Explain.

12. As the manager of Smith Construction, you need to make a decision on the number of homes to build in a new residential area where you are the only builder. Unfortunately, you must build the homes before you learn how strong demand is for homes in this large neighborhood. There is a 60 percent chance of low demand and a 40 percent chance of high demand. The corresponding (inverse) demand functions for these two scenarios are $P = 300,000 - 400Q$ and $P = 500,000 - 275Q$, respectively. Your cost function is $C(Q) = 140,000 + 240,000Q$. How many new homes should you build, and what profits can you expect?

13. Life insurance companies require applicants to submit to a physical examination as proof of insurability prior to issuing standard life insurance policies. In contrast, credit card companies offer their customers a type of insurance called "credit life insurance" which pays off the credit card balance if the cardholder dies. Would you expect insurance premiums to be higher (per dollar of death benefits) on standard life or credit life policies? Explain.

14. BK Books is an online book retailer that also has 10,000 "bricks and mortar" outlets worldwide. You are a risk-neutral manager within the Corporate Finance Division and are in dire need of a new financial analyst. You only interview students from the top MBA programs in your area. Thanks to your screening mechanisms and contacts, the students you interview ultimately differ only with respect to the wage that they are willing to accept. About 10 percent of acceptable candidates are willing to accept a salary of $70,000, while 90 percent demand a salary of $100,000. There are two phases to the interview process that every interviewee must go through. Phase 1 is the initial one-hour on-campus interview. All candidates interviewed in Phase 1 are also invited to Phase 2 of the interview, which consists of a five-hour office

visit. In all, you spend six hours interviewing each candidate and value this time at $900. In addition, it costs a total of $4,900 in travel expenses to interview each candidate. You are very impressed with the first interviewee completing both phases of BK Books's interviewing process, and she has indicated that her reservation salary is $100,000. Should you make her an offer at that salary or continue the interviewing process? Explain.

15. Congress enacted the Health Insurance Portability and Accountability Act (HIPAA) to potentially help millions of employees gain access to group health insurance. The key provision of HIPAA requires insurance companies and health insurance plans administered by employers who self-insure to provide all employees access to health insurance regardless of previous medical conditions. This provision is known as "guaranteed issue" and is a controversial topic in the insurance industry. Explain why this is controversial legislation.

16. Since the late 1990s, more than 25 domestic steel companies have filed for bankruptcy. A combination of low prices with strong competition by foreign competitors and so-called "legacy costs" of unions are cited as the primary reasons why so many steel companies are filing for bankruptcy. In 2002, as Brownstown Steel Corp. was in the process of restructuring its loans to avoid bankruptcy, its lenders requested that the firm disclose full information about its revenues and costs. Explain why Brownstown's management was reluctant to release this information to its lenders.

17. This past year, Used Imported Autos sold very few cars and lost over $500,000. As a consequence, its manager is contemplating two strategies to increase its sales volume. The low-cost strategy involves changing the dealership name to Quality Used Imported Autos to signal to customers that the company sells high-quality cars. The high-cost strategy involves issuing a 10-point auto inspection on all used cars on the lot and offering consumers a 30-day warranty on every used car sold. Which of these two strategies do you think would have the greatest impact on sales volume? Explain.

18. Pelican Point Financial Group's clientele consists of two types of investors. The first type of investor makes many transactions in a given year and has a net worth of over $1.5 million. These investors seek unlimited access to investment consultants and are willing to pay up to $20,000 annually for no-fee-based transactions, or alternatively, $40 per trade. The other type of investor also has a net worth of over $1.5 million but makes few transactions each year and therefore is willing to pay $120 per trade. As the manager of Pelican Point Financial Group, you are unable to determine whether any given individual is a high- or low-volume transaction investor. Design a self-selection mechanism that permits you to identify each type of investor.

19. CPT Inc. is a local manufacturer of conveyor systems. Last year, CPT sold over $2 million worth of conveyor systems that netted the company $100,000 in profits. Raw materials and labor are CPT's biggest expenses. Spending on structural steel alone amounted to over $500,000, or 25 percent of total sales. In an effort to reduce costs, CPT now uses an online procurement procedure that is best described as a first-price, sealed-bid auction. The bidders in these

auctions utilize the steel for a wide variety of purposes, ranging from art to skyscrapers. This suggests that bidders value the steel independently, although it is perceived that bidder valuations are evenly distributed between $8,000 and $25,000. You are the purchasing manager at *CPT* and are bidding on three tons of six-inch hot-rolled channel steel against four other bidders. Your company values the three tons of channel steel at $16,000. What is your optimal bid?

20. A few years ago PeopleSoft announced that its second-quarter net income was down by nearly 70 percent. The company's CEO attributed the poor performance to an ongoing hostile takeover battle against its rival, Oracle (PeopleSoft has reportedly spent over $10.5 million to defend itself). Analysts, however, were quick to note that PeopleSoft's revenue estimates were adjusted downward from approximately $680 million to $660 million. Suppose that Oracle perceives that there is a 70 percent probability that PeopleSoft's decline in net income is merely the transitory result of efforts to fight the takeover. In this case, the present value of PeopleSoft's stream of profits is $10 billion. However, Oracle perceives that there is a 30 percent chance that PeopleSoft's lower net income figures stem from long-term structural changes in the demand for PeopleSoft's services, and that the present value of its profit stream is only $2 billion. You are a decision-maker at Oracle and know that your current takeover bid is $7 billion. You have just learned that a rival bidder—SAP—perceives that there is an 80 percent probability that the present value of PeopleSoft's stream of profits is $10 billion and a 20 percent probability of being only $2 billion. Based on this information, should you increase your bid or hold firm to your $7 billion offer? Explain carefully.

21. You are considering a $500,000 investment in the fast-food industry and have narrowed your choice to either a McDonald's or a Penn Station East Coast Subs franchise. McDonald's indicates that, based on the location where you are proposing to open a new restaurant, there is a 25 percent probability that aggregate 10-year profits (net of the initial investment) will be $16 million, a 50 percent probability that profits will be $8 million, and a 25 percent probability that profits will be −$1.6 million. The aggregate 10-year profit projections (net of the initial investment) for a Penn Station East Coast Subs franchise is $48 million with a 2.5 percent probability, $8 million with a 95 percent probability, and −$48 million with a 2.5 percent probability. Considering both the risk and expected profitability of these two investment opportunities, which is the better investment? Explain carefully.

22. Online MBA programs significantly reduce the cost to existing managers of obtaining an MBA, as they permit students to maintain their existing residence and employment while working toward an advanced degree in business. Based on your knowledge of the economics of information and student characteristics, compare and contrast the likely characteristics of students enrolled in traditional MBA programs with those enrolled in online MBA programs, and discuss how potential employers might use information about where a candidate obtained his or her MBA degree to screen potential MBA job applicants.

23. Prosecutors representing the Securities and Exchange Commission recently announced criminal charges against 13 individuals for engaging in insider

trading. According to the SEC's director of enforcement, a trading ring acting on inside information "compromises the markets' integrity and investors' trust. . . ." Explain why.

CONNECT EXERCISES

If your instructor has adopted Connect for the course and you are an active subscriber, you can practice with the questions presented above, along with many alternative versions of these questions. Your instructor may also assign a subset of these problems and/or their alternative versions as a homework assignment through Connect, allowing for immediate feedback of grades and correct answers.

CASE-BASED EXERCISES

Your instructor may assign additional problem-solving exercises (called memos) that require you to apply some of the tools you learned in this chapter to make a recommendation based on an actual business scenario. Some of these memos accompany the Time Warner case (pages 561–597 of your textbook). Additional memos, as well as data that may be useful for your analysis, are available online at www.mhhe.com/baye8e.

SELECTED READINGS

Bikhchandani, Sushil, Hirshleifer, David, and Welch, Ivo, "A Theory of Fads, Fashion, Custom, and Cultural Change in Informational Cascades." *Journal of Political Economy* 100(5), October 1992, pp. 992–1026.

Cummins, J. David, and Tennyson, Sharon, "Controlling Automobile Insurance Costs." *Journal of Economic Perspectives* 6(2), Spring 1992, pp. 95–115.

Hamilton, Jonathan H., "Resale Price Maintenance in a Model of Consumer Search." *Managerial and Decision Economics* 11(2), May 1990, pp. 87–98.

Kagel, John, Levine, Dan, and Battalio, Raymond, "First Price Common Value Auctions: Bidder Behavior and the 'Winner's Curse.'" *Economic Inquiry* 27, April 1989, pp. 241–58.

Lind, Barry, and Plott, Charles, "The Winner's Curse: Experiments with Buyers and with Sellers." *American Economic Review* 81, March 1991, pp. 335–46.

Lucking-Reiley, David, "Auctions on the Internet: What's Being Auctioned, and How?" *Journal of Industrial Economics* 48 (3), September 2000, pp. 227–52.

Machina, Mark J., "Choice under Uncertainty: Problems Solved and Unsolved." *Journal of Economic Perspectives* 1, Summer 1987, pp. 121–54.

McAfee, R. Preston, and McMillan, John, "Auctions and Bidding." *Journal of Economic Literature* 25(2), June 1987, pp. 699–738.

McMillan, John, "Selling Spectrum Rights." *Journal of Economic Perspectives* 8(3), Summer 1994, pp. 145–62.

Milgrom, Paul, "Auctions and Bidding: A Primer." *Journal of Economic Perspectives* 3(3), Summer 1989, pp. 3–22.

Riley, John G., "Expected Revenues from Open and Sealed-Bid Auctions." *Journal of Economic Perspectives* 3(3), Summer 1989, pp. 41–50.

Salop, Steven, "Evaluating Uncertain Evidence with Sir Thomas Bayes: A Note for Teachers." *Journal of Economic Perspectives* 1, Summer 1987, pp. 155–59.

CHAPTER THIRTEEN

Advanced Topics in Business Strategy

Local Restaurateur Faces Looming Challenge from Morton's

Tom Jackson has been running a successful steakhouse that specializes in serving upscale steak dinners. His current marketing campaign targets residential households. Recently, it was announced that a new conference hotel was to open near his steakhouse, bringing in many potential business customers. Speculation followed that Morton's steakhouse—an upscale steakhouse chain currently marketing to business customers nationally—was considering opening one of its restaurants near the new hotel, and would therefore compete with Tom's restaurant.

In light of the potential threat from Morton's, Tom began considering the possibility of making a significant investment to change his marketing campaign and target businesses rather than households. In doing so, he estimated the following profit outcomes (in thousands of dollars) resulting from the strategies that he and Morton's might implement:

Learning Objectives

After completing this chapter, you will be able to:

LO1 Explain the economic basis for limit pricing, and identify the conditions under which a firm can profit from such a strategy.

LO2 Explain the economic basis for predatory pricing.

LO3 Show how a manager can profitably lessen competition by raising rivals' costs.

LO4 Identify some of the adverse legal ramifications of business strategies designed to lessen competition.

LO5 Assess whether a firm's profits can be enhanced by changing the timing of decisions or the order of strategic moves, and whether doing so creates first- or second-mover advantages.

LO6 Identify examples of networks and network externalities, and determine the number of connections possible in a star network with n users.

LO7 Explain why networks often lead to first-mover advantages, and how to use strategies such as penetration pricing to favorably change the strategic environment.

Tom	Morton's		
Marketing Target		**Enter**	**Don't Enter**
Businesses		−$200, −$50	$90, $0
Households		$50, $100	$105, $0

When analyzing this situation, Tom quickly noticed that his dominant strategy was to continue marketing to households, and was disappointed in the resulting profits. Then, an idea hit him, and he realized that much higher profits were possible. What did Tom decide to do?

INTRODUCTION

In our examination of the quest for profitable business strategies, we have generally taken the business environment (the number of competitors, the timing of decisions, and more generally, the decisions of rivals) as given and outside of the manager's control. This chapter changes all that. We identify strategies managers can use to change the business environment in order to enhance the firm's long-run profits. In short, this chapter's theme is: "If you don't like the game you're playing, look for strategies to change the game."

The first part of this chapter identifies three strategies that managers can use to change the business environment. Two pricing strategies—limit pricing and predatory pricing—are identified as potential tools for reducing the number of competitors. A third strategy lessens competition by raising rivals' fixed or marginal costs. Unfortunately, all these strategies involve economic trade-offs. Before implementing a given strategy, a manager must determine whether the potential benefits of the strategies exceed the associated costs.

One of the more important cost considerations is legal in nature: Business tactics that attempt to boost a firm's profits purely by eliminating competitors may result in your company being sued by one or more antitrust authorities. Antitrust laws are often complex and differ not only across countries but among states or provinces within a given country. A business tactic may be legal at the national level but illegal according to the antitrust laws of a particular state or in a different country. Additionally, different judges sometimes interpret the same antitrust law differently. Do not underestimate the potential costs of pursuing a strategy that is illegal in even one of the legal jurisdictions in which your company operates or competes. In addition to strong ethical reasons for abiding by federal and state antitrust laws, the potential costs of violating antitrust laws can swamp any profits achieved by the business strategies. These costs include legal fees, fines, adverse effects on a company's reputation, and even the forced breakup of a large company into smaller, independent firms.

The second part of this chapter focuses on first- and second-mover advantages and explains when it is profitable to change the business environment by altering the timing or sequence of decisions. We conclude by showing why first-mover advantages are typically strong in network industries (such as telecommunications, airlines, and the Internet). Penetration pricing is a strategy entrants can use to "change the game" in order to overcome these potential obstacles.

LIMIT PRICING TO PREVENT ENTRY

One of the unfortunate consequences of successful management is that it often leads to imitation or entry into the market by other firms. Of course, entry by competitors adversely affects the profits of existing firms. Faced with the threat of entry, a manager might consider a strategy like limit pricing. Limit pricing changes the business environment by reducing the number of competitors.

limit pricing
Strategy where an incumbent maintains a price below the monopoly level in order to prevent entry.

More formally, *limit pricing* occurs when a monopolist (or other firm with market power) prices below the monopoly price to prevent other firms from entering a market. As we will see, limit pricing is not always a profitable business strategy, and extreme care must be exercised when adopting such a strategy.

Theoretical Basis for Limit Pricing

Consider a situation in which a monopolist controls the entire market. The demand curve for the monopolist's product is D^M in Figure 13–1. Monopoly profits are maximized at the price P^M, and monopoly profits are given by π^M. Unfortunately for this incumbent, if a potential entrant were to learn about this profit opportunity and possesses the technological know-how to produce the product at the same cost as the incumbent, the profits enjoyed by the monopolist would be eroded if the potential entrant could profitably enter the market. Entry would move the industry from monopoly to duopoly and reduce the incumbent's profits. Over time, if additional firms entered the market, profits would be further eroded.

FIGURE 13–1 Monopoly Pricing

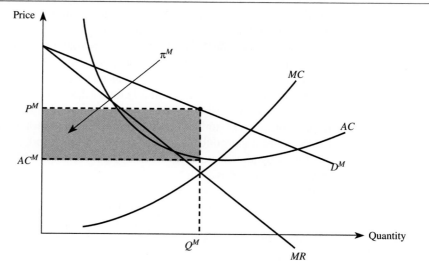

INSIDE BUSINESS 13–1

Business Strategy at Microsoft

On May 18, 1998, the United States Department of Justice filed suit against Microsoft—the world's largest supplier of computer software for personal computers— under Sections 1 and 2 of the Sherman Antitrust Act. The government alleged that Microsoft employed a number of anticompetitive business strategies, including tying other Microsoft software products to Microsoft's Windows operating system; exclusionary agreements precluding companies from distributing, promoting, buying, or using products of Microsoft's software competitors or potential competitors; and exclusionary agreements restricting the right of companies to provide services or resources to Microsoft's software competitors or potential competitors.

According to the government, Netscape enjoyed a 70 to 80 percent share of the Internet browser market during the early 1990s. Microsoft invested hundreds of millions of dollars to develop, test, and promote Internet Explorer, but it faced the serious challenge of getting consumers to switch from Netscape Navigator to Internet Explorer. According to the government, a top executive at Microsoft—its vice president of the Platforms

Group—summarized the company's strategy thusly: "We are going to cut off their air supply. Everything they're selling, we're going to give away for free." The government also alleged that Bill Gates made threats to Netscape and said, "Our business model works even if all Internet software is free . . . We are still selling operating systems. What does Netscape's business model look like? Not very good."

A lot has happened since 1998. Microsoft lost the suit; Netscape merged with America Online; America Online later merged with Time Warner, only to spin off again in 2009. And, in January of 2009, the European Commission ruled that Microsoft's practice of tying its browser to its operating system was illegal under European Union antitrust laws. Ultimately, only time will tell if Microsoft's strategies were successful.

Sources: Antitrust Complaint: *United States of America v. Microsoft Corporation,* May 18, 1998; *The Wall Street Journal Online Edition,* Front Page, October 9, 2001; "AOL Time Warner to Drop 'AOL' from Corporate Name," *The Wall Street Journal,* September 11, 2003; Robert Wielaard, "EU: Microsoft Must Unbundle Browser," Associated Press, January 17, 2009.

One strategy for an incumbent is to charge a price below the monopoly price in an attempt to discourage entry. To see the potential merits of this strategy, suppose for the moment that the entrant's costs are identical to those of the incumbent and that the entrant has complete information about the incumbent's costs as well as the demand for the product. In other words, imagine that the potential entrant knows all the information enjoyed by the incumbent.

To limit price, the incumbent produces Q^L (which exceeds the monopoly output of Q^M) and charges a price P^L that is lower than the monopoly price. This situation is shown in Figure 13–2. If the potential entrant believes the incumbent will continue to produce Q^L units of output if it enters the market, then the *residual demand* for the entrant's product is simply the market demand, D^M, minus the amount (Q^L) produced by the incumbent. This difference, $D^M - Q^L$, is the entrant's residual demand curve and is sketched in Figure 13–2. The entrant's residual demand curve starts out at a price of P^L (since $D^M - Q^L$ is zero at this price). For each price below P^L, the horizontal distance between the entrant's residual demand curve and the monopolist's demand curve is Q^L at each price.

Since the entrant's residual demand curve in Figure 13–2 lies below the average cost curve, entry is not profitable. To see this, note that the entrant loses money if it enters and produces more output or less output than Q units. By entering and

FIGURE 13–2 Limit Pricing and Residual Demand

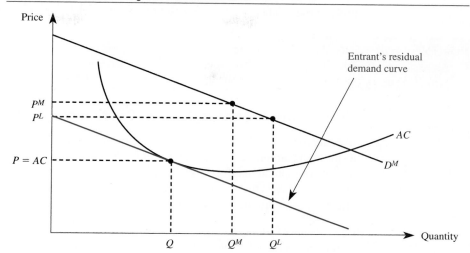

producing exactly Q units, total market output increases to $Q + Q^L$. This pushes the price down to the point where $P = AC$ for the entrant, so its economic profits are zero. Thus, the entrant cannot earn positive profits by entering the market. Furthermore, if entry involves any extra costs whatsoever (even one cent), the entrant will have a strict incentive to stay out of this market. Thus, limit pricing prevents entry and the incumbent earns higher profits than those earned in the presence of entry (but profits under limit pricing are lower than if it were an uncontested monopoly).

Limit Pricing May Fail to Deter Entry

Now that you understand the basic rationale for limit pricing, let's take a more critical look at this strategy. In our example, the potential entrant was assumed to have complete information about demand and costs, so the strategy of limit pricing did not "hide" anything about the profitability of the incumbent's line of business. In fact, the low price charged by the incumbent played no real role in preventing entry: The entrant opted to stay out because it believed the incumbent would produce at least Q^L units if it entered.

In light of this observation, a better strategy for the incumbent would be to charge the monopoly price (P^M) and produce the monopoly output (Q^M), but *threaten* to expand output to Q^L if entry occurs. If the potential entrant believes this threat and stays out of the market, the incumbent will earn higher profits from this strategy than under limit pricing. Unfortunately, it is not credible for the incumbent to produce an output of Q^L if entry occurs. In particular, entry reduces the incumbent's marginal revenue, leading to an optimal output that is less than Q^L. Thus, the incumbent has an incentive to renege on its threat to produce Q^L if entry occurs. Recognizing this, a rational entrant would find it profitable to enter the market if the incumbent sets its price at P^L.

In order to actually prevent entry, the incumbent must engage in an activity that lowers the postentry profits of the entrant. In the simple example considered above, postentry profits are completely independent of the preentry price charged by the incumbent. This, coupled with the fact that the "threat" to maintain output at Q^L in the face of entry is not credible, means that limit pricing will not protect an incumbent's profits unless other factors are present that link preentry prices to postentry profits.

Principle	**Effective Limit Pricing**
	For limit pricing to effectively prevent entry by rational competitors, the preentry price must be linked to the postentry profits of potential entrants.

Linking the Preentry Price to Postentry Profits

In many real-world business settings, the preentry price may be linked to postentry profits through commitments made by incumbents, learning curve effects, incomplete information, or reputation effects. As discussed below, limit pricing may be profitable if one or more of these conditions are met, but care must be taken in evaluating the dynamic effects of limit pricing to ensure that deterring entry is actually the best strategy.

Commitment Mechanisms

Returning to the example in Figure 13–2, the preentry price is not linked to postentry profits because rational entrants recognize that the incumbent does not have an incentive to maintain a postentry output of Q^L. The incumbent can overcome this problem by committing to produce at least Q^L units of output. More specifically, if the incumbent can somehow "tie its own hands" and credibly commit to not reducing output in the face of entry—and if this commitment is known by the potential entrant—then the strategy will indeed block entry.

The incumbent might make such a commitment by building a plant that is incapable of producing less than Q^L units of output. In this case, the incumbent may be able to produce more than Q^L units; the key is that all potential entrants know it cannot produce *less* than this amount. The incumbent can then set its price at P^L (which corresponds to the output Q^L), so that the preentry price is linked (through Q^L) to the postentry profits of the entrant. Since entrants realize that the incumbent will continue to produce at least Q^L units of output after entry, their residual demand curve lies below average costs. Therefore, it is not profitable for potential entrants to enter the market.

It may seem strange that the incumbent earns higher profits by "tying its hands" and committing to produce at least Q^L instead of maintaining the flexibility to adjust output as it sees fit should entry occur. To better understand why *commitment* is a profitable strategy, consider the extensive-form representation of the entry game presented in Figure 13–3. Here, the incumbent has a first-mover advantage that permits it to decide whether to (1) commit by building a plant that is incapable of producing less than Q^L units of output or (2) not commit by building a plant that can produce any range of output. Once this decision is made, the entrant decides to enter or not, given the decision of the incumbent. The payoffs in parentheses represent the profits the incumbent and entrant earn, respectively, in each possible scenario. For instance, if the incumbent does not commit to Q^L and the potential entrant does not enter, then the incumbent earns profits of $100 (the monopoly profits) and the potential entrant earns $0.

Notice in Figure 13–3 that the monopoly payoff of $100 is the highest possible payoff for the incumbent. However, any attempt by the incumbent to realize this

FIGURE 13–3 The Value of Commitment

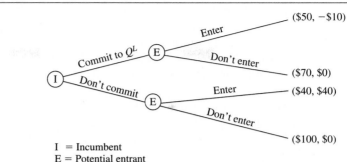

I = Incumbent
E = Potential entrant

payoff (by not committing to Q^L) provides the entrant an incentive to enter, since entry nets the entrant $40 instead of the $0 earned by not entering. Thus, we see that if the incumbent does not commit, it will earn $40 instead of the monopoly profits of $100 because it will end up sharing the market with the other firm.

In contrast, if the incumbent commits to produce Q^L, it alters the incentives confronting the potential entrant in a way that favorably changes the business environment. More specifically, commitment changes the postentry payoffs of the entrant and makes entry an unprofitable strategy. To see this, suppose the incumbent makes an irreversible decision to commit to produce Q^L. The potential entrant now earns a payoff of −$10 if it enters and $0 if it stays out of the market. In this case, the rational strategy by the entrant is to not enter, since this is better than the $10 loss that will occur if it enters the market. In the vernacular of game theory, the unique subgame perfect Nash equilibrium for the game in Figure 13–3 results in no entry; the incumbent earns an equilibrium payoff of $70 by committing to produce Q^L. While the incumbent's payoff is lower than the monopoly payoff of $100 (which cannot be achieved in equilibrium), it is greater than the $40 payoff that would have been earned absent commitment by the incumbent.

How might a firm commit to such a strategy? Suppose Applebee's is the first mid-priced restaurant to open in a small town and wishes to prevent entry by a rival. One way to do this is to build a restaurant that is relatively large. Once the restaurant is built, and the number of tables is set, Applebee's has a strong incentive to price in a way that fills all the tables with customers. Observing this, potential entrants (e.g., Chili's) will see that Applebee's is committed to a low-price, high-volume strategy in this particular town. If this reduces Chili's residual demand curve enough, it will discourage Chili's from entering this market.

Learning Curve Effects

learning curve effects
When a firm enjoys lower costs due to knowledge gained from its past production decisions.

In some production processes, the cost of producing a good or service depends on the firm's level of experience. Firms with greater historical levels of output have more experience and can produce more efficiently than firms with little or no past experience in producing the good. These effects are known as *learning curve effects*.

Learning curve effects provide a link between the preentry price and postentry profits and therefore may permit an incumbent to use limit pricing to block entry. To be concrete, consider an incumbent who has a one-period jump on a potential entrant.

This first-mover advantage permits the incumbent to produce and sell output for one period before the entrant has a chance to enter the market. In this case, the incumbent may find it profitable to produce more than the monopoly output in the first period. Doing so leads to lower first-period profits, but this extra output gives the firm more experience and therefore permits it to produce in the second period at a lower cost. If these learning curve effects are sufficiently strong, this cost advantage may induce the potential entrant to stay out of the market. Notice that by producing more output in the first period, the incumbent drives down the first-period price. Since this lower price is linked to postentry profits (through output and the learning curve effect), this form of limit pricing can be effective in discouraging entry.

Incomplete Information

The assumption that the entrant and incumbent enjoy complete information is clearly not applicable in all situations. It is usually costly for entrepreneurs and other potential entrants to find profitable business opportunities. To the extent that preentry prices or profits are a signal that lowers potential entrants' costs of identifying profitable opportunities, a link between price and postentry profits may be forged. Limit pricing may help "hide" information about profits from potential entrants, and this may delay or (in rare cases) completely eliminate entry, depending on how costly it is for potential entrants to obtain information from other sources.

To be concrete, imagine a small town with one attorney who is a monopolist in the local market for legal services. In the absence of entry, the attorney is able to earn a handsome salary of $500,000 per year. If the attorney has an impressive collection of sports cars and regularly travels to exotic places (because she charges the monopoly price), hometown kids who graduate from law school may decide to come back home to get a piece of this action. On the other hand, if the attorney lives a more modest lifestyle (because she charges less than the monopoly price), she is less likely to attract such attention. In this latter case, the attorney is practicing limit pricing in an attempt to "hide" information from potential entrants. To the extent that this tactic makes it more costly for new graduates from law school to recognize the excellent profit opportunities in this small town, the strategy may delay or eliminate entry.

Alternatively, consider a situation in which the potential entrant does not know for certain the incumbent's costs. If the potential entrant knows that the incumbent has high costs, it will find it profitable to enter the market. If the potential entrant knows the incumbent's costs are low, on the other hand, it will find the market unprofitable to enter. If the entrant does not know the incumbent's costs, it has an incentive to use whatever information is available to infer the incumbent's costs. For instance, when the incumbent charges a low price, the entrant might infer that costs are low and conclude that it does not pay to enter the market. In situations such as these, the incumbent may be able to induce the potential entrant to stay out of the market by pricing below the monopoly price. In this case, there is a link between the preentry price and postentry profits, and limit pricing can be used to profitably deter entry.

Reputation Effects

We learned in Chapter 10 that incentives in one-shot games are different than in repeated games. In games that are indefinitely repeated, trigger strategies link the past behavior of players to future payoffs. In the context of entry, such *reputation effects* can provide a link between the preentry price charged in a market and postentry profits. Permitting entry today is likely to encourage entry in future periods by other potential entrants. Depending on the relative costs and benefits of future entry, it may pay for a firm to invest in a reputation for being "tough" on entrants in order to deter future entry by other firms. To the extent that charging a low price today (to punish an entrant) discourages entry by other firms, such a strategy may increase long-run profits.

Dynamic Considerations

Even if the incumbent can forge a link between the preentry price and postentry profits to prevent entry, it may earn higher profits by allowing entry to occur. To see this, recall that when the interest rate is i and π^M represents the current profits a monopolist earns by charging P^M, the present value of current and future profits if the firm maintains its monopoly status indefinitely is

$$\Pi^M = \pi^M + \left(\frac{1}{1+i}\right)\pi^M + \left(\frac{1}{1+i}\right)^2\pi^M + \left(\frac{1}{1+i}\right)^3\pi^M + \cdots$$

$$= \left(\frac{1+i}{i}\right)\pi^M$$

Suppose that, upon observing the current period price (P^M), a new entrant decides to enter the market to compete with the (incumbent) monopolist. Entry fosters competition in the product market during the second and following periods, and this reduces the incumbent's profits from the monopoly level (π^M) to the duopoly level (π^D). While different oligopoly settings will lead to different duopoly profits, in all cases the duopoly profits are less than those enjoyed under monopoly: $\pi^D < \pi^M$. If entry occurs, the present value of the incumbent's current and future profits falls to

$$\Pi^{MD} = \pi^M + \left(\frac{1}{1+i}\right)\pi^D + \left(\frac{1}{1+i}\right)^2\pi^D + \left(\frac{1}{1+i}\right)^3\pi^D + \cdots$$

$$= \pi^M + \frac{\pi^D}{i}$$

In particular, the incumbent earns the monopoly profit during the first period, but this induces entry—which reduces profits to π^D in all remaining periods. The term π^D/i reflects the present value of the perpetuity of duopoly profits. It is clear that $\Pi^{MD} < \Pi^M$, so entry harms the incumbent.

Suppose that (through commitment, learning curve effects, incomplete information, or reputation effects) the incumbent can successfully thwart entry by charging a limit price. Is such a strategy profitable? Under the limit pricing strategy, the incumbent earns profits of π^L during each period, where $\pi^L < \pi^M$. Thus, under limit pricing, the present value of the firm's profit stream is

$$\Pi^L = \pi^L + \left(\frac{1}{1+i}\right)\pi^L + \left(\frac{1}{1+i}\right)^2\pi^L + \left(\frac{1}{1+i}\right)^3\pi^L + \cdots$$

$$= \left(\frac{1+i}{i}\right)\pi^L$$

A necessary condition for limit pricing to be an optimal strategy is for the present value of profits under limit pricing to exceed those under entry: $\Pi^L > \Pi^{MD}$. Rearranging the above equations for Π^L and Π^{MD} reveals that limit pricing is profitable ($\Pi^L > \Pi^{MD}$) whenever

$$\frac{(\pi^L - \pi^D)}{i} > \pi^M - \pi^L$$

The left-hand side of this inequality represents the present value of the benefits of limit pricing, and the right-hand side represents the up-front costs of limit pricing. Notice that a necessary condition for profitable limit pricing is for the per-period profits under limit pricing (π^L) to exceed the per-period duopoly profits (π^D). However, this alone is not enough to warrant limit pricing. In addition, the present value of these benefits must exceed the up-front costs of generating the profit stream. In this case, the up-front cost is the profit forgone by limit pricing in the first period rather than charging the monopoly price.

Based on this analysis, it is clear that limit pricing is more attractive in situations where (a) the interest rate is low, (b) profits under the limit price are close to the monopoly price, and (c) duopoly profits are significantly lower than profits under the limit price. Absent these conditions, it will not be in a firm's best interest to fight entry by limit pricing. When a firm faces entrants but opts against limit pricing, its price will gradually decline over time as more and more firms enter the market. U.S. Steel is an example of a firm that did not find it profitable to fight entry by limit pricing (see Inside Business 13–2).

Demonstration Problem 13–1

For a video walkthrough of this problem, visit www.mhhe.com/baye8e

Baker Enterprises operates a midsized company that specializes in the production of a unique type of memory chip. It is currently the only firm in the market, and it earns $10 million per year by charging the monopoly price of $115 per chip. Baker is concerned that a new firm might soon attempt to clone its product. If successful, this would reduce Baker's profit to $4 million per year. Estimates indicate that, if Baker increases its output to 280,000 units (which would lower its price to $100 per chip), the entrant will stay out of the market and Baker will earn profits of $8 million per year for the indefinite future.

1. What must Baker do to credibly deter entry by limit pricing?
2. Does it make sense for Baker to limit price if the interest rate is 10 percent?

Answer:

1. Baker must "tie its hands" to prevent itself from cutting output below 280,000 units if entry occurs, and this commitment must be observable to potential entrants before they make their decision to enter or not enter.

U.S. Steel Opts against Limit Pricing

In 1901, the United States Steel Corporation controlled almost 70 percent of the U.S. market and enjoyed profits (as a percentage of sales) of 25 percent. Rather than protect this market share through limit pricing, U.S. Steel adopted a strategy of setting the profit-maximizing price each period and enjoyed the higher short-term profits associated with such a strategy. As one would expect, this strategy resulted in entry by smaller firms who essentially took the price set by U.S. Steel as given and maximized their own profits. Over time, as the size of this competitive fringe grew, U.S. Steel gradually found it optimal to lower its price—not as a limit pricing strategy, but because its reduced market share and more elastic demand resulted in a lower optimal price. By the 1930s, U.S. Steel's market share had dropped to about 30 percent and its profits (as a percentage of sales) had fallen to less than 10 percent.

Looking at the discounted cash flows, most economists agree that U.S. Steel's policy of charging a high price and accepting entry by other firms was probably its best strategy. Among other things, U.S. Steel did not enjoy any significant cost advantages over rivals and could not credibly commit to maintain a high market share in the face of entry. Consequently, attempts to thwart entry by limit pricing would have reduced the firm's immediate profits without substantially retarding entry. Economists McCraw and Reinhardt have pointed out another reason why U.S. Steel did not attempt to limit price: It was concerned that legal (antitrust) actions would have resulted if it aggressively fought entry.

Sources: T. K. McCraw and F. Reinhardt, "Losing to Win: U.S. Steel's Pricing, Investment Decisions, and Market Share, 1901–1938." *Economic History* 49 (1989), pp. 593–619; H. Yamawaki, "Dominant Firm Pricing and Fringe Expansion: The Case of the U.S. Iron and Steel Industry, 1907–1930." *The Review of Economics and Statistics* 67, no. 3 (1985), pp. 429–37.

---

2. Limit pricing is profitable if

$$\frac{(\pi^L - \pi^D)}{i} > \pi^M - \pi^L$$

or in this case

$$\frac{(\$8 - \$4)}{.1} > \$10 - \$8$$

Since this inequality holds, limit pricing is profitable: The present value of the benefits of limit pricing (the left-hand side) is $40 million, while the up-front costs (the right-hand side) are only $2 million.

PREDATORY PRICING TO LESSEN COMPETITION

predatory pricing
Strategy where a firm temporarily prices below its marginal cost to drive competitors out of the market.

While limit pricing changes the business environment by preventing *potential* competitors from entering a market, predatory pricing lessens competition by eliminating *existing* competitors. More formally, *predatory pricing* arises when a firm charges a price below its own marginal cost in order to drive a rival out of business. Once the "prey" (the rival) leaves the market, the "predator" (the firm engaging in predatory pricing) can raise its price to a higher level, thanks to the dampened competition. Thus, predatory pricing involves a trade-off between current and future profits: It is profitable only when the present value of the higher future profits offsets the losses required to drive rivals out of the market.

Since predatory pricing hurts not only the prey but also the predator, its success critically depends on the presumption that the predator is "healthier" than the prey. A firm engaging in predatory pricing must have "deeper pockets" (greater financial resources) than the prey in order to outlast it. Reputation effects enhance the benefits of predatory pricing. Taking tough actions today to drive a competitor out of the market may, in a repeated play context, make it easier to drive future competitors out of the market. Establishing a reputation for playing tough against existing firms may induce other firms to stay out of the market. It may also provide smaller rivals an incentive to "sell out" to a large firm at a bargain price rather than risk being driven out of the market through predation.

A number of counterstrategies on the part of the prey can significantly reduce the profitability of predatory pricing. Since the predator is selling the product below its own cost, the prey might stop production entirely (in which case the predator will lose more money each period than the prey) or purchase the product from the predator and stockpile it to sell when predatory pricing ceases. The point is that a strategy of predatory pricing is typically more costly for the predator than for the prey. It is unlikely to be a profitable way of eliminating a rival that is similarly situated (in terms of size, costs, financial resources, and product appeal), but it can be successful in driving a small competitor (with "empty pockets") out of the market.

While businesses engaging in predatory pricing are vulnerable to prosecution under the Sherman Antitrust Act, predatory pricing is often difficult to prove in court. For example, in the early 2000s, American Airlines successfully defended itself against a charge from the Antitrust Division of the U.S. Department of Justice that it sought to drive small, start-up airlines out of Dallas/Ft. Worth International Airport by saturating its routes with additional flights and cutting fares. Even though the government alleged American Airlines raised fares after successfully driving out a new entrant, American Airlines prevailed at trial.

Many economists (and judges) believe that a number of practices that might be deemed "predatory" under legal definitions are, in fact, legitimate business practices. Entry generally heightens competition and results in more competitive pricing. In situations where there are substantial fixed costs, the end result of fierce price competition will be the departure of the weakest firms, and the surviving firm will raise its price. Efforts to prevent such competition would encourage entry by inefficient firms. Even worse, strict enforcement of rules against predatory pricing could lead to a collusive situation in which firms would be afraid to compete because such actions might be construed as predatory and lead to prosecution.

In addition, firms attempting to penetrate a market with a new product often find it advantageous to sell the product at a low price or even give it away for free initially, raising the price once consumers become aware of the product's value. As we will see toward the end of this chapter, the strategy of selling products below cost need not be motivated by a desire to drive rivals out of business. Quite to the contrary, such strategies are sometimes essential for new entrants to successfully compete against well-established firms.

We conclude by noting that the technical (legal) definition of predatory pricing requires the predator to price below its own marginal cost (and thus sustain losses in order to inflict damage on its prey). However, similar strategies can be used when the predator has a cost advantage over its prey. In this case, the predator does not have to price below its own marginal cost in order to drive a less efficient rival out of the market; it merely needs to set its price below the rival's cost. Similar to predatory pricing, the more efficient firm can raise its price after the less efficient firm exits the market.

Demonstration Problem 13-2

Baker Enterprises operates a midsized company that specializes in the production of a fairly unique type of memory chip. If Baker were a monopolist, it could earn $10 million per year for an indefinite period of time by charging the monopoly price of $115 per chip. While Baker could have thwarted the entry of potential rivals by limit pricing (see Demonstration Problem 13–1), it opted against doing so, and it is now in a duopoly situation, earning annual profits of $4 million per year for the foreseeable future. If Baker drops its price to $68 per chip and holds it there for one year, it will be able to drive the other firm out of the market and retain its monopoly position indefinitely. Over the year in which it engages in predatory pricing, however, Baker will lose $60 million. Ignoring legal considerations, is predatory pricing a profitable strategy? Assume the interest rate is 10 percent and, for simplicity, that any current period profits or losses occur immediately (at the beginning of the year).

Answer:

If Baker does not engage in predatory pricing, the present value of its earnings (including its current $4 million in earnings) will be Π^D, where

$$\Pi^D = \$4 + \left(\frac{1}{1+.1}\right)(\$4) + \left(\frac{1}{1+.1}\right)^2(\$4) + \left(\frac{1}{1+.1}\right)^3(\$4) + \cdots$$

$$= \left(\frac{1+.1}{.1}\right)(\$4)$$

$$= (11)(\$4)$$

$$= \$44 \text{ million}$$

If Baker uses predatory pricing, the present value of its current and future profits will be

$$\Pi^P = -\$60 + \left(\frac{1}{1+.1}\right)(\$10) + \left(\frac{1}{1+.1}\right)^2(\$10) + \left(\frac{1}{1+.1}\right)^3(\$10) + \cdots$$

$$= -\$60 + \frac{\$10}{.1}$$

$$= -\$60 + \$100$$

$$= \$40 \text{ million}$$

Since $\Pi^P < \Pi^D$, Baker earns less by engaging in predatory pricing than it does by not using predatory pricing (that is, maintaining its duopoly situation). It does not pay to use predatory pricing because it costs too much to drive the other firm out of the market.

RAISING RIVALS' COSTS TO LESSEN COMPETITION

raising rivals' costs
Strategy in which a firm gains an advantage over competitors by increasing their costs.

Another way a manager may be able to profitably change the business environment is by *raising rivals' costs*. By increasing rivals' costs, a firm distorts rivals' decision-making incentives, and this can ultimately affect their prices, output, and entry decisions. Provided the costs of implementing such a strategy are sufficiently low, the firm that raises rivals' costs may gain at the expense of other firms.

For instance, consider a large software manufacturer that is the sole producer of the most popular operating system. This firm also has a presence in other software markets; it competes against smaller rivals who sell different brands of word processing software. The large software maker might attempt to raise the costs of rivals who produce competing word processing software by making it difficult for them to access the operating system's code. In extreme cases, the large firm might refuse to release the operating system's code to firms that compete in other software markets. In both cases, this increases the cost to rivals of creating and updating their own word processing software, with little or no increase in the large firm's costs. In addition to increasing the rivals' fixed cost of producing software, this strategy may also increase the rivals' marginal cost of marketing their software, as customers are more likely to require their technical support to resolve conflicts and other problems.

A firm can also raise its rivals' costs by making it more costly for other firms to distribute their products through the retail chain. For instance, in the famous Microsoft case, the government alleged that Microsoft entered into exclusive contracts with PC suppliers, precluding them from loading Netscape's Internet browser on PCs loaded with the Windows operating system. This strategy presumably raised Netscape's cost of distributing its browser software relative to Microsoft's cost of distributing its own browser.

Strategies Involving Marginal Cost

To illustrate how a firm can gain by raising a rival's marginal cost, consider Figure 13–4, which shows a Cournot duopoly (see Chapter 9). Recall that r_1 and r_2 are the reaction functions of the two competing firms. The firms produce outputs of Q_1 and Q_2, and the reaction functions summarize each firm's profit-maximizing output given the output produced by the rival. For example, r_1 identifies the profit-maximizing output of firm 1 for each potential level of output by firm 2. These reaction functions are downward sloping because each firm produces its output simultaneously, and the market price adjusts to clear whatever output is brought to market. The greater the amount of output firm 2 brings to market, the lower the resulting market price and thus the lower the optimal output of firm 1.

FIGURE 13–4   Raising a Rival's Marginal Cost

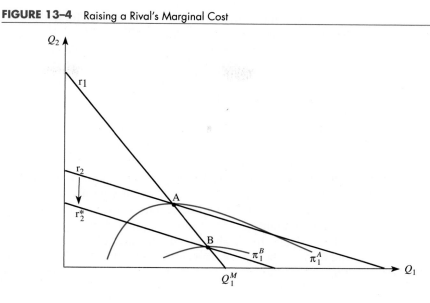

Point A in Figure 13–4 represents the initial Cournot equilibrium. Firm 1's profits are π_1^A and are associated with the isoprofit curve through point A. These profits are clearly lower than the profits that would result if firm 1 were a monopolist (the point where firm 1 produces Q_1^M units of output and firm 2 produces zero units of output).

Now suppose that firm 1 uses a business tactic that raises its rival's marginal cost of production. Due to the higher cost, firm 2 now has an incentive to produce less output than before. Geometrically, by raising its rival's marginal cost, firm 1 shifts its rival's reaction function down to r_2^* in Figure 13–4. The new equilibrium moves to point B. Due to its higher marginal cost, firm 2 reduces its output. This has the effect of raising the market price, and firm 1 takes advantage of this higher price by expanding its own output. Ultimately, firm 1 ends up with more market share and higher profits. In particular, notice that firm 1's profits at point B are π_1^B. Since this level of profits is associated with an isoprofit curve that is closer to the monopoly point, firm 1 has benefited by raising its rival's marginal cost.

Strategies Involving Fixed Costs

A firm may also gain by raising its rivals' fixed costs. Perhaps surprisingly, such benefits may accrue to a firm even when the strategy also raises the firm's own costs. To see this, consider an incumbent that earns monopoly profits of $200 if no other firms enter the market. However, if a rival enters the market, the competition that ensues reduces the incumbent's profit to $70, with the entrant also earning $70. Since the entrant earns zero if it does not enter but earns $70 by entering, the monopolist will be unable to sustain its monopoly profit unless it can successfully change the business environment.

Suppose the incumbent successfully lobbies for a regulation requiring any firm operating in the market (including itself) to obtain a license from the government that costs $90. Notice that the incumbent has raised its own fixed costs by $90, but more importantly, it also has raised its rival's costs by $90. Now if the rival enters the market it loses $20 (the original $70 less the $90 license fee). Since the rival earns $0 by not entering, this strategy of raising all firms' costs by $90 changes the rival's entry decision, and the incumbent maintains its monopoly position. Notice that the resulting profits of the incumbent are $110 (the original $200 monopoly profit less the $90 license fee). While this is not as profitable as before the license was required and the firm enjoyed a monopoly ($200), it is better than the $70 that would be earned if no license was required and the rival entered.

This scenario is depicted in the extensive form shown in Figure 13–5. Here, the incumbent has two strategies: support a $90 license fee, or do not support it. The potential entrant gets to observe whether there is a license fee before making its entry decision. In the absence of a license fee, the entrant has an incentive to enter and thus the incumbent earns profits of only $70. If the incumbent supports the $90 license fee, the entrant's best strategy is to stay out of the market (since $0 > −$20). In this case the incumbent earns $110. This is clearly the best strategy for the incumbent, and we see that the incumbent earns $110 in the unique subgame perfect equilibrium to this game.

Strategies for Vertically Integrated Firms

In Chapter 6 we learned that vertically integrated firms produce in both the upstream (input) market and the downstream (output) market. A vertically integrated firm with market power in an upstream market may be able to exploit this market power in order to raise rivals' costs in downstream markets. In particular, actions taken by the vertically integrated firm to increase input prices in the upstream market will increase the costs of rivals competing in downstream markets. In what follows, we discuss two strategies of this sort: vertical foreclosure and the price–cost squeeze.

FIGURE 13–5   Raising a Rival's Fixed Cost

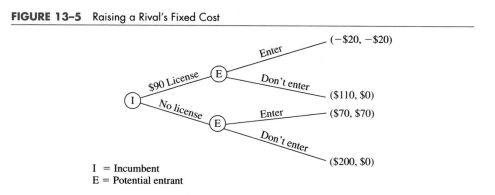

I = Incumbent
E = Potential entrant

Vertical Foreclosure

vertical foreclosure
Strategy wherein a vertically integrated firm charges downstream rivals a prohibitive price for an essential input, thus forcing rivals to use more costly substitutes or go out of business.

An extreme form of raising rivals' costs, called *vertical foreclosure,* occurs when a firm that controls an essential upstream input competes against other firms in the downstream market. By refusing to sell other downstream firms the needed input, it forces them to seek out less efficient substitutes. This increases their cost of production. When no substitutes are available, the rivals are completely driven out of the downstream market because they are unable to acquire the essential input.

While vertical foreclosure may be profitable in some instances, it is not always the most profitable strategy. In particular, by charging input prices so high that it drives nonintegrated firms out of the market, the vertically integrated firm forgoes upstream profits from the sale of the input. Vertical foreclosure is profitable only when the higher profits earned in the downstream market (due to the increased market power) more than offset the profits lost in the upstream input market.

The Price–Cost Squeeze

price–cost squeeze
Tactic used by a vertically integrated firm to squeeze the margins of its competitors.

In specialized circumstances, a vertically integrated firm may potentially benefit from raising rivals' costs through a *price–cost squeeze.* Here, the vertically integrated firm raises rivals' costs on the input side while holding constant (or even lowering) the price charged for the final product. This squeezes the margins of downstream competitors. The ultimate effect of a severe price–cost squeeze is similar to that under predatory pricing: It drives competitors out of the market. Since this tactic requires the vertically integrated firm to charge prices that do not maximize current profits in the upstream and downstream markets, the firm trades off lower short-term profits for the potential of higher future profits once rivals exit the downstream market. Depending on the magnitude of this trade-off and the level of interest rates, a price–cost squeeze may be profitable.

Price–cost squeezes also can be used by large vertically integrated firms to "punish" rivals who do not participate in market-sharing and other collusive arrangements in downstream markets. While the vertically integrated firm may lose short-term profits by using price–cost squeezes to discipline rivals, this investment in a reputation for being "tough" can generate higher future profits in markets where there is repeated interaction.

PRICE DISCRIMINATION AS A STRATEGIC TOOL

The profitability of predatory pricing, limit pricing, and raising rivals' costs depends on the relative benefits and costs of such strategies. The relative attractiveness of these tactics is enhanced when the perpetrator can effectively price discriminate among its various customers. Recall that price discrimination (discussed in detail in Chapter 11) is the practice of charging different customers different prices for the same product.

In the absence of price discrimination, it is more costly for a firm to engage in limit pricing or predatory pricing. By lowering its price to prevent entry or to drive a competitor from the market, a nondiscriminating firm must lower its price to all of its customers. In contrast, if the firm can price discriminate, it can "target" the price cuts to those consumers or markets that will inflict the most damage to the rival (in the case of predatory pricing) or potential entrants (in the case of limit pricing). Meanwhile, it can continue to charge the monopoly price to its other customers.

Likewise, a price discriminating firm using vertical foreclosure or a price–cost squeeze can target increases in input prices to those firms that pose the most serious threats in downstream markets. At the same time, it can continue to charge lower input prices to input buyers that pose no threat in downstream markets. This permits the firm to maximize profits from input sales to nonthreatening customers while raising the costs for those firms who are rivals in the downstream market.

For these reasons, price discrimination can be used as a strategic tool to facilitate limit pricing, predatory pricing, or raising rivals' costs.

CHANGING THE TIMING OF DECISIONS OR THE ORDER OF MOVES

Another way a manager can profitably change the business environment is by changing the timing of decisions or the order of moves. We formally illustrate this below.

First-Mover Advantages

A *first-mover advantage* permits a firm to earn a higher payoff by committing to a decision before its rivals get a chance to commit to their decisions. The Stackelberg model of oligopoly we examined in Chapter 9 is a classic example of a strategic environment in which the first mover enjoys an advantage. Recall that, in this setting, one firm (called the Stackelberg leader) gets to commit to a higher level of output before its rivals (followers) make their own output decisions. The Stackelberg leader earns higher profits than it would if it did not have the opportunity to move first.

The rationale for changing the timing of decisions to achieve a first-mover advantage can be easily illustrated. Consider two firms (firm A and firm B) that must make output decisions (low or high). We will consider two scenarios. In the first situation, both firms make their decisions simultaneously (and thus there is no scope for a first-mover advantage). We will see that the outcome of the game changes in the second situation, where firm A makes its decision before firm B.

The normal form representation for the simultaneous-move version of the game is presented in Table 13–1. For each pair of strategies by firm A and firm B, the first number in each cell represents the payoff to firm A, while the second entry represents firm B's payoff. For instance, if firm A produces a low level of output and firm B produces a low level of output, then firm A earns $30 and firm B earns $10.

TABLE 13-1 Simultaneous-Move Production Game

		Firm B	
	Strategy	**Low Output**	**High Output**
Firm A	**Low Output**	$30, $10	$10, $15
	High Output	$20, $5	$1, $2

In this simultaneous-move game, firm A has a dominant strategy: Regardless of whether firm B produces a low or high level of output, firm A's profits are highest if it produces a low level of output. Firm B, being rational, recognizes this and has an incentive to produce the high output (since the $15 earned from doing so exceeds the $10 that would be earned if it produced a low output). We conclude that the unique Nash equilibrium in this simultaneous-move production game is for firm A to produce a low output and firm B to produce a high output. In equilibrium, firm A earns profits of $10 and firm B earns profits of $15.

Now suppose firm A changes the timing of its decision so that it gets to move before firm B. Just as importantly, assume firm B actually observes firm A's decision before it makes its own decision, and firm A knows this. The extensive form for this sequential-move production game is given in Figure 13–6. Notice that the payoffs at the end of the game tree are identical to those in Table 13–1. The only difference between these two games is that, in Figure 13–6, firm A gets to move first and firm B gets to observe A's decision before making its own decision.

What should firm A do when it gets to move first? If it chooses a low level of output, firm B's best response would be to produce a high level of output. If it does so, firm A earns a payoff of $10. However, if firm A chooses a high level of output, firm B's best response is to produce a low level of output. In this case, firm A earns a payoff of $20. Thus, in the unique subgame perfect equilibrium to the game in Figure 13–6, firm A produces a high level of output. Firm B observes this and responds with a low level of output. Firm A's equilibrium payoff is $20, and firm B's equilibrium payoff is $5.

The fact that firm A's equilibrium payoff is higher ($20) when it gets to move first compared to its equilibrium payoff in the simultaneous-move game ($10) represents a

FIGURE 13-6 Sequential-Move Production Game

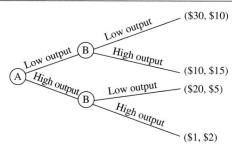

INSIDE BUSINESS 13–3

First to Market, First to Succeed? Or First to Fail?

During the early era of personal computers, companies were inaccurate in forecasting PC demand. As a result, many firms lost sales to competitors or were stuck with unsold inventories. This all changed in 1984, when Michael Dell founded the Dell Computer Corporation. Dell's business model permitted it to sell a 12-megahertz computer for $1,995, compared to the price of $3,995 that IBM was charging for a 6-megahertz machine. Ultimately, Dell pioneered the direct sales model for computers (selling computers directly to end users) and later expanded his direct sales model to the Internet. While many other businesses have attempted to imitate this strategy (Compaq began selling direct in 1998), Dell's first-mover advantage placed it at the top of the industry by the year 2000 in terms of sales and profit growth. Dell is an example of a firm that successfully capitalized on its first-mover advantage (although due to entry, the industry is becoming more and more competitive each day, which has led Dell to supply popular retail chains with its computers).

Unfortunately, being the first to market an idea or product does not guarantee success. A number of well-known companies have been first to introduce new products, but being first has not always formed the basis for an "advantage." The first disposable diaper—a product called Chux—lost out to Procter & Gamble, which later introduced Pampers. A company called Ampex pioneered the video recorder, but most remember Sony as being the first mover when it introduced VCRs based on the now defunct Beta format. Ultimately, JVC won the market with its VHS format. Prodigy Services was the main visionary regarding online services but ultimately lost out to a second mover (AOL).

Get the picture? Being first is not always an advantage; sometimes it pays to be patient. And even if you capitalize on a first- or second-mover advantage, remember that markets are dynamic. As illustrated by the longer-run experiences of Dell, AOL, and other companies, such advantages may not be sustainable in the long run.

Sources: "Being There First Isn't Good Enough," *The Wall Street Journal,* June 8, 1996; Michael Dell, *Direct from Dell,* Harper Collins, 1999; various company Internet sites.

---

first-mover advantage. In effect, the ability to move first gives firm A an advantage over its rival. In contrast, notice that firm B suffers from a second-mover disadvantage: It earns $5 when it moves second, which is lower than the $15 that is earned when both firms make decisions simultaneously.

It is important to stress that firm A's first-mover advantage in this example relies on three crucial things: (1) Firm A's decision to produce a high level of output is irreversible, (2) firm B observes this decision before making its own output decision, and (3) both of these facts are common knowledge (firm B knows firm A's decision is irreversible, firm A knows firm B knows this, and so on).

First-mover advantages are common in many business environments. Consider an innovator who is the first to market a new product. Being first may permit her to enjoy monopoly profits throughout the life of the patent. Due to learning curve effects, additional first-mover benefits may accrue in the form of lower costs. First-mover advantages due to learning curve effects can persist long after the patent expires, and also can be present even if there is not a patent in the first place. In the last part of this chapter, we will see that first-mover advantages are particularly strong in industries with significant network effects.

Second-Mover Advantages

Being first is not always advantageous; sometimes *second-mover advantages* are even greater. For example, being the second to introduce a new product can yield higher payoffs than being first if it permits the second mover to free-ride on investments made by the first mover. This permits the second mover to produce at a lower cost than the firm that moves first. In addition, a second mover may gain an advantage because it can learn from the first mover's mistakes. In this case, the second mover may be able to produce a better product at a lower cost than the firm that moves first. Inside Business 13–3 documents that, while many firms have benefited from being the first mover, some have benefited from being the second mover.

Demonstration Problem 13–3

Determine how much you would be willing to pay for the privilege of moving first in these two different games:[1]

1. There are two players, you and a rival. The player announcing the larger positive integer gets a payoff of $10, while the other player gets $0.
2. There are two players, you and a rival. The player announcing the smaller positive integer gets a payoff of $20, while the other player gets $2.

Answer:

1. This game has a second-mover advantage; the second player can guarantee a payoff of $10 by simply announcing a positive integer that is larger than that announced by the first mover. Since there is not a first-mover advantage, you should not be willing to pay anything to move first (but note that you would be willing to pay up to $10 for the right to move second).
2. This game has a first-mover advantage; the first mover can guarantee a payoff of $20 by announcing "1." Since there is a first-mover advantage and you stand to earn $18 more by moving first rather than second, you should be willing to pay up to $18 for the right to move first in this game.

PENETRATION PRICING TO OVERCOME NETWORK EFFECTS

In many industries (including airlines, electric power, and Internet auction markets), phenomena known as network effects give incumbents first-mover advantages that are difficult for potential entrants to overcome. In light of the growing importance of networks in the global economic landscape, we conclude with an overview of networks

---

[1]In working this problem, note that the positive integers consist of the numbers {1, 2, 3, 4, . . .}, and "infinity" is not an integer.

and explain why network externalities lead to significant first-mover advantages. We also show how entrants can use penetration pricing strategies to change the business environment and potentially overcome obstacles created by network externalities.

What Is a Network?

A *network* consists of links that connect different points (called *nodes*) in geographic or economic space. Networks play a profound role in the organization of many industries, including railroads, airlines, trucking, telecommunications, and a host of other sectors of the "new" economy, such as the Internet.

The simplest type of network is a *one-way network* in which services flow in only one direction. Residential water service is a commonly used example of a one-way network: Water typically flows one-way from the local water company to homes. Not surprisingly, one-way networks can lead to first-mover advantages because of economies of scale or scope. Since a network provider (the local water company) often enjoys economies of scale in creating a network to deliver service to its customers, new entrants typically find it difficult to build a network that supplants the network services of a well-established incumbent. The distinguishing feature of a one-way network is that its value to each user does not *directly* depend on how many other people use the new network.

As we will see, this is not the case for two-way networks (such as telephone systems, e-mail, or many facets of the Internet, including instant messages). In a *two-way network,* the value to each user depends *directly* on how many other people use the network. This may permit an existing two-way network provider to enjoy significant first-mover advantages even in the absence of any significant economies of scale.

An example of a two-way network is the *star network* shown in Figure 13–7. The points C_1 through C_7 represent nodes—for example, consumers who own a telephone. The point in the middle (denoted H) represents the *hub*—for example, a switch owned by the telephone company. Consumer C_1 can call consumer C_2 through the connection C_1HC_2. Star networks are common not only in telecommunications,

FIGURE 13–7 A Star Network

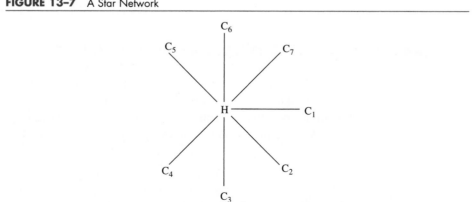

but also in other sectors of the economy, including the airline industry. For example, a consumer wishing to fly from Indianapolis to Philadelphia on Delta Airlines generally will first fly from Indianapolis to Atlanta (one of Delta's hubs) and then from Atlanta to Philadelphia.

Network Externalities

direct network externality
The direct value enjoyed by the user of a network because others also use the network.

Two-way networks that link users exhibit positive externalities called *direct network externalities:* The per-unit value of the services provided by a network increases as the size of the network grows. A telephone network with only one user is worthless. A telephone network that connects two users is more valuable, but worth less to each consumer than a network that connects three users, and so on. With only two users, there are two potential connection services created by the network: User 1 can call user 2, and user 2 can call user 1. Adding one more user increases the number of potential connection services from two to six: User 1 can call user 2, user 1 can call user 3, user 2 can call user 1, user 2 can call user 3, user 3 can call user 1, and user 3 can call user 2. More generally, if there are n users, there are $n(n - 1)$ potential connection services. Adding one user to the network directly benefits all users by adding $2n$ potential connections.

Principle	**Direct Network Externalities**
	A two-way network linking n users provides $n(n - 1)$ potential connection services. If one new user joins the network, all the existing users directly benefit because the new user adds $2n$ potential connection services to the network.

indirect network externality (network complementarities)
The indirect value enjoyed by the user of a network because of complementarities between the size of a network and the availability of complementary products or services.

In addition to these direct externalities present in two-way networks, *indirect network externalities* also can exist. Indirect externalities that stem from the growing use of a particular network are called *network complementarities* and can arise in both one-way and two-way networks. For instance, the growing use of the Internet has led to many complementary products and services, such as teleconferencing software. Due to the sizable fixed costs required to develop such software, a large number of Internet users is needed to justify the associated software development costs. As more and more software is developed for use on the Internet, the associated network complementarities make the Internet even more valuable to each user.

Similarly, the growing use of electricity in the early twentieth century led to the development of millions of different types of electrical appliances. The availability of these appliances and the associated network complementarities increased the value of electricity networks. Analogous indirect externalities arise in non-network industries. For example, growth in the number of cars using 85 percent ethanol fuel (E85) has led to an increase in the number of E85 gas stations in the United States.

Negative externalities such as *bottlenecks* also can arise in networks. As the size of a network grows, it may eventually reach a point where the existing infrastructure cannot handle additional users. Beyond this point, additional users create congestion. This makes it harder for users to make network connections, and the value per user of the services provided by the network declines. Examples of bottlenecks include traffic jams on highway networks, delays at airports, dropped calls on telecommunication networks, slow server responses on the Internet, and power outages on local electricity networks.

First-Mover Advantages Due to Consumer Lock-In

Because of network externalities, it is often difficult for new networks to replace or compete with existing networks—even if the new network is technologically superior to the existing one. In particular, since the established network is likely to have many users and complementary services, the total value of the existing network will be greater for each user (due to direct and/or indirect network externalities) than a new network with relatively few users or complementary services.

To see the nature of the problem, consider the simple two-way network shown in Figure 13–8(a) providing connection services between users C_1 and C_2. Imagine that this network is owned by the monopolist identified as the hub H_1 and that each user values these network services at $10 per month.

Now suppose another firm decides to enter the market to compete against the existing monopoly network. Since creating such a network will likely involve substantial fixed costs, let us suppose that the new firm has a superior technology such that, at full capacity, each user values the new network at $20 per month. Once the new network is built, the situation looks like that in Figure 13–8(b), where H_1 and H_2 represent the duopolists' hubs. In this figure, the two networks are exclusive. This means that both consumers must subscribe to the same network for the services of that network to be useful (see Inside Business 13–4).

Will the new entrant be able to enter the market with its superior technology? Table 13–2 illustrates the underlying issues. The players in this game are users who

FIGURE 13–8   Entry Creates a Competing (but Exclusive) Network

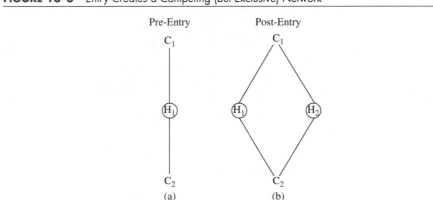

TABLE 13–2 A Network Game

		User 2	
	Network Provider	**H₁**	**H₂**
User 1	**H₁**	$10, $10	$0, $0
	H₂	$0, $0	$20, $20

must choose a network provider. Both users are initially using network provider H_1, thanks to its first-mover advantage. In the initial situation, each user receives $10 in value each month from the network. Notice that, when the new network becomes available, neither user has a unilateral incentive to change network providers. Given the choice of the other user, neither user has an incentive to change to H_2, even though, if both consumers switched simultaneously, each would be better off. This is a classic coordination problem (see Chapter 10). The network externalities create a consumer *lock-in:* The consumers are stuck in a situation (equilibrium) where they are using the inferior network.

INSIDE BUSINESS 13–4

Network Externalities and Penetration Pricing by Yahoo! Auctions

Online auctions are a classic example of an *exclusive network*. In particular, companies like eBay may be viewed as hubs that provide connections for buyers and sellers. The more buyers that visit the site, the more valuable the site is to sellers. Similarly, the more sellers that list items for sale at the site, the more valuable the site is to buyers.

Once a first-mover like eBay establishes itself as "the site" for buying and selling items on the Internet, it can be very difficult for a new entrant to gain a foothold with a competing auction site. After all, if no sellers list their products at the new site, buyers have no incentive to visit the site. And if no buyers visit the site, sellers have no incentive to pay for the privilege of listing items for sale at the new site. In this manner, a first mover into online auctions (such as eBay) may be able to sustain market power through network effects and its first-mover advantage.

This exact scenario presented a challenge for Yahoo! in the late 1990s. Yahoo! wanted to enter the market for online auctions to compete against eBay. Recognizing the problem of network effects and eBay's first-mover advantage, Yahoo! adopted a penetration pricing strategy, allowing both buyers and sellers to use its auction site for free. It reasoned that, since eBay was charging sellers a fee, this strategy would permit the Yahoo! auction site to grow to its critical mass. Once a sufficiently large number of buyers and sellers had begun using the site, the network effects would kick in and Yahoo! would be able to charge fees for its auction services.

Unfortunately for Yahoo!, this strategy did not permit it to overcome eBay's network effects and first-mover advantages. Ultimately, Yahoo! closed its U.S. online auction site in June 2007.

Sources: Michael R. Baye and John Morgan, "Information Gatekeepers on the Internet and the Competitiveness of Homogeneous Product Markets." *American Economic Review* 91, no. 3 (June 2001), pp. 454–74; Yahoo! Auction site at http://help.yahoo.com/help/auctions/asell/, accessed on October 6, 2001; "Yahoo! US Auction Sites Are Retired!" at http://auctions.shopping.yahoo.com/, accessed on March 7, 2009.

Using Penetration Pricing to "Change the Game"

While a lock-in with only two users might be easily resolved by communication between the two users (each consumer agreeing to switch to the other network), the transaction costs of such a strategy make it unfeasible when there are hundreds or potentially millions of users who do not know one another. In these more realistic settings, what can a business like firm 2 do to establish its network?

penetration pricing
Charging a low price initially to penetrate a market and gain a critical mass of customers; useful when strong network effects are present.

One strategy, called *penetration pricing,* entails charging an initial price that is very low—potentially even giving the product away for free or *paying* customers to try out the new product—to gain a critical mass of customers. This protects users from the risk that other users will not switch to the new technology: Users can maintain their use of the existing network while experimenting with the new network.

To see how a penetration pricing strategy can help firm 2 attract a critical mass of users on its network, notice that the value to users of having access to both networks is at least as large as the value of using either network individually. Consequently, if the new network provider actually pays users a small amount (say $1) to try out its service, then during this "trial" period the game facing consumers would change from the one in Table 13–2 to the one in Table 13–3. In this case, each consumer has an incentive to try the new network since the choice "H_1 & H_2" is a dominant strategy for each user.

Once consumers try the two networks, they will soon realize that H_2 is better and eventually quit using H_1. Once a critical mass of users (in this case, both users) begins using H_2, the owner of network H_2 can eliminate the $1 payment (and ultimately increase the price charged for access to its network), since each consumer now receives $20 in benefits from H_2, compared to the $10 in benefits when both consumers used H_1. In this manner, the new entrant can use penetration pricing to overcome the incumbent's first-mover advantage that stems from these network externalities. Looking again at Table 13–2, penetration pricing is exactly the tool needed to move consumers from the equilibrium in the top left cell to the bottom right cell.

TABLE 13–3   The Network Game with Penetration Pricing

		User 2	
	Network Provider	H_1	H_1 & H_2
User 1	H_1	$10, $10	$10, $11
	H_1 & H_2	$11, $10	$21, $21

Demonstration Problem 13–4

A firm is contemplating the establishment of a potential two-way network linking 100 users. A feasibility study reveals that each user is willing to pay an average of $1 for each potential connection service provided by the network. If the total cost of establishing the network is $500,000, should the firm establish the network? Explain.

Answer:

A network linking 100 users provides $100(100 - 1) = 9,900$ potential connection services. Valued at an average of $1 each, the firm can generate revenues of $9,900 from each user who subscribes to the network. If the firm gets all 100 users to subscribe to the network, its total revenues would be $990,000, which clearly exceeds the $500,000 in costs required to establish the network. However, note that the firm earns the $490,000 in profits only if all 100 users subscribe. Due to network effects and consumer lock-in, there is no guarantee that these profits will be realized. Penetration pricing or some other method will likely be needed to "jump start" the network. This will obviously impact the firm's revenues and profits in the short run.

ANSWERING THE HEADLINE

Tom's plan is to attempt to change the game from a simultaneous-move game (in which Tom and Morton's simultaneously announce their plans) to a sequential-move game in which Tom moves first. As shown in Figure 13–9, this will give Tom a first-mover advantage. By announcing as early as possible his plans to target business customers (and credibly commit to this strategy), Tom will get the jump on Morton's. Once Morton's observes this commitment, it will be too late: its best response will be to stay out of the market, since battling another upscale steakhouse for the same customers will be unprofitable. Obviously, this plan critically depends on Tom's ability to move very quickly (to make sure he preempts any entry commitment by Morton's) as well as his ability to credibly commit to and signal such a strategy. If Tom can do this, he will likely earn profits of $90,000—a marked improvement on the $50,000 he would expect to earn if he did not make this move.

FIGURE 13–9 First-Mover Advantage in Marketing

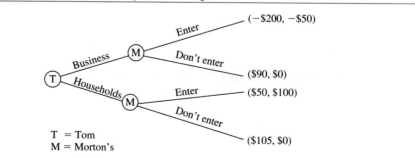

SUMMARY

In this chapter, we explored several strategies that businesses can use to change the environment in which they operate. Strategies such as limit pricing and predatory pricing are designed to eliminate competition in the market. For limit pricing to be effective, a firm must be able to link its preentry price to the postentry profits of potential entrants. Similarly, predatory pricing can be used to reduce the number of existing competitors. Both limit pricing and predatory pricing involve trade-offs between current and future profits, and therefore the profitability of such strategies depends on the interest rate and other variables. Additionally, since these practices are designed to boost profits by eliminating competitors, businesses that use these tactics run the risk of being sued by antitrust authorities for violating antitrust laws.

We also learned that, in situations where it is not possible to eliminate competition, other tactics may be used to change the environment in a manner that increases profits. Examples of such strategies include raising rivals' costs to lessen competition, changing the timing of decisions to create first- or second-mover advantages, and penetration pricing. Penetration pricing is particularly useful in network industries, where consumer lock-in due to direct and indirect network externalities gives existing firms a substantial advantage over new entrants.

KEY TERMS AND CONCEPTS

bottleneck	node
commitment	one-way network
direct network externality	penetration pricing
exclusive network	predatory pricing
first-mover advantage	price–cost squeeze
hub	raising rivals' costs
indirect network externality	reputation effects
learning curve effects	residual demand
limit pricing	second-mover advantage
lock-in	star network
network	two-way network
network complementarity	vertical foreclosure

END-OF-CHAPTER PROBLEMS BY LEARNING OBJECTIVE

Every end-of-chapter problem addresses at least one learning objective. Following is a nonexhaustive sample of end-of-chapter problems for each learning objective.

LO1 Explain the economic basis for limit pricing, and identify the conditions under which a firm can profit from such a strategy.

Try these problems: 1, 16

LO2 Explain the economic basis for predatory pricing.
Try these problems: 7, 12

LO3 Show how a manager can profitably lessen competition by raising rivals' costs.
Try these problems: 5, 18

LO4 Identify some of the adverse legal ramifications of business strategies designed to lessen competition.
Try these problems: 9, 21

LO5 Assess whether a firm's profits can be enhanced by changing the timing of decisions or the order of strategic moves, and whether doing so creates first- or second-mover advantages.
Try these problems: 3, 19

LO6 Identify examples of networks and network externalities, and determine the number of connections possible in a star network with n users.
Try these problems: 4, 20

LO7 Explain why networks often lead to first-mover advantages, and how to use strategies such as penetration pricing to favorably change the strategic environment.
Try these problems: 11, 14

CONCEPTUAL AND COMPUTATIONAL QUESTIONS

connect
|ECONOMICS

1. A potential entrant can produce at the same cost as the monopolist illustrated in the figure below. The monopolist's demand curve is given by D^M, and its average cost curve is AC.

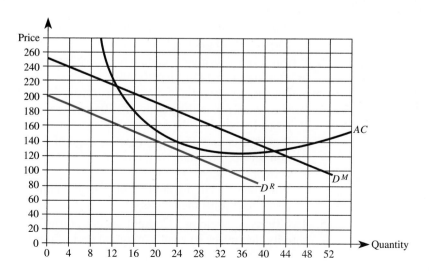

a. What level of output does the monopolist have to produce in order for the entrant to face the residual demand curve, D^R?
b. How much profit will the monopolist earn if it commits to the output that generates the residual demand curve, D^R?
c. Can the monopolist profitably deter entry by committing to a different level of output? Explain.

2. A monopolist earns $30 million annually and will maintain that level of profit indefinitely, provided that no other firm enters the market. However, if another firm enters the market, the monopolist will earn $30 million in the current period and $15 million annually thereafter. The opportunity cost of funds is 10 percent, and profits in each period are realized at the beginning of each period.
   a. What is the present value of the monopolist's current and future earnings if entry occurs?
   b. If the monopolist can earn $16 million indefinitely by limit pricing, should it do so? Explain.
3. Consider the following simultaneous move game:

		Player 2	
	Strategy	Yes	No
Player 1	Yes	400, 400	200, 375
	No	600, 500	300, 525

   a. What is the maximum amount player 1 should be willing to pay for the opportunity to move first instead of moving at the same time as player 2? Explain carefully.
   b. What is the maximum amount player 2 should be willing to spend to keep player 1 from getting to move first?
4. A firm is considering building a two-way network that links 12 users. The cost of building the network is $10,000.
   a. How many potential connection services does this network provide?
   b. If each user is willing to pay $150 to connect to the network, will the firm profit by building the network?
   c. If each user is willing to pay an average of $12 for each potential connection service provided by the network, will the firm profit by building the network?
   d. What happens to the number of potential connection services if one additional user joins the network?
5. Two firms compete in a Cournot fashion. Firm 1 successfully engages in an activity that raises its rival's marginal cost of production.

    a. Provide two examples of activities that might raise rivals' marginal costs.

    b. In order for such strategies to be beneficial, is it necessary for the manager of firm 1 to enjoy hurting the rival? Explain.

6. The market for taxi services in a Midwestern town is monopolized by firm 1. Currently, any taxi services firm must purchase a $40,000 "medallion" from the city in order to offer its services. A potential entrant (firm 2) is considering entering the market. Since entry would adversely affect firm 1's profits, the owner of firm 1 is planning to call her friend (the mayor) to request that the city change the medallion fee by $F thousand. The extensive form representation of the relevant issues is summarized in the accompanying graph (all payoffs are in thousands of dollars and include the current medallion fee of $40,000). Notice that when $F > 0$, the medallion fee is increased and profits decline; when $F < 0$, the fee is reduced and profits increase.

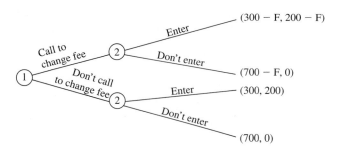

    a. What are firm 1's profits if it does not call to change the fee (that is, if it opts for a strategy of maintaining the status quo)?

    b. How much will firm 1 earn if it convinces the mayor to *decrease* the medallion fee by $40,000 ($F = -40) so that the medallion fee is entirely eliminated?

    c. How much will firm 1 earn if it convinces the mayor to *increase* the medallion fee by $300,000 ($F = 300)?

    d. Determine the change in the medallion fee that maximizes firm 1's profits.

    e. Do you think it will be politically feasible for the manager of firm 1 to implement the change in (*d*)? Explain.

7. Two firms compete in a homogeneous product market where the inverse demand function is $P = 20 - 5Q$ (quantity is measured in millions). Firm 1 has been in business for one year, while firm 2 just recently entered the market. Each firm has a legal obligation to pay one year's rent of $2 million regardless of its production decision. Firm 1's marginal cost is $2, and firm 2's marginal cost is $10. The current market price is $15 and was set optimally last year when firm 1 was the only firm in the market. At present, each firm has a 50 percent share of the market.

    a. Why do you think firm 1's marginal cost is lower than firm 2's marginal cost?

    b. Determine the current profits of the two firms.

     c. What would happen to each firm's current profits if firm 1 reduced its price to $10 while firm 2 continued to charge $15?

     d. Suppose that, by cutting its price to $10, firm 1 is able to drive firm 2 completely out of the market. After firm 2 exits the market, does firm 1 have an incentive to raise its price? Explain.

     e. Is firm 1 engaging in predatory pricing when it cuts its price from $15 to $10? Explain.

8. In this chapter's Headline, we learned that Tom Jackson benefits by announcing well in advance his new marketing plan to target businesses. Suppose you are an executive at Morton's, and by lucky happenstance you learn of Tom's plans before he implements them. What plan of action should you take? Explain.

9. You are the manager of an international firm headquartered in Antarctica. You are contemplating a business tactic that will permit your firm to raise prices and increase profits in the long run by eliminating one of your competitors. Do you think it would make economic sense to expend resources on legal counsel before implementing your strategy? Explain.

10. In the following game, determine the maximum amount you would be willing to pay for the privilege of moving (a) first, (b) second, or (c) third: There are three players, you and two rivals. The player announcing the largest integer gets a payoff of $10, that announcing the second largest integer gets $0, and that announcing the third largest integer gets $5.

PROBLEMS AND APPLICATIONS

11. UNIX is a powerful multiuser operating system designed for use with servers. UNIX's popularity has grown since it was developed by Bell Labs in 1969, as record numbers of users are logging onto the Internet. More recently, however, a branded version of another operating system has become available. This product, called Red Hat Linux, is a potential replacement for UNIX and other well-known operating systems. If you were in charge of pricing at Red Hat, what strategy would you pursue? Explain.

12. Between 1995 and 1997, American Airlines competed in the Dallas/Ft Worth Airport against several other low-cost carriers. In response to these low-cost carriers, American Airlines reduced its price and increased service on selected routes. As a result, one of the low-cost carriers stopped service, which led American Airlines to increase its price. Why do you think a lawsuit was filed against American Airlines? Why do you think American Airlines prevailed at trial?

13. Suppose that, prior to other firms entering the market, the maker of a new smartphone (Way Cool, Inc.) earns $80 million per year. By reducing its price

by 60 percent, Way Cool could discourage entry into "its" market, but doing so would cause its profits to sink to $-\$2$ million. By pricing such that other firms would be able to enter the market, Way Cool's profits would drop to $30 million for the indefinite future. In light of these estimates, do you think it is profitable for Way Cool to engage in limit pricing? Is any additional information needed to formulate an answer to this question? Explain.

14. During the early days of the Internet, most dot-coms were driven by revenues rather than profits. A large number were even driven by "hits" to their site rather than revenues. This all changed in early 2000, however, when the prices of unprofitable dot-com stocks plummeted on Wall Street. Most analysts have attributed this to a return to rationality, with investors focusing once again on fundamentals like earnings growth. Does this mean that, during the 1990s, dot-coms that focused on "hits" rather than revenues or profits had bad business plans? Explain.

15. A number of professional associations, such as the American Medical Association and the American Bar Association, support regulations that make it more costly for their members (for example, doctors and lawyers) to practice their services. While some of these regulations may stem from a genuine desire for higher-quality medical and legal services, self-interest may also play a role. Explain.

16. Barnacle Industries was awarded a patent over 15 years ago for a unique industrial-strength cleaner that removes barnacles and other particles from the hulls of ships. Thanks to its monopoly position, Barnacle has earned more than $160 million over the past decade. Its customers—spanning the gamut from cruise lines to freighters—use the product because it reduces their fuel bills. The annual (inverse) demand function for Barnacle's product is given by $P = 400 - .0005Q$, and Barnacle's cost function is given by $C(Q) = 250Q$. Thanks to subsidies stemming from an energy bill passed by Congress nearly two decades ago, Barnacle does not have any fixed costs: The federal government essentially pays for the plant and capital equipment required to make this energy-saving product. Absent this subsidy, Barnacle's fixed costs would be about $4 million annually. Knowing that the company's patent will soon expire, Marge, Barnacle's manager, is concerned that entrants will qualify for the subsidy, enter the market, and produce a perfect substitute at an identical cost. With interest rates at 7 percent, Marge is considering a limit-pricing strategy. If you were Marge, what strategy would you pursue? Explain.

17. During the dot-com era, mergers among some brokerage houses resulted in the acquiring firm paying a premium on the order of $100 for each of the acquired firm's customers. Is there a business rationale for such a strategy? Do you think these circumstances are met in the brokerage business? Explain.

18. Argyle is a large, vertically integrated firm that manufactures sweaters from a rare type of wool produced on its sheep farms. Argyle has adopted a strategy of selling wool to companies that compete against it in the market for

sweaters. Explain why this strategy may, in fact, be rational. Also, identify at least two other strategies that might permit Argyle to earn higher profits.

19. You are the manager of 3D Designs—a large imaging company that does graphics and web design work for companies. You and your only competitor are contemplating the purchase of a new 3-D imaging device. If only one of you acquires the device, that firm will earn profits of $20 million and the other firm will lose $9 million. Unfortunately, there is only one 3-D imaging device in the world, and additional devices will not be available for the foreseeable future. Recognizing this fact, an opportunistic salesperson for the company that makes this device calls you. She indicates that, for an additional up-front payment of $23 million (not included in the above figures), her firm will deliver the device to your company's premises tomorrow. Otherwise, she'll call your competitor and offer it the same deal. Should you accept or decline her offer? Explain.

20. Bank 1 and Bank 2 are considering entering a compatibility agreement that would permit the users of each bank's ATMs access to the other bank's ATMs. Bank 1 has a network of branches and automated teller machines (ATMs) extending from Connecticut to Florida. Bank 1's 12 million customers currently have access only to the 10,000 ATMs solely owned by the company on the East Coast. While Bank 2's core account holders are located on the West Coast and southwestern portion of the United States, the company is expanding to the East Coast. Bank 2 has 15 million customers who can use any of its 14,000 ATMs. Using the idea of network externalities, describe how such an agreement between Bank 1 and Bank 2 would benefit consumers.

21. By the end of 1995, Netscape's share of the browser market grew to 90 percent by continually upgrading its product to include new features such as e-mail and video capabilities. Shortly thereafter, Microsoft introduced and distributed a new version of its operating system that included its Internet Explorer browser at no cost. In addition, Microsoft allegedly imposed several restrictions on original equipment manufacturers (OEMs), Internet service providers (ISPs), and Internet content providers (ICPs) with the intention of (a) ensuring that almost every new computer had a version of Internet Explorer (IE) and (b) making it more difficult for consumers to get Netscape on new computers. On May 18, 1998, the government filed a complaint in District Court against Microsoft. Based on what you have learned in this chapter, briefly discuss the merits (if any) of the government's complaint against Microsoft.

22. The CEO of a regional airline recently learned that its only competitor is suffering from a significant cash-flow constraint. The CEO realizes that its competitor's days are numbered, but has asked whether you would recommend the carrier significantly lower its airfares to "speed up the rival's exit from the market." Provide your recommendation.

23. Evaluate the following: "Since a rival's profit-maximizing price and output depend on its *marginal* cost and not its fixed costs, a firm cannot profitably lessen competition by implementing a strategy that raises its rival's *fixed costs*."

CONNECT EXERCISES

If your instructor has adopted Connect for the course and you are an active subscriber, you can practice with the questions presented above, along with many alternative versions of these questions. Your instructor may also assign a subset of these problems and/or their alternative versions as a homework assignment through Connect, allowing for immediate feedback of grades and correct answers.

CASE-BASED EXERCISES

Your instructor may assign additional problem-solving exercises (called memos) that require you to apply some of the tools you learned in this chapter to make a recommendation based on an actual business scenario. Some of these memos accompany the Time Warner case (pages 561–597 of your textbook). Additional memos, as well as data that may be useful for your analysis, are available online at www.mhhe.com/baye8e.

SELECTED READINGS

Bental, Benjamin, and Spiegel, Menahem, "Network Competition, Product Quality, and Market Coverage in the Presence of Network Externalities." *Journal of Industrial Economics* 43(2), June 1995, pp. 197–208.

Bolton, Patrick, and Dewatripont, Mathias, "The Firm as a Communication Network." *Quarterly Journal of Economics* 109(4), November 1994, pp. 809–39.

Brueckner, Jan K., Dyer, Nichola J., and Spiller, Pablo T., "Fare Determination in Airline Hub-and-Spoke Networks." *RAND Journal of Economics* 23(3), Autumn 1992, pp. 309–33.

Economides, N., "The Economics of Networks." *International Journal of Industrial Organization* 14, October 1996, pp. 673–99.

Gabel, David, "Competition in a Network Industry: The Telephone Industry, 1894–1910." *Journal of Economic History* 54(3), September 1994, pp. 543–72.

Gilbert, Richard J., "The Role of Potential Competition in Industrial Organization." *Journal of Economic Perspectives* 3(3), Summer 1989, pp. 107–27.

LeBlanc, Greg, "Signaling Strength: Limit Pricing and Predatory Pricing." *RAND Journal of Economics* 23(4), Winter 1992, pp. 493–506.

Liebowitz, S. J., and Margolis, Stephen E., "Network Externality: An Uncommon Tragedy." *Journal of Economic Perspectives* 8(2), Spring 1994, pp. 133–50.

MacKie-Mason, Jeffrey K., and Varian, Hal, "Economic FAQs about the Internet." *Journal of Economic Perspectives* 8(3), Summer 1994, pp. 75–96.

Milgrom, Paul, and Roberts, John, "Limit Pricing and Entry under Incomplete Information: An Equilibrium Analysis." *Econometrica* 50(2), March 1982, pp. 443–60.

Salop, Steven C., "Exclusionary Vertical Restraints Law: Has Economics Mattered?" *American Economic Review* 83(2), May 1993, pp. 168–72.

Strassmann, Diana L., "Potential Competition in the Deregulated Airlines." *Review of Economics and Statistics* 72(4), November 1990, pp. 696–702.

Vickers, John, "Competition and Regulation in Vertically Related Markets." *Review of Economic Studies* 62(1), January 1995, pp. 1–17.

Weinberg, John A., "Exclusionary Practices and Technological Competition." *Journal of Industrial Economics* 40(2), June 1992, pp. 135–46.

CHAPTER FOURTEEN

A Manager's Guide to Government in the Marketplace

FTC Conditionally Approves $10.3 Billion Merger

The Federal Trade Commission (FTC) issued a complaint against Nestlé and Ralston Purina alleging that a proposed merger between the two companies would violate, among other things, Section 7 of the Clayton Act. While these two companies sell many products that raise no antitrust concerns, the FTC argued that Ralston and Nestlé controlled 34 percent and 11 percent of the dry cat food market, respectively, so a merger between these two companies would substantially increase concentration in this market. More specifically, the FTC alleged that the merger would increase the HHI by more than 750 points, to over 2,400, and increase the likelihood that the merged company could unilaterally exercise market power and raise prices in the market for dry cat food. Several months later, however, the FTC conditionally approved the $10.3 billion merger between the two companies. In light of the FTC's concerns, how do you think the parties ultimately obtained its approval?

Learning Objectives

After completing this chapter, you will be able to:

LO1 Identify four sources of market failure.

LO2 Explain why market power reduces social welfare, and identify two types of government policies aimed at reducing deadweight loss.

LO3 Show why externalities can lead competitive markets to provide socially inefficient quantities of goods and services; explain how government policies, such as the Clean Air Act, can improve resource allocation.

LO4 Show why competitive markets fail to provide socially efficient levels of public goods; explain how the government can mitigate these inefficiencies.

LO5 Explain why incomplete information compromises the efficiency of markets, and identify five government policies aimed at mitigating these problems.

LO6 Explain why government attempts to solve market failures can lead to additional inefficiencies because of "rent-seeking" activities.

LO7 Show how government policies in international markets, such as quotas and tariffs, impact the prices and quantities of domestic goods and services.

INTRODUCTION

Throughout most of this book, we have treated the market as a place where firms and consumers come together to trade goods and services with no intervention from government. But as you are aware, rules and regulations that are passed and enforced by government enter into almost every decision firms and consumers make. As a manager, it is important to understand the regulations passed by government, why such regulations have been passed, and how they affect optimal managerial decisions.

We will begin by examining four reasons why free markets may fail to provide the socially efficient quantities of goods: (1) market power, (2) externalities, (3) public goods, and (4) incomplete information. Our analysis includes an overview of government policies designed to alleviate these "market failures" and an explanation of how the policies affect managerial decisions. The power of politicians to institute policies that affect the allocation of resources in markets provides those adversely affected with an incentive to engage in lobbying activities. We will illustrate the underlying reasons for these types of rent-seeking activities. Finally, we will examine how these activities can lead politicians to impose restrictions such as quotas and tariffs in markets affected by international trade.

MARKET FAILURE

One of the main reasons for government involvement in the marketplace is that free markets do not always result in the socially efficient quantities of goods at socially efficient prices. In this section, we will consider why markets do not always lead to socially efficient outcomes and examine how government policies designed to correct "market failures" affect managerial decisions. We will begin by examining market failure due to the presence of market power.

Market Power

You learned in Chapters 2 and 8 that social welfare—defined as the sum of consumer and producer surplus—is maximized at the output where price equals marginal cost. The socially efficient price and output arises naturally if the industry is perfectly competitive. In contrast, a firm that has *market power* produces less than the socially efficient level of output because it charges a price that exceeds its marginal cost of production. In such instances, the value to society of another unit of the good is greater than the cost of the resources needed to produce that unit; there would be a net gain to society if additional output were produced. In these instances, government may intervene in the market and regulate the actions of firms in an attempt to increase *social welfare.*

market power
The ability of a firm to set its price above marginal cost.

To see the potential benefits of government intervention in a market, consider a market serviced by a monopoly. Figure 14–1 shows the monopolist's demand, marginal cost, and marginal revenue curves. Assuming the monopolist must charge the same price to all consumers in the market, the profit-maximizing output is Q^M units, and these units are sold at the monopoly price of P^M. At this price, consumers pay

FIGURE 14–1 Welfare and Deadweight Loss under Monopoly

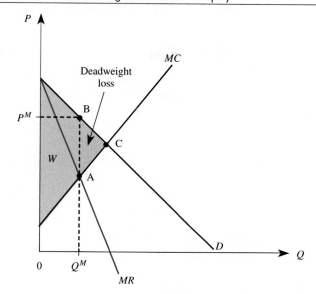

more for the last unit of output than it costs the producer to manufacture and sell it. Total social welfare under monopoly is the region labeled W in Figure 14–1.

Notice in Figure 14–1 that the area of triangle ABC is the *deadweight loss* of the monopoly—welfare that would have accrued to society if the industry were perfectly competitive but is not realized because of the market power the monopolist enjoys. The failure of the market to fully maximize social welfare is due to market power; the deadweight loss triangle provides a measure of this welfare loss to society.

The government uses antitrust policy to enact and enforce laws that restrict the formation of monopolies. The rationale for these policies is that by preventing monopoly power from emerging, the deadweight loss of monopoly can be avoided. In some instances, however, the presence of economies of scale makes it desirable to allow the formation of a monopoly. In these cases, government attempts to reduce the deadweight loss by regulating the price charged by the monopolist.

Antitrust Policy

antitrust policy
Government policies designed to keep firms from monopolizing their markets.

Antitrust policy attempts to eliminate the deadweight loss of monopoly by making it illegal for managers to engage in activities that foster monopoly power, such as price-fixing agreements and other collusive practices. The cornerstone of U.S. antitrust policy is contained in Sections 1 and 2 of the *Sherman Antitrust Act* of 1890:

Sec. 1

Every contract, combination in the form of trust or otherwise, or conspiracy, in restraint of trade or commerce among the several states, or with foreign nations, is hereby declared to be illegal. Every person who shall make any such contract or engage in any such combination or conspiracy shall be deemed guilty of a felony, and, on conviction thereof, shall be punished by fine not exceeding five thousand dollars (one million dollars if a corporation, or, if any other person, one hundred thousand dollars) or by imprisonment not exceeding one (three) years, or by both said punishments, in the discretion of the court.

Sec. 2
Every person who shall monopolize, or attempt to monopolize, or combine or conspire with any person or persons, to monopolize any part of the trade or commerce among the several States, or with foreign nations, shall be deemed guilty of a felony, and, on conviction thereof, shall be punished by fine not exceeding five thousand dollars (one million dollars if a corporation, or, if any other person, one hundred thousand dollars) or by imprisonment not exceeding one (three) years, or by both said punishments, in the discretion of the court.[1]

Among other things, the Sherman Act makes it illegal for managers of U.S. firms to collude with other domestic or foreign firms. Thus, even though OPEC is not bound by U.S. law (it is composed of foreign nations), the manager of a U.S. oil company cannot legally participate in the OPEC oil cartel.

The interpretation of antitrust policy is largely shaped by the courts, which rule on ambiguities in the law and previous cases. For example, the first successful use of the Sherman Antitrust Act was in 1897, when the Supreme Court held that rate agreements are illegal in *United States* v. *Trans-Missouri Freight Association*. This ruling was again upheld in *United States* v. *Joint Traffic Association* (1898). The court extended its interpretation to include collusive bidding in *Addyston Pipe & Steel Company* v. *United States* (1899). The full power of the Sherman Antitrust Act was not realized until the conclusion of *United States* v. *Standard Oil of New Jersey* in 1911. The last case is interesting and provides useful caveats to future managers.

Standard Oil of New Jersey, along with Standard Oil of Ohio, was charged with attempting to fix the prices of petroleum products and the prices at which the products would be shipped. Standard Oil, in particular, was accused of numerous activities designed to enhance monopoly power: using physical threats to shippers and other producers, setting up bogus companies, using espionage by bribing employees of other companies, engaging in restraint of trade, and making several attempts to monopolize the oil industry. Managers, of course, should avoid all of these practices; as a result of these actions, the court dissolved Standard Oil into 33 subsidiaries, many of which survive today under the names Exxon Mobil, Chevron, and BP America. More important than breaking up the Standard Oil Trust, however, was the Supreme Court's new *rule of reason,* as defined in Justice White's majority opinion:

> Thus not specifying, the indubitably contemplating and requiring a standard, it follows that it was intended that the standard of reason which had been applied at the common law and in this country in dealing with subjects of the character embraced by the statute was intended to be the measure used for the purpose of determining whether, in a given case, a particular act had or had not brought about the wrong against which the statute provided.

---

[1]The penalties have been amended twice, in 1955 and in 1970. The penalties in parentheses represent the 1970 change.

The rule of reason has since become the code of decision making used by the court for determining antitrust cases. Effectively, the rule of reason stipulates that not all trade restraints are illegal; rather, only those that are "unreasonable" are prohibited. For example, in applying this rule, the courts determined that the size of a firm alone is not sufficient evidence to convict a firm under Section 2 of the Sherman Act:

> To hold to the contrary would require the conclusion either that every contract, act, or combination of any kind or nature, whether it operated in restraint of trade or not, was within the statute.

Effectively, this means that a firm must take an explicit action designed to lessen competition before it can be found guilty of violating Section 2 of the Sherman Act. For example, the rule of reason was used in the decision against American Tobacco, which was found guilty of monopolizing the U.S. cigarette market by engaging in predatory pricing—pricing explicitly designed to harm other firms and thus enhance the firm's own monopoly power.

The problem with the rule of reason is that it makes it difficult for managers to know in advance whether particular pricing strategies used to enhance profits are in fact violations of the law. Congress attempted to clarify its intent by more precisely defining illegal actions in the *Clayton Act* (1914) and its amendment, the *Robinson-Patman Act* (1936). For example, Section 2(a) of the Robinson-Patman Act amends Section 2 of the Clayton Act and makes price discrimination illegal if it is designed to lessen competition or create a monopoly:

Sec. 2(a)

That it shall be unlawful for any person engaged in commerce, in the course of such commerce, either directly or indirectly, to discriminate in price between different purchasers of commodities of like grade and quality, . . . where such discrimination may be substantially to lessen competition or tend to create a monopoly in line of commerce, or to injure, destroy, or prevent competition.

Price discrimination that arises because of cost or quality differences is permitted under the act, as is price discrimination when it is necessary to meet a competitor's price in a market. Still, there is considerable ambiguity regarding whether a particular type of price discrimination is illegal under the law, and laws differ across countries. In the United States, for instance, legal actions against price discrimination are generally brought by private plaintiffs and relate to wholesale prices (but see Inside Business 14–1 for a glimpse of the European antitrust landscape).

The Clayton Act contains more than 20 sections that, among other things, make it illegal for firms to (1) hide kickbacks as commissions or brokerage fees; (2) use rebates unless they are made available to all customers; (3) engage in exclusive dealings with a supplier unless the supplier adds to the furnishing of the buyer and/or offers to make like terms to all other potential suppliers; (4) fix prices or engage in exclusive contracts if such a practice will lead to lessening of competition or monopoly; and (5) acquire one or more other firms if such an acquisition will lead to a lessening of competition.

The *Celler-Kefauver Act* (1950) strengthened Section 7 of the Clayton Act by making it more difficult for firms to engage in mergers and acquisitions without violating the law:

INSIDE BUSINESS 14–1

European Commission Asks Airlines to Explain Price Discrimination Practices

On 19 December 2003, the European Commission issued a press release indicating that it had written 18 European airlines, asking them if and why they charge different prices for identical flights to residents of different EU countries. The commission had received a number of complaints from EU citizens who felt they might have been discriminated against when buying plane tickets. According to the release, this practice within the EU *may* represent a ". . . breach of the Treaty provisions on non-discrimination and the internal market."

While the economic basis for price discrimination within the EU is clear—profit maximization dictates charging higher prices to customers in countries where demand is less elastic—the legal basis within Europe apparently is not. As of 9 June 2004, the European Commission indicated that the EU carriers stopped price discriminating as a result of the Commission's probe.

Sources: European Commission website; John Leyden, "Airlines Ground Online Ticket Gouging," *The Register,* June 9, 2004.

Sec. 7

That no corporation engaged in commerce shall acquire, directly or indirectly, the whole or any part of the stock or other share capital and no corporation subject to the jurisdiction of the Federal Trade Commission shall acquire the whole or any part of the assets of another corporation engaged also in commerce, where in any line of commerce in any section of the country, the effect of such acquisition may be substantially to lessen competition, or to tend to create a monopoly.

Merger policy changed, however, when new horizontal merger guidelines were written in 1982, amended in 1984, and revised in 1992, 1997, and 2010. In Chapter 7 you learned that these guidelines are based on the *Herfindahl-Hirschman index (HHI),*

$$HHI = 10{,}000 \sum_{i=1}^{N} w_i^2$$

where w_i is the market share of firm i. More precisely, w_i represents firm i's sales in the relevant market as a fraction of the total sales of all firms in that market. Under the *Horizontal Merger Guidelines*, a merger that increases HHI by less than 100 or leads to an unconcentrated market (post-merger HHI < 1,500) is ordinarily allowed. Markets in which the postmerger HHI is between 1,500 and 2,500 are considered moderately concentrated. In moderately concentrated markets, mergers that increase HHI by more than 100 points potentially raise antitrust concerns. Markets in which the postmerger HHI exceeds 2,500 are deemed highly concentrated. In highly concentrated markets, an increase in the HHI of between 100 and 200 points also potentially raises antitrust concerns. If a merger increases HHI by more than 200 and leads to a highly concentrated market, it is *presumed* to be likely to enhance market power.

It is important to stress that these are only guidelines; mergers are often allowed even when HHI indexes are large, provided there is a significant likelihood of potential entry into the market by domestic or foreign firms, an emerging new technology, increased efficiency, or one of the firms has financial problems.

As a practical matter, efficiencies make a difference in antitrust enforcement only when adverse competitive effects are not that great. As the 2010 revision to the *Horizontal Merger Guidelines* states, ". . . efficiencies almost never justify a merger to monopoly or near-monopoly."[2] Additionally, the *Guidelines* recognize that efficiencies are difficult to verify and quantify. Merging firms must substantiate any efficiency claims; "vague or speculative" claims do not count.

The *Antitrust Division of the Department of Justice (DOJ)* and the *Federal Trade Commission (FTC)* are charged with the task of enforcing antitrust regulations. The *Hart-Scott-Rodino Antitrust Improvement Act* of 1976 requires that parties to an acquisition notify both the DOJ and the FTC of their intent to merge, provided that the dollar value of the transaction exceeds a certain threshold (currently about $70 million). Following this premerger notification, the parties must wait 30 days before they may complete the merger. If the DOJ or FTC decides that further examination of the merger is warranted, a so-called second request is issued: The parties are asked to provide additional information to the government. A second request automatically extends the waiting period. Once the parties comply with the second request, the government has 30 days to review the information and either file a complaint to block the merger or permit the merger to take place.

In practice, less than 3 percent of all premerger notifications lead to a second request. In those cases where a second request is issued, the government and the parties usually reach an agreement before going to court. Typically, the firms sell to third parties assets in those product or geographic markets where there is considerable business overlap. This eliminates the government's antitrust concerns and allows the parties to consummate the merger. If the government and the parties cannot come to an agreement about which assets will be divested, the government may file suit to block the merger.

Price Regulation

In the presence of large economies of scale (as is the case for some utility companies), it may be desirable for a single firm to service a market. In these instances, government may allow a firm to exist as a monopoly but choose to regulate its price to reduce the deadweight loss. In this section, we will see how such regulation affects managerial decisions and social welfare.

---

[2]Department of Justice and the Federal Trade Commission, *Horizontal Merger Guidelines,* 2010.

FIGURE 14–2 Regulating a Monopolist's Price at the Socially Efficient Level

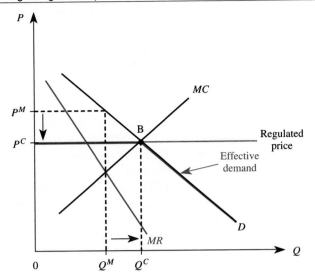

Consider the situation depicted in Figure 14–2, where an unregulated monopolist produces Q^M units of output at a price of P^M. A competitive industry would produce Q^C units, where marginal cost intersects the demand curve. Suppose the government imposed and enforced a regulated price of P^C, which corresponds to the price a competitive industry would charge for the product given identical demand and cost conditions. How should the manager respond to maximize the firm's profits?

The monopolist cannot legally charge a price above P^C, so the maximum price it can charge for units less than Q^C is P^C. For units above Q^C, the maximum price it can charge is the price along the inverse demand curve, since the amount consumers are willing to pay is less than the ceiling. As a consequence, the effective inverse demand curve of the monopolist is given by P^CBD. Notice that for points to the left of B, the demand curve is horizontal, just as it is for a perfectly competitive firm. But if the monopolist wishes to sell more than Q^C units of output, it can do so only by lowering price below P^C.

Since the monopolist can sell each unit up to Q^C at a price of P^C, the marginal revenue for these units is simply P^C: Each additional unit of output up to Q^C adds exactly P^C to the firm's revenue. In effect, the ceiling creates a situation where the demand curve the monopolist faces is just like that of a perfectly competitive firm for these output levels. To maximize profits, the regulated monopolist will produce where the marginal revenue of the effective demand curve (P^C) equals marginal cost, which in this case is at point B. This corresponds to an output of Q^C. Thus, when the monopolist's price is regulated at P^C in Figure 14–2, the firm maximizes profits by producing Q^C units and selling them at the regulated price of P^C.

FIGURE 14–3   Regulating a Monopolist's Price Below the Socially Efficient Level

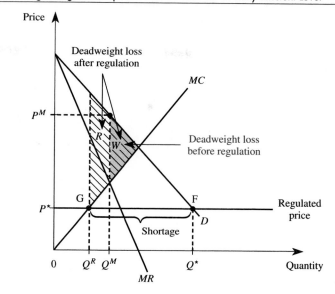

Notice that the impact of the price regulation is to induce the profit-maximizing monopolist to produce the perfectly competitive output at the perfectly competitive price. The result of the price regulation is to completely eliminate the deadweight loss of the monopoly. The government policy thus reduces monopoly profits but increases social welfare.

On the basis of Figure 14–2, one might be tempted to conclude that it is always beneficial to regulate the price charged by a monopolist. This is not the case, however. To see why, consider the monopoly situation in Figure 14–3. Suppose the government regulates the price at the level P^*. Given the regulated price, the effective demand curve for the monopolist is now P^*FD, and the corresponding marginal revenue curve for units produced below Q^* is given by line P^*F. To maximize profits, the regulated monopolist will produce where the marginal revenue of the effective demand curve (P^*) equals marginal cost, which is at point G. This corresponds to an output of Q^R, which is less than the output the monopolist would have produced in the absence of regulation. Moreover, the quantity demanded at a price of P^* is Q^*, so there is a shortage of $Q^* - Q^R$ units under the regulated price. Furthermore, the deadweight loss under this regulated price (regions $R + W$) is actually larger than the deadweight loss in the absence of regulation (region W). If the government lacks accurate information about demand and costs, or for some other reason regulates the price at too low a level, it can actually reduce social welfare and create a shortage of the good.

It is very important to note that the analysis in Figures 14–2 and 14–3 suppresses the position of the average total cost curve. To see why it is important to consider the position of the average total cost curve before reaching conclusions about the welfare

FIGURE 14–4 A Case Where Price Regulation Drives the Monopolist Out of Business

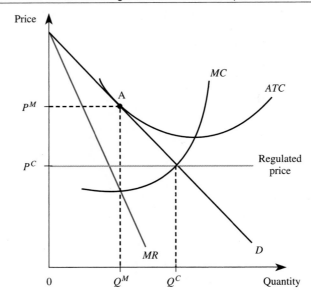

loss arising from monopoly, consider the situation in Figure 14–4, where the monopolist is just breaking even at point A. In this instance, an unregulated monopolist would produce Q^M units and charge a price of P^M. Since price is equal to the average total cost of production, this monopolist earns zero economic profits in the absence of regulation.

Now suppose the price is regulated at P^C. In the long run, how much output will the firm produce? The answer is zero output. To see why, note that under the regulated price, average total cost lies above the regulated price, so the monopolist would experience a loss if it produced. Thus, in the long run the monopolist in Figure 14–4 would exit the market if the price were regulated at P^C, and everyone in the market would be made worse off (there would be no product to consume). To keep this from happening, the government would have to subsidize the monopoly by agreeing to compensate it for any losses incurred. These funds would come from taxes, and thus consumers would indirectly be paying for the lower price through higher taxes. Moreover, the manager of a subsidized monopoly would have no incentive to keep costs low; any losses that resulted would be subsidized by the government. Consequently, the manager would have an incentive to spend enormous sums of money on plush offices, corporate jets, and the like, since losses would be reimbursed by the government.

The analysis in Figure 14–4 points out a very important caveat regarding comparisons of monopoly and perfect competition. One key source of monopoly power is the presence of economies of scale. These economies of scale may render it impossible for output to be produced in a competitive industry. For example, a competitive industry could not sustain an output of Q^C in Figure 14–4, because the intersection of the marginal cost and demand curves lies below the average total cost curve.

INSIDE BUSINESS 14–2

Electricity Deregulation

Historically, due to economies of scale in the capital-intensive electric power industry, prices of electricity have been regulated through "rate-of-return" regulation. These price restrictions allowed electric companies to earn a profit based on the value of their capital or rate base (but companies were not guaranteed a profit). More recently, however, the Public Utility Regulatory Policies Act (PURPA) of 1978 and the Energy Policy Act of 1992 opened the *wholesale* electricity market to unregulated independent power producers. By 1996, the Federal Energy Regulatory Commission (FERC) ordered that the bulk transmission lines that carried high voltage electricity geographically be opened to anyone wishing to supply power to an end user. Deregulation plans differed by state, but many required the once vertically integrated utilities to divest some or all of their generation capacity in an effort to promote competition.

Today, about 15 states allow choice for electricity consumers, but choice is limited solely to the generation of power. The *delivery* of electric power to end users remains a natural monopoly owing to the fact that the "poles and wires" used to transmit power are a substantial fixed cost. Consequently, what deregulation in the electric power industry has really boiled down to is a "restructuring" of the industry. For the states that have allowed deregulation, the power industry has become less vertically integrated. Generation is theoretically competitive, but regardless of who generates the customer's power, the local electric company still transmits and delivers that power, and charges for these services are still established under basic "rate-of-return" regulation.

Customers taking the fullest advantage of choice in electricity are mostly industrial facilities. Small commercial and residential customers find switching costs to be significant and, for the most part, the marginal benefits under choice (lower power prices) were small. Also, electricity marketers found that the acquisition costs to gain small customers were higher than originally expected, which lessened the incentive to sell power to small customers in new markets. Thus, in the states that have experimented with deregulated electricity, most small customers have few, if any, power suppliers to actually choose from.

Source: Interview with Vincent Marra, former rate analyst, Delmarva Power, February 28, 2007.

Demonstration Problem 14–1

Many firms that sell in small markets are effectively monopolies; they are the sole provider of a good in their geographic area. Most of these firms earn positive economic profits, yet they are allowed to operate as monopolies without regulation by government. Why?

Answer:

In situations where economies of scale are large relative to market demand, only a single firm will be able to service the market. In these instances, it is not desirable to break the firm up into smaller firms using antitrust policy. There would, however, be a potential gain in social welfare if the firm's price were regulated at the socially efficient level. This gain must be weighed against the cost of setting up a regulatory body to administer the regulation. If the cost of setting up and running the regulative body exceeds the deadweight loss of monopoly—as it likely will in small markets—there will be a net loss in social welfare by regulation. In these instances, social welfare would be better served by leaving the firm alone even though it creates a deadweight loss. In effect, it would cost more to fix the problem than would be gained by eliminating the deadweight loss.

Externalities

negative externalities
Costs borne by parties who are not involved in the production or consumption of a good.

Unfortunately, some production processes create costs for people who are not part of the production or consumption process for the good. These external costs are called *negative externalities.*

The most common example of a negative externality is pollution. When a firm creates wastes that either do not easily biodegrade or have harmful effects on other resources, it does not pay the full cost of production. For example, a firm that produces textiles usually creates waste products that contain dioxin, a cancer-causing chemical. When a textile manufacturer can dispose of this waste "for free" by dumping it into a nearby river, it has an incentive to dump more waste into the river than is socially optimal. While the firm benefits from dumping waste into the river, the waste reduces the oxygen content of the water, clogs normal waterway routes, and creates reproduction problems for birds, fish, reptiles, and aquatic animals. These results negatively affect people who are not involved in the production or consumption process.

To see why the market fails to provide the efficient level of output when there are externalities in production, consider Figure 14–5. If a firm emits pollutants into the water as a by-product of producing steel, a cost, or negative externality, is borne by members of society. Figure 14–5 shows the negative externality as the marginal cost of pollution to society. This cost represents the cost to society of dirtier water due to increases in steel production. The production of only a little steel results in only minor damage to water, but as increasing amounts of steel are produced, more and more pollutants collect in the water. The marginal cost of pollution to society thus increases as more steel is produced.

Assuming the market for steel is perfectly competitive, the market supply curve is S in Figure 14–5, which is the sum of the marginal costs of the firms producing in the industry. The supply curve is based on the costs paid by the steel firms; thus, if they are allowed to dump pollutants into the water for free, the market equilibrium is at point B, where the market demand and supply curves intersect. The result is that Q^C units will be produced and purchased at a price of P^C per unit of steel.

However, at this quantity of output, society pays a marginal price of A, on top of the price of P^C paid to the steel firms. This amount is the additional cost to society of the pollution. In particular, since the firms are dumping pollutants into the water for free, the cost of pollution is not internalized by those who buy and sell steel; rather, society pays for the dumping of pollutants by having to endure polluted water. If the firms were to take into account the cost of pollution to society, their marginal cost curves would become the vertical sum of the supply curve and the marginal cost of pollution to society. This sum is shown as the marginal cost to

FIGURE 14–5 The Socially Efficient Equilibrium in the Presence of External Costs

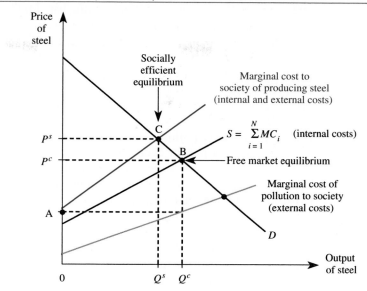

society of producing steel in Figure 14–5. The socially efficient level of output, which takes into account all the costs and benefits of producing steel, is at point C, where the marginal cost to society of producing steel intersects the market demand curve. The socially efficient level of steel output is Q^S, which is less than the output produced in the perfectly competitive market. The socially efficient price of steel is P^S, which is greater than the perfectly competitive price of P^C. In other words, in the presence of external costs, the market equilibrium output is greater than the socially efficient level, and the market price is below the socially efficient level. In effect, consumers get to purchase too much output at too low a price.

The basic reason for the "market failure" is the absence of well-defined *property rights;* the steel firms believe they have the right to use the river to dump waste, and environmentalists believe they have the right to a clean river. This failure often can be solved when government defines itself to be the owner of the environment. It can then use its power to induce the socially efficient levels of output and pollution.

To induce the socially efficient level of output, government may force firms to internalize the costs of emitting pollutants by enacting policies that shift the internal cost of production up to where it actually equals the social cost of production. A prime example of a government policy designed to do this is the Clean Air Act.

The Clean Air Act

To solve the externality problem caused by pollution, Congress passed the *Clean Air Act* in 1970 and a sweeping amendment in 1990. The amended Clean Air Act covers 189 toxic air pollutants and was the most comprehensive antipollution act passed by any country as of 1992. The Clean Air Act now covers any industry that releases over 10 tons per year of any of the listed pollutants or 25 tons per year of any combination of those pollutants. Previous law covered only industries that released 100 tons per year of a much smaller list of pollutants, but the new act covers a much broader set of industries. The amended Clean Air Act is so voluminous that guidelines for compliance usually comprise several hundred pages. Due to the comprehensive nature of the act, we will examine only one aspect of the new law that specifically uses the market as an enforcement mechanism.

A firm in an industry covered by the Clean Air Act is required to obtain a permit to be able to pollute. These permits are limited in availability and require the firm to pay a fee for each unit of pollutants emitted. For an existing firm, these permits increase both the fixed and variable costs of producing goods. They are a variable cost because as output increases, the level of pollutants emitted rises, and a fee must be paid on each of these units of pollution. The fixed-cost component is the fee required to obtain a permit in the first place. Along with the permit, the Clean Air Act requires new entrants into an industry to match or improve on the most effective pollution removal system used in the industry. Existing firms must follow suit and upgrade within three years. Once purchased from the government, the permits may be bought from and sold to other firms.

The Clean Air Act causes firms to internalize the cost of emitting pollutants, since a fee must be paid for each unit emitted. This raises each firm's marginal cost and therefore induces them to produce less output. As shown in Figure 14–6, this leads to a decrease in the market supply of the good; less of the product is available in the market at any price. Consequently, the Clean Air Act ultimately decreases the market equilibrium quantity from Q_0 to Q_1 in Figure 14–6 and raises

FIGURE 14–6   Impact of the Clean Air Act

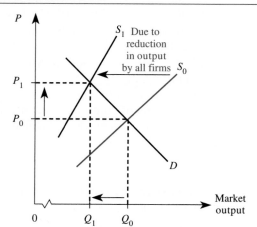

the market price from P_0 to P_1. The change caused by the permits is exactly what is called for in Figure 14–5 to solve the negative externality of pollution: less output at a higher price.

An interesting aspect of this new legislation is the fact that permits can be sold by one firm to another both within and across industries. This does two things that allow the market to reduce pollution. First, it allows new firms to enter an industry when demand increases. Second, it provides an incentive for existing firms to invest in new technology to create cleaner production methods.

To see this, suppose demand in a nonpolluting industry increases. As a result, the price increases, economic profits will be earned in the short run, and in the long run new firms will enter the market until economic profits return to zero. However, in a polluting industry that is not allowed to buy and sell permits to pollute, entry cannot occur; the fixed number of pollution permits are already allocated, and new entrants face a barrier to entry because of their inability to obtain a permit. In contrast, if the permits can be traded across industries, a potential entrant can purchase these rights from a firm in another industry or bring less polluting technology into the existing industry and buy some of the rights to pollute from existing firms. Thus, by making the pollution rights marketable, new firms can enter markets when consumer preferences indicate that more of the good is desired. Firms wishing to enter an industry that produces a highly valued product can purchase permits from firms that produce products that consumers do not value as highly.

The ability to sell the permits also provides an incentive for firms to develop and innovate new technologies that produce less pollution. In particular, a firm that develops a pollution-reducing technology can sell the pollution rights it no longer needs to firms in industries where the technology is not available. This allows the innovating firm to recover a portion of the cost of developing pollution-reducing technologies.

For a video walkthrough of this problem, visit www.mhhe.com/baye8e

Demonstration Problem 14–2

Suppose the external marginal cost of producing steel is

$$MC_{External} = 3Q$$

and the internal marginal cost is

$$MC_{Internal} = 6Q$$

The inverse demand for steel is given by

$$P = 100 - Q$$

1. What is the socially efficient level of output?
2. How much output would a competitive industry produce?
3. How much output would a monopoly produce?

Answer:

1. The socially efficient level of output occurs where the marginal cost to society of producing another unit equals demand. The social marginal cost is

$$MC_{Social} = MC_{External} + MC_{Internal} = 3Q + 6Q = 9Q$$

Equating this with price yields

$$9Q = 100 - Q$$

or $Q = 10$ units.

2. A competitive industry produces where the internal marginal cost equals price:

$$6Q = 100 - Q$$

or about $Q = 14.3$ units. Thus, a competitive industry produces too much steel because it ignores the cost society pays for the pollution.

3. A monopolist produces where marginal revenue equals the internal marginal cost. Since $MR = 100 - 2Q$, we have

$$100 - 2Q = 6Q$$

or $Q = 12.5$ units. Thus, given these demand and cost functions, a monopolist will produce more than the socially efficient level of steel with these cost conditions. Note, however, that since the monopolist has a tendency to restrict output, given these cost and demand functions it produces closer to the socially efficient level than does a competitive industry.

---

public good
A good that is nonrival and nonexclusionary in consumption.

nonrival consumption
A good is nonrival in consumption if the consumption of the good by one person does not preclude other people from also consuming the good.

nonexclusionary consumption
A good or service is nonexclusionary if, once provided, no one can be excluded from consuming it.

Public Goods

Another source of market failure is the provision of *public goods*—goods that are nonrival and nonexclusionary in nature and therefore benefit persons other than those who buy the goods. Public goods differ from most goods you consume, which are rivalrous in nature. This simply means that when you consume the good, another person is unable to consume it as well. For example, when you buy and wear a pair of shoes to protect your feet, you prevent someone else from wearing the same pair; the consumption of shoes is rivalrous in nature.

Nonrival goods include radio signals, lighthouses, national defense, and protecting the environment. When you receive a radio signal in your car, you do not prevent other drivers from picking up the same station in their cars. This is in sharp contrast to your purchasing a pair of shoes.

The second aspect of a public good is that it is *nonexclusionary:* Once a public good is made available, everyone gets it; no one can be excluded from enjoying the good. Most goods and services are by nature exclusionary. For example, when a car manufacturer produces a car, it can keep people from using the car by putting a lock on the door and giving the key only to the person who is willing to pay for the car.

Goods and services such as clean air, national defense, and radio waves are nonexclusionary goods. For example, when the air is clean, everyone gets to consume the clean air; it cannot be allocated to a single person.

What is it about public goods that leads the market to provide them in inefficient quantities? The answer is that since everyone gets to consume a public good once it is available, individuals have little incentive to purchase the good; rather, they prefer to let other people pay for it. Once it becomes available, they can "free ride" on the efforts of others to provide the good. But if everyone thinks this way, no one will buy the good and it will not be available. One person alone may be unable to afford to purchase the good.

Demonstration Problem 14–3

Every time you go to your firm's lounge to get a cup of coffee, the pot is empty. Why?

Answer:

There is a free-rider problem caused by the public-goods nature of making a pot of coffee. If you make a pot when it is empty, you benefit by getting a cup, but so do the next seven people who come into the lounge after you. Thus, people typically wait to let someone else make the coffee, which results in an empty coffee pot.

A concrete example will help you see why public goods are not provided in the socially efficient quantity. Suppose individuals value streetlights in their neighborhood because streetlights help prevent crime. Three people live in the neighborhood: A, B, and C. All three individuals have identical inverse demand functions for streetlights: $P_A = 30 - Q$, $P_B = 30 - Q$, and $P_C = 30 - Q$. The inverse demand curves reveal how much each person values another streetlight.

Because streetlights are nonexclusionary and nonrival in nature, everyone benefits once a streetlight is installed. For this reason, the total demand for a public good such as streetlights is the vertical sum of the individual inverse demand curves; it reveals the value of each additional streetlight to everyone in the neighborhood. Given A's, B's, and C's individual demands, the total demand for streetlights is given by

$$P_A + P_B + P_c = 90 - 3Q$$

The individual and total demand curves are graphed in Figure 14–7. Notice that the total demand curve is the vertical sum of all three individual demand curves, and thus every point on it is three times higher than each point on the individual demand curves.

The socially efficient level of streetlights is at point A in Figure 14–7, where the marginal cost of producing streetlights exactly equals the total demand for streetlights. Algebraically, if the marginal cost of providing streetlights is $54 per light, the socially efficient quantity of streetlights is the quantity that equates

$$54 = 90 - 3Q$$

which is 12 lights.

FIGURE 14–7 The Demand for a Public Good

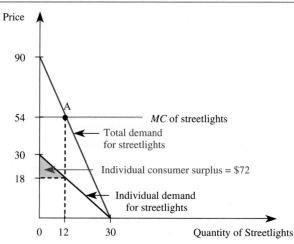

Since the marginal cost of each streetlight is $54 and lies above each individual's demand curve for streetlights in Figure 14–7, none of them will be willing to pay for even one streetlight on their own. However, if each person paid $18 per light, together they would pay $54 per light and could afford to purchase the socially efficient quantity of lights. The only way the people in this neighborhood can achieve the socially efficient quantity of lights is to pool their resources. If they accomplish this and each pays $18 per light, each will enjoy a consumer surplus of the shaded region in Figure 14–7, which is $72.

The problem, however, is that each individual would be better off by letting the other two install the streetlights. In particular, it is strategically advantageous for each person to misrepresent his or her true personal demand function (valuation of the public good). If A claimed she did not want streetlights, and let the others pay for them, she would get to enjoy the lights for free (due to the nonrival and nonexclusionary nature of the good). This is similar to "cheating" on a cooperative agreement and is called *free riding*.

To illustrate this idea, suppose that instead of revealing her true demand for streetlights, A stated that she does not value streetlights at all. If A is the only one who did this, the revealed demand function would be the vertical sum of B's and C's inverse demand functions, which is shown in Figure 14–8(a). Since this demand curve intersects the $54 marginal cost at three streetlights, B and C would each pay $27 per light and purchase three lights. A, on the other hand, would get to enjoy the three streetlights for free, because she misrepresented her true demand for streetlights. By consuming three streetlights for free, she would enjoy a consumer surplus of $85.50, which corresponds to the shaded region in Figure 14–8(b). In contrast, if she had truthfully revealed her demand for streetlights, her consumer surplus would be only $72—the shaded region in Figure 14–7. Thus A is better off by misrepresenting her true preferences for streetlights and letting B and C buy them.

FIGURE 14–8 The Free-Rider Problem

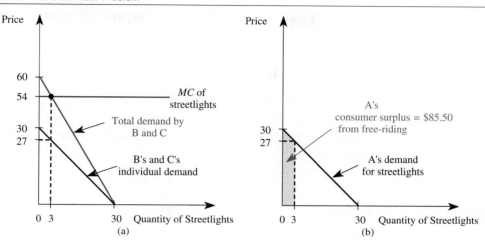

Of course, the same is true of the other two individuals: If they think the others will contribute to buying streetlights, they are better off claiming not to want them. And if they think no one else will pay for streetlights, they will not pay for even one, since the cost is greater than their own individual demand. In the end, no streetlights are provided; the market has failed to provide the public good.

Government solves the public-goods problem by forcing everyone to pay taxes regardless of whether or not a given taxpayer claims to want government services. Government then uses this revenue to fund public projects such as streetlights and national defense, which would not be provided in the absence of government intervention in the marketplace. Thus, while few of us enjoy paying taxes, it does provide a means for obtaining funds for public goods.

It is important to note that government may not provide the socially efficient quantity of public goods; it may in fact provide too much of them. The reason is that when a government official asks a citizen how much of a public good she or he desires, the person may misrepresent the quantity desired. Since most people believe their tax bill is an extremely small percentage of the total funds used to provide public goods, they perceive that the personal cost of the goods is zero and report to the official how many units of the public good they would desire if it were free. In our streetlight example, this means that all three people would tell the official they wanted 30 streetlights—more than twice the socially efficient quantity.

Demonstration Problem 14–4

A firm has 20 employees, each of whom desires a more pleasant work environment. Accordingly, they are considering planting shrubs near the firm's parking lot. Each employee has an inverse demand for shrubs of $P = 10 - Q$, where Q is the number of shrubs. The marginal cost of planting shrubs is $20 each.

1. What is the socially efficient quantity of shrubs to plant?
2. How much would each person have to pay per shrub to achieve the efficient quantity?
3. How many shrubs are likely to be planted? Why?

Answer:

1. The total demand for shrubs (a public good) is

$$P = 200 - 20Q$$

Equating this with the marginal cost of planting shrubs yields the socially efficient quantity of shrubs:

$$200 - 20Q = \$20$$

or $Q = 9$ shrubs.

2. If each person paid his or her marginal valuation of another shrub, which is

$$P = 10 - 9 = \$1$$

the 20 employees together would pay $20 for each shrub.

3. Since there is a free-rider problem, no shrubs are likely to be planted unless the boss exerts "moral suasion" and collects $9 from each employee to plant nine shrubs.

We conclude by pointing out that it may be advantageous for a firm to contribute to public goods in its market area. Doing things such as cleaning up a local park or giving money to public television creates goodwill toward the firm and as a result may create brand loyalty or increase the demand for the firm's product. Since public goods are nonrival and nonexclusionary, $1 spent on cleaning up a park or subsidizing public TV is $1 spent on everyone who finds a clean park or public TV appealing. This makes the provision of public goods an inexpensive way for a firm to "benefit" numerous consumers and thus may be a useful advertising strategy in some situations. Another advantage is that it may put the firm on more favorable terms with politicians, who have considerable latitude in affecting the environment in which the firm operates. Unfortunately, there is no easy way to explicitly calculate the optimal amount that a firm should voluntarily contribute to public goods. But ultimately, if the firm's goal is to maximize profits, the last dollar spent on contributions to public projects should bring in one additional dollar in revenue.

Incomplete Information

For markets to function efficiently, participants must have reasonably good information about things such as prices, quality, available technologies, and the risks associated with working in certain jobs or consuming certain products. When participants in the market have *incomplete information* about such things, the result will be inefficiencies in input usage and in firms' output.

Consider the consumption of cigarettes. If individuals are not told that cigarettes are hazardous, some people who currently do not smoke because of the known health risks would smoke out of ignorance of the dangers of smoking. The decision to smoke would be based on incomplete information about the dangers of smoking.

For reasons such as these, government serves as a provider of information in many markets, dispensing information to consumers about the ingredients of certain foods, the dangers of certain products and drugs, and the like. Firms print some of this information on the labels of their products due to regulations imposed by government. Government even regulates the work environment by ensuring that workers are aware of the dangers of chemicals such as asbestos and the benefits of precautions such as wearing hard hats in construction jobs. In these instances, the regulations are carried out by the Occupational Safety and Health Administration (OSHA).

One of the more severe causes of market failure is asymmetric information, a situation where some market participants have better information than others. As we saw in Chapter 12, the presence of asymmetric information can lead buyers to refuse to purchase from sellers out of fear that the seller is willing to get rid of the product because it is worth less than they are willing to pay. In the extreme case, the market can collapse altogether. For this reason, several government policies are designed to alleviate the problems caused by asymmetric information. A few of the policies that affect managers are discussed next.

Rules against Insider Trading

One example of a government regulation designed to alleviate market failures due to asymmetric information is the law against *insider trading* in the stock market. The purpose of the law is to ensure that asymmetric information (better information by insiders) does not destroy the market by inducing outsiders to stay out of it.

For example, suppose Jane Insider has just learned that her research staff has made a discovery that will revolutionize the industry. If Jane can keep the discovery quiet for a short time while she purchases some of her company's stock at its present price, she will make a bundle. When the announcement of the discovery is made public and the market price of the stock increases dramatically, she can resell the stock and make a large profit. Unfortunately, if potential investors believe the market is dominated by insiders who buy and sell stock based on inside information, they will stay out of the market. The only time the insiders will sell is when they know the price will fall, and they will buy only when they know the price will rise. There is no way for outsiders to earn money in a market dominated by insiders, and they will refuse to buy or sell stock. This reduces the marketability of assets in markets dominated by insiders, which decreases the welfare of all potential market participants.

To prevent insider trading from destroying the market for financial assets, the government has enacted rules against insider trading. The regulations on insider trading come from Section 16 of the *Securities and Exchange Act* (1934). They were amended in 1990 and again in 2002. Most recently, Section 16 was amended by the Sarbanes-Oxley Act of 2002, which made sweeping changes in governance and reporting obligations.

Certification

Another policy government uses to disseminate information and reduce asymmetric information is the certification of skills and/or authenticity. The purpose of *certification* is to centralize the cost of gathering information. All licensing done by the government falls under certification; this includes all nonprofit organizations, such as charities. Certification can also be a set of minimum standards, such as those for schools and physicians. The purpose is to assure consumers that the products or services have been certified as meeting a certain set of minimum standards. Without a central authority to fulfill this information-gathering role, each individual would have to pay the cost of gaining knowledge about the quality of a product or service. This would lead to inefficiencies due to duplication of information-gathering efforts.

Schools are an example of a potential asymmetric information problem. Without the government certifying a school as satisfying some minimum standard, anyone could open a school. Parents who wanted to educate their children would choose a school based on appearance, cost, proximity to their home, advertising, and reputation. When the school first opened, it might look like a very good deal. But to save money, the school might choose to use unsafe equipment, hire undereducated teachers, and crowd classrooms far beyond a size that is conducive to learning. In the long run, the market would correct these problems; their reputation for poor quality would drive bad schools out of business. In the short run, however, parents who had enrolled their children would lose their investment in education, and the students would have wasted potentially valuable time.

Physician certification is another example of the short-run benefits of government certification. In the absence of physician certification, some less than reputable person could hang a sign stating "Medical Service Here." If improperly trained, this person might prescribe a medicine that could make a patient worse, cause a drug addiction, or even lead to death. In the presence of a government-enforced set of standards, however, this short-run scenario is less likely to happen.

Truth in Lending

A set of legislation over the years has made gathering information for borrowing purposes less difficult. Confusion caused by the *Truth in Lending Act* (1969) led Congress to pass the *Truth in Lending Simplification Act (TLSA)* in 1980. TLSA is enforced by the Federal Reserve Board (FRB) and has been revised several times. In 1980, the FRB passed *Regulation Z* to provide guidelines for enforcement; it amended Regulation Z in 1982.

Regulation Z and TLSA require that all creditors comply with the act. A creditor is defined as anyone who loans money subject to a finance charge, where the money is to be paid back in four or more installments. A creditor must also be the person to whom the original obligation is payable. TLSA has some exemptions regarding the types of loans covered, the most notable being business, agricultural, and commercial loans.

TLSA requires that creditors disclose certain information to debtors in writing before the consummation of loans. This information includes an itemization of all finance charges, the total purchase price, the annual interest rate charged, and over a dozen other items. The purpose of this law is to ensure that all debtors are given an opportunity to understand all aspects of borrowing money from a specific creditor, thus creating more symmetric information between borrowers and lenders.

The Truth in Lending Act affects both the supply of and the demand for credit. Potential borrowers now have more complete information about what a loan involves. This increased knowledge reduces the risk involved in repayment for the borrower. The reduced risk shifts the demand curve for loans to the right. The suppliers of loans (creditors) are affected mainly by the increased cost of complying with the government regulations. This shifts the creditors' supply curve to the left. Since the demand curve for loans shifts to the right and the supply curve shifts to the left, the effect of this law is to increase the price of loans (the interest rate).

The financial crisis of 2009 led to additional changes in regulations related to credit and financial markets. In particular, Congress passed the *Dodd-Frank Wall Street Reform and Consumer Protection Act* in 2010. One piece of this law is designed to increase investor protection in a manner similar to the way TLSA increases protection of borrowers. Specifically, it grants the Securities and Exchange Commission (SEC) the power to issue "point-of-sale disclosure" rules when retail investors purchase investment products or services. Such disclosures include information on costs, risks, and whether there is a conflict of interest. The specific rules to be implemented by the SEC are yet to be determined, so stay tuned.

Truth in Advertising

Often firms have better information about their products than do consumers. This advantage may give firms an incentive to make false claims about the merits of their products to capitalize on consumers' lack of information. In some instances, such practices can lead consumers to switch from one firm's product to a competitor's product. In extreme cases, the asymmetric information can induce consumers to ignore advertising messages altogether, out of fear that the messages are false. Government often can alleviate these market failures by regulating the advertising practices of firms.

Advertising regulation, which encourages *truth in advertising,* usually is enforced by civil suits. Under Section 43 of the *Lanham Act,* false and misleading advertising is prohibited. Technically, the FTC can bring suit against any false advertising using the Lanham Act, although most cases are filed in civil court by those harmed by deceptive advertising rather than by the FTC.

The Lanham Act, in concert with the Clayton Act, allows someone who is harmed by false or misleading advertising to stop the deceptive practice and receive treble damages. If a firm finds that a competitor's deceptive advertising reduces the demand for its product, it may sue under the Lanham Act. The plaintiff first must prove that the advertisement is either false or misleads consumers. The plaintiff also must prove that the misleading or false advertising harmed it. If the plaintiff wins, the defendant must cease running the advertisement, recall any units of the product that have the false or misleading claim on their label, and pay the plaintiff three times the damages the advertisement caused the plaintiff.

Enforcing Contracts

Another way government solves the problems of asymmetric information is through *contract enforcement.* In Chapters 6 and 10, we learned that contracts are written to keep the parties from behaving opportunistically in the final period of a game. For example, suppose your boss "promised" you payment for labor services at the end of the month. After you have worked for a month, your boss refuses to pay you—in effect gaining a month's worth of your labor for free. In Chapters 6 and 10 we saw that these types of problems do not arise when reputation is important or when there is the potential for repeated interaction among the parties. In these instances, the one-time gain to behaving opportunistically will be more than offset by future losses.

INSIDE BUSINESS 14–3

Canada's Competition Bureau

The Competition Bureau is an independent law enforcement agency responsible for promoting and maintaining fair competition in Canada. Its authority stems from *The Competition Act*, a federal law that contains both criminal and civil provisions aimed at preventing anticompetitive practices in the marketplace. The Competition Bureau's principal responsibilities are divided among seven branches:

- *The Civil Matters Branch* is responsible for detecting and deterring restrictive trade practices that have a negative impact on competition, such as abuse of dominance, refusal to deal, exclusive dealing, tied-selling, and price maintenance.

- *The Compliance and Operations Branch* is responsible for ensuring that branches work within approved policies and procedures and have the necessary tools to conduct their work.

- *The Criminal Matters Branch* is responsible for detecting, investigating, and deterring hard-core cartels, including conspiracies, agreements, or arrangements among competitors and potential competitors to fix prices, allocate markets, or restrict supply, and bid-rigging.

- *The Economic Policy and Enforcement Branch* is responsible for providing expertise on leading economic theory, advice on enforcement matters and policy activities of the Bureau, and developing and disseminating economic knowledge to the Bureau.

- *The Fair Business Practices Branch* is responsible for promoting a competitive marketplace by discouraging deceptive business practices, which include: misleading representations, deceptive marketing practices, and the adequacy and accuracy of information provided to consumers in labeling, packaging, and marketing certain consumer goods.

- *The Legal Support Branch* is responsible for providing legal services to the Commissioner of Competition and for initiating and conducting criminal prosecutions on behalf of the attorney general of Canada. It also advises the Competition Bureau on criminal investigations.

- *The Legislative and International Affairs Branch* is responsible for input into legislative proposals relating to the Competition Act and other legislation administered and enforced by the Bureau for providing competition policy input into departmental and government wide legislative and regulatory proposals.

- *The Mergers Branch* is responsible for reviewing merger transactions, and taking remedial action where necessary, to protect and promote competitive markets in Canada.

- *The Public Affairs Branch* is responsible for providing leadership, support, and advice in communicating to the public the Bureau's contribution to competition in the marketplace.

Source: Competition Bureau website, July 31, 2012.

In short-term relationships, however, one or more parties may take advantage of the "end period" by behaving opportunistically. If you knew your boss would not pay you at the end of the month, you would refuse to work. The problem, however, is that you do not know what your boss will do at the end of the month—only she does. In effect, you are uncertain whether your boss is honest (will keep a promise) or dishonest (will break a promise). This asymmetric information can destroy the ability of individuals to use contracts to solve the problem of opportunism; even if a contract is written, a boss may not honor it. Because of this, you may refuse to work for your boss even if she is honest, because you do not *know* whether she is honest.

One solution to this problem is for government to enforce contracts. By enforcing contracts, government effectively solves the "end-of-period" problem by requiring dishonest people to honor the terms of contracts. In this case, even if you do not know whether your boss is honest, you will be willing to work under contract. If she turns out to be dishonest, the government will force her to pay you. Thus, government enforcement of contracts can solve market failures caused by the end-of-period problem.

RENT SEEKING

rent seeking
Selfishly motivated efforts to influence another party's decision.

The preceding analysis shows how government policies can improve the allocation of resources in the economy by alleviating the problems associated with market power, externalities, public goods, and incomplete information. It is important to note, however, that government policies generally benefit some parties at the expense of others. For this reason, lobbyists spend considerable sums in attempts to influence government policies. This process is known as *rent seeking*.

To illustrate rent seeking and its consequences, suppose a politician has the power to regulate the monopoly in Figure 14–9. The monopoly currently charges a price of P^M, produces Q^M units of output, and earns profits described by the shaded region A. At the monopoly price and output, consumer surplus is given by triangle C.

If consumers could persuade the politician to regulate the monopolist's price at the competitive level (P^C), the result would be an output of Q^C. If this happened, the monopoly would lose all of its profits (rectangle A). Consumers, on the other hand, would end up with total consumer surplus of regions A, B, and C.

Since the monopolist stands to lose rectangle A if the regulation is imposed, it has an incentive to lobby very hard to prevent the regulation from being imposed. In fact, the monopolist is willing to spend up to the amount A to avoid the regulation. These expenditures may be in the form of legal activities, such as campaign contributions or wining and dining the politician, or illegal activities such as bribes.

FIGURE 14–9 The Incentives to Engage in Rent-Seeking Activities

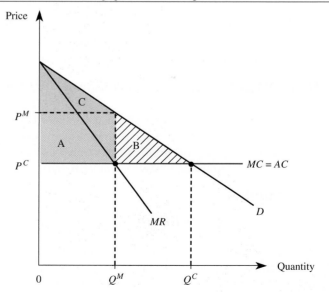

Notice that the consumers in Figure 14–9 also would be willing to spend money to persuade the politician to regulate the monopoly. In fact, as a group they would be willing to spend up to A + B to impose the competitive solution, since this is the additional consumer surplus enjoyed when the price is P^C. Of course, each individual consumer stands to gain much less than the group (regulation is a public good in that it benefits all consumers). Consequently, each consumer has an incentive to "free ride," and in the end the amount the consumers spend as a group will be very low. The monopolist, on the other hand, is a single entity. Avoiding regulation is not a public good to the monopolist; the monopolist will receive private gains if it can avoid the legislation. As a result, the monopolist generally will spend much more on lobbying activities than the consumers and thus will often avoid legislation by engaging in rent-seeking activities.

Demonstration Problem 14–5

You are the manager of a monopoly that faces an inverse demand curve of $P = 10 - Q$ and has a cost function of $C(Q) = 2Q$. The government is considering legislation that would regulate your price at the competitive level. What is the maximum amount you would be willing to spend on lobbying activities designed to stop the regulation?

Answer:

If the regulation passes, your firm's price will be regulated at marginal cost ($2) and the firm will earn zero profits. If not, the firm can continue to produce the monopoly output and charge the monopoly price. The monopoly output is determined by the point where $MR = MC$:

$$10 - 2Q = 2$$

Solving for Q yields the monopoly output of $Q^M = 4$ units. The monopoly price is obtained by inserting this quantity into the demand function to obtain

$$P^M = 10 - (4) = 6$$

Thus, your firm stands to lose monopoly profits of $P^M Q^M - C(Q^M) = \$16$ if the regulation is imposed. The most you would be willing to spend on lobbying activities thus is $16.

GOVERNMENT POLICY AND INTERNATIONAL MARKETS

Sometimes rent seeking manifests itself in the form of government involvement in international markets. Such policies usually take the form of tariffs or quotas that are designed to benefit specific firms and workers at the expense of others. In this section, we will examine how government tariff and quota policies affect managerial decisions.

Quotas

quota
A restriction that limits the quantity of imported goods that can legally enter the country.

The purpose of a *quota* is to limit the number of units of a product that foreign competitors can bring into the country. For example, a quota on Japanese automobile imports limits the number of cars Japanese automakers can sell in the United States. This reduces competition in the domestic automobile market, which results in higher car prices, higher profits for domestic firms, and lower consumer surplus for domestic consumers. Domestic producers thus benefit at the expense of domestic consumers and foreign producers.

FIGURE 14–10 The Impact of a Foreign Import Quota on the Domestic Market

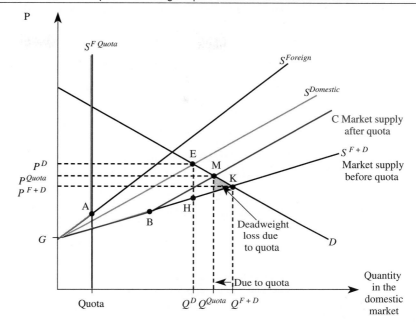

To see why these results occur, consider Figure 14–10, which shows the domestic market for a product. Before the imposition of a quota, the domestic demand curve is D, the supply curve for foreign producers is $S^{Foreign}$, the supply curve for domestic producers is $S^{Domestic}$, and the market supply curve—the horizontal summation of the foreign and domestic supply curves—is S^{F+D}. Equilibrium in the absence of a quota is at point K, where the equilibrium price is P^{F+D} and the equilibrium quantity is Q^{F+D}.

Now suppose a quota is imposed on foreign producers that restricts them from selling more than the quota in the domestic market. Under the quota, foreign supply is $GAS^{F\ Quota}$, while the supply by domestic firms remains at $S^{Domestic}$. Thus, market supply in the domestic market after the quota is GBC, resulting in an equilibrium at point M. The quota increases the price received by domestic producers to P^{Quota}, and domestic firms now earn higher profits. The shaded triangle in Figure 14–10 represents the deadweight loss due to the quota. Total welfare declines as a result of the quota even though domestic producers earn higher profits. The reason for the decline in total welfare is that domestic consumers and foreign producers are harmed more than domestic producers gain from the quota. Domestic producers therefore have a strong incentive to lobby for quotas on foreign imports into their market.

Demonstration Problem 14–6

Suppose the supply of a good by domestic firms is $Q^{SD} = 10 + 2P$ and the supply by foreign firms is $Q^{SF} = 10 + P$. The domestic demand for the product is given by $Q^d = 30 - P$.

1. In the absence of a quota, what is the total supply of the good?
2. What are the equilibrium price and quantity of the good?

3. Suppose a quota of 10 units is imposed. What is the total supply of the product?
4. Determine the equilibrium price in the domestic market under the quota of 10 units.

Answer:

1. The total supply is the sum of foreign and domestic supply, which is

$$Q^T = Q^{SD} + Q^{SF} = (10 + 2P) + (10 + P) = 20 + 3P$$

2. Equilibrium is determined by equating total demand and supply:

$$30 - P = 20 + 3P$$

Solving for P yields the equilibrium price of $P = \$2.50$. Given this price, domestic firms produce

$$Q^{SD} = 10 + 2(2.5) = 15 \text{ units}$$

and foreign firms produce

$$Q^{SF} = 10 + 2.5 = 12.5 \text{ units}$$

for a total equilibrium output of $Q^T = 27.5$ units.

3. With a quota of 10 units, foreign firms will sell only 10 units in the domestic market. Thus, total supply is

$$Q^T = Q^{SD} + Q^{SF} = (10 + 2P) + 10 = 20 + 2P$$

4. Equilibrium is determined by equating total demand and total supply under a quota:

$$30 - P = 20 + 2P$$

Solving for P yields the equilibrium price of $P = \$3.33$. The quota increases the price of the good in the domestic market due to the reduction in foreign competition.

---

lump-sum tariff
A fixed fee that an importing firm must pay the domestic government in order to have the legal right to sell the product in the domestic market.

per-unit (or excise) tariff
The fee an importing firm must pay to the domestic government on each unit it brings into the country.

Tariffs

Tariffs, like quotas, are designed to limit foreign competition in the domestic market to benefit domestic producers. The benefits to domestic producers accrue at the expense of domestic consumers and foreign producers.

We will address two types of tariffs: lump-sum tariffs and excise or per-unit tariffs. A *lump-sum tariff* is a fixed fee that foreign firms must pay the domestic government to be able to sell in the domestic market. In contrast, a *per-unit* or *excise tariff* requires the importing firms to pay the domestic government a fee on each unit they bring into the country.

Lump-Sum Tariffs

Figure 14–11 shows the marginal and average cost curves for an individual foreign firm before and after the imposition of a lump-sum tariff. The first thing to notice about the lump-sum tariff is that it does not affect the marginal cost curve. This is because the importer must pay the same amount of tariff regardless of how much of the product it brings into the country. Since the lump-sum tariff raises average costs

FIGURE 14–11 Impact of a Lump-Sum Tariff on a Foreign Firm

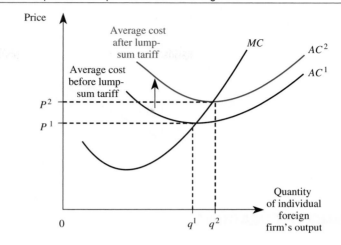

from AC^1 to AC^2, an importer is unwilling to pay the tariff to enter the domestic market unless the price in the domestic market is at least P^2.

Figure 14–12 shows the effect of a lump-sum tariff on the market. Before the tariff is imposed, the supply curve for foreign competitors is ES^F, that for domestic producers is ES^D, and the market supply curve—the summation of domestic and foreign supply—is ES^{D+F}. After the lump-sum tariff is imposed, the foreign supply curve becomes AS^F, because importers will not pay the lump-sum tariff to enter the domestic market unless the price is above P^2. Thus, the market supply curve in the presence of a lump-sum tariff is given by $EBCS^{D+F}$. The overall effect of this policy is to remove foreign competitors from the domestic market if the demand curve crosses the domestic supply curve at a price below P^2. A lump-sum tariff increases the profits of domestic producers if demand is low but has no effect on their profits if demand is high.

Excise Tariffs

If an excise tariff is imposed on foreign producers instead of a lump-sum tariff, domestic producers benefit at all levels of demand. To see this, consider Figure 14–13, which shows the effect of an excise tariff. S^F is the supply by foreign producers before the tariff, S^D is the supply by domestic producers, and ABS^{D+F} is the market supply curve before an excise tariff. Equilibrium in the absence of a tariff is at point H.

When a tariff of T is imposed on each unit of the product, the marginal cost curve for foreign firms shifts up by the amount of the tariff, which in turn decreases the supply of all foreign firms to S^{F+T} in Figure 14–13. The market supply under a per-unit tariff is now ACS^{D+F+T}, and the resulting equilibrium is at point E. The tariff raises the price domestic consumers must pay for the product, which raises the profits of domestic firms at the expense of domestic consumers and foreign producers.

FIGURE 14–12 Impact of a Lump-Sum Tariff on Market Supply

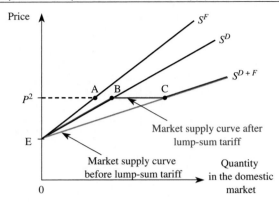

ANSWERING THE HEADLINE

How did Nestlé and Ralston obtain conditional approval for their merger? As we learned in this chapter, the most common way for merging parties to alleviate antitrust concerns is by agreeing to divest assets in those markets where the business overlap would lead to a significant increase in market power. This is precisely what happened in this case. The overlap of concern was the market for dry cat food, and the parties ultimately obtained conditional approval by agreeing to divest Ralston's Meow Mix and Alley Cat brands of cat food to another company. The parties recognized that their merger increased levels of concentration above those permitted by the *Horizontal Merger Guidelines* and that divesting these assets to gain approval made more sense than spending millions of dollars on a costly legal battle.

FIGURE 14–13 Impact of an Excise Tariff on Market Supply

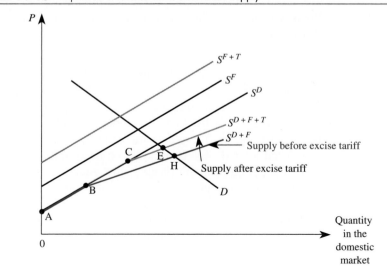

SUMMARY

In this chapter, we focused on government's activity in the market to correct market failures caused by market power, externalities, public goods, and incomplete information. The government's ability to regulate markets gives market participants an incentive to engage in rent-seeking activities, such as lobbying, to affect public policy. These activities may extend to international markets, where government imposes tariffs or quotas on foreign imports to increase the profits of special interests.

In the United States, the government influences markets through devices such as antitrust enforcement and legislation, price regulation, insider-trading restrictions, and truth-in-advertising/truth-in-lending regulations, as well as policies designed to alleviate market failure due to externalities or public-goods problems. The rules that affect the decisions of future managers are spelled out in documents such as the Sherman Antitrust Act, the Clayton Act, the Robinson-Patman Act, the Celler-Kefauver Act, the Lanham Act, the Securities and Exchange Act, Regulation Z, and the Clean Air Act.

KEY TERMS AND CONCEPTS

Antitrust Division of the Department of Justice (DOJ)
antitrust policy
Celler-Kefauver Act (1950)
certification
Clayton Act (1914)
Clean Air Act (1990)
contract enforcement
deadweight loss
Dodd-Frank Wall Street Reform and Consumer Protection Act (2010)
Federal Trade Commission (FTC)
free riding
Hart-Scott-Rodino Antitrust Improvement Act (1976)
Herfindahl-Hirschman index (HHI)
Horizontal Merger Guidelines
incomplete information
insider trading
Lanham Act

lump-sum tariffs
market power
negative externalities
nonexclusionary consumption
nonrival consumption
per-unit (excise) tariffs
property rights
public goods
quotas
Regulation Z
rent seeking
Robinson-Patman Act (1936)
rule of reason
Securities and Exchange Act (1934)
Sherman Antitrust Act (1890)
social welfare
truth in advertising
Truth in Lending Act (1969)
Truth in Lending Simplification Act (TLSA) (1980)

END-OF-CHAPTER PROBLEMS BY LEARNING OBJECTIVE

Every end-of-chapter problem addresses at least one learning objective. Following is a nonexhaustive sample of end-of-chapter problems for each learning objective.

LO1 Identify four sources of market failure.

Try these problems: 1, 21

LO2 Explain why market power reduces social welfare, and identify two types of government policies aimed at reducing deadweight loss.

Try these problems: 2, 23

LO3 Show why externalities can lead competitive markets to provide socially inefficient quantities of goods and services; explain how government policies, such as the Clean Air Act, can improve resource allocation.

Try these problems: 3, 15

LO4 Show why competitive markets fail to provide socially efficient levels of public goods; explain how the government can mitigate these inefficiencies.

Try these problems: 4, 14

LO5 Explain why incomplete information compromises the efficiency of markets, and identify five government policies aimed at mitigating these problems.

Try these problems: 9, 16

LO6 Explain why government attempts to solve market failures can lead to additional inefficiencies because of "rent-seeking" activities.

Try these problems: 5, 17

LO7 Show how government policies in international markets, such as quotas and tariffs, impact the prices and quantities of domestic goods and services.

Try these problems: 6, 19

CONCEPTUAL AND COMPUTATIONAL QUESTIONS

connect
|ECONOMICS

1. You are the manager in a market composed of eight firms, each of which has a 12.5 percent market share. In addition, each firm has a strong financial position and is located within a 100-mile radius of its competitors.
   a. Calculate the premerger Herfindahl-Hirschman index (HHI) for this market.
   b. Suppose that any two of these firms merge. What is the postmerger HHI?
   c. Based only on the information contained in this question and on the *Horizontal Merger Guidelines* described in this chapter, do you think the Justice Department (or FTC) would attempt to block a merger between any two of the firms? Explain.

2. Use the accompanying graph to answer the questions that follow.
   a. Suppose this monopolist is unregulated.
      (1) What price will the firm charge to maximize its profits?
      (2) What is the level of consumer surplus at this price?
   b. Suppose the firm's price is regulated at $80.
      (1) What is the firm's marginal revenue if it produces 7 units?
      (2) If the firm is able to cover its variable costs at the regulated price, how much output will the firm produce in the short run to maximize its profits?
      (3) In the long run, how much output will this firm produce if the price remains regulated at $80?

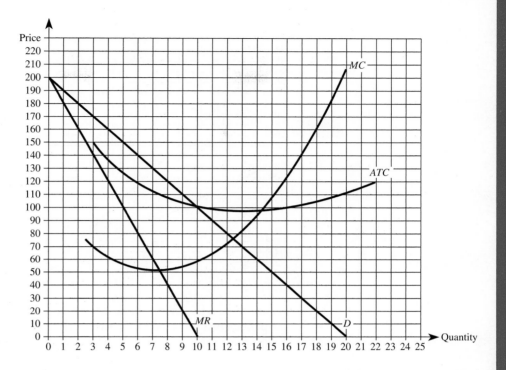

3. You are an industry analyst who specializes in an industry where the market inverse demand is $P = 200 - 4Q$. The external marginal cost of producing the product is $MC_{External} = 6Q$, and the internal cost is $MC_{Internal} = 12Q$.
    a. What is the socially efficient level of output?
    b. Given these costs and market demand, how much output would a competitive industry produce?
    c. Given these costs and market demand, how much output would a monopolist produce?
    d. Discuss actions the government might take to induce firms in this industry to produce the socially efficient level of output.
4. There are two workers. Each worker's demand for a public good is $P = 20 - Q$. The marginal cost of providing the public good is $24. The accompanying graph summarizes the relevant information.
    a. What is the socially efficient quantity of the public good?
    b. How much will each worker have to pay per unit to provide the socially efficient quantity?
    c. Suppose the two workers contribute the amount needed to provide the quantity of public good you identified in parts (a) and (b). A third worker values the public good just like the two contributing workers, but she claims *not* to value the good because she wants to "free ride" on the payments of the other two workers.

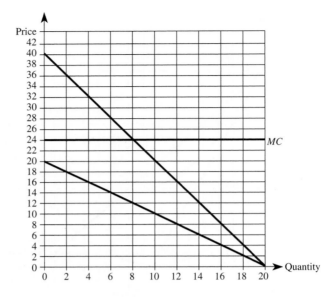

(1) Given the three workers' true demands for the public good, is the amount of the public good provided by the two workers socially efficient?

(2) Compare the level of consumer surplus enjoyed by these three workers. Which worker(s) enjoys the most surplus?

5. As the manager of a monopoly, you face potential government regulation. Your inverse demand is $P = 40 - 2Q$, and your costs are $C(Q) = 8Q$.

   a. Determine the monopoly price and output.

   b. Determine the socially efficient price and output.

   c. What is the maximum amount your firm should be willing to spend on lobbying efforts to prevent the price from being regulated at the socially optimal level?

6. Consider a competitive market served by many domestic and foreign firms. The domestic demand for these firms' product is $Q^d = 600 - 2P$. The supply function of the domestic firms is $Q^{SD} = 200 + P$, while that of the foreign firms is $Q^{SF} = 250$.

   a. Determine the equilibrium price and quantity under free trade.

   b. Determine the equilibrium price and quantity when foreign firms are constrained by a 100-unit quota.

   c. Are domestic consumers better or worse off as a result of the quota?

   d. Are domestic producers better or worse off as a result of the quota?

7. Suppose that the U.S. Congress passes legislation that imposes a one-time lump-sum tariff on the product that a foreign firm exports to the United States.

   a. What happens to the foreign firm's marginal cost curve as a result of the lump-sum tariff?

   b. Will the lump-sum tariff cause the foreign firm to export more or less of the good? Explain carefully.

8. The accompanying diagram depicts a monopolist whose price is regulated at $10 per unit. Use this figure to answer the questions that follow.

     a. What price will an unregulated monopoly charge?

     b. What quantity will an unregulated monopoly produce?

     c. How many units will a monopoly produce when the regulated price is $10 per unit?

     d. Determine the quantity demanded and the amount produced at the regulated price of $10 per unit. Is there a shortage or a surplus?

     e. Determine the deadweight loss to society (if any) when the regulated price is $10 per unit.

     f. Determine the regulated price that maximizes social welfare. Is there a shortage or a surplus at this price?

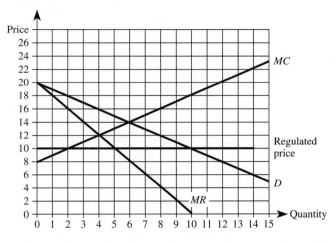

9. Explain, using precise economic terminology, the economic rationale for laws against insider trading.

10. Is "fairness" the economic basis for government laws and regulations designed to remedy market failures? If so, why; if not, what is the economic basis?

PROBLEMS AND APPLICATIONS

11. Attorneys for Eastman Kodak argued before the U.S. Supreme Court to defend the company against charges levied by several independent firms that provided service for machines sold by Eastman Kodak. At issue was a decision by Kodak to limit the availability of replacement parts to these firms, making it more difficult for them to compete against Kodak in servicing Kodak machines. The suit alleged that Kodak unlawfully tied the sale of service for its machines to the sale of parts and, therefore, unlawfully monopolized and attempted to monopolize the sale of service and parts for such machines. Under which act do you think Kodak was charged?

12. Between 1972 and 1981, Texaco sold gasoline to independent Texaco retailers at "retail tank wagon prices" but granted substantial discounts to distributors Gull and Dompier. Gull resold the gas under its own name. Dompier resold the gas under the Texaco brand name to retail stations and entered the retail

market directly. Since neither Gull nor Dompier had significant storage facilities, both distributors picked up gas directly from the Texaco plant and delivered it to their retail outlets. As a result, the sales volume increased substantially at the retail stations purchasing gas from these distributors, while independent Texaco retailers suffered a corresponding sales decline. In 1976, independent Texaco retailers filed suit against Texaco. In 1990, the Supreme Court of the United States found that Texaco had indeed violated antitrust law. Which law do you think Texaco was found guilty of violating?

13. Social Dynamo Corporation earned profits last year of $49 million on sales of $500 million. During the same period, its major competitor—EIO Corp.—enjoyed sales of $490 million and earned profits of $52 million. Currently, Social Dynamo is negotiating a deal in which it would acquire the assets of EIO in a transaction Wall Street values at $120 million. A successful merger between the two companies is expected to raise prices in the market by 2 percent. Is Social Dynamo obligated to notify the U.S. Justice Department and the Federal Trade Commission of its merger intentions? Explain.

14. A well-known conglomerate that manufactures a multitude of noncompeting consumer products instituted a corporatewide initiative to encourage the managers of its many divisions to share consumer demographic information. However, since the initiative was implemented, the CEO has noticed that less information is available than ever. Why do you think the CEO's plan backfired?

15. You are the manager of a paper mill and have been subpoenaed to appear before a joint session of the Senate Consumer Affairs and the Senate Environmental subcommittees. The Consumer Affairs Subcommittee is interested in your testimony about the pricing practices of your company because a recent news magazine reported that your markups are 250 percent. The Environmental Subcommittee is interested in exploring ways to reduce the pollution associated with your paper mill. In particular, you know that one senator on the Environmental Subcommittee will ask you to justify why the firm should not be charged a per-unit tax on the firm's output to compensate for the pollution it discharges into a major river. Devise a game plan for responding to the questions that will be raised in the joint session of the subcommittees.

16. Section 16(a) of the Securities and Exchange Act of 1934, as amended in 1990, requires that the officers, directors, and principal shareholders of companies disclose the extent of their ownership of equity securities of the company and any changes in the ownership. Section 16(b) permits companies to recover trading profits realized by such people arising from short-swing transactions in the company securities. Do you think that, as a result of these laws, the government will be forced to spend more money on its auditing and enforcement efforts? Explain.

17. Enrodes is a monopoly provider of residential electricity in a region of northern Michigan. Total demand by its 3 million households is $Q^d = 1,500 - 2P$, and Enrodes can produce electricity at a constant marginal cost of $4 per megawatt-hour. Consumers in this region of Michigan have recently complained that Enrodes is charging too much for its services. In fact, a few consumers are so upset that they are trying to form a coalition to lobby the local government to regulate the price Enrodes charges. If all the consumers of this

region joined the coalition against Enrodes, how much would each consumer be willing to spend to lobby the local government to regulate Enrodes's price? Do you think the consumers will be successful in their efforts? Explain.

18. China's entry into the World Trade Organization (WTO) in 2001 created more competition between local and foreign firms, and also provided China greater access to the market for exports. This was particularly true in the market for rubber since, at the time, China was the world's second largest consumer of rubber (China is now the world's largest consumer of rubber). Shortly after joining the WTO, China eliminated its import quota on rubber. What impact do you think the import quota reduction likely had on the price of rubber and the quantity of rubber exchanged in China? What implications do you think the elimination of the quota on rubber had on China's social welfare?

19. The U.S. International Trade Commission's committee in charge of the global safeguard investigation involving imports of steel has announced its recommendations to be forwarded to the president. Of the 33 steel product categories investigated, 12 have experienced a significant increase in the quantity of imported steel, causing serious injury or the threat of serious injury to the U.S. steel industry. The commission has recommended that the president impose a 20 percent tariff on these 12 categories of imported steel. If the president follows the commission's recommendations, what will happen to the supply of foreign steel in these categories? What impact will this have on the equilibrium quantity of steel sold (in these categories) in the United States? Will the equilibrium price for these categories of steel in the United States market increase or decrease? Explain.

20. Canada's forestry industry (composed mainly of those involved in the lumber industry) directly employs about 370,000 workers and indirectly employs an additional 510,000 people in support services. Forestry products account for nearly 3 percent of Canada's gross domestic product (GDP) and 14.1 percent of its exports. Lobbyists for the U.S. lumber and timber producers recently filed a complaint with the U.S. International Trade Commission (ITC) and the U.S. Department of Commerce (DOC) alleging that the Canadian government provided a subsidy to its lumber producers and caused harm to U.S. lumber and timber producers. As a result of these concerns, one U.S. lobbyist proposed the imposition of a 15 percent excise tariff on all Canadian forestry products. Determine the likely impact of the proposed 15 percent excise tariff on the equilibrium price and quantity of lumber exchanged in the United States. Would domestic consumers and producers benefit from the proposed tariff? Explain carefully.

21. Suppose that, prior to the passage of the Truth in Lending Simplification Act and Regulation Z, the demand for consumer loans was given by $Q^d_{pre-TILSA} = 12 - 100P$ (in billions of dollars) and the supply of consumer loans by credit unions and other lending institutions was $Q^S_{pre-TILSA} = 5 + 100P$ (in billions of dollars). The TILSA now requires lenders to provide consumers with complete information about the rights and responsibilities of entering into a lending relationship with the institution, and as a result, the demand for loans has increased to $Q^d_{post-TILSA} = 18 - 100P$ (in billions of dollars). However, the TILSA also imposed "compliance costs" on lending institutions, and this reduced the supply of consumer loans to $Q^S_{post-TILSA} = 3 + 100P$ (in billions of dollars). Based on

this information, compare the equilibrium price and quantity of consumer loans before and after the Truth in Lending Simplification Act.

22. Evaluate this statement: "If the U.S. imposed a uniform excise tariff on *all* foreign imports, all U.S. businesses and workers would benefit. Consequently, if a bill to impose a uniform excise tariff were introduced in the U.S. Congress, it would unanimously pass."

23. Moses Inc. is a small electric company that provides power to customers in a small rural area in the Southwest. The company is currently maximizing its profits by selling electricity to consumers at a price of $0.15 per kilowatt-hour. Its marginal cost is $0.05 per kilowatt-hour, and its average cost is $0.15 per kilowatt-hour. A government regulator is considering a proposal to regulate the firm's price at $0.05 per kilowatt-hour. Would such a policy improve social welfare? Explain.

CONNECT EXERCISES

If your instructor has adopted Connect for the course and you are an active subscriber, you can practice with the questions presented above, along with many alternative versions of these questions. Your instructor may also assign a subset of these problems and/or their alternative versions as a homework assignment through Connect, allowing for immediate feedback of grades and correct answers.

CASE-BASED EXERCISES

Your instructor may assign additional problem-solving exercises (called memos) that require you to apply some of the tools you learned in this chapter to make a recommendation based on an actual business scenario. Some of these memos accompany the Time Warner case (pages 561–597 of your textbook). Additional memos, as well as data that may be useful for your analysis, are available online at www. mhhe.com/baye8e.

SELECTED READINGS

Economides, Nicholas, and White, Lawrence J., "Networks and Compatibility: Implications for Antitrust." *European Economic Review* 38(34), April 1994, pp. 651–62.

Elzinga, Kenneth, and Breit, William, *The Antitrust Penalties: A Study in Law and Economics.* New Haven: Yale University Press, 1976.

Formby, John P.; Keeler, James P.; and Thistle, Paul D., "X-efficiency, Rent Seeking and Social Costs." *Public Choice* 57(2), May 1988, pp. 115–26.

Gradstein, Mark; Nitzan, Shmuel; and Slutsky, Steven, "Private Provision of Public Goods under Price Uncertainty." *Social Choice and Welfare* 10(4), 1993, pp. 371–82.

Inman, Robert P., "New Research in Local Public Finance: Introduction." *Regional Science and Urban Economics* 19(3), August 1989, pp. 347–52.

McCall, Charles W., "Rule of Reason versus Mechanical Tests in the Adjudication of Price Predation." *Review of Industrial Organization* 3(3), Spring 1988, pp. 15–44.

Rivlin, A. M., "Distinguished Lecture on Economics in Government: Strengthening the Economy by Rethinking the Role of Federal and State Governments." *Journal of Economic Perspectives* 5(2), Spring 1991, pp. 3–14.

Steiner, R. L., "Intrabrand Competition—Stepchild of Antitrust." *Antitrust Bulletin* 36(1), Spring 1991, pp. 155–200.

Those who cannot remember the past are condemned to repeat it—

George Santayana

Managers who cannot apply managerial economics are destined for failure—

Michael Baye and Jeffrey Prince

The case-study method is a useful pedagogy for applying managerial economics to real business scenarios. Two things are required for this approach to yield optimal results. First, since hindsight is always 20–20, put yourself in the shoes of decision-makers at the time of their decisions—January 2003 in this case—rather than at the time you read the case. This is your job. Second, the case being studied must involve economic issues that transcend time. That's our job.

Challenges at Time Warner is a timeless case that was written especially for *Managerial Economics and Business Strategy.* Regardless of whether you've covered a single chapter or every chapter in the text, the case provides an opportunity to apply tools from managerial economics to a real-world business situation. The case includes a plethora of issues and may be used in a variety of ways to hone your decision-making skills.

For example, your instructor may choose to use the case as a capstone experience where you and/or team members present your analysis and make recommendations for the company. For this reason, when you read the case you will observe that it provides information about the company and its business environment, but it does not identify specific problems or ask specific questions. As in the business world, the onus is on you to identify key issues and to defend your recommendations. Different students are likely to focus on different issues and to make different recommendations, depending on the chapters covered and their mastery of the material.

Alternatively, or in addition, your instructor may use this case as "an extended problem" throughout the course to illustrate concepts developed in specific chapters. The case includes a variety of memos—some at the end of the case and others available online at www.mhhe.com/baye8e—that permit you to apply concepts on a chapter-by-chapter basis.

We hope you enjoy the case. Remember that an important component of any case exercise is to use the information provided along with your knowledge of managerial economics and business strategy to identify key issues and to guide your recommendations and decisions. Consider this a practice run for when you leave the classroom and enter the business world.

Challenges at Time Warner[1]

Note to Students: Please read the information on page 561 before working through this case.

In January 2003, AOL Time Warner, Inc., announced that it would be posting a loss of $98.7 billion for the year ended December 31, 2002, the largest corporate loss in U.S. history. While company executives described the loss as a result of accounting changes rather than problems with ongoing operations, the media conglomerate clearly faced significant challenges. The stock price closed the month of January at $11.66, down from $71 in January 2000, when it announced its merger with America Online (AOL).

The gravity of the events of the past few years hit TJ like a hammer. TJ was coming down from the high she felt when the CEO called last week to promote her to a new position within Time Warner—effective today, September 1, 2004. TJ set aside her morning coffee and *The Wall Street Journal* to review the company's operations before replying to the first memo in her inbox.

---

[1]This case was prepared with Kyle Anderson and Dong Chen for use as a teaching tool rather than to illustrate Time Warner Inc.'s effective or ineffective handling of difficult managerial challenges. The information contained in this case is based on information that is publicly available and that was collected from a variety of industry sources. The memos contained at the end of this case—as well as those available online at www.mhhe.com/baye8e—were written by the authors of the case purely for use as a teaching tool; they do not represent actual company memos. Any relation between these memos and memos actually sent by personnel at Time Warner or any other company is purely coincidental.

BACKGROUND

Time Warner, Inc., was formed in 1990 by the merger of magazine publisher Time, Inc. and Warner Communications, primarily a producer of film and television programming. To reduce debt, Time Warner sold 25 percent of Time Warner Entertainment (which included HBO, Warner Bros., and part of Time Warner Cable) to Media One Group. In 1996, Time Warner acquired Turner Broadcasting Systems, expanding its cable programming networks significantly. By the end of 1999, Time Warner had revenues in excess of $27 billion and net income of almost $2 billion.

In January 2000, AOL and Time Warner announced their intent to merge, and the merger was completed a year later. The merger was the largest in U.S. corporate history, with AOL's preannouncement value at $163 billion, and Time Warner's preannouncement value of $100 billion. However, by the time the merger was completed, the value of the combined firm had dropped to $165 billion. Both companies hoped that the combination of Time Warner's content and AOL's Internet base would provide increased opportunities for the merged company to grow. Many ideas were presented to show how AOL and Time Warner would be able to combine their Internet and media operations to enhance the value of the combined entity.

By 2003, AOL Time Warner had achieved few successes in merging the products. Cooperation between the AOL and Time Warner divisions was nonexistent, and advertising deals were lost due to internal conflicts. The decline in the value of technology stocks and a sluggish economy forced AOL Time Warner to take a $98.7 billion loss in 2002, primarily due to the write-down of the value of AOL. Gerald Levin, the chairman and CEO of Time Warner prior to the merger, stepped down as the CEO of AOL Time Warner in 2002. Steve Case, former chairman and CEO of AOL, resigned as chairman of AOL Time Warner in early 2003. Richard Parsons was promoted from COO of the Time Warner side to the position of CEO of the firm. Parsons, who was also appointed chairman of the board when Case resigned, promoted several senior Time Warner executives and accepted the resignations of some of the top AOL management.

Several commentators and numerous Time Warner investors considered the AOL merger a mistake, some even calling it the "worst deal in history." Many believed that AOL misled Time Warner prior to the merger about the outlook in online advertising and overstated its revenues. In 2003, the Securities and Exchange Commission announced an investigation into allegations that AOL used aggressive and illegal methods for recognizing revenue leading up to the merger. By early 2003, the prospect of splitting AOL and Time Warner and undoing the largest merger in U.S. history was a real possibility.

However, Parsons declined to shed AOL and instead focused on reducing the company's debt and integrating the businesses. The company announced agreements to sell its music recording and publishing operations, Warner Music Group, for $2.6 billion and its CD and DVD manufacturing and distribution business, Warner Manufacturing, for $1.05 billion. It also reached agreements to sell Time Life operations, a direct-marketing business with 2003 net operating losses of $82 million, and its Turner winter sports teams (the NHL's Atlanta Thrashers and NBA's Atlanta Hawks), which posted operating losses of $37 million. In September 2003, the company dropped AOL from its corporate name and resumed operations as Time Warner, Inc.

While 2003 saw improvement in operations and a return to profitability (see Exhibits 1A and 1B in the Appendix), Time Warner executives still face numerous challenges in managing the largest media company in the world. America Online is facing declining revenues, Time Warner Cable is seeing saturated markets and increased competition, and the publishing industry is soft due to low advertising levels. Success in its filmed entertainment and cable programming networks has provided the only encouragement.

OVERVIEW OF THE INDUSTRY AND TIME WARNER'S OPERATIONS

Subsequent to the AOL merger, Time Warner, Inc., is the largest media company in the world, with revenues in excess of $38 billion. However, Disney, Viacom, News Corp., and Sony are all huge media competitors, with various assets in the television, publishing, music, Internet, and film markets. (See Exhibit 2 for an overview of selected competitors in the media industry.) In 2004, General Electric agreed to merge its NBC property with Universal, owned by French firm Vivendi, to create NBC Universal. The new entity is 80 percent owned by GE and 20 percent owned by Vivendi. Currently there is speculation that Sony is attempting to acquire MGM.

Media consolidation is expected to continue due to recent revisions of media ownership restrictions by the Federal Communications Commission (FCC). In 2003, the FCC relaxed several regulations that restricted the number of media outlets a company could own in any local market and increased the national audience that any one company can reach. Media ownership regulations are designed to prevent any one company from controlling too much of the media; they represent an effort to ensure some level of diversity in the media. Proponents of the stricter media regulations fear that increased concentration will lead to greater homogeneity in media content and will be a disservice to consumers. Those favoring relaxing the guidelines argue that the fast pace of technological change makes it impossible for any company to control the flow of information to consumers. The status of regulatory changes is still uncertain, as Congress is considering legislation that would affect ownership rules.

Time Warner, Inc., operations include five principal business areas: AOL, filmed entertainment, publishing, programming networks, and cable systems. Figure 15–1 provides a snapshot of how these business areas contributed to Time Warner, Inc.'s 2003 net income and sales. These operations are discussed in more detail below.

AMERICA ONLINE

Introduced in 1989, America Online (AOL) was among the earliest companies in the United States to provide Internet service to households. AOL provided not only a connection to the Internet, but also significant Internet-related content. In the early and mid 1990s, the World Wide Web was in its infancy, and much of the content on the Internet was difficult to find or unreliable. AOL's proprietary content provided great value to new users who were unfamiliar with the new technology of

FIGURE 15–1 Contributions by Business Area to Time Warner's Overall Net Income and Sales, 2003

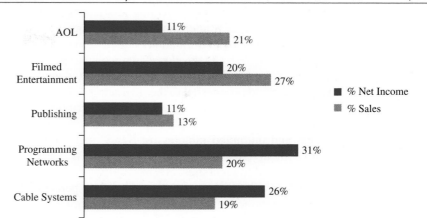

■ % Net Income	
■ % Sales	

AOL — 11% / 21%
Filmed Entertainment — 20% / 27%
Publishing — 11% / 13%
Programming Networks — 31% / 20%
Cable Systems — 26% / 19%

Source: Hoover Online, company reports, and author calculations.

the Internet. AOL became the pioneer of mass-marketing Internet services by distributing millions of disks with its software and offering free minutes to new users.

By the end of 1995, AOL had almost 5 million members and had launched AOL Europe in partnership with Bertelsmann AG, a German media conglomerate. In 1996, AOL began charging a flat rate for its service, which increased its popularity greatly but also resulted in busy signals and network congestion. Also that year, AOL launched its AOL Canada subsidiary and, through a joint venture, expanded to Japan. Rapid growth in subscribers continued through the end of the 1990s, and AOL had over 20 million members by the end of 2000. By 2003, it appeared that AOL's membership had peaked; membership actually declined from 24.7 million to 24.3 million during the fourth quarter.

Market Conditions

U.S. households have several options for obtaining Internet service. They can use a traditional dial-up service from any number of providers, including AOL. Alternatively, they can obtain a broadband connection, generally provided through a cable company with a cable modem or through a digital subscriber line (DSL) connection through their phone company. Approximately 63 percent of U.S. households with an Internet connection use a dial-up connection, while the remaining 37 percent have a broadband connection.

The Internet service provider (ISP) market has enjoyed incredible growth during its brief 10-year history. National companies such as AOL, Prodigy, and CompuServe were the first large providers. Exhibit 3 in the Appendix provides subscription data for the largest traditional ISPs.

Due to several factors, AOL is now suffering declining membership. First, the growth in the Internet and the number of free services available on it have reduced the value of AOL's proprietary content. Second, discount ISPs, such as United Online's brands and Earthlink, have successfully competed with AOL for dial-up customers by cutting monthly fees and providing less content. Consumers are also switching to broadband Internet connections in order to increase the speed with which they can access and download information on the Internet. As more consumers have switched to broadband, Web site developers and content providers have increased the amount of graphics and content designed for high bandwidth users. By 2003, 23.5 million U.S. households connected to the Internet via a broadband service.

AOL's revenues are derived from subscription services and advertising. Subscribers can choose varying plans for service, but the most popular includes dial-up access and unlimited minutes for $23.95 per month. Advertising revenues come from both advertisements shown on the screen and fees that companies pay to have users directed to their sites.

AOL's advertising revenues declined 40 percent between 2002 and 2003. Due to weakening economic conditions, many large companies reduced their general advertising budgets, especially targeting online advertising. In addition, many Internet businesses that previously provided significant advertising and click-through revenues to AOL either cut advertising or ceased operations altogether.

To combat the decline in subscribers, AOL has worked to offer several new products, including bring your own access (BYOA), which allows consumers to connect to the Internet through other means and then use AOL's content and services. The BYOA plan generally has lower fees because customers must pay separately to obtain their own Internet connection. However, AOL has attempted to increase its value to broadband users by building up its high bandwidth content (e.g. music and video). It is not clear how many customers are willing to pay separately for an Internet connection and subscribe to AOL's content.

AOL Operations

In addition to its branded online service, AOL operations include CompuServe, Netscape, Moviefone, Mapquest, and AOL Instant Messenger. CompuServe, acquired by AOL in 1998, offers a discounted ISP product through its own name and through Wal-Mart Connect Internet Service.

Netscape offers a variety of products, including search services, Web-based e-mail, and opportunities for electronic commerce. AOL acquired Netscape in 1999 for about $10 billion. Netscape software was once the dominant tool in the Internet browser software market, but Microsoft's Internet Explorer has overtaken the market. As of 2002, less than 4 percent of Internet users chose Netscape. In January 2002, Netscape filed suit against Microsoft for antitrust violations following a federal court ruling that Microsoft had engaged in anticompetitive practices. The lawsuit was settled in May 2003, with Microsoft agreeing to pay AOL $750 million and allowing AOL to use its Internet Explorer browser on AOL without charge for seven years.

AOL launched its popular AOL Instant Messenger (AIM) in 1996. Instant messaging services allow users to send short instant messages to other users, facilitating an online e-mail "conversation." Initially, use of AIM was restricted to AOL subscribers, but competition from other services, first ICQ and eventually others such as Yahoo! and Microsoft, forced AOL to make its messenger service available without charge to any Internet user. In 1999, Microsoft attempted to make its MSN messenger service compatible with AIM, but AOL blocked Microsoft by changing the settings on its servers. AOL cited security reasons for the blockage, while Microsoft stated that AOL was trying to prevent Microsoft's messenger customers from communicating with AIM users. The disagreement was settled in 2003 as part of the Netscape settlement, and both firms agreed to make AIM and MSN instant messaging compatible.

AOL Europe

AOL Europe was launched in 1996 in partnership with Bertelsmann AG, which received 49.5 percent ownership in the entity. Growth in Europe was much slower than in the United States. Language and cultural differences across Europe made it difficult for AOL to create content with broad appeal. On top of that, AOL had difficulty gaining access since European customers generally had to pay phone companies by the minute for online time, as well as paying AOL. These higher costs have resulted in a smaller fraction of households with Internet access in Europe than in the United States. Competing national telecommunications companies, such as Deutsche Telekom, France Telecom, Spain's Telefonica, and Telecom Italia are now bundling phone and Internet services, and they have gained an advantage over AOL.

In 2001, AOL Europe suffered losses of $600 million on revenues of $800 million and 2.5 million subscribers. To make matters worse, it was forced to buy out Bertelsmann for $6.75 billion, a significant premium, due to antitrust concerns between the music and publishing groups of Time Warner and Bertelsmann. There was considerable debate within Time Warner whether AOL Europe was a viable entity.

However, subsequent to the Bertelsmann buyout, AOL Europe has made significant gains. Subscribership has increased to 6.4 million, with annual revenues of $1.5 billion (in part due to favorable exchange rates). These gains stemmed from several strategic moves. First, AOL Europe lobbied for open access laws and secured guarantees for parity in the prices for broadband services in Britain, France, and Germany. These guarantees have enhanced the company's ability to compete with European national telecommunications companies. Second, AOL Europe entered into an agreement with Dixons Group (the largest computer retailer in Britain) to be the company's exclusive marketing partner. Finally, AOL Europe has worked hard to tailor its content to the customs and languages of specific countries and regions within the European Union.

FILMED ENTERTAINMENT

In the early 1900s, the four Warner brothers, Jack, Abe, Harry, and Sam, created the company that eventually became Warner Bros. Entertainment. They started with one movie theater in the early 1900s in New Castle, Pennsylvania, and soon expanded into movie production and distribution. Their company, then named Warner Bros. Studio, first had its headquarters in New York City and later moved to Burbank, California. Warner Bros. was the producer of the first widely released motion picture with sound, *The Jazz Singer,* in 1927. It was followed by a series of big successes in the 1930s and 40s, including *Casablanca* (1942). Like other major movie studios of that time, Warner Bros. also owned large assets in theater chains.

The Paramount Decree of 1948 made it illegal for movie studios to own the-aters, and this ultimately led to the downturn of Warner Bros. In 1966, the company was sold to Seven Arts Productions and was renamed Warner Brothers–Seven Arts, which was shortly thereafter acquired by entrepreneur Steven Ross and became Warner Communications. The movie production business picked up under this name and the company released hits like *Superman* (1978) and the Academy Award–winning film *The Color Purple* (1985).

In 1990, Warner Communications merged with Time Inc. and became part of Time Warner Inc. The movie production and distribution businesses were operated under Time Warner Entertainment, a limited partnership between Time Warner and AT&T (whose interest was later purchased by Comcast). From the early 1990s until the company's restructuring in 2003, the company released some of the most suc-cessful movies in the industry. Successful movies during this era included *The Fugitive* (1993), *Twister* (1996), and the *Batman* films (1989–97).

In March 2003, Time Warner completed its restructuring. Under the new struc-ture, Time Warner Inc. obtained complete ownership of Time Warner Entertain-ment's content business, including movie production and distribution. Currently, this part of the business is operated by Warner Bros. Entertainment Inc.

Motion Picture Production and Distribution

Motion picture production and distribution are core businesses of Time Warner and are conducted mainly by Warner Bros. Entertainment, Inc.—a wholly owned sub-sidiary of the company. New Line Cinema Corporation is the other movie produc-tion and distribution arm of Time Warner, and it is fully owned by the company through Turner Broadcasting System (TBS).

Today, Warner Bros. Entertainment, Inc., is one of the leading movie distribu-tors in the world. Every year it releases about 20 theatrical movies, some financed by Warner Bros. Entertainment, and others produced and financed by other parties. Recent blockbusters include *The Matrix* trilogy (1999–2003), the *Harry Potter* series (2001–04), *Scooby Doo* (2002), and *The Last Samurai* (2003).

New Line Cinema Corporation is a leading independent movie producer and distributor. Its operations are conducted through two divisions: New Line Cinema and Fine Line Features. New Line Cinema distributed the highly successful *Lord of the Rings* trilogy (2001–03), Academy Award–winning *About Schmidt* (2002), and box-office blockbusters like *Rush Hour 2* (2002) and *Elf* (2003). Fine Line Features specializes in the production and distribution of art house films. It released the Oscar-winning films *Shine* (1996) and *Dancer in the Dark* (2000).

The Film Industry

In 2003, U.S. domestic box office revenues from motion pictures reached $9.45 billion. As shown in Figure 15–2, U.S. domestic box office receipts have steadily increased over the past 20 years. In addition to revenues at the box office, movies also gener-ate revenues from subsequent sales of video products, television licensing, and other types of media and related merchandise. On average, these sources account for over 50 percent of total revenues from a film release.

FIGURE 15–2 U.S. Domestic Box Office Admissions and Revenues, 1983–2003

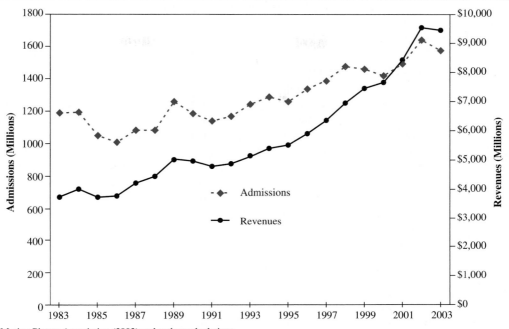

Source: Motion Picture Association (2003) and author calculations.

Most of the revenues from theatrical movies released in the United States are generated by seven major movie studios, collectively known as the "Hollywood Studios." These companies are members of the Motion Picture Association of America (MPAA) and include Buena Vista Pictures Distribution (The Walt Disney Company), Sony Picture Entertainment Inc., Metro-Goldwyn-Mayer Studios Inc. (MGM), Paramount Pictures Corporation, Twentieth Century Fox Film Corporation, Universal City Studios LLP, and Warner Bros. Entertainment Inc.

These seven companies consistently dominate the production and the distribution of major films. Out of the 459 new films released in 2003, the major studios distributed 194 films. The average box office receipts for a movie released by a major studio were $41.6 million, compared with $8.21 million for films distributed by smaller studios. Of the top 20 highest grossing movies of 2003, 16 were distributed by major studios (see Exhibit 4).

Movie studios serve as *distributors* of motion pictures. By providing financing, distribution, and marketing services, they largely determine strategies related to the release of a movie, such as the types of movie produced, its budget, and the timing of its release. A movie studio may produce a movie itself or provide financing to independent producers. In both cases, the studio maintains a high level of control over production. Sometimes, a studio may acquire movies that have been completed by other parties.

Studios not only distribute movies to theaters, but typically retain rights for other forms of media distribution as well. They assume the responsibility for negotiating exhibition contracts with theaters, carrying out marketing campaigns, and distributing movies on DVDs and other types of media.

Independent movie distributors are also players in this market. Although independent studios collectively distribute more films each year than major studios, individually they generally release fewer films per year, and the movies they release are usually low-budget films targeted toward niche markets. However, a few independent studios have grown quite large. These include New Line Cinema, Miramax, and DreamWorks. As noted earlier, however, some of these independents are actually affiliated with the major distributors. For example, New Line Cinema and Fine Line Features are wholly owned subsidiaries of Time Warner; Miramax is owned by Walt Disney.

In 2003, the seven major distributors accounted for about 75 percent of total box office revenues. Disney had the largest share (17 percent), followed by Sony and Warner Bros. (13 percent each), Universal (12 percent), Twentieth Century Fox (10 percent), Paramount (7 percent), and MGM (4 percent). The leading independents are New Line Cinema (with a 10 percent share of the overall market), Miramax (4 percent), and DreamWorks (3 percent). As shown in Figure 15–3, when one takes into account the fact that the largest two of these three independents are subsidiaries of Time Warner and Disney, Time Warner enjoyed the largest share of the 2003 market (23 percent), followed closely by Disney (21 percent).

Competition

Unlike many industries where firms compete through price, companies in the movie industry mainly compete by improving product quality. Studios pay increasingly greater amounts to obtain the services of top writers, directors, and actors. They also incur high costs to create more splendid sets and more realistic special effects. During the 15 years from 1988 to 2002, the average production cost of a feature film in the

FIGURE 15–3   Market Shares Based on 2003 Gross Box Office Receipts of Companies and Their Subsidiaries

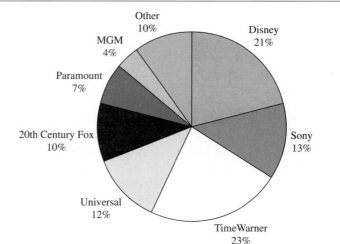

Source: Annual reports, Motion Picture Association (2003), Box Office Mojo, and author calculations.

United States increased over 312 percent—significantly more than the 262 percent increase in average box office receipts. Exhibit 5 provides more detailed historical data on the average production costs and revenues for new release feature films.

The demand for theatrical movies varies dramatically during the course of the year and tends to follow seasonal patterns. In the United States, the demand for movies is highest during the summer and the Christmas periods. The summer season starts around Memorial Day and ends around Labor Day, peaking around July 4th. The Christmas season is shorter, starting at Thanksgiving and ending in early January.

Movie demand also tends to vary with the movie's life cycle. For example, for the 20 highest-grossing movies of 2003, the average box office receipts during the first weekend accounted for about 30 percent of total box office revenues. The percentage is even higher for less successful movies. The seasonality of the demand, combined with the fact that the bulk of box office revenues are derived from the early stage of a movie's life cycle, makes the release date of a movie extremely important.

Players in this market sometimes act strategically to avoid releasing movies with similar themes at the same time. This is mainly achieved by publicly announcing production plans in trade magazines and other channels well before a movie is ready to be released. However, coordination and commitment are rarely perfect; collisions in the release dates of movies appealing to similar segments of the market inevitably occur from time to time.

Television Programming

Time Warner is also a leading provider of television programming. This part of the business is conducted through Warner Bros. Television, which has produced some of the most popular TV series in U.S. history. These include the Emmy Award–winning comedy series *Friends* and drama series *The West Wing*.

Home Video Distribution

Time Warner distributes movies, television series, professional sports events, and other entertainment materials on DVDs and VHS cassettes. The programming may be produced (or otherwise acquired) by Time Warner's various content-producing subsidiaries, such as Warner Bros. Pictures, Warner Bros. Television, HBO, or New Line Cinema. Or, it may be produced by other content producers, such as the BBC, PBS, or National Geographic. In 2003, Time Warner's total revenues from video sales (including movies and television series) reached $425 million worldwide.

Time Warner's video distribution business is conducted mainly by Warner Home Video. Warner Home Video has released nearly 2,000 titles on DVD, including the top-selling *Harry Potter* series. Sales of *Harry Potter and the Sorcerer's Stone* and *Harry Potter and the Chamber of Secrets* have exceeded over 40 million copies worldwide.

PUBLISHING

Time, Inc., the publishing subsidiary of Time Warner, has about 135 magazine titles, including *Time, People, Sports Illustrated, Money, Fortune,* and *Entertainment Weekly.* In addition, Warner Books and Little, Brown and Company offer a full range of book publishing, including 50 titles on *The New York Times* bestseller list in 2003. Time, Inc. generated revenues of $5.5 billion and net income of $664 million in 2003.

Magazine Publishing

While Time, Inc., publishes a large number of different magazines, four titles (*People, Time, Sports Illustrated,* and *Fortune*) account for about 80 percent of Time Inc.'s advertising revenues. Collectively, Time, Inc.'s magazine sales account for almost 25 percent of the industry's revenues, making it the leader in U.S. market share.

Several publishers with a broad line of magazines compete with Time, Inc. Advance Publications operates Conde Nast Publications (17 magazines including *Vogue, Wired,* and *The New Yorker*), Fairchild Publications (*Details*), and Golf Digest Companies. Hearst Magazines publishes 19 titles, including *Good Housekeeping, Cosmopolitan, Esquire,* and *Popular Mechanics.*

The economic downturn in the early 2000s adversely impacted industry advertising revenues and, to a lesser extent, reduced the circulation of most magazines in the United States. In addition, major publishers have been plagued by a number of recent trends. Consumers increasingly have many more choices for obtaining news and information, including a large amount of free content on the Internet and on television. This increased competition contributed to a 6.5 percent decline in newsstand sales of magazines in 2003. Currently, about 4,000 different magazine titles are sold on newsstands in the United States, including over 900 new titles launched in 2003 alone. In light of the large number of titles, it is a significant challenge to obtain shelf space for a new or niche magazine.

Class action lawsuits, as well as legal actions by attorneys general in several states over deceptive and illegal marketing practices, have hampered the industry's ability to gain subscribers through the "publisher's sweepstakes" that traditionally generated 25 to 50 percent of new magazine subscriptions. In addition, "do-not-call" legislation constrains the ability of telemarketers to sell subscriptions on behalf of publishers. Thus far, the publishing industry has not identified a way to supplant these mechanisms for generating new subscribers.

Some within the magazine industry are concerned that cable channels such as Home & Garden Television (HGTV) may ultimately become the primary information source for consumers who otherwise would have subscribed to several home and gardening magazines. Likewise, multiple cable channels devoted to sports, news, and entertainment may have a lasting impact on the circulation rates of *Sports Illustrated, Time,* and *Entertainment Weekly.*

Retail space for magazines has declined over the past few years. Supermarkets now use space once reserved for magazines to create self-checkout lanes and to experiment with different items near checkout lanes (e.g., rotisserie chicken). While most magazines rely on subscriptions rather than newsstands for the bulk of their sales, margins for newsstand sales are significantly higher due to the impulse nature of consumer purchase decisions.

In addition to a declining readership, the publishing industry has been hurt by allegations that its circulation numbers are inaccurate. In the fall of 2003, a legal dispute between a small publisher, Gruner + Jahr, and the editor of one of its magazines, Rosie O'Donnell, led to allegations that publishers regularly inflate their circulation numbers. The Audit Bureau of Circulations is currently addressing these concerns, and advertisers are increasingly demanding more information from publishers regarding the circulation and selling rates for each issue of a publication.

Despite all this bad news, there is some cause for optimism. Advertising executives have expressed concerns about the productivity of television advertising, due to the projected growth in use of digital video recorders (DVRs). Many fear that television viewers will fast forward through commercials, making television a less reliable source for advertising. While this could have a negative impact on programming networks and cable companies, it may give magazine publishers an advantage.

Magazines Online

Many magazine publishers upload content to the Internet. With a few notable exceptions, the content is generally free to anyone who chooses to access it through the magazine's Web site. *Consumer Reports* has been successful in building a pay Web site; however, its content provides data that is unavailable elsewhere. Other magazines attempting to restrict access to paying users have had limited success.

In May 2003, Time, Inc., announced that it would begin restricting access to the Web sites of 13 titles, including *People* and *Entertainment Weekly,* to paying subscribers and AOL members. While traffic at the *People* Web site declined 30 to 40 percent, the number of online magazine subscribers increased several fold. AOL promotes access to the magazine through its content, and in return pays Time Inc. $40 million. In return, AOL is permitted to sell advertising around the magazine's content, and users viewing the magazine's site are offered a trial AOL subscription. Time Warner hopes to expand this type of cross-promotion throughout the company.

Book Publishing

Time Warner publishes books under the brands of Warner Books and Little, Brown and Company. Revenues for the book publishing group were about $400 million in 2002. By contrast, sales at Random House (a subsidiary of Bertelsmann AG) were over $2.2 billion. Similarly, Harper Collins (a subsidiary of News Corp.) posted revenues of $1.1 billion over the same time period. In 2003, total revenue for the top 20 book publishers in the United States was over $5.5 billion, up 5 percent over the previous year.

The distribution channels for book publishers include online and traditional bookstores (48 percent), jobbers and wholesalers (42 percent), special sales (6 percent), and direct-to-consumer sales (4 percent). By most estimates, about 10 percent of books are sold over the Internet. However, sales of books directly from publishers' Web sites represent only 0.1 percent of overall sales. Time Warner Books does not sell any books directly to consumers from its Web site, instead directing customers to an online retailer. Sales of e-books—electronic books that are downloaded to a computer—increased 27 percent in 2003 to $7.3 million.

PROGRAMMING NETWORKS

Time Warner's programming network division is divided into three units: Turner Broadcasting System, Home Box Office, and the WB Network. The cable programming networks collectively generate $8.4 billion in revenues, with Turner and HBO generating about 54 percent and 37 percent, respectively.

Turner focuses primarily on its basic cable programming networks, including general interest networks (such as TNT and TBS), news networks (CNN networks), and special interest networks (such as Cartoon Network and Turner Classic Movies). Including international networks, Turner has over 20 network properties. In addition, it operates the CNN news Web site and owns the Atlanta Braves Major League Baseball team.

Home Box Office (HBO) operates 18 premium cable programming networks under the HBO and Cinemax brand names. In addition, HBO produces movies, mini series, and programs. About 75 percent of HBO's revenues come from subscriber fees. The remaining revenues derive from content sales, including video sales of hit shows such as *The Sopranos* and *Sex and the City*. Despite the popularity and critical acclaim of HBO's programming, the number of subscribers has remained flat over the last two years, due in part to the fact that HBO has implemented price increases of about 5 percent per year. Operating income for the cable network division declined 2 percent in 2003.

Basic cable programming networks rely on two main revenue sources: subscription fees charged to cable and satellite carriers, and advertising. Subscription fees are charged on a per-subscriber, per-month basis, ranging from over $1 for high-demand programming networks such as ESPN to as little as $.03 for smaller networks. TBS has the highest average charge for any Time Warner basic programming network at $.61 per subscriber per month. Subscription revenues account for about half of Turner's total programming network revenues; advertising revenues account for about 40 percent. Television viewers have shifted from broadcast to cable networks over the past few years. This shift, especially among young viewers coveted by advertisers, contributed to a 10 percent increase in Turner's advertising revenues in 2003.

Each year, dozens of new programming networks are launched and a few go out of business. In 1994, there were only 106 programming networks delivered via national satellites in the United States, compared to nearly 340 today (see Exhibit 6). Although cable systems have invested heavily over the past decade to upgrade infrastructure, the increase in channel capacity has not caught up with the number of available programs. As a result, cable programming networks have to compete to be carried by a cable system. A cable system may have to drop one programming network to be able to carry a new one. Time Warner has benefited from the fact that most cable companies view its TNT and TBS programming networks as "essential" offerings. Subscription fees charged to cable and satellite carriers have increased at a rate of about 5 percent per year over the last several years.

Time Warner's cable programming networks (such as TBS, CNN, and HBO) are vertically integrated with its cable systems (its Time Warner Cable operations). Industrywide, about 32 percent of all cable programming networks are vertically integrated with multiple system operators (MSO). (See Exhibit 6.) The vertical relations between cable programming networks and MSOs have raised concerns about potential foreclosure. In many markets, cable systems are monopolists, and it is possible that, in allocating limited channel space, the cable system tends to favor its affiliated programming networks at the expense of the others. However, cable operators argue that such a practice is uncommon and that, when it occurs, it is done for efficiency rather than strategic reasons.

CABLE SYSTEMS

Time Warner cable system operations form the core of its offerings of services such as analog and digital cable TV, high-speed Internet access, and telephone services. Time Warner's cable system units are facing a variety of challenges that stem from competitive pressures as well as technological and regulatory changes. Many of these challenges are common to the entire cable industry. Whether Time Warner has the ability to meet these challenges and outperform its rivals will determine the future standing of these units.

Analog and Digital Cable TV

Industry growth in traditional analog-based cable services has been flat in recent years, and the market base is almost saturated. (See Exhibit 7.) As of December 2003, Time Warner Cable's systems passed by approximately 18.8 million homes in 27 states. Among these homes, 10.9 million subscribed to their basic video service, which represents a 58 percent penetration rate.

With stagnant growth in traditional analog-based cable services, Time Warner Cable has turned to new products, such as digital services, for revenue growth. Due to more efficient use of the spectrum, robust resistance to noise, and flexibility, digital technology permits cable operators to deliver a wide range of new services. While traditional analog-based technology allows only one-way communication, digital networks permit two-way communications. This has opened the door for interactive services such as video on demand and high-speed Internet.

Time Warner Cable started upgrading its infrastructure in the early 1990s. Improvements included the use of fiber optics for backbone networks, which greatly improved both the quality of and capacity for video programming transmission and permits the company to provide broadband services. In 1994, Time Warner Cable was the first company to receive an Emmy Award for its outstanding achievement in technological development. The build-out was completed in 2001, after a total investment of over $5 billion. By the end of 2003, 99 percent of the cable systems operated by Time Warner were able to carry two-way broadband services. As a result, the company is now able to offer digital cable, video on demand, high-definition television (HDTV), cable Internet, and digital telephony in most of its service areas.

Time Warner charges additional fees for a digital upgrade, and it is capable of using digital ancillary services (such as pay-per-view) to generate additional revenues. The penetration rate for digital upgrades will be a key driver of revenue growth going forward. Furthermore, since digital signals are 10 times more compact to transmit, cable companies will free up significant bandwidth once they convert all customers to digital receivers.

High-Speed Internet Service

Presently, about 63 percent of U.S. households with an Internet connection use a dial-up service to access the Internet. Broadband Internet usage is growing rapidly, especially in major cities. The total number of subscribers to high-speed Internet service in the United States was 23.5 million in 2003, a 45 percent increase over the previous year.

Cable access is the most popular method of securing broadband access, and it accounts for 58 percent of all household high-speed Internet connections. However, cable broadband providers face increased competition from DSL (digital subscriber line), which accounts for about 33 percent of the broadband Internet connection market. (See Exhibit 8.) In the summer of 2003, several DSL service providers launched an aggressive marketing campaign in an attempt to grab more market share. One of the main tactics used by DSL providers is price. Verizon Communications, SBC Communications, and EarthLink offered an introductory rate of $29.95 for their DSL service, compared to rates charged by cable providers that range from $40 to $45. During the second half of 2003, the number of DSL subscribers increased 27 percent, compared to 24 percent for cable modems and 23 percent for the broadband industry as a whole. (See Exhibit 8.)

In 2003, Time Warner Cable was the second largest broadband Internet operator in the United States, after Comcast. Time Warner Cable accommodates multiple ISPs on its network, including its own Road Runner brand and other services such as EarthLink and some smaller regional ISPs. Time Warner Cable's share of the broadband market is about 14 percent.

Historically, AOL's main service has been dial-up (narrowband) access. Consequently, when Time Warner Cable began aggressively marketing its Road Runner broadband service, it competed directly with AOL. AOL lost nearly a half million subscribers in the fourth quarter of 2003 alone. In an attempt to remedy the problem, Time Warner Inc. launched an AOL–Road Runner cross-promotion plan in April 2004.

Telephone Service

Voice over Internet protocol (VoIP) is a technology that allows telephone calls to be transmitted over the Internet. In 2003, Time Warner tested its VoIP product, Digital Phone, in Portland, Maine. Penetration rates exceeded all expectations, and within a year Time Warner had signed up nearly 10 percent of its basic cable subscribers to its phone service. To assist with the rollout, Time Warner has agreed to a multiyear deal with MCI and Sprint. The phone companies will assist by providing termination of voice traffic to the public switched phone network, 911 and operator assistance services, local number portability, and long distance service. By the end of 2004, Time Warner plans to introduce Digital Phone in all of its cable markets.

Digital Phone is priced at $44.95 per month for unlimited local and long distance calling, and includes popular features such as call waiting and caller ID. It is available to customers who subscribe to either Time Warner's cable or high-speed Internet service and comes with free installation and a $5.00 discount for customers who subscribe to all three services. While there have been a few complaints about the service, such as difficulties in reaching 800 numbers or connecting with fax machines, most customers have noticed no difference in the connection quality of Internet phone calls compared to traditional phone services.

Estimates of market penetration rates for VoIP phone service vary widely. However, if Time Warner can eventually achieve a 10 percent penetration rate, revenues from phone services will significantly boost annual revenues. Competition is keen, though; currently over 20 companies provide or are planning to provide VoIP service. Many of these companies do not provide any sort of Internet connection; customers must secure their own broadband access.

Competition

Direct Broadcast Satellite Operators

Time Warner Cable competes in the video programming distribution market with direct broadcast satellite (DBS) operators like DirecTV and EchoStar. The costs of DBS equipment have dropped dramatically in recent years, allowing DBS operators to offer services at attractive prices. In 1999, DBS operators obtained the legal right to deliver over-the-air broadcast signals from local TV stations to their subscribers. Many of these local broadcast stations are affiliates of national broadcast networks, such as ABC, CBS, Fox, and NBC. These networks are considered among the "must-have" channels due to their high programming quality and their local content. The inclusion of local broadcast stations significantly strengthened DBS operators' competitive position. This, combined with the low pricing strategies of DBS operators, has resulted in a rapid growth in DBS subscriptions (see Exhibit 9).

The prices of cable television services have increased 53.1 percent since 1993, compared to a 25.5 percent increase in the overall consumer price index (CPI). In light of this, DBS operators have successfully used low pricing strategies to attract customers. Compared to the average subscription fee of about $35 for basic cable service, Dish Network (owned by EchoStar Communications) offers its basic package at less than $25.

The largest DBS operator in the United States—DirecTV with over 12 million subscribers—was acquired by News Corp. in 2003. One of the world's largest media conglomerates, News Corp. has assets in publishing, filmed entertainment, broadcasting, and cable distribution. It owns Fox Entertainment Group, which controls Fox broadcast TV network, Twentieth Century Fox, and other entertainment assets. News Corp's acquisition of DirecTV makes its strong financial support and its extensive holdings in video programming available to DirecTV.

Recently, telephone companies have responded to Time Warner's move into telephone services by partnering with DBS providers to provide their own bundled package of video, Internet, and telephone services. Verizon, Qwest, and Bell South are partners with DirecTV in marketing and have cross-promotional relationships. SBC and EchoStar have entered into a more complex relationship, in which SBC handles all installation, service, and billing for Dish Network subscribers in its 13-state service area.

Overbuilders

In some markets, Time Warner Cable also faces competition from overbuilders—new entrants who built their own infrastructure in the presence of an incumbent cable company. In the early days of cable television, local cable systems were granted exclusive franchises, largely based on the "natural monopoly" assumption. It was widely believed that, due to large fixed costs, it was not viable to permit more than one cable system to operate in one local market. In exchange, cable operators were under stringent government regulations. Cable operators remained local monopolists until 1992, when the *Cable Television Consumer Protection and Competition Act* was passed. This act prohibited franchising authorities from unreasonably refusing to award additional franchises. Further, the *1996 Telecommunication Act* now allows telephone companies and electric companies to enter the video distribution market to compete with the existing cable operators.

In several notable markets, Time Warner Cable faces competition from other wire-based cable companies. For instance, in New York City, Time Warner competes head-to-head with RCN—a company that entered in 1996 by acquiring Liberty Cable. Ironically, when Time Warner unveiled its Time Warner Center in Manhattan in February 2004, the cable TV and broadband Internet service for the new building was being provided by RCN. Likewise, Time Warner Cable faces competition from Everest Connection (a subsidiary of energy firm Aquila Inc.) in Kansas City, Missouri.

Unlike incumbent cable operators whose networks obtained digital capabilities through upgrades, overbuilders typically build their infrastructure from scratch. This allows them to design network architecture with the idea of "digital convergence" in mind from the very beginning—providing cable television, high-speed Internet, and digital telephony together. As a result, some overbuilders are able to provide more dedicated bandwidth and better performance at lower prices. Despite these advantages, overbuilders have not expanded into most U.S. markets. The collapse in the prices of telecommunication stocks has all but dried up the capital the companies need to build new networks. In addition, potential competition from DBS operators makes overbuilders hesitant to enter markets to compete with existing wire-based operators. Of the over 10,000 cable franchise areas in the United States, only about 2 percent have more than one wire-based cable operator.

Bundling

Cable system operators have bundled multiple programming services since the beginning of cable television. In general, programming networks that cable systems distribute fall into three categories. The first is *broadcast networks*. These include major national networks such as ABC, CBS, NBC and Fox, as well as local television programming. Signals for these networks are transmitted through the air, picked up by a cable system, and then redistributed to their subscribers. The second type is *advertisement-supported* (or *basic*) *cable networks*. These include well-known channels such as MTV and ESPN. The third type is *payment-based* (or *premium*) *cable networks,* which include HBO, Cinemax, and Showtime. Usually, broadcast and basic cable networks are offered by a cable system as a bundle (called the basic cable package), and premium networks are provided on an à la carte basis.

Recently, consumer advocates have criticized the bundling practices of cable companies, arguing that consumers should have the right to purchase only those programs they are willing to buy rather than be forced to pay for channels they never watch. Since cable networks are not subject to the same FCC regulations as broadcast networks, many cable shows have adult content in their programming. Conservative groups have advocated that families should not be forced to pay for material they find obscene or inappropriate. These views have been echoed by government officials. In May 2004, several key members of the Commerce Committee of the House of Representatives, led by Chairman Joe Barton, wrote to FCC Chairman Michael Powell requesting that his agency examine this issue and evaluate the feasibility of à la carte pricing.

Minority groups, on the other hand, have argued that without bundling, programming diversity would decline, as new and minority-targeted networks might not be able to attract enough viewers and advertisers and thus could not survive. For these reasons, the current bundling practices of cable companies have been supported by groups such as the Minority Media & Telecommunications Council (MMTC) as well as minorities in Congress.

Although cable operators oppose à la carte pricing, some cable companies have started to prepare for possible changes in regulation. Comcast is planning to test a variant of à la carte programming in its Washington–Baltimore market. Several other cable operators are considering similar plans.

Regulatory Considerations

Prior to the enactment of the 1996 Telecommunication Act, cable operators were largely local monopolists. In exchange for the monopolistic position, cable operators were under stringent government regulations. In particular, the subscription fees were regulated by franchise authorities. The price regulation was relaxed in 1984 by the *Cable Communication Policy Act*. The 1996 Telecommunication Act further phased out all regulation of expanded-basic service prices by March 1999.

However, due to the sharp increase in cable rates in recent years, many consumer groups have started pushing for re-regulation of cable rates, as well as à la carte pricing. Since deregulation, cable prices have increased two to three times faster than the rate of inflation. Critics use these sorts of statistics as evidence that cable operators have monopoly power and have been able to raise prices without losing customers. Cable operators cite the increased fees paid to cable networks, especially sports networks, as necessitating the price increases.

Technological Considerations

High-Definition Television (HDTV)

Industry growth for HDTV has been slow, with only about 6 million U.S. households owning high-definition television sets. The primary inhibitor to growth has been the high cost of the television sets, which ranges from $1,000 to as much as $7,000. Adding to the problem, less than one-third of all cable networks carry any high-definition programming. Consumers generally have been unwilling to spend a significant amount of money for new HDTV sets when there is little programming to justify their expenditures. Likewise, networks and program producers have been reluctant to incur the increased costs of high-definition broadcasting when only a small percentage of households have HDTVs.

Due to superior viewing quality, HDTV is likely to make gains over the next few years. HDTV offers much higher screen resolution (at least 1280×720 pixels) than conventional analog TV in National Television System Committee (NTSC) format (525×427 pixels). In addition, HDTV is broadcast in an aspect ratio of 16:9, the same as a wide-screen motion picture, compared with the aspect ratio of 4:3 for conventional TV. Finally, HDTV signals are digital rather than analog and thus contain significantly more information. Combined with Dolby digital surround sound, HDTV provides viewers with a greatly enhanced TV viewing experience.

High-definition technology first emerged in the early 1980s, although development and implementation were significantly delayed due to the absence of a standard. In 1996, the FCC adopted a technology standard for digital TV based on an industrial consensus reached by players in broadcasting, equipment manufacturing, and computer industries. By May 1999, the FCC required major broadcast TV networks (ABC, CBS, Fox, and NBC) to begin airing programming in HDTV format in 10 markets representing about 30 percent of TV households.

Time Warner Cable was among the first to explore HDTV technology and, as of 2003, carried more HDTV programming than any other cable operator in the United States. In addition to the broadcast networks, in certain areas it also carried cable networks such as HBO, Showtime, PBS, WB, UPN, Discovery HD Theater, and Fox Sports regional sports networks in HDTV format at no additional charge. Time Warner also offered premium HD channels at an additional charge.

Although major DBS operators such as DirecTV and EchoStar also provide HDTV programming, due to bandwidth limitations they generally do not include local channels in high-definition format. Bandwidth limitations can cause digital signals to freeze or go blank when too few data packets are successfully transmitted. Exploiting customer frustration over satellite transmission problems is one of the key marketing tactics of cable companies.

Digital Video Recorders (DVRs)

DVRs allow consumers to record TV programs and watch them at another time. DVRs have superior functionality compared to traditional VCRs and are simpler to operate. The devices allow consumers to record multiple programs simultaneously, record entire seasons of shows, and allow pausing, fast-forwarding, and rewinding live events. Some DVRs (for example, those provided by TiVo) memorize a consumer's tastes and record programs automatically based on viewing habits.

Cable companies initially shunned DVRs. The conventional wisdom was that if large numbers of consumers began skipping commercials, advertising revenues would drop. For several reasons, however, cable operators reluctantly have begun to embrace DVRs. First, DBS operators began offering DVRs in 1999. Second, DVRs represent a potential source of revenue; they are typically rented for about $7.00 per device per month, and customers using them must pay to be upgraded to digital cable in order to use a DVR.

Time Warner Cable was the first major player in the cable industry to offer and promote DVRs to its customer base. It introduced the DVR service in July 2002 and by the end of 2003, nearly 370,000 recorders had been installed. Time

Warner Cable was soon followed by other major operators such as Comcast, Cox, and Charter. Cable companies are now downplaying their concerns about commercial-skipping technology, citing studies that show that a significant number of consumers do not use the feature and that others are able to retain information even as they fast-forward through commercials. In addition, studies suggest that consumers increase their time spent viewing television as a result of the product.

CHALLENGES

While Time Warner survived its record-setting losses, it still faces a number of challenges. It has failed to realize the anticipated synergies from combining AOL with the traditional Time Warner media. AOL faces a declining subscriber base and a business model that may not be sustainable. The film production business is volatile, with success based on being able to secure and produce successful films in a fickle market. Even though Time, Inc. is the market leader in magazine publishing, the industry faces declining readers and increased competition. The company's programming networks, such as TNN and CNN, have enjoyed success but face growing competition from Fox News and other programming networks. Time Warner's cable system units face a saturated market and increased competition. The manner in which Time Warner manages its day-to-day operations, develops strategies to deal with these threats, and develops new opportunities will determine whether it survives as the largest media company in the world.

TJ took another sip of coffee from the mug that displayed the logo of the business school where she earned her MBA. She glanced at the raindrops pounding her new corner office windows and quickly focused on the first memo in her inbox. TJ recognized that her response would impact the future of the company—and her career.

CASE-BASED EXERCISES

The attachments referred to in the following memos are available online at www.mhhe.com/baye8e. This site also contains additional data that may be useful in your analysis of the case, as well as additional memos that your instructor may choose to assign as problem-solving exercises.

MEMOS

Read the following memos and use the attachments available online at www.mhhe. com/baye8e to provide the information requested.

Memo 1

To: Pricing Manager, Region 1

From: Regional Manager, Region 1 Cable System

Re: Revenue from STARZ

We recently added the STARZ Network to our premium cable tier. Currently, 852 of our basic service subscribers purchase this service. At the current price of $10.50, our revenues from this new channel are $8,946 per month.

As you know, our penetration rate for STARZ is not as high as we expected. Compared with the other two pay services we offer (HBO and Showtime), the number of subscribers for STARZ is still rather low. Some of our customers have indicated that the main reason they haven't signed up is the price.

To boost revenues, I am thinking that we might want to offer a promotional price for STARZ starting in July. Since this offer will be part of our summer promotion plan and will be well publicized, the same deal has to be offered to our existing subscribers as well. My concern is that the additional subscriptions generated by the lower price may not fully offset the revenues lost from our existing base of subscribers.

The marketing department provided the attached data on the demand and costs for this channel in our Region 1 service area. Please evaluate our current pricing strategy for STARZ based on these data. I am particularly interested (1) in whether lowering the price will yield higher revenues, and (2) in an estimate of the maximum monthly revenues we can achieve through this channel.

Attachment: Starz.xls

Memo 2

To: Pricing Manager, Kansas City

From: Vice President, Marketing

Re: How Low Can We Profitably Go?

Recent reports reveal that Everest has started a new wave of construction in the Kansas City area, after having stopped their expansion one year ago. Their financial health has apparently improved over the past year, allowing them to expand their fiber network beyond their current service areas. Although it's still unclear whether the new expansion is only limited to a few neighborhoods or is part of a broader effort to cover the entire metropolitan area, I'm trying to wrap my head around the worst-case scenario.

As you know, we invested over $500 million to upgrade our infrastructure in the Kansas City area. This enables us to provide a full line of services, including cable television, broadband Internet and digital telephony. So, if Everest indeed expands throughout the entire area, we should be able to compete with them by offering bundled services as well. Currently, in the neighborhoods that Everest serves, they provide bundled services starting at $84.95 per month. At present, there are approximately 321,000 households in the entire Kansas City area, and we plan to price in order to maintain a market share of about 65 percent.

In addition to monthly costs associated with the $500 million (which is being amortized over 20 years at 8.7 percent), agreements with program providers stipulate that we pay them monthly programming fees of $32.50 per subscriber. On top of all this, our monthly maintenance, service and billing costs are about $7.60 per subscriber.

I am concerned that if we get into a price war with Everest, pricing in the market may move to unprofitable levels. If things turn for the worse, we need an exit strategy. How low should we be willing to go with our pricing before it makes sense for us to write off our operations in KC?

Please provide your input on this matter as soon as possible. Thanks.

Memo 3

To: National Sales Manager, Cable Operations

From: Vice President, Cable Operations

Re: HDTV Promotion

The provision of high-definition TV (HDTV) service is an important component of our digital cable strategy. As you know, it provides significant improvements in visual and audio quality compared to traditional cable TV, and the value added is a promising new source of revenue for the company.

Currently, we offer HD programming with standard definition counterparts for free to our digital service subscribers. In certain areas, we also offer a separate package devoted exclusively to HD programming for a monthly price of $5.99. Although we do not charge extra fees for some HD channels, we still benefit because of the higher advertising revenues it generates. According to estimates by our product development division, the extra advertising revenue that each HDTV subscriber brings us is about $10/month, compared to a traditional TV customer.

The development of our HDTV business remains slow. According to a recent survey by the product development department, two major factors contribute to the sluggish market. The first is the high price of HDTV sets. Currently, a typical HDTV set costs well over $1,000, and this keeps many customers from upgrading their equipment. The second factor is the lack of HDTV programming. Customers indicate a very strong preference for viewing sporting events (such as NFL and NBA games) in HD format. We expect that more HDTV programming will boost the sales of HDTV sets, and in turn, stimulate subscriptions to our HDTV services.

My goal is that, within three years, a significant fraction of our digital cable subscribers will be equipped with HDTV sets and signed up for our new program tier devoted to HDTV programming. Please formulate a plan that will permit us to profitably achieve this goal.

Memo 4

To: Vice President, Global Strategy

From: President, Network Television Division

Re: Possible Acquisition

To help strengthen our position in the U.S. and abroad, we are considering Fox News as a potential target for acquisition. As you know, our CNN division is the largest cable news service in the U.S, with over 87.5 million subscribers and over $900 million in revenue. Fox News would offer us an additional 83.6 million subscribers. Perhaps more relevant is the fact that Fox News enjoyed a whopping 67.8 percent increase in revenues last year, compared to the 12.5 percent growth of our CNN division.

The potential synergies here are phenomenal, and the acquisition of Fox News would put us in an excellent position to grow our European and Asian markets.

I'm attaching a relevant spreadsheet file. I'd appreciate your thoughts on the matter. Thanks!

Attachment: Networks.xls

Memo 5

To: Assistant Director, Strategy

From: Director, Strategy

Re: Strategic Analysis

As we discussed last week during lunch, I am performing a strategic analysis of our business lines. To assist in this process, please provide a detailed competitive analysis of our five major business lines. I'm particularly interested in answers to the following:

- Which of our lines provide the best opportunity to grow the profitability of the company?

- Which business lines are most susceptible to competitive pressure, or are unlikely to be able to sustain current growth and profitability? What other risks to profitability and/or growth are present for each of the business lines?

- What strategic moves would you recommend to position the company for long-term growth?

As always, please justify your recommendations. Thanks!

Memo 6

To: Pricing Manager, Region 1

From: Regional Manager, Region 1 Cable System

Re: Profits from STARZ

We recently added the STARZ Network to our premium cable tier. Currently, 852 of our basic service subscribers purchase this service at our current price of $10.50 per month.

As you know, our current contributions from STARZ are not as high as we expected. I would like you to evaluate our current price to see if we might be able to raise or lower it to enhance the contributions of STARZ to our bottom line.

In an earlier study of the feasibility of adding STARZ, the marketing department obtained the attached data on the demand and costs for this channel in our Region 1 service area. Please use these data to provide your recommendation. I am particularly interested in (1) an estimate of our profit-maximizing price, and (2) an estimate of how much our monthly profit will increase if we adjust price to your recommended level.

Attachment: Starz.xls

Memo 7

To: Pricing Manager, District 6SW

From: Vice President, Marketing

Re: Strategic Pricing Decision

Our only competitor in District 6SW currently provides bundled services at $84.95. We are currently charging a 10 percent premium over their price, but there are unsubstantiated rumors that they are contemplating a 10 percent price increase. We don't know their cost structure, so we don't know whether their potential price increase is driven by cost increases or is merely a strategic move on their part.

Historically, when we both charge the same price, our market share is about 65 percent. When we charge a 10 percent premium over their price, our market share declines to about 60 percent. It appears that in those instances where they have charged a 10 percent premium over our price, our market share is about 70 percent.

Please provide a recommendation regarding whether we should maintain our current price or reduce our price to $84.95. Please factor into your recommendation that we pay programming fees to providers that amount to $32.50 for each subscriber. In addition, maintenance, service and billing costs are about $7.60 per subscriber. At present, there are about 110,000 households in the relevant area.

Memo 8

To: Strategy Group

From: COO

Re: Ramifications of AOL Divestiture

I need your immediate input regarding the potential impact on our bottom line of selling our AOL unit. For obvious reasons, it is imperative that you treat this request as confidential.

Memo 9

To: Strategy Group

From: COO

Re: Ramifications of Spinning off our Publishing Units

I need your immediate input regarding the potential sale of our publishing units. Would such a move make sense from the perspective of our overall bottom line?

For obvious reasons, it is imperative that you treat this request as confidential.

Memo 10

To: President, Global Operations

From: COO

Re: AOL Europe

As you know, some of your colleagues have privately recommended that we sell our holdings in AOL Europe. While I have yet to form an opinion on this matter, an important issue is how such a deal might be put together. In particular, if we move in this direction, how do you envision selling these assets—individually or in one big deal?

Memo 11

To: Strategy Group

From: COO

Re: Ramifications of Divestitures in Filmed Entertainment

I need your immediate input regarding the potential impact on our bottom line of selling our filmed entertainment units. For obvious reasons, it is imperative that you treat this request as confidential.

Memo 12

To: Pricing Department

From: Regional Manager, Region 3

Re: New Channel Lineup

We are thinking of adding three networks to our basic cable lineup: Bravo, ESPNews, and MTV2. Each of these networks would charge us programming fees on a per subscriber basis, as follows:

- Bravo—8 cents per subscriber per month

- ESPNews—10 cents per subscriber per month

- MTV2—7.5 cents per subscriber per month

To offset a portion of these fees, each network would allow us to sell some local advertising time on their networks. Based on current network ratings, our advertising department estimates that the monthly advertising revenues earned would amount to $1,200 on Bravo, $1,500 on ESPNews, and $1,200 on MTV2.

Approximately 46 percent of the 110,000 customers in our Region 3 market currently subscribe to our basic services. Anytime the basic channel lineup is adjusted, there is a shift in the number of customers who take the basic cable package. We tend to lose a few channel loyal customers anytime we drop a channel, and likewise, gain a new group when a channel is added. Our marketing department has provided estimates of the number of loyal customers for each channel. This represents an estimate of the number of cable customers we will lose if we drop a particular network. Likewise, it also provides an estimate of the number we can gain by adding a new channel. Currently, we do not have the capacity to add new channels to our basic lineup without dropping existing channels. Our marketing department estimates the following increases in subscribers by adding these new channels: Bravo—150, ESPNews—300, and MTV2—225. Our current pricing (not including taxes) for the basic package is $34.99 per month. Our programming fees for the basic package total $14.55 per month.

The current basic cable lineup is attached. The list only includes networks that could feasibly be replaced. It excludes channels that must be retained due to governmental regulation (local access channels, etc.) as well as broadcast networks.

Using this information, please make a recommendation for whether we should add any of the proposed new networks to our basic package.

Attachment: Potential_Changes.xls

Memo 13

To: Sales Manager, Region 3

From: Regional Manager, Region 3

Re: Recession Question

One of your MBA interns sent the attached spreadsheet in response to a question I asked regarding the potential impact of the 2.85 percent decline in income that has been forecasted for our Region 3 market. This is nuts—do they not teach people how to speak in words any more?

What do the numbers mean? Can you help me out? All I need to know is this: If income declines by 2.85 percent as forecasted, how much will we have to cut price in order to maintain our existing base of customers?

Attachment: Output.xls

Memo 14

To: Pricing Manager, Midwest Region

From: Vice President, Marketing

Re: Pricing New Program Tiers

In response to increased requests for a la carte pricing, we have decided to start a trial offering of smaller program tiers. As the first step of the trial, two small program packages will be offered to those using our basic package. The first is a sports package which includes NBA TV and the Soccer Channel. The second is a music package that includes MTV2 and GAC.

The trial offering will be limited to our Region 1 and Region 2 markets only. We estimate that our relevant incremental costs for the sports package are $1.45 per subscriber and the incremental costs for the music package are $1.20 per subscriber.

I am attaching a preliminary survey conducted by our marketing team that indicates anticipated sales at various pricing points. I would appreciate your recommendations regarding the pricing of these new program tiers. Thanks.

Attachment: Sports&Music.xls

SELECTED READINGS AND REFERENCES

Angwin, J., "Road Runner, America Online Wage Unsisterly Rivalry." *The Wall Street Journal,* November 21, 2002, p. B1.

Angwin, J., "Road Runner, AOL Are to Cooperate after Barrier Lifts." *The Wall Street Journal,* April 23, 2004, p. B4.

Angwin, J., "Time Warner Considers Return to Acquisitions." *The Wall Street Journal,* April 28, 2004, p. C1.

Angwin, J.; Grant, P.; and Wingfield, N., "In Embracing Digital Recorders, Cable Companies Take Big Risk—Viewers Flock to the Devices, but Advertisers May Flee; Debating Ad-Skip Feature—Time Warner's 'Meteorite'." *The Wall Street Journal,* April 26, 2004, p. A1.

Ahrens, F., "FCC Asked to Examine À la Carte Cable TV." *BizReport.Com,* May 20, 2004.

Barnhart, A., "Everest Mounts a Cable Takeover in Kansas City." *Electronic Media,* October 14, 2002.

Barnhart, A., "Everest Emerges as Competitor for Area Cable, Phone and Web Providers." *Kansas City Star,* October 27, 2002.

Bates, R. J., *Broadband Telecommunications Handbook.* Boston: McGraw-Hill, 2002.

Belson, K. and Richtel, M., "Hoping to Attract Callers to the Internet." *New York Times,* May 3, 2004, p. 10.

Consumers Union, "Cable 'À la Carte' Amendment Major Step in Giving Consumers Choice and Control over Bills, Programming." Consumer Union News Release, April 28, 2004.

Consumers Union, "Consumers Union Tells Senate Panel 'A la Carte' Option Needed for Lower Cable TV Bills, Real Choice." Consumer Union News Release, March 25, 2004.

Earthlink, Inc., *Annual Report 2003.*

Eggerton, J., "MMTC Opposes À la Carte." *Broadcasting & Cable,* May 13, 2004.

Everly, S., "Everest Restarts Area Expansion: With Financial Condition Improving, Aquila Subsidiary Sees Brighter Future." *Kansas City Star,* November 19, 2003.

Fabrikant, G., "Looking Past Cable's Profits to the Rivals on Its Heels." *New York Times,* May 3, 2004. p. C 10.

Federal Communications Commission, *Annual Assessment of the Status of Competition in the Market for the Delivery of Video Programming.* 2004.

General Accounting Office, *Subscriber Rates and Competition in the Cable Television Industry.* March 25, 2004.

General Accounting Office, *Wire-Based Competition Benefited Consumers in Selected Markets.* February, 2004.

Grant, P., "What's On? The Battle among Broadband Providers Has Moved to a New Arena: Content." *The Wall Street Journal,* March 22, 2004, p. R5.

Grant, P. and Young, S., "Time Warner Cable Expands Net-Phone Plan." *The Wall Street Journal.* December 9, 2003, p. A19.

Kirkpatrick, D., "AOL Europe Emerges as a Bright Spot." *International Herald Tribune.* September 8, 2003.

Latour, A. and Grant, P., "Verizon May Set Off Price War—Decision to Cut DSL Rates May Put Pressure on Cable Firms." *The Wall Street Journal,* May 5, 2003, p. B2.

Love, B., "Time Inc./AOL Restrict Access to Magazine Sites: A Breakthrough?" *Circulation Management.* May 1, 2003.

Mara, Janis, "AOL, Road Runner Do Broadband Cross-Promotion." *ClickZNews,* April 23, 2004.

Microsoft Corporation, *Annual Report, 2003.*

Motion Picture Association, *US Entertainment Industry: 2003 MPA Market Statistics*.

Parker, A., "Comcast Asks Government to Forgo Cable-TV Regulation." *Philadelphia Inquirer,* May 4, 2004.

Pasztor, A. and Lippman, J., "Finally, Murdoch Wins DirecTV, but His Prize Has Pitfalls." *The Wall Street Journal,* April 10, 2003, p. B1.

Reuters News Service, "AOL, Time Warner Cable to Launch Cable Channel," April 22, 2004.

Sayre, A., "Time Warner Chief Doubts Price Controls." *Associated Press Newswire,* March 3, 2004.

Shook, D., "AOL Europe: Well, It's Not America." *BusinessWeek Online.* February 1, 2002.

SBC Communications Inc., *Annual Report 2003.*

Time Warner Inc., *Annual Reports, 1993–2003.*

Time Warner, Inc., "Time Warner Cable and Fox Sports Net Team Up to Bring High-Definition NBA and NHL Games throughout the Season to Major Markets from Coast to Coast Beginning Dec. 5." *Time Warner News Release,* November 24, 2003.

Time Warner, Inc., "Pioneer & Time Warner Cable Launch National HDTV Retail Promotion." Time Warner News Release, November 24, 2003.

Time Warner, Inc., "Time Warner Cable Partners with MCI and Sprint for Nationwide Rollout of Digital Phones." Time Warner News Release, December 8, 2003.

Time Warner, Inc., "Time Warner Cable Adds HDNet and HDNet Movies to High-Def Lineup." Time Warner News Release, December 16, 2003.

Waterman, D., *Hollywood's Road to Riches.* Cambridge, MA: Harvard University Press, 2005.

APPENDIX: EXHIBITS

EXHIBIT 1A Time Warner, Inc.—Consolidated Statement of Operations Year Ended December 31 (millions except per share amounts)

	2003	2002	2001
Revenues:			
Subscriptions	$ 20,448	$ 18,959	$ 15,657
Advertising	6,182	6,299	6,869
Content	11,446	10,216	8,654
Other	1,489	1,840	2,327
Total revenues	39,565	37,314	33,507
Costs of revenues	(23,285)	(22,116)	(18,789)
Selling, general and admin.	(9,862)	(8,835)	(7,486)
Merger and restructuring costs	(109)	(327)	(214)
Amortization of intangible assets	(640)	(557)	(6,366)
Impairment of goodwill	(318)	(44,039)	–
Net gain on disposal of assets	14	6	–
Operating income (loss)	5,365	(38,554)	652
Interest expense, net	(1,844)	(1,758)	(1,316)
Other income (expense)	1,210	(2,447)	(3,458)
Minority interest income (expense)	(214)	(278)	46
Income tax provision	(1,371)	(412)	(145)
Discontinued operations, net of tax	(495)	(1,012)	(713)
Cumulative effect of accounting change	(12)	(54,235)	–
Net income (loss)	2,639	(98,696)	(4,934)
Average diluted common shares	4,623.7	4,454.9	4,429.1
Diluted net income per share	$ 0.57	$ (22.15)	$ (1.11)

EXHIBIT 1B Time Warner, Inc.—Consolidated Balance Sheet Year Ended December 31 (millions)

	2003	2002	2001
Assets			
Cash and equivalents	$ 3,040	$ 1,730	$ 719
Receivables, less allowances	4,908	4,846	6,054
Inventories	1,390	1,376	1,791
Prepaid expenses and other current assets	1,255	1,130	1,687
Current assets of discontinued operations	1,675	1,753	–
Total current assets	12,268	10,835	10,251
Noncurrent inventories and film costs	4,465	3,739	3,490
Investments	3,657	5,094	6,886
Property, plant, and equipment	12,559	11,534	12,669
Intangible assets	43,885	40,544	44,997
Goodwill	39,459	36,986	127,420
Other assets	2,858	2,418	2,791
Noncurrent assets of discontinued operations	2,632	4,368	–
Total assets	$ 121,783	$ 115,518	$ 208,504
Liabilities and Shareholders' Equity			
Accounts payable	$ 1,629	$ 2,244	$ 2,266
Participations payable	1,955	1,689	1,253
Royalties and programming costs payable	778	600	1,515
Deferred revenue	1,175	1,159	1,451
Current debt	2,287	155	48
Other current liabilities	6,120	5,887	6,443
Current liabilities of discontinued operations	1,574	1,730	–
Total current liabilities	15,518	13,464	12,976
Long term debt	23,458	27,354	22,792
Deferred income taxes	13,291	9,803	11,231
Deferred revenue	1,793	1,839	1,048
Mandatorily convertible preferred stock	1,500	–	–
Other liabilities	3,883	3,867	4,839
Minority interests	5,401	5,038	3,591
Noncurrent liabilities of discontinued operations	901	1,336	–
Shareholders' equity			
Common stock	46	45	44
Paid-in capital	155,578	155,134	155,172
Accum. other comprehensive loss, net	(291)	(428)	49
Accum. deficit	(99,295)	(101,934)	(3,238)
Total shareholders' equity	56,038	52,817	152,027
Total liabilities and shareholders' equity	$ 121,783	$ 115,518	$ 208,504

EXHIBIT 2 Time Warner and Selected Competitors—Overview

| | Financial Data | | | | |
| | Revenues ($ millions) | | Net Income ($ millions) | | |
Company	2003	2002	2003	2002	Key Business Areas
Disney	$27,061	$25,329	$1,267	$ 1,236	Networks (ABC, ESPN, Disney, A&E), Film/TV Production (Buena Vista, Miramax), Theme Parks (Disney World), Local TV Stations (10 ABC affiliates)
Viacom	$26,585	$24,606	$1,417	$ 726	Networks (CBS, UPN, MTV, BET, Nick, ShowTime), Film/TV Production (Paramount), Publishing (Simon & Schuster)
News Corp.	$19,848	$16,221	$ 948	($8,269)	Broadcast/Cable Networks (Fox, Fox News), Film/TV Production (Fox, 21st Century Fox), Newspapers (*New York Post, The Times* [UK]), Satellite Television
Comcast	$18,348	$12,460	$3,240	($274)	Cable (Comcast), Sports Teams (Philadelphia 76ers [NBA])
NBC Universal*	$13,000	$ 3,000	na	na	Broadcast/Cable Networks (NBC, Bravo, USA), Film/TV Production (NBC, Universal Studios), Theme Parks (Universal Studios), Local TV Stations (14 NBC affiliates)
Sony	$12,657	$11,993	$ 521	$ 419	Film (Sony Pictures, Columbia Pictures, Tristar), TV Production (Columbia Tristar), Music (Columbia, Sony, Epic Records)

*NBC Universal is the result of a 2004 merger of the NBC operations owned by General Electric and the Universal operations owned by the French firm, Vivendi. GE owns 80 percent of the new company, Vivendi 20 percent. Revenue estimates for 2003 are based on the joint assets of the two companies. The figure stated for net income reflects an estimate of EBITDA and is not comparable to the other net income figures.

Source: Company Annual Reports.

EXHIBIT 3 Number of Subscribers and Revenues for Selected ISPs in 2003

Internet Service Provider	Number of Subscribers (thousands)	Revenues ($ millions)
AOL	24,300	$8,600
MSN	9,000	$1,953
Earthlink	5,500	$1,400
United Online (Juno, Netzero)	2,900	$ 185
Source: Company annual reports.		

EXHIBIT 4 Highest Grossing Movies, 2003*

Rank	Title	Distributor	2003 Gross Box Office Receipts ($ millions)	Percentage Received during Opening Weekend
1.	*Finding Nemo*	Buena Vista	$340	20.7%
2.	*Pirates of the Caribbean*	Buena Vista	$305	15.3%
3.	*Lord of the Rings: Return of the King*	New Line	$290	25.0%
4.	*The Matrix Reloaded*	Warner Bros.	$282	32.6%
5.	*Bruce Almighty*	Universal	$243	33.7%
6.	*X2: X-Men*	Fox	$215	39.8%
7.	*Elf*	New Line	$171	18.2%
8.	*Chicago*	Miramax	$161	**
9.	*Terminator 3: Rise of the Machines*	Warner Bros.	$150	29.3%
10.	*Bad Boys II*	Sony	$138	33.6%
11.	*The Matrix Revolutions*	Warner Bros.	$138	34.6%
12.	*Anger Management*	Sony	$134	31.5%
13.	*Bringing Down the House*	Buena Vista	$133	23.5%
14.	*The Hulk*	Universal	$132	47.0%
15.	*2 Fast 2 Furious*	Universal	$127	39.7%
16.	*Seabiscuit*	Universal	$120	17.4%
17.	*S.W.A.T.*	Sony	$117	31.8%
18.	*Spy Kids 3-D: Game Over*	Miramax	$112	29.9%
19.	*Freaky Friday*	Buena Vista	$110	20.1%
20.	*Scary Movie 3*	Paramount	$110	43.9%

*Box office receipts reflect 2003 gross only.

**Released prior to 2003.

Source: Motion Picture Association (2004).

EXHIBIT 5 Average Production Costs and Average Revenues for New Release Feature Films, 1988–2002

Year	Number of Films Released	Average Production Cost ($ millions)	Average Box Office Receipts ($ millions)	Consumer Price Index
1988	202	$10.3	$16.4	118.3
1989	277	$10.2	$14.7	124
1990	192	$15.9	$22.3	130.7
1991	197	$16.1	$21.4	136.2
1992	174	$18.3	$24.9	140.3
1993	149	$16.6	$25.4	144.5
1994	141	$23.3	$30.7	148.2
1995	163	$23.7	$29.4	152.4
1996	179	$23.6	$26.6	156.9
1997	170	$29	$33.7	160.5
1998	168	$30.9	$34.1	163
1999	216	$30.3	$37.7	166.6
2000	167	$36.1	$44.6	172.2
2001	151	$38.4	$52	177.1
2002	118	$42.4	$59.4	179.9

Sources: Motion Picture Association (2004); Bureau of Labor Statistics (CPI—Series CUUS0000SA0).

EXHIBIT 6 Number of National Satellite-Delivered Networks, Number of Vertically Integrated Networks, and the Percent of Vertically Integrated Networks, 1994–2003

Year	Total Number of Networks	Number of Vertically Integrated Networks	Percentage of Vertically Integrated Networks
1994	106	56	52.8%
1995	129	66	51.2%
1996	145	64	44.1%
1997	172	68	39.5%
1998	245	95	38.8%
1999	283	104	36.7%
2000	281	99	35.2%
2001	194	104	53.6%
2002	308	92	29.9%
2003	339	110	32.4%

Source: Federal Communications Commission (2004).

EXHIBIT 7 Cable Industry Growth, 1994–2003

Year	TV Households* (millions)	Homes Passed** (millions)	Basic Subscribers (millions)	Cable Penetration***
1994	95.4	91.6	59.5	0.650
1998	99.4	95.6	65.1	0.681
1999	100.8	97.6	65.9	0.675
2000	102.2	99.1	66.6	0.672
2001	105.4	100.6	66.9	0.665
2002	106.7	102.7	66.1	0.644
2003****	106.7	103.5	65.9	0.637

*Number of U.S. homes with at least one television.

**Total number of households capable of receiving cable television service.

***Ratio of the number of basic cable subscribers to the number of residential cable homes passed.

****As of June, 2003.

Source: Federal Communications Commission (2004).

EXHIBIT 8 Number of U.S. Broadband Internet Subscriptions by Connection Type, 2001–2003

	2001	2002	2003
DSL	2,693,834	5,101,493	7,675,114
Other wireline	1,088,066	1,186,680	1,215,713
Coaxial cable	5,184,141	9,172,895	13,684,225
Fiber	455,593	520,884	575,613
Satellite	194,707	220,588	309,006
Totals	9,616,341	16,202,540	23,459,671

Source: Federal Communications Commission (2004).

EXHIBIT 9 Competing Technologies, Percentage of Multichannel Video Programming Distributor (MVPD) Households Served, Selected Years

	1993	1998	2003
Cable	94.89%	85.34%	74.87%
Direct broadcast satellite (DBS)	0.12%	9.40%	21.63%
Other MVPDs	4.99%	5.26%	3.50%

Source: Federal Communications Commission (2004).

Additional Readings and References

Chapter 1

Arnold, R. Douglas, "Political Control of Administrative Officials." *Journal of Law, Economics and Organization* 3(2), Fall 1987, pp. 279–86.

Balachandran, Kashi R. and Srinidhi, Bin, "A Stochastic Planning Model for Manufacturing Environments." *Atlantic Economic Journal* 20(1), March 1992, pp. 48–56.

Beck, Paul J. and Zorn, Thomas S., "Managerial Incentives in a Stock Market Economy." *Journal of Finance* 37(5), December 1982, pp. 1151–67.

Bryan, William R.; Gruca, Thomas; and Linke, Charles M., "The Present Value of Future Earnings: Contemporaneous Differentials and the Performance of Dedicated Portfolios." *Journal of Risk and Insurance* 57, September 1990, pp. 530–39.

Cannings, Kathleen and Lazonick, William, "Equal Employment Opportunity and the 'Managerial Woman' in Japan." *Industrial Relations* 33(1), January 1994, pp. 44–69.

Chan, Anthony and Chen, Carl R., "How Well Do Asset Allocation Mutual Fund Managers Allocate Assets?" *Journal of Portfolio Management* 18(3), Spring 1992, pp. 81–91.

Episcopos, Athanasios, "Investment under Uncertainty and the Value of the Firm." *Economics Letters* 45(3), July 1994, pp. 319–22.

Gaughan, Patrick; Lerman, Paul; and Manley, Donald, "Measuring Damages Resulting from Lost Functionality of Systems." *Journal of Legal Economics* 3(2), July 1993, pp. 11–24.

Gegax, Douglas; Gerking, Shelby; and Schulze, William, "Perceived Risk and the Marginal Value of Safety." *Review of Economics and Statistics* 73(4), November 1991, pp. 589–96.

Giordano, James N., "A Trucker's Dilemma: Managerial Behavior under an Operating Ratio Standard." *Managerial and Decision Economics* 10(3), September 1989, pp. 241–51.

Lange, Mark; Luksetich, William; and Jacobs, Philip, "Managerial Objectives of Symphony Orchestras." *Managerial and Decision Economics* 7(4), December 1986, pp. 273–78.

Ling, David C., "Optimal Refunding Strategies, Transaction Costs, and the Market Value of Corporate Debt." *Financial Review* 26, November 1991, pp. 479–500.

Marcus, Richard D.; Swidler, Steve; and Zivney, Terry L., "An Explanation of Why Shareholders' Losses Are So Large after Drug Recalls." *Managerial and Decision Economics* 8(4), December 1987, pp. 295–300.

Prasnikar, Janez and Svejnar, Jan, "Workers' Participation in Management vs. Social Ownership and Government Policies: Yugoslav Lessons for Transforming Socialist Economics." *Comparative Economic Studies* 33(4), Winter 1991, pp. 27–45.

Ravenscraft, David J. and Wagner, Curtis L., III, "The Role of the FTC's Line of Business Data in Testing and Expanding the Theory of the Firm." *Journal of Law and Economics* 34(2), Part 2, October 1992, pp. 703–39.

Saltzman, Cynthia; Duggal, Vijaya G.; and Williams, Mary L., "Income and the Recycling Effort: A Maximization Problem." *Energy Economics* 15(1), January 1993, pp. 33–38.

Sanghvi, Arun P. and Dash, Gordon H., Jr., "Core Securities: Widening the Decision Dimensions." *Journal of Portfolio Management* 4(3), Spring 1978, pp. 20–24.

Strong, John S. and Meyer, John R., "An Analysis of Shareholder Rights Plans." *Managerial and Decision Economics* 11(2), May 1990, pp. 73–86.

Tuckman, Howard P. and Chang, Cyril F., "Cost Convergence between For-Profit and Not-for-Profit Nursing Homes: Does Competition Matter?" *Quarterly Review of Economics and Business* 28(4), Winter 1988, pp. 50–65.

Chapter 2

Barzel, Yoram, "Rationing by Waiting." *Journal of Law and Economics,* April 1974, pp. 73–96.

Bell, Frederick W. and Leeworthy, Vernon R., "Recreational Demand by Tourists for Saltwater Beach Days." *Journal of Environmental Economics and Management* 18(3), May 1990, pp. 189–205.

Bohanon, Cecil E.; Lynch, Gerald J.; and Van Cott, T. Norman, "A Supply and Demand Exposition of the Operation of a Gold Standard in a Closed Economy." *Journal of Economic Education* 16(1), Winter 1985, pp. 16–26.

Burrows, Thomas M., "Pesticide Demand and Integrated Pest Management: A Limited Dependent Variable Analysis." *American Journal of Agricultural Economics* 65(4), November 1983, pp. 806–10.

Chaloupka, Frank J. and Saffer, Henry, "Clean Indoor Air Laws and the Demand for Cigarettes." *Contemporary Policy Issues* 10(2), April 1992, pp. 72–83.

Crafton, Steven M.; Hoffer, George E.; and Reilly, Robert J., "Testing the Impact of Recalls on the Demand for Automobiles." *Economic Inquiry* 19(4), October 1981, pp. 694–703.

Craig, Ben and Batina, Raymond G., "The Effects of Social Security on a Life Cycle Family Labor Supply Simulation Model." *Journal of Public Economics* 46(2), November 1991, pp. 199–226.

Duncan, Kevin C.; Prus, Mark J.; and Sandy, Jonathan G., "Marital Status, Children and Women's Labor Market Choices." *Journal of Socio Economics* 22(3), Fall 1993, pp. 277–88.

Englander, Valerie and Englander, Fred, "The Demand for General Assistance in New Jersey: A New Look at the Deterrence Effect." *Journal of Behavioral Economics* 13(2), Winter 1984, pp. 53–65.

Gillespie, Robert W., "Measuring the Demand for Court Services: A Critique of the Federal District Courts Case Weights." *Journal of the American Statistical Association* 69(345), March 1974, pp. 38–43.

Gulley, O. David and Scott, Frank A., Jr., "The Demand for Wagering on State-Operated Lotto Games." *National Tax Journal* 46(1), March 1993, pp. 13–22.

Kasulis, Jack J.; Huettner, David A.; and Dikeman, Neil J., "The Feasibility of Changing Electricity Consumption Patterns." *Journal of Consumer Research* 8(3), December 1981, pp. 279–90.

Knowles, Glenn; Sherony, Keith; and Haupert, Mike, "The Demand for Major League Baseball: A Test of the Uncertainty of Outcome Hypothesis." *American Economist* 36(2), Fall 1992, pp. 72–80.

Kridel, Donald J.; Lehman, Dale E.; and Weisman, Dennis L., "Option Value, Telecommunications Demand, and Policy." *Information Economics and Policy* 5(2), July 1993, pp. 125–44.

Martin, Randolph C. and Wilder, Ronald P., "Residential Demand for Water and the Pricing of Municipal Water Services." *Public Finance Quarterly* 20(1), January 1992, pp. 93–102.

Max, Wendy and Lehman, Dale E., "A Behavioral Model of Timber Supply." *Journal of Environmental Economics and Management* 15(1), March 1988, pp. 71–86.

Millner, Edward L. and Hoffer, George E., "A Re-examination of the Impact of Automotive Styling on Demand." *Applied Economics* 25(1), January 1993, pp. 101–10.

Munley, Vincent G.; Taylor, Larry W.; and Formby, John P., "Electricity Demand in Multi-Family, Renter-Occupied Residences." *Southern Economic Journal* 57(1), July 1990, pp. 178–94.

Nickerson, Peter H., "Demand for the Regulation of Recreation: The Case of Elk and Deer Hunting in Washington State." *Land Economics* 66(4), November 1990, pp. 437–47.

O'Neill, June; Brien, Michael; and Cunningham, James, "Effects of Comparable Worth Policy: Evidence from Washington State." *American Economic Review* 79(2), May 1989, pp. 305–9.

Parker, Darrell F. and Rhine, Sherrie L. W., "Turnover Costs and the Wage Fringe Mix." *Applied Economics* 23(4A), Part A, April 1991, pp. 617–22.

Ramagopal, K. and Ramaswamy, Sunder, "Measuring the Efficiency Cost of Wage Taxation with Uncertain Labor Productivity." *Economics Letters* 42(1), 1993, pp. 77–80.

Saffer, Henry, "Alcohol Advertising Bans and Alcohol Abuse: An International Perspective." *Journal of Health Economics* 10(1), May 1991, pp. 65–79.

Scahill, Edward, "The Determinants of Average Salaries of Professional Football." *Atlantic Economic Journal* 13(1), March 1985, pp. 103–4.

Siegfried, John J. and Scott, Charles E., "Recent Trends in Undergraduate Economics Degrees." *Journal of Economic Education* 25(3), Summer 1994, pp. 281–86.

Vedder, Richard K. and Gallaway, Lowell, "Racial Differences in Unemployment in the United States, 1890–1990." *Journal of Economic History* 52(3), September 1992, pp. 696–702.

Watkins, Thomas G., "The Shortage of Math and Science Teachers: Are Financial Aid Incentives Enough?" *Journal of Economics (MVEA)* 18(0), 1992, pp. 29–34.

Wilson, John Sullivan, "The U.S. 1982–93 Performance in Advanced Technology Trade." *Challenge* 37(1), January–February 1994, pp. 11–16.

Wu, Mickey T. C. and Monahan, Dennis, "An Experimental Study of Consumer Demand Using Rats." *Journal of Behavioral Economics* 12(1), Summer 1983, pp. 121–38.

Yen, Steven T., "Cross Section Estimation of U.S. Demand for Alcoholic Beverage." *Applied Economics* 26(4), April 1994, pp. 381–92.

Zuber, Richard A. and Gandar, John M., "Lifting the Television Blackout on No-Shows at Football Games." *Atlantic Economic Journal* 16(2), June 1988, pp. 63–73.

Chapter 3

Brooking, Carl G. and Taylor, Patrick A., "The Effect of Stochastic Variables on Estimating the Value of Lost Earnings." *Journal of Risk and Insurance* 58(4), December 1991, pp. 647–56.

Chressanthis, George A., "The Impacts of Tuition Rate Changes on College Undergraduate Headcounts and Credit Hours over Time. A Case Study." *Economics of Education Review* 5(2), 1986, pp. 205–17.

Combs, J. Paul and Elledge, Barry W., "Effects of a Room Tax on Resort Hotel/Motels." *National Tax Journal* 32(2), June 1979, pp. 201–7.

Dubin, Jeffrey A. and Henson, Steven E., "An Engineering/Econometric Analysis of Seasonal Energy Demand and Conservation in the Pacific Northwest." *Journal of Business and Economic Statistics* 6(1), January 1988, pp. 121–34.

Dumas, Edward B. and Sengupta, Jati K., "Fundamentals and Fads in Asset Pricing: An Empirical Investigation." *Applied Financial Economics* 4(3), June 1994, pp. 175–80.

Fox, William F. and Campbell, Charles, "Stability of the State Sales Tax Income Elasticity." *National Tax Journal* 37(2), June 1984, pp. 201–12.

Heinen, D., "The Structure of Food Demand: Interrelatedness and Duality." *American Journal of Agricultural Economics* 64(2), May 1982, pp. 213–21.

Hsing, Yu, "Estimation of Residential Demand for Electricity with the Cross Sectionally Correlated and Time-Wise Autoregressive Model." *Resource and Energy Economics* 16(3), August 1994, pp. 255–63.

Jones, Clifton T., "A Single Equation Study of U.S. Petroleum Consumption: The Role of Model Specification." *Southern Economic Journal* 59(4), April 1993, pp. 687–700.

Lange, Mark D. and Luksetich, William A., "Demand Elasticities for Symphony Orchestras." *Journal of Cultural Economics* 8(1), June 1984, pp. 29–47.

Lee, Joe W. and Kidane, Amdetsion, "Tobacco Consumption Pattern: A Demographic Analysis." *Atlantic Economic Journal* 16(4), December 1988, pp. 92–94.

Lee, Tong Hun and Kong, Chang Min, "Elasticities of Housing Demand." *Southern Economic Journal* 44(2), October 1977, pp. 298–305.

Lin, An loh; Botsas, Eleftherios N.; and Monroe, Scott A., "State Gasoline Consumption in the USA: An Econometric Analysis." *Energy Economics* 7(1), January 1985, pp. 29–36.

Loeb, Peter D., "Automobile Safety Inspection: Further Econometric Evidence." *Applied Economics* 22(12), December 1990, pp. 1697–1704.

Matulich, Scott C.; Workman, William G.; and Jubenville, Alan, "Recreation Economics: Taking Stock: Problems and Solutions in Estimating the Demand for and Value of Rural Outdoor Recreation." *Land Economics* 63(3), August 1987, pp. 310–16.

Newman, Robert J. and Sullivan, Dennis H., "Econometric Analysis of Business Tax Impacts on Industrial Location: What Do We Know, and How Do We Know It?" *Journal of Urban Economics* 23(2), March 1988, pp. 215–34.

Nguyen, Hong V., "Energy Elasticities under Divisia and Btu Aggregation." *Energy Economics* 9(4), October 1987, pp. 210–14.

Raffiee, Kambiz and Wendel, Jeanne, "Interactions between Hospital Admissions, Cost per Day and Average Length of Stay." *Applied Economics* 23(1), Part B, January 1991, pp. 237–46.

Ramin, Taghi, "A Regression Analysis of Migration to Urban Areas of a Less Developed Country: The Case of Iran." *American Economist* 32(2), Fall 1988, pp. 26–34.

Raymond, Richard D.; Sesnowitz, Michael L.; and Williams, Donald R., "The Contribution of Regression Analysis to the Elimination of Gender-Based Wage Discrimination in Academia: A Simulation." *Economics of Education Review* 9(3), 1990, pp. 197–207.

Reaume, David M., "Migration and the Dynamic Stability of Regional Econometric Models." *Economic Inquiry* 21(2), April 1983, pp. 281–93.

Stine, William F., "Estimating the Responsiveness of Local Revenue to Intergovernmental Aid." *National Tax Journal* 38(2), June 1985, pp. 227–34.

Tashman, Leonard J. and Leach, Michael L., "Automatic Forecasting Software: A Survey and Evaluation." *International Journal of Forecasting* 7(2), August 1991, pp. 209–30.

Taube, Paul M.; Huth, William L.; and MacDonald, Don N., "An Analysis of Consumer Expectation Effects on Demand in a Dynamic Almost Ideal Demand System." *Journal of Economics and Business* 42(3), August 1990, pp. 225–36.

White, Michael D. and Luksetich, William A., "Heroin: Price Elasticity and Enforcement Strategies." *Economic Inquiry* 21(4), October 1983, pp. 557–64.

Wilder, Ronald P.; Johnson, Joseph E.; and Rhyne, R. Glenn, "Income Elasticity of the Residential Demand for Electricity." *Journal of Energy and Development* 16(1), Autumn 1990, pp. 1–13.

Chapter 4

Colburn, Christopher B., "Work Requirements and Income Transfers." *Public Finance Quarterly* 21(2), April 1993, pp. 141–62.

Danziger, Sheldon and Taussig, Michael K., "The Income Unit and the Anatomy of Income Distribution." *Review of Income and Wealth* 25(4), December 1979, pp. 365–75.

Giertz, J. Fred and Sullivan, Dennis H., "On the Political Economy of Food Stamps." *Public Choice* 33(3), 1978, pp. 113–17.

Goodfellow, Gordon P., Jr. and Sweeney, Vernon E., "Vertically Parallel Indifference Curves with a Non-Constant Marginal Utility of Money." *American Economist* 13(2), Fall 1969, pp. 81–86.

Goodman, Allen C., "Estimation of Offset and Income Effects on the Demand for Mental Health Treatment." *Inquiry* 26(2), Summer 1989, pp. 235–48.

Johnston, Richard S. and Larson, Douglas M., "Focusing the Search for Giffen Behavior." *Economic Inquiry* 32(1), January 1994, pp. 168–74.

Kaun, David E., "Writers Die Young: The Impact of Work and Leisure on Longevity." *Journal of Economic Psychology* 12(2), June 1991, pp. 381–99.

Klingaman, David, "A Note on a Cyclical Majority Problem." *Public Choice* 6(0), Spring 1969, pp. 99–101.

Senauer, Ben and Young, Nathan, "The Impact of Food Stamps on Food Expenditures: Rejection of the Traditional Model." *American Journal of Agricultural Economics* 68(1), February 1986, pp. 37–43.

Chapter 5

Caves, Douglas W.; Herriges, Joseph A.; and Windle, Robert J., "The Cost of Electric Power Interruptions in the Industrial Sector: Estimates Derived from Interruptible Service Programs." *Land Economics* 68(1), February 1992, pp. 49–61.

Coates, Daniel E. and Mulligan, James G., "Scale Economies and Capacity Utilization: The Importance of Relative Fuel Prices." *Energy Economics* 10(2), April 1988, pp. 140–46.

Corman, Hope; Joyce, Theodore J.; and Grossman, Michael, "Birth Outcome Production Function in the United States." *Journal of Human Resources* 22(3), Summer 1987, pp. 339–60.

Dobitz, Clifford P., "Energy Substitution in Irrigation." *Regional Science Perspectives* 14(1), 1984, pp. 25–29.

Duchatelet, Martine, "A Note on Increasing Returns to Scale and Learning by Doing." *Journal of Economic Theory* 27(1), June 1982, pp. 210–18.

Eckard, E. Woodrow, "Cost Competition: New Evidence on an Old Issue." *Applied Economics* 24(11), November 1992, pp. 1241–50.

Griffin, Peter, "The Substitutability of Occupational Groups Using Firm Level Data." *Economics Letters* 39(3), July 1992, pp. 279–82.

Grosskopf, Shawna and Yaisawarng, Suthathip, "Economies of Scope in the Provision of Local Public Services." *National Tax Journal* 43(1), March 1990, pp. 61–74.

Harris, R. Scott, "Planning, Flexibility, and Joint Specificity of Inputs: The Use of First Refusal Rights." *Zeitschrift fur die Gesamte Staatswissenschaft (JITE)* 141(4), December 1985, pp. 576–85.

Hayashi, Paul M. and Ziegler, Lawrence F., "Separability and Substitutability of Inputs in the Production of Police Services and Their Implications for Budgeting." *Journal of Economics (MVEA)* 19(1), Spring 1993, pp. 23–30.

Holcomb, James H. and Evans, Dorla A., "The Effect of Sunk Costs on Uncertain Decisions in Experimental Markets." *Journal of Behavioral Economics* 16(3), Fall 1987, pp. 59–66.

Huckins, Larry E., "Capital Labor Substitution in Municipal Government." *Public Finance Quarterly* 17(4), October 1989, pp. 357–74.

Huettner, David A. and Landon, John H., "Electric Utilities: Scale Economies and Diseconomies." *Southern Economic Journal* 44(4), April 1978, pp. 883–912.

Johnson, Dennis A., "Opportunity Cost: A Pedagogical Note." *Southern Economic Journal* 50(3), January 1984, pp. 866–70.

Kim, H. Youn and Clark, Robert M., "Economies of Scale and Scope in Water Supply." *Regional Science and Urban Economics* 18(4), November 1988, pp. 479–502.

Koshal, Rajindar K. and Koshal, Manjulika, "Economies of Scale of State Road Transport Industry in India." *International Journal of Transport Economics* 16(2), June 1989, pp. 165–73.

Lichtenberg, Frank R. and Siegel, Donald, "The Impact of R&D Investment on Productivity: New Evidence Using Linked R&D LRD Data." *Economic Inquiry* 29(2), April 1991, pp. 203–29.

MacDonald, James M., "R and D and the Directions of Diversification." *Review of Economics and Statistics* 67(4), November 1985, pp. 583–90.

Maxwell, W. D., "Production Theory and Cost Curves." *Applied Economics* 1(3), August 1969, pp. 221–24.

McDonald, J. R. Scott; Rayner, Tony J.; and Bates, John M., "Productivity Growth and the U.K. Food System 1954–84." *Journal of Agricultural Economics* 43(2), May 1992, pp. 191–204.

Mullen, John K. and Williams, Martin, "Convergence, Scale and the Relative Productivity Performance of Canadian–U.S. Manufacturing Industries." *Applied Economics* 26(7), July 1994, pp. 739–50.

Niroomand, Farhang and Sawyer, W. Charles, "The Extent of Scale Economies in U.S. Foreign Trade." *Journal of World Trade* 23(6), December 1989, pp. 137–46.

Okunade, Albert Ade, "Production Cost Structure of U.S. Hospital Pharmacies: Time Series, Cross-Sectional Bed Size Evidence." *Journal of Applied Econometrics* 8(3), July–September 1993, pp. 277–94.

Olson, Dennis O. and Jonish, James, "The Robustness of Translog Elasticity of Substitution Estimates and the Capital Energy Complementarity Controversy." *Quarterly Journal of Business and Economics* 24(1), Winter 1985, pp. 21–35.

Robison, H. David and Silver, Stephen J., "The Impact of Changing Oil Prices on Interfuel Substitution: Ethanol's Prospects in the United States to 1995." *Journal of Policy Modeling* 8(2), Summer 1986, pp. 241–53.

Sengupta, Jati K. and Okamura, Kumiko, "Scale Economies in Manufacturing: Problems of Robust Estimation." *Empirical Economics* 18(3), 1993, pp. 469–80.

Sexton, Robert L.; Graves, Philip E.; and Lee, Dwight R., "The Short- and Long-Run Marginal Cost Curve: A Pedagogical Note." *Journal of Economic Education* 24(1), Winter 1993, pp. 34–37.

Thomas, Janet M. and Callan, Scott J., "An Analysis of Production Cost Inefficiency." *Review of Industrial Organization* 7(2), 1992, pp. 203–25.

Toda, Yasushi, "Estimation of a Cost Function When the Cost Is Not Minimum: The Case of Soviet Manufacturing Industries, 1958–1971." *Review of Economics and Statistics* 58(3), August 1976, pp. 259–68.

Wen, Guanzhong James, "Total Factor Productivity Change in China's Farming Sector: 1952–1989." *Economic Development and Cultural Change* 42(1), October 1993, pp. 1–41.

Williams, Martin and Moomaw, Ronald L., "Capital and Labour Efficiencies: A Regional Analysis." *Urban Studies* 26(6), December 1989, pp. 573–85.

Chapter 6

Allen, Bruce T., "Merger Statistics and Merger Policy." *Review of Industrial Organization* 1(2), Summer 1984, pp. 78–92.

Arnold, Michael A., "The Principal–Agent Relationship in Real Estate Brokerage Services." *American Real Estate and Urban Economics Association Journal* 20(1), Spring 1992, pp. 89–106.

Aron, Debra J. and Olivella, Pau, "Bonus and Penalty Schemes as Equilibrium Incentive Devices, with Application to Manufacturing Systems." *Journal of Law, Economics and Organization* 10(1), April 1994, pp. 1–34.

Atkinson, Scott E.; Stanley, Linda R.; and Tschirhart, John, "Revenue Sharing as an Incentive in an Agency Problem: An Example from the National Football League." *Rand Journal of Economics* 19(1), Spring 1988, pp. 27–43.

Bull, Clive; Schotter, Andrew; and Weigelt, Keith, "Tournaments and Piece Rates: An Experimental Study." *Journal of Political Economy* 95(1), February 1987, pp. 1–33.

Byrd, John W. and Hickman, Kent A., "Do Outside Directors Monitor Managers? Evidence from Tender Offer Bids." *Journal of Financial Economics* 32(2), October 1992, pp. 195–221.

Cardell, Nicholas Scott and Hopkins, Mark Myron, "Education, Income, and Ability: A Comment." *Journal of Political Economy* 85(1), February 1977, pp. 211–15.

Cordell, Lawrence R.; MacDonald, Gregor D.; and Wohar, Mark E., "Corporate Ownership and the Thrift Crisis." *Journal of Law and Economics* 36(2), October 1993, pp. 719–56.

Cornwell, Christopher; Dorsey, Stuart; and Mehrzad, Nasser, "Opportunistic Behavior by Firms in Implicit Pension Contracts." *Journal of Human Resources* 26(4), Fall 1991, pp. 704–25.

Dearden, James; Ickes, Barry W.; and Samuelson, Larry, "To Innovate or Not to Innovate: Incentives and Innovation in Hierarchies." *American Economic Review* 80(5), December 1990, pp. 1105–24.

Erekson, O. Homer and Sullivan, Dennis H., "A Cross Section Analysis of IRS Auditing." *National Tax Journal* 41(2), June 1988, pp. 175–89.

Hansen, Robert S. and Torregrosa, Paul, "Underwriter Compensation and Corporate Monitoring." *Journal of Finance* 47(4), September 1992, pp. 1537–55.

Hirao, Yukiko, "Task Assignment and Agency Structures." *Journal of Economics and Management Strategy* 2(2), Summer 1993, pp. 299–323.

Honig Haftel, Sandra and Martin, Linda R., "The Effectiveness of Reward Systems on Innovative Output: An Empirical Analysis." *Small Business Economics* 5(4), December 1993, pp. 261–69.

Ingberman, Daniel E., "Privatization as Institutional Choice: Comment." *Journal of Policy Analysis and Management* 6(4), Summer 1987, pp. 607–11.

Janjigian, Vahan and Bolster, Paul J., "The Elimination of Director Liability and Stockholder Returns: An Empirical Investigation." *Journal of Financial Research* 13(1), Spring 1990, pp. 53–60.

Kalt, Joseph P. and Zupan, Mark A., "The Apparent Ideological Behavior of Legislators: Testing for Principal–Agent Slack in Political Institutions." *Journal of Law and Economics* 33(1), April 1990, pp. 103–31.

Karpoff, Jonathan M. and Rice, Edward M., "Organizational Form, Share Transferability, and Firm Performance: Evidence from the ANCSA Corporations." *Journal of Financial Economics* 24(1), September 1989, pp. 69–105.

Louie, Kenneth K. T.; Fizel, John L.; and Mentzer, Marc S., "CEO Tenure and Firm Performance." *Journal of Economics (MVEA)* 19(1), Spring 1993, pp. 51–56.

Lyon, Thomas P. and Hackett, Steven C., "Bottlenecks and Governance Structures: Open Access and Long–Term Contracting in Natural Gas." *Journal of Law, Economics and Organization* 9(2), October 1993, pp. 380–98.

Majumdar, Sumit K. and Ramaswamy, Venkatram, "Explaining Downstream Integration." *Managerial and Decision Economics* 15(2), March/April 1994, pp. 119–29.

Mulherin, J. Harold; Netter, Jeffry M.; and Overdahl, James A., "Prices Are Property: The Organization of Financial Exchanges from a Transaction Cost Perspective." *Journal of Law and Economics* 34(2), Part 2, October 1992, pp. 591–644.

Nantz, Kathryn and Sparks, Roger, "The Labor Managed Firm under Imperfect Monitoring: Employment and Work Effort Responses." *Journal of Comparative Economics* 14(1), March 1990, pp. 33–50.

Shogren, Jason F. and Kask, Susan B., "Exploring the Boundaries of the Coase Theorem: Efficiency and Rationality Given Imperfect Contract Enforcement." *Economics Letters* 39(2), June 1992, pp. 155–61.

Singh, Nirvikar and Thomas, Ravi, "User Charges as a Delegation Mechanism." *National Tax Journal* 39(1), March 1986, pp. 109–13.

Zorn, Thomas S. and Larsen, James E., "The Incentive Effects of Flat Fee and Percentage Commissions for Real Estate Brokers." *American Real Estate and Urban Economics Association Journal* 14(1), Spring 1986, pp. 24–47.

Chapter 7

Adrangi, Bahram; Chow, Garland; and Gritta, Richard, "Market Structure, Market Share, and Profits in the Airline Industry." *Atlantic Economic Journal* 91(1), March 1991, pp. 98–99.

Amato, Louis and Wilder, Ronald P., "Market Concentration, Efficiency, and Antitrust Policy: Demsetz Revisited." *Quarterly Journal of Business and Economics* 27(4), Autumn 1988, pp. 3–19.

Bradley, James W. and Korn, Donald H., "Bargains in Valuation Disparities: Corporate Acquirer versus Passive Investor." *Sloan Management Review* 20(2), Winter 1979, pp. 51–64.

Carroll, Sidney L. and Scott, Loren C., "The Modification of Industry Performance through the Use of Government Monopsony Power." *Industrial Organization Review* 3(1), 1975, pp. 28–36.

Carter, John R., "Concentration Change and the Structure Performance Debate: An Interpretive Essay." *Managerial and Decision Economics* 5(4), December 1984, pp. 204–12.

Chang, Winston W. and Chen, Fang Yueh, "Vertically Related Markets: Export Rivalry between DC and LDC Firms." *Review of International Economics* 2(2), June 1994, pp. 131–42.

Crane, Steven E. and Welch, Patrick J., "The Problem of Geographic Market Definition: Geographic Proximity vs. Economic Significance." *Atlantic Economic Journal* 19(2), June 1991, pp. 12–20.

Deily, Mary E. and Gray, Wayne B., "Enforcement of Pollution Regulations in a Declining Industry." *Journal of Environmental Economics and Management* 21(3), November 1991, pp. 260–74.

Diamond, Charles A. and Simon, Curtis J., "Industrial Specialization and the Returns to Labor." *Journal of Labor Economics* 8(2), April 1990, pp. 175–201.

Dranove, David; Shanley, Mark; and White, William D., "Price and Concentration in Hospital Markets: The Switch from Patient-Driven to Payer-Driven Competition." *Journal of Law and Economics* 36(1), Part 1, April 1993, pp. 179–204.

Evans, William N. and Kessides, Ioannis, "Structure, Conduct, and Performance in the Deregulated Airline Industry." *Southern Economic Journal* 59(3), January 1993, pp. 450–67.

Hannan, Timothy H. and McDowell, John M., "The Impact of Technology Adoption on Market Structure." *Review of Economics and Statistics* 72(1), February 1990, pp. 164–68.

Hartley, Keith and Corcoran, William J., "Short-Run Employment Functions and Defence Contracts in the U.K. Aircraft Industry." *Applied Economics* 7(4), December 1975, pp. 223–33.

Haworth, Charles T. and Reuther, Carol Jean, "Industrial Concentration and Interindustry Wage Determination." *Review of Economics and Statistics* 6(1), February 1978, pp. 85–95.

Hiebert, L. Dean, "Cost Flexibility and Price Dispersion." *Journal of Industrial Economics* 38(1), September 1989, pp. 103–9.

Jarrell, Stephen, "Research and Development and Firm Size in the Pharmaceutical Industry." *Business Economics* 18(4), September 1983, pp. 26–39.

Kyle, Reuben; Strickland, Thomas H.; and Fayissa, Bichaka, "Capital Markets' Assessment of Airline Restructuring Following Deregulation." *Applied Economics* 24(10), October 1992, pp. 1097–1102.

Lane, Sylvai and Papathanasis, Anastasios, "Certification and Industry Concentration Ratios." *Antitrust Bulletin* 28(2), Summer 1983, pp. 381–95.

Levin, Sharon G.; Levin, Stanford L.; and Meisel, John B., "Market Structure, Uncertainty, and Intrafirm Diffusion: The Case of Optical Scanners in Grocery Stores." *Review of Economics and Statistics* 74(2), May 1992, pp. 345–50.

Mallela, Parthasaradhi and Nahata, Babu, "Effects of Horizontal Merger on Price, Profits, and Market Power in a Dominant Firm Oligopoly." *International Economic Journal* 3(1), Spring 1989, pp. 55–62.

Norton, Seth W., "Vertical Integration and Systematic Risk: Oil Refining Revisited." *Journal of Institutional and Theoretical Economics* 149(4), December 1993, pp. 656–69.

Peoples, James; Hekmat, Ali; and Moini, A. H., "Corporate Mergers and Union Wage Premiums." *Journal of Economics and Finance* 17(2), Summer 1993, pp. 65–75.

Salinger, Michael, "The Concentration Margins Relationship Reconsidered." *Brookings Papers on Economic Activity,* Special Issue, 1990, pp. 287–321.

Sandler, Ralph D., "Market Share Instability in Commercial Airline Markets and the Impact of Deregulation." *Journal of Industrial Economics* 36(3), March 1988, pp. 327–35.

Walsh, Carl E., "Taxation of Interest Income, Deregulation and the Banking Industry." *Journal of Finance* 38(5), December 1983, pp. 1529–42.

Yandle, Bruce and Hite, Arnold, "Branded Competition and Concentration Measures." *Southern Economic Journal* 43(4), April 1977, pp. 5176–81.

Chapter 8

Benson, Bruce L. and Faminow, M. D., "The Impact of Experience on Prices and Profits in Experimental Duopoly Markets." *Journal of Economic Behavior and Organization* 9(4), June 1988, pp. 345–65.

Besanko, David and Perry, Martin K., "Exclusive Dealing in a Spatial Model of Retail Competition." *International Journal of Industrial Organization* 12(3), 1994, pp. 297–329.

Brastow, Raymond and Rystrom, David, "Wealth Effects of the Drug Price Competition and Patent Term Restoration Act of 1984." *American Economist* 32(2), Fall 1988, pp. 59–65.

Brown, John Howard, "Airline Fleet Composition and Deregulation." *Review of Industrial Organization* 8(4), August 1993, pp. 435–49.

Chen, Yu Min and Jain, Dipak C., "Dynamic Monopoly Pricing under a Poisson-Type Uncertain Demand." *Journal of Business* 65(4), October 1992, pp. 593–614.

Cheng, Doris and Shieh, Yeung Nan, "Bilateral Monopoly and Industrial Location: A Cooperative Outcome." *Regional Science and Urban Economics* 22(2), June 1992, pp. 187–95.

De Bondt, Raymond; Slaets, Patrick; and Cassiman, Bruno, "The Degree of Spillovers and the Number of Rivals for Maximum Effective R & D." *International Journal of Industrial Organization* 10(1), 1992, pp. 35–54.

Feinberg, Robert M. and Shaanan, Joseph, "The Relative Price Discipline of Domestic versus Foreign Entry." *Review of Industrial Organization* 9(2), April 1994, pp. 211–20.

Gegax, Douglas and Nowotny, Kenneth, "Competition and the Electric Utility Industry: An Evaluation." *Yale Journal on Regulation* 10(1), Winter 1993, pp. 63–87.

Gupta, Barnali; Kats, Amoz; and Pal, Debashis, "Upstream Monopoly, Downstream Competition and Spatial Price Discrimination." *Regional Science and Urban Economics* 24(5), October 1994, pp. 529–42.

Holahan, William L. and Schuler, Richard E., "Competitive Entry in a Spatial Economy: Market Equilibrium and Welfare Implications." *Journal of Regional Science* 21(3), August 1981, pp. 341–57.

Kats, Amoz, "Monopolistic Trading Economies: A Case of Governmental Control." *Public Choice* 20, Winter 1974, pp. 17–32.

Kripalani, G. K., "Monopoly Supply." *Atlantic Economic Journal* 18(4), December 1990, pp. 32–37.

Lau, Lawrence and Ma, Barry K., "The Short-Run Aggregate Profit Function and the Capacity Distribution." *Scandinavian Journal of Economics* 96(2), 1994, pp. 201–18.

Levy, David T. and Gerlowski, Daniel A., "Competition, Advertising and Meeting Competition Clauses." *Economics Letters* 37(3), November 1991, pp. 217–21.

Magas, Istvan, "Dynamics of Export Competition in High-Technology Trade: USA, Japan, and Germany 1973–1987." *International Trade Journal* 6(4), Summer 1992, pp. 471–513.

Mirman, L. J.; Tauman, I.; and Zang, Y., "Cooperative Behavior in a Competitive Market." *Mathematical Social Science* 54(3), October 1991, pp. 227–49.

Oster, Clinton V., Jr. and Strong, John S., "The Worldwide Aviation Safety Record." *Logistics and Transportation Review* 28(1), March 1992, pp. 23–48.

Peck, J. and Shell, K., "Liquid Markets and Competition." *Games and Economic Behavior* 2(4), December 1990, pp. 362–77.

Phillips, Owen R. and Schutte, David P., "Identifying Profitable Self-Service Markets: A Test in Gasoline Retailing." *Applied Economics* 20(2), February 1988, pp. 263–72.

Rock, Steven M. and Hall, W. Clayton, "Advertising and Monopoly Power: The Case of the Electric Utility Industry: Comment." *Atlantic Economic Journal* 15(1), March 1987, pp. 67–70.

Sattler, Edward L. and Scott, Robert C., "Price and Output Adjustments in the Two-Plant Firm." *Southern Economic Journal* 48(4), April 1982, pp. 1042–48.

Schroeter, John R.; Smith, Scott L.; and Cox, Steven R., "Advertising and Competition in Routine Legal Service Markets: An Empirical Investigation." *Journal of Industrial Economics* 36(1), September 1987, pp. 49–60.

Seldon, Barry J. and Doroodian, Khrosrow, "Does Purely Predatory Advertising Exist?" *Review of Industrial Organization* 5(3), Fall 1990, pp. 45–70.

Suslow, Valerie Y., "Estimating Monopoly Behavior with Competitive Recycling: An Application to Alcoa." *Rand Journal of Economics* 17(3), Autumn 1986, pp. 389–403.

Zietz, Joachim and Fayissa, Bichaka, "R&D Expenditures and Import Competition: Some Evidence for the U.S." *Weltwirtschaftliches Archiv* 128(1), 1992, pp. 52–66.

Chapter 9

Benson, Bruce L. and Hartigan, James C., "An Explanation of Intra-industry Trade in Identical Commodities." *International Journal of Industrial Organization* 2(2), June 1984, pp. 85–97.

Buschena, David E. and Perloff, Jeffrey M., "The Creation of Dominant Firm Market Power in the Coconut Oil Export Market." *American Journal of Agricultural Economics* 73(4), November 1991, pp. 1000–1008.

Cremer, Helmuth and Cremer, Jacques, "Duopoly with Employee-Controlled and Profit-Maximizing Firms: Bertrand vs. Cournot Competition." *Journal of Comparative Economics* 16(2), June 1992, pp. 241–58.

Darrat, A. F.; Gilley, O. W.; and Meyer, D. J., "Petroleum Demand, Income Feedback Effects, and OPEC's Pricing Behavior: Some Theoretical and Empirical Results." *International Review of Economics and Finance* 1(3), 1992, pp. 247–59.

Friedman, Daniel, "Producers' Markets: A Model of Oligopoly with Sales Costs." *Journal of Economic Behavior and Organization* 11(3), May 1989, pp. 381–98.

Fuess, Scott M., Jr. and Loewenstein, Mark A., "On Strategic Cost Increases in a Duopoly." *International Journal of Industrial Organization* 9(3), 1991, pp. 389–95.

Hamilton, James L., "Joint Oligopsony Oligopoly in the U.S. Leaf Tobacco Market, 1924–39." *Review of Industrial Organization* 9(1), February 1994, pp. 25–39.

Hartigan, James C.; Kamma, Sreenivas; and Perry, Philip R., "The Injury Determination Category and the Value of Relief from Dumping." *Review of Economics and Statistics* 71(1), February 1989, pp. 183–86.

Hwang, Hae Shin and Schulman, Craig T., "Strategic Non-Intervention and the Choice of Trade Policy for International Oligopoly." *Journal of International Economics* 34(12), February 1993, pp. 73–93.

Karikari, John A., "Tariffs versus Ratio Quotas under Oligopoly." *International Economic Journal* 6(3), Autumn 1992, pp. 43–48.

Katz, Barbara G. and Nelson, Julianne, "Product Availability as a Strategic Variable: The Implications of Regulating Retailer Stockouts." *Journal of Regulatory Economics* 2(4), December 1990, pp. 379–95.

Mai, Chao cheng; Yeh, Chiou nan; and Suwanakul, Sontachai, "Price Uncertainty and Production Location Decisions under Free Entry Oligopoly." *Journal of Regional Science* 33(4), November 1993, pp. 531–45.

Roufagalas, John, "Price Rigidity: An Exploration of the Demand Side." *Managerial and Decision Economics* 15(1), January/February 1994, pp. 87–94.

Chapter 10

Ahlseen, Mark J., "The Impact of Unionization on Labor's Share of Income." *Journal of Labor Research* 11(3), Summer 1990, pp. 337–46.

Basu, K., "Duopoly Equilibria When Firms Can Change Their Decisions Once." *Economic Letters* 32(3), March 1990, pp. 273–75.

Blair, Douglas H. and Crawford, David L., "Labor Union Objectives and Collective Bargaining." *Quarterly Journal of Economics* 99(3), August 1984, pp. 547–66.

Bowman, Gary W. and Blackstone, Erwin A., "Low Price Conspiracy: Trade Regulation and the Case of Japanese Electronics." *Atlantic Economic Journal* 18(4), December 1990, pp. 59–67.

Burgess, Paul L. and Marburger, Daniel R., "Do Negotiated and Arbitrated Salaries Differ under Final Offer Arbitration?" *Industrial and Labor Relations Review* 46(3), April 1993, pp. 548–59.

Cheung, Francis K. and Davidson, Carl, "Bargaining Structure and Strike Activity." *Canadian Journal of Economics* 24(2), May 1991, pp. 347–71.

Conrad, Cecilia and Duchatelet, Martine, "New Technology Adoption: Incumbent versus Entrant." *International Journal of Industrial Organization* 5(3), September, 1987, pp. 315–21.

Hackett, Steven; Schlager, Edella; and Walker, James, "The Role of Communication in Resolving Common Dilemmas: Experimental Evidence with Heterogeneous Appropriators." *Journal of Environmental Economics and Management* 27(2), September 1994, pp. 99–126.

Holcomb, James H. and Nelson, Paul S., "Cartel Failure: A Mistake or Do They Do It to Each Other on Purpose?" *Journal of Socio Economics* 20(3), Fall 1991, pp. 235–49.

Horowitz, I., "On the Effects of Cournot Rivalry between Entrepreneurial and Cooperative Firms." *Journal of Comparative Economics* 15(1), March 1991, pp. 115–21.

Koeller, C. Timothy, "Union Activity and the Decline in American Trade Union Membership." *Journal of Labor Research* 15(1), Winter 1994, pp. 19–32.

Chapter 11

Beard, T. Randolph and Sweeney, George H., "Random Pricing by Monopolists." *Journal of Industrial Economics* 42(2), June 1994, pp. 183–92.

Benson, B. L.; Greenhut, M. L.; and Norman, G., "On the Basing Point System." *American Economic Review* 80(3), June 1990, pp. 584–88.

Blair, Roger D. and Fesmire, James M., "The Resale Price Maintenance Policy Dilemma." *Southern Economic Journal* 60(4), April 1994, pp. 1043–47.

Bosch, Jean Claude and Eckard, E. Woodrow, Jr., "The Profitability of Price Fixing: Evidence from Stock Market Reaction to Federal Indictments." *Review of Economics and Statistics* 73(2), May 1991, pp. 309–17.

Braid, Ralph M., "Uniform versus Peak Load Pricing of a Bottleneck with Elastic Demand." *Journal of Urban Economics* 26(3), November 1989, pp. 320–27.

DeSerpa, Allan C., "A Note on Second-Degree Price Discrimination and Its Implications." *Review of Industrial Organization* 2(4), 1986, pp. 368–75.

Greenhut, John G. and Smith, Dean H., "An Operational Model for Spatial Price Theory." *Review of Regional Studies* 23(2), Fall 1993, pp. 115–28.

Halperin, Robert and Srinidhi, Bin, "The Effects of the U.S. Income Tax Regulations' Transfer Pricing Rules on Allocative Efficiency." *Accounting Review* 62(4), October 1987, pp. 686–706.

Horsky, Dan and Nelson, Paul, "New Brand Positioning and Pricing in an Oligopolistic Market." *Marketing Science* 11(2), Spring 1992, pp. 133–53.

Koller, Roland H., II, "When Is Pricing Predatory?" *Antitrust Bulletin* 24(2), Summer 1979, pp. 283–306.

Malko, J. Robert; Lindsay, Malcolm A.; and Everett, Carol T., "Towards Implementation of Peak Load Pricing of Electricity: A Challenge for Applied Economics." *Journal of Energy and Development* 3(1), Autumn 1977, pp. 82–102.

Nahata, Babu; Ostaszewski, Krzysztof; and Sahoo, P. K., "Direction of Price Changes in Third-Degree Price Discrimination." *American Economic Review* 80(5), December 1990, pp. 1254–58.

Ormiston, Michael B. and Philips, Owen R., "Nonlinear Price Schedules and Tied Products." *Economica* 55(218), May 1988, pp. 219–33.

Page, Frank H. and Sanders, Anthony B., "On the Pricing of Shared Appreciation Mortgages." *Housing Finance Review* 5(1), Summer 1986, pp. 49–57.

Sass, Tim R. and Saurman, David S., "Mandated Exclusive Territories and Economic Efficiency: An Empirical Analysis of the Malt Beverage Industry." *Journal of Law and Economics* 36(1), Part 1, April 1993, pp. 153–77.

Shaanan, Joseph, "A Method for the Estimation of Limit Prices without Entry Data." *Managerial and Decision Economics* 11(1), February 1990, pp. 21–29.

Taylor, Thomas N. and Schwarz, Peter M., "The Long-Run Effects of a Time-of-Use Demand Charge." *Rand Journal of Economics* 21(3), Autumn 1990, pp. 431–45.

Wirl, F., "Dynamic Demand and Noncompetitive Pricing Strategies." *Journal of Economics* 54(3), 1991, pp. 105–21.

Young, A. R., "Transactions Cost, Two-Part Tariffs, and Collusion." *Economic Inquiry* 29(3), July 1991, pp. 581–90.

Chapter 12

Albrecht, James W. and Vroman, Susan B., "Dual Labor Markets, Efficiency Wages, and Search." *Journal of Labor Economics* 10(4), October 1992, pp. 438–61.

Ballantine, John W.; Cleveland, Frederick W.; and Koeller, C. Timothy, "Profitability, Uncertainty, and Firm Size." *Small Business Economics* 5(2), June 1993, pp. 87–100.

Balvers, Ronald J. and Miller, Norman C., "Factor Demand under Conditions of Product Demand and Supply Uncertainty." *Economic Inquiry* 30(3), July 1992, pp. 544–55.

Biglaiser, Gary, "Middlemen as Experts." *Rand Journal of Economics* 24(2), Summer 1993, pp. 212–23.

Bodvarsson, Orn B., "Educational Screening with Output Variability and Costly Monitoring." *Atlantic Economic Journal* 17(1), March 1989, pp. 16–23.

Butler, Richard J. and Worrall, John D., "Claims Reporting and Risk Bearing Moral Hazard in Workers' Compensation." *Journal of Risk and Insurance* 58(2), June 1991, pp. 191–204.

Cabe, Richard and Herriges, Joseph A., "The Regulation of Non-Point Source Pollution under Imperfect and Asymmetric Information." *Journal of Environmental Economics and Management* 22(2), March 1992, pp. 134–46.

Camerer, Colin and Weigelt, Keith, "Information Mirages in Experimental Asset Markets." *Journal of Business* 64(4), October 1991, pp. 463–93.

Charles, Joni S. James, "Information Externalities: Information Dissemination as a Policy Tool to Achieve Efficient Investment Decisions in a Two-Firm Oil Drilling Industry." *Studi Economici* 44(39), 1989, pp. 29–49.

Copeland, Thomas E. and Friedman, Daniel, "The Market Value of Information: Some Experimental Results." *Journal of Business* 65(2), April 1992, pp. 241–66.

Cotter, Kevin D. and Jensen, Gail A., "Choice of Purchasing Arrangements in Insurance Markets." *Journal of Risk and Uncertainty* 2(4), December 1989, pp. 405–14.

Dionne, Georges and Doherty, Neil A., "Adverse Selection, Commitment, and Renegotiation: Extension to and Evidence from Insurance Markets." *Journal of Political Economy* 102(2), April 1994, pp. 209–35.

Eaker, Mark; Grant, Dwight; and Woodard, Nelson, "International Diversification and Hedging: A Japanese and U.S. Perspective." *Journal of Economics and Business* 43(4), November 1991, pp. 363–74.

Engelbrecht Wiggins, Richard and Kahn, Charles M., "Protecting the Winner: Second Price versus Oral Auctions." *Economics Letters* 35(3), March 1991, pp. 243–48.

Fu, Jiarong, "Increased Risk Aversion and Risky Investment." *Journal of Risk and Insurance* 60(3), September 1993, pp. 494–501.

Giliberto, S. Michael and Varaiya, Nikhil P., "The Winner's Curse and Bidder Competition in Acquisitions: Evidence from Failed Bank Auctions." *Journal of Finance* 44(1), March 1989, pp. 59–75.

Hausch, Donald B. and Li, Lode, "A Common Value Auction Model with Endogenous Entry and Information Acquisition." *Economic Theory* 3(2), 1993, pp. 315–34.

Hayes, James A.; Cole, Joseph B.; and Meiselman, David I., "Health Insurance Derivatives: The Newest Application of Modern Financial Risk Management." *Business Economics* 28(2), April 1993, pp. 36–40.

Hoffer, George E.; Pruitt, Stephen W.; and Reilly, Robert J., "Market Responses to Publicly Provided Information: The Case of Automotive Safety." *Applied Economics* 24(7), July 1992, pp. 661–67.

Holt, Charles A., Jr. and Sherman, Roger, "Waiting Line Auctions." *Journal of Political Economy* 90(2), April 1982, pp. 280–94.

Horowitz, John K. and Lichtenberg, Erik, "Insurance, Moral Hazard, and Chemical Use in Agriculture." *American Journal of Agricultural Economics* 75(4), November 1993, pp. 926–35.

Kamma, Sreenivas; Kanatas, George; and Raymar, Steven, "Dutch Auction versus Fixed Price Self Tender Offers for Common Stock." *Journal of Financial Intermediation* 2(3), September 1992, pp. 277–307.

Kogut, Carl A., "Recall in Consumer Search." *Journal of Economic Behavior and Organization* 17(1), January 1992, pp. 141–51.

McCabe, Kevin; Rassenti, Stephen; and Smith, Vernon, "Auction Institutional Design: Theory and Behavior of Simultaneous Multiple Unit Generalizations of the Dutch and English Auctions." *American Economic Review* 80, December 1990, pp. 1276–83.

Meador, Joseph W.; Madden, Gerald P.; and Johnston, David J., "On the Probability of Acquisition of Non-Life Insurers." *Journal of Risk and Insurance* 53(4), December 1986, pp. 621–43.

Meurer, Michael J. and Stahl, Dale O., II, "Informative Advertising and Product Match." *International Journal of Industrial Organization* 12(1), 1994, pp. 1–19.

Rosenman, Robert E. and Wilson, Wesley W., "Quality Differentials and Prices: Are Cherries Lemons?" *Journal of Industrial Economics* 39(6), December 1991, pp. 649–58.

Schlarbaum, Gary C. and Racette, George A., "Measuring Risk: Some Theoretical and Empirical Issues." *Journal of Business Research* 2(3), July 1974, pp. 349–68.

St. Louis, Robert D.; Burgess, Paul L.; and Kingston, Jerry L., "Reported vs. Actual Job Search by Unemployment Insurance Claimants." *Journal of Human Resources* 21(1), Winter 1986, pp. 92–117.

Swaim, Paul and Podgursky, Michael, "Female Labor Supply Following Displacement: A Split Population Model of Labor Force Participation and Job Search." *Journal of Labor Economics* 12(4), October 1994, pp. 640–56.

Tenorio, Rafael, "Revenue Equivalence and Bidding Behavior in a Multiunit Auction Market: An Empirical Analysis." *Review of Economics and Statistics* 75(2), May 1993, pp. 302–14.

Vanderporten, Bruce, "Strategic Behavior in Pooled Condominium Auctions." *Journal of Urban Economics* 31(1), January 1992, pp. 123–37.

Wiggins, Steven N. and Lane, W. J., "Quality Uncertainty, Search, and Advertising." *American Economic Review* 73(5), December 1983, pp. 881–94.

Woodland, Bill M. and Woodland, Linda M., "The Effects of Risk Aversion on Wagering: Point Spread versus Odds." *Journal of Political Economy* 99(3), June 1991, pp. 638–53.

Zorn, Thomas S. and Sackley, William H., "Buyers' and Sellers' Markets: A Simple Rational Expectations Search Model of the Housing Market." *Journal of Real Estate Finance and Economics* 4(3), September 1991, pp. 315–25.

Chapter 13

Bagwell, Kyle and Ramey, G., "Oligopoly Limit Pricing." *Rand Journal of Economics* 22(2), Summer 1991, pp. 155–72.

Bagwell, Kyle; Ramey, G.; and Spulber, D. F., "Dynamic Retail Price and Investment Competition." *Rand Journal of Economics* 28(2), Summer 1997, pp. 207–27.

Baumol, William J., "Predation and the Logic of the Average Variable Cost Test." *Journal of Law and Economics* 39(1), April 1996, pp. 49–72.

Biglaiser, Gary and DeGraba, Patrick, "Downstream Integration by a Bottleneck Input Supplier Whose Regulated Wholesale Prices Are above Costs." *Rand Journal of Economics* 32(2), Summer 2001, pp. 302–15.

Bolton, Patrick; Brodley, J. F.; and Riordan, M. H., "Predatory Pricing: Response to Critique and Further Elaboration." *Georgetown Law Journal* 89(8), August 2001, pp. 2495–2529.

Capra, C. M.; Goeree, J. K.; and Gomez, R., et al., "Predation, Asymmetric Information and Strategic Behavior in the Classroom: An Experimental Approach to the Teaching of Industrial Organization." *International Journal of Industrial Organization* 18(1), January 2000, pp. 205–25.

Chen, C. P., "Consumer Self-Generation and Monopoly Limit-Pricing under Timing Uncertainty of Deregulation in the Electricity Market." *Journal of Regulatory Economics* 15(3), May 1999, pp. 309–22.

Christian, S., "Limit Pricing When Incumbents Have Conflicting Interests." *International Journal of Industrial Organization* 17(6), August 1999, pp. 801–25.

Cooper, D. J.; Garvin, S.; and Kagel, J. H., "Signaling and Adaptive Learning in an Entry Limit Pricing Game." *Rand Journal of Economics* 28(4), Winter 1997, pp. 662–83.

Depken, C. A. and Ford, J. M., "NAFTA as a Means of Raising Rivals' Costs." *Review of Industrial Organization* 15(2), September 1999, pp. 103–13.

Elzinga, Kenneth G. and Mills, D. E., "Predatory Pricing and Strategic Theory." *Georgetown Law Journal* 89(8), August 2001, pp. 2475–94.

Fishman, A. and Gandal, N., "Experimentation and Learning with Network Effects." *Economics Letters* 44(1–2), 1994, pp. 103–8.

Granitz, E. and Klein, B., "Monopolization by 'Raising Rivals' Costs': The Standard Oil Case." *Journal of Law and Economics* 39(1), April 1996, pp. 1–47.

Guiltinan, J. P. and Gundlach, G. T., "Aggressive and Predatory Pricing: A Framework for Analysis." *Journal of Marketing* 60(3), July 1996, pp. 87–102.

Hawker, N. W., "Wal-Mart and the Divergence of State and Federal Predatory Pricing Law." *Journal of Public Policy and Marketing* 15(1), Spring 1996, pp. 141–47.

Holmes, T. J., "Can Consumers Benefit from a Policy Limiting the Market Share of a Dominant Firm?" *International Journal of Industrial Organization* 14(3), May 1996, pp. 365–87.

Katz, Michael L. and Shapiro, C., "Systems Competition and Network Effects." *Journal of Economics Perspectives* 8(2), Spring 1994, pp. 93–115.

LeBlanc, G., "Signaling Strength—Limit Pricing and Predatory Pricing." *Rand Journal of Economics* 23(4), Winter 1992, pp. 493–506.

Lopatka, J. E. and Godek, P. E., "Another Look at Alcoa—Raising Rivals' Costs Does Not Improve the View." *Journal of Law and Economics* 35(2), October 1992, pp. 311–29.

Lu, D., "Limit Pricing under a Vertical Structure." *Canadian Journal of Economics* 29, Part 1 Special Issue, April 1996, pp. S288–S292.

Majumdar, S. K. and Venkataraman S., "Network Effects and the Adoption of New Technology: Evidence from the U.S. Telecommunications Industry." *Strategic Management Journal* 19(11), November 1998, pp. 1045–62.

Martin, S., "Oligopoly Limit Pricing—Strategic Substitutes, Strategic Complements." *International Journal of Industrial Organization* 13(1), March 1995, pp. 41–65.

Norton, R., "The Myth of Predatory Pricing—Exposed." *Fortune* 141(3), February 7, 2000, p. 49.

Salonen, H., "Entry Deterrence and Limit Pricing under Asymmetric Information about Common Costs." *Games and Economic Behavior* 6(2), March 1994, pp. 312–27.

Sartzetakis, E. S., "Raising Rivals' Costs Strategies via Emission Permits Markets." *Review of Industrial Organization* 12(5–6), December 1997, pp. 751–65.

Sawyer, W. C., "NAFTA as a Means of Raising Rivals' Costs: A Comment." *Review of Industrial Organization* 18(1), February 2001, pp. 127–31.

Werden, G. J., "Network Effects and Conditions of Entry: Lessons from the Microsoft Case." *Antitrust Law Journal* 69(1), 2001, pp. 87–111.

Wolf, H., "Network Effects of Bilaterals: Implications for the German Air Transport Policy." *Journal of Air Transportation and Management* 7(1), January 2001, pp. 63–74.

Chapter 14

Anthony, Peter Dean, "Regulation and Supply Externalities." *Atlantic Economic Journal* 13(2), July 1985, pp. 86–87.

Banaian, King and Luksetich, William A., "Campaign Spending in Congressional Elections." *Economic Inquiry* 29(1), January 1991, pp. 92–100.

Bender, Bruce and Shwiff, Steven, "The Appropriation of Rents by Boomtown Governments." *Economic Inquiry* 20(1), January 1982, pp. 84–103.

Blackstone, Erwin A. and Bowman, Gary W., "Antitrust Damages: The Loss from Delay." *Antitrust Bulletin* 32(1), Spring 1987, pp. 93–100.

Butler, Richard V. and Maher, Michael D., "The Control of Externalities in a Growing Urban Economy." *Economic Inquiry* 20(1), January 1982, pp. 155–63.

Dearden, James A. and Husted, Thomas A., "Do Governors Get What They Want? An Alternative Examination of the Line Item Veto." *Public Choice* 77(4), December 1993, pp. 707–23.

Falkinger, J., "On Optimal Public Good Provision with Tax Evasion." *Journal of Public Economics* 45(1), June 1991, pp. 127–33.

Fon, Vincy, "Free Riding versus Paying under Uncertainty." *Public Finance Quarterly* 16(4), October 1988, pp. 464–81.

Formby, John P.; Smith, W. James; and Thistle, Paul D., "Economic Efficiency, Antitrust and Rate of Return." *Review of Industrial Organization* 5(2), Summer 1990, pp. 59–73.

Gallo, Joseph C.; Craycraft, Joseph L.; and Bush, Steven C., "Guess Who Came to Dinner? An Empirical Study of Federal Antitrust Enforcement for the Period 1963–1984." *Review of Industrial Organization* 2(2), 1985, pp. 106–31.

Greenway, D. and Milner, C., "Fiscal Dependence on Trade Taxes and Trade Policy Reform." *Journal of Development Economics* 27(3), April 1991, pp. 95–132.

Hanemann, W. M., "Willingness to Pay and Willingness to Accept: How Much Can They Differ?" *American Economic Review* 81(3), June 1991, pp. 635–47.

Huang, Peter H. and Wu, Ho Mou, "Emotional Responses in Litigation." *International Review of Law and Economics* 12(1), March 1992, pp. 31–44.

Hwang, H. and Mai, C.-C., "Optimum Discriminatory Tariffs under Oligopolistic Competition." *Canadian Economic Journal* 24(3), August 1991, pp. 693–702.

Jianakoplos, Nancy Ammon and Irvine, F. Owen, "Did Financial Deregulation Help Consumers? Access to Market Yield Instruments." *Applied Economics* 24(8), August 1992, pp. 813–32.

Laband, David N. and Sophocleus, John P., "An Estimate of Resource Expenditures on Transfer Activity in the United States." *Quarterly Journal of Economics* 107(3), August 1992, pp. 959–83.

Lee, Eric Youngkoo and Szenberg, Michael, "The Price, Quantity and Welfare Effects of U.S. Trade Protection: The Case of Footwear." *International Economic Journal* 2(4), Winter 1988, pp. 95–110.

Lott, John R., Jr. and Bronars, Stephen G., "Time Series Evidence on Shirking in the U.S. House of Representatives." *Public Choice* 76(12), June 1993, pp. 125–49.

Lozada, Gabriel A., "The Conservationist's Dilemma." *International Economic Review* 34(3), August 1993, pp. 647–62.

Marshall, L., "New Evidence on Fiscal Illusion: The 1986 Tax 'Windfalls.'" *American Economic Review* 81(5), December 1991, pp. 1336–44.

Mayshar, J., "On Measuring the Marginal Cost of Funds Analytically." *American Economic Review* 81(5), December 1991, pp. 1329–35.

Millner, Edward L. and Pratt, Michael D., "Risk Aversion and Rent Seeking: An Extension and Some Experimental Evidence." *Public Choice* 69(1), February 1991, pp. 81–92.

Murthy, N. R. Vasudeva, "Bureaucracy and the Divisibility of Local Public Output: Further Econometric Evidence." *Public Choice* 55(3), October 1987, pp. 265–72.

Nollen, Stanley D. and Iglarsh, Harvey J., "Explanations of Protectionism in International Trade Votes." *Public Choice* 66(2), August 1990, pp. 137–53.

Pratt, Michael D. and Hoffer, George E., "The Efficacy of State-Mandated Minimum Quality Certification: The Case of Used Vehicles." *Economic Inquiry* 24(2), April 1986, pp. 313–18.

Rittennoure, R. Lynn and Pluta, Joseph E., "Theory of Intergovernmental Grants and Local Government." *Growth and Change* 8(3), July 1977, pp. 31–37.

Romer, Thomas; Rosenthal, Howard; and Munley, Vincent G., "Economic Incentives and Political Institutions: Spending and Voting in School Budget Referenda." *Journal of Public Economics* 49(1), October 1992, pp. 1–33.

Stanton, Timothy J., "Regional Conflict and the Clean Air Act." *Review of Regional Studies* 19(3), Fall 1989, pp. 24–30.

Thistle, Paul D., "United States versus United Shoe Machinery Corporation: On the Merits." *Journal of Law and Economics* 36(1), Part 1, April 1993, pp. 33–70.

NAME INDEX

Page numbers followed by n refer to footnotes.

GENERAL INDEX

Page numbers followed by n refer to footnotes.